Excavations at Dryslwyn Castle
1980–95

WITHDRAWN

by
Chris Caple

with contributions by
Edward Besley, Ian Betts, Ray Caple, Mark Copley, John Daniell, Stephanie Dudd, David Dungworth, Richard Evershed, Louisa Gidney, Alison Goodall, Ian Goodall†, Jacqui Huntley, Oliver Jessop, Alison Locker, Jennifer Miller, Sonia O'Connor, Chris Phillpotts, Clare Pickin, Susan Ramsay, Jeremy Reid, Carol Spence, Alice Thompson, Rachel Tyson, Catherine Vinson, Peter Webster and Hugh Willmott

Illustrations by
Oliver Jessop

Llywodraeth Cynulliad Cymru
Welsh Assembly Government

✛Cadw

THE SOCIETY FOR MEDIEVAL ARCHAEOLOGY
MONOGRAPH 26

ISBN 978 1 905981 88 5

Edited by Christopher Gerrard
Published by The Society for Medieval Archaeology
Printed in England by Maney Publishing, Leeds

This publication has been made possible by a grant from Cadw

The Society for Medieval Archaeology
www.socmedarch.org / publications

Cover: Dryslwyn Castle from the air, Terry James of Cambria Archaeology

CONTENTS

LIST OF FIGURES

GLOSSARY

anrheg	A gift of food designed to impress the recipient, usually meat.
arglwydd	Lord. The use of the term *brenin* (king) to describe the leaders of the traditional kingdoms of Gwynedd, Powys and Deheubarth ceased during the mid 12th century with the acceptance of the overlordship of Henry II and the term *arglwydd* came into use (Pierce 1972, 28). Llywelyn ap Iowerth (d. 1240) and Llywelyn ap Gruffudd (d. 1282), Lords of Gwynedd, used the term prince (*princeps*) when they effectively controlled *pura Wallie*.
commote	Traditional local land division, a sub division of the cantref (Davies 1987, 20–21).
cantref	Traditional Welsh land division (pl: cantrefi). Legal, economic and social structures were based on the cantref and its sub divisions (Davies 1987, 20–21).
commorth	Periodic render of cattle to the lord.
dawnbywd	Food render to the lord, normally from bondmen (*taeogs*).
Deheubarth	Lands of the modern day counties of Carmarthenshire, Ceredigion and parts of east Pembrokeshire (Turvey 2002, xxv; Rees 1951, plate 30).
dofraeth	Food render to the lord, often oats, normally from freemen.
golwython	An impressive dish of food at the start of the feast.
gwestfa	Food render to the lord's court normally from freemen (Charles-Edwards *et al* 2000, 567: Rees 1924, 10–12).
hendre-hafod	Winter valley pastures and summer mountain grazing, the system of transhumance, moving cattle between these feeding grounds.
llu	The lord's host or army, comprising all those (freemen) who were required to serve their lord (Davies 2004, 50–84).
llys	Lord's court. It may refer both to the physical (hall, lords chamber and associated buildings within a defensive perimeter) and the social structure (people and rituals of the court).
maerdref	The lord's settlement associated with working the lord's demesne land.
marchia Wallie	Lands along the eastern and southern sides of Wales held by Anglo-Norman lords following the Norman invasion (Turvey 2002, xxvi).
neuadd	Hall.
pannage	Grazing of pigs during the Autumn in the lord's woods, and the payment in pigs due for this.
pura Wallia	Lands under Welsh control during the 13th century prior to 1283, where Welsh law and social structures were present (Turvey 2002, xxvi).
rhaglaw, rhingyll	Officer of the commote, collecting rents, later known as the beadle (Rees 1924, 95–103).
teulu	Lord's household warriors, his war band (Davies 2004, 14–49).
tref	Settlement and associated land.
uchelwyr	Noble householder, significant freeman, minor aristocracy.
Welshry	Areas of Welsh control, where welsh laws were implemented, the term would be applied to Wales as a whole and individual lordships.
ystafell	The chamber or private living space of the lord.

Place names

A confusing mixture of English and Welsh spellings of place names are used in almost all modern publications: Cardiff rather than Caerdydd, but the River Tywi rather than Towy. In this publication place names are used with either English or Welsh spelling depending on normal usage *c*2000–06. Castle names are normally from Avent's *Castles of the Princes of Gwynedd* and King's *Castellarium Anglicanum*. The cantref and commote names are from Rees's *An historical atlas of Wales: from early to modern times*.

In his book *The age of conquest*, Prof R R Davies commented on this subject that 'The existence of alternative place names and of alternative spelling of place names is a reflection of the emergence of that duality of culture and language within Wales which is one of the themes of this volume' (Davies 1987, xiv). This duality of language and culture continues to evolve into the third millennium and is reflected in this publication.

SUMMARY

Excavations at Dryslwyn between 1980 and 1995 uncovered a masonry castle, founded in the late 1220s by Rhys Gryg for his son Maredudd ap Rhys, the first Lord of Dryslwyn. The first castle was a simple round tower and polygonal walled enclosure, which subsequently included a kitchen, prison and wood-framed, clay-floored great chamber beside a great hall. In the mid 13th century a second ward was added and the great chamber rebuilt in stone. This castle was greatly expanded in the period 1283–87 by Rhys ap Maredudd, the second and final Lord of Dryslwyn, who added an Outer Ward and gatehouse. He also rebuilt much of the Inner Ward, adding an extra storey to the great hall and great chamber and a series of apartments and a chapel along the south side of the great hall. Thus at the end of the 13th century a large three-ward castle stretched along the eastern and southern edge of the hill while the rest of the hilltop was occupied by a settlement defended by a wall and substantial ditch with access through a gatehouse. This castle and its associated settlement were besieged and captured in 1287 by an English royal army of over 11,000 men following damage inflicted by a trebuchet and mining of the walls.

During the Welsh lordly period, the castle was the home of the lords of Dryslwyn, their family and retainers, as well as the administrative centre of a lordship, which between 1285 and 1287 was as large as present day Carmarthenshire. Throughout the 14th century the English Crown garrisoned and repaired the castle, supervised by an appointed constable. This castle was surrendered to Owain Glyn Dŵr in 1403 and at some point in the early to mid 15th century was deliberately walled up to deny its use to a potential enemy. It was subsequently looted, burnt and deliberately demolished.

By the late 13th century, though possibly from its initial construction, the castle had a white rendered and lime-washed appearance, creating a very dramatic and highly visible symbol of lordship. Internally, the lord's and guest apartments had decorative wall paintings and glazed windows. Evidence from charred beams still *in situ*, the sizes, shapes and distribution of nails, sheet lead, slates and postholes recovered during excavation has enabled some of the wooden as well as masonry buildings to be reconstructed. Waterlogged deposits had preserved a rich assemblage of seeds, birds, fish and animal bone which reveal evidence of the dining habits of Welsh lords, their guests and household. They frequently consumed young veal calves and sucking pig, marine and fresh water fish, wild birds and shellfish, oatcakes and breads as well as local and imported fruit. A unique example of a 15th-century quill from a pen, together with the published 14th-century accounts of the castle (Rhys 1936) and unpublished records collected by E A Lewis (*NLW Add MS 455D*) demonstrate the administrative role of the site.

Though crossbows dominate in the castle armoury accounts after 1287 and throughout the 14th century, the recovery of 92 armour-piercing arrowheads from Dryslwyn Castle indicates that the longbow was the principal weapon in use. These were almost certainly 'personal' weapons owned by individual bowmen, whereas crossbows were supplied by the state for the use of troops. A rare bronze knop-headed mace was also recovered from a mid 13th-century context whilst two of the three spearheads and the majority of arrowheads come from contexts associated with the siege. Damage and repairs to the castle walls can be correlated with historic accounts while three stone balls recovered by the excavation were undoubtedly thrown by the trebuchet, details of whose construction are recorded in the royal accounts of expenditure during 1287. Lithic projectiles, from slingstones to the trebuchet balls, provide evidence for both defence and attack.

RESUMEN

Las excavaciones desarrolladas entre 1980 y 1995 en Dryslwyn descubrieron el castillo de piedra construido a finales de los años 1220 por Rhys Gryg para su hijo Maredudd ap Rhys, primer señor de Dryslwyn. El primer castillo consistió en una simple torre redonda y un área poligonal murada que incluiría la cocina, prisión y una gran sala, de suelo de tierra batida y paredes de tapial, situada junto al gran salón. A mediados del siglo XIII se añadió un segundo patio a la vez que la gran sala se reconstruyó a base de piedra. Durante 1283 y 1287 Rhys ap Maredudd, el segundo y último señor de Dryslwyn, agrandó el castillo, añadiendo un patio exterior y torreón de entrada. Además reconstruyó parte del patio interior, añadiendo un piso superior al gran salón y sala, junto con una serie de habitaciones y capilla en el lado sur del gran salón. A finales del siglo XIII el castillo de Dryslwyn con sus tres patios se eregía en el extremo de una colina, cuya pendiente estaba ocupada por un asentamiento defendido por muros y una gran zanja, con acceso a través de una entrada defendida. En 1287 el castillo y su población adjunta fueron sitiados y capturados por un ejército real inglés de más de 11.000 hombres, con la ayuda de zapas y ataques con catapultas.

Durante el señorío galés, el castillo fue tanto residencia de los señores de Dryslwyn, sus familias y séquito, como fue también centro administrativo del señorío, tan grande entre 1285 y 1287 como el actual condado de Carmarthenshire. Durante el siglo XIV la corona inglesa ocupó y reparó el castillo bajo la supervisión de un condestable. El castillo se rindió en 1403 a Owain Glyn Dŵr, y seguidamente sus muros fueron recrecidos deliberamente para evitar que fuera utilizado por un posible enemigo. Poco más tarde fue saqueado, quemado y demolido deliberamente.

En el siglo XIII, y posiblemente ya desde el momento de su construcción, el castillo estuvo lavado en yeso y recubierto de cal blanca, creando así un símbolo de señorío muy dramático y visible. En cuanto al interior, las habitaciones del señor y visitantes estuvieron decoradas con pinturas murales y ventanas con cristales. Gracias a los restos de vigas quemadas *in situ*, tamaños, formas y distribución de los clavos encontrados, piezas de plomo, pizarras y elementos excavados se han podido reconstruir los edificios que integraron el castillo, tanto los de madera como los de piedra. Además, los depósitos anegados han preservado una rica colección de semillas y restos de fauna que pone en evidencia los hábitos de la mesa del señor del castillo, sus invitados y sirvientes. Ellos se sirvieron frecuentemente de ternera lechal y cochinillo, pescado fresco y marino, pájaros, marisco, panes y fruta importada. En cuanto al papel administrativo del castillo, éste queda claramente evidenciado gracias al ejemplar único de una plumilla del siglo XV, junto con las cuentas del siglo XIV (publicadas por Rhys 1936) y otros documentos recogidos por E A Lewis (*NLW Add MS 455D*).

Aunque son las ballestas las que dominan en las cuentas del castillo tras 1287 y durante todo el siglo XIV, durante las excavaciones se encontraron 92 puntas de flecha cuya presencia indica que el arco fue el arma predilecta. Éstas serían seguramente armas de uso personal, propiedad de cada arquero, mientras que las ballestas eran suministradas por el estado para el uso de las tropas. También se encontró una maza de bronce, ejemplar muy raro, en un contexto de mediados del siglo XIII, mientras que las tres punta de lanza y la mayoría de las puntas de flecha aparecieron en contextos asociados con el asalto de 1287. Daños y reparos acaecidos en los muros del castillo pueden ser asociados con sucesos históricos específicos; no hay duda, por ejemplo, que las tres bolas de piedra encontradas durante la excavación fueron lanzadas por una catapulta cuya construcción ha quedado documentada en los gastos de 1287. Los proyectiles de piedra recuperados ofrecen evidencia clara tanto del ataque como de la defensa del castillo.

RÉSUMÉ

Les fouilles archéologiques de Dryslwyn entre 1980 et 1995 ont mis au jour un château maçonné, fondé à la fin des années 1220 par Rhys Gryg pour son fils Maredudd ap Rhys, le premier seigneur de Dryslwyn. Le premier château était constitué d'une simple tour circulaire et d'une enceinté murée polygonale qui renferma plus tard une cuisine, une prison et une camera en bois dont le sol était en terre battue, située à côté d'une aula. Au milieu du XIIIe siècle, une seconde salle fut ajoutée et la camera fut reconstruite en pierre. Ce château fut largement agrandi au cours de la période 1283–87 par Rhys ap Maredudd, le second et dernier seigneur de Dryslwyn, qui fit ajouter une Salle Extérieure et une guérite. Il fit aussi reconstruire la majeure partie de la Salle Intérieure, ajoutant un étage supplémentaire à l'aula et à la camera, ainsi qu'une série d'appartements et une capella le long du côté sud de l'aula. Ainsi, à la fin du XIIIe siècle, un grand château à trois salles s'étendait le long des flancs est et sud de la colline tandis que le reste du sommet de la colline était occupé par un établissement défendu par une enceinte et un fossé avec un accès par la guérite. Ce château et l'établissement qui lui était associé furent assiégés et pris en 1287 par une armée royale anglaise de plus de 11000 hommes, suite aux dommages infligés par un trébuchet et à la sape des murs.

Au cours de la période de règne galloise, le château fut la résidence des seigneurs de Dryslwyn, de leur famille et de leurs domestiques, ainsi que le centre administratif de la seigneurie, qui, entre 1285 et 1287, fut aussi importante que l'actuel Carmarthenshire. Au cours du XIVe siècle la Couronne Anglaise mit en garnison et répara le château, dirigé par un gouverneur nommé. Ce château fut cédé à Owain Glyn Dŵr en 1403 et dans la première moitié du XVe siècle, il fut intentionnellement bloqué pour éviter qu'il ne soit pris par tout ennemi potentiel. Il fut par la suite pillé, brûlé et volontairement démoli.

A la fin du XIIIe siècle, l'aspect blanchi à la chaux du château produisait un symbole relativement dramatique et ostentatoire de la seigneurie. A l'intérieur, les appartements du seigneur et de ses hôtes disposaient de peintures murales décoratives et de vitraux. Des indices de poutres carbonisées toujours *in situ*, les dimensions, les formes et la répartition des clous, des plaques de plomb, des ardoises et des trous de poteaux mis au jour lors de la fouille ont permis la reconstitution de bâtiments en bois, ainsi que de ceux en pierre. Des dépôts imbibés d'eau ont conservé un ensemble riche de graines, d'ossements d'oiseaux et d'animaux et des arêtes de poisson qui ont révélé le mode alimentaire des seigneurs gallois, de leurs hôtes et des gens du logis. Ils consommaient fréquemment de jeunes veaux et du porc, du poisson marin et d'eau douce, des oiseaux sauvages et des fruits de mer, des gâteaux à base d'orge, du pain, ainsi que des fruits locaux et importés. L'exemple unique de plume à écrire du XVe siècle, ainsi que les comptes publiés du XIVe siècle du château (Rhys 1936) et les documents non-publiés réunis par E A Lewis (*NLW Add MS 455D*), témoigne du rôle administratif du site.

Bien que les arbalètes dominent les comptes de l'arsenal du château après 1287 et au cours du XIVe siècle, la découverte à Dryslwyn Castle de quatre-vingt douze pointes de flèche pouvant percer une armure indiquent que l'arc était l'arme la plus employée. Il s'agissait presque certainement d'armes personnelles appartenant individuellement aux archers, tandis que les arbalètes étaient fournies aux troupes par l'état. Une massue exceptionnelle avec un bouton en bronze fut aussi mise au jour dans un contexte du milieu du XIIIe siècle. Deux des trois fers de lance et la majorité des pointes de flèche proviennent de contextes associés au siège. Les dommages et réparations des murs du château peuvent être corrélés avec les comptes historiques. Trois boulets de pierre mis au jour lors des fouilles ont sans aucun doute été lancés par le trébuchet, dont des détails de la construction sont consignés dans les comptes royaux des dépenses de 1287. Les projectiles lithiques, des lance-pierre aux boulets de trébuchets, constituent des indices sur les aspects défensifs et offensifs de ce site.

ACKNOWLEDGEMENTS

This work is dedicated to my father Raymond Francis Caple who fired my enthusiasm for archaeology and whose energy and commitment has done so much both to aid this excavation and archaeology in Wales.

Thanks must be personally accorded to Peter Webster, the initial director of excavations at Dryslwyn, for giving me the opportunity to take over this project; Peter has continued to act as my mentor throughout this endeavour. Thanks also go to Cadw and its inspectors Sian Rees and Rick Turner who supported the excavation from first to last. It is a tribute to Cadw's commitment to the archaeology of Wales that this project has been fully funded from its humble beginnings through to final publication. The Department of Archaeology, Durham University, has also contributed significantly to the project, providing scientific and conservation facilities, authors for several sections and especially funding and staff time to complete the final stages of the report. At this point I would like to pay particular tribute to the late Richard Avent, Principal Inspector of Ancient Monument at Cadw, who tragically died whilst the editing of this report was taking place. Richard was a great friend and supporter of the excavation; for a number of years Dryslwyn and Richard's excavation at Laugharne shared accommodation at Trinity College Carmarthen and many evenings of stimulating discussion. He provided advice and encouragement throughout the project; his support, friendship and guidance will be greatly missed.

In undertaking this work I have been greatly aided by a number of colleagues. In particular Tony Spence, for many years my deputy director, and Olly Jessop who was site assistant, post-excavation assistant and draughtsman. They have provided the energy, enthusiasm, logical order and the sheer variety of archaeological skills necessary to get this project from the earth to the word. Over the years we have been assisted by many other individuals; excavation supervisors Carol Spence, Norman Redhead, Brian Williams and Alan Thomas laboured physically and mentally to make sense of this site. Our finds supervisors Roz Cooper and, in particular Norma Hancock, kept the excavation going in a million and one ways and provided the voice of humanity and sanity that we all need to hear sometimes. I am grateful to all the authors of the specialist reports, their efforts and expertise, which have yielded a great deal of additional information about the site. Only through the work of colleagues such as the late Ian Goodall does an accurate and detailed picture of life in the medieval past emerge. I would like to thank colleagues Christopher Gerrard and Simon Draper for editing and correcting my manuscript, their efforts have been essential in creating a readable report.

Finally I must especially thank all the volunteers who laboured so long and hard on what has often been a demanding site. The spirit of the excavation volunteer was undoubtedly best exemplified by the late Russ Taylor whose enthusiasm as a volunteer from the very early years of this project never waned even on the longest and hottest day. It is a tribute to him and every other volunteer who worked on this site that this was such an enjoyable excavation over so many years.

EXCAVATION HISTORY AND PROCESSES

1.1 INTRODUCTION

The picturesque ruin of Dryslwyn Castle, perched at the southern end of Dryslwyn hill overlooking the River Tywi has attracted antiquarians, visitors and artists from the 18th century to the present day. The hill on which the ruins lie is located 22km east of Carmarthen and 12km west of Llandeilo (SN554203; Figure 1.1) and virtually the whole of the valley between these two towns is visible from the summit. The antiquity of the site, particularly as the castle stronghold of the Lords of Dryslwyn, who played such an important role in the late 13th-century history of Wales, has long been recognised. The site features in almost every history of the county (Lloyd 1935), as well as in accounts of medieval Wales and Britain in the 13th century (Davies 1987; Morris 1901; Prestwich 1988; Powicke 1962). Though much of the available medieval documentary evidence related to this site was collected and collated in 1907 by the historian E A Lewis and is now lodged in the National Library of Wales (*NLW Add MS 455D*), no archaeological excavation had been undertaken prior to 1980.

This monograph describes the results of the excavation of Dryslwyn Castle undertaken between 1980 and 1995, which provided a large volume of new historical and archaeological detail about life in, and the construction of, a castle in 13th- and early 14th-century Wales. In contrast to the limited archaeological data from Welsh castles such as Dolwyddelan (Conwy) or Castell-y-Bere (Gwynedd) (Butler 1974, 80), which suffered poorly recorded excavation and restoration work in the 19th and earlier 20th century, the medieval archaeological deposits at Dryslwyn were fortuitously preserved intact beneath the castle's destruction. This allowed modern excavation to reveal the full sequence of construction and occupation activity on this site while coins, imported ceramics and details of architectural form have enabled this sequence to be dated. Detailed recording, including stone by stone drawings

of every upstanding masonry wall, has ensured this record remains for future generations to study, since the act of preservation and restoration of extant remains invariably results in the loss of information.

Briefly, excavation and historical research indicate that Dryslwyn Castle was founded in the late 1220s by Rhys Gryg to provide a protected home for his new son Maredudd. The castle was then developed by Maredudd ap Rhys (1220s–71), the first Lord of Dryslwyn, and further enlarged by his son Rhys ap Maredudd (1240s–92), the last Lord of Dryslwyn. By 1287 Rhys had gained lands due to his support of the English Crown in the war between Edward 1 and Llywelyn ap Gruffudd equivalent to modern day Carmarthenshire and had developed Dryslwyn into a large three-ward castle, with an associated defended town, similar to many large English baronial castles. Surviving archaeological evidence creates a picture of Rhys and his entourage seated in a great hall feasting on a wide range of local animals, birds and fish, eating imported fruits and drinking imported wine in fine French ceramics. Some rooms had wall-paintings. The sophisticated nature of the military architecture, such as the castle gatehouse, which alone of the Welsh castles had an entrance guarded with double gate and portcullis either end of a gate passage, betrays a blend of both Marcher and Welsh influences.

The Welsh lordly period of construction and occupation ended in 1287 when Rhys rose in revolt against the Crown. The records of the English Crown detail the costs of men and materials used in this siege, which can be compared to the archaeological evidence, for the physical reality of this event and its aftermath. This has enabled a detailed picture of the longest siege of any Welsh castle to be established. Later, Dryslwyn became a garrisoned castle of the English Crown. Historic records and archaeological evidence for food consumption, repairs and construction reveal a castle in gentle decline, being minimally maintained throughout the 14th century. After the hiatus of the revolt of Owain Glyn Dŵr, the historical record falls silent.

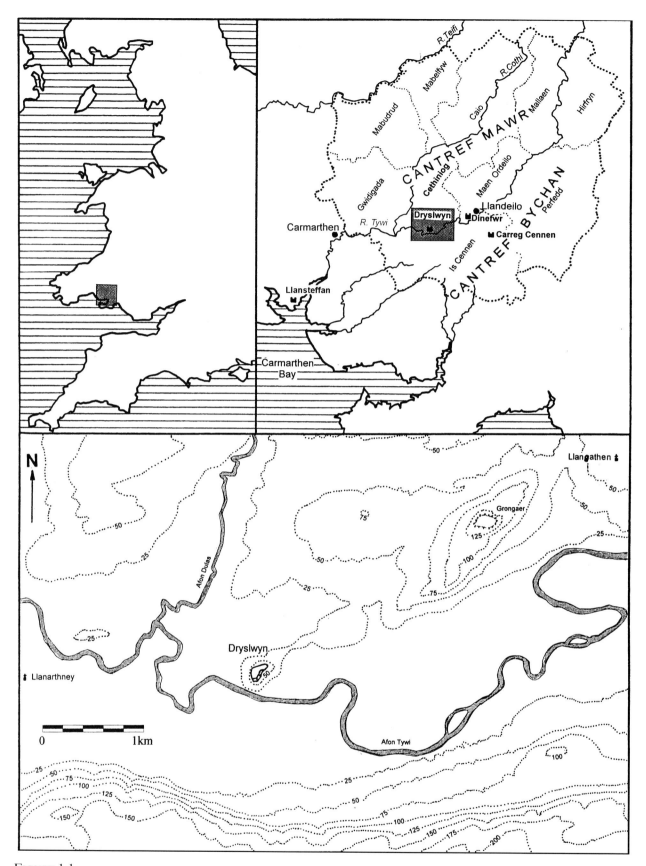

FIGURE 1.1

Location of Dryslwyn Castle, the Tywi Valley, Cantref Mawr and Cantref Bychan

The archaeology, however, reveals a detailed picture of closing the castle, including the blocking of gateways and entrances, followed by looting, then an all-consuming fire, before the castle was deliberately demolished, so sealing its medieval occupation. On the hilltop beside the castle, historical evidence indicates a defended settlement or town prior to 1287 to which archaeological evidence adds the detail of a complex sequence of house and defence construction. By 1300 this was the borough of Dryslwyn, a township of around 200 souls, the third largest town in Carmarthenshire and Cardiganshire.

As we shall see, perhaps the most remarkable evidence to emerge from this excavation is the sheer size, scale and speed of the construction at Dryslwyn, which developed from a bare hillside in the 1220s to a highly sophisticated castle and associated town in only 70 years. This indicates not only the power and position of the lords of Dryslwyn, but is indicative of the economic expansion of Wales as a whole in the 13th century. The development of other Welsh sites such as Dolforwyn (Powys), Castell-y-Bere (Gwynedd) and Newcastle Emlyn (Carmarthenshire) may be equally rapid, whilst existing centres such as Carmarthen and Cardigan also show expansion.

1.2 THE EXCAVATION

Dryslwyn Hill with its attendant ruined castle was transferred from the Cawdor estate into the care of the Secretary of State for Wales as an Ancient Monument in 1979. The Welsh Office, Ancient Monuments Branch, as Cadw (Welsh Historic Monuments) after 1984, then funded archaeological excavation under the directorship of Peter Webster, lecturer in Archaeology, Department of Extra Mural Studies at University College Cardiff, University of Wales, in 1980, ahead of consolidation of the masonry. The author of this report, originally the deputy director, directed the excavations from 1984 until 1995. Excavation work was carried out for three to four weeks every summer. The volunteers were initially adult education students attending Peter Webster's classes. In later years students, principally from the Department of Archaeology, Durham University, undertook much of the work. Their efforts revealed a castle buried in several metres of masonry rubble with substantial walls still standing and 13th- and 14th-century archaeological deposits. Though a mechanical excavator removed some of the rubble between the 1981 and 1982 seasons, almost all the excavation was by hand.

The hill itself is composed of Ordovician limestone interleaved with thin bands of shale. The limestone from the hillside was quarried for stone for the castle and burnt to make the lime mortar that adhered the masonry together. Limited remains of stonework were visible on the southern edge of the hill when the excavation commenced (Webster 1981b, 34). At that time survey work by Ray Caple and Peter Webster suggested a substantial castle extended across the eastern ridge of the hill with a substantial fortified town covering the rest of the hilltop (Webster 1987, 103).

The aims of the excavation were to completely excavate the Inner Ward of the castle to reveal a visitable monument and to conduct excavations throughout the castle and town in order to determine the date and nature of the occupation and construction activity on the site. It was also considered important for the present and future management of this site to reveal the extent and nature of the archaeological deposits on the site and to excavate any areas which might be damaged by the construction of paths and steps, required to facilitate visitor access.

Initially a series of rectangular trenches, numbered 01 to 13, were laid out across the site between 1980 and 1983 over areas of potential archaeological interest (Caple and Jessop 1997, fig 5). Individual contexts (features/layers) were numbered for each trench. In 1984 the site was reorganised using the existing buildings and areas of the castle, which were given alphabetic letters again with numbered contexts (Figures 1.2 and 1.3). This facilitated excavation of the Inner Ward of the castle room by room, building by building but meant that some dividing walls have two or even three area/context codes. All the records of the 1980–83 excavation were converted into the new site code system and the finds were re-labelled. All contexts (walls, layers, postholes) were recorded on context sheets and, where appropriate, were photographed and recorded on plans and sections. The plans, sections, photographs and details of finds recovered from each context, plus a day diary kept by each area supervisor, have been bound together in files for each area, to form an accessible and usable archaeological archive. Alphabetical area and numerical context codes have been employed throughout this report e.g. (C16), together with the descriptive name of the building to facilitate accuracy and understanding (for example, Round Tower D). Significant finds, such as arrowheads, were given a unique small find numbers comprising: the year, the initials SF and a sequential number (90SF9). In this report they are referred to also by their catalogue number, e.g. [M79]. Throughout the excavation regular interim reports on the progress of the excavation were provided to Cadw and published in a variety of locations (Webster 1980; 1981a; 1981b; 1982a; 1982b; 1982c; 1983a; 1983b; 1984; 1987; Webster and Caple 1983; Caple 1985a; 1985b; 1990a; 1990b; 1991; 1992a; 1992b; 1993a; 1993b; 1993c; 1994a; 1994b; 1996a; 1996b; Caple and Denison 1994; Caple and Jessop 1996). The castle fully opened to the public in August 1996, and a guidebook was published in 1999 (Rees and Caple 1999).

The Inner Ward was fully excavated, consequently clear conclusions regarding the sequence of construction and dating have been reached. The limited excavation possible in the Middle and Outer Wards

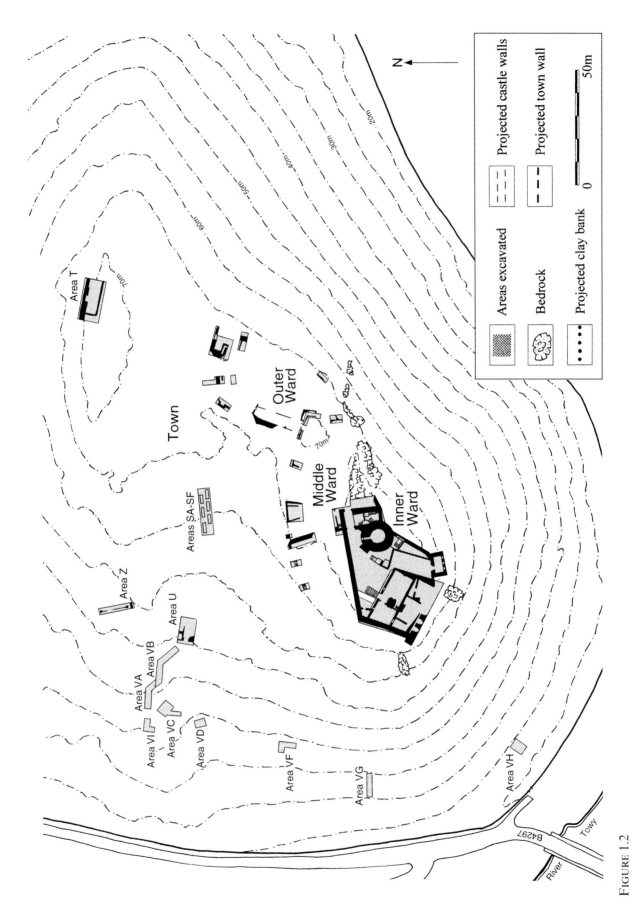

FIGURE 1.2

Dryslwyn Castle and township. Excavated areas 1980–95

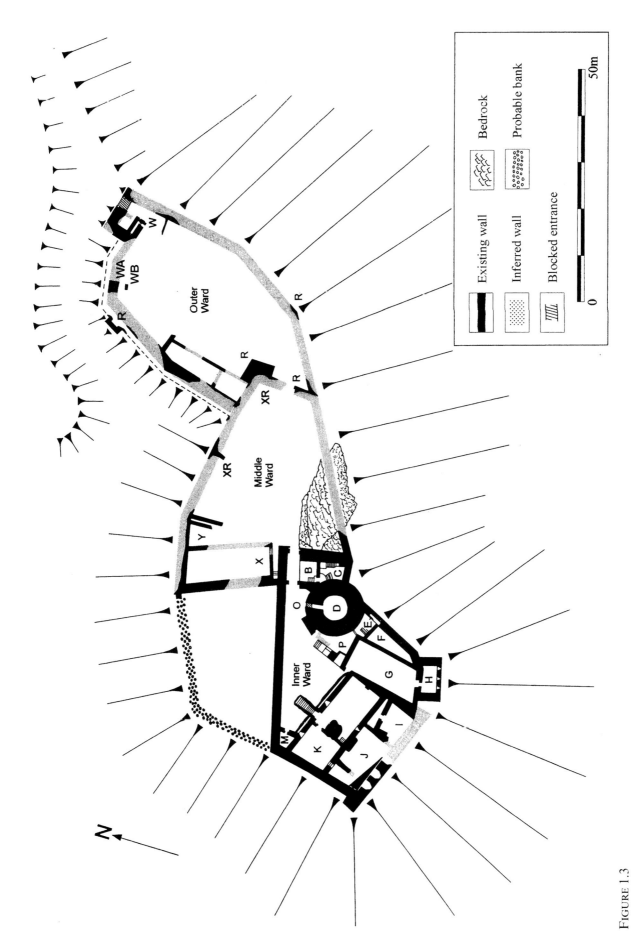

FIGURE 1.3

Dryslwyn Castle. Excavated areas 1980–95

Key to plans:

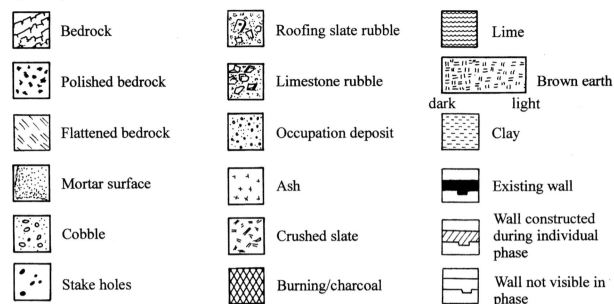

Bedrock	Roofing slate rubble	Lime
Polished bedrock	Limestone rubble	Brown earth — dark / light
Flattened bedrock	Occupation deposit	Clay
Mortar surface	Ash	Existing wall
Cobble	Crushed slate	Wall constructed during individual phase
Stake holes	Burning/charcoal	Wall not visible in phase

Key to sections:

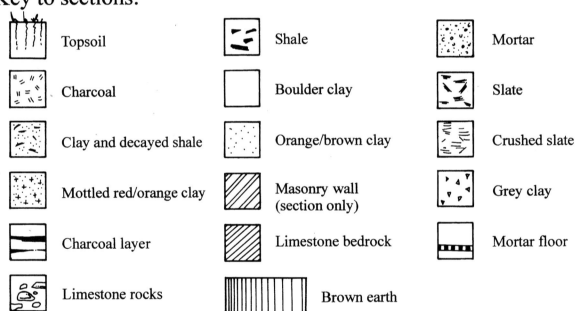

Topsoil	Shale	Mortar
Charcoal	Boulder clay	Slate
Clay and decayed shale	Orange/brown clay	Crushed slate
Mottled red/orange clay	Masonry wall (section only)	Grey clay
Charcoal layer	Limestone bedrock	Mortar floor
Limestone rocks	Brown earth — dark / light	

Key to elevations:

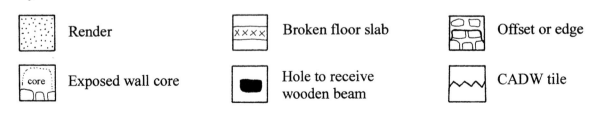

Render	Broken floor slab	Offset or edge
Exposed wall core	Hole to receive wooden beam	CADW tile

FIGURE 1.4

Drawing conventions

and township has meant that only tentative conclusions regarding the development of these parts of the site have been possible. Only bone, stone, ceramic and highly corroded metal finds survived buried in the thin aerated limy soil and limestone building rubble of the site. However, seeds (some charred or mineralised) and small bones were recovered from pockets of waterlogged soil present in a number of pits and late 13th-century kitchen middens above the clay-floored buildings in Area F. Very lightly corroded metal artefacts and charred seeds were also preserved in the oxygen-free soil conditions created by the burning deposits which formed in the base of the Great Hall K/L, Round Tower D and Great Chamber G when the castle was set alight prior to demolition in the 15th century.

Small finds were principally conserved in the laboratories at Cardiff University (1980–85) and Durham University (1988–95). All the upstanding walls were recorded on stone-by-stone drawings. With the exception of the architectural stone fragments, which were drawn, photographed and recorded on site before being re-buried in the Prison M, all the ceramic, glass, metal, stone and bone artefacts, plus a sample of the animal bone and seed evidence, were deposited in Abergwilli Museum after study.

The responsibility of primary editing and interpretation of all the specialist reports, the analysis of the site and all its evidence and then creating the excavation report which follows has fallen to its principal author. It is acknowledged that every excavator and interpreter of the past is biased by their own experience, the physical remains they recover, the culture in which they live and work and the state of knowledge at the time in which they are writing (Stocker 1992). The full detailed accounts of the excavation, area by area, plus the phased Harris matrices and the full specialist reports were assembled in 2002 into a three-volume archive level report entitled *A Welsh lord's castle of the 13th century: Dryslwyn Castle excavations 1980–1995*, by Chris Caple. Copies of which were deposited with Cadw and Abergwilli Museum. All excavation archive, including specialist reports, has been deposited at Abergwilli Museum.

1.3 PHASING

Construction and occupation activities, as recorded through the excavated contexts, were revealed in a series of Harris matrices (Barker 1979). These were created for every area (room or building) on the site. Related activities and contexts were then grouped into phases and these 'area' phases were related to a series of seven major phases (1 to 7) and 26 sub-phases (1a, 1b, 2a–d, 3a–d, 4a–d, 4a–d, 5a–d, 6a–d, 7a–d) of construction and occupation activity stretching across the site. In Phases 1 to 5, sub-phases a and c are mainly construction activity whilst sub-phases b and d

are mainly occupation activity. The dating was provided by the coins but also obtained from typological analysis of the metal objects, ceramics, glass and architectural features. Only in the final phase of writing up has the historical information been used to interpret the archaeological evidence, consequently the major siege of the castle in 1287 lies in the midst of Phase 4. This results in the Welsh lordly occupation and construction period lasting from Phase 1a to Phase 4b and the English garrison occupation lasted from Phase 4b to 6a, with the destruction of the castle occurring in Phases 6b to 6d. The full sequence is outlined in Figure 1.5 and described in detail in Sections 2.2 and 3.2.

— **Phase 1** was the initial construction of the castle, a large round tower (Round Tower D) and curtain wall forming a polygonal enclosure (Inner Ward) at the highest point on the hill.

— **Phase 2** involved the construction of a hall (Great Hall K/L) in the enclosure followed by a sequence of wooden buildings against its eastern side. A hearth to the south of the hall became a masonry kitchen building (Kitchen I) and in the angle between the curtain wall and the hall a single cell prison was constructed (Prison M).

— **Phase 3** saw the expansion of the castle with the construction of a large masonry building beside the hall (Great Chamber G) replacing the earlier wooden structures. A second ward (Middle Ward) was added to the castle, increasing its defensive capability and the volume of accommodation. A hall (Guest Hall X) and a couple of phases of buildings (Building Ya later replaced by Building Yb) were constructed against the walls of the new ward. There was extensive occupation of all these buildings.

— **Phase 4a–b** saw the redevelopment of the castle. A third ward (Outer Ward), incorporating a small gatehouse (Castle Gatehouse W), was added. The Inner Ward had a new series of apartments (Apartments I/J) constructed alongside the south side of the Great Hall K/L, which was itself altered, receiving an extra storey and lowering the level of the first floor. A chapel (Chapel H) was constructed at the south end of the Great Chamber G, which itself had an additional floor inserted. The Gateway Area B into the Inner Ward was remodelled and a new outer gateway added.

— **Phase 4b–c** incorporates the siege of 1287. The damaged castle was subsequently repaired followed by a period of occupation.

— **Phase 5** was a long period with occupation and a series of repairs. A new wooden floor was inserted into the Great Chamber G and a small new timber framed guardhouse added into the Gateway Area B.

PHASE	DATE	Castle: Inner Ward	Castle: Middle & Outer Wards & Town
1a	1220–30	Round Tower D & initial castle curtain wall	
1b		Occupation	
2a	1230–50	Great Hall K/L & dividing wall (E4)	
2b		Occupation	
2c		Kitchen I, Prison M & clay-floored buildings in Areas F & G	
2d		Occupation	
3a	1250–80	Great Chamber G & Middle Ward	Middle Ward & Welsh town
3b		Occupation & latrine (F23)	Occupation
3c			Guest Hall X
3d		Occupation & kitchen midden (F19)	Building Ya, occupation
4a	1280–87	Great Hall K/L altered, Apartments I/J, Gateway B altered	Outer Ward, Castle Gatehouse W & Building Yb. Possible town expansion & town walls & Town Gatehouse U
4b		Occupation, kitchen midden (F16)	
4c	1287–1300	Siege repairs (F2), passage into round tower (D10)	Town expansion & town walls & Town Gatehouse U in or before this period
4d		Occupation	
5a	1338–1405	Repairs to Great Hall K/L, crosswalls in I/J	
5b		Occupation	
5c		Wood frame gatehouse (B21, B22), posts in Great Chamber G	
5d		Occupation	
6a	1405–30	Decommissioning	
6b		Looting	
6c		Burning	
6d		Demolition & rubble deposition	
7a	1430–1700	Late & post-medieval activity	
7b	1430–1980	Late & post-medieval soil build up	
7c	1700–1980	Post-abandonment activity, eg animal burial	18th & 19th century visiting of the site
7d	1980–95	Excavation	

FIGURE 1.5

Dryslwyn Castle and town: phasing and dating summary

— **Phase 6** saw the decommissioning of the castle, with entrances being blocked, followed by looting and the pulling out of freestone from the walls, after a substantial fire which engulfed the whole of the Inner Ward. The castle was deliberately demolished.

— **Phase 7** includes the possible re-use/rebuilding of at least one building in the Outer Ward. Occupation continued in the town. After abandonment of the site there is evidence from the 18th century to the present day of picnicking and casual visitation to the hilltop ruins.

1.4 CASTLE STUDIES IN WALES

The state of scholarship of English castles has recently been outlined by Wheatley (2004, 4–14). She suggests that the excavation and interpretation of Dryslwyn

Castle occurs at a time when almost all masonry castles with upstanding remains in England and Wales have been identified (King 1983) and the sequence of development for the castle in England has been established (Clark 1884; Armitage 1912; Brown 1954; King 1988; Thompson 1987; 1991b; Kenyon 1990). Initial work on castles which focused on the functional, defensive qualities of remaining masonry (Stocker 1992), is now being reinterpreted as castles are increasingly seen as signifiers in a wider social and cultural context. This approach appreciates castles as devices which define lordship (Coulson 2003), are mechanisms for the display of power, wealth and status, form part of much larger physical and cultural landscapes (Johnson 2002; Liddiard 2005), constitute part of the medieval intellectual landscape (Wheatley 2004) and act as both drivers and products of economic and political development (Pounds 1990). This approach has been principally focused on 'English' castles, whether in England, Wales, Ireland or Scotland, for which there are extensive historical records and which can be readily appreciated as part of the fabric of a clearly comprehended late medieval society.

The situation for castles built by Welsh princes and lords is far less well understood (Avent 1983; Butler 2003), since there is limited historic and archaeological information. A situation which has also been noted for the castles of the native lords in Ireland (McNeill 1997). Texts from pre-14th-century Wales, such as the chronicle *Brut-y-Tywysogyon*, the Welsh law codes (Charles-Edwards *et al* 2000), literature such as the *Mabinogion* (Jones and Jones 1949), descriptions such as the *Journey through Wales* and the *Description of Wales* by Giraldus Cambrensis (Thorpe 1978) and the legal documents and letters of Welsh princes and lords (Edwards 1935; Pryce 2005), provide little meaningful information about Welsh castles. There are no building accounts for Welsh castles such as those for the Edwardian castles of North Wales (Brown *et al* 1963) and no household accounts. The Welsh texts do describe the activities in the *llys*, the traditional court of the Welsh lord and the physical structure in which it was located (Charles-Edwards *et al* 2000). Masonry castles are, however, barely mentioned in these documents since the texts derive in large part from an earlier period of Welsh history and they have a focus on traditional social structures in which the masonry castles of the 1180s–1280s do not yet have a distinctive role. In comparison to England and France, there is also a dearth of information on the nature of 12th- and 13th-century Welsh society as few contemporary documents were ever created and even fewer survive. There has been only limited advance, principally through the works of Griffiths (1994), Smith (1998), Davies (2004), and Pryce (2005), from the picture drawn of 11th to 14th century Wales by Prof R R Davies in his 1987 work *Conquest, coexistence and change: Wales 1063–1415* (reissued in paperback in 1991 as *The age of conquest: Wales 1063–1415*). Evidence from the art and literature of Wales indicates regional activity and distinctive styles that fit into wider European literary and artistic traditions (Huws 2000; Lord 2003).

Castles were undoubtedly key symbols of status and lordship for Welsh princes and lords by the early 13th century. In 1216, the *Brut-y-Tywysogyon* describes the Treaty of Aberdyfi, in which the lands of the Lord Rhys were divided up amongst his most prominent sons. Each smaller 'lordship' was described in terms of the cantrefs and commotes that formed the lordship plus a named castle. The equating of lands, lordship and a castle is unmistakable and also occurs in England and France (Coulson 2003, 205). However, as Giraldus Cambrensis observes, 'The Welsh value distinguished birth and noble descent more than anything else in the world. They would rather marry into a noble family than a rich one. Even the common people know their family tree by heart and can recite from memory the list of their grandfathers, great grandfathers, great great grandfathers back to the sixth or seventh generation.' (Thorpe 1978, 251). Thus lordship in Wales was engendered through lineage; castles were a representation and product of that lordship in the late 12th and 13th century. The limited Welsh historical sources include Iolo Goch's late 14th-century poem on Owain Glyn Dŵr's castle at Sycharth (Denbighshire) (Hague and Warhurst 1966). This initially describes the palatial nature of an aisled wooden hall behind a wide gateway surrounded by a moat but principally focuses on praising the fishponds, rabbit warren, orchard and other resources and natural advantages of the site. The only building comparison made is between a stone tower and the towers of Westminster Abbey. A similar description, focussing on the abundant natural and man made resources available at a site, is given by Giraldus Cambrensis in his late 12th-century description of the castle at Manorbier (Pembrokeshire) (Thorpe 1978, 150). Though both authors could eulogise over architecture making numerous classical or biblical references such as those seen elsewhere in English and French literature to describe castles, such as the description by Lambert of Ardres of the domus (castle) of Count Baldwin II of Guines (Coulson 2003, 73), they do not do so. This might suggest that such classical analogies were not part of the thinking of Welsh lords and their acolytes when contemplating castles. There was, however, cultural virtue in placing your castle in a location with abundant natural resources, which you then further enhanced. Awareness of other more powerful architecture, especially the Marcher castles of south Wales, is evident as Giraldus Cambrensis hesitates to describe Manorbier (Pembrokeshire) as a castle in comparison to such fortresses. The fact that wealth was displayed by even modest wooden buildings in the Wales of 1390, says much about the changes in political and economic fortune which took place in Welsh society between 1280 and 1380. Tellingly, the hall at Sycharth (Denbighshire) is described in the manner of an early medieval hall, indicative of the increasingly traditional, backward looking, cultural reference points of Welsh society by this later date. The extent of the much greater cultural confidence in the Wales of the 13th century, however, remains unclear. Since Welsh castles do not simply copy earlier Marcher forms, but develop some elements which are architecturally distinctive, it would suggest that between 1180 and 1280 some form of 'Welsh' architecture had developed, perhaps based on Welsh social structures and an appreciation of the resources of the site (Section 2.3).

Like the historical information, the physical evidence also has limitations. Welsh masonry castles are, with the exception of Ewloe (Flintshire), situated on hilltop sites, seemingly defensive locations with high visibility. Many of their physical features could be considered to have limited military effectiveness: towers which do not provide flanking fire across the walls, arrowloops which do not provide an effective field of fire, weak gateways and walls which are thin and have limited resistance to siege engines, thus they could be interpreted as merely having a 'marshal appearance'. However, it could equally convincingly be argued that these were functional defensive structures, designed to be effective against siege by the forces of neighbouring lords. They *were* clearly both attacked and defended since Carmarthenshire is one of the counties with the highest recorded instances of siege (Liddiard 2005, 71). Defences, it should be remembered, are often constructed through fear of violence, rather than an accurate and detailed appreciation of the threat.

The masonry castles built by Welsh princes and lords now lie in isolated rural locations (Avent 1983; Davis 1988); a consequence of the movement of power and people, during and after the conquest of Wales (1093–1283), to present day population centres around the ports of the north and south Wales coast. Though this potentially left most Welsh castles, such as Castell-y-Bere (Gwynedd) and Dinas Bran (Denbighshire), as substantial 13th-century remains devoid of later buildings and alterations, their remote location, ruined appearance and lack of later use led many to appear as romantic ruins, visited from the 18th century onwards and described and drawn in 18th- and 19th-century books on tours of Wales (Pennant 1773; Gastineau 1830; Black 1864). The role of these castles as visitable monuments has often determined their subsequent history. Some, such as Dolwyddelan (Conwy), were uncovered and restored in the 19th century (Avent 1994b) or amended for the ease and comfort of visitors as exemplified by the installation of the tea house at the top of the round tower at Dinefwr (Carmarthenshire) (Rees and Caple 1999, 20–21). Many were cleared in the early to mid 20th century and consolidated to improve them as legible monuments. The clearance of monuments such as Castell-y-Bere (Gwynedd) and Carreg Cennan (Carmarthenshire) continued up to the late 20th century, leaving little or no archaeological record (Butler 2003, 149; 1974, 80–81). Though a limited number, including Caergwrle (Flintshire), Dolforwyn (Powys) and Dryslwyn, survived intact to become the subject of modern excavation projects (Manley 1994; Butler 1990; 1994;1997; Webster 1987; Caple 1990b), others such as Carndochan (Gwynedd), Dinas Bran (Denbighshire) and Dinefwr (Carmarthenshire), have yet to be investigated.

Those castles which were subject to earlier excavation such as Criccieth (Gwynedd) (O'Neil 1944–45) and Deganwy (Conwy) (Alcock 1967) provided valuable but limited published information. Excavation invariably revealed complex sequences of construction with only limited stratified archaeological deposits.

It often proved difficult to relate the archaeological deposits to the associated walling sequences. Dating evidence in the form of coins, ceramic sequences and architectural fragments was scarce. Due to funding constraints excavations such as those at Dinas Emrys (Gwynedd) (Savory 1960) and Dyserth (Denbighshire) (Glenn 1915) were often of limited scale. Dating was frequently by stylistic comparison to English examples, as in the case of the gatehouse at Criccieth (Gwynedd) which was dated by comparison to those at Beeston (Cheshire) and Montgomery (Powys) castles (Avent 1983, 17; 1989, 10). Combinations of these factors have made it difficult to achieve a refined chronology for the construction of Welsh castles, especially since the construction of masonry castles occurs over such a short period between the 1180s and 1280s. Indeed much of the focus of Welsh castle studies has been to distinguish accurately between the work of the Welsh princes and subsequent Edwardian construction.

Excavation work has also been undertaken at a number of Marcher castles: Laugharne (Carmarthenshire) (Avent 1981), Loughor (Swansea) (Lewis 1994), Montgomery (Powys) (Knight 1993; 1994; 1996) and Rumney (Cardiff) (Lightfoot 1992) and there is ongoing reassessment, by Cadw, of the surviving masonry at many Marcher castles: Chepstow (Monmouthshire) (Turner 2002a; Turner and Johnson 2006), Cilgerran (Pembrokeshire) (Hilling 2000) and Kidwelly (Carmarthenshire) (Kenyon 2002). This is seeking to provide improved accuracy and dating for castle building in south Wales and the Marches.

During the excavation and subsequent post-excavation work on Dryslwyn Castle the legacy of 19th- and early 20th-century excavation of Welsh castles and its lack of detailed archaeological record has loomed large. Consequently this author has endeavoured to record the excavation in as much detail as was practical, to recover and analyse as much evidence as possible, from measuring the nails and weighing all rounded stones to analysing the pottery for organic residues and identifying tens of thousands of pieces of bone. That evidence is placed in context in this report, though the quality and quantity of the environmental evidence has resulted in a more substantial appreciation of the evidence of food production and consumption in 13th–15th-century Wales (Section 10.1). No apology is made for what may still seem to some an excess of detail. The vast majority of the books on Welsh castles frequently do little more than produce an uncritical echo of the old ideas about one tower form developing after another, or ascribe building activities to one or other of the named historical figures recorded in the *Brut-y-Tywysogyon*. What Welsh castles need is hard information and not more recycled ideas. Even serious scholars such as Roger Turvey (1997) have created complete landscapes of history filled with castles, strategies, campaigns and battles, whilst the supposed, castle remains have not even been accurately surveyed, let alone excavated or dated.

1.5 DEVELOPMENT OF WELSH CASTLES

Masonry castles were an expression of political, military, social and economic power, in built form. They were often constructed initially as one means of exercising control over a localised area and employed later as part of a wider national social and legal control system. As such, castles frequently mark the end of tribal, clan-centred society and the emergence and development of a hierarchical, centralised 'modern' state (Pounds 1990, 295). Whilst elements in a castle's design and construction may represent the taste and ideas of an individual lord or mason, they were usually built in a form that corresponds to the military and architectural thinking of the period. They were designed to defend and accommodate those who owned the castle and impress those viewing or visiting it. Individuals or societies that created such buildings must have possessed the economic resources and the constructional skills necessary to erect them, as well as the appropriate social and economic structures to maintain them and their associated military and domestic organisations. The presence and operation of masonry castles in 13th-century Wales indicates that these resources, skills and social and economic structures were all present within that society.

Following the Norman incursions into Wales during the 11th century, the Welsh learnt to adapt and use earth and wood motte and bailey or ringwork castles, for example at Cymer (Gwynedd) (Avent 1983, 4; 1992, 11; King 1988, 130). The role and influence of existing 'native' building forms, whether the rath, crannog, hillfort or *llys*, has rarely been discussed, due to a lack of evidence. McNeill (1997, 234) notes that, even after the appearance of English-built masonry castles in Ireland, with only a few exceptions the Irish kings and chieftains did not start to use castles, since substantial permanent defensive structures had no role in their society. Kings or chieftains were chosen as the member of a noble family who commanded widespread respect and support from the clan. Personal ownership of a substantial building had no part to play in this process. It is interesting to note, however, that castle-building did emerge in Welsh society.

Masonry castle construction was not utilised by Welsh princes in the 11th and early 12th centuries, despite the presence of early Norman masonry castles, such as Cardiff and Chepstow (Monmouthshire). Welsh masonry castles appear to have been constructed only from the late 12th century. Giraldus Cambrensis identifies only two Welsh masonry castles in his tour through Wales in 1188 (Avent 1983, 7), although there were almost certainly more than this. With evidence of more than 25 Welsh masonry castles

by the 1280s (Avent 1994b, 11; Davis 1988; King 1983) (Figure 2.1), it can be suggested that by the end of the13th-century Welsh society, or at least sections of it, had evolved from a clan or family basis to a more aristocratic, hierarchical system that retained personal wealth; in other words, one which had both the need and the social and economic means to construct and maintain functioning castles. The presence of well-developed 'kingdoms' (Deheubarth, Gwynedd and Powys), the proximity of feudal Marcher lordships and constant military threat, in addition to increasing economic prosperity and social development, all aided this development.

Welsh masonry castles

Welsh castles constructed by the princes and lords of Gwynedd, Deheubarth and Powys all conform to wider traditions of castle architecture in 12th- to 14th-century England. From the late 12th century, square keeps inside curtain walls began to be superseded by round keeps, for example at Conisborough Castle (South Yorkshire). Flanking towers projecting from the curtain wall also changed from the square forms, seen at Dover (Kent) and Framlingham (Suffolk), to semi-circular forms, for example at Skenfrith (Monmouthshire) (Forde-Johnston 1979, 28; Kenyon 1990, 72). The traditional keep and curtain wall castle was also superseded by castles without keeps, like Bolingbroke (Lincolnshire), where a series of towers set within a curtain wall formed a strongly defended ward. This form had evolved by the late 13th century into the classic concentric castles found at Caerphilly (Caerphilly) and Harlech (Gwynedd), in addition to the more irregularly shaped strongholds seen at Caernarfon (Gwynedd) and Conwy (Conwy) (Forde-Johnston 1979, 97).

Welsh castles, such as Castell-y-Bere (Gwynedd), Dolforwyn (Powys) and Dryslwyn, were not ersatz copies of Marcher castles. They developed distinctive architectural forms that must be seen as a response to the military and social needs of their own society. With the exception of Carndochan (Gwynedd) and Ewloe (Flintshire), they do not have the form of a central keep and surrounding curtain wall, but form an irregular, polygonal walled enclosure with a substantial tower or towers. These towers act primarily as a series of small donjons, rather than as flanking towers, since they were not positioned to provide effective covering fire for the curtain wall. Significantly, they provided domestic occupation in a defendable form and, as such, they correspond with Thompson's classification of the 'solar keep' (Thompson 1991b, 39). They also provided a 'visible permanent architectural statement of lordship in an age when the feudal lord might, in practice, be absent for most of the time' (Marshall 2002, 34)

Military service by feudal vassals in England during the 12th and 13th centuries was increasingly replaced with financial contributions (scutage), leading to the rise of professional soldiery. The corresponding evolution of military architecture, influenced by European siege warfare and the Crusades, led to large and increasingly specialised forms, culminating by the late 13th century in the concentric castle. In Wales, however, armed conflict was largely between lords and princes engaged in family feuds or fighting over landholdings. The societies of Wales, Scotland and Ireland, which retained tribal/clan and family loyalties (McNeill 1997, 234; Pierce 1972), controlled much smaller amounts of land and had smaller populations with lower levels of currency, so that castles continued to act as personal strongholds long into the 13th century.

Welsh castles probably evolved from both the traditional Welsh *llys* and Norman motte and bailey castles of the 11th and 12th centuries. The defensive circuits of the bailey and *llys* are present in the form of timber stockades or curtain walls and surrounding ditches. These protected the hall, which, as is shown by Edward's removal of the timber hall from the *llys* at Ystumgwern to Harlech Castle (Smith 1998, 235), remained the focus for social and political activity in Welsh medieval society. Activities, such as cooking, stabling and sleeping, were ranged around the hall of the *llys*, many in separate buildings (Johnstone 1999; Longley 1996). The rising level of wealth in Wales, as well as in England, in the 13th century led to an increased desire for privacy and new emphasis was placed on the construction of private chambers and apartments. The increasing utilisation of masonry in Welsh castles of the late 12th and 13th century enabled the private chambers and defensive requirement to be incorporated to form towers such as the round tower at Dolbadarn. This dual defence and accommodation role was common for mural towers in 13th century English and Marcher castles as in the case of the Martens Tower at Chepstow Castle (Turner and Johnston 2006, 151–167). In some cases private chambers and defence may have also been merged with a hall function as seen in the masonry tower-hall seen at Dolwyddelan (Conwy).

The format of the tower on the perimeter wall may derive from the earlier Norman motte-and-bailey castle forms where the first building constructed in masonry were the keeps/towers erected on the motte, such as the shell keep at Cardiff. In the case of Nevern we can see an early Welsh masonry castle incorporating a masonry tower on a Norman motte as part of its defensive perimeter (Caple forthcoming). The architecture of Welsh castles, such as Dinas Bran (Denbighshire) and Dolforwyn (Powys), clearly emphasises the importance of the tower, which would have been a culturally important symbol as well as a functional residential and defensive structure. In comparison to towers (round, square or apsidal and almost always part of the defensive circuit), gateways and low thin curtain walls have minimal visual emphasis. Most Welsh castles comprise several towers connected by a curtain wall, for example, Castell-y-Bere (Gwynedd), Dinas Bran (Denbighshire) and Dolforwyn (Powys). These towers acted as discrete foci; each may have accommodated different individuals and their families who co-operated in a joint castle defence. The hypothesis that the towers of a Welsh castle (Criccieth) were occupied by different branches of a single family clan was initially proposed by Dr Douglas Simpson (Hemp 1942, 112) who observed separate houses occupied by different branches of the same family clustered around a single farmyard, the unit system, in the late 17th century farmstead of Park Llanfrothen in Gwynedd. However, since there was no historical basis for this arrangement, Hemp was reported to have abandoned the idea (O'Neil 1944–45, 20).

Faulkner (1958) noted the occurrence of multiple suites of accommodation within a defensive wall as an emerging theme in castle architecture of England in the 14th century. As in the case of Goodrich Castle, the accommodation was often based in a mural tower with associated hall (Faulkner 1958, 224) with access to central facilities such as chapel, kitchen and stables. Dixon also noted the presence of separate households in the castles of north-western France. The idea of 'separate households' within a defensive perimeter has been present since the Iron Age hillfort, and is perhaps an obvious and rational explanation for any defended settlement with multiple suites of accommodation such as the Romano-British defended village of Din Lligwy (Anglesey).

The key question is the nature of the 'separate household' and its relationship to the owner of the castle. In a feudal society the separate households may be others of social rank such as the king, bishop or another lord and their attendant retinue, although in a family- or clan-based society this household would have been kinsmen of the lord. Social rank and kinship were often combined in an aristocracy or elite. In the case of Welsh castles, there is little evidence of fellow Welsh lords of the 12th and 13th centuries visiting and entertaining each other, consequently the presence of separate towers as suites of accommodation may be argued as demonstrating the continuing elements of the clan or family structure. In the case of castles with only one tower, such as Dryslwyn, it may suggested that only a single dominant individual or group was present within the castle when it was constructed.

Although the prime importance of towers in Welsh castles is generally accepted (Avent 1994b, 13), other interpretations for the multiple tower forms, such as hosting or performing different functions or being constructed at different times (Avent 1983), or as an indicator of wealth or prestige (Butler 2003), are also possible. No evidence of differing function has yet been produced and it has been argued that Castell-y-Bere (Gwynedd) (Butler 1974) and Dolforwyn Castle (Powys) (Butler 1997), for example, were largely built in one phase (Avent 1994b, 14).

It is interesting to note that the towers characterising the initial phases of Welsh masonry castle construction generally contained a basement, a small hall or public room at first-floor level, private rooms on the upper floors and a first-floor entrance. This arrangement is very similar to the tower-houses that were developed by the native aristocracy in 15th- to 17th-century Scotland and Ireland (Thompson 1987, 22), in addition to the keeps of 12th-century English castles. Thus, it appears to be an almost generic form of masonry castle construction developed by every society as it experimented with defensive masonry structures. It is reasonable to suggest that, as different parts of Britain developed social and economic structures at different rates, so they spawned these early masonry tower-house castles in different centuries.

Construction

The Welsh lords and princes of the 12th century perceived clear threats from each other, the English Crown and their Marcher neighbours. As a result, there were periods of relative peace interspersed with periods of armed conflict, which might have induced castle-building. The written record of the *Brut-y-Tywysogyon* (Section 2.1) indicates that there was a high level of armed conflict in 12th-century Wales in which castles were often captured. This would suggest not only that the castles were made of wood, but also that their number increased (Kenyon 1996). It was only during the late 12th and 13th centuries that they started to be built in stone, giving advantages of greatly improved defences and a significant display of power and wealth, but at high cost.

The conditions for the construction of a masonry castle are, even in the 13th and 14th centuries, a rare combination of circumstances that fulfil King's paradox of castle building: 'war supplied the need for castles, but they could only be built in conditions of peace' (King 1983, xxxix). Since walls may take several years to build, stability and control of an area must be maintained over a number of years. However, the resources and manpower available also determine the time taken to construct a castle: the keep at Scarborough (North Yorkshire) required ten seasons of work, Newcastle (Tyne and Wear) eight and Dover (Kent) nine (Rowland 1996, 155). Simple tower keeps, like Dryslwyn, could have been constructed in two or three seasons, though since the curtain wall could have been constructed simultaneously, the first castle (Phase 1) at Dryslwyn might have only taken two to three years to build. With the main defences established, internal buildings, such as the hall block and great chamber, could safely be added at a later date, giving the castle the appearance of a building site for much of its early life.

The major limitation in the creation of masonry castles was funding. A number of factors needed to be in place in order to raise sufficient funds. Firstly, the traditional dues and renders of the *gwestfa* had to be consolidated into a single financial payment (Rees 1924; Turvey 2002, 107), thereby raising taxation that provided the necessary funding for construction projects. It would have been impossible to fund a major programme of building through a stream of food renders in the form of a variety of small animals presented at irregular intervals throughout the year. Secondly, dependent towns or villages were required to provide revenue for the lord. It is no coincidence that the origins of many Welsh townships (*trefi*) can be traced to the late 12th and early to mid 13th centuries, when castles were also being constructed (Soulsby 1983, 130). Thirdly, an expansion in the use of coinage was needed, not only to enable the payment of the *gwestfa* in coin, but also to acquire easily the wide range of materials and specialist services required for castle-building. This process was started by the princes of Gwynedd and lords of Deheubarth in the early to mid 13th century (Davies 1987, 139–171), but Edward I greatly accelerated it in north Wales by paying the workers on his castles in silver coin. The money was then spent in markets and fairs in nearby towns and villages, which in turn fostered the growth of these settlements into centres of taxable wealth.

Pounds' (1990, 18) 'Wild West' model of castles as bases for hostile invaders who projected their will over the local population through the use of cavalry is clearly inappropriate for the castles of Welsh lords, who already controlled the local population. His suggestion that castles were located with regard to centres of population, securing services to support the castle and future tax revenue, and not with regard to rivers and roads, since these routeways need not be used by armed raiders, is certainly interesting (Pounds 1990, 56–57). Nevertheless, given the limited urban development in Wales, it is doubtful that Welsh castles had many large centres of population to control. All Welsh castles, with the exception of Ewloe (Flintshire), are situated on naturally defensive sites, thus, the combination of military advantage and visual prominence was almost certainly key to their location. Several examples, Dryslwyn and Dolforwyn (Powys) included, also lie within or close to major river valleys, which may have contained important routeways. Unfortunately, our lack of knowledge concerning the roads and tracks of 13th-century Wales is such that no definitive statement can be made concerning their overall relationship to communications routes. The valleys below the castles may have had greater importance for supporting agriculture than acting as routeways.

Castles in England were initially built by the Norman kings, lords and their knightly tenants in locations where they needed to control an existing town and its associated existing social, political and economic systems or an area of land (Liddiard 2005, 18). In the 11th and 12th century, Wales was still largely ruled according to tradition and codified law, overseen by minor princely families. Although often at war with each other, there was only a limited tradition of physical defences, conflict being based on open armed combat. There were few, if any, existing settlements of any great size or economic importance to dominate. Beneath the princes, who after the mid 12th century were normally termed *arglwydd* or lord (Pierce 1972, 28), there was no established class of aristocracy with sufficient wealth to develop castles. King (1983, xxxvi) confidently asserts that both princes and freemen (*uchelwyr*) who had risen to hold the title of lord (*arglwydd*) could build castles, these being primarily of earth and timber. Avent (1983, 28–36), however, suggests the princes of Gwynedd were responsible for constructing almost all the castles in north Wales. The paucity of historical documentation precludes any confident statement on this point.

The suggestion has been put forward by Avent (1983, 13) that, by the early 13th century, the princes of Gwynedd were building castles in order to mark and defend the edge of their territory. Turvey (1997, 105), meanwhile, proposes that the Lord Rhys constructed a series of castles to expand a̶ date the boundaries of late 12th-century D Davies (2004, 198–207) echoes this theory, that Welsh castles were designed only to short sieges, since they were only erected as part of a system of frontier control by major lords and princes, who would quickly dispatch a relieving force to any besieged castle. Whilst it is widely accepted that castles could be instruments of regional control, crucially it is their dating that indicates which lord had them constructed and whether at the time the region concerned had been recently annexed. The limited number of well excavated and dated Welsh castles makes any such interpretation premature. The limitations of the argument are demonstrated by Pounds (1990, 164), who suggests that Dryslwyn Castle and the castle of Newcastle Emlyn (Carmarthenshire) were outlying fortresses of the lands of Rhys ap Gruffudd, the Lord Rhys. Since these castles were not built for another 50 years, however, they are in fact quite unconnected with the Lord Rhys's control of the territory of Deheubarth.

The lack of control by the Crown over castles built in Marcher lands (Pounds 1990, 38) may have influenced Welsh lords and princes and there is no evidence of any formal controls being exercised over the construction of Welsh castles. The walls of such castles were invariably located on the break of slope that defined the top of a hill; thus, the size and shape of the hill and any associated prehistoric earthwork governed the size and shape of the castle (Kenyon 1990, 47; King 1988, 134). Both Dinas Bran (Denbighshire) and the Phase 1 castle at Dryslwyn demonstrate this point clearly. Working with the slope of the ground and using the natural defensive qualities of the site were thus inherent characteristics of Welsh castles. This was, by the mid 13th century, in marked contrast to English and Marcher castle construction, which, in response to castle sieges of the early 13th century, favoured the imposition of predetermined castle plans onto the landscape, for example at Beaumaris (Anglesey) and Caerphilly (Caerphilly).

By the 13th century, Wales was increasingly using the commote, a sub-division of the cantref, for administrative purposes. In a number of the commotes of north Wales, castles co-existed with *llys* (Longley 1996, 205), suggesting that, for a time, they fulfilled different roles. Castles represent strong defensive sites with an architecture designed to resist attack, whilst the traditional *llys* sites of Gwynedd, for example Rhosyr and Aberffraw, were lightly defended centres for the lord's court and commotal centre, with activities usually based in the hall (*neuadd*). In many commotes, however, especially those in the frontier region, it is probable that the role of commotal centre and stronghold were combined in a single site, such as at Dinefwr (Carmarthenshire), Deganwy (Conwy) and Dryslwyn. Goronwy Evans has suggested that a Norman (earth and timber) castle was present in every (Avent 1994b, 12). In the 13th- ds of Wales, this was invariably the ligham 1988, 64; King 1983, xxxvii). Given their superior defensive qualities, it is probable that castles had effectively displaced *llys* by this date in these regions. McNeill (1997, 52) argues that most of the early masonry castles of Ireland were built for administration and display and had limited expectation of serious attack. Many of the lesser elite built out-of-date motte-and-bailey castles on the same basis. The careful itemisation of the castles with their land divisions in the 1216 Treaty of Aberdyfi, as recorded in the *Brut-y-Tywysogyon*, indicates that, for the Welsh too, castles were as important as symbols of power as they were in physical reality.

Much of the success that the Welsh had previously enjoyed against the armies of English kings, such as John and Henry III, had been based on fighting using guerrilla 'hit-and-run' tactics. Lost in the vastness of the Welsh forests, English kings had found that fighting the Welsh was almost unwinable (Davies 2004, 89–111). However, the establishment of castles by the Welsh in the 13th century, together with their associated settlements, now created fixed points in the landscape, places where the wealth and power of Wales could be concentrated. As a result, it was perhaps the establishment of these castles and settlements that made Wales both vulnerable to and worthy of capture by the late 13th century. Furthermore, the emergence of professional soldiers, paid for through the financial levy (scutage), enabled Edward I to keep a professional army in the field against the Welsh 365 days a year (Morris 1901, 68). This allowed him to campaign through the year and not solely in the summer, when he was able to call upon his feudal levies. This, together with the development of towns and castles made it possible to wage a successful war against the Welsh for the first time.

The development of Welsh masonry castles, untrumpeted by written history, reflects a substantial change in the social and economic fabric of Wales: the ability to centralise and husband resources. Castles did not merely reflect this change passively, but played an active role, an agency fostering urbanism and the development of a cash economy. This made Wales worth invading and possible to hold. Urban development and masonry building ran ahead of and were part of the reason for the English invasion, rather than its consequence.

WELSH LORDSHIP PERIOD (1197–1287): HISTORICAL AND ARCHAEOLOGICAL SUMMARY

2.1 HISTORY OF THE LORDSHIP AND CASTLE OF DRYSLWYN 1197–1287

by Chris Caple and Chris Phillpotts

This chapter presents a history of the military and political activities of the lords of Dryslwyn, including their forebears and relatives. It also incorporates the principal references to the foundation and development of Dryslwyn Castle. The information has been collated primarily from two near-contemporary sources: the *Brut -y-Tywysogyon* in its various versions (*BT*) and the *Annales Cambriae* (*AC*). The *Annales Cambriae* contains sections derived from an original native Latin chronicle, which is itself thought to have been compiled towards the end of the 13th century at the Cistercian abbey of Strata Florida (Cardiganshire/Ceredigion) as a continuation of Geoffrey of Monmouth's *Historia Regum Britannie*, which has since been lost. The *Brut-y-Tywysogyon* is a 14th-century Welsh translation of the same lost chronicle.

Additional primary and secondary works provide further context and explanation for the events recorded in the chronicles, whilst the castles, towns, religious houses, cantrefi and commotes referred to below are located on Figures 2.1–2.3. The term Ystrad Tywi is used in the historical sources to refer to the middle and upper reaches of the valley of the River Tywi, above Carmarthen.

The legacy of the Lord Rhys

In the year 1197, Rhys ap Gruffudd, lord of the lands of Deheubarth, known as the Lord Rhys (*AC* 60–61; *BT* 76–78), died. He had been remarkably successful in restoring the fortunes of his principality and maintaining its integrity in the face of intermittent pressure from the Anglo-Norman Marcher lords. From his principal and ancient power centre of Dinefwr, he ruled over Ceredigion, Cantref Mawr and Cantref Bychan, together with some peripheral commotes. He achieved his success through astute and flexible diplomacy, and by establishing a working relationship with King Henry II of England in 1171–72. During Rhys' final years, his numerous sons also began to compete for power and for their shares of the inheritance, which would come to them by the Welsh principle of male partibility (Davies 1987, 120). In this system of division, descendants in the male line divided the ancestral lands into fractions, which were determined by their representation of the shares of the founding father's sons (*per stirpes*). The struggles between the Lord Rhys' sons and their descendants framed the political history of south-west Wales in the 90 years after his death. In the Tywi valley, the main competition was between two branches of the progeny of his son Rhys Gryg (Figure 2.4). One branch was descended from Rhys Mechyll and based at Dinefwr; the other comprised in succession Maredudd ap Rhys Gryg and his son Rhys ap Maredudd, who were lords of Dryslwyn. Their contest was profoundly influenced by pressure from the princes of Gwynedd and the kings of England. As lords of Deheubarth, both families would have sought to maintain a court (Charles-Edwards *et al* 2000) and band of warriors (*teulu*). Both families were conscious of their ancestry and aimed to emulate the Lord Rhys in the traditions of the court, power and landholding.

Rhys Gryg

After the death of the Lord Rhys, the feuds between his sons became murderous (Davies 1987, 224). Between 1202 and 1209, two of them, Rhys Gryg and Maelgwyn, and their nephews Rhys Ieuanc and Owain ap Gruffudd, were locked in armed struggle for the possession of all the lands and castles of Deheubarth.

FIGURE 2.1

Principal English and Welsh masonry castles of the mid to late 13th century, in Wales and the Marches (after Avent 1994b; King 1983)

Rhys Gryg mostly held Dinefwr Castle and Cantref Mawr, but spent much of his time battling with his nephews and brother over Llandovery Castle and Cantref Bychan (*AC* 66; *BT* 82–83; Lloyd 1912, 619; 1935, 160–162; Smith 1964, 263).

Llywelyn ap Iowerth brokered and enforced a settlement of the land disputes of south-west Wales in the Treaty of Aberdyfi of 1216, which apportioned the lands of the late Lord Rhys in Deheubarth amongst his most warlike sons. This process took place in the

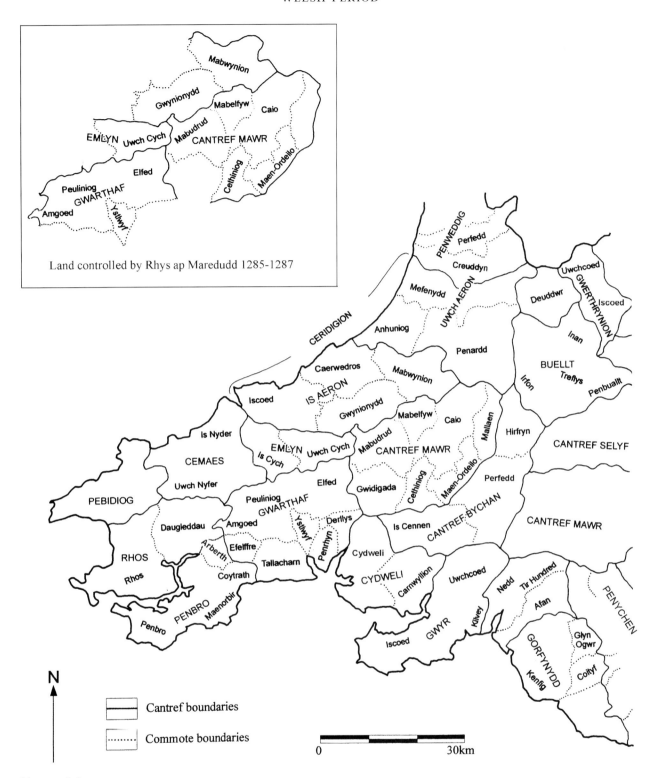

Land controlled by Rhys ap Maredudd 1285-1287

N

Cantref boundaries

Commote boundaries

0   30km

FIGURE 2.2

Principal administrative divisions (commotes and cantrefi) of west Wales in the late 13th century (after Rees 1951)

presence of his counsellors of Gwynedd and all the Welsh princes. Rhys Gryg was formally given Dinefwr Castle, Cantref Mawr and Cantref Bychan (except the commotes of Mallaen and Hirfryn, but probably including the commote of Gwidigada) and the cantref of Cydweli (consisting of the commotes of Cydweli and Carnwyllion). Maelgwyn gained the cantrefs

of Emlyn, Gwarthaf and Cemaes, Peuliniog, and the castle of Cilgerran; the castle of Llandovery with its associated commotes of Mallaen and Hirfryn; the commotes of Gwynionydd and Mabwynion; and the castle of Carmarthen. Rhys Ieuanc and his brother Owain gained the three cantrefs of Ceredigion (excluding the commotes of Gwynionydd and

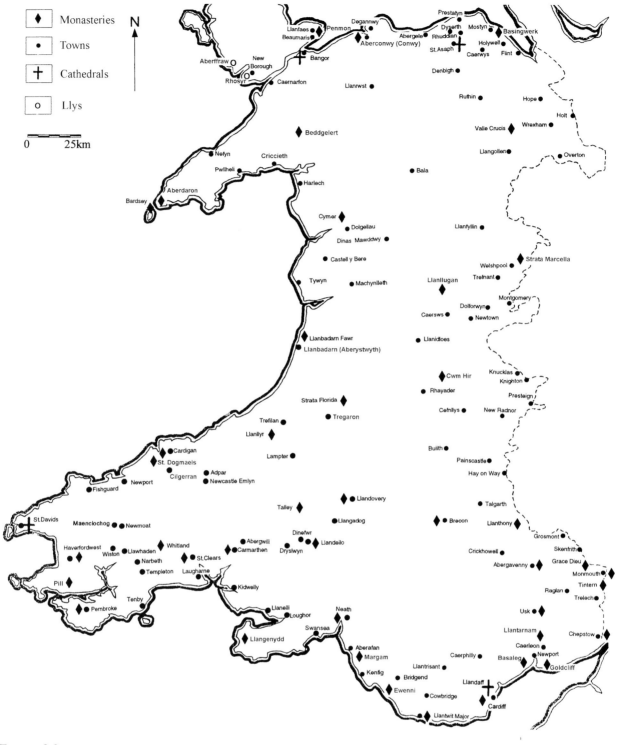

FIGURE 2.3

Principal towns and monasteries in mid to late 13th century Wales (after Soulsby 1983; Davies 1987)

Mabwynion) and the castle of Cardigan (*BT* 92; Lloyd 1912, 649; 1935, 167; Smith 1964, 264–265). This division proved to be an enduring one. When Rhys Ieuanc died in 1222, Llywelyn ap Iowerth divided his lands between his brother Owain and his uncle Maelgwyn. There is no record of any of his lands coming into the hands of his other uncle Rhys Gryg (*AC* 75; *BT* 99; Lloyd 1935, 173; Smith 1964, 265).

There is no mention of Dryslwyn in these divisions, although the other castles of the area were specifically named. Each of the three areas was centred on at least one castle. The naming of the castles in the *Brut-y-Tywysogyon* indicates that they were an important component of any inheritance and served as a status symbol for these lords of west Wales. By the early 13th century, castles must already have played a crucial role

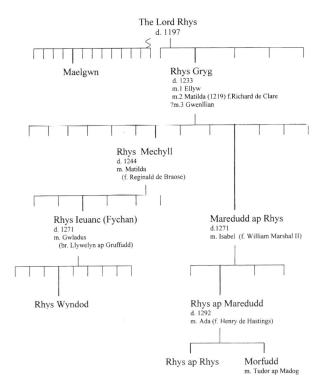

FIGURE 2.4

Genealogy of the lords of Dryslwyn (after Bartrum 1974)

in controlling and maintaining landholdings in Welsh society.

In 1219, Rhys Gryg married Matilda, daughter of Richard de Clare, Earl of Hertford (brother of Gilbert de Clare, Earl of Gloucester and Lord of Glamorgan), and the widow of William de Braose (*BT* 97; Bartrum 1974, iv R ap T 8) (Figure 2.4). Rhys' first wife, the mother of his eldest son Rhys Mechyll, must have died, leaving him free to seek an advantageous match. He was evidently of sufficient standing to marry a daughter of one of the most powerful Marcher families. After the death of William de Braose, the bulk of his estates had passed to his brother Reginald. William's widow Matilda and her son John inherited estates around Bramber (Sussex) and the Gower. Since 1216, Rhys Gryg had effectively controlled the lands of the Gower; by his marriage to Matilda, he probably sought to legitimise his occupation of them, whilst Matilda gained the effective ownership of lands to which she had only a titular claim. Any future offspring of this marriage would have a strong claim to the Marcher lordship of the Gower, leaving John de Braose with only Bramber (Altschul 1965, 30–31, 47). By Rhys' control of the Gower and the commote of Carnwyllion, his lands separated the English at Carmarthen geographically from their countrymen in Glamorgan.

In 1227, Rhys Gryg was taken prisoner by his son 'Rhys Fychan' and only released on the surrender of a castle (*BT* 101). This son must have been 18 years of age or older and therefore the issue of his first marriage. Genealogical records indicate that Rhys Gryg's first wife Ellyw was of noble Welsh stock and that they were probably married in the late 12th century. The eldest son of this marriage was Rhys Mechyll (Bartrum 1974, iv R ap T 8). This Rhys and his mother Ellyw were almost certainly the wife and son who had been held hostage in Rhys Gryg's place in 1213. Although there is little evidence for paternal or filial affection in the history of the Welsh lords and princes of the 12th and 13th centuries, some dispute must have been necessary to trigger such an event. Perhaps the son's demand for the surrender of the father's castle was the action of an insecure heir, who needed to have his own base. He may have doubted he would get his true inheritance, because Rhys had had another son by his second wife Matilda.

Llywelyn ap Iowerth campaigned throughout south Wales in 1220, confining the most powerful Marcher lord of west Wales, William Marshal, Earl of Pembroke, to his castle of Pembroke (*BT* 97; Lloyd 1935, 172–173). Between 1218 and 1220, Llywelyn compelled Rhys Gryg to return the commotes of Gwidigada, Cydweli and Carnwyllion to the English (Davies 1987). It is also possible that Llywelyn forced Rhys to return the Gower to John de Braose, who had married Llywelyn's daughter Margaret in 1219 (Lloyd 1912, 658–659). The surrender of these commotes was part of Llywelyn's fulfilment of his commitment to enforce the Treaty of Worcester (1218), in which he and the English Crown had agreed a return to pre-dispute boundaries. The enforcement of this surrender and his role in brokering the Treaty of Aberdyfi were demonstrations of Llywelyn's assumed role as overlord of all Wales, for which he sought acceptance from the king of England (Smith 1998, 23–24). Whilst they illustrate the power and pre-eminence that Llywelyn ap Iowerth wielded throughout Wales at this time, these actions are unlikely to have endeared Rhys to Llywelyn and they not only sowed the seeds of the future enmity of the Dinefwr dynasty towards the house of Gwynedd, but also provoked its subsequent collaboration with the Earls Marshal.

William Marshal II, Earl of Pembroke, returned to Wales from his conquests in Ireland in the spring of 1223 with a large army. He used it to capture Cilgerran, Cardigan and Carmarthen, which had previously been under the control of Llywelyn ap Iowerth and his allies, and appears to have annexed much of Ceredigion, although he had no legitimate claim to these territories and castles. There was an indecisive battle on the bridge at Carmarthen with the forces of Llywelyn, led by his son Gruffudd and Rhys Gryg. Both sides came into the king's peace later in the year, but were not reconciled (*AC* 75–76; *BT* 99–100; Lloyd 1912, 661, 663; 1935, 173–174). Although there was good cause for further conflict between William Marshal and Rhys Gryg, there is no record of any. Both remained powerful men with considerable economic resources, but a need for defence. Both may have been wary of the power of Llywelyn ap Iowerth and did not wish to give him a reason to return to west Wales. It is therefore likely that peace was maintained between them. William Marshal surrendered Carmarthen and Cardigan to the Crown in August 1226, acknowledging its right to them (Lloyd 1935, 176).

King John's successor, Henry III, led an expedition into Wales in 1228, but he and his army were defeated at Ceri by Llywelyn ap Iowerth (*BT* 101). This defeat reinforced the power that Llywelyn continued to wield throughout Wales. In 1231, Llywelyn, with the aid of Maelgwyn Ieuanc ap Maelgwyn and Owain ap Gruffudd, waged war through all of south and west Wales, seizing land, burning towns and capturing castles, including Kidwelly, Neath and Cardigan, which they took with catapults. Llywelyn renewed his raids in 1233, with the support of his new ally Richard Marshal, Earl of Pembroke. Rhys Gryg, Maelgwyn Ieuanc ap Maelgwyn and Owain ap Gruffudd all joined Llywelyn in ravaging south and west Wales, burning Cardiff and besieging Carmarthen for three months (*AC* 79; *BT* 102–103; Bridgeman 1876, 110; Lloyd 1912, 680; 1935, 179–80).

In 1234, the king granted Carmarthen and Cardigan back to Gilbert Marshal, who had succeeded his brother Richard, although Cardigan was still in the actual power of Llywelyn ap Iowerth (Lloyd 1935, 180).

Maredudd ap Rhys

Rhys Gryg died at Llandeilo Fawr from wounds received at the siege of Carmarthen and was buried next to his father at St David's (*AC* 80; *BT* 103; Bridgeman 1876, 110; Lloyd 1935, 180). His lands, which presumably still comprised Cantref Mawr and Cantref Bychan (except the commotes of Mallaen and Hirfryn), descended to his sons, of whom two — Rhys Mechyll (often referred to in the chronicle texts as 'Rhys Fychan') and Maredudd ap Rhys — gained substantial inheritances.

The obvious division of land between the two half-brothers would have been into the two cantrefi, plus or minus the odd commote. Certainly, later references suggest that Maredudd ap Rhys held the bulk of the lands in Cantref Mawr, whilst Rhys Mechyll and his successors held much of Cantref Bychan. It might be expected that each landholding would be centred on a castle, as in the Treaty of Aberdyfi. Presuming that Llandovery and the commotes of Mallaen and Hirfryn did not form part of Rhys Gryg's lands, no major castle was definitively recorded in Cantref Bychan by this time (there is no record of Carreg Cennan prior to 1248); the only known castle in Cantref Mawr at this date was Dinefwr. Dinefwr Castle appears to have been included in the lordship of Rhys Mechyll, who was the oldest son and therefore

received the ancient seat of power and prominence. By this time, however, there may have been a new castle at Dryslwyn to serve as Maredudd's principle seat in Cantref Mawr. Projecting backwards from the later landholdings detailed in the 1270s and 1280s, it can be suggested that Rhys Gryg's estates were distributed between his two sons as follows: Rhys Mechyll received the commotes of Caio and Maen-Ordeilo, Perfedd and Is Cennan, and perhaps also Mabelfyw; Maredudd ap Rhys was assigned the commotes of Cethiniog, Mabudrud and Gwidigada, and probably Mabelfyw (Figure 2.2). The commote of Gwidigada was later regarded as part of the Welshry lands associated with the town of Carmarthen and therefore Maredudd's hold on it was always tenuous. On his father's death, Maredudd was not yet of an age to take up his inheritance and Gilbert Marshal, Earl of Pembroke, was appointed as his guardian. Such a powerful guardian undoubtedly helped keep at bay his acquisitive and warlike brother Rhys Mechyll.

There are almost no references to Maredudd ap Rhys prior to the 1250s. A reference to Rhys Gryg and his son Maredudd in 1222, when Talley Abbey was confirmed in its rights to hold lands at Llandeilo Fawr, is almost certainly inaccurate (Griffiths 1994, 259). It is likely that Maredudd was the offspring of Rhys Gryg's second marriage to Matilda de Braose and therefore that he was born after 1219 (Smith 1998, 103 n50). Consequently, he would have been too young to receive the chroniclers' attention until the 1240s and 1250s, when he reached maturity and entered into the Welsh arena of politics and warfare.

Maredudd ap Rhys' mother was recorded as being the niece of the last Marshal Earl of Pembroke and also related to the Earl of Gloucester, the Earl of Warenne and the Earl Marshal, which indicates that she was Matilda de Braose (formerly Matilda de Clare) (Smith 1964, 266 n4; Griffiths 1966). However, Bartrum suggests that Maredudd was the son of Gwenllian, daughter of Elidir ap Owain and the third wife of Rhys Gryg (Bartrum 1974, iv R ap T 8). The important Marcher lord connections that Maredudd had throughout his life suggest it is more likely that he was closely related to some of the major Marcher families and therefore the son of Matilda, rather than a lady of the minor Welsh nobility. It is likely that Matilda de Braose survived Rhys Gryg. If so, she probably retained a settlement of land agreed in the marriage contract, perhaps consisting of the commotes of Perfedd and Is Cennan.

In order to ensure a smooth succession to his principality of Gwynedd and his overlordship of the other Welsh lords, Llywelyn ap Iowerth summoned all the Welsh lords to Strata Florida to swear fealty to his second son Dafydd in 1238 (*BT* 104). Henry III issued a mandate addressed to the barons of south and west Wales instructing them not to transfer their homage to Dafydd. The Crown was content to let Dafydd succeed to Llywelyn's hereditary lands, but not to those acquired by conquest. The addressees of this mandate included Rhys Mechyll and Maredudd ap Rhys (Smith 1964, 266; *CCR 1237–42*, 123–124). This was the first mention of the name of Maredudd ap Rhys in the historical record.

Llywelyn ap Iowerth died on 11 April 1240 and power passed to his son Dafydd ap Llywelyn, who agreed that the homages of the lords of Wales should remain to the English Crown. Since 1216, Llywelyn had exerted a level of control over the lords of Deheubarth, effectively keeping their disputes in check. On 18 June 1240, Maredudd ap Rhys performed homage to King Henry III at Westminster for his lands. Gilbert Marshal was ordered to render to Maredudd *rationabilem partem suam de terris et tenementis que ipsum contingunt de honore de Calverdin*, 'a reasonable portion of his lands and holdings which belong to him from the honour of Carmarthen'. The other lords of Deheubarth, including Rhys Mechyll, did homage a few days later for their lands as tenants-in-chief of the Crown (*AC* 82–83; *BT* 105; *CCR 1237–42*, 198; Smith 1964, 266).

Maredudd was swift to take advantage of the removal of Llywelyn's guiding hand. In late 1240 or early 1241, he occupied the lands held by his half-brother Rhys Mechyll in Ystrad Tywi and, on 7 February 1241, he was ordered by the king to appear at Woodstock (Oxfordshire) to receive justice regarding these lands. This instruction was also conveyed to Gilbert Marshal, as he was still acting as Maredudd's guardian. Smith has convincingly argued that, after the death of Llywelyn ap Iowerth, Gilbert and Maredudd acted in concert. Gilbert seized the lands around St Clears and took control of lands in Ceredigion. Walter Marshal seized the commotes of Ystlwyf and Emlyn from Cynan ap Hywel on behalf of his brother Gilbert, who then sold them to Maredudd ap Rhys for 300 marks (Bridgeman 1876, 115, 187). Maredudd subsequently held Ystlwyf under the Marshals' overlordship (*CPR 1247–58*, 63). Meanwhile, Maredudd himself seized his half-brother's remaining lands in the Tywi valley and the commote of Cydweli from Hawise de Londres. Since Gilbert already held the custody of Cardigan and Carmarthen, which included the commotes of Derllys, Elfed and Gwidigada (which he gave to Maredudd), these seizures consolidated almost all of the land on the eastern flank of his hereditary landholding under Maredudd's control. By exploiting the power vacuum created by Llywelyn's death, Gilbert and Maredudd had effectively acquired control of much of south-west Wales, with Gilbert's lands now largely shielded behind the lands of Maredudd ap Rhys (Smith 1964, 267–268; *CCR 1237–42*, 280, 348–349; *Cal Inq Misc*, i 410, no. 1443).

Subsequently, the cantref of Emlyn was formally partitioned by King Henry between Walter Marshal and Maredudd ap Rhys. Walter acquired the commote of Emlyn Is Cych with its castle of Cilgerran, whilst Maredudd retained Emlyn Uwch Cych and

constructed a new castle. This new castle of Newcastle Emlyn was sited on a long peninsular projecting into the River Teifi (Soulsby 1983, 196; Parry 1987; King 1983, 59, 561–562).

In the spring of 1241, Maredudd married Isobel or Isobella, the daughter of William Marshal II and niece of Gilbert Marshal (Bartrum 1974, iv R ap T 11). The match was probably made while Maredudd was still Gilbert's ward (Lewis 1998, 22). This marriage alliance provided mutual reinforcement for the recent bold territorial acquisitions of both Gilbert and Maredudd. In addition to helping Gilbert secure the eastern edge of the Marshal lands in Pembrokeshire, the marriage gave Maredudd powerful connections with the Marcher lords.

Gilbert Marshal died unexpectedly at a tournament in June 1241 and Maredudd lost his guardian and protector (*BT* 84). It was unlikely that Maredudd could retain the lands he acquired earlier in the year without Gilbert to support him, although he did retain the commote of Emlyn Uwch Cych and pressed on with the construction of his new castle. King Henry reclaimed Cardigan and Carmarthen from Marshal control and these towns were subsequently held for him by his seneschal, John of Monmouth (Lloyd 1935, 182). The king marched into north Wales with a substantial armed force and pushed back the borders of Dafydd ap Llywelyn's inheritance, constructing a new castle at Dyserth. The king then kept Dafydd's brother Gruffudd ap Llywelyn as a hostage in the Tower of London (*AC* 83–84; *BT* 105–106).

The following year, Maredudd was required to surrender the commote of Gwidigada, which he had acquired from Gilbert Marshal, since it was found by inquisition to belong to the king's demesne as an integral part of the royal lordship of Carmarthen (*CPR 1232–47*, 289; Daniel-Tyssen 1878, 43). This commote was transferred to the control of the new royal seneschal of Carmarthen town and castle. Maredudd was also required to give up the commote of Cydweli to Hawise de Londres (the widow of Walter de Braose), who married Patrick de Chaworth in 1243 (Lloyd 1912, 699; 1935, 183).

Rhys Mechyll died in 1244, barely eleven years after his father (*BT* 106). He was survived by his widow Matilda de Braose, to whom the protection of the Crown was extended (Lloyd 1935, 183). This Matilda was the daughter of Reginald de Braose and a niece of the Matilda de Braose who had been married to Rhys Gryg. Rhys Mechyll's eldest son Rhys Ieuanc, also known as Rhys Fychan, took over all his father's lands. He was probably only a few years younger than his uncle Maredudd ap Rhys.

Following the death of Gruffudd ap Llywelyn on 1 March 1244, his brother Dafydd ap Llywelyn rose in revolt. All the Welsh lords followed him, including Maredudd ap Rhys and Rhys Fychan. They confined the English to their castles and Dafydd and his forces burned Carmarthen (*AC* 84–85; *BT* 106; Lloyd 1912, 703n). On 27 December 1244, Richard de Clare was empowered to receive Maredudd back into the king's peace and service, offering him the promise that the king would provide him with justice in his courts about the lands which he said should fall to him by hereditary right (*CPR 1232–47*, 447). The following year, an English army commanded by Henry III came to Wales to quell the rebellion, but suffered heavy casualties as they pushed the Welsh back to the River Conwy. Henry had to content himself with reconstructing the castle at Deganwy on the eastern side of the river (*AC* 85; *BT* 107).

The rebellion lost its momentum when Dafydd ap Llywelyn died on 25 February 1246. Maredudd ap Rhys was received to the king's peace on 27 April, followed by Rhys Fychan and the other lords of Deheubarth at various dates between April and November (Smith 1964, 269; *CPR 1232–47*, 479, 485). Maredudd ap Rhys and Rhys Fychan were both confirmed in their territories: Maredudd ap Rhys retained the commotes of Emlyn Uwch Cych and Ystlwyf, as well as his commotes in Cantref Mawr, and he was recognised as Lord of Cethiniog (Lloyd 1935, 185). This settlement was brokered by the seneschal Nicholas de Molis, who afterwards led a largely Welsh and Marcher army northwards with Maredudd ap Rhys and Maredudd ap Owain to subdue the final vestiges of Dafydd's revolt. It may have been on this expedition that Dryslwyn Castle was captured for Maredudd ap Rhys by Molis. The two Maredudds dispossessed Maelgwyn Fychan of his lands, acting in the name of the king (*AC* 86; *BT* 107). It is unclear who gained control of these lands, which included the castle of Llandovery and the associated commotes of Hirfryn and Mallaen, but they were probably seized by Maredudd ap Rhys.

Court actions in 1250 show that Maredudd was certainly in possession of the commote of Cethiniog and Llandovery Castle in that year. In a surviving legal document, Maredudd was recorded as being in dispute with the Bishop of St David's over the appointment of the incumbent of the church at Llandovery. It is clear from this court case that Maredudd still had interests in the town of Llandovery and that he was willing to engage in legal actions to defend his rights (Edwards 1935, 52; Davies 1940, 19–21).

In 1248, Rhys Fychan regained the castle of Carreg Cennan, 'which his mother had treacherously placed in the hands of the French' (*BT* 108). This event confirms the presence of Rhys Fychan in Cantref Bychan, lands he had inherited from his father Rhys Mechyll. Rhys Mechyll had married Matilda or Maud, daughter of Reginald de Braose (Bridgeman 1876, 126–127; Lloyd 1935, 185; Bartrum 1974, iv R ap T 8). She survived her husband and probably retained the castle and its associated lands. She then passed them to her Braose kinsmen, an action later described by a Welsh scribe or translator as 'treacherously given to the French', a term habitually applied to any

foreigner. An alternative interpretation of the chronicle entry is that it was Rhys Fychan's grandmother, another Matilda de Braose and the widow of Rhys Gryg, who acquired these commotes on the death of Rhys Gryg and subsequently passed them to the Braose family.

In 1251, an alliance was sworn at Caernarfon between Llywelyn ap Gruffudd with his brother Owain Goch and Maredudd ap Rhys with his nephew Rhys Fychan, in which each party agreed to help and maintain the other against all living men as though they were sworn brothers (Edwards 1940, 160–161; Smith 1964, 269; 1998, 68; Davies 1987, 309). This arrangement marks the start of the relationship between Llywelyn, the emerging Prince of Gwynedd, and the lords of Deheubarth. The alliance formed part of the network of contacts and alliances that Llywelyn was developing to protect himself against the activities of the Marcher lords and the other Welsh lords as he built up his power in north Wales. Llywelyn's system of alliances was further extended and reinforced in the 1250s. His sister Gwladus married Rhys Fychan, linking the royal families of Gwynedd and Deheubarth (*BT* 112). Consequently, Rhys Fychan increased his power and reputation, expanding from his lands around Dinefwr apparently with the support of the English Crown (Lloyd 1935, 186, 187).

Following the death of Anselm Marshal in 1246 the male line of the Marshals had now failed entirely and the estates were broken up amongst co-heiresses (*AC* 86–88). After this division, there was no single powerful lord controlling and representing Marcher interests in the west of Wales. In 1254, the royal possessions in Wales, including Cardigan and Carmarthen, were granted to the Lord Edward, the 15-year-old son of Henry III (Lloyd 1935, 186). Contact was also maintained with Maredudd ap Rhys, as he was given a safe-conduct to visit Henry III at Westminster at Easter 1255 (*CPR 1247–58*, 393). It is not known if he made the trip.

By 1256, Maredudd had been ejected from what he regarded as his hereditary lands of Hirfryn, Perfedd, Mallaen, Caio, Cethiniog, Emlyn Uwch Cych and Ystlwyf through the combined efforts of Rhys Fychan and Stephen Bauzan, the Lord Edward's officer in south-west Wales (*AC* 91; Smith 1998, 92). Left landless, he went north to assist Llywelyn ap Gruffudd in regaining the lands of Meirionydd and Perfeddwlad (Rees 1951, plate 28) in north and mid Wales from Edward, who had been taxing the local people so heavily that they had appealed to Llywelyn for aid (Lloyd 1912, 717; Smith 1998, 85). In return, Llywelyn's forces were instrumental in the reinstatement of Maredudd in both his own territory and the lands of Rhys Fychan, which he claimed by hereditary right (*AC* 91; *BT* 110). Together, these probably comprised the whole of Cantref Mawr and Cantref Bychan, reconstituting the lordship of Ystrad Tywi, to be ruled from the castle of Dinefwr. His nephew Rhys Fychan was expelled and fled to England (Smith 1964, 269–270; 1998, 91–93; Griffiths 1994, 260). Maredudd was now a powerful lord equipped with an effective alliance with Llywelyn ap Gruffudd, currently the most powerful lord in Wales. These actions were undertaken under the terms of the agreement made between them in 1251.

The alliance was employed with deadly effect in the spring campaign of 1257. Llywelyn ap Gruffudd, Maredudd ap Rhys and Maredudd ap Owain captured much of southern Powys, burned Welshpool and threatened the upper Severn valley, before raiding as far south as the Gower peninsula (Smith 1998, 94–95). On 31 May, Rhys Fychan, together with a number of English nobles and an army of approximately two thousand men led by Stephen Bauzan, marched up the Tywi valley in an attempt to recapture the castle of Dinefwr. The objective of the expedition was to reinstate Rhys in the territory in which Llywelyn had installed Maredudd ap Rhys. This army was defeated on 2 June by Welsh forces, led by Maredudd ap Rhys and Maredudd ap Owain, in a running fight, which commenced at Llandeilo Fawr and continued through Coed Llathen to Cymerau (the positions of the last two locations are uncertain). Most of the English soldiers and many Welshmen were killed. Amongst the casualties was Stephen Bauzan (*AC* 92–95; *BT* 110–111; Lloyd 1912, 720–721; 1935, 188–189; Griffiths 1994, 260; Lewis 1998, 23–25; Smith 1998, 97–99). This was a considerable victory for the Welsh and a significant defeat for the English. Following the troubles of the 1230s and the defeat of Henry III at Ceri, it perpetuated the idea that it was difficult to defeat the Welsh by force of arms, as King Edward I was never to forget the death of his captains at Cymerau (Davies 1987, 355).

Rhys Fychan deserted the English camp before the decisive battle and presented himself at Dinefwr Castle, so saving his own fortunes (*AC* 94; *BT* 111). He was subsequently reconciled with Llywelyn ap Gruffudd and Maredudd ap Rhys, but his change of sides created a challenging dilemma for the alliance between them. It is probable that he regained some of his lands from his uncle Maredudd at this point, including Dinefwr Castle, almost certainly at Llywelyn's insistence (Smith 1964, 270; 1998, 99–100, 107; Griffiths 1994, 261). The fact that Rhys was Llywelyn's brother-in-law may have had some bearing on the decision. There had been a previous enmity between Maredudd and his half-brother Rhys Mechyll as a result of the uneven distribution of their father's lands in 1233 and this feud was undoubtedly fuelled by later conflicts between Maredudd and his nephew Rhys Fychan (Smith 1998, 92). However, from 1257 onwards, Maredudd and his son Rhys were firm in their belief that they were the rightful lords of the whole of Cantref Mawr by conquest and by law. All of their subsequent actions were governed by their desire to regain control of this inheritance; their future relationship with

Llywelyn ap Gruffudd was therefore poisoned by the return of part of these patrimonial lands to Rhys Fychan, which he enforced in this year. Llywelyn probably took Maredudd's son Rhys hostage at this time in order to guarantee his cooperation.

Following the defeat at Coed Llathen/Cymerau, and probably in response to it, Henry III marched into Wales with an army, but stopped at Deganwy, having advanced just far enough to remind Llywelyn ap Gruffudd of his power, and then retreated. A second army, under Richard de Clare, maintained a presence in Glamorgan to check any advance from the Welsh forces in Deheubarth, who were commanded by Maredudd ap Rhys and Rhys Fychan (*BT* 111; Lloyd 1912, 721–722; Prestwich 1988, 18; Smith 1998, 101–102, 104–105). The English Crown made fewer military interventions in Welsh affairs after this date, appearing to regard it as too dangerous, costly and unrewarding to send armies into Wales.

In the late summer of 1257, the Crown sought to undermine Llywelyn's power and position by purchasing the loyalty of Maredudd ap Rhys. Discussions were held between Maredudd and his cousin Richard de Clare, Earl of Gloucester, during September (Smith 1998, 103–105). He was pardoned by the Crown and confirmed in his title to the commotes of Gwynionydd (formerly held by Maredudd ap Owain) and Perfedd (formerly held by Rhys Fychan) on 4 September (*CCR 1256–59*, 91; *CPR 1247–58*, 577). He was received back into the king's peace on 18 October, paying homage and swearing fealty to the king in London. He was then confirmed in his existing lands, specified as the commotes of Mallaen, Hirfryn, Perfedd and Is Cennen. Additionally, he was granted the commotes of Mabwynion and Gwynionydd, together with the lands of Rhys Fychan, specified as the commotes of Mabudrud, Mabelfyw, Caio, Cethiniog and Maen-Ordeilo, with the castles of Dinefwr and Carreg Cennen (these lists of landholdings appear to have been drafted the wrong way round in the English Chancery). His total landholding potentially comprised the whole of Cantref Mawr and Cantref Bychan (excluding the commote of Gwidigada, which was considered as part of the demesne of Carmarthen), plus the commotes of Emlyn and Ystlwyf. These widespread lands included the castles of Dinefwr, Dryslwyn, Llandovery, Carreg Cennan and Newcastle Emlyn. The Crown also agreed not to receive Llywelyn ap Gruffudd into the king's peace until his son Rhys ap Maredudd had been released; and neither Maredudd ap Owain or Rhys Fychan would be received into the king's peace without Maredudd's counsel (*AC* 96; Bridgeman 1876, 135; Smith 1964, 270; *CPR 1247–58*, 577, 582; *CChR 1226–57*, 475). The Crown was not in a sufficiently powerful position in west Wales to implement the territorial aspects of this bargain (Smith 1998, 106–107). Nevertheless, the promise had been made and, from this time onwards, Maredudd and later his son Rhys invariably took sides with the English Crown against the princes of Gwynedd.

The defection of Maredudd to the English Crown was initially regarded as a secret, although rumours of it impelled Llywelyn ap Gruffudd to a response. Later in October, he imprisoned Maredudd and also kept his son hostage. This suggests that Llywelyn was well aware of Maredudd's discussions with the English Crown, although he may have been unaware of the details of the agreement that had been reached (Smith 1998, 107 n65). Maredudd was still at the court of Llywelyn ap Gruffudd on 18 March 1258, when he was a party to a treaty between Scotland and Wales, devised by Llywelyn as part of the establishment of Wales as a separate and united nation state (Smith 1998, 111–112). Llywelyn began to use the title 'Prince of Wales'. On 26 April, all the lords of Wales gave their oaths of allegiance to Llywelyn under pain of excommunication (Lloyd 1912, 723–724). This was an oath of full feudal homage and fealty and indicates the power that Llywelyn now wielded. As part of this agreement, Llywelyn provided Maredudd with unique guarantees regarding his rights in return for his fealty and homage. He agreed never to imprison Maredudd, nor to take his son hostage, nor to take possession of his castles. This emphasises the importance that Llywelyn attached to gaining Maredudd's homage; it is likely that Maredudd's only motivation in paying the homage was to obtain the release of his son (Edwards 1940, 168–169; Smith 1964, 271; 1998, 107–108, 115, 297–298). The deal also underlines the importance of the possession of castles as guarantors of lordship.

Although Henry III had been planning to renew his campaign in north Wales, a dispute with his barons caused him to conclude a truce with Llywelyn on 17 June 1258, which was renewed several times in the succeeding years, thus perpetuating the status quo and leaving Llywelyn in control of his gains (Lloyd 1935, 191; Smith 1998, 118–120). However, by mid-summer, Llywelyn had become fully aware of Maredudd's agreement with the English Crown and marched into Deheubarth with an army, accompanied by Maredudd ap Owain and Rhys Fychan. They occupied Maredudd's lands, although they may not have taken control of his castles (Bridgeman 1876, 136–137). Their troops were hunting for Maredudd, who fled to Kidwelly and the protection of Patrick de Chaworth, seneschal of Carmarthen. Later in the summer, Llywelyn's brother Dafydd ap Gruffudd returned with the army and won a skirmish against the forces of Chaworth and Maredudd (Smith 1998, 108). In September, there was a meeting under a flag of truce between Maredudd ap Rhys (accompanied by Chaworth), Maredudd ap Owain, Rhys Fychan and Dafydd ap Gruffudd in an attempt to resolve the dispute. This meeting ended in conflict and Chaworth was killed (*AC* 96–7; *BT* 111–112; Lloyd 1912, 725; 1935, 192). Maredudd was said to have disturbed

all Wales by his treachery. He was back in Llywelyn's custody by the end of the year (Smith 1998, 121).

At a meeting at the ford of Montgomery on 25 November 1258, the representatives of Henry III demanded the return of Maredudd ap Rhys, but Llywelyn would not accede to this request (Lloyd 1935, 192). Late in 1258, Maredudd's brother Hywel ap Rhys did homage to Llywelyn for the commote of Mabelfyw, indicating that Llywelyn had now confiscated Maredudd's lands and was granting them to others (Edwards 1940, 45). On 28 May 1259, Maredudd was tried and convicted on a charge of treachery (*infidelitas*) at Llywelyn's court, held at Arwystli (Davies 1987, 254, 316; Smith 1964, 271; 1998, 298). He was then imprisoned at Criccieth Castle until Christmas, when he was released, although his son was held hostage in his stead (Johns 1970, 5). His lands were entirely expropriated and he was required to surrender the castles of Newcastle Emlyn and Dinefwr (almost certainly an error for Dryslwyn) and the adjacent commotes of Emlyn Uwch Cych and Maen-Ordeilo (*AC* 97; Lloyd 1912, 725–726; 1935, 192; Smith 1964, 271). The English king had no power to prevent this treatment to his ally and vassal, underlining the degree of control that Llywelyn ap Gruffudd exercised during this period in both west and north Wales. On 25 June, Llywelyn concluded a truce extension with the English Crown (*AC* 99). This left him free to exercise control over all the 'Welsh' areas of Wales.

It has been suggested that Maredudd remained imprisoned at Criccieth until December 1261 (Smith 1998, 121). At this date, Llywelyn ap Gruffudd imposed further terms on Maredudd, who had dared to 'withdraw from the prince's unity' and was only now readmitted to his 'peace and benevolence'. Maredudd and all his forces were required to serve Llywelyn unreservedly in fighting his enemies in south Wales. He was also required to consult with Maredudd ap Owain regarding joint action to recover his father Owain's inheritance in west Wales and to comply with a series of details regarding military cooperation with Rhys Fychan. In return, Maredudd was restored to his lands of Cethiniog, Mabudrud, Mabelfyw and Gwidigada and his title to them was confirmed (Edwards 1940, 104–105; Smith 1964, 268, 271; 1998, 293, 299; Davies 1987, 311, 319). Llywelyn also required a further 24 hostages from Maredudd as a surety for his good behaviour (Prestwich 1988, 172). The consistent antagonism that Maredudd and his son Rhys later displayed towards Llywelyn ap Gruffudd stemmed from this conflict and the humiliation it inflicted upon them. The demeaning nature of these terms contrasts the relative power of Llywelyn with the impotent plight of Maredudd at this time.

In 1262, upon rumours of the death of Llywelyn ap Gruffudd, the English Crown ordered the Marcher lords to ensure that Maredudd and the other lords of Deheubarth did not perform homage to his son Dafydd ap Llywelyn (*CCR 1261–64*, 142–144; Smith 1964,

272; 1998, 137–138). This order was reminiscent of the events of 1238. However, Llywelyn had not died and the following year he invoked the conditions of armed support he had imposed in exchange for Maredudd's release in 1261. In March 1263, Maredudd participated in skirmishes in the Usk valley and the lordship of Abergavenny in the south-eastern March (Edwards 1935, 52; Smith 1964, 272; 1998, 151–152). This was probably at the behest of Llywelyn, since there was no other obvious reason for Maredudd's involvement.

In the war that followed over the next two years between Henry III and his barons, Llywelyn ap Gruffudd sided with the barons. He used this excuse to capture the royal castle of Deganwy, but refrained from sending Welsh troops to aid Simon de Montfort and the baronial forces at the Battle of Evesham (*AC* 101; *BT* 113). An accord in the form of an exchange of letters patent was reached in 1265 between Llywelyn and Henry III, whilst he was in the power of Montfort. For a fee or fine of £20,000, Henry granted Llywelyn the 'lordship of the barons of Wales' (*magnates Wallie*) (Smith 1998, 167).

Shortly afterwards, Henry attempted to persuade Maredudd ap Rhys to challenge the power of Llywelyn in west Wales. In September 1265, he was confirmed by the English Crown in all the lands granted to him by the king in 1257 (Edwards 1940, 107; Smith 1964, 272). This confirmation and the instruction of 1262 show that, although the English Crown realised that in practice Maredudd was bound in allegiance to Llywelyn ap Gruffudd, the lure of obtaining his patrimony in Cantref Mawr and Cantref Bychan might persuade him to break with the prince of Gwynedd.

In the Treaty of Montgomery of September 1267, sworn in front of a papal legate, Henry III accepted Llywelyn ap Gruffudd as 'Prince of Wales' for a fee of 25,000 marks (Lloyd 1912, 739). This title was almost certainly conceded by Henry because he needed the money and possibly because of the restraint that Llywelyn had shown in the baronial war. As an adjunct of this title, Llywelyn was to receive the homage of all the lords of Wales, except Maredudd ap Rhys; he alone was exempted and still owed his fealty directly to the king. Llywelyn was given the option of buying his homage later. As part of the treaty, Llywelyn also agreed that Maredudd should be restored to his former territories (Edwards 1940, 2; Lloyd 1935, 194; Smith 1998, 180–182). This might suggest that Maredudd gained control of the commotes of Emlyn Uwch Cych, Ystlwyf, Cethiniog, Mabudrud, Mabelfyw and Gwidigada. In 1268, he held a barony of two and a half commotes from Edmund, Earl of Lancaster's lordship of Carmarthen (Smith 1998, 182 n165, from Longleat MSS 268). Several reasons may be advanced for the conclusion of this treaty. The need for unity in the kingdom following the damaging baronial conflicts was probably paramount. The treaty ensured that Llywelyn would not support any future baronial opposition to the king, it provided funding for the impoverished English Crown, it regularised the agreement of 1265 about the lands of Maredudd, and it provided the papal legate Ottobuono with a peace-making achievement (Smith 1998, 185–186).

In 1270, Henry III acquired further potential funds from Llywelyn by selling him the homage of Maredudd ap Rhys for 5,000 marks, as foreseen in the Treaty of Montgomery (*CPR 1266–72*, 457). Llywelyn had been keen to acquire Maredudd's homage since 1267 and the high price reflects the value he placed on it. This sale was urged on the king by his son Edward, who needed the money to help fund a pilgrimage to the Holy Land (Edwards 1935, 209–210; Smith 1998, 348–349, 410). The money may never have been paid, however. Against the background of the enmity that existed between Maredudd and Llywelyn, Maredudd probably felt the transaction to be both a great indignity and an act of betrayal by the English Crown.

The origin of Dryslwyn Castle

Under the year 1227, the *Brut-y-Tywysogyon* records that Rhys Gryg was seized at 'Llanarthnau' by his son 'Rhys Fychan' and was only released when he had surrendered the castle of Llandovery to his son (*BT* 101). Although the name 'Rhys Fychan' was used, this was an error for Rhys' son Rhys Mechyll; it was Rhys Mechyll's son who was called Rhys Fychan. This nomenclature occurs several times in the various versions of the *Brut-y-Tywysogyon*.

There are a number of possible interpretations of this annal. Since there is no record of Rhys Gryg owning the castle of Llandovery (part of Maelgwyn's share in 1216), it is possible that the name of the castle is incorrectly recorded. It is conceivable that Rhys was seized at a new castle at Llanarthney, which might have been Dryslwyn Castle, for it is barely 4km to the east. As the name Llanarthney was unfamiliar to the author of *Brut-y-Tywysogyon*, he may have substituted the nearest known castle name of Llandovery. If this interpretation of the passage is accepted, it is the earliest reference to Dryslwyn Castle. This would place its initial construction between 1216 and 1227 and most probably between 1223 and 1227, after the loss of Carmarthen to William Marshal and subsequently to the English Crown.

It may have been the birth of Maredudd ap Rhys in the 1220s that provoked Rhys Mechyll's kidnap of his father in 1227. The knowledge that he would have to divide the inheritance of his lands into two parts by the rule of partibility may have inspired Rhys Gryg to construct a new castle at Dryslwyn in Cantref Mawr, so that each of his sons could both receive and retain their separate inheritances. By the early 13th century, it was the expectation of any major Welsh lord that his landholding should be centred on a castle. A son of Rhys Gryg and Matilda de Braose would expect to gain a substantial inheritance with a castle; a presumption reinforced by Matilda's connections to the de Clares and other prominent Marcher families. Since there are references to Maredudd ap Rhys as lord of Dryslwyn from the 1250s onwards, this castle was almost certainly the focus of his inheritance from his father, surrounded by associated lands on the western side of Cantref Mawr.

The castle of Dryslwyn was first mentioned by that name in the one version of the *Annales Cambriae* under the year 1245 or 1246, when the seneschal of Carmarthen laid siege to the castle, to regain it for its rightful owner (*AC* 86). If this siege was undertaken before 1 November, this seneschal must have been John of Monmouth; if it was after that date, the reference was to Nicholas de Molis. This confirms that a substantial castle had been constructed at Dryslwyn by this date. It was probably garrisoned by Maredudd as part of the final actions of Dafydd ap Llywelyn's rebellion, although there are no specific details as to who held it, or whom the seneschal regarded as the rightful owner. From this point onwards, it became the subject of frequent dispute between Maredudd ap Rhys and Rhys Fychan (Smith 1964, 269).

Rhys ap Maredudd

On 6 August 1271, Maredudd ap Rhys died in his castle of Dryslwyn and was buried in front of the high altar of Whitland Abbey (*BT* 116). This statement in the *Brut-y-Tywysogyon* definitively connects Maredudd with the possession of Dryslwyn. His burial at Whitland (a Cistercian monastery founded by King John and supported by the Lord Rhys), rather than at Strata Florida or another Welsh religious foundation, was symbolic of his political position straddling the societies of the native Welsh dynasties and the English Marcher lords. He was succeeded by his son Rhys ap Maredudd. It is reasonably certain that Rhys inherited the castle and town of Dryslwyn, together with the commotes of Cethiniog and Mabudrud (Smith 1964, 272). He probably also retained the commotes of Emlyn Uwch Cych and Ystlwyf, although there is no extant evidence for this. The commote of Mabelfyw, part of Maredudd's confirmed lands in 1261, was in the possession of Rhys Wyndod by 1277 and had probably been lost by Maredudd in the turbulence of 1258 and not returned, although this return had been implied by the terms of the Treaty of Montgomery. The commote of Gwidigada had probably been under the control of the seneschal of Carmarthen since 1242, although it may have been reincorporated into Maredudd's landholding after the conflict of 1257, but it is unlikely that he retained or acquired it in the 1260s. Rhys ap Maredudd also inherited his father's ambition for the renewed lordship of all of Ystrad Tywi and his resentment towards Llywelyn ap Gruffudd.

Three weeks after the death of Maredudd, on 27 August 1271, Rhys Fychan died in his castle of Dinefwr and was buried in Talley Abbey (*BT* 116). His son Rhys Wyndod inherited Dinefwr and the bulk of his father's lands, including the commotes of Maen-Ordeilo, Mallaen, Caio, and Mabelfyw (Smith 1964, 272). A second son, Llywelyn ap Rhys, became lord of the commote of Is Cennan and presumably master of Carreg Cennan Castle. The commotes of Is Cennen and Perfedd did not figure in the later disputes between Rhys ap Maredudd and Rhys Wyndod, although Rhys Fychan (presumably Rhys Wyndod) was cited as holding the commote of Perfedd in a court case of 1279. They were therefore not regarded as part of the disputed inheritance of Rhys Gryg, but as the separate inheritance of Llywelyn ap Rhys (Bridgeman 1876, 179–180; Bartrum 1974, iv R ap T 8).

In England, Edward I succeeded his father Henry III as king in 1272. Edward was in a stronger position as king than his father and was determined to avenge the political and military humiliations of his father's reign (Prestwich 1988, 170). In Wales, it was the attitude of Llywelyn ap Gruffudd to the new king, which precipitated the conflict. He failed to do homage to Edward in 1275. Consequently, Edward declared Llywelyn a rebel in November 1276 and prepared to invade Wales the following year.

In the spring of 1277, Pain de Chaworth, the commander of the royal forces in west Wales, and John Giffard moved their forces into Ystrad Tywi, but before the military hostilities commenced, diplomatic preparations were made. Following lengthy discussions and an exchange of letters between the king and Chaworth during March, on 11 April 1277 Rhys ap Maredudd came to terms with the English Crown, although an outline agreement had already been reached at Carmarthen before 21 March (Edwards 1940, 36–37, 48; 1935, 55–56, 71–72; Smith 1964, 281–282; 1998, 419–421; Griffiths 1966, 122; Prestwich 1988, 176–177). This negotiated agreement confirmed Rhys in his existing landholding and ownership of Dryslwyn Castle and promised judicial consideration of his claim to the lands and castle of Rhys Wyndod (the commotes of Maen-Ordeilo, Mallaen, Caio and Mabelfyw, with Dinefwr Castle) if they should come into the king's hands, in fulfilment of the promise made to his father by Henry III. He was no longer to do homage to the 'Prince of Wales', but directly to the king, and he was to be answerable only in royal courts. In return, Rhys granted the English forces the right to march through his lands unhindered and they were permitted entry into his castles. This document was witnessed by notables, including the Bishop of St David's (Lloyd 1935, 197; Smith 1964, 273). This was a carefully negotiated settlement exclusively concerning Rhys ap Maredudd.

It is probable that, because Rhys had come early into the king's peace and because of the preceding agreement made with Pain de Chaworth and the long-standing arrangement with his father Maredudd, the king granted him the commotes of Maen-Ordeilo and Mabelfyw (Griffiths 1966, 123 n10). This increased Rhys' landholding and income, but it was a long way short of what he wanted and expected, namely the honouring of his father's full title to the whole of Cantref Mawr and Cantref Bychan. The extent to which the king could reward Rhys ap Maredudd was limited by the swift accession of Rhys Wyndod to the king's peace and a subsequent settlement with Llywelyn.

The other principal Welsh lords of Deheubarth, Rhys Wyndod and the brothers Gruffudd and Cynan ap Maredudd ap Owain quickly followed Rhys' lead and surrendered to the Crown on 24–25 April, although they did so without negotiated settlements. They were 'stumbling over one another in their anxiety to turn surrender to the English into a means for furthering their ambitions at the expense of other members of their own family' (Davies 1987, 333). Rhys Wyndod retained the commotes of Mallaen, Caio, Hirfryn, Perfedd and Is Cennen. On 1 July, Rhys ap Maredudd, Rhys Wyndod, Gruffudd and Cynan ap Maredudd ap Owain all rendered their homage to Edward I at Worcester (*BT* 118; Griffiths 1966, 123; Prestwich 1988, 177). The Treaty of Aberconwy, signed by Llywelyn ap Gruffudd in November, ensured that these lords of Deheubarth would all continue to swear fealty directly to the king (Prestwich 1988, 180–181). This greatly reduced Llywelyn's power, effectively reducing him to the lordship of Gwynedd, despite his retention of the title 'Prince of Wales'. The loss of Deheubarth, largely stemming from Rhys ap Maredudd's change of allegiance, and the loss of military control of mid Wales, following the fall of Dolforwyn Castle, were the key factors in Llywelyn ap Gruffudd's loss of his principality.

Rhys Wyndod's surrender had placed his lands in the hands of the Crown. On 5 June, Pain de Chaworth was ordered to retain in the king's possession the castle of Dinefwr, together with the castles of Llandovery and Carreg Cennan (*CPR 1272 81*, 212). This was an instance of Edward's policy of controlling the Welsh through the occupation of existing castles, even where the surrounding lands were returned to the native rulers (Davies 1987, 337, 339). Elsewhere in north and mid Wales, there were fewer Welsh castles and they were not in locations so useful to the English Crown; Edward therefore had castles such as Llanbadarn and Rhuddlan built at appropriate locations. It is unclear whether Rhys Wyndod received a royal pardon immediately after the end of the rebellion of 1277, with reinstatement in his lands of Caio, Mallaen and Hirfryn, or if he had to wait until 1279 (Bridgeman 1876, 161; Griffiths 1966, 123). Whichever is correct, Rhys Wyndod would undoubtedly have felt highly aggrieved at losing his castle to the Crown in 1277, depriving him of a central stronghold from which to control his much-reduced landholding. In May 1278, Rhys Wyndod, Gruffudd and Cynan ap Maredudd ap Owain were present with other Welsh nobles at the court of Llywelyn ap Gruffudd at Dolwyddelan, indicating their continuing loyalty to the Prince of Wales. Rhys ap Maredudd, however, was absent, remaining loyal to the English king (Edwards 1940, 43; Davies 1987, 343).

The acquisition of Dinefwr Castle meant that the king now held demesne lands in Carmarthenshire. Under the terms of the agreements with the king of 1246 and 1277, Rhys was henceforward obliged to answer on legal matters in the county court. In July, Pain de Chaworth implemented the agreement of 1277 and asserted the royal right of entry into Dryslwyn Castle (Griffiths 1966, 123–124). On 7 January 1278, the king issued an order that Rhys ap Maredudd and his men were not to be troubled for any trespass that they might have committed prior to their admission to the king's peace (*Cal Chancery Rolls Various* 161; Davies 1940, 41). This effectively wiped the slate clean for Rhys in return for his support in 1277. As part of Edward's policy of improving his access and control in Wales, Rhys and several other Marcher and Welsh lords were required in this month to widen the roads by tree clearance, in his case between Carmarthen and Brecon (Bridgeman 1876, 159; Davies 1940, 40; Davies 1987, 339). On 10 January, Edward re-established the king's courts and justices to hear all disputes. These had been in abeyance since Llywelyn's rise to power in 1258. Both Welsh and Marcher lords appeared before these courts and received English royal justice (*Cal Chancery Rolls Various* 163, 171; Edwards 1940, 199; Davies 1987, 340).

On 8 November 1279, Rhys ap Maredudd was accused of seizing lands in Caio that were also claimed by Hywel and Rhys ap Gruffudd. Justices were appointed to resolve the conflict (Davies 1940, 94). It is clear that Rhys was continuing the attempt to increase his landholding, but without success. In June 1280, Edward I annexed the commote of Maen-Ordeilo from Rhys, in order to provide financial support for the royal castle of Dinefwr. Rhys was supposed to be compensated by receiving other lands in Carmarthenshire (*Cal Chancery Rolls Various* 182, 185; Smith 1964, 273; Davies 1987, 339–340). On 1 May 1281, Goronwy Goch, currently serving as Rhys' constable of Dryslwyn Castle, witnessed a grant of land at Brechfa to Rhys from Talley Abbey (Griffiths 1972, 279). This strengthening of his links with Talley may be related to the lands he was to obtain in compensation for relinquishing Maen-Ordeilo.

In June 1281, Robert de Tibetot was appointed Justiciar for West Wales. Tibetot had been one of Edward's household knights before his accession to the throne and so he doubtless arrived with both personal and professional royal support (Griffiths

1972, 91). Tibetot has been described as 'an assertive personality and an efficient administrator' (Griffiths 1966, 129), or more simply as 'powerful and ruthless' (Davies 1987, 366). As the king owed money to him for war expenses dating from 1282, Tibetot was allowed to collect the revenues of west Wales, as well as being its justiciar, thereby making him virtually its viceroy. The actions of Tibetot over the next few years, and the reactions to them of Rhys ap Maredudd, were to draw them into a destructive collision course.

Following his brother Dafydd's capture of Hawarden Castle, Llywelyn ap Gruffudd was drawn into another war against Edward I in 1282. Rhys Wyndod, Gruffudd and Cynan ap Maredudd ap Owain, together with many other Welsh lords, supported Llywelyn. Rhys ap Maredudd was the only lord of west Wales to support the English king. On 26 March, Llywelyn's troops ravaged the Tywi valley, capturing the castles of Llandovery and Carreg Cennen and badly damaging the latter (Lloyd 1935, 199; Prestwich 1988, 182). Whilst these forces may have been commanded by Dafydd ap Llywelyn, it is more likely that the local lords Rhys Wyndod, his sons Gruffudd and Llywelyn, and Gruffudd and Cynan ap Maredudd ap Owain played the major role in this raid (*AC* 106; *BT* 120; Smith 1964, 275). On 16 and 17 June, these forces successfully ambushed an English relief column commanded by Earl Gilbert at Llandeilo Fawr; many were killed, including William de Valence the Younger. This defeat caused considerable concern to the English Crown, but Llywelyn's forces subsequently retreated. On 28 July, Rhys ap Maredudd was granted the commotes of Mabwynion and Gwynionydd, previously the property of Gruffudd and Cynan ap Maredudd ap Owain, in addition to the commotes of Mallaen and Caio, formerly the property of Rhys Wyndod (Edwards 1940, 165–166; *Cal Chancery Rolls Various*, 236–237). During August, armies of English and Marcher forces approached Ystrad Tywi from Brecon and Carmarthen to support Rhys, whose forces played an active part in taking control of the region. On 17 August, Rhys' men were financially rewarded for their fighting at or near Llangadog by William de Valence, Earl of Pembroke, who was commanding the royal forces in west Wales and who was related to Rhys by marriage (Smith 1998, 523–525). In August or September, Rhys cooperated with Robert de Tibetot and Pain de Chaworth in a surprise night attack on Gruffudd and Cynan ap Maredudd ap Owain at Trefilan (Edwards 1935, 132; Prestwich 1988, 190). The rebels escaped, but Rhys and his allies captured cattle and released prisoners. Local skirmishes of this sort were typical of much of the action of the Welsh Wars, but Rhys' participation demonstrates his commitment to the cause of the English Crown.

The rebellion effectively ceased after Llywelyn ap Gruffudd was killed on 11 December 1282, although resistance by Dafydd ap Gruffudd continued into 1283. The English forces captured most of the Welsh lords who had sided with Llywelyn; many were imprisoned in the Tower of London until they died (including Rhys Wyndod) and Edward retained many of the captured lands as Crown property (*AC* 107; Davies 1940, 173; Prestwich 1988, 203, 205; Davies 1987, 361; Griffiths 1994, 261). The castle of Llandovery and the disputed commotes of Perfedd and Hirfryn were granted to John Giffard and his wife Matilda, along with the commote of Is Cennen (the property of Rhys Wyndod's brother Llywelyn), constituting the whole of Cantref Bychan. In November 1283, Giffard was formally confirmed in possession of the commote of Is Cennan (Davies 1987, 363; Prestwich 1988, 204). In north Wales, substantial castles were constructed at Harlech, Caernarfon and Conwy and some existing Welsh castles, such as Castell-y-Bere and Criccieth, were repaired and garrisoned in order to retain tight control of the region and access into it. Few Welsh lords with any substantial landholdings remained after the rebellion. Gruffudd ap Gwenwynwyn and Rhys ap Maredudd had both sided with the English Crown in the conflict of 1282–83 and were now the two most prominent surviving Welsh lords (Davies 1987, 361).

Rhys was somewhat precipitant in occupying not only his new possessions, but also the adjacent lands of the royal ward Llywelyn ap Owain. He subsequently appeared before Edward in a full council meeting at Acton Burnell (Shropshire) in June 1283, to be tried and convicted of the charges of 'taking seisin of lands in Wales without waiting for formal investiture by a royal official contrary to the custom of the realm' (Davies 1987, 381; Prestwich 1988, 218; Griffiths 1994, 261). This was a public humiliation for the impetuous Rhys, particularly when he was made to quitclaim his rights to the castle of Dinefwr and its associated lands (the commote of Maen-Ordeilo) to the king (Edwards 1940, 122). However, on 3 October, he was finally confirmed as lord of all Cantref Mawr (except the commote of Maen-Ordeilo with its associated castle of Dinefwr, and the commote of Gwidigada, associated with Carmarthen Castle), plus his two commotes north of the River Teifi (Mabwynion and Gwynionydd). These lands made Rhys a substantial landowner and one of the principal lords of the southern Marches. It allowed him to entitle himself proudly as 'Lord of Ystrad Tywi', but he had been obliged to abandon his central aim of regaining Dinefwr Castle (*AC* 107; *CPR 1281–92*, 84; Smith 1965, 156; Davies 1987, 380). Without the rivalry of the lords of Dinefwr or the princes of Gwynedd, his position was far more firmly established than in earlier years. He was important not just because of his Welsh royal lineage, but also because of his present landed power, although he was now a royal vassal answerable to the English Crown for his lands. However, he was probably unable to win the trust of the leading men of Mallaen and Caio, the former commotes of Rhys Wyndod (Smith 1965, 160–161). On 20 October, he was granted a pardon for his earlier transgression on condition that he restored the lands of Llywelyn ap Owain, together with any profits he had received whilst in possession of those lands. In return, he was given the right to determine whether the Welshmen of his lands and any others he brought into the king's peace should live under English or Welsh laws (Edwards 1940, 160; Smith 1965, 156). He was also knighted. The question of the costs and compensation for his temporary occupation of the lands of Llywelyn ap Owain subsequently provided the material for a long-running legal dispute with the justiciar, Robert de Tibetot.

Disputes and jurisdiction

It was through English justices using English law that the King of England exerted his new control of Wales. Throughout the land there was hostility to the introduction of English laws and customs (Prestwich 1988, 188). In 1241, the English Crown had established the county of Carmarthenshire (Smith 1998, 62). It is unclear how quickly the county's legal and administrative system was set up and the extent to which it actively operated in Ystrad Tywi. From 1246 onwards, the royal justices of Carmarthen had jurisdiction over all the lands of Ystrad Tywi in the county court, although whether they should use English or Welsh law remained a point of uncertainty (Smith 1964, 269; Davies 1987, 227). Henceforward, the English Crown's representative in Carmarthen, the seneschal Nicholas de Molis, had far greater influence over the events in Ystrad Tywi (Smith 1965, 152).

In 1278, the royal courts were re-established after the events of Llywelyn ap Gruffudd's rebellion. On 14 January 1279, a prolonged court case was opened by John Giffard and his wife Matilda against Rhys Wyndod, claiming the commote of Perfedd, the castle and vill of Llandovery (later modified to just the vill of Llandovery, since the Crown held the castle) and reiterating Matilda's claim to Hirfryn, which she held in her own right. The claims were based on English law, because English rule now extended to this land. The claim to Perfedd derived from Matilda's grandfather Walter de Clifford, who had held the land briefly in the 12th century, when English rule had temporarily penetrated this far into Wales; the claim to Hirfryn derived from Matilda's father Walter de Clifford, who had been granted these lands by Henry III in the early 13th century. The claim to Perfedd continued through the courts, but the claim to Hirfryn was complicated by the fact that Rhys Wyndod only held one third of the commote. Rhys Wyndod initially argued that these were Welsh lands and subject only to Welsh law; then Clifford successfully counter-claimed that they were Marcher land and therefore subject to Marcher or English law. The case then moved down to the local court, where it was much delayed by the non-appearance of Rhys Wyndod or his representatives, and eventually the local court referred the matters

back to the king (summarised in Davies 1940, 163–173). However, on 27 January 1282, before the case could be heard, the Welsh again rose up in revolt.

The general tone of this case was quite clear: Welsh lands could be subjected to English claims of ownership on very tenuous historical grounds. Whichever side held political control of an area would rule it under their own laws and, so, the Welsh could not expect to retain their lands where English rule now applied. During the fluctuating fortunes of the conflict between the English Marcher lords and the Welsh in west Wales, much of the land had had a variety of owners in the past two centuries and was therefore wide open to such challenges. It appeared that, unless the Welsh held military control over an area, they were unlikely to retain legal title to their lands there. This message would not have been lost on the other Welsh lords of north and west Wales.

On 5 January 1280, a justiciar was appointed for west Wales, bringing all the royal estates there under a unified civilian and military command (*Cal Chancery Rolls Various* 182; Davies 1987, 340). This was an officer with the highest political and judicial authority. Through such appointments, Edward tightened the straitjacket of English law on the people of Wales. Jurisdictional control was now to be exercised over the native rulers with increasing pressure. Edward gave the justiciar a free hand for the insensitive bullying of Welsh society and its lords (Davies 1987, 348). Following on from the earlier court case between John Giffard and Rhys Wyndod, on 8 July an order was sent to Rhys ap Maredudd to be in court on 29 July with Rhys Wyndod and Morgan ap Maredudd to answer the claim of John Giffard and his wife Matilda to the lands of Hirfryn, which these three Welsh lords held jointly, and which Matilda claimed through her father. Due to Rhys ap Maredudd's non-appearances, the case continued to be deferred, but at his fourth non-appearance on 22 June 1281, he automatically forfeited the case and lost his claim to the lands (Davies 1940, 328–329). This might have shown Rhys the folly of not defending himself in court, although it is debatable whether such cases could be successfully defended.

In June and July, Rhys' steward Llywelyn ap Madog and Goronwy Goch used force to prevent John Giffard and his wife from taking control of the lands they had won in the recent court case (Davies 1940, 171, 332). These lands can be presumed to lie in the commote of Hirfryn.

In 1284, Edward I issued the Statute of Wales, which specified that, henceforward, English laws would apply in Wales for criminal acts and Welsh laws would still apply for minor matters, in particular land disputes. Over the course of the next three years, Rhys ap Maredudd presented a series of petitions to the king for what he regarded as his just territorial rights. He sought the return of Dinefwr Castle or an equivalent compensation, basing his claim on the settlement he had made with Pain de Chaworth in 1277. He requested the king to command Hywel ap Gruffudd to do suit to him for the lands he held at Llansadwrn in the commote of Mallaen and that the king should command his bailiffs at Dinefwr, in order to allow the Abbot of Talley to render his service to Rhys for the abbey lands (Smith 1965, 154, from PRO SC8/63/3122). Rhys was having a frustrating time trying to exercise his expanded lordship.

Just as Talley enjoyed the benefactions of the Welsh princes, it was also to suffer from the English conquerors. The Abbey suffered losses in the war of 1277 and the king took it into his hands the following year, supposedly because of its poverty. In 1284, the Welsh canons were accused of living immorally; the king expelled then and replaced them with English canons (Smith 1964, 278; Smith and O'Neil 1967, 8).

On 7 June 1285, Rhys married Ada de Hastings in the presence of many of the principal lords of the March. This marriage required a papal dispensation, as they were related by blood, which was obtained with the king's support. Ada's dowry was the barony of St Clears, which included the lands of St Clears, Amgoed and Peuliniog to the west of Elfed and Ystlwyf (Edwards 1940, 92–93, 101, 167–168) (Figure 2.2). This recovered some of the lands which Maredudd ap Rhys and Gilbert Marshal had tried to annex in their pact of 1241. Rhys granted Ada the commotes of Ystlwyf and Mabwynion as dower land for life, should she outlive him. These contracts were witnessed by the Bishop of Bath and Wells, the Bishop of St David's, Gilbert Earl of Gloucester, Lord William de Valence, John Earl Warrene and many other Marcher lords, who were presumably present at the marriage.

The dispute between Rhys and the justiciar Robert de Tibetot over the money that Rhys had collected during his illegal occupation of the lands of Llywelyn ap Owain ran on into 1286 and 1287. There was another concurrent dispute over the commote of Emlyn Uwch Cych. In both cases, Tibetot attempted to prosecute Rhys under English law in the Carmarthenshire county court. In both cases, Rhys denied the jurisdiction of this court and any other court over him, effectively claiming that he was only obliged to appear before the king himself and that he was only subject to Welsh law. Rhys communicated directly with the king on these matters; he may even have gone to Gascony to see him. It was stated by the Hagnaby chronicler that Rhys journeyed to France to see Edward I in person (BL Vespasian Bxi f32; Prestwich 1988, 218). This may explain both the safe conducts that were issued to Rhys in this year and Edward's conciliatory tone in his letter to his regent, the Earl of Cornwall, about this matter, asking that Rhys should not be molested and that the earl should attend to his grievances (Edwards 1940, 169–170; CChR vi 290, 297–298; Smith 1965, 157–159, 162–163).

It appears that Rhys was the victim of a campaign of administrative and judicial harassment, largely at

the hands of Robert de Tibetot. Tibetot, like other English officials recently appointed in Wales, was not restrained by the king. He had little appreciation of the effect that these summonses would have on the status of the last surviving lord of Deheubarth, and probably did not care. His mission was to exploit Carmarthenshire and Ystrad Tywi for himself and his royal master.

2.2 ARCHAEOLOGICAL OUTLINE, PHASES 1A–4B: THE WELSH LORD'S CASTLE

Pre-castle

The earliest evidence of activity on the site are nine fragments of prehistoric flintwork (White 2002) and a few Roman finds, including a piece of glass (Section 9.6) from layer (G348) and two coins ([C1 and C2], Section 9.3). No prehistoric or Roman features were recorded on the hilltop and it is likely that these finds were brought to the site during the medieval period. One of the Roman coins was worn and pierced, indicating its re-use as a pendant.

Founding Dryslwyn Castle

Dryslwyn Castle is not mentioned in the Treaty of Aberdyfi of 1216, when a full list of the lands and castles of Lord Rhys was recorded, but does appear in the *Brut-y-Tywysogyon* in 1246, strongly suggesting a start-date for construction and occupation somewhere between these two dates. Perhaps the likeliest time for the foundation of Dryslwyn Castle is in the mid 1220s, as mentioned above.

First, there is the question of historical context (Section 2.1). Maredudd ap Rhys, first lord of Dryslwyn, was probably the son of Rhys' second wife Matilda, daughter of Richard de Clare and widow of William de Braose. If this were the case, since they were married in 1219, Maredudd would probably have been born in 1221 or 1222; thus, at the death of Rhys Gryg, Maredudd was only 11 or 12 years old. Maredudd's youth would account for the fact that he does not appear in historical records much before 1240, when he is recorded as doing homage to Henry III for his lands. His older brother Rhys Mechyll is mentioned frequently during the late 1220s and 1230s and is clearly aggressive and much older.

Rhys Gryg would have been under some pressure to secure the inheritance of the son he had by Matilda, given the influence of her relatives. Uncles in the de Clare family would have applied pressure to see that their nephew was well treated in any 'inheritance' struggle. Rhys Gryg would have been painfully aware of the turmoil that followed his father's death, when a clear succession and division of lands were not established. He was also aware of the predatory nature of the other lords of the area and that his sons could end up with nothing. Consequently, it is likely that he established a clear inheritance for Rhys, with a castle to defend his landholding and a powerful guardian.

Rhys Mechyll's capture of his father in 1227, illustrates a particularly low point in their relationship. What could have caused such a rift? Perhaps the answer lies with the construction of the castle at Dryslwyn, which might explain the garbled reference in the *Brut-y-Tywysogyon* suggesting that Rhys Gryg surrendered his castle of 'Llandovery' to Rhys Mechyll to secure his release. Since Llandovery Castle was not in Rhys Gryg's possession, the castle referred to may have been that of 'Llanarthnau', *alias* Dryslwyn, since the village of Llanarthney was the nearest significant settlement to the emerging castle.

The 1230s saw the death of Rhys Gryg, when Maredudd was still only his teens. Since castles are normally seen as expensive to build, requiring a considerable amount of organisation and a period of calm over several years to ensure their completion, it is perhaps unlikely that such a turbulent time saw building work start at Dryslwyn.

Second, we must consider important parallels between the architecture of the castles at Dryslwyn and Dinefwr. If, as the documentary sources suggest, Rhys was forced to dismantle his castle at Dinefwr in around 1220 and rebuild it in the 1220s, he was probably responsible for the earliest surviving masonry structure there: the flared-based round tower. This is strikingly similar to Round Tower D at Dryslwyn Castle, perhaps suggesting that both were built by Rhys Gryg at roughly the same time in the 1220s.

Lastly, there is archaeological evidence in the form of four coins (Section 9.3): two from the period *c*1205–17 [C4 and C5], one from *c*1194–1204 [C3] and another minted between *c*1230 and *c*1236 [C6]. Coins are rare finds on Welsh sites and thus four coins of this early date from a Welsh castle are perhaps indicative of early activity on the site. Admittedly, the possibility that they had remained in circulation for several years before they were lost must be considered, together with their presence in redeposited contexts, but their presence at Dryslwyn does appear to suggest an earlier rather than a later date for the construction of the first castle.

Most likely, then, is that a castle at Dryslwyn was built by Rhys Gryg for his young son Maredudd in the mid or late 1220s, perhaps in 1225–26 ahead of his capture by Rhys Mechyll. This stronghold, together with the provision of guardianship for the young Maredudd under Gilbert Marshal, would appear the best way to secure the child's future, avoiding the internecine strife that blighted Rhys' own youth. Creating a second castle, a second power base, was undoubtedly a risky strategy, as his struggle with his eldest son Rhys Mechyll confirms. Nevertheless, Dryslwyn Castle flourished in the period after his death, playing a key role in the divided lands of Cantref Mawr.

Phase 1: The establishment of Dryslwyn Castle

Phase 1a

The earliest feature of the castle is the flared-based Round Tower D (D3), constructed on the highest point of the hill (Figure 2.5). The bedrock here was first levelled and a distinctive foundation of flat stones laid to support the south-east side. Adjoining Round Tower D was a curtain wall (B1, K60, J10, J29 and

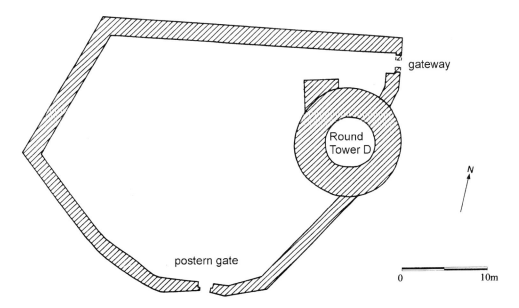

FIGURE 2.5

Dryslwyn Castle: Phase 1

33

O24), which enclosed the sloping ground to the west, overlooking the River Tywi. This curtain wall was battered at an angle of 8–10° at the base and cemented with the same poor-quality earthy mortar as the Round Tower. A flat-laid foundation of stone, identical to that of Round Tower D, supported the south-west corner of the curtain wall, suggesting that both were built in a single phase of construction. On the north and west sides of the early castle, the original curtain wall survived later changes associated with the development of the Inner Ward. On the south side, however, only the lower courses of the Phase 1a curtain wall (H41–42, I110 and J10) were revealed by excavation, whilst, on the east side, the curtain wall (F12) had been partially rebuilt or obscured by later building work.

The main entrance to the early castle was through a small gateway or doorway in the curtain wall on the north-east side, adjacent to Round Tower D. Welsh castles of the late 12th and early 13th centuries often have narrow entrances situated close to substantial towers, for example at Dolwyddelan (Conwy). Such entrances would only have permitted single-file access to people and animals: wheeled vehicles could not enter. Access to the main entrance at Dryslwyn was over exposed bedrock that had been worn smooth by the passage of feet (B125). An associated area of cobbling (B118), which filled in clefts in the bedrock, was similarly eroded. On the south side of the early castle was another small doorway or postern gate (H41–42), positioned directly above the fording point of the river. Whilst the main north-east entrance was later demolished and rebuilt several times, the lower half of this southern postern gateway remained intact. Once inside the postern gate, a flight of stone steps set into a gully in the hillside led upwards to the interior of the castle.

Round Tower D most likely rose two storeys above a basement level and was therefore similar in many respects to other surviving flared-based round towers in west Wales (Renn 1961) (Section 4.1). A row of stones in Courtyard O (O228) indicates the presence of a stone platform on the north-west side of the Round Tower that would have supported a wooden stairway running up from Area P to a first-floor doorway. The absence of entrances at ground-floor level is another characteristic of 'Welsh' flared-based round towers, including those at Dolbadarn (Gwynedd) and Dolforwyn (Powys), since this was a crucial element of their defensive design. Round towers could function as places of refuge in times of siege, in much the same way as more traditional keeps, and so first-floor entrances were harder for attackers to reach. Traditionally, flared-based round towers are dated to the early 13th century (Renn 1961; Avent 1983) and, for the historical and archaeological reasons already discussed above, it is most likely that Round Tower D was constructed in the 1220s.

Phase 1b

Evidence of Phase 1b occupation comprises wear on the bedrock (B125) outside the castle entrance, occupation debris in Area G and stakehole structures in Areas F, G and I (Figure 1.3). No clear building outlines could be discerned from the pattern of stakeholes, although the presence of structures sited directly on the natural clay immediately behind the postern gate is implied. It is likely that the stakeholes were originally far greater in extent, since evidence from further up the slope in Area G has been lost as a result of later levelling of the bedrock and the construction of Great Hall K/L. The Area F stakeholes (F121–125) cut through a mortar layer (F110), which rested up against the curtain wall (F12). This confirms that they are the earliest internal structures of the castle, possibly temporary buildings constructed during or after the erection of the curtain wall.

In Area J, a crude courtyard surface was present in this early occupation phase, on top of which occupation material (J18) was deposited. In part, this layer (J18) was sealed beneath the wall of Great Hall K/L, which was constructed in Phase 2a. As a result, we can be confident that it relates to the occupation of the stake-built structures in Phase 1b. The only other accommodation certainly present during this period lay within Round Tower D.

Phase 2: The development of Dryslwyn Castle

Phase 2a

Great Hall K/L was constructed of masonry and butted up against the curtain wall at its western end (Figure 2.6). The rock on which the Great Hall was built had been levelled prior to construction. Much of the earth and stone derived from this process was dumped in the western half of Area O. Small deposits of lime, reddened earth and charcoal (K63 and K69), the debris from burning lime used as mortar in the construction of the new building, were present on the surfaces inside and outside the Great Hall in Areas K and J. Following the construction of the walls of Great Hall K/L, the bedrock ground surface inside was further quarried downwards, leaving the walls on raised rock steps. Adjoining the eastern side of the building in Area G, a series of stake-built structures (G406–410, G417–419, G420–438 and G439–442) was erected.

Great Hall K/L originally comprised a first-floor hall with an undercroft beneath. Entry to the hall was gained through a door in the east end of the north wall, where a terrace (O96) continued the level of the courtyard surface in Area O to give access at first-floor level. There was a central hearth in the hall, which was supported by a masonry pillar (K55) in the undercroft below. Assuming that the hall was arranged along

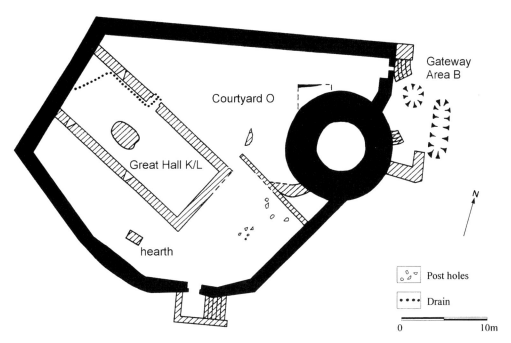

FIGURE 2.6

Dryslwyn Castle: Phase 2a–b

traditional lines, there would have been a raised dais for the lord at the west end, whilst towards the east end a screen would have hidden two opposing entrances: the first in the north wall led into Area O, whilst the second in the south wall gave access to cooking and service facilities located in Area I, where a large hearth was certainly present by Phase 2b. The undercroft below the first-floor hall contained at least one arrow-loop, although it is likely that three had once existed in the south wall, with a further one located towards the western end of the north wall. These arrowloops served not only to illuminate the undercroft, but also, in the case of the three on the south side, to give a field of fire over the open courtyard in Area J.

In Area O, to the north of Great Hall K/L, the bedrock was quarried away to give a level rock shelf that provided access from Gateway Area B to the rest of the castle, including the Great Hall. Running east–west across the castle from the curtain wall to the north east corner of Great Hall K/L were traces of a wall (P85). This divided the lower ground of Area G with its timber structures and associated occupation from the area of raised bedrock containing Round Tower D to the north. This dividing wall may have served a defensive purpose, allowing Great Hall K/L and the developing Courtyard O to be defended, even if attackers had gained access to Areas F, G, I and J to the south. Alternatively, it may represent a social and functional divide, separating the menial tasks of food preparation and stockbreeding, conducted south of this wall, from the receiving of visitors and guests, which occurred to the north. A platform (P57), which probably supported a series of steps up to a wall-walk on the northern side of wall (P85), perhaps supports

the defensive interpretation, although it is equally likely that both functions were served.

In the final building activity of this phase, the bedrock of much of Area G was made level to receive wooden buildings, whilst Area P was revetted with a wall (P18), which improved access along the bedrock shelf between Gateway Area B and Great Hall K/L. Area P continued to give access to the wall-walk (P85) and, via the buttress (O228), up wooden steps to the first-floor entrance of Round Tower D.

The main entrance to the castle was developed with the addition of a rock-cut trench (A19) and scoop (B122) across the bedrock ridge to the east of Round Tower D. A short wall was added along the top of the bedrock ridge, projecting forward from the Round Tower and then turning at a right angle. A flight of steps (C23 and C24) curved around the exterior of Round Tower D to give access into the area enclosed by the projecting wall, which thus acted as an external bastion overlooking the way into the castle. These structures increased the defensive nature of the site against attack. Access to the castle's entrance was later improved by the construction of a curved flight of steps (B106) and a wall (B11) in front of the existing eastern entrance. This would have made access easier than traversing the worn bedrock. These defensive structures in front of the entrance were paralleled at the postern gate in Area H, where an L-shaped wall (H62) defended and revetted a series of steps or perhaps a ramp, which descended east from the exterior of the postern gate.

The date of the construction of Great Hall K/L is uncertain, although it clearly followed the construction of the Phase 1a curtain wall, onto which it butted, and overlay the occupation material of Phase 1b. The recovery of a coin dated 1218–42 from deposits (K35) associated with the construction of the drain in Great Hall K/L suggests a date in the 1230s or 1240s for this phase.

Phase 2b

Considerable wear on the bedrock of Courtyard O (O236) indicates a long period of use of this eastern edge of the castle courtyard as a routeway into Great Hall K/L. The western side of Courtyard O appears to have remained relatively open with few features, save the occasional rocky outcrop. Within this area, a single line of stakeholes (O164–174) indicates the presence of a fence, which was probably used for penning animals. Immediately alongside is the northern entrance to the undercroft within Great Hall K/L, which appears to be contemporary with the construction of the rest of the building. The lack of an obvious access down to this entrance, combined with its large size and the fact that it led out to the probable animal pen in Courtyard O, perhaps suggests that valuable animals, such as horses or cattle, were stabled in the undercroft.

In the area to the south of Great Hall K/L lay a large stone hearth (I72), which was probably used to cook food. No evidence for an associated building was found, although it is possible that a wooden lean-to structure set against the curtain wall may once have existed. This hearth may have replaced some of the stake-built structures in Areas G and I, which could have supported cooking activities in the preceding period, since there were traces of fires and burning

associated with some of the stakeholes. The exact east–west alignment of the hearth appears simply fortuitous.

Phase 2c

This phase saw additional building to support the activities being undertaken in Great Hall K/L (Figure 2.7). Immediately south of the Great Hall, a small rectangular stone building, Kitchen I, was constructed in Area I around the earlier hearth. Kitchen I probably butted up against the curtain wall, taking up the same orientation as the hearth and incorporating a drain (O43 and O100), which removed excess rainwater pouring off the southern roof of Great Hall K/L, thus preventing flooding within the kitchen. The line of the drain was carefully positioned to avoid the existing hearth (I72). Access from Kitchen I to the lord and his guests in Great Hall K/L was probably up a series of wooden steps, later replaced in stone, and through a small doorway in the south wall of Great Hall K/L, opening directly into the west end of the first-floor hall. The construction of Kitchen I severely limited the amount of light entering the arrowloop (I171) at the east end of the south wall of Great Hall K/L and, at this stage, it may have been widened to its present form.

In the north-west angle between Great Hall K/L and the north curtain wall, a crosswall (M35) was constructed, creating a small room with a sunken floor. This isolated but secure location with a door opened from the exterior is interpreted as Prison M. Holding wealthy and influential prisoners hostage was an important function of Welsh castles. Maredudd ap

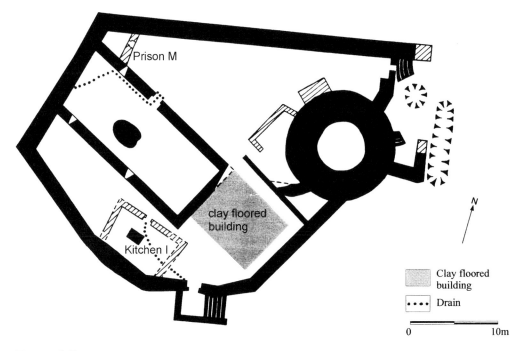

FIGURE 2.7

Dryslwyn Castle: Phase 2c–d

Rhys was held by Llywelyn ap Gruffudd at Criccieth Castle between 1258 and 1261.

A sequence of buildings was constructed on the eastern side of Great Hall K/L in Area G. The first was a timber post-built structure with post pits cut into the bedrock. This was then replaced by at least two major phases and several minor phases of clay-floored timber buildings. The bedrock to the north was sculpted to receive the wooden beams supporting the superstructure of the buildings and, on the eastern side, traces of a trench (dug out stone foundation or beam slot) remained. Evidence from the south side was lost due to later activity, but enough survives to show that these buildings were on the same alignment as Great Hall K/L (Figure 2.10). Their location and the presence of a central hearth indicate that they provided domestic habitation.

Minor alterations to Gateway Area B were carried out, most notably with the addition of a wall (B77) protecting the curved steps leading up to the main castle entrance. There is no evidence that specifically dates this construction period. Minor or ancillary buildings, such as Kitchen I and Prison M, could have been constructed at any time after the completion of Great Hall K/L. Given the length of subsequent occupation in Phase 2d, however, it would appear most likely that they were erected shortly after the Great Hall, early in the 1240s.

Phase 2d

The extensive evidence of wear and rebuilding of the clay-floored buildings east of Great Hall K/L indicates that this was a period of intensive occupation in the castle. Substantial deposits around the hearth in Kitchen I suggest extensive use of this feature.

Phase 3: The expansion of Dryslwyn Castle

Phase 3a

At the eastern end of Great Hall K/L, the latest clay-floored timber building was replaced by an altogether grander structure built of stone (Figure 2.8). Construction of Great Chamber G involved the removal of most of the existing deposits in the southern half of Area G, since the new building was butted onto the existing curtain wall at its southern end, set at right angles to Kitchen I. In the course of construction, the crosswall (P85) was removed, whilst the east wall of Great Hall K/L was partially demolished and reconstructed (G169). Two narrow windows (G540 and G541) were incorporated within the north wall of Great Chamber G, whilst a small entrance accessed from Courtyard O was present in the northwest corner. Both the size and location of this building adjacent to Great Hall K/L suggest secular use as a solar or chamber providing accommodation either for the lord of Dryslwyn or his important guests. The floor was of high quality mortar (G57) with stakeholes (G65–G111 and G125–G146) indicating the lines of internal partitions.

Kitchen I was now altered; its eastern wall being rebuilt as part of the western wall of Great Chamber G. A stone pier (I14) was also added to the north-west corner of the building and a new high-quality mortar floor (I19) laid down. Stone steps (I15) led from the

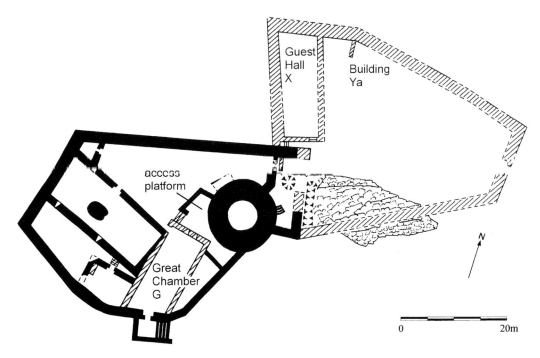

FIGURE 2.8

Dryslwyn Castle: Phase 3

entrance of Kitchen I to the south-east doorway in Great Hall K/L.

The location of the narrow entrance in the north-west corner of Great Chamber G gave it direct access to the worn bedrock path, which ran along the eastern side of Area O in Phases 1 and 2. This may have been the principal, indeed possibly the only, access route from Gateway Area B to the main buildings of the castle during this period. Building activity in Phase 3a resulted in the deposition of substantial dumps of cobble, earth and rubble in Courtyard O.

Also at this time, an additional ward was added to the castle (Figure 2.8). This is referred to as the Middle Ward, since it occupied this position in the final castle form. For the duration of Phase 3, however, it functioned as the outer ward of a two-ward castle. The buildings excavated in the Middle Ward include rectangular masonry structures interpreted as houses and halls (Section 5.1), evidently constructed to accommodate more people. This larger household almost certainly derived from increased administrative and social activities. The structure and people would have increased the overall defensive capacity of the castle. This expansion also appears to reflect the improved fortunes of the lords of Dryslwyn, since it must have required considerable investment. It is most likely to have occurred in the 1250s, following victory at the Battle of Coed Llathen/Cymerau.

The addition of a second ward was accompanied by modifications to the existing castle, reflecting its new status as an Inner Ward. Gateway Area B was remodelled with the previous stepped entrance being covered up and a gentle ramp created with a new single substantial step (B69) built in front of the entrance. The wall to the north of this ramp (B15) was extended, as was the walled and defended promontory (C16) to the south, thus creating an outer entrance at the base of the ramp. Traces of this first outer gateway are scant, since they were covered up by subsequent building work.

Outside the castle walls, it is likely that a small town started to develop during this period. Since the earliest houses appear to butt onto a town wall beyond, it appears that the settlement was enclosed even at this early date.

Phase 3b

Following the construction of Great Chamber G, there was an extended phase of occupation in the castle. Within the Great Chamber itself, a succession of stake-holes indicates that the internal partitions were replaced several times. In Courtyard O, meanwhile, a substantial midden accumulated in the western half of this area, whilst against the northern wall a latrine (O50) was constructed, which produced a bronze macehead (Section 7.3). Area F, beside Great Chamber G, initially housed a latrine (F23) yielding a copper-alloy spur [A33], before the area was used as a

kitchen midden (F19). Gateway Area B gained a few dump deposits, whilst the steps (I15) from Kitchen I up to Great Hall K/L showed considerable wear, indicative of a long period of use.

This extensive period of occupation appears to represent an episode of calm and measured activity, with little disruption or alteration to the castle fabric. If the expansion of the castle in Phase 3a is related to the emergence of Rhys ap Maredudd as a powerful lord of Dryslwyn, then this period of calm that followed may have encouraged the development of the town outside the castle. This phase may have continued when Rhys ap Maredudd succeeded his father. The conflicts of 1277 and 1282–83 that caused disruption elsewhere in Wales appear to have had little effect on Dryslwyn Castle.

Phases 3c and 3d

These phases were only represented in the Middle Ward and in the town. The construction of Guest Hall X and Buildings Ya against the Middle Ward wall is perhaps indicative of more extensive building activity.

Phases 4a and 4b: The rebuilding of Dryslwyn Castle

Phase 4a

This phase saw not only a major remodelling of the Inner Ward, but also the addition of an Outer Ward to the castle (Figure 2.9). In Great Hall K/L, the wooden first floor was lowered and the main entrance to the hall was moved to the centre of the north wall. The arrowloops on the south side were filled in to provide better structural support for the floor beams, whilst, either in this phase or Phase 5a, the arrowloop on the west end of the north wall was expanded to create a window. The large masonry pier supporting the first-floor hearth was also enlarged and it is probable that an extra storey was added to the building. This created an impressive façade to Great Hall K/L, which would immediately have greeted visitors entering the Inner Ward through Gateway Area B. Damaged glazed floor tiles, from the destruction rubble, may have formed a tile surround to a hearth on either the first or second floor.

To the south of Great Hall K/L, the Phase 1a curtain wall (J10) overlooking the River Tywi was demolished and a substantial new wall (J7) took its place. Between this wall and the Great Hall was built the two-storey building known as Apartments I/J. The existing Kitchen I was slighted and the whole of Areas I and J was covered in clay and cobble deposits, which raised the ground level to match that of the newly lowered first floor in Great Hall K/L. The central arrowloop in the south wall of the Great Hall had a

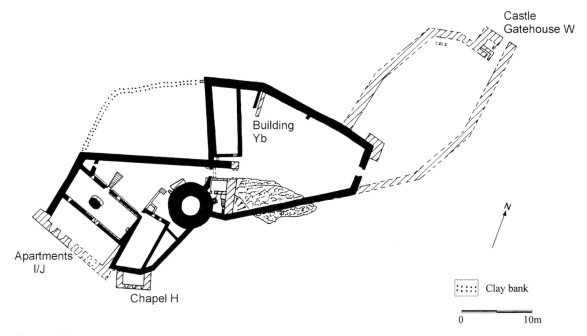

FIGURE 2.9

Dryslwyn Castle: Phase 4a–b

FIGURE 2.10

Reconstruction of Dryslwyn Castle during Phase 2d, c1240 (drawn by Chris Jones-Jenkins)

doorway inserted into its upper half, which provided access between Great Hall K/L and Apartments I/J.

In Area H, a projecting tower was built on top of the former access to the postern gateway. This building, Chapel H, is believed to have housed the castle's chapel at first-floor level, as is perhaps indicated by the presence of three lancet windows. The adjacent Great Chamber G may well have received an upper storey in this phase, the evidence for which is a raised platform (P8) and steps (P30), which were added to Area P presumably to give access to an upper storey from Courtyard O.

Courtyard O itself gained new rubble spreads before a good mortar surface was laid down. A flight of steps was inserted leading down to the undercroft entrance (L60) of Great Hall K/L. A pair of revetting walls ensured that rubble did not rest up against the north wall of the Great Hall and that a drain was able to run between the building and Courtyard O in order drain rainwater from the Courtyard.

Gateway Area B was strengthened with the construction of a substantial new outer gateway and wall (B3). A ramped entrance now ran between the outer and inner gateways, both of which were defended by double-leafed gates with substantial drawbars: the outer gateway also had a portcullis. Both inner and outer gateways were nearly 2m wide and thus permitted the access of wheeled vehicles into the Inner Ward. West of the outer gate wall (B3) was a guard chamber, which was lit by two arrowloops in its south wall. A flight of steps gave access to the wall-walk of wall (B3) and the presence of the springing for an arch suggests that there was a new first-floor entrance into Round Tower D on its eastern side.

Round Tower D and the external walls of Gateway Area B were rendered and it is likely that much of the rest of the castle was now rendered in order to make it more weatherproof. A new buttress (O22) to support the wooden steps from Area P up to the first-floor entrance of Round Tower D was built hard up against the freshly rendered masonry of the Round Tower. Elsewhere on Round Tower D (O24) and on the new Outer Ward wall (R7) there is evidence of numerous coats of limewash (R10).

The addition of the Outer Ward substantially increased the amount of accommodation that the castle could offer. The new Castle Gatehouse W was a two-storey construction with a guardhouse on one side of the gate-passage, a portcullis and double-leafed gates on both inner and outer gateways. In the Middle Ward building Ya was demolished and building Yb constructed.

Following the remodelling of Phase 4a, the castle was now a fitting symbol of the power and wealth of the lord of Dryslwyn. A two-storey hall and apartment block with a prominent chapel tower rose high above the hillside, whilst the new limewash on many of the castle walls would have shone bright white in the sunlight. Those visiting the castle were forced to pass through the town, then through an elaborate gatehouse with double gates and portcullis, on through two wards and finally through a double gateway into the Inner Ward, where Great Hall K/L stood with elaborate tracery windows. The presence of window glass and wall-paintings within many of the buildings of the Inner and Middle Wards further added to the impression of luxury and sophistication.

This building programme, with its emphasis on accommodation and opulence, is unlikely to have been undertaken by the English Crown, given its extensive financial commitments to castle-building in north Wales, and no English noble appears likely to have lavished this level of expenditure on a distant Welsh castle: certainly, no such expenditure or benefactor is recorded in documents. Instead, the man behind the Phase 4a changes at Dryslwyn Castle is almost certainly Rhys ap Maredudd, who had both the means and the motive for such construction work. The culmination of the war of 1282–83 had left Dinefwr in the hands of the Crown; Rhys had effective control of Ystrad Tywi, the ancestral lands of Rhys Gryg, but had been made to quitclaim this castle and was now without any realistic possibility of regaining his ancestral family seat. From 3 October 1283, he was the most powerful Welsh lord of royal lineage left in south and west Wales, without Dinefwr, however, he had the need to establish an impressive castle befitting his status as a 'prince' of Deheubarth. The only realistic option was to expand and redevelop his castle of Dryslwyn. This led to a substantial building campaign, newly constructed defences, an enlarged castle and the provision of high-quality accommodation.

After the siege of Dryslwyn Castle in 1287, its new constable Alan de Plucknet was able to raise £40 12s 10¼d in rents, dues and fines from the six commotes of Cantref Mawr in 1288–89 (Rhys 1936, 43). In the following year, when agricultural production had recovered from the devastation of the revolt, Plucknet raised between £50 and £70, suggesting that in a good year over £100 could be raised from Cantref Mawr. In the early and mid 1280s, Rhys could have raised revenue not only from Cantref Mawr, but also from his commotes north of the River Teifi and the lands he acquired with the barony of St Clears by his marriage to Ada de Hastings (Figure 2.2). His total landed income may have amounted to well over £200 *per annum* (Pounds 1990, 145–148). This revenue stream would have provided either sufficient funds over a number of years to undertake substantial building work at his castle of Dryslwyn, or against which he could borrow larger sums for more intensive periods of building activity (Davies 1987, 168).

The archaeological evidence from Phase 4a provides a series of nine coins dated to early–mid 1280s associated with much of this building work. This appears to confirm the dating of Phase 4a construction to between 1283 and 1287.

Phase 4b

There is limited evidence of any occupation phase following the Phase 4a building work and preceding Phase 4c construction. A further kitchen midden in Area F (F16) appears likely, since it overlies the building rubble from the preceding construction in Phase 4a. There are also minor rubble spreads where construction had taken place in Areas B and C.

ENGLISH GARRISON PERIOD (1287–1455): HISTORICAL AND ARCHAEOLOGICAL SUMMARY

3.1 HISTORY OF THE ENGLISH GARRISON PERIOD (1287–1455)
by Chris Caple and Chris Phillpotts

After the siege of 1287 (Section 7.1), Rhys ap Maredudd's castle at Dryslwyn was confiscated and occupied by the English Crown, garrisoned and refurbished as a component in its defensive network in Wales. It was to remain garrisoned and subject to intermittent repair programmes for at least a century and was a sufficiently significant stronghold to play a part in the Glyn Dŵr revolt in the early 15th century. Its military role then ended, although it continued to be rented out to notable local figures for some years afterwards. What follows is a detailed account of the castle's development during this period.

Garrisons and repairs

Alan de Plucknet was appointed constable of Dryslwyn Castle at the end of the siege on 8 September 1287. On 24 September, he was formally granted the right to hold the castle for the Crown and with it the former lands of Rhys ap Maredudd, comprising the commotes of Caio, Cethiniog, Mabelfyw, Mabudrud, Maen-Ordeilo and Mallaen (Figure 2.2) (*CFR 1272–1307*, 242; *Cal Chancery Rolls Various* 311; Griffiths 1972, 7). Half of the commote of Mallaen Uwchcoed was at first retained by the Earl of Hereford for his role in the campaign of 1287 on the borders of his own lordship of Brecon, only finally coming under Plucknet's control in November 1289.

The substantial garrison that initially occupied Dryslwyn Castle in 1287–88 comprised Plucknet as constable, 2 knights, 11 mounted squires, 7 mounted sergeants-at-arms, 16 crossbowmen, 80 archers with their leader (*vintener*), 3 janitors and 5 watchmen, 125

men in all (Morris 1901, 214–215 gives different figures). The presence of three gatekeepers could suggest that there were three gatehouses to guard. Amongst those who formed the initial English garrison at Dryslwyn were Richard de la Mote and John Braz, both soldiers of the besieging army. It is possible that the occupying troops were entirely drawn from the campaign force. One of the soldiers was called Iorwerth the Doctor (*Ieruarth Medicus*), but as he was an archer serving for 2d a day, this seems likely to have been a nickname. Two twenties of archers were withdrawn from the garrison on 26 October 1287. There may have been similar reductions in the forces at the other castles in west Wales, as the pacification of the country was completed.

Perhaps encouraged by these troop reductions, Rhys ap Maredudd emerged from the woods and restarted the war on 2 November 1287 with the capture of Newcastle Emlyn. Gruffyn Gough, the beadle of Cethiniog commote, was probably one of those who joined Rhys's renewed revolt. The garrison at Dryslwyn was immediately reinforced with contingents of local Welsh horsemen and archers. Extra crossbowmen were added in late November, with contingents of horsemen and crossbowmen from London and Kent arriving in mid December. When the danger was over, the numbers of the garrison were again reduced during February and March 1288 (PRO E101/4/20, printed in Rhys 1936, app 4). Alan de Plucknet wrote to William de Hamilton in April or May 1288 informing him that he could not leave Dryslwyn as Rhys was still at large (Edwards 1935, 135–136). Evidently the fear of Rhys retaking the castle was still very real, no doubt provoked by his recent capture of the castle at Newcastle Emlyn.

On 3 December, armaments were supplied from the Tower of London to Alan de Plucknet and the garrison of Dryslwyn. These included 18 crossbows, 12 of wood and 6 of horn; 2 bows of 1 yard width, 2 bows of

2 feet width and 2 bows of 1 foot width; and 2000 quarrels (crossbow bolts) (Rhys 1936, 53). All the weapons recorded as supplied to the castle after this date were crossbows and quarrels. Crossbows were the most effective weapon for defending a castle because of their ease of use, especially when crouching behind a low battlement or parapet. They certainly did not require the skill, strength and training needed to use a longbow effectively. There are later accounts of maintaining stocks of crossbows and quarrels at Dryslwyn and also of their repair and maintenance. Crossbowmen were paid 4d per day, whilst archers, who used their own longbows and were only paid half as much, were most likely drawn from Wales and the Marches.

The payment of the garrison during this first year of the English occupation required continued funding from the Italian moneylender Ricardo Guicciardini, who represented a consortium of merchants and bankers from Lucca. Money was paid both through the Exchequer in London and directly to Plucknet, just as it had been during the campaign and siege of 1287. Lesser sums were drawn from the sheriffs of Herefordshire, Gloucestershire and Somerset, as well as the merchants of Carmarthen.

Supplies of food and other goods were found in Dryslwyn Castle when the besiegers took it over from Rhys ap Maredudd's men in September 1287. They included apples, baskets of nuts, quantities of mixed grain (wheat and rye), second-grade wheat, oatmeal and salt. There were also cattle and horse hides. It is unclear if these provisions were the normal complement of foodstuffs held in the castle for the household and garrison, or if they had been specifically gathered in preparation for the looming siege. Whichever, it is clear that Rhys's garrison were not on the verge of being starved out.

From the beginning, Plucknet evidently took over the local machinery of government, both its personnel and courts, and collected its rents, tolls and mill renders in kind. Rents from the commotes of Cantref Mawr totalled £15 9s, a lower sum than in subsequent years, no doubt due to the ravages of the revolt. There is a suggestion of punitive action against some of Rhys's associates. Salted pig carcasses (bacons), which Rhys had prepared and sold, were confiscated by Plucknet and sold again, whilst a fee that Rhys had paid for reaping his corn was also retrieved from the recipient. On the other hand, some of the rent payments for 1287–88 were postponed because war damage in the countryside left its inhabitants too poor to pay.

The accounts presented for the period 8 September 1287 to 8 September 1288 indicate that Plucknet was raising money by selling off part of the contents of the castle. Amongst Rhys' possessions sold for profit by the victors were his herds of cattle, which were found in the countryside around Dryslwyn, probably by foraging parties during the siege. Some of these animals were sold in 1287–88, but others were only sold off in 1289–90, when there was a need for ready cash at the castle to pay wages. The sales included 147 cattle that year, as well as produce, such as bacon, hay, apples, nuts and cattle and horse hides.

Expenses included extensive work on the castle and the town: £129 4s 10d were spent on workmen, quarrymen and masons, presumably undertaking repairs to the castle; £109 3s 8d on carpenters, smiths and charcoal burners constructing a new mill; £36 5s 1d on felling wood from around the castle, renovating the town ditches *circa villam*, cleaning the castle and breaking a rock at the castle entrance; and 16s 2d on putting up a fence around the fair and repairs to a newly constructed bakehouse and granary. These may have been temporary buildings, required because of damage sustained during the siege; they were certainly replaced by new buildings in 1305/06 (Webster 1987; PRO E101/4/20, printed in Rhys 1936, app 4; summary version on the Pipe Roll at E372/134 m1, printed at Rhys 1936, 38–43). Suggestions by Lloyd (1935, 282) of expenditure of £338 13s 4d for repairs to the fabric of the castle arise from an incomplete reading of the sources of income and expenditure.

Accounts for the periods 8 September 1288 to 8 September 1289 and 8 September 1289 to 29 September (Michaelmas) 1289 show that Alan de Plucknet was again selling oats, lambs, pigs, wheat, mixed grain (wheat and rye), malt, apples, hay and cattle from the castle. The accounting date now changed from 8 September (the anniversary of when Plucknet became custodian of the castle) to 29 September, which was the usual Michaelmas quarter day for the settling of accounts. The yearly rents from Cantref Mawr had increased to £40 12s 10¼d. Repairs to the castle included the work of Simon the mason and his assistants for 41 weeks at a total cost of £21 19s. Those receiving wages included a man to care for the king's stud, for which horses had been bought in the previous year, and an enclosure was made for these horses. This 'stud' probably comprised horses stabled at the castle and retained for the king's business, particularly for messengers taking documents and information to the king's justiciar in Carmarthen, part of the early warning system to allow news of any trouble in the Welsh heartlands to be quickly communicated to the English authorities. The bulk of the expenditure was still on the garrison, although by now this had been reduced to 77 men, including the constable, plus another eight archers for part of the year. One of the mounted sergeants present in the garrison of this period was mentioned by name as Einion Goch. One of the crossbowmen went absent without leave, but with his crossbow. Some additional funding was still required from Guicciardini and the royal purse. A stock check of the 'dead garnisture', or stores of the castle in this period, noted supplies of wheat, oatmeal, malt, two tuns (barrels) of salt, pipes of honey, casks of wine, as well as a quern and two quernstones. A silver cup with a gilded cover and four drinking horns had been acquired as booty from the Welsh of Cantref Mawr. There were ample supplies of armour and weapons, including 45 standard crossbows, 5 large crossbows and over 6600 quarrels. The use of 700 quarrels during the year indicates a continuing level of military activity (Rhys 1936, 43–55, 456).

In the accounting period 29 September 1289 to 16 February 1290, Plucknet spent no more money on the fabric of the castle: presumably all the damage had been successfully repaired by this time. As the continuing presence in the area of Rhys ap Maredudd was still a cause for concern, the castle must have been returned to a defensible state as quickly as possible. There was a slightly reduced garrison of 73 men, including the constable and a chaplain, John de Cerezie, who had been attached to the castle establishment since its capture. Those paid as archers included a slinger, and also a smith and a sawyer, who perhaps doubled as craftsmen. Alan de Plucknet and his entourage were frequently absent on trips to the royal court.

The rental income from Dryslwyn and the rest of the cantref had continued to rise as the six commotes slowly recovered from the devastation of 1287 and arrears of rent from 1287/88 were paid. Income also came from rents for mills at Henllys (near the castle), Brechfa and Cilsan; the pannage of pigs in the woods; the sale of agricultural produce and other castle stores, including the former possessions of Rhys ap Maredudd; and from the court cases and land sales (perquisites of the court) (PRO E101/4/23, printed in Rhys 1936, app 5; summary account on Pipe Roll at E371/135 m1, printed and translated by Rhys 1936, 58–63). At the close of the pannage season each year, all tenants with swine in the forest of Glyncothi were required by custom to bring them to Dryslwyn Castle (Rees 1924, 125, from PRO SC6/1158/3).

On 27 January 1290, Philip ap Owain ap Meurig was appointed constable of Dryslwyn Castle in succession to Plucknet (Griffiths 1972, 255) and a few months later, on 13 July, the six commotes of Cantref Mawr were united under a single stewardship and absorbed into the financial and judicial system of Carmarthenshire. These lands and Dryslwyn Castle were initially granted to Robert de Tibetot, Justiciar of West Wales for Edward I, and the income was specifically to be used for maintaining and defending the castle. The constable of Dryslwyn was therefore placed under the authority of the justiciar (Griffiths 1966, 140 n101). Tibetot had his own supplies of victuals and weapons at Dryslwyn and the other west Wales castles. Much of his stock was rotten or worn-out by the time of his death in 1298, when the prior of Carmarthen took over responsibility for what remained. The nature of Tibetot's regime in west Wales may be indicated by the stores of shackles and locks that he had at Dinefwr and Dryslwyn (PRO E101/8/29). Following his death, Ralph le Blunt was appointed constable of Dryslwyn

Castle in May 1298, with a garrison of 24 men (Griffiths 1972, 255).

A detailed set of accounts for west Wales presented by Tibetot's successor as justiciar, Walter de Pederton, survives for the period 1298 to 1300. Because of the administrative changes of 1290, the income from Cantref Mawr and the expenses of the garrison at Dryslwyn Castle were not presented as a single account, but rather included together with the other income and expenditure for the whole of west Wales. Much of the food and other supplies for all the castles in west Wales were now purchased centrally and distributed. In these accounts, the maintenance of the garrison of Dryslwyn at 24 men is noted, with only 49s 10d being spent on minor works and repairs, possibly to the town walls and gates, or to the castle itself. By comparison, 26s 3d was spent annually on cutting and carrying away the hay from the twelve acres of meadow in the Tywi valley below the castle. A supervisor of crossbows toured the royal castles of Carmarthen, Dinefwr, Dryslwyn and Emlyn, ensuring that all the crossbows were in a good state of repair and, presumably, that the men were properly trained. He was paid 31s 8d for half a year. The Crown was therefore active in ensuring the security of the area, garrisoning and repairing the castles and reviewing their equipment (Rhys 1936, 121–123, 131–135).

Further accounts indicate that £4 9s 10d was spent on re-roofing the buildings in Dryslwyn Castle that were damaged by a great wind in January 1300. Payments continued to the constable Ralph le Blunt, his garrison of 24 men, and the supervisor of crossbows. Other named individuals who received payment included Roger de Bergh, as 'keeper of the dead garnisture' (quartermaster of the castle stores). He was also a burgess in Dryslwyn town (Rhys 1936, 135, 147–149; Griffiths 1966, 142).

The accounts for the year 1300/01 were drawn up by the prior of Carmarthen as Chamberlain of West Wales. Ralph le Blunt was still constable at Dryslwyn with a garrison of 24 men, at an annual cost of £20. A further 40s 8d was spent on 'divers works in Dryslwyn castle' (Rhys 1936, 66, 221, 225). A stock account covering the overlapping period of July 1300 to July 1301 lists various categories of supplies in the castles of west Wales, including Dryslwyn Castle. It contained supplies of wheat, oatmeal, oats, beef, bacon, suet, wine and honey, hay and firewood. Amongst the items listed were brass jars and pans, a hammer, a crowbar and a hand-mill. The equipment of the castle chapel is also listed (PRO E101/8/29, printed at Rhys 1936, app 6).

In 1301, Gerard del Espiney (de la Spine) was appointed constable of Dryslwyn Castle and leased the mill there (Griffiths 1972, 242, 255; Lewis 1923–95, 73, 79). On 6 October 1303, Dafydd ap Hywel ap Dafydd (Dafydd Bongham) was appointed steward of Cantref Mawr (Griffiths 1972, 279). Accounts presented by William de Rogate, the new Chamberlain of West Wales, for the period 1303/04 indicate that he himself was appointed constable of Dryslwyn at an annual fee of £40 (Griffiths 1972, 168, 255). This is comparable to the fees paid to the other constables of royal castles in west Wales (£60 for Carmarthen, £60 for Llanbadarn (Aberystwyth), £33 6s 8d for Dinefwr, £20 for Newcastle Emlyn and £10 for Cardigan) suggesting that Dryslwyn was the third most important castle in the strategic defence of west Wales at this period. Other expenses included 104s 11d spent on building work at the castle, 71s 5½d for a new mill and 4s 6d for an armourer to burnish and repair the armour at the castles of Dryslwyn and Dinefwr. Roger the crossbowman continues his surveying and servicing of crossbows in all the royal castles of west Wales at a rate of 2d per day. William de la Marche (probably also known as William of Hereford) was keeper of the castle stores (Rhys 1936, 323, 325, 329, 333; Griffiths 1972, 256). In the year 1304/05, the constable and garrison were identical to the previous year and £12 10¾d was spent on repairs to the castle (Rhys 1936, 397, 399, 409).

Investment in construction

In the accounting year 1305/06, further investment was made in the buildings of the castle: a new granary and bakehouse were constructed at costs of £25 16s ½d and £25 1s 11d respectively. Both buildings, probably located in the Outer Ward, seem to have consisted of timber-framed superstructures resting on stone walls, the timber being cut in the woods of Glyncothi. Lime was burnt to make mortar at the foot of the castle hill, indicating that local limestone was probably used, whilst slates were cut from a quarry in Carmarthen to cover the roofs of both buildings. The granary required a foundation trench 8 feet (2.44m) deep and 82½ feet (25.15m) in total length. Between the stone walls, earth was rammed to make a level platform and steps built to climb up to it. The building required joists 26 and 16 feet (7.92m and 4.88m) long, which were probably the dimensions of the building in plan, and rafters in 19 feet (5.79m) lengths. The roof was covered with 58 cartloads of slates. The bakehouse required a trench-built foundation wall recorded as 396 feet (120.7m) in total length, although this may be an error, as it took no longer to make than the granary foundation. Rocks had to be broken to make room for it, whilst the adjacent castle wall was trimmed down to be level with the new bakehouse wall, in order to take the wall-plate that now supported the roof timbers. The roof needed rafters 20 feet (6.1m) long and 92 cartloads of slates. The new structure contained a kiln and an oven with a plastered partition over them. An arch over the well was also constructed. This is the only reference to a source of water for the castle (PRO E101/486/18; Salzman 1952, 203; Webster 1987, 92–94) and, since no well was discovered during the

excavation of the Inner Ward (Section 5.1), it probably lies either in the unexcavated areas of the Middle or Outer Wards, or in the town.

William de Brebelschete, one of the joint leaseholders of the mill at Dryslwyn, was appointed constable of Dryslwyn Castle in 1307, the other joint lessee, Sir Thomas de Roshale (Roshall), succeeding him on 3 March 1308, only to be succeeded again exactly a year later by John Giffard the younger. On 22 October 1309, Giffard was also granted the town and its demesnes (Griffiths 1972, 256). A new constable, Sir Thomas le Blunt, was appointed on 20 May 1312, having been aided to take possession of the castle by the justiciar from Carmarthen on 23 March. Perhaps Giffard's men were trying to withhold it from him, a hint of the troubles to come later in Edward II's reign. Blunt was also granted the town of Dryslwyn and its demesnes, as well as the stewardship of Cantref Mawr. After 30 August, he held the town and demesne lands freely in order that their income should be devoted to the keeping of the castle (Griffiths 1972, 257).

In August 1312, the chamberlain of Carmarthen was required to repair and provision the castle (*CCR 1307–13*, 476). The resulting refurbishment comprised repairs to the gutters and roofs of the stables and constable's office, which apparently lay near the new bakehouse; making a new opening in the castle wall near the stables; making and hanging a new door for the hall (in Great Hall K/L); repairing the three windows in the undercroft beneath the hall; whitewashing the undercroft walls; repairing the plank flooring of the middle storey of the high tower (*altae turris*) (Round Tower D); and binding in iron the chest in which the chapel ornaments were kept. The stonemason is named as Simon of Ibernia. The undercroft beneath the first-floor hall is described as 'where the victuals and garnisture of the castle are stored', suggesting that it was the principal food store of the castle at this period. Wooden shingles were used for roofing the constable's office (PRO E101/486/27; *NLW Add MS 455D*; Webster 1987, 94; Lewis 1998, 45).

In August 1314, King Edward II wrote to the chamberlain of west Wales, ordering the repair of walls, towers and other buildings within the castle of Dryslwyn. Up to 20 marks was allowed to the constable, Thomas le Blunt, for this work (Lewis 1998, 46). In August 1315, further minor repairs were carried out in response to the orders of the previous year (*CCR 1313–18*, 240).

In 1316, additional men were requested and added to the garrison during the revolt of Llywelyn Bren (*CCR 1313–18*, 283; Griffiths 1972, 257; Webster 1987; Lewis 1998, 49). Bren was active from January to March in the Marcher lordship of Glamorgan. His raids extended as far west as Dinefwr, which he burnt (Lloyd 1935, 342; Davies 1987, 388). An allowance was also made in the accounts of Richard Mustlewyk, chamberlain of west Wales, in 1318, for his expenses in repairing or improving the defences of Dryslwyn Castle at the time (Fryde 1974, 46).

Conflict and neglect

After surviving this episode unscathed, Dryslwyn now became a minor pawn in the political game of Edward II's reign. On 18 November 1317, the town and castle of Dryslwyn and the stewardship of Cantref Mawr were granted for life to Hugh le Despenser the younger in lieu of an annual fee of 600 marks due to him by the king (*CPR 1317–21*, 56, 130; *CCR 1313–18*, 534–535). Walter Box became his constable of Dryslwyn and steward of Cantref Mawr on 4 July 1318 (*CFR 1307–19*, 364). Despenser resigned his grant on 14 September 1318, when Dryslwyn was granted by Edward II to Sir Giles de Beauchamp, one of the king's household knights (Griffiths 1972, 259). Despenser's grant was then re-issued to him on 21 November 1318 (*CPR 1317–21*, 255–256; Griffiths 1972, 258).

The political stresses of England now found expression in open fighting in Wales and the Marches (Davies 1987, 403–405). In 1320, Despenser authorised his men of Cantref Mawr to 'take distress' on John Giffard's tenants in Cantref Bychan, amounting to a virtual licence for Marcher warfare (Davies 1978, 242). When war broke out between Despenser and his opponents in 1321, Giffard advanced from Cantref Bychan to capture the Despenser lands, towns and castles in Cantref Mawr, including Dryslwyn (Lewis 1998, 51). Despenser went into exile shortly afterwards. On 30 September, Walter de Beauchamp was appointed constable of Dryslwyn Castle and steward of Cantref Mawr, replacing the previous constable, Rhys ap Gruffydd (Griffiths 1972, 260; Rees 1975, 80–81).

The next year, when Edward II gained the upper hand in his struggle with his baronial opponents at the Battle of Boroughbridge, John Giffard lost his lands. The king granted the castle and town of Dryslwyn back to Despenser on 7 May 1322 (*CPR 1321–24*, 115; Griffiths 1972, 261); however, the castle was captured and sacked by his enemies on 8 May. Despenser was subsequently able to regain control of the castle and town. This was a small part of his construction of a vast territorial hegemony in the Marches in the early 1320s, an empire which stretched from the River Wye across south Wales to the River Teifi (Davies 1978, 279–280; 1987, 405–406). Despenser leased his holding of Cantref Mawr for seven years to Rhys ap Gruffydd, together with the castles of Dinefwr and Dryslwyn (Lloyd 1935, 244).

After the execution of Despenser, Llywelyn Du ap Gruffydd ap Rhys was appointed constable on 7 November 1326. By 2 December, he had been succeeded by John Laundrey, followed swiftly by Sir Roger Pychard (or Picard), who also leased the town (Griffiths 1972, 246, 261). He, in turn, was succeeded on 8 November 1328 by Richard de Pembrugg (or Pembridge) of Clehonger in Herefordshire (Griffiths 1972, 262).

There are frequent references in the Memoranda Rolls between 1325/26 and 1335/36 to requirements for Llywelyn Du ap Gruffudd ap Rhys to account 'for the issues' (expenditures) of the castles of Dryslwyn and Dinefwr (Fryde 1974, 66, 70, 78, 82, 84, 89, 96). It is unclear whether he had a continuing role in their finances throughout this period, or if he was being pursued for arrears dating from his brief period as constable in 1326. Clearly he had to be pressed to present his accounts. This indolence and the lack of any detailed accounts from the other constables of this period suggests that little repair work was done to the castle. In 1329, the constable was instructed to 'use some of the revenue of Dryslwyn Castle for the repair of the castle', implying a need for remedial works (Fryde 1974, 74).

On 20 December 1330, Rhys ap Gruffydd was reappointed constable and acted in that capacity from the following 2 January (*CFR 1327–37*, 209–210; Griffiths 1972, 262). His post was renewed on 6 August 1333, naming him as constable of Dryslwyn Castle, steward of Cantref Mawr and forester of Glyncothi and Pennant forests for life, for his 'good services at Berwick' (*CFR 1327–37*, 370). Rhys dominated the holding of royal offices in south-west Wales in the first half of the 14th century, and was frequently appointed to array the armed men of Carmarthenshire for military expeditions from 1310 to 1341. His lands and his accumulated offices made him too powerful in the area to be ignored by the Crown, which regularly fined him for exploiting his position, but also rewarded him handsomely for his loyalty and service. He was knighted in about 1346 and died in 1356 (Lloyd 1935, 247, 249; Davies 1987, 415–417).

In 1337, the commotes of Cethiniog, Mabudrud and Mabelfyw were fined for not carrying timber to Dryslwyn Castle (PRO SC2/215/21; Rees 1924, 77n). This may have been a pretext for raising revenue through the imposition of a punitive fine for the non-performance of an obsolete custom (Davies 1987, 439). By 1338/39, the castle had suffered two decades of neglect and had unrepaired damage, which probably dated back to the Despenser period. Extensive remedial works were now undertaken. The west gable of the 'King's Hall' (Great Hall K/L) had decayed through old age and fallen, and the tops of its two side walls under the wall-plates were also broken down. These were all built up again and corbels inserted beneath the gutters for additional roof support. The timber was again brought from Glyncothi and the roof covered with slates. Although the stone used for most of this building work came from a quarry near the castle, presumably at the base of the hill, freestone from a quarry in Is Cennen was used for the doorway into the 'King's Hall' and a new window in the same building. Lime for the works was burned using seacoal. In addition, there were repairs to other buildings in the castle, including the repointing of the bakehouse and kitchen and works on 'the large tower damaged and ruined in the inner ward of the castle' (Round Tower D). Lead was used on the roofs and for the guttering, and the total cost for the work was £33 13s 2d (PRO E101/487/9; Webster 1987, 95–96).

In 1342, Edward III granted a ten-year lease of Carmarthen and Cantref Mawr to his cousin Henry of Grosmont, later Duke of Lancaster (Davies 1978, 285 n35). Edward III's son Edward, the Black Prince, took possession of the lordship of Dryslwyn in 1343 as part of his principality of Wales. On 5 May, the keepers of the castles of Dinefwr and Dryslwyn were ordered to surrender them to him (*CChR 1341–1417*, 16). At this time, the curtain wall was repaired and rebuilt, and the 'Great Tower' at the end of the hall, called the *Appeltour* (Round Tower D), was restored at a total cost of £41 (Lewis 1998, 52). This was part of a general programme of refurbishment of the prince's castles in Wales, Cornwall and elsewhere, and just one aspect of the rigorous exploitation of his lordship in Wales (Lloyd 1935, 245; Davies 1987, 403). He was content that the area should remain in the control of local Welsh gentry, providing that the revenue kept coming to his coffers.

In June and December 1355, Sir Rhys ap Gruffydd was ordered to protect the castle during the Black Prince's absence in France (*Register of the Black Prince* iii, 492, 495). In 1356/57, Gilbert de Felmersham was appointed constable (Griffiths 1972, 262). In this year also, £25 1s 11d was spent on carpenters, masons and tilers undertaking repairs to the castle and the enclosure of the park. Local control was soon reasserted. On 3 April 1358, Rhys ap Gruffudd II, son of the above Sir Rhys ap Gruffydd, was appointed constable for life, and he may have been appointed as early as 1353. In 1359/60, he took a lease of the demesnes of Dinefwr and Dryslwyn (Griffiths 1972, 262–263). On 26 November 1359, John Langley and William de Norton were appointed joint storekeepers of Carmarthen, Cardigan and Dryslwyn Castles, and Rhys ap Gruffydd was ordered to ensure the defence of Dryslwyn Castle whilst the Black Prince was overseas, and to provide two watchmen on its walls at night. In July 1377, he was paid for taking arms to the castle (*Register of the Black Prince* iii, 378; Griffiths 1972, 196, 263).

In the mean time, William Houghton had been appointed constable of Dryslwyn Castle, on 9 June 1374, and on 5 June 1380 he was reappointed as constable for life, a grant that was repeated several times (Griffiths 1972, 263). On 8 May 1385, he was ordered to repair the castle in advance of the invasion that was being prepared by King Charles VI of France in Flanders (*CCR 1381–85*, 549). An inventory drawn up in this year indicates that there were provisions and armaments for a garrison of 12 men-at-arms at Dryslwyn Castle, of whom 4 were armed with crossbows. Whilst it was no longer a front-line fortress, the castle and its garrison were still being maintained as a defensive strong-point (PRO SC6/1221/16; Webster

1987, 96). In 1387/88, Philip ap Madog, a merchant and burgess of Cardigan, bought 40s worth of putrid honey, which was found to be unfit for the provision store at the castle (Griffiths 1972, 419). The chapel of Dryslwyn Castle was dependent on the parish church of Llangathen, which had been granted to St Mary's Abbey in Chester by the Black Prince. By 1388, however, the poverty of the nuns there was so great that they were released from the burden of finding a chaplain to celebrate services at the castle three days a week (Lloyd 1935, 299). Presumably, there was no longer a need to provide as many services for the garrison. On 11 February 1399, William Houghton and William Bradewardyn (a surgeon) were appointed constables of Dryslwyn Castle for life 'in survivorship' and, on the following 12 December, Bradewardyn was reappointed (Griffiths 1972, 263, 264).

Revolt and destruction

There was no immediate response in the Tywi valley to the declaration of revolt by Owain Glyn Dŵr in northeast Wales in September 1400. Following the capture of Conwy Castle for Glyn Dŵr by Owain ap Rhys and Gwilym ap Tudur in May 1401, the revolt gained wider support and there were reports of rebels assembling in Carmarthenshire. Consequently, the garrison at Kidwelly Castle was strengthened, as were the garrisons of other unspecified castles, almost certainly including Dryslwyn. By the closing decades of the 14th century, little use had been made of many of the castles for some time and, as a result, programmes of repair had not been maintained. Some showed signs of partial abandonment and dilapidation; even notable strongholds, such as Harlech (Davies 1995, 105).

In October 1401, Henry IV arrived in the upper reaches of the Tywi valley, from Strata Florida to Llandovery, at the head of a punitive expedition to suppress the supporters of Owain Glyn Dŵr. There was clearly a requirement for well-garrisoned and secure castles to hold out against the rebels. The fact that Henry did not proceed further down the valley as far as Carmarthen may suggest that no signs of rebellion were yet apparent there (Lloyd 1935, 252). In November, the men of Carmarthenshire and Cardiganshire accepted a pardon from the king (Davies 1995, 106).

Following the defeat of the English at Bryn Glas on 22 June 1402, increased attention was paid to strengthening some castles, such as Kidwelly, and garrisoning others, including Carreg Cennan. This defensive action was the only clearly distinguishable coherent policy of the English and Marcher authorities to the emerging rebellion (Davies 1995, 107–108). Dryslwyn almost certainly received extra garrison troops at this time and it is possible that minor improvements to the state of the castle were effected. The appointment of a new constable, Rhys ap

Gruffydd ap Llywelyn Foethus, on 2 March 1402 appears to have been a further move to ensure that a loyal man was safeguarding the castle (*CPR 1401–05*, 57; Griffiths 1972, 264).

On 2 July 1403, Henry Don of Cydweli and other local Welsh leaders, including Rhys ap Gruffydd of Dryslwyn, rose in revolt for Owain Glyn Dŵr and laid siege to Dinefwr Castle. Glyn Dŵr himself entered the Tywi valley the following day and the new constable surrendered Dryslwyn Castle to him (Griffiths 1972, 264; Davies 1995, 312). A letter from John Scudamore (or Skidmore), constable of Carreg Cennan Castle, relates that Owain Glyn Dŵr spent the night of 4 July at Dryslwyn Castle. Scudamore visited him there to seek safe passage for his wife and her mother, but was refused (Solomon 1982, 67). On 5 July, Glyn Dŵr captured the town of Carmarthen, killing 50 of the defenders; the castle surrendered to him the following day. All Carmarthenshire, Cydweli, Carnwyllion and Is Cennen pledged their loyalty to Glyn Dŵr and he planned to take all the castles in the region (Lloyd 1935, 253; Davies 1995, 111–112, 151, 274). Glyn Dŵr's progress through west Wales was subsequently halted by the forces of Lord Carew near St Clears. In mid September, Henry IV again marched down the Tywi valley, recaptured Carmarthen and installed a substantial garrison of 550 men. This garrison was later strengthened and commanded by the king's cousin Edward, Duke of York. Whilst this helped to secure and retain the important castle and town of Carmarthen, probably the second largest town in Wales during this period, English control was otherwise only effective in the castles and walled boroughs of the region, such as Kidwelly and Llanstephan; the native rural population retained its loyalty to Glyn Dŵr (Lloyd 1935, 254; Davies 1995, 114).

If Dryslwyn Castle and town were recaptured by the English forces at this time, there is no surviving record, although it could have occurred as early as mid September during the march of the forces of Henry IV down the Tywi valley, or in the subsequent months by the forces of the Duke of York in Carmarthen. Most probably, however, Dryslwyn remained under Welsh control and loyal to Owain Glyn Dŵr. The Duke was given the custody of Dryslwyn Castle and all the other royal castles in south Wales on 29 November 1403, as an adjunct to his post of Lieutenant of All Wales (Griffiths 1972, 127, 264). This appointment was for three years, but the custody of Dryslwyn was titular; there is no indication that he was able to take actual control of the castle.

In August 1404, the town of Kidwelly was captured and burnt by the Welsh of the region (Davies 1995, 116). A year later, Glyn Dŵr received military assistance from an expedition of French troops sent by his ally Charles VI and, in August 1405, the joint Franco-Welsh forces marched through south Wales from Milford Haven, burning the town of Haverfordwest,

capturing Carmarthen and destroying part of the town, before moving on to burn towns and besiege castles in south-east Wales, marching almost as far as Worcester. This campaign penned up the English garrisons in their castles and the followers of Owain Glyn Dŵr continued to dominate the Tywi valley. The French troops withdrew in 1406 (Davies 1995, 117).

Prince Henry of Wales was made Lieutenant of All Wales in succession to the Duke of York on 29 January 1406 and, as part of his lieutenancy, he was given the custody of Dryslwyn Castle and all other royal castles in south Wales. This appointment was thereafter periodically extended (Griffiths 1972, 127–128, 264). It is unlikely that the prince ever paid a visit to Dryslwyn during his service in Wales. Following the commencement of his command, there was a gradual return to English control over many parts of Wales during the year 1406. By 1407, almost all of Cantref Mawr and Cantref Bychan were again in English hands, paying a communal fine of £1000 and further sums in subsequent years as the price of their rebellion (Davies 1995, 124, 305). Many rebels were eventually pardoned, including Rhys ap Gruffydd ap Llywelyn Foethus, who returned to the king's peace in 1409. Many paid large fines and, suffered impoverishment for the rest of their lives.

The re-establishment of English control in the Tywi valley was signalled by the appointment of Rhys ap Thomas ap Dafydd as beadle of the commotes of Maen-Ordeilo and Cethiniog in 1407. He was probably a descendant of Goronwy Goch and had been retained as an 'esquire' by Richard II. He had remained loyal to the Crown throughout the revolt and his lands in Carmarthenshire were ravaged by the rebels. After the end of the rebellion, he became a key figure in the royal government of the south part of the principality. He was granted an exemption from anti-Welsh legislation, becoming 'true English' (Davies 1995, 225). On 2 October 1407, Rhys was granted Dryslwyn Castle and the income from Dryslwyn town and demesne lands for ten years at a rent of ten marks in the first year and £10 per annum every subsequent year (Griffiths 1972, 143, 264–265).

There is no further record of repairs or garrisoning of the castle after the period of the revolt. The castle almost certainly ceased to be used and may have been deliberately destroyed. It has been suggested that it was set ablaze by the retreating troops of Owain Glyn Dŵr (Lewis 1998, 66): Talley Abbey, for example, was also damaged in the rebellion (Smith and O'Neil 1967, 8). The title normally used for the occupier of the castle from this date onwards was 'farmer of Dryslwyn castle and town'. This suggests a considerable change in the way in which Dryslwyn was held: it was no longer granted by the king to a favoured individual, who received both the income from the town and a stipend as constable in return for ensuring the castle remained in a defensible condition. Under the new arrangement, the farmer paid the Crown a fixed annual rent and extracted rents and fees from the town and associated lands as best he could. This was probably the point at which the castle ceased to be a military stronghold.

The castle farmers

John Wodehouse was granted the farm of the town of Dryslwyn for 20 years at a rent of £10 *per annum* on 15 February 1409. The grant made no specific mention of the castle, although it is probable that he occupied it (Griffiths 1972, 265). In 1415, Rhys ap Thomas ap Dafydd was granted the title of steward of Cantref Mawr and keeper of Glyncothi forest (Lloyd 1935, 256). Rhys acted as Wodehouse's deputy at Dryslwyn and remained in control of the area until 1446. On 15 February 1422, he received a grant in the name of Henry, Prince of Wales, of five marks per year out of the fee farm of the town, to be paid by John Wodehouse (Griffiths 1972, 265). Sir John Scudamore was granted Dryslwyn for eight years on 5 May 1429, although John Wodehouse was almost immediately reinstated and continued as farmer of Dryslwyn until his death in 1431. On 12 May 1432, Rhys ap Thomas ap Dafydd was granted Dryslwyn for 20 years at an annual rent of £10 6s 8d (Griffiths 1972, 265).

On 4 March 1439, Thomas Staunton was appointed as constable of Dryslwyn Castle and custodian of the Glyncothi forest for life. This was almost certainly the grant of an obsolete title to give Staunton an income from the Crown. He was a prominent member of the king's household and later served as Member of Parliament for Leicestershire (Griffiths 1972, 264, 398). His appointment does not necessarily imply that there was still a defensible castle at Dryslwyn at that date. In 1446, Rhydderch Rhys ap Gruffydd and Thomas ap Thomas Fychan were granted the farm of Dryslwyn for 24 years (Griffiths 1972, 265). The succession of farmers continued until at least 1522, by which time the annual rent had declined from £10 to £8 (Griffiths 1972, 265–266).

Dryslwyn Castle played no part in the Wars of the Roses, although every other functioning castle in the region is noted in the written records of the period, and it may safely be concluded that the castle was no longer defended by the mid 15th century. It was certainly not involved in any later conflict, such as the Civil War, and had effectively ceased to be a military stronghold in about 1407 and a defensible structure by 1455.

Discussion

In the initial years of occupation following the revolt of 1287, the Crown maintained a military presence at Dryslwyn and the other castles of west Wales. It invested in their repair, maintained the equipment they contained and retained considerable garrisons. This was a prudent precaution against Welsh revolt, but the level of manning was always consistent with the level of threat. The constable and garrison of Dryslwyn and the upkeep of the structures of the castle represented a cost to the Crown, against which could be set a variable rental income from the town and district, and the sale of war booty and surplus supplies in the early post-siege period.

However, as early as the 1320s, after the grant of the castle to Hugh le Despenser, little further interest was shown in its development. There were periods without building works, when the castle's fabric, and presumably its equipment, suffered considerable decay. The occasional programmes of essential repairs, such as that in 1338–39, proved costly, whilst the garrison costs remained high and rent returns were variable. In the second half of the 14th century, local figures were in control of the castle and the garrison and equipment were maintained at a reduced level.

In the 15th century, the Crown farmed out Dryslwyn, receiving a fixed rent. Any improvements to the castle and town were now an investment decision for the farmer and had ceased to be a Crown responsibility. The appointment of minor Welsh knights or local officials as farmers of Dryslwyn and other Crown properties in the principality formed part of the development of a new class of gentry in Wales in the late medieval period. The money collected in rents stayed in the local economy, but there is no evidence of local investment and development. There had been a change of emphasis from the security of the area to its exploitation as a source of profit.

3.2 ARCHAEOLOGICAL OUTLINE, PHASES 4C–7D: THE ENGLISH GARRISON CASTLE

Phase 4c

Many of the deposits from this phase of activity are rich in finds indicative of armed conflict, such as arrowheads, lithic projectiles and links of chain mail, and, since they post-date construction in the early 1280s, they almost certainly derive from the siege of 1287. Two substantial spherical limestone projectiles, one from between the north wall (K59) of Great Hall K/L and the revetting wall (O181) of Courtyard O, the other from the Area F middens (F16 and F19), clearly date to this phase and could only have been fired by a large trebuchet of the type documented as being in use at the 1287 siege.

The building work of Phase 4c at Dryslwyn Castle is characterised by the use of squared limestone blocks and hard white mortar (Sections 6.1 and 6.3). The only substantial walls and masonry features built using these materials are the east wall (E2 and F2) of the Inner Ward, together with its associated garderobes (E9 and E17) and steps (E5) (Figure 3.1). This limited building work, which is concentrated on the east side

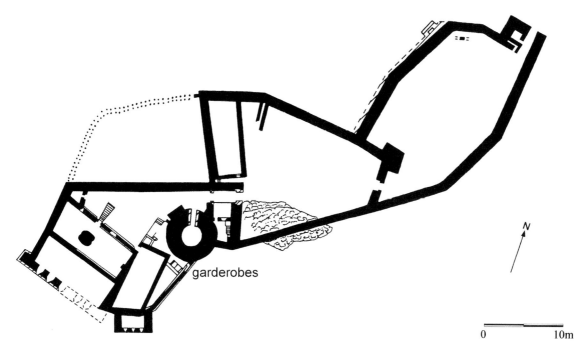

garderobes

0   10m

FIGURE 3.1

Dryslwyn Castle: Phase 4c–d

of the Inner Ward, appears to partially overlie the Phase 4a walls of Chapel H and cuts through the middens in Area F, which date to Phases 3b and 4b. Thus, this squared stone-block construction post-dates the building work of Rhys ap Maredudd and any evidence of a late 'Welsh' occupation phase and is almost certainly the work of English-trained masons from north Wales in the late 1280s and early 1290s, after the siege (Section 6.1). Further dating evidence is offered by a coin ([C14], Section 9.3) from the foundation (F120) of wall (F3), which was minted between 1282 and 1289. The revetting wall and bastion of the north-west corner of the Outer Ward is also constructed of squared stone. The limited extent of this work, restricted to a single corner of the Outer Ward, tallies with its interpretation as a repair carried out soon after the siege and suggests also that this north-west corner is where the Outer Ward wall was breached by the besieging English forces in 1287.

The hard white mortar that bonds the squared stone walls of this phase was also used in the construction of the passageway (O10), which was inserted into the base of Round Tower D from Courtyard O at ground level. This eliminated the Round Tower as a stronghold of last resort and meant that it was probably thereafter used as a lookout tower, becoming part of an integrated defensive strategy for the castle as a whole. Passageway (O10) gave easy access into the ground-floor level of Round Tower D, which was probably used for storage. The jambs of the two doors located at either end of the passage indicate that they were normally opened from the exterior, as one would expect for a storeroom, but could also be bolted from the inside in case of defence. The round towers in the

castles of Cilgerran (Pembrokeshire) and Dinefwr (Carmarthenshire) were also breached with a ground-floor passageway and this would appear to be a deliberate change in the defensive form of all the castles of this area by their new English occupants. The original flagstone floor (D11) of Round Tower D was torn up when the passageway (O10) was inserted.

The hard white mortar was also used on a new buttress (P5), which was added to support a platform giving access to the upper storey of Great Chamber G, and again to form a new floor (P33) over Area P, where a door now controlled access between Areas P and E. This necessitated the construction of a door jamb in the exterior wall (E14) of Round Tower D and a door reveal (E49) with hinge pillars built into the corner of Great Chamber G. The new arrangement controlled access to the newly constructed garderobes and the wall-walk in Area E.

At roughly the same time, a revetting wall (B18) in Gateway Area B was constructed, which butted onto the walls of the Phase 4a inner and outer gateways. The area to the north of this wall was filled and covered with a mortar surface (P44, P51 and P63), which formed a raised platform north of the passageway between the two gateways. Subsequent wear occurred on these surfaces, although no building can be discerned. Any form of more elaborate guardhouse, which is perhaps indicated by the Phase 4a arrowloops (B24) in the wall (B5) between Areas B and C, was either never built or demolished without trace by the time the revetting wall and platform were constructed.

There are extensive areas of squared stone on the outer face of the substantial southern wall (J2) of the

Inner Ward, particularly around the windows. Given the prevalence for using squared stone blocks in Phase 4c, it thus appears likely that this wall had its exterior face extensively repaired. These repairs appear to have wrapped around to the west side of this wall to form a buttress, which reinforced the corner, although it is possible that it was added in the later Phase 5a construction work. This buttress, when erected, blocked a west-facing window in the Phase 4a wall (J2) of Apartments I/J.

Following Edward's victory over the princes of Gwynedd in 1283, Edwardian policy actively encouraged urban development, resulting in the construction of such towns as Conwy (Conwy) and Caernarfon (Gwynedd) in north Wales and encouraging urban expansion throughout Wales (Soulsby 1983, 13). It appears possible that this same period saw a substantial expansion of the town of Dryslwyn. Historical records indicate that, by 1300, it had been expanded to take 45 burgage plots. The existing town wall (T20) was certainly thickened (T16), with access probably created for a wall-walk, but also the town wall (Z22) and ditch (Z34) were extended to encompass the whole of the hilltop with a substantial gatehouse (Town Gatehouse U) with gates and a portcullis on its western side. There is also evidence that a palisade (Z31) was constructed to protect those at work on the town wall and ditch. Though these developments can be attributed to the Edwardian policy of urbanisation of Wales after 1283, that fact that the Town Gatehouse U has an identical plan to that of the Castle Gatehouse W could well argue that the expansion of the town derives from Rhys's redevelopment of the site in Phase 4a.

Phase 4d

Following the siege and reconstruction of the castle, there was a period of occupation. Rubble (O52), flooring (O58) and occupation deposits (O51) were laid down in Courtyard O, whilst occupation debris (G25) was deposited on a poor-quality mortar and clay and cobble surface (G27 and G29) that, together with a platform (G24), was constructed on top of siege deposits in Great Chamber G. Most activity would have taken place on the upper floors of the Inner Ward buildings, explaining the scarcity of occupation material from this phase when compared to others.

Phase 5a

The south-west corner of Great Hall K/L was remodelled (Figure 3.2) with the west end of the southern wall (J83, K57 and K58) being rebuilt from ground level. A doorway (K57), built into an earlier arrowloop opening, provided direct access from the undercroft of Great Hall K/L to Apartments I/J. The lower part of the southern side of this rebuilt wall was not faced, since it was below the clay and cobble dump in Area J that supported the first-floor level. Wall (J21), constructed of poor-quality shale, was built in this phase of activity to revet the clay and cobble around the rising passageway, which ran up from the steps (J76 and K58) into the most westerly first-floor apartment. The foundations of wall (J5), which ran between Areas I and J and rested on the partially demolished wall of Kitchen I, were similarly constructed of shale and contained at least one lithic projectile

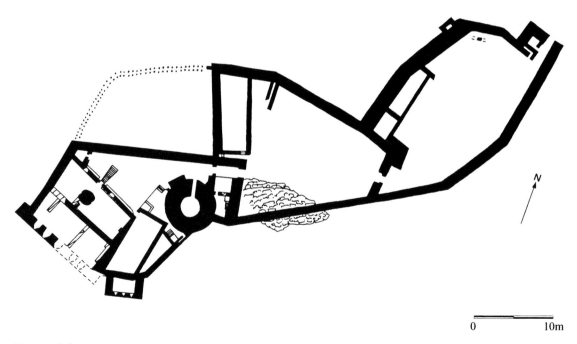

0   10m

FIGURE 3.2

Dryslwyn Castle: Phase 5a–b

50

from the 1287 siege. The crosswall (K52 and L6) was constructed to support the south-west corner of Great Hall K/L during this rebuilding. A wooden pillar with a red sandstone base (L22) was also added to support the central wooden beam, which in turn supported the wooden first floor. Subsequently, a set of steps (L7) was built against the crosswall (L6), which allowed the undercroft to be entered from a trapdoor in the floor of the hall above. On the north side of Great Hall K/L, the arrowloop (K72) was altered to form a window (K73). This allowed much more light to enter the western end of the undercroft, which now acted as a thoroughfare between Courtyard O and Apartments I/J. The increase in traffic through this area resulted in the deposition of the first of several floor surfaces (K19 and K20). There is evidence that one or more cinque-foil mullioned windows, carved in red sandstone, were inserted into the north wall of the Great Hall K/L. It is possible that this construction activity relates to the repair and rebuilding of the south-west corner of the 'King's Hall', which was recorded in 1338 (Section 3.1) (Figure 3.3).

A further resurfacing (O45) of Courtyard O also occurred in this phase of rebuilding, and a drain (I12), possibly replacing an earlier one, was constructed against the east wall of Area I, suggesting that this most easterly room of Apartments I/J may have been used as a kitchen. Much of the stone used for construction work in this phase was shale, a poor-quality building stone indicative of a decline in the standard of building work in the 14th century.

A large building (R) was constructed in the Outer Ward.

Phase 5b

There is little evidence of activity during the 14th-century occupation of Dryslwyn Castle. Presumably, the garrison was operating at a reduced level and there was little requirement for further building work, save minor repairs to surfaces and the occasional deposit of occupation material. Additional flooring (K13 and K18) was deposited in the western end of Great Hall

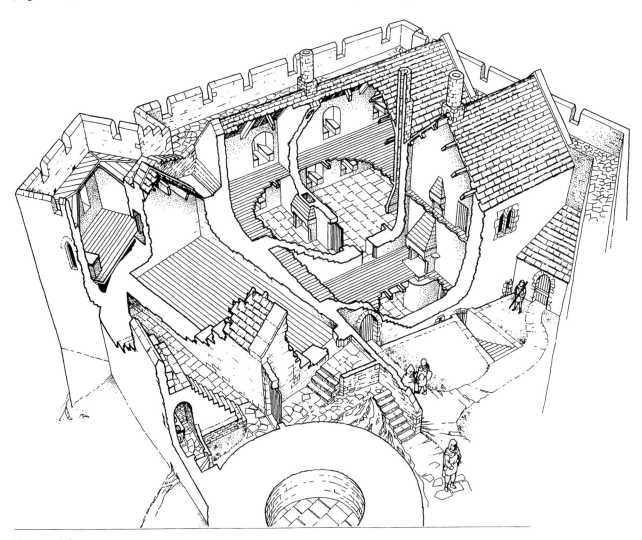

FIGURE 3.3

Reconstruction of the Great Hall and apartments as they appeared in the mid 14th century (drawn by Chris Jones-Jenkins)

K/L. Two coins (nos 13 and 20), recovered from the crushed slate floor layer (K18), were of the 1280s and the early 14th century respectively and help to confirm a mid 14th-century date. The drain (K16) continued in use throughout this period, with silts (K30 and K31) from this drain producing coins of the early and mid 14th century (nos 17 and 19, Section 9.3). Dumps of occupation material (O44) and roofing slate (O25) were excavated in Courtyard O.

Phase 5c

A number of minor building works were carried out in stone during this phase (Figure 3.4). These included the construction of a platform in Area J, possibly to support a fireplace in an upper storey of Apartments I/J. Also, in Area P, the route through to the garderobes of Area E was blocked (P13) and a new mortar floor (P19) laid.

The major development in this phase was the construction of a timber-framed guardhouse on the raised platform of Gateway Area B. This may have replaced an earlier masonry structure of Phase 4a or 4c. The guardhouse was constructed using wooden sill beams (B21 and B22), as there was insufficient soil to use earthfast posts. A door probably stood in the centre of the building's north wall, its location marked by an exterior step and the findspot of iron hinges that had fallen from their working positions when the building was burnt to the ground. The window blocking (C42) was inserted and a stone step (B33) added in front of the guardhouse as part of this building activity.

A series of postholes (G15–G19), dug into the floor of Great Chamber G, held wooden posts supporting a new upper storey to replace the one built during Phase 4a. In addition, a wooden sill beam (L49) was laid east–west down the centre of the undercroft in Great Hall K/L. This appears to have supported a timber-framed partition that now divided up the space within the eastern room of the undercroft (Area L).

These timber-framed buildings must have been cheaper to construct, although they were less substantial defensive structures than the earlier masonry buildings. Together with the use of poor-quality shale stone in Phase 5a and records of repair rather than new construction, the impression is that, during the 14th century, Dryslwyn Castle was being maintained in a cost-effective manner.

There is no direct dating evidence for this phase, although, since it follows the mid 14th-century occupation of Phase 5b, it is presumed to be late 14th-century in date.

Phase 5d

This phase of activity in the castle is marked by a series of occupation deposits and dumps of soil and stone. The accumulation of soil (E48) in Area E is interpreted as a period of abandonment, probably following the blocking of the doorway linking Areas E and P in the preceding period. Minor repairs (B36) to surfaces were undertaken in Gateway Area B, in addition to minor modifications, such as the steps (B40) between Areas B and C. In Great Chamber G and Courtyard O, crushed

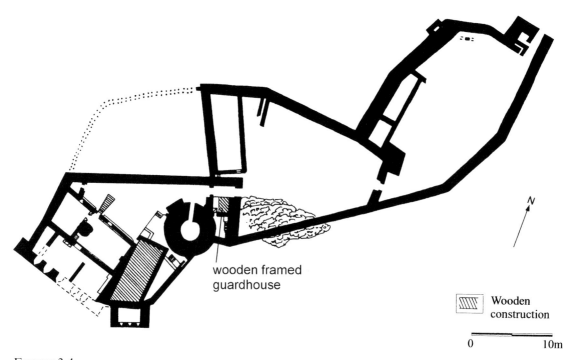

wooden framed guardhouse

| ▨ | Wooden construction |

0   10m

FIGURE 3.4

Dryslwyn Castle: Phase 5c–d

shale flooring layers (G13 and O28) were deposited, which were very similar to the Phase 5b layer (K18) seen in the undercroft of Great Hall K/L. Crushed shale seems to have been a favoured flooring material in the 14th century castle, probably because it could be quarried locally and provided a cheap alternative to crushed slate.

A spread of coal (P9) found in Arca P indicates that this part of the Inner Ward acted as a coal store in Phase 5d, suggesting that a change had by now taken place in the preferred fuel used within the castle, from wood to coal or a mixture of both. This presumably reflects the cheapness and availability of coal in the Tywi valley at this time, since it could be sourced locally from the outcrops on the western edge of the south Wales coalfield, a few miles to the east of Dryslwyn.

There is little, if any, independent dating evidence for this phase of occupation. It appears likely to correspond with the later half of 14th and early 15th centuries, since it precedes the phase of the castle's destruction in the early to mid 15th century.

Phase 6a

Several attempts were made to block up entrances at different locations around the castle in this phase (Figure 3.5). The main passageway through Castle Gatehouse W had a substantial wall (W12) built into it, completely sealing it. Similarly, the passageway into Round Tower D was walled up (O216) and filled with rubble (O211). A wall (J85) was also constructed, blocking the doorway (J84) between Areas I and J,

and a blocking (J49) was inserted into the doorway between Great Hall K/L and Apartments I/J. Burnt stones (E47) appear to have been pushed down the garderobe chutes (E9 and E17) in order to block them, although it also possible to interpret this evidence as part of the later castle destruction in Phase 6d.

Taken together, these appear to be deliberate measures to 'decommission' the site and they would have effectively denied the use of the castle as a defensive structure to any armed forces. There is no archaeological dating evidence associated with this phase of activity, but the capture of the castle by the forces of Owain Glyn Dŵr presents the most likely event to have triggered such actions. The castle was surrendered intact to Glyn Dŵr's forces in 1405, but, since their revolt was unsustainable, they quit the castle around 1407. Perhaps they decommissioned the castle prior to abandoning it; however, it is far more likely that the castle was decommissioned by the English forces once they had regained control of the Tywi valley around 1408. It is likely that the English forces were, at that stage, unable to afford to garrison the castle and probably not yet prepared to make the commitment to demolish it. Therefore, in order to deny Dryslwyn Castle as a defendable stronghold or place of refuge to any future forces of revolt, they decommissioned it.

Phase 6b

Several locations in the castle display clear evidence for a phase of looting prior to the castle's destruction

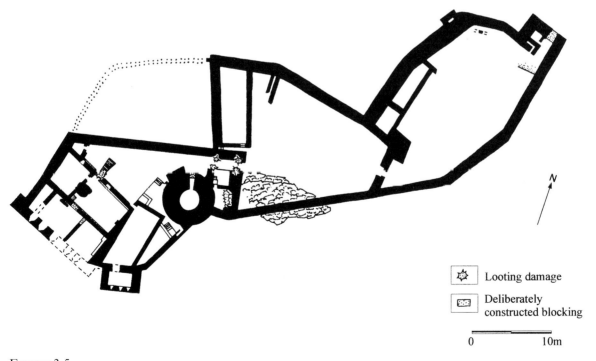

Looting damage

Deliberately constructed blocking

0 ——— 10m

FIGURE 3.5

Dryslwyn Castle: Phase 6

(Figure 3.5). In Gateway Area B, the hinges that supported the outer gates of the Inner Ward had been hastily removed (B128), leaving broken stones and burning against the wall where fires had been lit to melt the lead holding the iron hinge pillar supports in place. Similar damage is also seen where the hinges of the inner gates had been present in the wall.

In Area C, the stone treads of steps (C7) had been removed, leaving holes in the face of the adjoining wall (C6). As a result, charcoal from the subsequent burning of the castle (Phase 6c) lay directly on the stone rubble core of these steps. Also missing was an iron grill that covered the drain (O185) at the base of the steps (O152) in Courtyard O. All that remained to show the existence of this feature were iron stains (O197) on the side of the drain. In Area G, the wooden posts that had been erected in Phase 5c to support an upper wooden floor appear to have been removed prior to the burning. They were clearly not burnt *in situ*, as burnt roof debris had filled the empty postholes.

The lack of carved freestone in upstanding walls or within the layers of stone rubble of the castle's demolition indicates that almost all the freestone from the window and doorway surrounds was removed prior to demolition (Phase 6d). Several of the capstones of the drain (K16) that ran through the undercroft in Great Hall K/L had even been removed.

This looting may either have lasted several years, whilst the castle was abandoned, or for a short time just ahead of the castle's burning and demolition. The fact that a number of doors and their hinges remained in Great Hall K/L, in addition to the wooden gatehouse in Gateway Area B, suggests that the looting had not finished when the castle was set alight. In Round Tower D, the discovery of a pile of iron roves, apparently dropped and never retrieved, gives the impression of looting brought to a halt by the burning of the castle. Perhaps the fires laid to melt the lead retaining the iron hinge pillars set the castle ablaze unintentionally.

It appears that almost all of the ironwork, freestone and even much of the timber was removed offsite. The thoroughness with which this was done indicates an organised stripping process prior to burning and demolition. Such a deliberate policy strongly suggests a commercial contract similar to that granted in 1649 for the deliberate stripping and demolition of Montgomery Castle (Powys) (Knight 1993, 121; Thompson 1987, 186–193).

Phase 6c

Following its looting, the castle was set alight, burning down the wooden structures within the masonry walls. Buildings with slate roofs, such as Gateway Area B, Great Chamber G and Great Hall K/L, filled with collapsed roofing material, which also scattered into adjoining areas, including the passageway of Gateway Area B and the eastern and southern sides of Courtyard O. In many other un-roofed areas, such as Area C, there was just a fine layer of charcoal, but there was a considerable depth (up to 0.7m in places) of a burning deposit in Great Hall K/L. In addition to the slates from the roof and associated nails, extensive deposits of clay probably represented make-up from the two floors above the undercroft. The lack of clay in the burnt debris from Great Chamber G suggests it may not have had any internal floor left and that it was removed, together with its supporting posts, during earlier looting in Phase 6b. The heat during the burning was intense and, in places, temperatures had become high enough to create a natural glazing process, forming glassy slag within the burnt debris. This process may occasionally have been aided by the pieces of lead used for waterproofing and water drainage from the roof. The heat was most intense within Round Tower D, which, once it lost its roof, drew air up through the passageway (O10), thereby acting like a huge furnace. The very high temperatures generated reddened the limestone blocks within the tower to a depth of several centimetres. There was no slate in the burning layer of Round Tower D, suggesting that its roof was instead covered with lead.

The discovery of an early 15th-century jetton ([C22], Section 9.3) at the base of the burning deposit (K12) in Great Hall K/L suggests that both the looting and burning of the castle happened in the early to mid 15th century, only a few years after its decommissioning. As we have already seen, the documentary evidence does not record Dryslwyn Castle playing any part in any later armed conflict, the castle appears to have been decommissioned and burned down by the second quarter of the 15th century.

Phase 6d

Following the burning of the castle, all the walls were demolished. A deliberate and swift act of demolition is indicated by clean breaks in the un-weathered rubble, in stark contrast to Town Gatehouse U, where slow weathering leading to a build-up of rubble took place. In the western face of wall (B3) in Gateway Area B, a small hole was uncovered that had been picked through the rendered surface into the rubble core of the wall. Evidence of burning within the hole can be interpreted as a deliberate attempt to undermine the masonry using a wooden prop that was subsequently burnt in order to topple the wall. In this instance it failed and the wall survived, but it does provide evidence for the mechanics of the demolition process.

The substantial depth of rubble, over 5m thick in places, completely buried all but a few of the walls of the castle. Substantial sections of masonry were dislodged in this demolition process, such as a large part of Round Tower D (O24), which fell outwards, pushing back the foundations of the northern curtain wall by over 0.65m. Similarly massive pieces of masonry did considerable damage to the surfaces and steps in Courtyard O, whilst a substantial section of the southern curtain wall was sent crashing down into the River Tywi, causing slumping and disruption to the archaeological deposits in Areas G, H and I.

Phase 7a

There was no evidence of very late medieval or post-medieval activity in the Inner Ward, but a building (R2 and R4–6) in the Outer Ward with split stone roof tiles is probably a house or barn. A layer of stone (Z6) in the town ditch indicates a deliberate attempt to create a crudely surfaced roadway in this shallow depression.

Phase 7b

There was a gradual build-up of soil over the ruined castle and its rubble, from the point of its demolition to the start of excavations in 1980. In some areas, such as Area J, the soil cover was thin due to the exposed nature of the hillside and it is probable that there had been active erosion of the archaeological deposits during the very late medieval and post-medieval periods. In other areas, for example Areas K and L, where there was a dip in the hillside, there had been a considerable accumulation of soil, up to 0.3m deep in places.

Phase 7c

Following the abandonment of Dryslwyn town, the site was regularly visited in the 18th and 19th centuries by tourists, poets and artists. By the 19th century Dryslwyn hill and castle regularly featured in published scenic tours of Wales (Pennant 1773; Gastineau 1830; Black 1864). Ceramic sherds, including 18th- and 19th-century porcelain, particularly from Castle Gatehouse W, perhaps indicate that picnics were consumed at this scenic beauty spot. At the western end of the hill in Areas H and K, two mining tokens of the late 18th century ([C23–24], Section 9.3) were recovered from the topsoil, again probably dropped by visitors. Still later activity is attested by a substantial pit (H33), 2m deep, which was dug in the south-eastern corner of Area H alongside the eastern wall of Chapel H. At its base was the partial skeleton of a horse. A halfpenny ([C25], Section 9.3) and fragments of a beer bottle from pit fill (H10) indicate a date after 1917.

4

INNER WARD: EXCAVATION EVIDENCE

Though each area of the Inner Ward was excavated separately (Figure 1.3), the information recovered has been summarised in composite plans and phased descriptions of the archaeology for adjoining areas. Discussion of the key features in the areas follows the description, elevation drawings and plans. The individual area excavation details and phased matrices are available in the archive level report (Caple 2002).

4.1 AREAS D, E AND P: ROUND TOWER

Areas D, E and P are situated in the north-eastern quarter of the Inner Ward and are dominated by the flared-based round tower or cylindrical keep, here referred to as Round Tower D (Figure 1.3). This building was the first to be constructed on the hill at Dryslwyn and it occupied the whole of Area D, perched high on a ridge of bedrock that also extended into Area C. Areas E and P lie on the southern slope of this bedrock ridge, surrounding the base of Round Tower D. They remained devoid of buildings throughout the castle's occupation, their main purpose being to facilitate access between Courtyard O, Round Tower D, Great Chamber G and the wall-walk of the curtain wall.

Phase 1

Before building work on Round Tower D could begin, the natural bedrock (D9/E25/P15) was quarried to form a level foundation and obtain building stone. This quarrying activity created a small scoop (P90) and flat-bottomed gully (P94) in Area P, which were both formed out of a natural crack in the bedrock. Where the bedrock platform was not wide enough, limestone slabs (D16 and P66) were used to extend it, creating a raised level surface for the foundation (P44) and wall (D3/E14/P14) of the Round Tower

itself (Figure 4.1). This wall (D3/E14/P14), which had a rubble core, was built using naturally split limestone and a yellow earthy mortar, typical features of Phase 1a construction within the castle (Section 6.1). A slight offset of 20–30mm in the lower courses of masonry suggests that it was constructed in two stages, probably over two consecutive seasons.

Inside Round Tower D, a yellow earthy mortar sub-floor (D7) was laid, covering traces of original soil (D8) and natural boulder clay (D14), which were still present in small hollows in the bedrock (D9). This acted as a base for a flagstone floor (D11), which was built into the Round Tower wall (D3/E14/P14). Only the lowest 2m of masonry of Round Tower D now remain, but comparison with other flared-based round towers at Bronllys Castle (Powys) (Smith and Knight 1981), Cilgerran Castle (Pembrokeshire) (Hilling 2000, 12–15) and Dolbadarn Castle (Gwynedd) (Avent 1994a, 30–33) indicates that such buildings were normally three storeys high (Figure 4.2): the ground floor acted as a storage room for provisions, whilst the upper two storeys served as accommodation for the lord and his family. Round towers were generally accessed at first-floor level and Round Tower D was no exception, with an external wooden staircase leading up to a first-floor doorway from Area P (Figure 4.2).

Ephemeral traces of three openings (D22–24) were observed in the remains of the Round Tower wall (D3) (Figure 4.3). These were not sufficiently well preserved to identify their form or function with confidence. Openings (D23 and D24), however, were fully contained within wall (D3) and did not project through to the exterior. They may have formed the lower parts of light wells or ventilation shafts that enabled both light and air to enter the basement of the tower from external openings located higher up: such features have been identified within other Welsh round towers, including those at Dinefwr Castle (Carmarthenshire), Dolbadarn Castle (Gwynedd) and Dundrum Castle

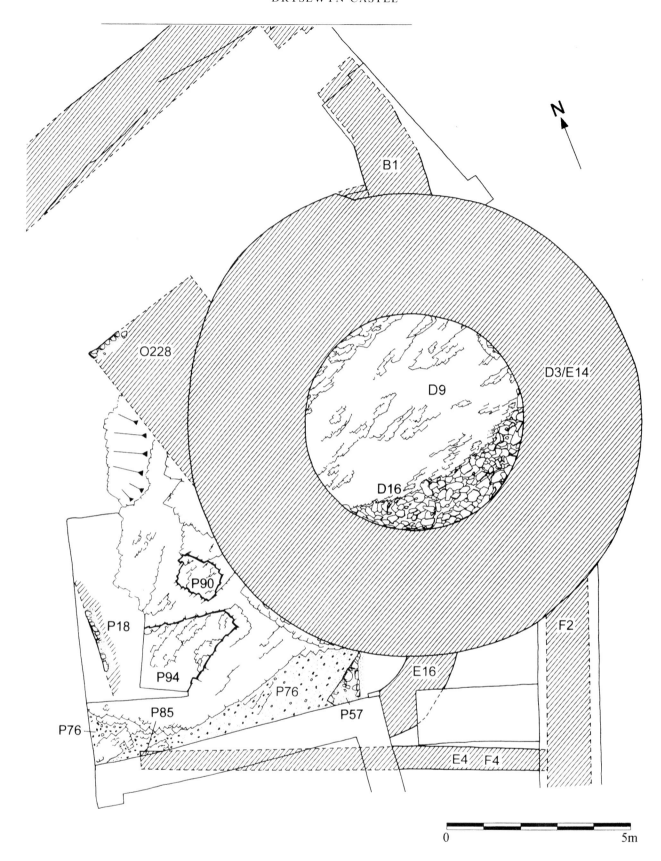

FIGURE 4.1

Areas D, E and P: Phases 1 and 2a (O228 = Phase 2c). For general location see Figure 2.6

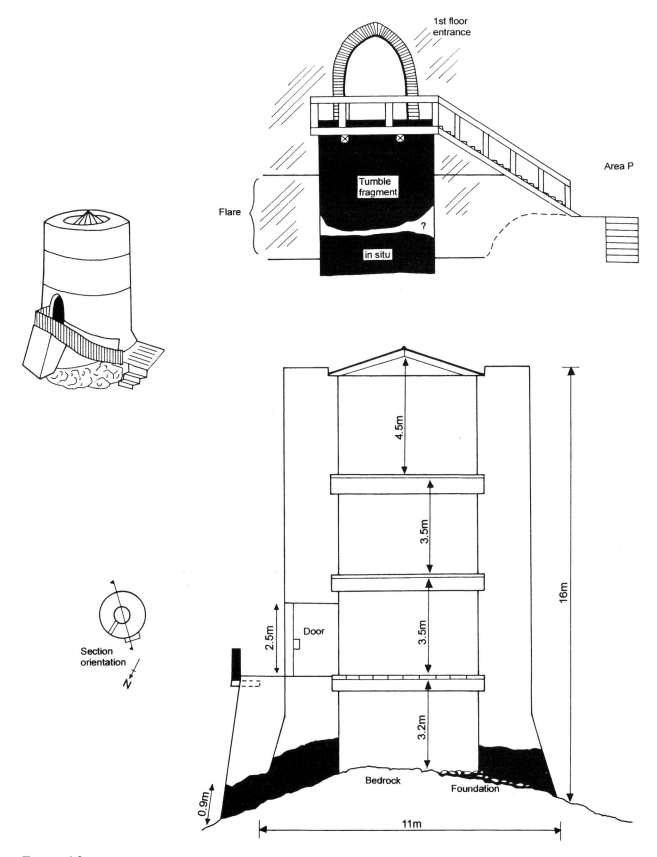

FIGURE 4.2

Areas D, E and P: reconstruction of the Round Tower D (not to scale)

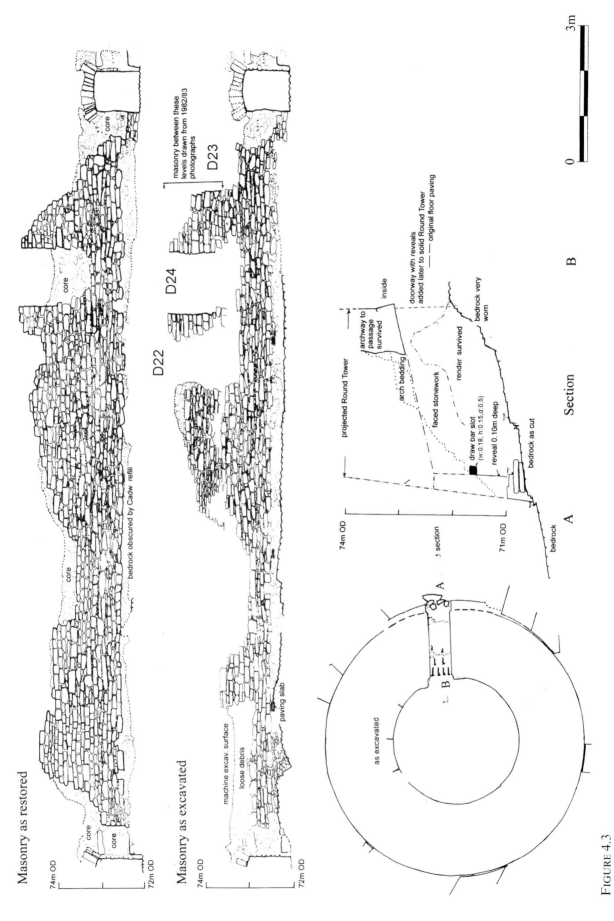

Masonry as restored

Masonry as excavated

D22

D24

D23

masonry between these
levels drawn from 1982/83
photographs

core

core

core

core

core

core

core

bedrock obscured by Cadw refill

machine excav. surface

loose debris

paving slab

74m OD

72m OD

74m OD

72m OD

projected Round Tower

inside

archway to
passage
survived

doorway with reveals
added later to solid Round Tower

original floor paving

arch bedding

faced stonework

render survived

bedrock very
worn

draw bar slot
(w: 0.18, h: 0.15, d: 0.5)
reveal 0.10m deep

bedrock as cut

74m OD

section

71m OD

bedrock

A

Section

B

A

B

as excavated

0

3m

FIGURE 4.3

Internal elevation of Round Tower D

60

(County Down) (Avent 1994a, 30). Alternatively, they could have been parts of entrances to spiral stairs within the Round Tower wall (D3), similar to those seen at Bronllys Castle (Powys) (Smith and Knight 1981, 15). A fourth, fully preserved opening (D25) was square in shape, measuring only 0.3 by 0.3m, and located on the exterior of Round Tower D, adjacent to Area C (Figure 4.4). Its regularity suggests that it was a feature original to the building, although it did not extend far back into the rubble core of wall (D3). It may be a drain or garderobe outlet that emptied outside the Phase 1a curtain wall, or possibly a putlog hole, similar to those in the round tower at Dolforwyn Castle (Powys) (Butler 1997, 142), although this might be expected to penetrate deep into or through the wall.

Phase 2

In Phase 2a, masonry structures were built in Areas E and P, several of which were later altered or demolished, leaving only fragmentary remains. An 11m-long crosswall (E4/P85) was built along the southern edge of Areas E and P, running from the curtain wall (F2) in the east towards the north-east corner of newly constructed Great Hall K/L in the west (Figure 4.1). This wall served a defensive purpose, dividing the early castle in two, but it also functioned as a retaining wall, enabling timber buildings to be built on its southern side in Areas F and G. In Area E, a stone foundation (E16, E36 and P57) was constructed between the south side of Round Tower D and the crosswall (E4). Its function is uncertain, but it may be the base of a flight of steps leading up to a wall-walk behind the crosswall (E2). A further new wall (P18) was constructed against the western edge of Area P (Figure 4.1). This was orientated at right angles to the bedding plane of the bedrock and may have originally formed part of a flight of wooden steps leading from Area O up to Area P. Alternatively, the wall (P18) could have been built as a retaining wall, designed to hold back the soil and stones of Area P in advance of quarrying in Area O to create a level pathway between Gateway Area B and Great Hall K/L (Figure 4.63).

In Area E, spilt mortar (E39) from the construction of the wall (E4/P85) was overlain by clay and cobble dumps (E28, E38, E42, E53 and E54), deposited in Phase 2b to form an improvised surface. At the same time in Area P, drain deposits (P61, P65 and P69) accumulated in the bedrock gully (P94). These were composed of fine clay, suggesting their origin in a relatively pure flow of rainwater, possibly from the roof of Round Tower D, which drained westwards into Area O. A later Phase 2b deposit (P65) in Area P was more organic in nature and contained a quantity of large whelk shells (Section 9.4). This perhaps suggests that kitchen waste was now being disposed of in this area.

In Phase 2c, a low wall (P4) was constructed in Area P. This enclosed the southern and western sides of the area and turned east at its northern end to butt onto Round Tower D as wall (P23) (Figure 4.64). A 1m-wide gap between the southern end of wall (P4) and the pre-existing wall (P85) may have served as a ramp to provide access up to Area P from developing Courtyard O. Walls (P4 and P23) thus acted as revetments for a platform in Area P, from which it was possible to ascend a new wooden staircase up to the first-floor entrance of Round Tower D (Figure 4.2). These steps were supported on a purpose-built stone buttress (O228), which was constructed in Phase 2c against the Round Tower wall (D3/E14/P14) in adjacent Courtyard O (Section 4.5).

Evidence was found in the wall (P4) for an outlet, which could indicate the continued use of the gully (P94) to drain waste water into Courtyard O. This gully (P94) contained a single course of stone (P40 and P62), which is perhaps best interpreted as the side of a drain, which subsequently collapsed and was then partially robbed. Also during Phase 2c, soil with mortar and small pebbles (P36) was spread to the area north of the gully (P94), whilst charcoal (P50) and organic soil (P35), probably kitchen waste, was deposited immediately to the south of this feature (Figure 4.64). Over the course of Phase 2d, mortar, stone and earth deposits (P74, P77 and P87) were laid down in the area to the north of the wall (E4/P85).

Phase 3

Phase 3a saw the construction of Great Chamber G (Section 4.4), the north wall (E11/P3) of which abutted Areas E and P. This required the demolition of most of the stone foundation (E16 and E36), the revetment wall (P18) and the foundation wall (P57), in addition to a large section of wall (E4/P85), although its eastern half, forming the division between Areas E and F, was left intact. The building of the Great Chamber wall (E11/P3) with its foundation (P79) resulted in a large quantity of mortar (P58) being spilt over the remains of the demolished wall (P57), which then hardened at the foot of the new wall (E11/P3) to form a mortar fillet (P75). Also in Phase 3a, a mortared stone platform (E51), which had an associated mortar layer (E34), was built on the eastern side of Area E. Its purpose is uncertain, but it may relate to a structure adjoining the curtain wall (F2), of which there is now no remaining trace. In Courtyard O, a new masonry buttress (O227) was built in Phase 3a, suggesting that the wooden steps leading from Area P up to Round Tower D were also replaced at this time.

In Phase 3b, a clay layer (P70) was deposited in Area P, which was followed by extensive dumps of earth and building rubble (P52 and P67–68), including stone chips from the construction of Great Chamber

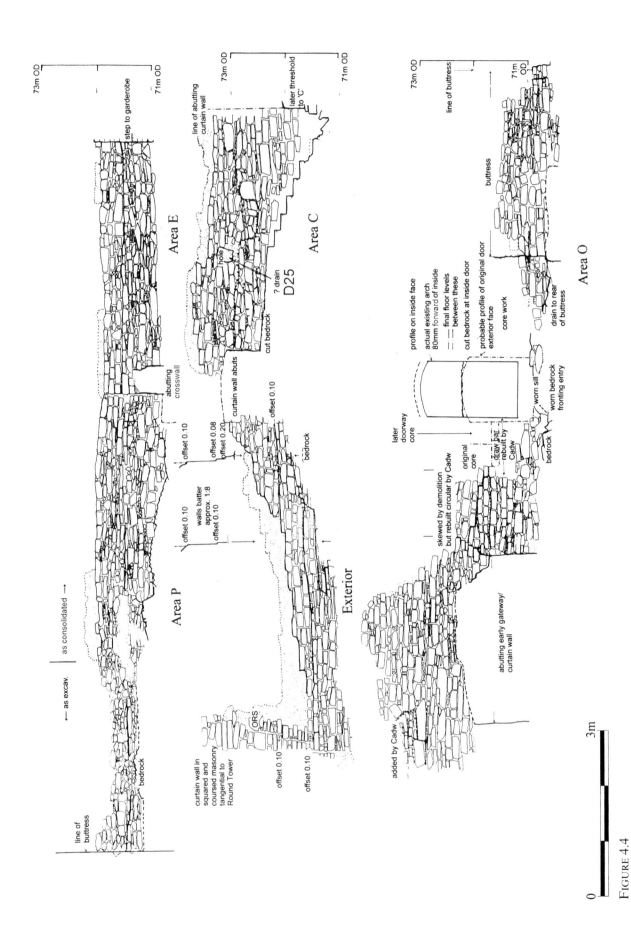

FIGURE 4.4

External elevation of Round Tower D

G. Traces of mortared masonry (P88) beside the north-west corner of this building, in addition to the mortar deposit (P84) and large stones (P80), probably formed part of a flight of stone steps, which led up to Area P from Courtyard O at this time (Figure 4.54).

Phase 4

Phase 4a witnessed a series of developments in Area P, mostly connected with providing access up to the new first-floor doorway inserted into the north wall (E11/P3) of Great Chamber G (Figure 4.5). The western

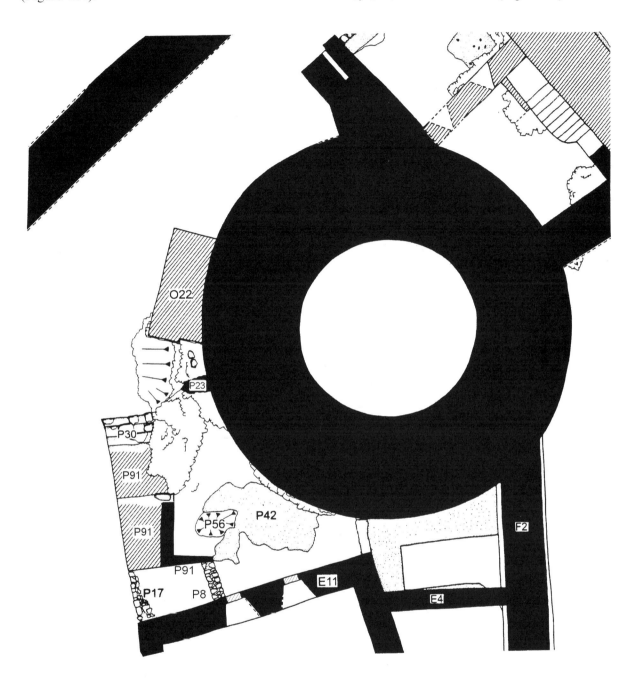

FIGURE 4.5

Areas D, E and P: Phase 4a. For general location see Figure 2.9

side and southern end of the low wall (P4) was first altered (P91), so that its southern face became parallel to the Great Chamber wall (E11/P3). Then, a short wall (P8) was built, which spanned the gap between the walls (E11/P3 and P4/P91) and formed the eastern side of what was to become a raised platform abutting the Great Chamber wall (E11/P3) at the same level as the first-floor doorway. This wall (P8) was deliberately constructed to one side of the two lancet windows (G540 and G541) in order to avoid blocking out light. The western side of the platform was formed by another new wall (P17), which acted as a revetment for fills (P26–28, P51, P78 and P81–83): these were now dumped in the area between the two walls (P8 and P17) to form the raised platform itself. In adjacent Courtyard O, a new stone buttress (O22) was built in Phase 4a, indicating that the wooden steps leading up to Round Tower D from Area P were replaced once again. This buttress protected part of the exterior face of the Round Tower wall (D3/E14/P14), which had been rendered as part of the Phase 4a refurbishment of the castle.

Leading down from the western edge of the revetment wall (P4) into Courtyard O, a flight of stone steps (P30) was built in Phase 4a. These steps now allowed people to reach the raised platform in Area P and also the first-floor entrance to Great Chamber G directly from Courtyard O; however, they also provided access to a new landing in Area P, which enabled freer movement in and out of Areas E and F to the south.

This landing was created by dumping large amounts of soil and building rubble (P12, P43, P46, P49, P59–60 and P63–64) in the area to the north of the Great Chamber wall (E11/P3), against the eastern side of the platform wall (P8). This led to the collapse of the drain (P40 and P62) in the gully (P94), whilst it also raised the ground level here to such an extent that it was now necessary to block the lower parts of the lancet windows (G540 and G541) in the Great Chamber wall (E11/P3) (Figure 4.6). The new landing was given a mortar surface (P42, P48 and P53), in which a mortar-lined pit (P56), containing organic material (P55), may have functioned as a soak-away. It received much use in the following Phase 4b, causing extensive wear to the mortar surface (P42) and leading to repair with a mortar patch (P38) and a layer of earth (P47).

The siege of 1287, which saw the lodging of a stone projectile in the earthen deposit (P47) (Section 7.4), was followed in Phase 4c by an intense period of post-siege repairs and modifications in Areas D, E and P (Figure 4.7). Nothing concerning the development of Round Tower D in Phases 2 and 3 is known, mainly because the original Phase 1a flagstone floor (D11) was removed (D25) in Phase 4c in preparation for the insertion of an arched stone passageway (D10) at ground level through the Round Tower wall (D3/E14/P14) (Figures 4.3, 4.4 and 4.7).

The passageway (D10) was poorly constructed and off-centre. It sloped uphill from Courtyard O and entered Round Tower D at a level below that of the

FIGURE 4.6

The lancet windows in the north wall of the Great Chamber G. The blocking is still present in the right-hand lancet widow

FIGURE 4.7

Areas D, E and P: Phases 4c–5c. For general location see Figure 3.1

former flagstone floor (D11). Rebates located at both ends of the passageway indicate that it had an inward-opening door at the interior end and an outward-opening door to the exterior. A short 0.5m-deep slot in the wall on the northern side of the passageway at the exterior end contained the degraded remains of

a wooden beam, possibly the remains of a drawbar (Figure 4.3). Hard white mortar was used in the construction of the passageway and this formed a mortar apron (D12 and D17) overlying the Phase 1a earthy mortar layer (D7), which now acted as the principal basement floor (Figures 4.8 and 4.9). No features were

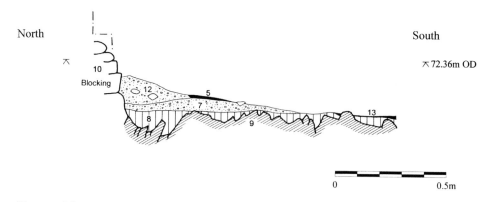

FIGURE 4.8

Section D1, N–S section through the floor layers in the base of the Round Tower D

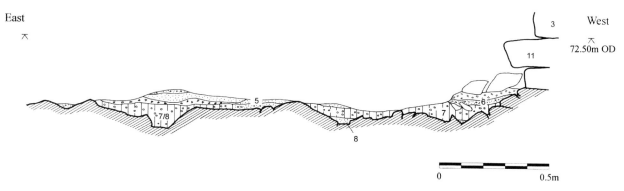

FIGURE 4.9

Section D2, E–W section through the floor layers in the base of the Round Tower D

recovered from this floor surface (D7), which was repaired using patches of hard white mortar (D6), and very few occupation deposits lay above it. This would support an interpretation of the Round Tower basement as a storage area, rather than a living space.

In Area E, Phase 4c saw the slighting of the remaining portion of the wall (E4/P85) to a low level and the replacement of the Phase 1a curtain wall (F2) with a substantial new curtain wall (E2), which was constructed of squared limestone blocks bonded together with hard white mortar (Section 6.1). Within this new wall (E2), a passage was built containing twin garderobe chutes (E9 and E17) (Section 4.5). Traces of the recesses for the wooden boarding that formed the seat and front board (E40) over the top of these chutes were recovered (Figures 4.10 and 4.11). The garderobes were reached by a short flight of six spiral steps (E12) within the wall (E2) leading up from Area E.

Also in Area E, a flight of stone steps (E5) was built in Phase 4c, which provided access up to the wall-walk of the new curtain wall (E2) (Figure 4.11). These steps were seated on mortared foundations (E15 and E35), which in turn sat on a loose stone foundation (E33). They were constructed with a wet mortar, some of which spilt, forming a fillet (E31) around the base of the steps. The area between Round Tower D and the steps (E5) was filled with brown soil (E24 and E26) and given a crude stone and mortar surface (E23, E32 and E46).

In Area P, the earthen deposit (P47) was covered over in Phase 4c by the extensive mortar surface (P33), which was 0.15m thick in places, notably beside Round Tower D. This surface contained several layers of repeated wear and repair. Its inception may have coincided with the construction of the garderobes (E9 and E17) and steps (E5) in Area E. As a further part of the Phase 4c alterations, a new wall (P5) was constructed to support the revetment wall (P4/P91), whilst part of the curving Round Tower wall (D3/E14/P14) was straightened in order to fashion a jamb for a new doorway between Areas E and P. The reveal (E49) of this doorway, which contained evidence for a hinge, was created by altering the north-east corner of the Great Chamber wall (E11/P3).

Phase 5

During Phase 5a, new mortar surfaces were laid both in Area E (E20 and E21) and also on the landing in

FIGURE 4.10

Garderobe in wall (E2), with chutes (E9 and E17) and socket for the front board of the wooden commode

garderobe chutes (E9 and E17) themselves, whilst an accumulation of soil (E48) covered the mortar surface (E8 and E18–19) leading towards them.

Phases 6 and 7

Abandonment of the garderobes in Area E was followed by a concerted effort to block their chutes (E9 and E17) by wedging in fire-reddened stones (E47). Part of a wider effort to decommission the castle, this is most likely to have taken place in Phase 6a, although a date in Phase 6c, following the devastating castle fire, is not impossible. Since no other traces of burning were present, it appears that there were no wooden structures or quantities of flammable materials here at the time that fire took hold.

The narrow passageway (O10) into Round Tower D was walled up (O216) in Phase 6a and then filled with rubble (O211) in Phase 6b in an attempt to seal the basement of this building from use. The Round Tower D, suffered badly in the Phase 6c fire. Some organic materials were preserved as carbonised remains (D13 and D15). These included straw and other plant stems used to cover the basement floor (Section 9.5). Also in the burnt layer (D15) were fragments of coal and a collection of 68 iron roves that had probably once been contained within a bag or box (Figure 4.7; Section 6.5). Above these deposits (D13 and D15) was a thick layer of debris (D5), representing the burnt remains of the roof and upper floors of the Round Tower. This contained a large quantity of clay, some of which had been fired to a hard, red brick-like consistency by the heat of the blaze. The clay may have served as a sound- and spark-proof flooring material on top of wooden floorboards and may also have acted as a fire-protection within the roof space (Section 6.1). That the roof itself was covered with sheets of lead is suggested by nails recovered from the debris (D5) (Section 6.6). Much of this lead may have been looted in Phase 6b. Looting of ironwork almost certainly took place within the Round Tower at this time, since, in contrast to Great Hall K/L, no iron wall furniture, such as hinges or light brackets, was recovered.

In Phase 6d, the remaining walls of the castle were demolished and Areas D, E and P were each covered with large quantities of mortared rubble (D2, D4, E6, P6 and P7). In Area D, much of the broken masonry was burnt red on its internal face, often to a depth of 50–60mm, suggesting that the fire had been particularly intense within Round Tower D. The Round Tower itself collapsed into Areas O and P, causing extensive damage to the wall (P4), in addition to the raised platform and stone steps (P30). Walls (P5), (G3) were knocked off vertical (Figure 4.12). Large sections of walling (O19–21) from Round Tower D were recovered in Courtyard O. In Phase 7b, Area D was covered by a layer of topsoil (D1). Area E gained its topsoil (E10) in Phase 7d.

Area P (P29). Those in Area E were heavily worn and replaced later in Phase 5a by a more coherent mortar surface (E8 and E18–19), which formed a deposit up to 0.75m thick. This surface was thinnest where the greatest level of activity had taken place, around the base of the steps (E5) and within the doorway created in Phase 4c between Areas E and P. It was at the same level as the top of the slighted wall (E4) (Figure 4.7).

In Phase 5b, a series of dumps (P10, P20, P21, P25 and P34) and a further mortar surface (P24) were laid down in Area P. In Phase 5c, however, these were followed by the construction of a blocking wall (E13/P13), which sealed the doorway between Areas E and P, (Figure 4.7), and a final mortar surface (P19). Since access was no longer possible from Area P into Areas E, Area P now became a coal store: in Phase 5d, after a period of soil accumulation (P22), a thin layer of anthracite coal and coal dust (P9) was deposited here (Section 9.11). Meanwhile, in Area E, the stone steps (E5) leading down from the wall-walk received continued use in Phase 5d, as was shown by wear in the mortar surface (E8 and E18–19) at their base. The garderobes, however, appear to have fallen into disrepair, since soil layers (E1 and E3) were present within the

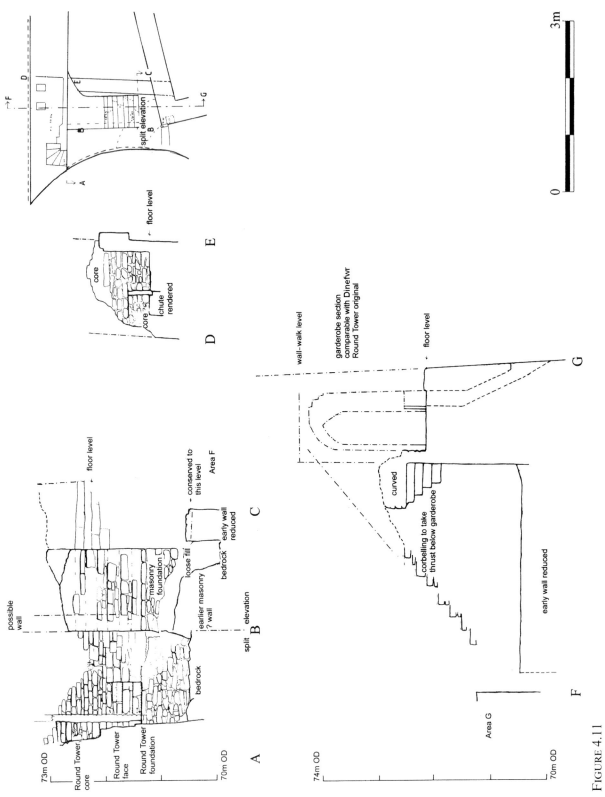

FIGURE 4.11

Elevation of the west face of wall (F2), N–S and E–W cross sections through the garderobe

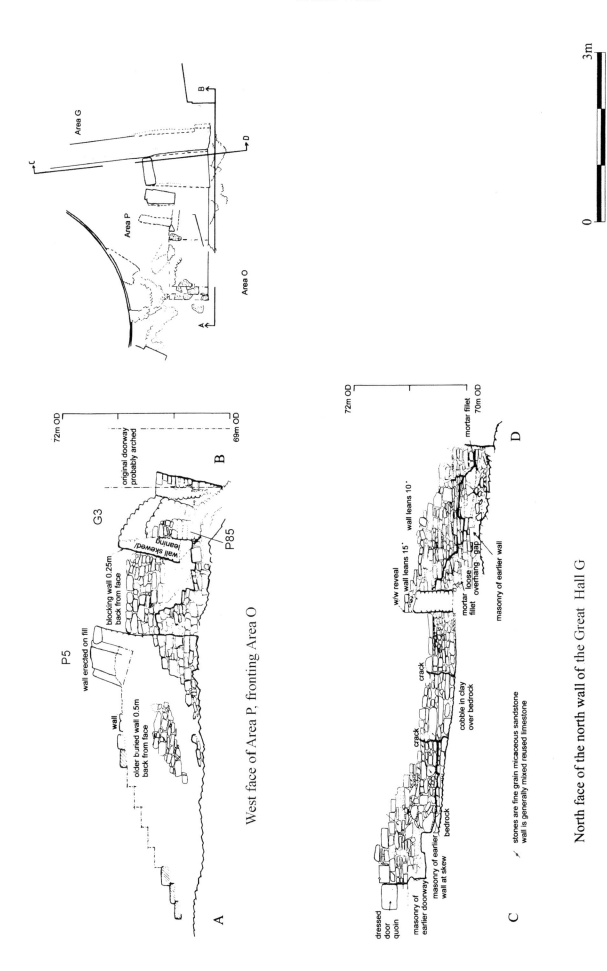

0   3m

West face of Area P, fronting Area O

72m OD

original doorway probably arched

69m OD

B

G3

wall skewed/ leaning

P85

blocking wall 0.25m back from face

P5

wall erected on fill

wall

older buried wall 0.5m back from face

A

North face of the north wall of the Great Hall G

72m OD

70m OD

D

wall leans 10°

mortar fillet

w/w reveal

wall leans 15°

mortar loose overhang gap fillet

masonry of earlier wall

crack

crack

crack

cobble in clay over bedrock

masonry of earlier doorway

wall at skew

bedrock

dressed door quoin

masonry of earlier doorway

stones are fine grain micaceous sandstone wall is generally mixed reused limestone

C

FIGURE 4.12

Elevation of the west face of the revetment wall (P4) and the exterior face of the north wall of the Great Chamber G and the exterior face of the north wall of the Great Hall G

69

Round Tower

Square and rectangular plan keeps and towers were erected in Britain throughout the late 11th and 12th century. They declined in popularity in the late 12th century, when circular keeps and towers became the norm. Traditionally it is suggested this was due to an appreciation of the weaknesses of the square form; vulnerability of the corners to collapse when undermined and the creation of 'dead zones' at the corners where defenders could not easily fire on attackers (King 1988, 98; Renn 1961, 129). Consequently, novel polygonal keeps, such as Orford (Suffolk) and Tickhill (South Yorkshire), were built in England by c1180 and a buttressed circular keep was erected at Conisbrough (South Yorkshire) in c1180 (Johnson 1989, 21). Eventually full circular form keeps, with their increased stability, improved visibility and the ability to deflect missiles, were developed (Thompson 1991b, 43). Cylindrical keeps or round towers, often with flared bases, in medieval castles, have generally been ascribed a French origin, since there are early to mid 12th-century examples at Courcy (Aisne) and Houdan (Yvelines) (Brown 1984, 44). By the end of the 12th century, large cylindrical donjons, such as those at the Louvre (Paris) (Avent 2006), Falaise (Calvados) and Rouen (Seine-Maritime) (Brown 1984, 45), were regularly being constructed in France by King Philip Augustus. Free-standing round towers, used as a final refuge (*bergfried*), were also present in Germany by the late 12th century (Renn 1961, 133). More recently Liddiard (2005, 47–50) has suggested that the military obsolescence of square keeps may have been exaggerated by earlier authors since square keeps continued to be constructed in Britain during the 13th century, as at Dolforwyn (Powys) which was built between 1273 and 1277 (Butler and Knight 2004, 26). Both Liddiard and McNeill (2003, 98) suggest that the change may be due to aristocratic fashion, regarding round donjons as highly desirable powerful, prestigious modern buildings, rather than as a result of any observed weakness of square keeps.

In the 13th century the keepless castle, a polygonal ward with several substantial towers as part of a defensive circuit, exemplified by Framlingham (Suffolk) (1180s) and Bolingbroke (Lincolnshire) (1220s), became the dominant castle form in England. In these castles, the round tower is seen in the form of mural towers such as those that flank the walls of the Middle and Lower Wards of Chepstow Castle (Monmouthshire), constructed by William Marshal in the 1190s (Turner 2002a, 32–33; Turner and Johnson 2006). In some instances one of the round mural towers was of a larger form: a donjon. Examples include Barnard Castle in Durham (1170–85) (Austin 1988a), Bothwell in South Lanarkshire (1242–78) (Simpson *et al* 1990, 5) and Kildrummy in Grampian (mid 13th century) (Tabraham 1986).

The round tower keep is traditionally considered to have been introduced to south Wales by William Marshal. He married Isabella de Clare, heiress of Pembroke, in 1189 and after using the round tower form for mural towers at Chepstow in the 1190s (Turner 2002a), he constructed the round tower keep at Pembroke (Pembrokeshire) between 1201 and 1207 or 1211 and 1219 (Rowland 1996). In reality several lords were constructing round tower keeps in the final decades of the 12th century. McNeill (1997) has suggested that the round tower keep at Dundrum (Down) was probably built by John de Courcy in the 1180s or 1190s, certainly before 1211–12, when it is recorded as being repaired, and Nenagh (Tipperary) which was probably constructed after lands were given to Theobald Walter in 1185 and before his death in 1206. The flared-based round tower was constructed at Longtown (Herefordshire) in the period c1180–90 (King 1988, 98, 105; Renn 1961, 133).

In the decades that followed it appears likely that the round tower became a fashionable form of military architecture throughout the Welsh Marches and Ireland and between 1220–40 many of the castles built in Wales and the Welsh Marches incorporated a flared-based round tower keep. This architectural form was particularly prevalent in the Brecon region, where it is principally seen as a separate keep, for example at Skenfrith (Monmouthshire) and Bronllys (Powys) (Smith and Knight 1981). It was also used in the castles of Welsh princes and lords at Castell-y-Bere (Gwynedd), Dolbadarn (Gwynedd) and Dolforwyn (Powys), where it was invariably constructed as part of the defensive circuit, acting partly as a flanking tower (often near the entrance though without the arrowslits to provide flanking fire), partly as a stronghold and partly to provide domestic accommodation. In north and mid Wales, the round tower was often used in addition to the earlier Welsh rectangular and apsidal tower forms, for example at Castell-y-Bere (Gwynedd). In west Wales, it was more often used as the sole or principal tower, as at Dinefwr (Carmarthenshire).

Round towers, as discussed by Renn (1961), usually have a series of recurrent features: flared base, first-floor entrance, stair access within the wall, basement lit by steeply shelving loops and window loops on upper floors. Many also have a roll-moulded string-course. Whilst Kenyon (1990, 54) describes the Welsh Marcher round towers, such as Bronllys (Powys), as having a basement plus three upper storeys, Avent (1994a, 31) suggests that round tower keeps, like Dolbadarn (Gwynedd), comprise a basement or ground level plus two storeys. The incomplete nature of many surviving examples, including Dryslwyn, means that it is frequently difficult to establish the original height of the tower and also to ascertain the number of floors it once possessed. Wooden plank floors within the round tower would have been supported on beams set into the wall (McNeill 2003) and evidence from Dryslwyn suggests a clay floor was sometimes present above the wooden planking (Section 6.1).

In the case of Round Tower D at Dryslwyn, documentary evidence suggests construction in the 1220s (Section 2.1). As discussed above, the round tower as part of the defensive circuit is typical of a castle constructed during this period in Wales and the Marches. The recovery of a fragment of glass (Section 6.7) indicates the presence of glazed windows in the Round Tower by at least the 15th century, although they were probably present far earlier. This, together with the fragments of wall plaster (Section 6.4), points to a high-status use, probably as the lord's chamber (solar). The Dryslwyn Round Tower therefore falls within Thompson's solar-keep category of private apartments within a defensive masonry form (Thompson 1991b, 65–67). At approximately 6m internal diameter, it is, like Bronllys (Powys), much smaller than those Thompson considers capable of performing a hall/keep function and, given the presence of Great Hall K/L within the early castle, it is unlikely that Round Tower D had any hall functions. The damaged traces of openings on the inside face of the Round Tower wall indicate the presence of steeply shelving light loops and stair access within the wall. The presence of fireplaces in round towers at Dolbadarn (Gwynedd) and Dinefwr (Carmarthenshire) indicates how they were heated and although the absence of walls above basement level means there is no such evidence present at Dryslwyn, the presence of the clay floor indicates the potential the use of a brazier in the centre of the room to provide warmth. This heating provision plus the presence of the garderobe in the tower at Dolbadarn (Gwynedd) and in the adjacent building at Dolforwyn (Powys) (Butler 1997, 150) and Dryslwyn (Area F) emphasises the residential nature of round towers in Welsh castles.

Access to Round Tower D was at first-floor level, via a series of external wooden steps supported on a masonry pier, which had at least three phases of construction and replacement. Traces of stone walls to support wooden stairs were also uncovered at Dolforwyn (Powys). Here, Butler (1997, 198) suggests that there may have been a drawbridge or lifting platform to give access from the round tower to the top of the stairs. A movable wooden bridge, which could be pushed out to provide access to the round tower, has also been postulated for Pembroke (Pembrokeshire) (Renn 1967–68, 39). Unfortunately, the masonry remains at Dryslwyn were not preserved to a height that would permit the detection of any such features, but traces of render or harling were found on the tower exterior, as they were at Dolforwyn (Powys) (Butler 1997, 199). The render and subsequent limewash coats detected at Dryslwyn (Figure 4.71) would have created a highly visible monument (Section 6.1).

The presence of later entrances forced through at ground-floor level into round towers at Cilgerran (Pembrokeshire), Dinefwr (Carmarthenshire) and Pembroke (Pembrokeshire), as well as Dryslwyn, indicates just how far defence and access priorities changed at these sites. The fact that this change can be dated to the period 1287–1300 at Dryslwyn indicates the extent to which the concept of a defensible keep had already become redundant for royal garrison castles by the 14th century.

4.2 AREAS B, C AND A: GATEWAY

Areas B, C and A together form the main zone of entry into the early castle and the later interface between the Inner and Middle Wards (Figure 1.3). Area B, also known as Gateway Area B, contained the principal gateway entrance and its associated structures. Area C, to its immediate south, was developed as a defensive platform, providing access from Gateway Area B to Round Tower D and up to the wall-walk of the curtain wall. Area A initially lay outside the castle, but contained a rock-cut ditch that formed part of its outer defences. In Phase 3a, the whole of Area A was taken into the new Middle Ward and a description of its subsequent development can be found in Section 5.1, together with the rest of the excavated Middle Ward (Areas X, Y and XR).

Phase 1

Phase 1a saw the construction of the first castle at Dryslwyn. In Areas B and C, this comprised Round Tower D (B14/C3) and the curtain wall (B1/C30 and B114) (Figure 4.13), both of which flared outwards at the base at an angle of 8–10° from the vertical, a characteristic of Phase 1a walling within the castle. It can be suggested with some confidence that the Round Tower was completed first, since the masonry of the curtain wall (B1/C30) displayed evidence of being deliberately bonded into the pre-existing Round Tower wall (B14/C3) in order to secure this potential weak-point in the castle's defensive circuit.

Access into the Phase 1a castle was primarily gained through a narrow gateway between the two sections of the curtain wall (B1/C30 and B114). The subsequent widening of this entrance in Phase 3a removed all traces of its previous form, but it is likely that the earliest castle entrance consisted of a small doorway, probably closed by a heavy single-leafed wooden door, wide enough only to permit the access of a man or a horse. Its position beside Round Tower D ensured greater protection.

On the eastern side of Gateway Area B, access was gained over an outcrop of bedrock (B125), which was quarried away to create a pathway: this had been

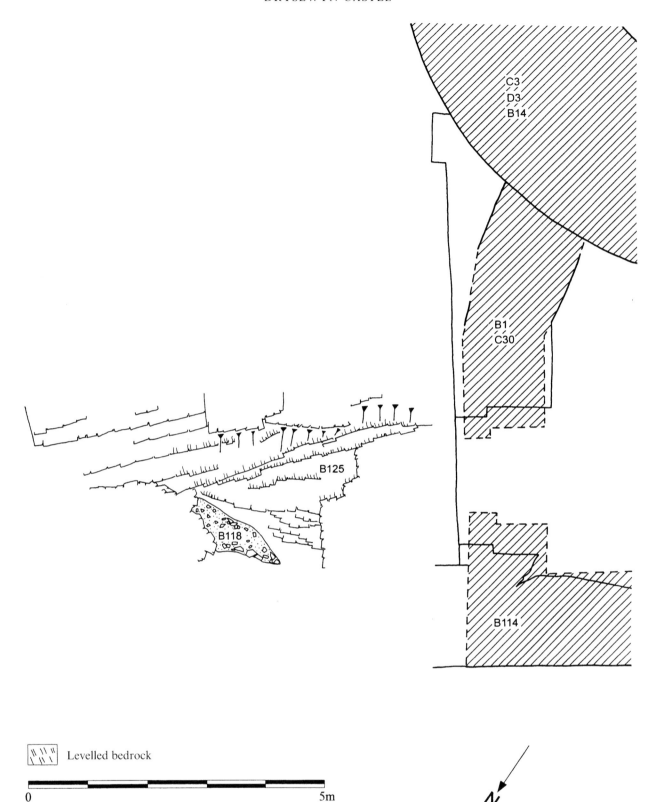

Levelled bedrock

0   5m

FIGURE 4.13

Areas B, C and A: Phase 1. For general location see Figure 2.5

polished smooth due to the passage of numerous feet. The pathway continued as a layer of worn cobbles (B118), although dumps of soil (B107 and B117) were made over the rock and cobbles in Phase 1b in an attempt to repair the worn surface.

Phase 2

Phase 2a saw a number of important modifications to Gateway Area B (Figure 4.14). A wall (B11) was built, which extended the northern section of the curtain

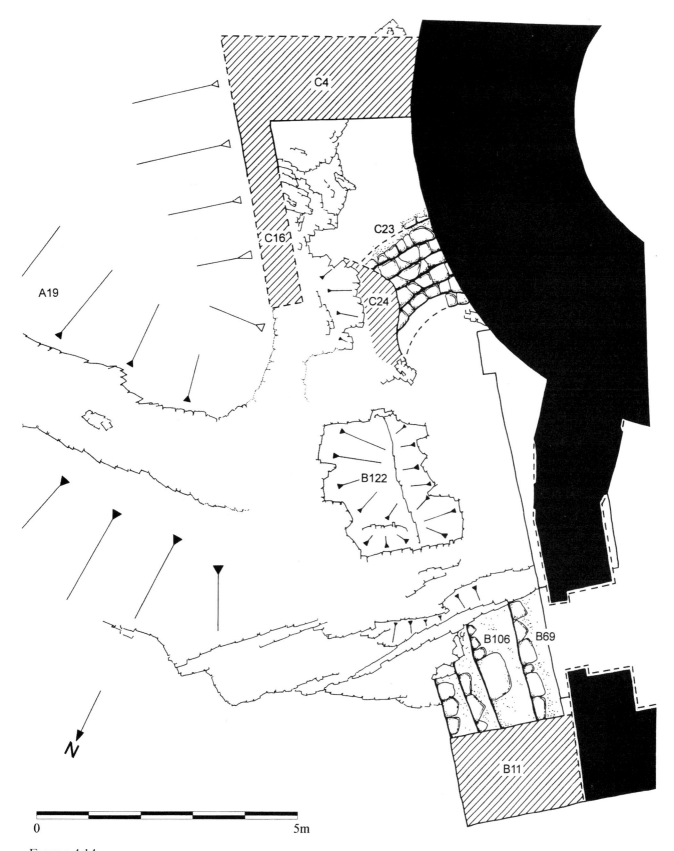

FIGURE 4.14

Areas B, C and A: Phase 2a. For general location see Figure 2.6

wall (B114) out beyond the existing entrance. Beside this wall, leading up to the entrance, a flight of well-mortared stone steps (B106) was constructed, which partially overlay the earlier worn bedrock surface. Of the original five steps, the lowest and highest were subsequently removed (Figure 4.15). A piece of polished limestone from the earlier smoothed bedrock surface (B125) was re-used in the construction of the central step. To the south of the steps, a rock-cut hollow (B122) may have served a dual function as a quarry and defensive feature.

In Area C, a wall (C4) was added in Phase 2a, which ran east along the rocky ridge from Round Tower D. This wall then turned north (C16) to form an L-shaped enclosure behind a rock-cut ditch (A19) in Area A, which had been newly created by quarrying out stone from a natural cleft in the bedrock (A8). These features guarded the approach up the ridge to the Round Tower and were important elements in enhancing the outer defences of the early castle. The full extent of the ditch (A19) and wall (C16) are not known, as they were lost under the later wall (A2/B3/C6), which was constructed in Phase 4a.

Against Round Tower D (B14/C3), a set of seven mortared stone steps (C23) was uncovered in Area C. These steps were originally part of a much longer flight, but were truncated by the later construction of walls (C21 and C22) in Phases 4a and 5a. The steps were accompanied by a fragmentary flanking wall (C24), which may have formed part of a more complex masonry structure, perhaps associated with wall (C16). Both the steps (C23) and flanking wall (C24) could date to Phase 2a and represent a means of access to the defensive position behind wall (C16). There are structural similarities between these worn curved steps (C23) and those in Gateway Area B (B106). Alternatively, the steps (C23) may be associated with the single step (B34), which was not constructed until Phase 3a.

In Phase 2c, the stepped castle entrance in Gateway Area B was modified by the addition of a wall (B77), which ran south-east from the extended curtain wall (B11 and B114). This wall effectively blocked access to the steps (B106); its original extent and purpose is unknown, obscured by later construction. At the base of this wall, a foundation (B108) suggests the existence of a replacement step at the foot of the flight (Figure 4.16). There are no surfaces that can be unequivocally connected with this phase of entrance walling. Most of the wall (B77) was subsequently demolished (B127).

Phase 3

Phase 3a saw both the addition of the Middle Ward to the castle at Dryslwyn and the construction of a ramped access, which led in turn to an enlarged Inner Ward entrance in Gateway Area B (Figure 4.17). First,

FIGURE 4.15

The mortared stone step (B106) at the entrance to the Phase 2a castle

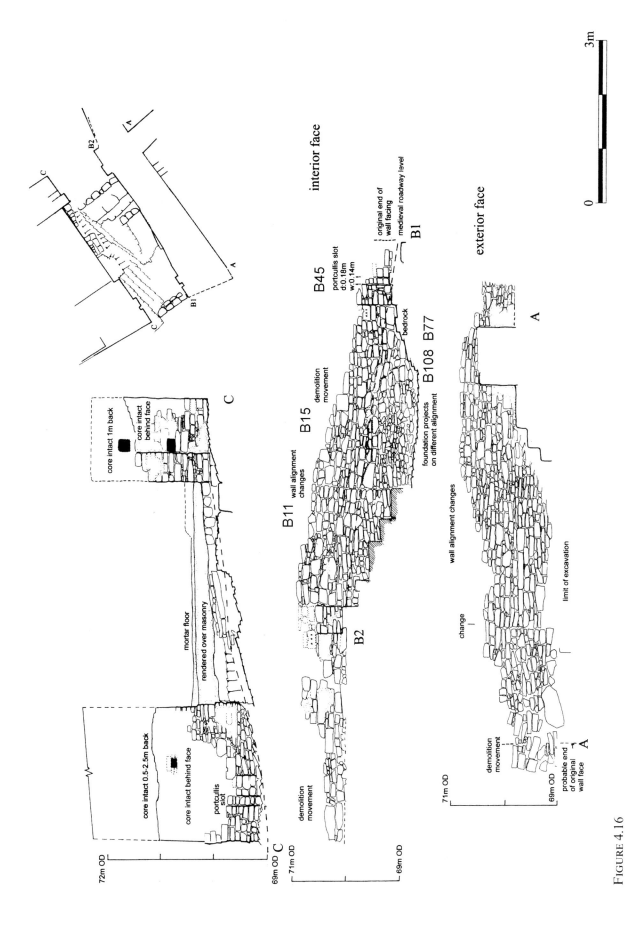

FIGURE 4.16

Internal elevations of the passageway of the Gateway Area B

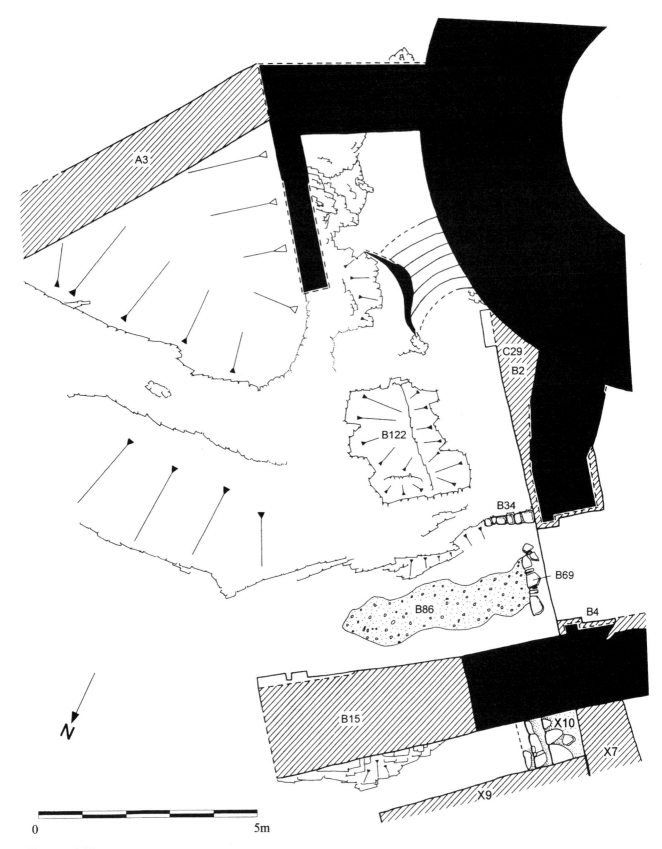

FIGURE 4.17

Areas B, C and A: Phase 3. For general location see Figure 2.8

a wall (B15) was constructed, which replaced the demolished wall (B77) in extending the eastward line of the curtain wall (B11 and B114). It was built in one episode on a mortared foundation (B105), which formed a flat platform on top of the bedrock. Together with the wall (C16), it is possible that this new wall (B15) formed part of an outer gateway, a precursor of what was to follow in Phase 4a. The full extent of both walls (B15 and C16) is, however, unknown and this suggestion must remain conjecture.

Wall (B15) served an additional purpose, as a revetment for the material making up the new ramped passageway leading up to the Inner Ward entrance. This ramp, constructed on top of the mortared foundation (B105), replaced the flight of steps (B106) and consisted at first of a dump of large stones (B99 and B104), topped by a crude cobbled surface (B100). Later, dumps of cobble (B103) and orange clay (B101) were added and this was followed by the laying of the first substantial cobbled surface (B86), still in Phase 3a. An additional line of larger stones was placed in the passageway surface in front of the Inner Ward entrance in order to create a threshold (B69). This was probably formed from stones taken from the upper step of the former steps (B106). The threshold (B69) was located at the break of slope, where the passageway surface, sloping up from the putative outer gateway, levelled off to go through the Inner Ward entrance into Courtyard O. Since the front of this threshold was faced (Figures 4.14 and 4.15), it is possible that it was originally intended to be a single step up at this point. However, since the threshold (B69) was partially buried by a surface layer (B100), it was not possible to gauge whether its depth would have prevented the admission of wheeled transport.

The Inner Ward entrance itself also underwent reconstruction during Phase 3a: the alignment and extent of the threshold (B69) point toward a much larger and slightly re-aligned gateway. The north side of the gateway (B114) was widened and remodelled (B4) and this process also took place on the north side, where the existing curtain wall (B1/C30) was made thicker and refaced (B2/C29). The result was an entrance nearly 2m wide, closed by a twin-leafed gate supported on stout iron hinges. These hinges were housed in matrices carved into large blocks of freestone set into the flanking walls (B2/C29 and B4) and fixed using lead, traces of which survived in wall (B4). In wall (B2/C29) there was also a drawbar slot for securing the gate by means of a wooden beam (Figure 4.16).

Within the rock-cut hollow (B122), to the east of the ramped passageway, dumps of clay and cobble (B62 and B67–68) were made in Phase 3a, which were overlain by a short-lived surface layer (B48). Further dumps of mortar and burnt material (B49, B54 and B65–66) were made on top of this surface (B48) at a slightly later date. Another mortar surface (B47), on the western side of the hollow (B122), was associated with a step (B34), which was constructed from a single line of stones. The original form and function of this surface (B47) and step (B34) is unclear, but it is possible that they represent part of an access route leading from Gateway Area B into Area C, via the steps (C23). Both the step (B34) and the threshold (B69) displayed evidence of wear, suggesting a lengthy period of use. Deposits of clay with charcoal (B96 and B98), mortar (B92 and B95) and burnt material with charcoal (B90–91 and B97) were later made here in Phase 3b.

Phase 4

Clay soil layers (B93 and B94) and an extensive mortar deposit (B80 and B88) mark the start of major rebuilding in Phase 4a. This included the construction of a double-gated entrance with a guard chamber in Gateway Area B and a new outer gateway wall with steps leading up to Round Tower D and a wall-walk in Area C (Figure 4.18).

In order to construct this new outer gateway the rock cut ditch (A19) was filled (A18, A16, A11) and the earlier walls (B15 and C16) were partially demolished and substantial limestone walls (A2/B3/C6 and B45) erected in their place. The outer gateway entrance itself was marked by a threshold (B74), which rested on an existing stone foundation (B105). Slots cut into the opposing faces of walls (A2/B3/C6 and B45), measuring 120–150mm wide and 150–200mm deep, betray the presence of a portcullis, set back at a distance of 0.55–0.7m from the gateway façade. Set a further 0.45m back, behind a 200mm-deep reveal, were matrices for the hinges of a twin-leafed gate. The end of a drawbar slot was also present in wall (A2/B3/C6) (Figure 4.16, C–C). In order to ease access to the new outer gateway, an outcrop of bedrock to its south and west was partially quarried away (B126). A document written shortly after the siege of 1287 records the 'breaking of a rock at the castle entrance' (Webster 1987, 91) and this may indicate that further quarrying was required here at a later date (Figure 4.19).

Marking the boundary between Gateway Area B and Area C was a crosswall (B5/C43 and C22), which butted up against the outer gateway wall (A2/B3/C6) to its east and the remodelled curtain wall (B2/C29) to the west. This crosswall (B5/C43 and C22) contained at least one arrowloop (B24), which faced southwards into Area C, and the implication seems to be that it formed the back wall of a Phase 4a guard chamber in Gateway Area B, which fronted onto the passage linking the inner and outer gateways to the north. Traces of lime plaster were found on all the walls of this room, showing that they were once rendered (Figure 4.20); a recurring feature of Phase 4a construction throughout the castle. The gateway

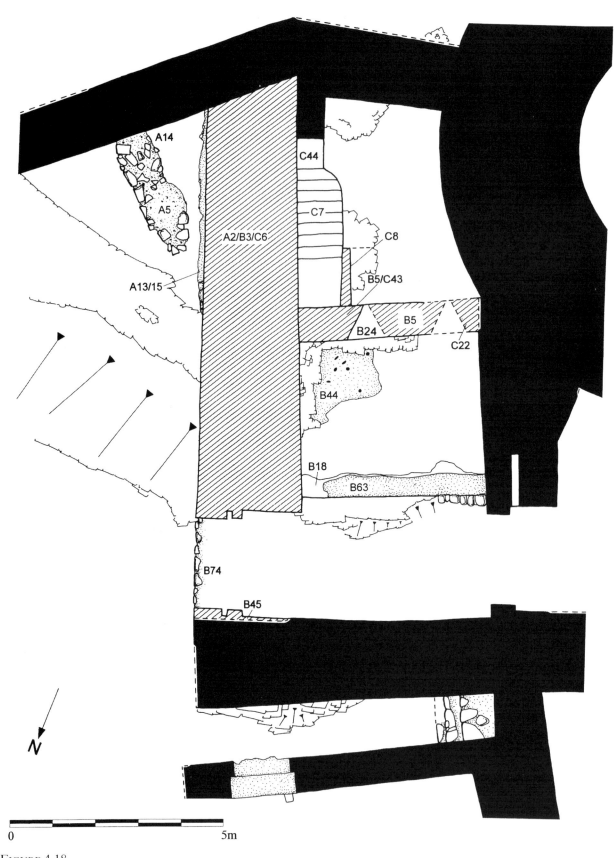

FIGURE 4.18

Areas B, C and A: Phase 4. For general location see Figure 3.1

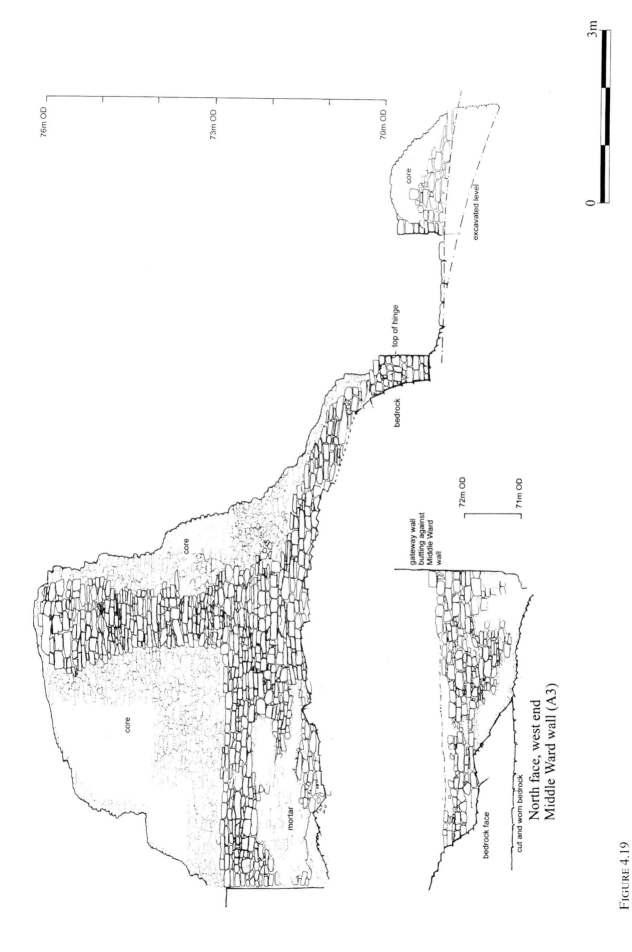

FIGURE 4.19

Elevation of the external east face of the east wall (A2) of the Inner Ward

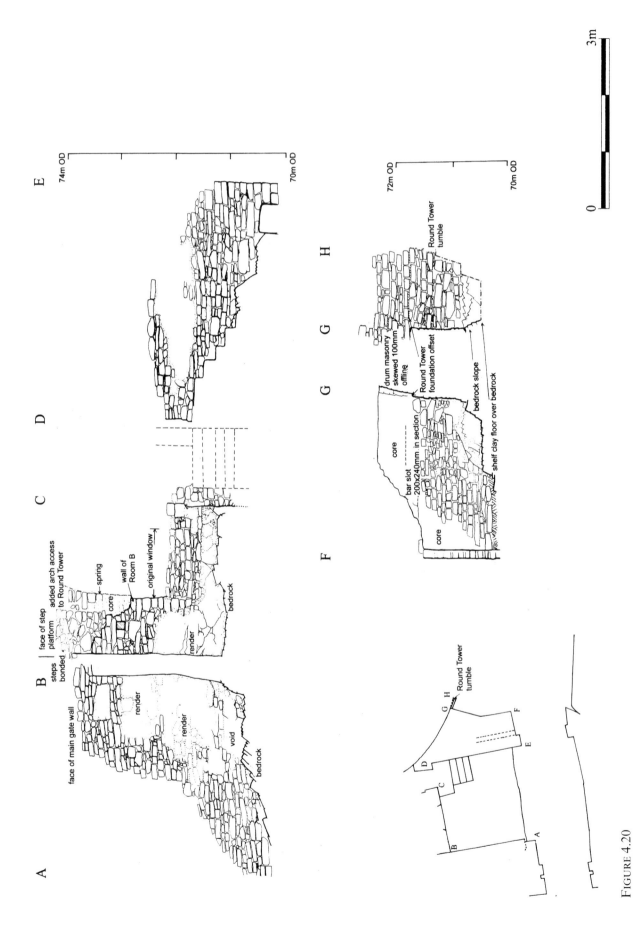

FIGURE 4.20

Internal elevations of the raised platform area of the Gateway Area B with location plan for elevations (bottom left)

passage itself appears to have had a cobbled surface (B70) in Phase 4a, which overlay a patchy deposit of crushed shale (B89).

A further Phase 4a addition, located in Area C, was a flight of stone steps (C7) with a quarter landing (C44) at its base. These steps not only provided access up to the wall-walk of wall (A2/B3/C6), from where the portcullis within the outer gateway was operated, but they also led to an arched walkway, partially supported by a stone pier (C8). This walkway, it is believed, connected with a specially inserted first-floor doorway in Round Tower D. The shape and position of the stone pier (C8) (Figures 4.21 and 4.18) suggests that every effort was made to avoid blocking the arrowloop (B24) in the crosswall (B5/C43), which must have already existed at this time.

Phase 4b evidence in Areas B and C was confined to a few layered deposits associated with occupation and general use in the gateway passage and at the base of the stone steps (C7). Those seen in the passage consisted of clay soil (B83 and B87), burnt material (B85) and mortar (B82), whilst those in Area C (C36, C38 and C43) were composed primarily of soil and mortar.

In Phase 4c, following the castle siege of 1287, the sloping floor of the guard chamber in Gateway Area B was levelled off and built up as a platform (Figure 4.16, C–C). First, a low wall (B18) was constructed, which incorporated the earlier wall (B34) and ran between walls (B2/C29 and A2/B3/C6). The floor was then made up to the level of the top of the wall (B18) with infill deposits (B52 and B53) covered with layers of mortar (B44, B51 and B63). Deposits (B52 and B53) contained antler-working waste, probably derived from earlier castle occupation. Repairs to the gateways may also have been carried out in Phase 4c: the squared stones in the walls flanking the inner and outer gateway entrances (Figure 4.16) are very similar to post-siege 'English' masonry elsewhere in the castle (Section 6.1).

Evidence for use of the platform in Phase 4c comes from a series of stakeholes (B55–B61) in the mortar floor, which indicates that there was some form of wooden structure in the north-east corner. There were also signs of wear and repair of the mortar flooring in the form of a dumps of clay and cobble (B26 and B43). Similar minor repairs were made to the floor of the gateway passage (B71–72, B75–76, B79 and B112).

Phase 5

During Phase 5a, remodelling of the guard chamber in Gateway Area B included a stepped landing, which gave access into Area C (Figure 4.22). There is no evidence that the original crosswall (B5/C43 and C22) contained an entrance; however, following its partial collapse, perhaps as a result of damage inflicted during the siege of 1287, a replacement wall was built in Phase 5a, which did incorporate an entrance (C49) linking Areas B and C. This new wall (B124/C21) was of poor-quality construction and the western side of the existing arrowloop opening (B24) was rebuilt differently with a much shallower splay. The result was a new wider arrowloop (B129), but one with an asymmetrical form.

On the north side of the entrance (C49), a landing (B10/C46) was constructed in Phase 5a using mortared stone with a clay and stone filling. This landing was reached from the gateway passage by a flight of steps (B123), which were the same width as the landing. These were later replaced in Phase 5c and could have been constructed in either stone or wood. From the southern side of the landing (B10/C46) in Area C, the pre-existing steps (C23) were re-used with a soil fill (C40) and capped with a mortar floor (C28) to provide a flat access from the entrance (C49) to the steps (C23). The area at the top of the steps received considerable wear and was subsequently given a mortar surface (C25–26 and C33) with an underlying brown earth layer (C32) in Phase 5b.

In Phase 5c, a detached timber-framed guardhouse was constructed on the mortar platform in Gateway Area B, adjacent to the landing (B10/C46). A mortar seating (B46) for a sill beam (B22) was first laid on the existing low wall (B18). Then, a second sill beam (B21) was cut into the sub-floor (B26) and a stone step (B33) was constructed beside wall (B18) in order to improve access up into the guardhouse from the gateway passage (Figures 4.22 and 4.23). The presence of a step in this location strongly suggests that the guardhouse had a door facing the gateway passage and this was confirmed in excavation by the recovery of iron hinges still *in situ*. At the back of the guardhouse, against the rebuilt crosswall (B5/C43 and B124/C21), a shelf of clay (B30) was built up, perhaps as a support for seating or a raised platform. By this time, the arrowloop (B129) was redundant and so it was blocked (B8/C42) (Figure 4.20, B–C). The finished guardhouse was given a mortar floor (B25) (Figure 4.22).

To the west of the new guardhouse, the stepped landing linking the gateway passage with Area C remained in use. In Phase 5d, the pre-existing steps (B123) were replaced with a new flight of mortared stone steps (B40/C31), which were slightly narrower than their predecessors. This reduction in width was echoed in the addition of a thin wall (C45) to wall (B124/C21), thereby reducing the entrance (C49) to the same width as the new steps. At the base of these steps (B40/C31), a new mortar floor was laid (B121), which was very similar in composition to that of the neighbouring guardhouse (B25).

There is also evidence for occupation in Phase 5d. Within the guardhouse, a layer of green sand (B23 and B28) is probably all that remains of a poor-quality mortar floor that was laid over the existing floor (B25),

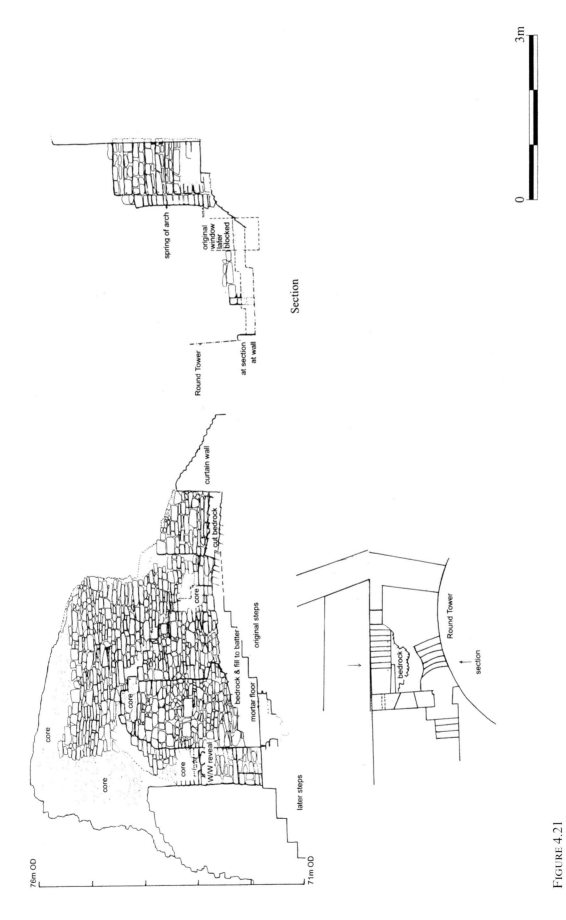

FIGURE 4.21

Elevation of the north wall (C6) south face and N–S cross section, Area C

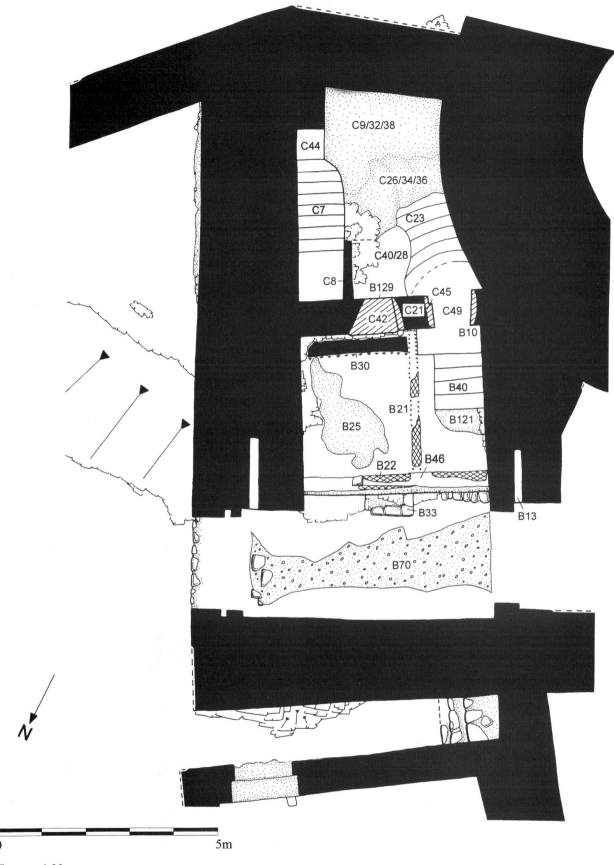

FIGURE 4.22

Areas B, C and A: Phase 5. For general location see Figure 3.2

FIGURE 4.23

Mortar-floored guardhouse with charred timber sill beams (B21 and B22) and stone steps (B10)

whilst a pile of stone projectiles, recovered from the area in between the guardhouse and steps (B40/C31), is also likely to be from this period of occupation (Section 7.2). In Area C, brown earth and rubble fills (C10, C13, C15 and C19) at the top of the steps (C23) are best interpreted as a series of spreads to level out this platform area. The uppermost layer (C10) had become hard-packed from its continued trampling by those moving between floors.

Phases 6 and 7

Following a period of abandonment and decommissioning in Phase 6a, looting took place across the castle in Phase 6b. In Gateway Area B, the iron hinge pillars were ripped out of the inner and outer gates (B128) and, to assist in this process, fires were lit beneath the hinges in order to melt the lead that held them in place. In Area C, the stone treads of the steps (C7) were forcibly removed, thereby exposing the core rubble beneath and causing extensive damage to the face of wall (A2/B3/C6) (Figure 4.24).

Looting was followed in Phase 6c by a catastrophic fire. This completely destroyed the timber-framed guardhouse in Gateway Area B, leaving charred beams *in situ* (Figure 4.23) and deposits 200–400mm thick of charcoal and red clay (B19, B32 and B78) over the mortar platform beneath and the adjacent gateway passage. Traces of wind-blown charcoal (C2 and C27) were also found in Area C, whilst patches of yellow clay (B16, B31 and C37) on the steps (B40/C31) and mortar platform probably came from the roof or perhaps an upper storey of the guardhouse. Within the destruction deposits, several iron hinges were found; four [**M79, M82–84**] at the entrance to the guardhouse in the gateway passage appear to have been burnt

in situ. An even layer of slate (B50) from the roof of the guardhouse was then deposited over a large part of Gateway Area B. The gatehouse passage was most likely open to the sky, since no evidence was found here for a collapsed roof or stone vault.

Above the Phase 6c destruction layers were large quantities of rubble and mortar from the demolition of the castle walls in Phase 6d. In Gateway Area B, the rubble deposit (B7) included many large pieces of fallen masonry (B9, B13, B17, B20 and B38), one of which (B38) can be identified as part of the outer gateway arch. At the base of the wall (A2/B3/C6), a void had been deliberately picked into the stonework and subsequently reddened by fire (B130) (Figure 4.20, A–B). This appears to be evidence of an attempt — in this instance unsuccessful — to undermine the wall, then prop it up with timber supports and set fire to the props, which then caused the wall to collapse. In Area C, Phase 6d rubble deposits were identified as layers (C12, C17–18, C35 and C37). These were subsequently covered in Phase 7b by topsoil (C1), which was also present in Gateway Area B (B6).

Gateway

The initial stepped entrance to Dryslwyn indicates that admission to this early 13th-century castle was to man or horse, but not wheeled vehicles. Such vehicles may either have been unable to ascend the steep hill or were not permitted entry to the castle. Although they are often now lost due to the development of larger later entrances, narrow stepped entrances with single-leafed doors may originally have been present at many Welsh castles. A narrow entrance, which, given the fall of the ground, was probably entered via a series of steps, is present at Dolwyddelan (Conwy), whilst at

FIGURE 4.24

The steps (C7) from which the stone treads have been removed (C48), leaving damaged areas in the face of wall (C6)

Cilgerran (Pembrokeshire) the narrow entrance was protected with a portcullis (Hilling 2000, 21): both were probably constructed in the period 1220–50. A wider stepped entrance still exists at Castell-y-Bere (Gwynedd) (Butler 1974, fig 1). This may suggest limited use of wheeled transport at this period, since access to many sites could only be gained across steeply sloping ground with no metalled surface. Consequently, most goods, even agricultural produce and building stone, were locally sourced and were moved by water, manpower or pack-horse. This would impact on the level, volume and nature of trade, which tended to be principally in small luxury goods, so that castles only needed small entrances closed with single-leafed doors. At Dryslwyn, the appearance of a wider ramped entrance by Phase 3 may be symptomatic of a wider change in transport, with wheeled carts and wagons becoming more widely used by the mid 13th century in west Wales.

The surviving sequence of gateway construction, illustrated in Figure 4.25, shows development from a simple narrow entrance in Phase 1, accessed on foot up a series of steps, to one with an external defensive ditch and walls in Phase 2, leading to a wider ramped entrance in Phase 3. The extent of the projecting walls is uncertain in Phases 2 and 3, but they are clearly enhancing the defence of the entrance leading to a

fully developed double-gated entrance with guard-chamber beside the gatepassage and a portcullis in the outer gate in Phase 4. This final arrangement is not directly paralleled elsewhere. However, most Marcher castles constructed or rebuilt after the early 13th century, such as Caerphilly (Caerphilly) or Montgomery (Powys) have large gatehouses which contain these elements. Welsh castles such as Dolforwyn (Powys) (Butler 1997), Dinas Bran (Denbighshire) (King 1974) and Criccieth (Gwynedd) (O'Neil 1944–45) often have idiosyncratic gatehouses adapted to the geography of the site. At Dryslwyn, the necessity for a substantial Inner Ward gatehouse was removed by the narrow confines of the site, coupled with the development of Middle and Outer Wards. The gateway arrangement developed for the Inner Ward is seen in more compact form in the Castle Gatehouse W and the Town Gatehouse U.

The most common location for a castle entrance was either next to or beneath a large tower, such as the Middle Ward Gate at Chepstow Castle (Monmouth-shire) (Turner 2002a, 32). A tower projecting beyond the curtain wall provided flanking fire across the front of the entrance, often making it the best-defended point on the perimeter. This form of defended entrance was used extensively in Welsh castles during the 13th century, for example Castell-y-Bere (Gwynedd),

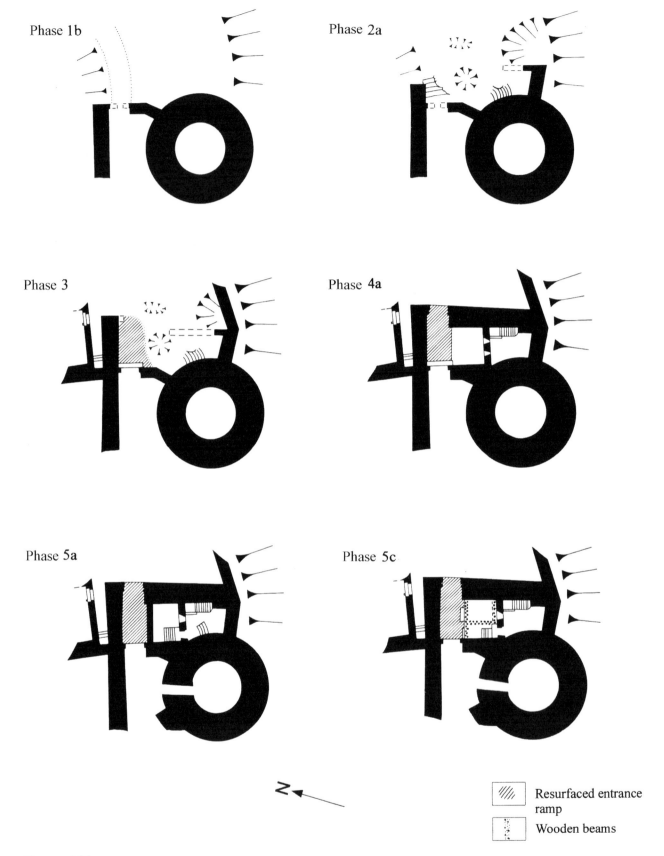

Phase 1b

Phase 2a

Phase 3

Phase 4a

Phase 5a

Phase 5c

Z

///// Resurfaced entrance ramp

Wooden beams

FIGURE 4.25

Areas B, C and A: development sequence of the Castle/Inner Ward gateway

Dolforwyn (Powys) and Dolwyddelan (Conwy), and was employed for the Inner Ward entrance at Dryslwyn, though these towers often lack the arrowslits to provide flanking fire.

The remodelling of the existing gateway at Dryslwyn in the 1280s to a double-gateway form demonstrates a clear appreciation of the essential elements of a castle gatehouse, albeit achieved with modest means. Unusually, the lack of later development of the castle at Dryslwyn has left this double gateway with traces of its development still visible. A similar adaptation to local circumstances exists at Dinas Bran (Denbighshire), where a long, narrow gatehouse, dictated by the contours of the site, was constructed with the rest of this castle in the 1260s (Avent 1983, 33; King 1974, 125).

The final significant development of the Dryslwyn Castle gateway was the construction of a timber-framed guardhouse, represented by the charred remains of beams, in Phase 5c. This use of cheaper, quicker and less durable timber box-frame construction is paralleled in the 15th–16th century castle gatehouse at Brockhampton (Herefordshire) (Howarth 1991) and the 17th-century gatehouse at Stokesay Castle (Shropshire) (Munby 1993, 32).

4.3 AREAS I, J, K AND L: GREAT HALL, KITCHEN AND APARTMENTS

Areas I, J, K and L lie together in the south-western quarter of the Inner Ward (Figure 1.3). Initially open areas within the early castle, from Phase 2a, Areas K and L formed the western and eastern portions of Great Hall K/L, a substantial masonry building containing a first-floor hall. From Phase 4a, this building was abutted in Areas I and J by another large stone building: a residential apartment block (Apartments I/J). Prior to its construction, Area J was open and largely empty, without a specific function. Area I, however, saw a series of stake-built structures in Phases 1 and 2, which were replaced in Phase 2c by a small masonry building (Kitchen I). This was demolished in Phase 4a in advance of construction work on Apartments I/J.

Phase 1

The earliest structure in Areas I, J and K is the curtain wall (I110/J10/J29/K60) surrounding the early castle (Figure 2.5). This was erected in Phase 1a either directly on top of the bedrock (I45/J9/K25) or, in the south-west corner, on limestone slabs (J38), identical to the foundation (D16) of Round Tower D. Several deposits (I107, J12, J19, J23, J35, J39–43, J50 and K36) relating to its construction were identified, including stone chippings, earthy mortar, charcoal and lime. Against the inner face of the curtain wall (I110) in Area I, an oval stone pier (I106) was also erected in Phase 1a. Its function is uncertain, although it presumably supported a structure associated with the curtain wall (I110).

Among the early features in Area I was a pit (I59) and various stakeholes (I62 and I111–162) dug into the natural clay (I45). Similar stakeholes were identified in Area G, all of which probably derive from temporary shelters erected either during the construction of the first castle or in its initial occupation in Phase 1b. Further stake-built structures may have been present in Areas K and L prior to the construction of Great Hall K/L in Phase 2a, which destroyed all trace of previous activity here.

Phase 1b activity in Area J was represented by a thick accumulation of occupation material (J18, J36–37 and J72) containing substantial quantities of bone, pottery and organic remains. These deposits almost certainly relate to the stake-built structures in Area I. Traces of the layer (J18) were found to underlie the south wall (I4/J4/K66/L4) of Great Hall K/L.

Phase 2

Phase 2a saw the construction of Great Hall K/L, whose west wall was formed by the pre-existing curtain wall (K60) (Figure 4.26). The north (K59/L3), south (I4/J4/K66/L4) and east (L2) walls were erected directly on the bedrock (K25/L20) without foundation, but were soon left perched on small rock shelves following the quarrying away of bedrock within the building (Figures 4.27 and 4.28). A layer of small cobbles (L21) was then hammered into the crevices of the bedrock in Area L, creating an even ground surface on which construction work could continue; dumps of yellow soil (K32, K38 and K69) performed the same function in Area K. On top of these surfaces, deposits of lime (K49, K63 and L43) and burnt materials (K61–62 and K67) indicate the production of mortar.

Great Hall K/L initially had two storeys: a hall at first-floor level, whose wooden floor rested on offsets in the walls (K59/L3 and I4/J4/K66/L4), and a ground-floor undercroft, lit by at least four (probably five) arrowloops (K72, L52/J74, L54 and L65) and entered from Courtyard O via an archway (L60) in the north wall (K59/L3). The hall above gained both heat and some of its light from a central hearth supported on a stone pier (K55/L8), the base of which was recovered on top of the cobbled layer (L21) at the western end of Area L. A crescent of mortar (K50/L42), dropped during the creation of the pier, was deposited around its foot. The pier base itself was rendered and all the internal wall faces of Great Hall K/L were probably similarly finished in Phase 2a.

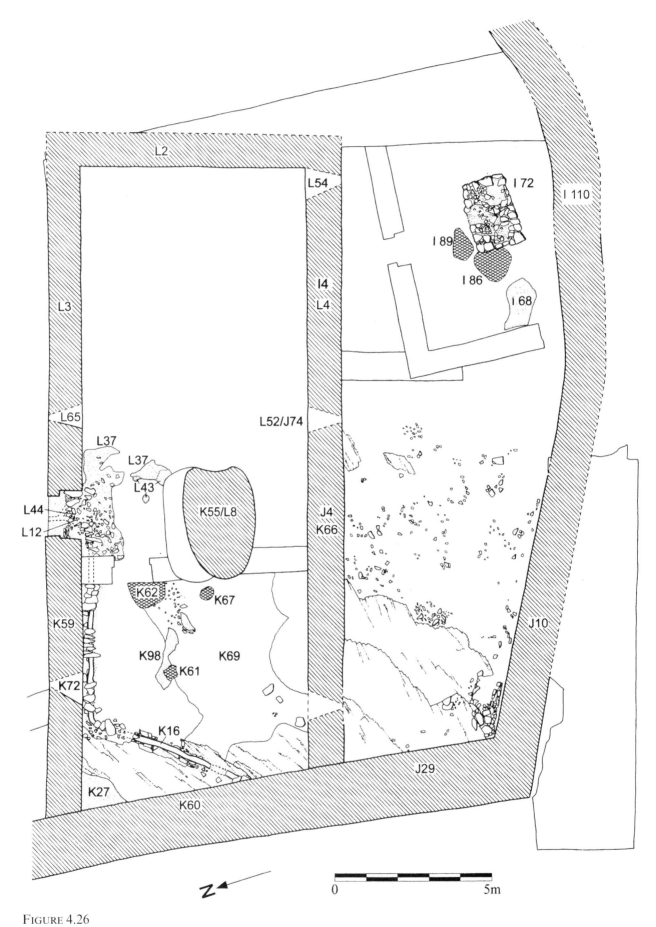

FIGURE 4.26

Areas I, J, K and L: Phase 2a. For general location see Figure 2.6

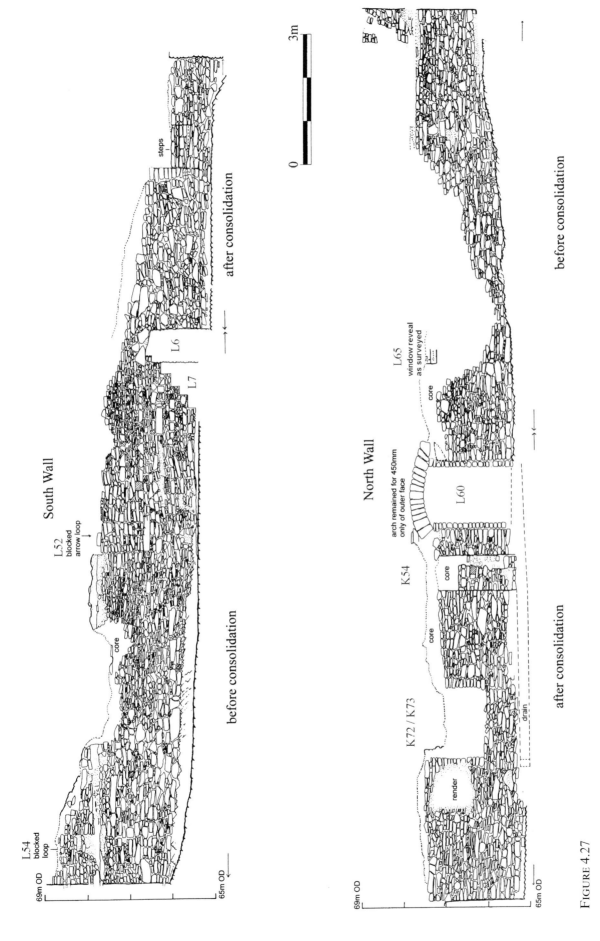

FIGURE 4.27

Elevation of the interior of the Great Hall K/L, north and south walls

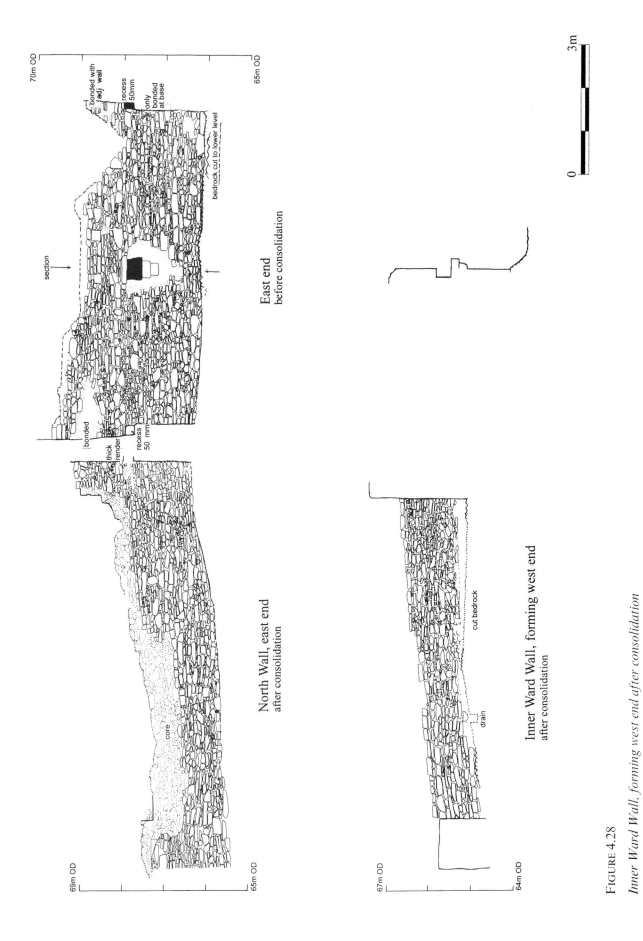

FIGURE 4.28

Inner Ward Wall, forming west end after consolidation

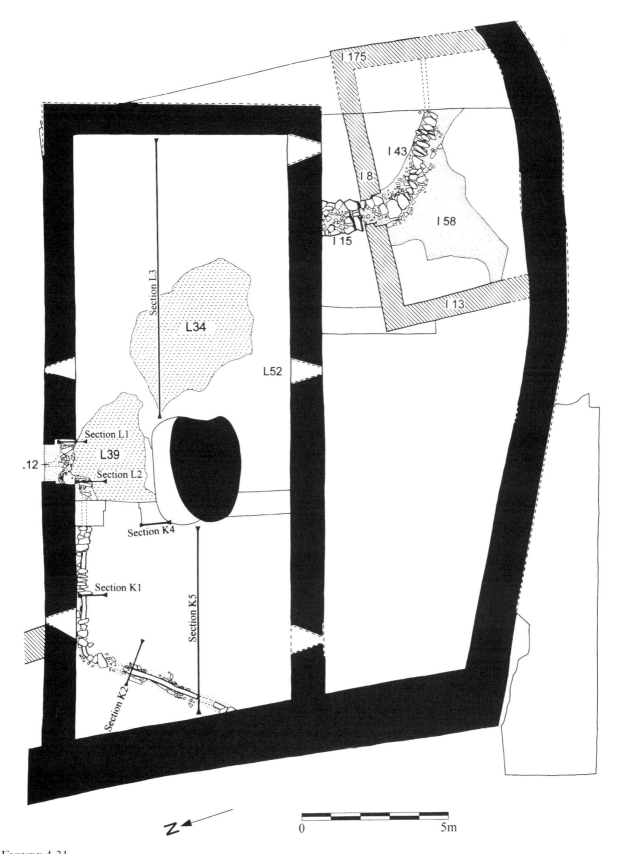

FIGURE 4.31

Areas I, J, K and L: Phases 2c–3a, sections L1 and L2 not illustrated. For general location see Figures 2.7 and 2.8

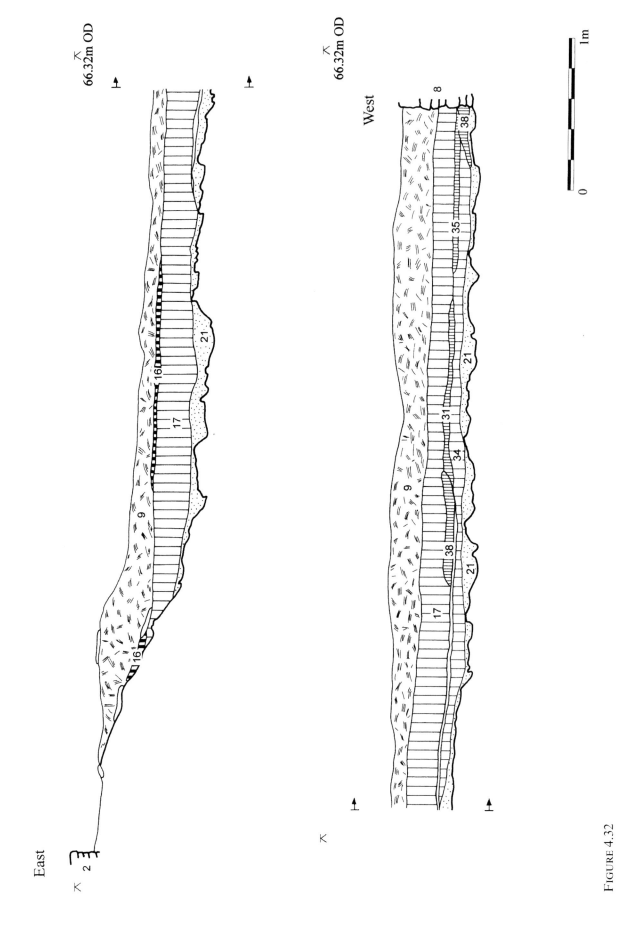

FIGURE 4.32

South-facing Section L3 through the thin flooring and sub flooring layers of the undercroft of the Great Hall K/L

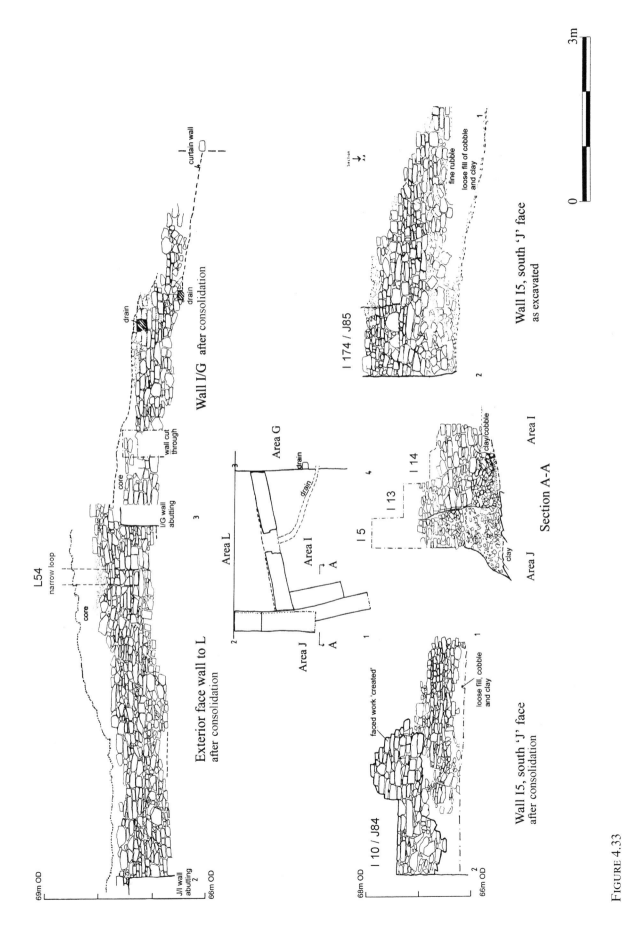

FIGURE 4.33

Elevations. East end of the external face of the south wall of the Great Hall K/L, the west face of I/G wall (I171) and the west face of I/J wall (I5)

FIGURE 4.34

Remains of the steps (I15) leading up from the entrance to the Kitchen I (left) up to the original first-floor level of Great Hall K/L (right)

first necessitated the partial demolition of the existing curtain wall (I110/J10), before its replacement with a substantial new wall (J7) of well-mortared limestone, which was topped with battlements. The eastern end of Apartments I/J was created by the addition of a new wall (I171) to the existing walls (I2 and I175).

The ground-floor rooms of Apartments I/J were at the level of the first floor of adjacent Great Hall K/L. To achieve the required floor height, Areas I and J were filled with clay and stone (I6, I11, I20–22, I26–27, I31, I38–39, J6, J14–16, J20, J24 and J31) (Figure 4.37). A wide range of material was represented, including building rubble, some of which came from the demolished walls of Kitchen I, and occupation debris, comprising pottery, bone and charcoal. The floor surface that ultimately rested on top of this dumped material was above the level of surviving archaeological deposits. In the north-east corner of Area J, however, a flattened area (J89) was identified, which may have formed part of the sub-floor. Broken flagstones in the south wall (J7) (Figure 4.36) indicate that the lost floor surface was certainly paved. The upper floor of Apartments I/J was evidently made of wood with rafters supported on a wooden sill beam, which rested on a step built into the width of the wall (J7). This step was 300mm deep and was located above the shallow ground-floor window arches (J86–87) (Figure 4.39). Fragments of red sandstone found in the surviving masonry (J7) indicate that these south-facing windows had fine red sandstone mullions when constructed (Section 6.2).

In Great Hall K/L, Phase 4a was characterised by a major re-ordering of the building. The existing central stone pier (K55/L8) was first enlarged with new masonry (K56/L50). This sat directly on top of bedrock that had first been exposed by the digging of a construction trench (L36). This enlarged pier incorporated a stone corbel, which supported one end of a wooden beam spanning the full length of Area L. The other end of this beam slotted into a hole with a supporting corbel (L56) built into the east wall (L2) (Figure 4.28).

The new wooden floor carried on this beam replaced the original Phase 2a upper floor, but it did so at a level 0.5m lower, thereby creating headroom for a third storey, most likely of chambers or apartments (Figures 4.38 and 4.39). It is not clear how the first and second floors of the building were now heated; the creation of an additional storey would almost certainly have rendered the central hearth in the first-floor hall redundant. It is possible, however, that fireplaces and chimneys were now constructed within the walls of the building.

As part of the process of lowering the first-floor level within Great Hall K/L, the south-facing arrowloops (J74/L52 and L54) were blocked (J75/L53 and L55). The blocked arrowloop (J75/L53) was incorporated into a doorway (J48), which cut through at first-floor level from the ground floor of Apartments I/J. Conversely, the north-facing arrowloop (L65) was widened in Phase 4a to form a small window (L57), which continued to light the undercroft of Area L. In

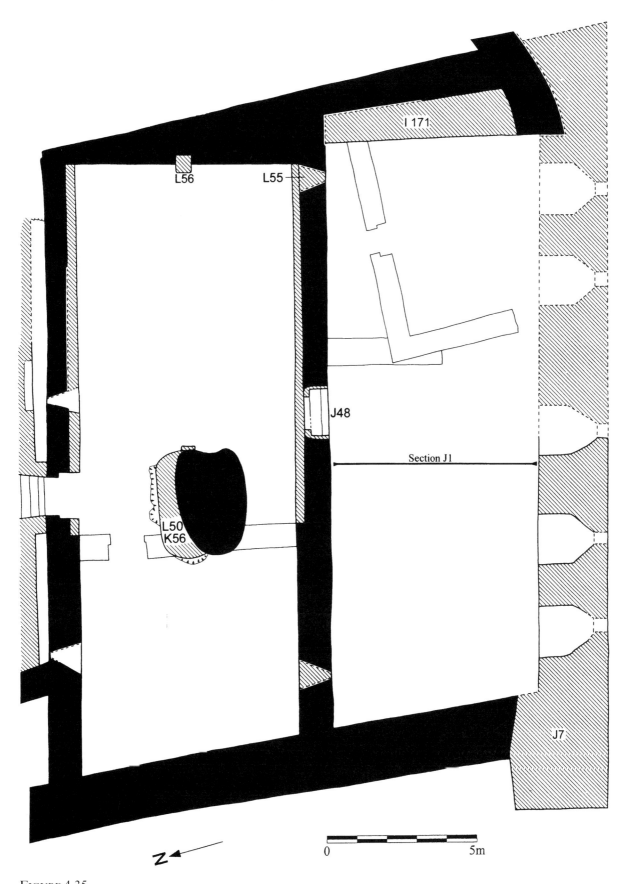

FIGURE 4.35

Areas I, J, K and L: Phase 4a. For a general location see Figure 2.9

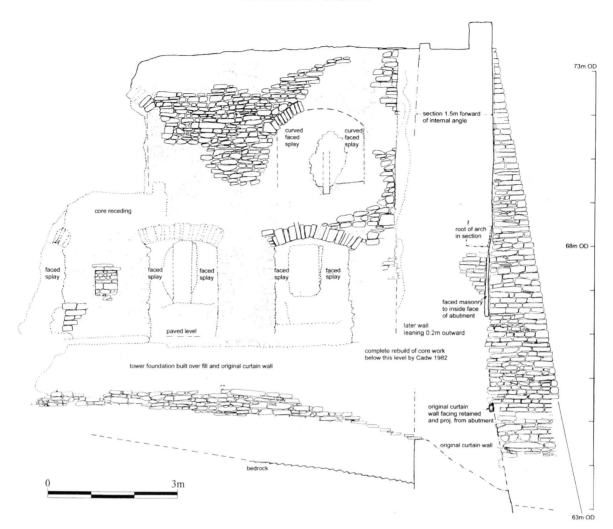

FIGURE 4.36

Elevation of the interior (north) face of the south wall of Area J

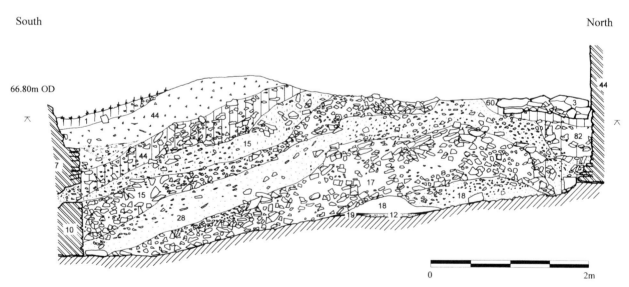

FIGURE 4.37

Section J1 through the numerous deposits of clay and stone in Area J

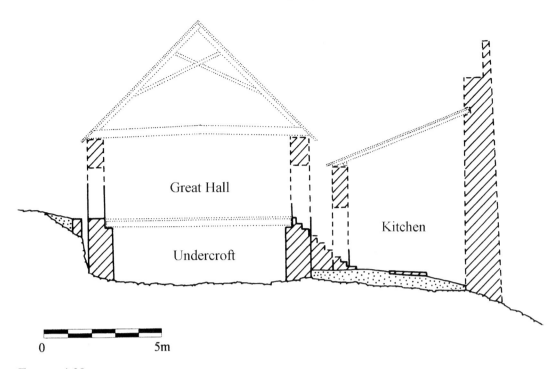

FIGURE 4.38

Reconstructed cross section through the Great Hall K/L and associated surfaces in Phase 2c

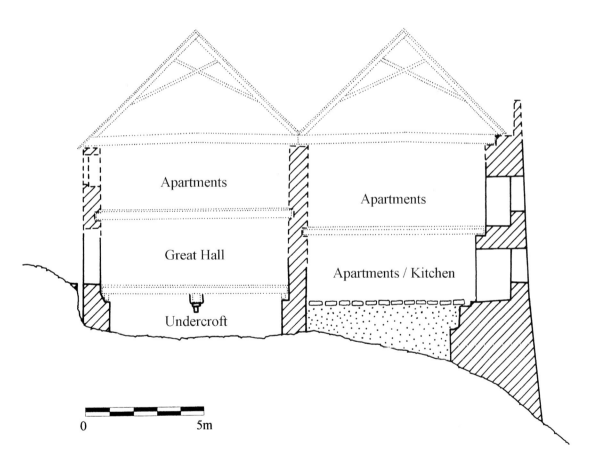

FIGURE 4.39

Reconstructed cross section through the Great Hall K/L, Apartments I/J and associated surfaces in Phase 4a

addition, new offsets in the north (K59/L3) and south (I4/J4/K66/L4) walls were created, 0.5m below the original Phase 2a offsets, to hold timber beams supporting the new wooden floor. A hole (L59) in the east wall (L2) received the eastern end of the southern timber beam (Figures 4.40 and 4.28). The offsets themselves and the wall faces above them were re-pointed with a hard white mortar, which was absent from the lower parts of the north (K59/L3) and south (I4/J4/K66/L4) walls. This appears to have been an attempt to make good the interior of the upper two storeys of Great Hall K/L, following completion of the Phase 4a alterations.

In Phase 4c, changes were made to the undercroft floor of Great Hall K/L in the area to the south of the archway (L60). A layer of crushed shale (L27) was laid down, which was followed by further deposits (L24, L28 and L29). These are best interpreted as repairs made to the worn floor surface, which had become damaged as a result of moving around heavy goods and victuals stored in the undercroft during the post-siege period (Section 3.1). In Apartments I/J, there were further post-siege repairs, which were conspicuous by their squared stone-block construction (Section 6.1). These included a buttress at the western end of the south wall (J7), which partially blocked a

FIGURE 4.40

Offset in wall (L4) and socket (L59) in wall (L2) to support the wooden beam which carried the first floor level of the Great Hall K/L. Note the socket for the beam of the original floor level, at a higher level

west-facing window (Figure 4.36), in addition to sections of masonry surrounding some of the south-facing window openings.

Phase 5

In Phase 5a, Apartments I/J were divided internally by a crosswall (I5/J5), which now formed the boundary between Areas I and J (Figure 4.41). This crosswall was built on a foundation of poor-quality shale (J11), the partially demolished west wall (I13/J64) of Kitchen I and incorporated at least one stone projectile from the 1287 siege (Figures 4.42 and 4.33). A doorway (I10/J84) was included at the northern end of the crosswall (I5/J5), linking Areas I and J, the threshold of which was set at the same level as the first floor of neighbouring Great Hall K/L.

To the east of the crosswall (I5/J5) in Area I, a drain (I12) was cut into the floor in the north-east corner of Apartments I/J. Seated in soil-filled trench (I30, I41 and I172), it emptied through a hole (I3) in the east wall (I171), which appears to have been an original feature of its construction. Given the stratigraphic position of the drain (I12) and the fact that it did not line up correctly with the hole (I3), it is very likely that it replaced an earlier Phase 4a drain here. With its large square troughs at one end, the Phase 5a drain (I12) parallels those found in other castle kitchens, for example at Chepstow (Monmouthshire) (Rick Turner pers comm). It would thus appear that the easternmost ground-floor room of Apartments I/J inherited the function of Kitchen I, following its demolition in Phase 4a.

To the west of the crosswall (I5/J5) in Area J, a drystone revetment wall of shale (J21) was built in Phase 5a in order to hold back the clay and stone levelling deposits of Area J during extensive alterations to the western end of the south wall (I4/J4/K66/L4) of Great Hall K/L. This revetment wall (J21), similar in materials and construction to the foundation (J11) of the crosswall (I5/J5), could have supported a partial crosswall at a higher level. A crosswall (K52/L6) existed in Area K and may also have been built in Phase 5a in order to provide structural stability during building work.

Evidence for the Phase 5a alterations to the western end of the wall (I4/J4/K66/L4) was seen in both Areas J and K and this activity may correspond to the building repair on the west side of the 'King's Hall' recorded in an account of 1338/9 (Webster 1987, 95). The western section of wall (I4/J4/K66/L4) was demolished and a pit was subsequently dug beside the curtain wall and filled with stone (K28). This provided a foundation for the replacement wall (J83/K58), which contained a flight of stone steps (J76/K57) leading up from the undercroft of Great Hall K/L into the ground floor of Apartments I/J. The north face of the

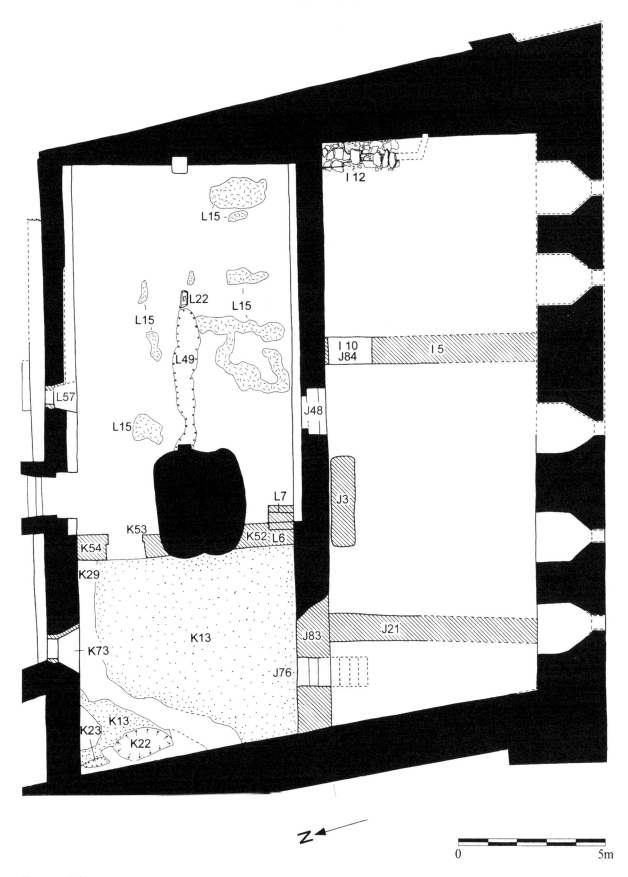

FIGURE 4.41

Areas I, J, K and L: Phase 5. For a general location see Figure 3.2

FIGURE 4.42

Smooth rounded stone, a lithic projectile from the 1287 siege in the foundations (J21) of wall (J5), looking south

new wall (J83/K58) was finished to appear continuous with the remaining stretch of the undercroft wall (I4/J4/K66/L4) within Great Hall K/L. The bottom portion of the south face of wall (J83/K58), however, had only a crude finish, where it was hidden below the ground-floor level of Apartments I/J. The Phase 5a alterations were accompanied in Area K by the widening of the arrowloop (K72) in the north wall (K59/L3) of Great Hall K/L to form a window (K73). Fragments of fine red sandstone tracery from an ogee cinquefoil window were recovered from Areas L and O (Figure 6.6). Given the likely dating of this window form (Section 6.2) and the documentary reference to the construction of a new window in the 'Kings Hall' in the building accounts of 1338 (Section 3.1), it is likely that this window was inserted into one of the upper storeys of the north wall of Great Hall K/L at this time. Partial traces of a contemporary mortar floor (K19 and K20), which had been extensively worn, were also recovered throughout Area K.

In Area L, a flight of stone steps (L7) was constructed to lead up to the newly built crosswall (K52/L6), which itself was now altered to accommodate the top step. These steps presumably gave access to the undercroft of Great Hall K/L from a trapdoor in the floor of the hall above and they may have replaced an earlier wooden ladder in the same location. The stone steps (L7) were constructed on top of a mortar floor surface

(L35), which may correlate with the Phase 5a mortar floor (K19 and K20) observed in Area K.

Also at this time, Area L received a series of occupation and rubble deposits (L17, L19, L23 and L31) (Figure 4.32), one of which (L17) contained a piece of red freestone (L22). Originally a corbel, it was now re-used as a padstone for a wooden pillar, which rose up to support the longitudinal floor beam running between the corbel (L56) and the stone pier extension (K56/L50). The padstone (L22) had a mortise cut into its upper surface, which received a tenon at the base of the wooden post. This wooden support appears to have been an afterthought, added only once the floor beam above had shown signs of weakening. One further Phase 5a feature of the floor layer (L17) was a depression (L49), which marked the position of a sill beam. This would have supported an internal partition running down the spine of Area L to the stone pier (K55/L8 and K56/L50), thus subdividing the existing floor space within the undercroft.

In Phase 5b, Area K of the undercroft in Great Hall K/L received two new floor surfaces: the first was a hard-wearing layer of crushed slate or shale (K18), which was thickest in the area of the through-route between Courtyard O and Apartments I/J, whilst the second was formed from mortar (K13) (Figure 4.43). At the same time, the drain (K16/L12/L37), which had remained in constant service since its construction in Phase 2a, began to fill with silt (K30, K31, L11 and L12). Excavation of this material in Area K produced two coins [C19 and C17] dated to 1317–20 and 1344–51 respectively.

Phase 5c saw the building of two new crosswalls (K53 and K54) in the undercroft of Great Hall K/L, which together formed a doorway to the north of the central stone pier (K55/L8 and K56/L50) (Figure 4.44). These now restricted access between Areas K and L at ground-floor level and provided an extra level of privacy for the steps (J76/K57) leading up into adjacent Apartments I/J. Construction of the crosswall (K54) over the drain (K16/L12/L37) caused the builders to remove several of the drain's capstones and then to mortar them back in place (K29), presumably to support the new wall (Figure 4.30, Section K1). At first-floor level, the crosswalls (K52/L6, K53 and K54) may have been extended upwards in Phase 5c, thereby shortening the hall to the dimensions of Area L. If this did take place, the central stone pier (K55/L8 and K56/L50) could now have supported a fireplace and chimney set against the new western wall of the room. Part of a circular chimney (L63) was recovered from the Phase 6d demolition rubble overlying Area L; however, this could derive from other fireplaces in Great Hall K/L or Apartments I/J.

In Phase 5d, a stone pier (J3 and J52) was placed in a foundation trench (J2, J55 and J60) in Area J, against the south wall (I4/J4/K66/L4) of Great Hall K/L (Figure 4.44). The function of this pier is unknown, but its size, shape and position suggest a support for a

North   South

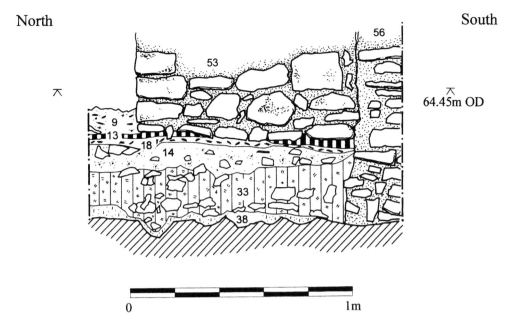

64.45m OD

0   1m

FIGURE 4.43

Section K4, through the floor layers beneath wall (K53)

fireplace, located on either the ground or first floor of Apartments I/J.

Phases 6 and 7

In Phase 6a, many of the doorways within the castle were blocked up when the site was decommissioned: these include two (J48 and I10/J84) within Apartments I/J, both of which received blocking walls (J49 and I174/J85). Decommissioning was followed in Phase 6b by looting. In Apartments I/J, this episode probably saw the removal of the flagstones covering the ground floor, whilst in Great Hall K/L, some of the capstones from the undercroft drain (K16/L12/L37) were removed as well as items of architectural stone-work and some of the larger iron fittings. The fact that several large iron objects, particularly door hinges, did survive *in situ* in Great Hall K/L, however, may suggest that the fire that followed in Phase 6c took hold before looting was complete (Section 6.5).

Traces of the fire in Phase 6c that devastated much of the castle were hard to find in Apartments I/J. In the demolition that followed in Phase 6d, most of the deposits forming the ground floor of this building were lost down the side of the hill. In Great Hall K/L, however, the extent and ferocity of the Phase 6c fire was plain to see. In Area L, burnt material consisted primarily of charred floor timbers (L14) and roof debris (L9 and L13). A similar range of material was recovered in Area K in a deep destruction deposit (K9), 0.3–0.4m deep in places where it had collapsed into the undercroft (Figure 4.45). Fragments of large roofing slates were found close to the walls of the building, whilst smaller slates were present towards

the centre. This suggests that the roof of Great Hall K/L had larger slates near its base and smaller slates nearer its apex. No ridge tiles were found, although there were significant traces of lead flashings and mortar apex cappings (Figure 6.2).

Accompanying the charred timbers in layers (K12 and L14) was a mixture of red burnt and yellow unburnt clay, which was probably used either as a fire-resistant coating for the roof beams or, more probably, as a flooring material for the upper two storeys of Great Hall K/L. Some of this red burnt clay ended up in the drain (K47), which had been left open following the looting of several capstones (Figure 4.30, Section K2). Numerous iron artefacts were also present in the burnt layers, including loop-ended door hinges with their support pivots, lamp holders, wallhooks and timber dogs (Section 6.5). These were particularly well preserved due to the initial lack of oxygen in the soil and rubble deposits, which had been consumed during the fire. Indeed, the ferocity of the fire within the building was demonstrated by the natural glazing of masonry and mortar, which happened as the heat fused the alkali content of the wood ash with the silica present in the stone and mortar. Many thousands or iron nails survived in near perfect condition and their presence may be taken as evidence for the use of plank-ing, probably in the upper two floors, within Great Hall K/L. Plant materials, perhaps the remnants of reed or straw floor coverings, were also recovered as carbonised remains (Sections 10.5 and 10.6).

In Phase 6d, both Great Hall K/L and Apartments I/J were demolished. Some loose rubble that had not been lost down the hillside in Area J was present as layers (J47, J51 and J53–54), whilst further rubble

FIGURE 4.44

Elevations. Interior of the Great Hall K/L, central stone pier (K55 and K56) and internal walls (K52, K53 and K54)

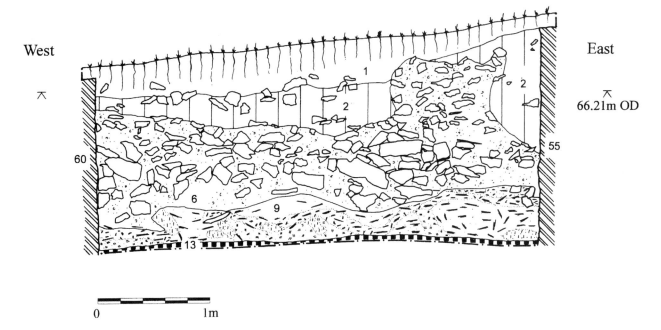

West   East

66.21m OD

0   1m

FIGURE 4.45

Section K5, through the lower rubble (K6) and the burning deposits (K9) filling the undercroft of the Great Hall K/L

existed in layers (J44–46 and J61), although these had been affected by erosion and appear to contain redeposited material. Very little rubble survived in Area I. In Areas K and L, rubble deposits (K6 and L1), averaging 1.5–2m deep but sometimes reaching 3.5m in thickness, filled the undercroft. Only a few pieces of freestone remained; much of the useful building stone had been looted both before and after the fire in Phase 6c.

During Phase 7b, topsoil (J1, K3, K5, K7–8 and L62) formed above the demolition layers in Area J, K and L. In Area K, this was followed in Phase 7c by a sheep burial (K68). Modern disturbance of exposed archaeological layers by rabbits was noted in Area I, whose burrows were recorded as features (I44, I48, I65 and I77).

Great Hall

Halls were the principal spaces for social display and control throughout the medieval period. The Welsh law books show that they were the first buildings which villeins were responsible for constructing for their lord (Jones 2000, 296; Willis-Bund 1902, 201, 213). Lying at the heart of the lord's *llys* or castle, it was in this prominent building that the lord held court, dispensed law, exercised power, celebrated with his followers and entertained guests. In smaller castles it may have provided accommodation and been the principal space for eating and living, in larger castles the hall was principally used for feasting, administration and ceremonial roles (Kenyon 1990, 97). The symbolic importance of the seat of power, especially for the

Welsh, was recognised by Edward I who moved the timber hall from the *llys* at Ystumgwern to Harlech castle and the timber building known as the 'Hall of the Prince' (Llywelyn?) at Conwy, which may have originally derived from Gronant, into his new castle at Caernarfon (Smith 1998, 235).

The Great Hall K/L at Dryslwyn is, due to the slope of the ground, located above an undercroft at first floor level. Blair (1993) has argued that first-floor halls, as described by Wood (1983, 16–34) and Faulkner (1958) were rare and, since the hall is at the same level as the Inner Ward courtyard (Figure 4.38), Dryslwyn can be regarded as hall which is merely at first-floor level rather than a first-floor hall. Among the best parallels for the Great Hall K/L at Dryslwyn is the example at Christchurch Castle (Dorset) (Wood 1983, 17–18), to which it bears a strong resemblance. Constructed around 1160, Christchurch was owned by Hubert de Burgh, who also built the hall at Grosmont (Monmouthshire) between 1201 and 1204 (Knight 1980, 13). This latter example may well have been seen by Rhys Gryg or Maredudd ap Rhys, in turn influencing the form of Great Hall K/L at Dryslwyn, erected in *c*1230.

In common with other first-floor buildings, including the hall at Christchurch Castle, the ground-floor undercroft at Dryslwyn was lit by arrowloops (Figure 4.26). Access into the hall above was gained at first-floor level through opposed north and south entrances set at the east end of the building: the north entrance opened onto Courtyard O, whilst the south entrance led to Kitchen I. In order to hide both doorways from view by the lord, seated at the west end of the hall on a raised dais, it is likely that a screen was erected parallel with the east wall, thus creating a screens passage, an arrangement typical after the 1190s (Blair 1993, 13). Windows in the north and south walls provided daylight, the most important of which was probably located at the west end in the south wall, immediately adjacent to the lord's dais.

The Welsh law books (Charles-Edwards *et al* 2000, 570), which can be described as 'antique when written in the 14th century' (Pierce 1972, 20), show that the physical form of the hall (*neuadd*) influenced its role as a social space. The central cruck of the three-cruck form of the wooden medieval Welsh hall often supported a wooden structure which at least partially divided the hall into the privileged, near the lord, in the upper part of the hall (*uwch cyntedd*) and the less privileged in the lower part of the hall (*is cyntedd*), with the fire near the centre of the hall. Though the dividing wall was no longer present in masonry halls, or had moved to the far end to become the screen, the social divisions remained. In the centre of the hall at Dryslwyn was a hearth, supported at first-floor level on a substantial stone pier, similar to examples at Ludlow Castle (Shropshire), Bletchingly Castle (Surrey) and Launceston Castle (Cornwall) (Kenyon 1990, 120), as well as Dolforwyn Castle (Powys) and Castell-y-Bere (Gwynedd) (Butler and Knight 2004, 33). The presence of a louvre in the roof to permit the smoke to escape can reasonably be inferred. The central hearth at Dryslwyn is a rare survival, since many have been lost, replaced by later fireplaces built into the long walls of the hall.

Kitchen

Preparation of the food served in the first-floor hall at Dryslwyn may once have taken place outside Great Hall K/L on a substantial hearth, open to the elements. Such external cooking arrangements have also been proposed at Northolt Manor (Greater London) (Hurst 1961). Perhaps a more likely scenario, however, is that the hearth in Area I was originally sheltered within a wooden kitchen building, similar to that uncovered at Weoley (Warwickshire) (Oswald 1962–63), of which no trace was detected during excavation. In Phase 2c, the hearth was incorporated within Kitchen I, a stone-walled building constructed at a slight angle against the curtain wall. This building is almost identical in plan to the kitchen uncovered at Sandal Castle (West Yorkshire) (Mayes and Butler 1983). Access from Kitchen I, up three or four steps to Great Hall K/L at first-floor level, was almost certainly covered by some form of pentice, as was common between kitchen and hall (Wood 1983, 248). Subsequently, Kitchen I was joined to the newly erected Great Chamber G, making an unusual L-shaped solar and service block. A masonry pier (I14) may mark the presence of a second hearth against the west wall.

Following the remodelling of the Inner Ward in Phase 4a, the location of the main castle kitchen is uncertain, although the presence of a drain (I12) in the north-east corner of Area I does suggest that the kitchen function continued within this part of the new Apartments I/J. This continuity of function in a specific location is not unusual and would have allowed ready access to both Great Hall K/L and private rooms within Apartments I/J. It is probable that the ground-floor level of the Great Chamber G, which adjoins Area I, may have had food preparation or storage role in this period with accommodation on the upper floor.

A kitchen (*kegyn*) (or food-house or *buetty*) was a key component of any castle or *llys*, and was amongst the first buildings which villeins were responsible for constructing for their lord (Jones 2000, 296). However, they can be difficult to detect or identify archaeologically as seen at Rhosyr (Johnstone 1999, 265), the Welsh phases at Dolforwyn or Phase 1 at Caerphilly. Often it is only with the presence of substantial masonry remains such as the ovens at Dolforwyn (Butler and Knight 2004, 28–29) and the Phase 2 Kitchen Tower at Caerphilly (RCAHMW 2000, 94), which belong to the later phases of castle construction and occupation which provides clear evidence of kitchen activities. These have often obliterated evidence of earlier kitchen buildings. At Dryslwyn, the sequence of development from an open hearth, through existence as a separate stone building connected via steps (and pentice) to the Great Hall K/L, to part of a service block with accommodation, may be typical for kitchens in 13th-century castles (Kenyon 1990, 138–150). Though the absence of ovens is probably due to the later castle demolition, the presence of a bakestone [**S16**] (Section 9.8) reminds us of the traditional baking of flat breads and cakes in Welsh cookery (Section 10.1).

Apartments and Great Hall

When the castle was remodelled in Phase 4a, limitations of space meant that the development of an additional solar block to form the normal H-shaped plan was not possible. Instead, a two-storey apartment block with large south-facing windows was constructed in Areas I and J, along the south side Great Hall K/L, whilst both Great Hall K/L and Great Chamber G were almost certainly raised by one storey. New facilities, such as garderobes and a chapel, greatly increased the range and quality of accommodation in the Inner Ward of the castle. At the same time, the addition of an Outer Ward, incorporating the new Castle Gatehouse W, further enhanced the size and appearance of Dryslwyn Castle.

At some point prior to the Phase 4a remodelling, perhaps as the result of a water-flow problem, Courtyard O was extended and the entrance to Great Hall

K/L moved to a more central position. Ephemeral remains of a raised platform or step were found in front of the entrance, although no evidence was recovered to suggest the presence of a porch (Section 4.5).

Whilst the lowered first-floor level is clear on the eastern side of Great Hall K/L, with a refurbished offset and beam socket visible (Figure 4.40), the situation is more uncertain on the western side, due to a lack of surviving masonry. The alteration of the arrowloop (K72) to a wider window form (K73) could have occurred in Phase 4a, but a Phase 5a date is also possible, along with the rebuilding of the south-west wall, the insertion of steps (J76) and the addition of crosswalls. Certainly by 1340, the undercroft of Great Hall K/L was used primarily as a through-route between Courtyard O and Apartments I/J and it is also likely that the first-floor hall above had been shortened by this time with the construction of a crosswall supported on walls K52, K53 and K54. This crosswall may have incorporated a fireplace and it is perhaps no coincidence that a cylindrical chimney was recovered from the rubble in Area L. This same chimney form can be found at Manorbier (Pembrokeshire) and a number of other sites in the Pembrokeshire area, where it is referred to as a Flemish chimney. The presence of a short flight of steps (L7), built against the crosswall (L6), indicates that a trapdoor was inserted into the wooden floor of the hall to give access to the undercroft below. A pivoting strap hinge (81SF31) from just such a trapdoor was recovered from the burnt debris in Area K.

If, as appears likely, the first-floor hall of Great Hall K/L was greatly reduced in size by the mid 14th century, this is a clear indication of the reduction in the level of public ceremony and entertainment performed at Dryslwyn Castle by this date. This reduced hall may, by now, have served as little more than a grand entrance lobby to the private apartments in neighbouring Apartments I/J, Great Chamber G and above the hall itself in Great Hall K/L.

Apartments I/J, a building of two storeys, was undoubtedly a substantial construction, indicating the prominence of private apartments in high-status medieval buildings even by the late 13th century. The windows of Apartments I/J share many characteristics with those of the initial 14th-century phase of the Bishop's Palace in Dunfermline (Fife) (Fawcett 1990, 23), both have shallow arched windows with window seats built in either side. The need for light for needlework, reading and writing in private accommodation led to an increase in the number and size of windows and also the provision of window seats in the late 13th and 14th centuries. Almost all windows were rebated for shutters and increasing numbers of windows, even in secular high-status buildings, were glazed by the late 13th century. Given their position and status, it is highly likely that the windows in the south wall of Apartments I/J were glazed. The lack of archaeological deposits of post 1280s date in Areas I and J explains the total absence of any window glass, lead cames or tracery from these areas (Section 6.7 for similar material recovered elsewhere on the site). Following the construction of Apartments I/J, daylight was no longer able to enter windows on the south side of Great Hall K/L. This was rectified in the early 14th century by the addition of ogee cinquefoil windows in the north wall of the building (Section 6.2), which were rebated (K73) to allow fenestration and/or shutters.

The development of a Great Hall of the early 13th century into a complex series of private apartments, service areas and an entrance hall is typical of a rising tide of domesticity seen in private castle development in the period 1200–1500. It articulates the desire for increasing levels of privacy and stratification within society (Pounds 1990, 272–275). At Dryslwyn, as at Kenilworth (Warwickshire) (Thompson 1991a), the later development of an expanded hall block, solar and apartments was retained within the initial curtain wall. The need for the defensive protection of the curtain wall encouraged the construction of upper storeys, building upwards rather than outwards (Thompson 1991b, 160), and two-storey accommodation eventually became the norm in the post-medieval period.

It is unclear if the lords of Dryslwyn who had previously occupied rooms in the Round Tower D in the period 1220s–1250s and in the Great Chamber G 1250s–1280s moved to occupy the Apartments I/J or whether these were intended as guest accommodation. The dumping of siege material on the ground floor level of the Great Chamber G in the post-1287 building work, may suggest that during the English Garrison period the principal accommodation was in the Round Tower G, the upper storey of the Great Chamber G and the Apartments I/J. One of these locations was probably occupied by the constable and his family the others were probably retained for guests.

4.4 AREAS G, H AND F: GREAT CHAMBER AND CHAPEL

Areas G, H and F together occupy the south-east quarter of the Inner Ward, south of Round Tower D and east of Great Hall K/L (Figure 1.3). Both Areas F and G contained clay-floored timber buildings in the initial phases of the castle's occupation, but these were replaced in Area G by a large masonry building, Great Chamber G, constructed in Phase 3a. Area F was subsequently used as a midden area and also contained a latrine pit. Area H initially contained a postern gateway to the castle through the curtain wall. In Phase 4a, this was replaced by a two-storey tower butting onto Great Chamber G. This tower housed the castle's chapel at first-floor level and is referred to as Chapel H.

Phase 1

Phase 1a saw the construction of the curtain wall (F12/G524/G525/H30/H41/H42), which, together with Round Tower D, formed the initial castle at Dryslwyn (Figure 4.46). The curtain wall contained a small postern gateway on the threshold of Areas G and H (G537/H69), leading out and down a steep slope to a ford across the River Tywi. In Area F, a series of clay (F107 and F113) and ash/charcoal (F98–99 and F114) deposits were excavated, one of which (F113) contained sherds of Ham Green pottery dating to the late 12th or early 13th century (Section 9.2). Covering these deposits was a layer of brown soil (F115), on top of which was built the stone foundation (F103 and F104) and the curtain wall (F12) itself.

Curtain wall (F12/G524/G525/H30/H41/H42) displayed the key characteristics of Phase 1a masonry in the castle, being constructed of naturally split limestone bonded with a poor-quality earthy mortar and possessing a battered exterior face and vertical inner face. It had been built in two phases, since there was a near-vertical joint in Area F where the two portions met (Figure 4.47). The postern gateway in Area H contained a single-leafed gate. The eastern face of the western gateway wall (H42) was damaged (Figure 4.48), strongly suggesting that a hinge pillar had originally been seated in the wall here and then forcibly removed. The west face of the eastern gateway wall (H41) was also damaged and it may be that a drawbar across the postern gate was forced from its socket.

Immediately inside the postern gateway (G537/H69) was a small cobbled area (G493), in addition to a shallow drain (G492), which had been roughly chipped into the bedrock and drained from the west. Other Phase 1a features in Area G were ephemeral traces of early castle occupation set on a steep bank of natural clay rising up behind the curtain wall: they comprised stakeholes (G487–488, G490, G494–511 and G514–516), dark earths (G354, G378 and G384) and an occupation deposit (G491). It was not possible to discern the form or function of any structures.

In Phase 1b, occupation continued in Areas F and G, with a further row of five stakeholes (F121–125) being sunk close to the curtain wall (F12) and a gully dug (G358 and G523), running north-east from the postern gateway (G537/H69). This gully was filled with clay containing occupation material (G480) and two flat stones (G535) were then set within it, seemingly forming steps leading up a steep bank. Large quantities of soil and stones (G351, G367, G376, G468, G475, G479 and G481) were later dumped on the bank, thereby extending the area of flat ground southwards towards the curtain wall.

Phase 2

Following the building of adjacent Great Hall K/L, Phase 2a saw the construction of two masonry walls in Areas F, G and H. The first (F4/G538) defined the boundary between Areas E and F, butting up against the curtain wall (F12) at its eastern end and running for 11m west into Area G towards the newly built Great Hall K/L. It acted both in a defensive capacity, dividing the early castle in two, and as a retaining wall, enabling buildings and other structures to be safely erected in Areas F and G.

The second wall (H57 and H62) to be built was L-shaped, projecting out from the curtain wall (H42) in front of the postern gateway in Area H. As the level of the postern entrance (H69) was at least 1m above that of the steeply sloping exterior ground surface, it is likely that this L-shaped wall (H57 and H62) was designed to protect either a ramp or a series of stone steps leading down to the ground. The original form of this construction is unclear as it was partially overlain by the Chapel wall (H60) in Phase 4a (see below).

Other excavated Phase 2a features included stakeholes (G406–410, G417–419, G420–438, G439–442, G446–453, G457–465, G476 and G522) and cobbled surfaces (G455 and G456) in Area G, all associated with continued domestic activity in this part of the early castle. As Figure 4.49 shows, some stakeholes formed straight lines perpendicular with the end wall (L2) of Great Hall K/L and it is possible to interpret them as evidence for a rectangular animal pen, which butted up against the Great Hall. Other stake-built features are harder to discern from the available evidence, although windbreaks, animal pens and structures for hanging or drying cloth are all possibilities. Cooking also cannot be ruled out, as the large patch of burnt material (G416) clearly attests the presence of fires.

Later in Phase 2a, the stake-built structures in Area G were dismantled and a layer of cobbles and earth (G398) deposited, rich in organic and possibly faecal material. Clay and soil was then excavated from Areas F and G and the bedrock quarried away (F129/G536) to create a platform of flat ground, onto which a large timber building could be placed. This building was represented by a series of post pits (F130–131, G203–204, G345, G380, G385, G387, G389, G396–397, G402, G404, G443 and G528–529) and may have been constructed as additional castle accommodation alongside Great Hall K/L (Figure 4.50). In Phase 2b, however, it was pulled down and layers of clay and cobbles (G361 and G362) deposited in the centre of Area G, filling the now redundant postholes. Limited use of this area, represented by minor deposits (G395 and G401), a pit (G411 and G414) and a pair of stakeholes (G382 and G394), was then succeeded by two mortar surfaces (G355 and G366), sandwiched above and below a layer of occupation debris (G371). It is

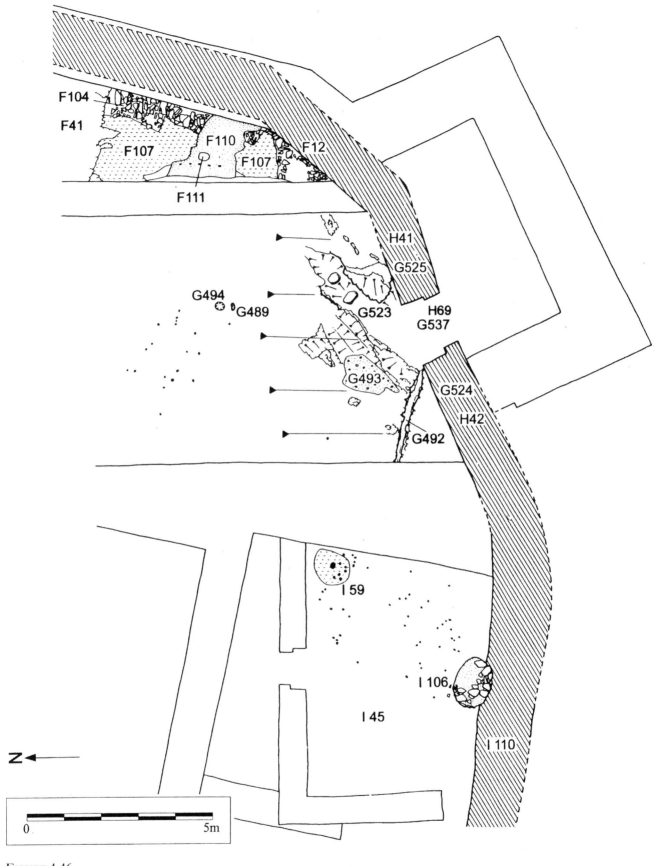

FIGURE 4.46

Areas F, G, H and I: Phase 1. For a general location see Figure 2.5

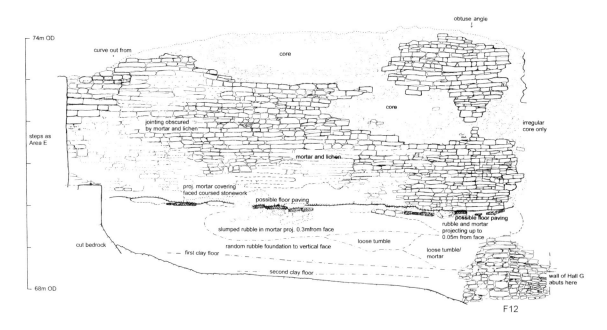

0   3m

FIGURE 4.47

Elevation of the west face of the east wall (F2) of Area F

FIGURE 4.48

The eastern face of the western postern gate wall (H42) damaged by the removal of the hinge pillar

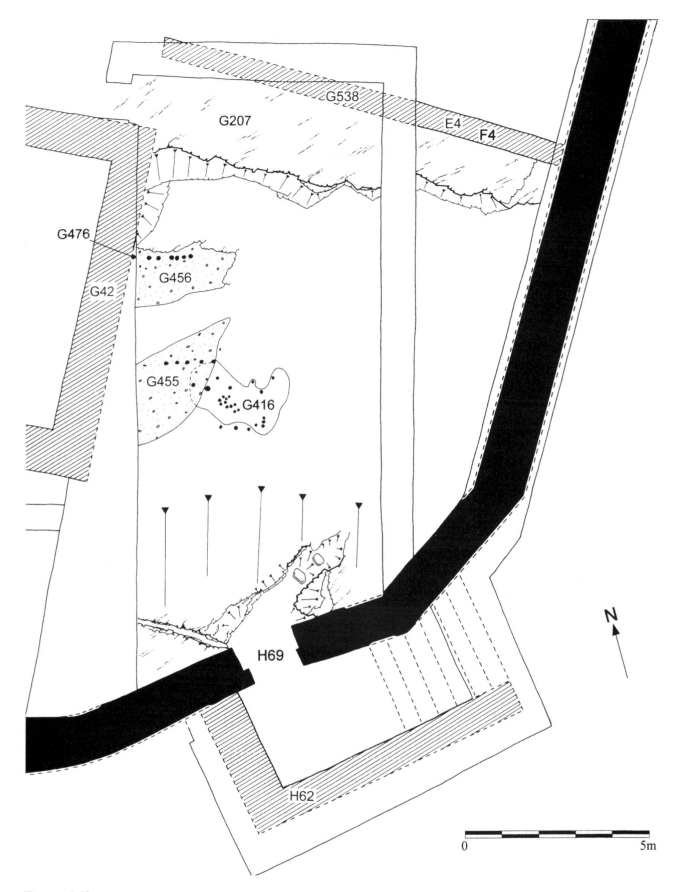

FIGURE 4.49

Areas F, G and H: Phase 2a. Stakehole structures. For a general location see Figure 2.6

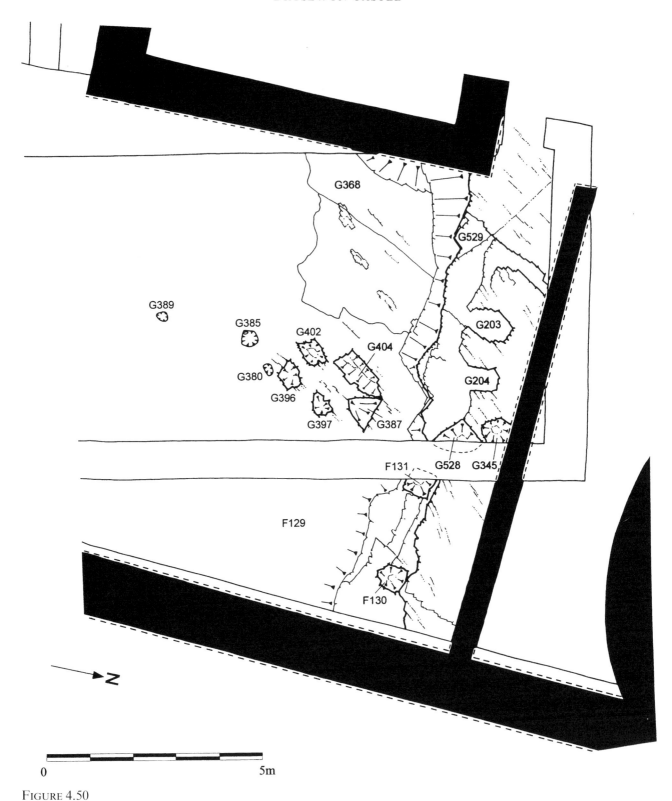

FIGURE 4.50

Areas F, G and H: Phase 2a. Post-built structures. For a general location see Figure 2.6

not clear whether these surfaces had buildings associated, since they were of limited extent and contained no distinctive features or diagnostic material culture.

In Phase 2c, a large timber building was constructed on an east–west axis in Areas F and G, mainly resting on a foundation of rubble (G195, G346, G350 and G352). The floor of this building, the Lower Clay Floor, was formed from puddled clay with stone and patches of burnt daub and was 100–200mm thick (F84/F88/G194) (Figure 4.51). It contained a number of stakeholes (F91–92, F94, G291–344 and G347–349) indicative of internal structures or divisions, but they give little clue as to the building's arrangement or function. The western end of the building butted up

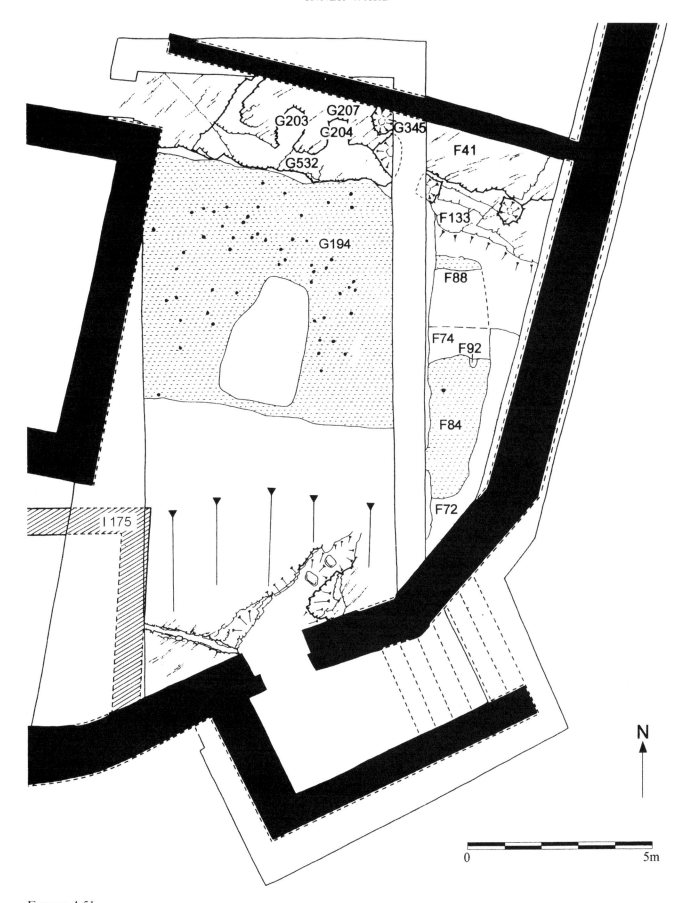

FIGURE 4.51

Areas F, G and H: Phase 2c. Lower Clay Floor building. For general location see Figure 2.7

against the end wall (L2) of Great Hall K/L and it may have been a lean-to structure, rather than free-standing. The northern wall appears to have been of timber-framed construction, resting on a sill beam situated on a step (F133/G532) which had been cut into the quarried bedrock (F129/G536) through the post pits (G203 and G204) of the preceding timber building (Figure 4.52). The only trace of the east wall was a shallow trench (F134), possibly designed to hold a sill beam, which contained a later rubble fill (F72). The south wall had mostly been lost as a result of Phase 3a activity in Area G.

Later in Phase 2c, the large timber building represented by the Lower Clay Floor was pulled down and succeeded by a second timber building in the same location, which was substantially larger than its predecessor and possessed a new clay floor, the Upper Clay Floor (Figure 4.53). Once again, this building adjoined Great Hall K/L to its west, but the presence of a sill beam impression (G174) in front of the wall (L2) suggests that it was freestanding and had a timber-framed west wall. The eastern and northern walls were also timber-framed, since a construction trench (F135) for an eastern sill beam was identified in Area F, whilst the northern sill beam step (F133/G532) was re-used and a drip trench (F128) cut into the bedrock alongside it in order to prevent rainwater from running into the building. The Upper Clay Floor was again formed of burnt daub and puddled clay and was 100–150mm thick (F33, F57, F69, G166, G179 and G182), containing a complex series of stakeholes (F65, F67, F79–82, F89, G191–192, G205–206, G212, G216–218 and G219–289) and a beam slot (G215) relating to various unidentified internal features. Towards the end of Phase 2c, the Upper Clay Floor was renewed using

grey clay (F36, F55, F58, G172, G180 and G214). The drip trench (F128), meanwhile, filled up with mortar (F60).

In Phase 2d, the second timber building continued to be occupied for a time. Layers of charcoal (G187 and G198), burnt clay (G173 and G208) and ash (G177, G181, G197 and G213) all indicate the presence of a hearth located towards the centre of the Upper Clay Floor. Subsequently, however, the building fell out of use and its floor was covered with a series of dumps of soil (G161, G178 and G183), whilst the northern and eastern sill beam trenches (F133/G532 and F135) filled with earth, mortar and rubble (F34, F64, F68, F70–71, F95, G176, G189, G200 and G202). At some point later in Phase 2d, an open drain (G186) was cut through these deposits, although this too eventually silted up (G184 and G190). It is unclear why waste-water was allowed to spill across this area, but it was clearly unoccupied and used primarily for dumping rubbish. One possible interpretation is the deliberate despoilation of the castle during 1246 when forces held the castle for Dafydd ap Gruffudd, before it was recaptured for the Lord of Dryslwyn by the seneschal of Carmarthen (Section 2.1).

Phase 3

Phase 3a was dominated in Area G by the construction of a large masonry building interpreted as Great Chamber G due to its position alongside Great Hall K/L and its fine stone walls rendered with lime plaster (Figure 4.54). At its northern end, foundations (F56, G199 and G201) for the east wall (F1/G1) cut through earlier deposits, including the Upper and Lower Clay

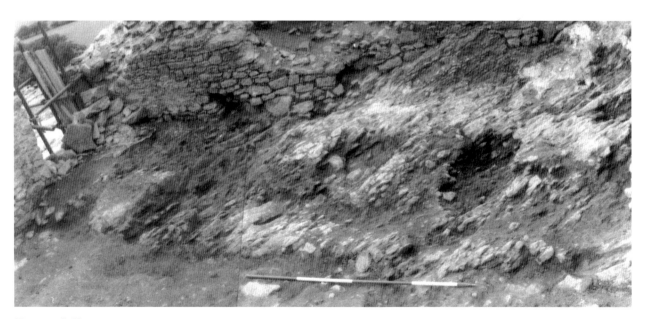

FIGURE 4.52

Step cut in the bedrock (G32) to create a flat seating for a sill beam cutting through the earlier post pits including (G203) and (G204)

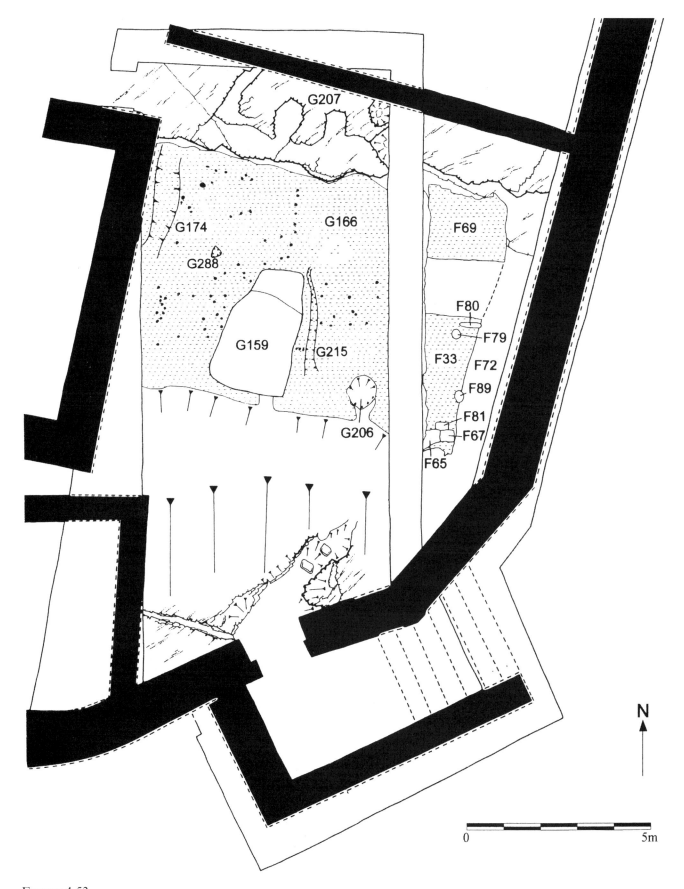

FIGURE 4.53

Areas F, G and H: Phase 2c. Upper Clay Floor building. For general location see Figure 2.7

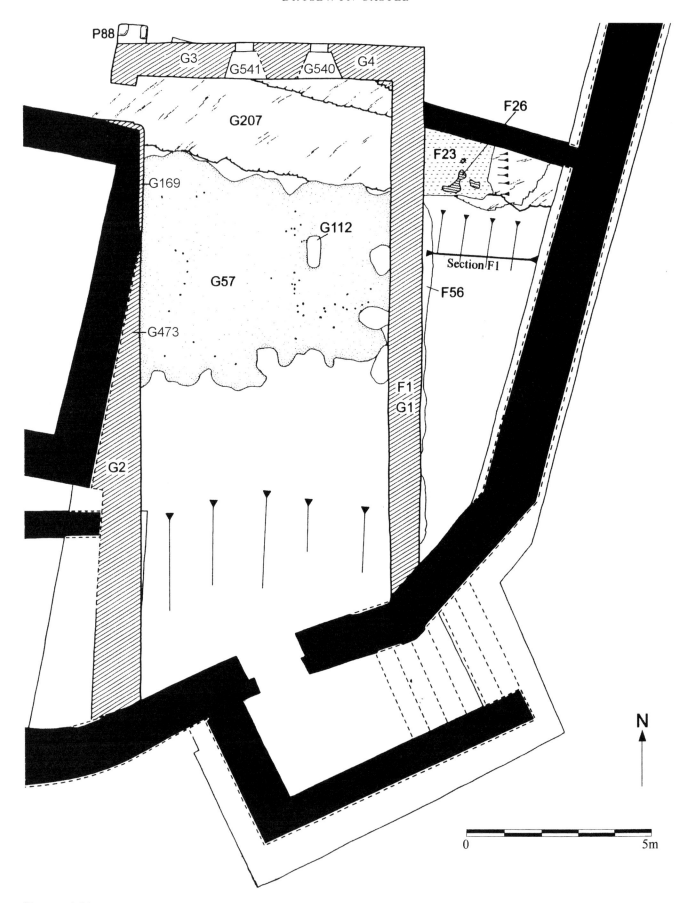

FIGURE 4.54

Areas F, G and H: Phase 3. Great Chamber G. For general location see Figure 2.8

Floors. This wall (F1/G1) contained putlog holes at regular intervals (Figure 4.55) and offers good evidence that the building had high walls. The west wall (G2) was largely built on top of the partially demolished east wall (G513) of Kitchen I. At its northern end, a loose stone foundation (G473) was laid and the end wall (L2) of Great Hall K/L was substantially altered (G169) in order to support the wall (G2). The north wall (G3 and G4) of Great Chamber G was of continuous build with the east wall (F1/G1) and its construction necessitated the partial demolition of the earlier wall (F4/G538). Incorporated within the north wall was a pair of narrow lancet windows (G540 and G541) (Figure 4.55), whilst a narrow doorway leading into Courtyard O was situated in the very north-west corner of the building.

In order to build the southern sections of walls (F1/G1 and G2), which butted up against the curtain wall (G524/H42 and G525/H41), it was first necessary to dig considerable foundations (G467 and G533). This activity removed much of the earlier deposits at the southern end of Area G, including the southern walls of the two Phase 2c timber buildings. Following the completion of wall (G2) and the infilling of its foundation trench (G375, G466, G472, G482 and G484), the excavated southern half of Area G was filled up again

with a variety of deposits. The main part of this fill was material that had previously been excavated from this area, including layers (G347–349 and G359).

The initial floor surface laid within Great Chamber G was a limited mortar spread (G160). Following dumps of clay (G165 and G168), however, an extensive levelling operation was undertaken, using mortar and rubble (G157). This acted as a base for a more substantial mortar floor (G57, G119 and G148), which was composed of several different layers reflecting constant patching and repair. Originally, this mortar surface extended to all four corners of Great Chamber G, but later activity (G383/H70) in Phase 4a resulted in its destruction in the southern half of the building.

In Area F, substantial dumps of charcoal (F50), brown and grey clay (F51 and F54), mortar (F52) and earthy rubble (F21, F31–32, F44–45 and F47–48) were first made in Phase 3a, before a latrine pit (F23) was cut into them in Phase 3b. This pit measured 1.5×2m and was 100–150mm deep; however, it is likely that it was once much deeper, the upper section having been dug out later, possibly in Phase 4a. The pit (F23) contained a dark clay-rich earth with an unmistakable odour and frequent small patches of lime (F26), which had periodically been thrown in, in an attempt to reduce the smell (Figure 4.56). Other contents of the

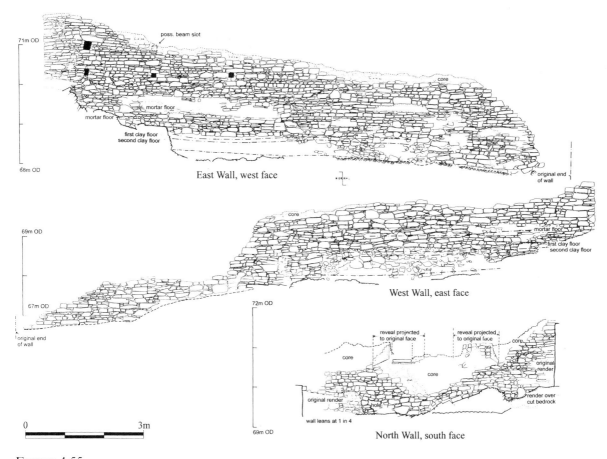

FIGURE 4.55

Internal elevations of the west, north and east walls of the Great Chamber G

FIGURE 4.56

Base of the latrine pit (F23) showing the shovel full of white lime, thrown into the latrine to reduce the odour

latrine, which had probably served the high-status residents of Round Tower D and Great Chamber G, included various bird and fish bones and plant remains, in addition to a spur [A33] (Chapter 10 and Section 9.5).

In Phase 3c, there is evidence, in the form of stake-holes (G65–111, G113, G125–146, G150–151 and G156) in the mortar floor (G57, G119 and G148), that Great Chamber G was divided into a series of 'rooms' by the erection of internal partitions (Figure 4.54). These were most likely of wattle-and-daub construction and observed groupings of stakeholes include an 'east room' (G80–110 and G145–150) with an associated sill beam (G63), a 'south-west room' (G76–79 and G130–140), a 'west room' (G69–75 and G130–131) and a 'north-west room' (G66–68 and G125–129). These internal divisions, however, were not necessarily all contemporary with each other and it is apparent from the repairs made to the mortar floor that Great Chamber G enjoyed a long period of use throughout Phase 3.

In Phase 3d, the greater part of Area F was covered with a black earth deposit (F19, F22, F25 and F28), which was rich in decayed organic matter. Many bones, seeds and pips were recovered from the sieved soil of this deposit (Section 10.5) and it is therefore reasonable to assume that it was a kitchen midden, although the source of the waste is unclear. The most likely building in the castle to have been a kitchen at this time is Kitchen I, but it is difficult to see how it had access to Area F following the construction of Great

Chamber G. Whatever the source of the kitchen waste, it appears that it was laid down in stages over a period of time, as layers were observed within the midden material.

Phase 4

Whilst Area F continued its previous role as a rubbish dump in Phases 4a and 4b, receiving several layers of building rubble (F11, F17–18, F20 and F24) and further kitchen waste (F15 and F16) (Figure 4.57), Great Chamber G gained a wooden first floor in Phase 4a, which was supported in the centre of the building by a substantial wooden post seated in posthole (G20) (Figures 4.58 and 4.59). Access to this new upper floor was through a doorway inserted in the north wall (G3 and G4) which led out onto a specially built raised platform and down into Courtyard O via a set of stone steps (Section 4.1). Construction of this raised platform and associated landing in Area P necessitated the blocking of the lower portions of the two lancet windows (G543) (Figures 4.6 and 4.55).

Phase 4a also saw the construction of Chapel H (Figure 4.58). In order to create a stable foundation, the existing ramp or staircase in Area H was removed and the walls (G524/H42, G525/H41, H57 and H62) partially dismantled. This work also required the digging of a large pit (G383/H70) through the mortar floor (G57, G119 and G148) at the southern end of Great Chamber G. Only when the masonry walls of

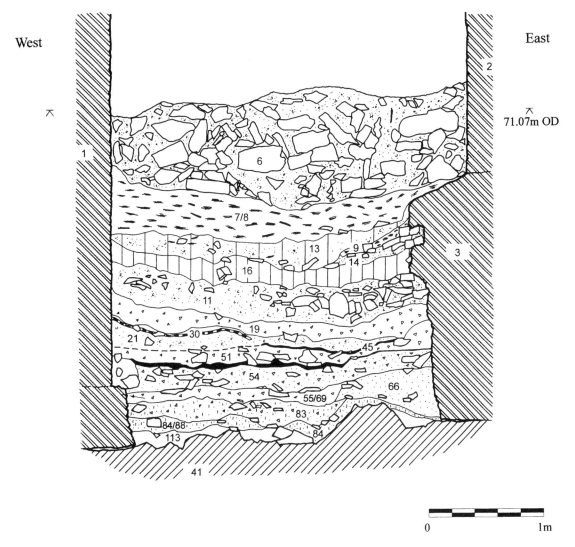

West   East

71.07m OD

FIGURE 4.57

Section F1, through the middens (F16 and F19) above the clay-floored buildings (F55/69) and (F84/88)

Chapel H had been completed was this pit (G383/H70) backfilled. Whilst this process almost certainly began later in Phase 4a, when a mixture of earth and rubble (H40, H45–46 and H49) was deposited, it was not completed until after the castle siege in Phase 4c (see below).

Chapel H took the form of a two-storey tower, which butted onto the curtain wall (G524/H42 and G525/H41) and also Great Chamber G on its northern side. A poor-quality drystone wall (H63) was first built across the open eastern side of the L-shaped wall (H57 and H62), blocking access to the postern entrance, which was now decommissioned. Then a more substantial wall (H60) was erected, which sat on top of both the drystone wall (H63) and the damaged L-shaped wall (H57 and H62), forming the east, south and west sides of the new tower. Little is known of activity within the lower room of the tower, since the medieval floor here was at a higher level than the surviving archaeological deposits. The upper room,

however, was almost certainly accessed directly from the first floor of Great Chamber G and was lit by three narrow lancet windows (H66–68) (Figure 4.60). It is this room that is interpreted as a chapel.

In Phase 4c, Great Chamber G appears to have lost its wooden first floor, since the posthole (G20), which held its central supporting timber, was now filled with earth (G116 and G117). This action may perhaps be associated with the castle siege of 1287, since there is further evidence that the building suffered neglect and even damage at this time. Covering the mortar floor (G57, G119 and G148) and completing the backfilling of the pit (G383/H70) — perhaps a suggestion that Chapel H was not yet complete in 1287 — were deposits of black organic-rich soil (G45, G50, G59, H35, H50 and H59) and grey sand (G56 and G58), both of which contained direct evidence for the siege, including stone projectiles, corroded iron links from chain-mail, arrowheads and a spearhead (Sections 7.2 and 7.4). There was no relationship between these

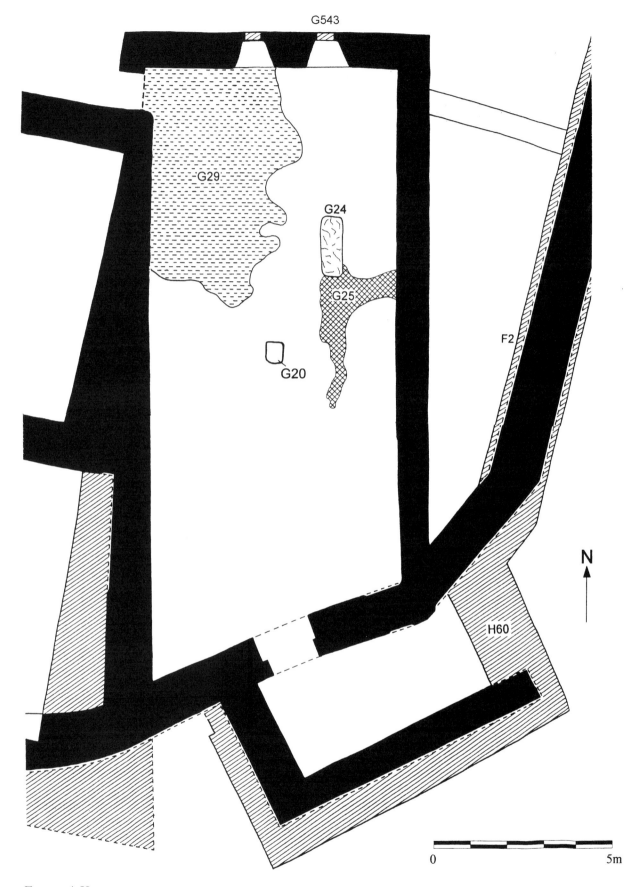

FIGURE 4.58

Areas F, G and H: Phase 4. For a general location see Figure 2.9

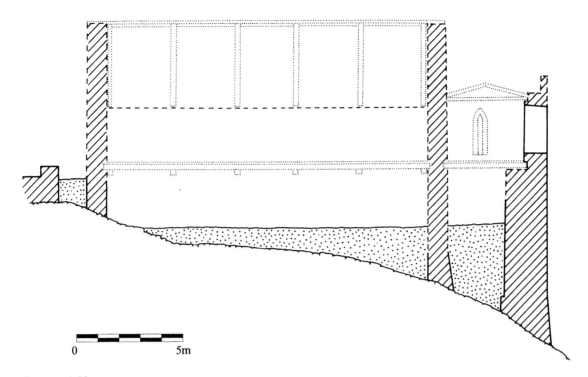

0   5m

FIGURE 4.59

Reconstruction of the long section through the Great Chamber G and Chapel H: Phase 4

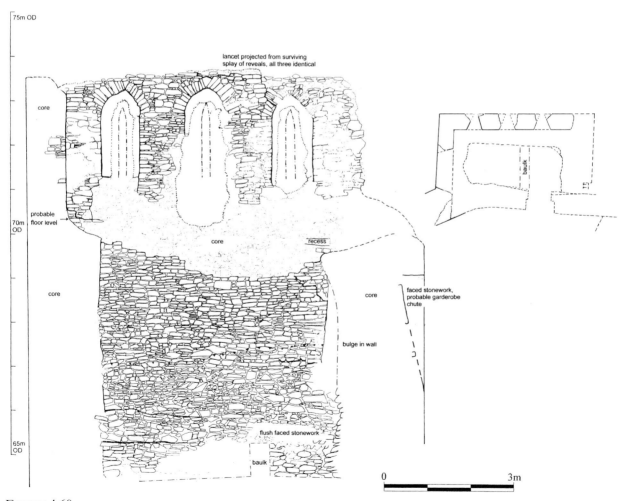

FIGURE 4.60

Elevation of the north face of the south wall (H60) of Chapel H

121

new deposits and the various 'rooms' identified within Great Chamber G in Phase 3c and it would thus appear that the internal partitions had been removed, perhaps at the same time as the wooden first floor, both possibly as a result of trebuchet ball damage.

Overlying the siege deposits in Great Chamber G were further dumps of brown earth and stone (G38–39, G43–44, G46–49 and G60). These lacked the organic content of contexts (G45 and G59) and appear to represent crude levelling layers, probably from a single phase of post-siege consolidation in Phase 4c. In the north-west corner was an ephemeral layer of mortar (G41 and G42) containing traces of charcoal, which had clearly acted as a temporary floor surface. Partially covering it, and running into a depression in the centre of the building, was a thick deposit of mottled yellow clay (G29) with a thin veneer of grey clay (G27). This surface (G27 and G29), on which traces of a waxy deposit were found (Section 9.10), represented yet another floor within Great Chamber G and was evidently the result of a concerted effort to make the building usable again following the damage and disruption caused by the siege. A pier (G24), formed from re-used stone and situated to the east of the clay floor remains (G27 and G29), may have supported a hearth. Given its position it is possible that the ground floor level was used for food preparation activities as an extension of the kitchen in Area I.

Area F did not escape the effects of the 1287 siege. Slingshots were recovered from the rubble layer (F18), whilst a trebuchet ball [LP44], weighing 52kg, had impacted with great force, bursting through the rubble deposits into the lower Phase 3d midden layer (F19) (Section 7.4). The curtain wall (F12) had evidently also sustained damage, since it was rebuilt (F2) on a substantial new foundation (F3) in Phase 4c, using high-quality white mortar and limestone in the squared stone-block construction typical of 'English' post-siege repairs carried out across the castle (Figure 4.47) (Section 6.1). Associated with this new wall (F2) was a flagstone floor (later removed) that covered much of Area F, the only remains of which were broken flagstone fragments present in the top of foundation (F3).

Phase 5

Following the removal of the flagstone floor in Area F, two crude and inexpensive surfaces were laid, befitting its reduced status as an open storage area: the first, laid in Phase 5a, consisted of large roof slates (F8), whilst the second, dating to Phase 5c, was made up of earth and crushed slate or shale (F7). Traces of anthracite were found on part of this second surface (F7) and it is therefore possible that Area F was being used for coal storage.

In Phase 5c, Great Chamber G gained a new upper wooden floor to replace the original one lost in Phase 4c. It was supported by a series of wooden posts set against the east and west walls of the building (Figure 4.61). On the eastern side, earth and stone deposits (G22–23, G26, G28 and G31) were first dumped, through which six pits (G32–37) were dug for six wooden posts, seated to a depth of 0.5m in postholes (G15–17 and G517–519). A padstone (G530), located at the southern end of these eastern postholes, may have supported a seventh post. On the western side, three smaller postholes (G18, G520 and G521), typically 0.15m deep, were recovered, whilst one central posthole (G19) was excavated to the west of posthole (G519). Covering the earth and stone deposits (G22–23, G26, G28 and G31), into which the eastern posts were sunk, was an ephemeral layer of mortar (G21), topped by a layer of crushed slate and shale (G13). This constitutes the Phase 5d floor surface, in use at the same time as the wooden first floor above, and it was also the latest floor recovered in Great Chamber G.

Phases 6 and 7

Above the floor (G13 and G21) in Great Chamber G was a layer of broken slates (G12), which had fallen from the roof of the building during the devastating fire that swept through the castle in Phase 6c (Figure 4.62). The slates were predominantly of two sizes: a larger form (0.27×0.3m) with two nail holes and a smaller form (0.13×0.15m) with only one nailhole. There was no evidence of decayed or burnt wooden posts *in situ* in the postholes (G15–19 and G517–521) and the timbers of the wooden first floor must have been removed or looted before the fire, perhaps in Phase 6b. The absence of a first floor in Phase 6c is further suggested by the lack of yellow clay in the burnt deposits of Great Chamber G; in contrast to Great Hall K/L, for example, where it had clearly been used as a flooring surface above planking in the two upper floors. The discovery of a charred and compressed mat of vegetation (G539), lying on the floor (G13 and G21) beneath the broken slates (G12), might even suggest that the building functioned as a stable in its last phase of use (Section 9.5).

In Area F, no trace of the castle fire was present in the excavated deposits and we may thus conclude that it remained an open space in Phase 6c, with no wooden superstructure or roof to catch light. In Chapel H, partial and disturbed layers of charcoal (H15) and burnt slate (H12 and H13) suggest the presence of a slate and timber roof. Following the fire, most of the remaining walls of the castle were swiftly demolished in Phase 6d, causing large amounts of rubble to build up across the site. In Areas F and G, thick rubble layers (F6, G6–7, G11 and G14) were encountered, but, in the very south of Area G and in Area H, this demolition material had either been lost down the side

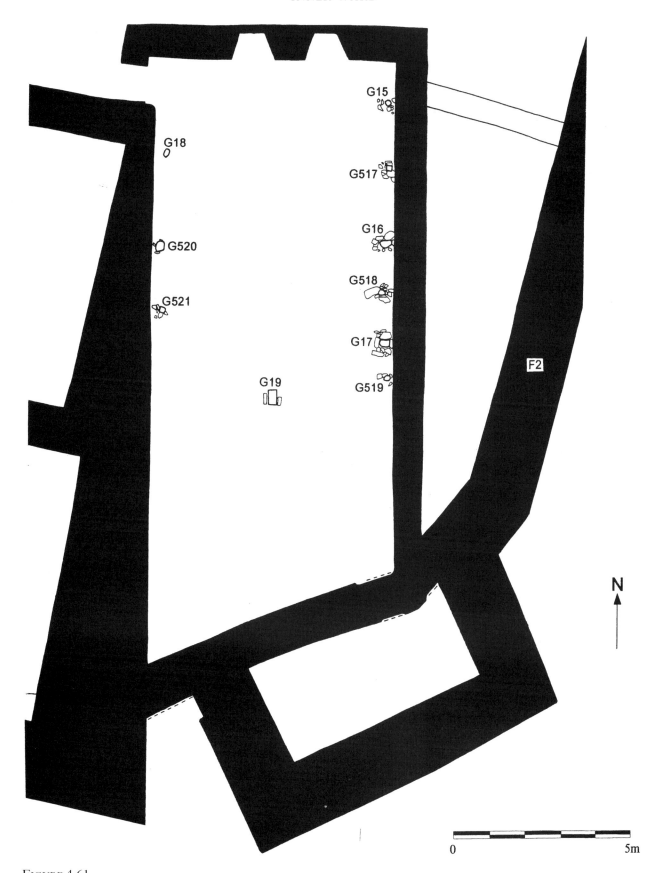

F2

G15

G18

G517

G520

G16

G521

G518

G17

G19

G519

N

0   5m

FIGURE 4.61

Areas F, G and H: Phase 5. For a general location see Figure 3.2

FIGURE 4.62

Collapsed slate roof layer (G12), looking south-west

of the hill or removed by mechanical excavator in 1981–82.

In the south-east corner of Area H, against the interior of wall (H60), a pit (H33) was cut in the early 20th century. In its base were a large number of horse bones, although not enough to form a complete skeleton (Section 10.2). It is far from clear what activity led to the creation of this deposit. Artefacts found within the fill of the pit together point towards a date between *c*1917 and *c*1930 for its excavation and backfill. Included within the upper pit fill layers (H4, H10 and H24–25) was a 1917 halfpenny ([C25], Section 9.3), whilst the lower layers (H22 and H26–29) contained fragments of glass bottles (Section 9.6).

Great Chamber

In high-status medieval buildings, private accommodation for the lord and his family was typically built onto the 'high' end of the Great Hall (Grenville 1997, 90). At Dryslwyn, however, as at Christchurch Castle (Dorset) and Grosmont Castle (Monmouthshire), limitations of space meant that this was not possible. Instead, accommodation was built adjacent to the 'low' end of the hall, beyond the entrances and screens passage, in Area G. This area was eventually filled by a large masonry building, which, on account of its ground-floor living-space, can most accurately be described as a great chamber or *camera*, rather than a solar (Wood 1983, 67). The Welsh law books were less specific describing the lord's chamber (*ystafell*) as normally a separate building beside the hall (*neuadd*) (Charles-Edwards *et al* 2000, 575). Prior to the

construction of Great Chamber G, however, Area G possessed two clay-floored timber buildings, which can perhaps be interpreted as predecessors to the Great Chamber, serving the same purpose of lordly accommodation.

The presence of a large double lancet window in the north end of Great Chamber G argues for a large open-hall arrangement during the initial occupation phase of this building, although stakeholes in the mortar floor (G57) indicate that this space was later partitioned into a series of smaller rooms, perhaps private apartments. The lancet windows were possibly glazed, the lancet form designed to admit the maximum amount of light for the minimum aperture and expense. The absence of any evidence for a fireplace suggests that there was instead a central hearth, the smoke escaping through a louvre in the roof.

Access into Great Chamber G from the first-floor hall of Great Hall K/L seems to have been gained via Courtyard O, since no trace of a connecting doorway was found: the lord and his family would exit through the north doorway of Great Hall K/L, before turning sharp right to enter through a door in the north-west corner of Great Chamber G. This arrangement parallels that at the Prebendal House, Nassington (Northamptonshire), where a great chamber/solar block was also constructed beyond the screens passage (Wood 1983, 127). At Dryslwyn, the presence of Kitchen I and the undercroft beneath Great Hall K/L removed the need for additional services. Consequently, Great Chamber G was an uncompromising great chamber construction, which, like the solar at Hadleigh (Essex), was only slightly smaller than the Great Hall.

The Phase 4a remodelling of the Inner Ward result-ed in the insertion of a first-floor level into Great Chamber G, which necessitated the blocking of the lower part of the double lancet window in the north wall. This was almost certainly part of a wider effort to increase the amount of private accommodation within the castle, coinciding with the construction of Apart-ments I/J and the creation of a second floor in adjacent Great Hall K/L. The new first floor of Great Chamber G was entered from Courtyard O via a flight of stone steps, constructed on a raised platform in Area P. This platform may also have formed the base to a porch built onto the north end of Great Chamber G, thus furnishing the building with an imposing first-floor entrance.

Chapel

In the 13th century, chapels were often plain, rectan-gular buildings (Thompson 1991b, 134) with triple lancet windows, similar to those in the west front of Llandaff Cathedral (Cardiff), constructed *c*1220 (Hilling 1975, 40). Chapel H is no exception, being a two-storey tower projecting beyond the curtain wall and housing the chapel (identified by its triple lancets) at first-floor level. The lancets (H66, H67 and H68), which are similar to those at the east end of Cymer Abbey (Gwynedd) (Robinson 2006, 103, 236), were constructed with the rest of the chapel wall (H60) as part of the Phase 4a remodelling of the Inner Ward and there are traces of a further single lancet window in the north wall (Figure 4.60). The creation of a chapel was part of the improvements to castle accom-modation for the lord and his guests and first-floor chapels, such as that at Kidwelly (Carmarthenshire) (Kenyon 2002, 43–44), closely associated with halls and domestic apartments, were relatively common during the late 13th century (Grenville 1997). A chapel at Dryslwyn is first documented in accounts relating to the castle siege of 1287 (Section 7.1).

Whilst chapels are often found in English and Marcher masonry castles, such as Kidwelly (Carm-arthenshire) and Ludlow (Shropshire), they are rarely identified in Welsh castles. No chapel building has been unambiguously identified at any of the major Welsh castles, although fragments of fine carved masonry, interpreted as being from a chapel, were recovered from Castell-y-Bere (Gwynedd) (Butler 1974, 99), whilst a bronze statuette from the western apsidal tower of the Inner Gatehouse at Criccieth (Gwynedd) provides a tenuous chapel attribution (Avent 1989, 22; O'Neil 1944–45, 23, 38). This is in marked contrast to Edwardian castles in Wales, such as Caernarfon (Gwynedd), where clear evidence for four chapels exists (Kenyon 1990, 151). This may simply be a case of differential survival, but may also reflect a different relationship between Church and State in England and Wales. The Welsh appear to have been as devout a people as their English counterparts, but their religion was based in traditional centres, often associated with early Celtic saints (Davies 1987, 172–210). Many Welsh churches in use in the 13th century were early medieval foundations, often of 5th- to 7th-century date and the population continued to use these traditional religious centres. Even in the early years of the 20th century, the villagers of Drysl-wyn, just like the occupants of the medieval town, journeyed every Sunday to the 7th-century church at Llangathen (Figure 8.11) in order to pray. In stark contrast, English castles and settlements typically established new chapels and parish churches. This suggests that the establishment of a castle chapel in the Phase 4a remodelling at Dryslwyn may have been a novel 'English' feature introduced by Rhys ap Maredudd.

The projecting nature of Chapel H beyond the curtain wall is unusual, although not unique, and there are comparable examples in castles at Framling-ham (Suffolk) (Raby and Reynolds 1987, 15) and Restormel (Cornwall) (Radford 1986, 10). Perhaps the closest parallels may be found at Kidwelly (Carm-arthenshire), dated to *c*1300 (Kenyon 2002, 43–44), where the chapel (perhaps inspired by that at Drysl-wyn) overhangs the river, and Kildrummy (Aberdeen-shire), where the mid to late 13th-century chapel has three large lancet windows and projects beyond the castle's defensive circuit (Tabraham 1986, 29; Apted 1963–64, 214). It is unclear why, when efforts were made not to breach a curtain wall with domestic buildings, such a defensive weakness was permitted with chapels. Perhaps there was a wish to preserve the traditional east–west orientation of these buildings. At Dryslwyn, the answer may lie instead with the desire to provide a first-floor chapel as an integral part of the residential accommodation in the southern half of the Inner Ward, despite little obvious room for expansion. The earlier foundation of the postern gate steps provided a convenient projecting base for Chapel H, but it also gave the first-floor chapel a very poor east–west alignment. Similar laxity in the orientation of chapels has been noted at several other castle sites (Pounds 1990, 240).

Chapel H continued in use throughout the English garrison period, although it is unlikely to have pos-sessed either a font or a churchyard. The chapel had probably been endowed with an income to pay for a priest or chaplain shortly after dedication in *c*1280, but, by 1388, it had been joined to the parochial seat at Llangathen and granted as a living (an income in exchange for religious service) to the nuns of St Mary's, Chester (Cheshire). Such little money was generated from this endowment, however, that the nuns were released from the financial burden of supplying a priest to Dryslwyn (Section 3.1). The Nunnery at Chester subsequently endowed the church at Llangathen with land value £40 (Briggs 1999, 245).

4.5 AREAS O AND M: COURTYARD, PRISON AND LATRINES/GARDEROBES

Areas O and M together occupy the north-western quadrant of the Inner Ward, lying to the north of Great Hall K/L and to the west of Gateway Area B and Round Tower D (Figure 1.3). Initially, both areas were little more than exposed bedrock and grassy hillside bounded to the north by the curtain wall. Throughout Phase 2, however, following the construction of Great Hall K/L along its southern side, Area O gradually acquired a man-made surface, taking on its later role of Courtyard O. In Phase 2c, Area M was divided off from Area O by a small lean-to building against the curtain wall, interpreted as Prison M.

Phase 1

The earliest features identified in Areas O and M were foundations for the Phase 1a curtain wall (M10/M18/O11/O24) (Figure 4.63). In Area M and the western half of Area O, these foundations (M45 and O161) were of mortared stone, resting on top of the bedrock (M44/O12), some of which had been levelled in advance. In the eastern half of Area O, where the ground sloped sharply away, foundations (O110, O124, O136 and O143) were built up using loose stones. Where the two foundation types met, there was a step in the bedrock and a mortared stone foundation wall (O90) which retained the loose stone foundation at its upper level. In the north-eastern corner of Area O, the curtain wall circuit was pierced by the main entrance to the early castle (O233) (Section 4.2).

Phase 2

The construction in Phase 2a of Great Hall K/L, whose north wall (M17/O1) defined the southern extent of Areas O and M, created large amounts of rubble and earth, which were redeposited in Area M and the western half of Area O as layers (M54 and O193–195). On top of these deposits was laid a stone surface of cobbles and clay (M60/O113/O192) (Figure 4.63). This was the first man-made surface to be created in the emergent courtyard.

In Phase 2b, the rocky outcrop west of Round Tower D was quarried level along its north and west sides, forming a second man-made surface: a bedrock shelf (O244). This allowed easier access from Gateway Area B to Great Hall K/L and had been polished through wear (O236). In order to reach the first-floor entrance into Great Hall K/L, a ramp was constructed, comprising an L-shaped limestone wall (O96) with a rubble and soil infill (O239). The upper stones of this wall (O96) were also polished smooth (O245), as were the stones of a further Phase 2b courtyard surface

(O156, O218, O221 and O230), which was created in the eastern half of Area O by hammering cobbles into natural gaps in the bedrock slope leading up to Round Tower D. Phase 2b occupation features observed within Area O comprised a small pit (O231), a posthole (O175) and a series of stakeholes (O164–174). The latter were aligned at right angles to the curtain wall (O24) and may represent an animal pen.

In Phase 2c the first in a series of three stone buttresses was constructed against the north side of Round Tower D in Area O. Only ephemeral traces of this early buttress (O228) remain, as it was destroyed in the building of the later two buttresses, but it is clear that the bedrock was first quarried level in order to provide a firm foundation. The exact form and function of the buttress are unclear, but it was probably very similar to its successors, with a rectangular section and supporting a flight of wooden steps, which led from the first-floor entrance of Round Tower D down into Area P (Section 4.1).

A further event of Phase 2c was the construction of Prison M (Figure 4.64). This effectively divided off Area M from Area O, leaving Area O alone to develop into Courtyard O. A trench was first dug down into the rubble and earth layer (M54) along the eastern side of Area M and a loose stone foundation (M46) built within it to a height of 0.6–0.8m. On top of this foundation sat a wall (M35 and M49), which butted up against the curtain wall (M10) and the north wall of Great Hall K/L (M17) and contained a doorway (M23), which was rebated so that the door could only be opened from the outside (Figure 4.65). The erection of this eastern wall now created a secure room, entered from Courtyard O, which was defined on its other three sides by existing walls (M10, M17 and M18). It was carefully positioned so as to avoid blocking the arrowloop (M19) in the Great Hall wall (M17).

Phase 3

During Phase 3a, soil, slate, cobble and mortar was dumped in Courtyard O. In the west these comprised deposits (O137–139, O153, O158 and O163), whilst in the east a thin occupation earth (O121) was laid down. This material probably originated in part from building works taking place in Area G (Section 4.4). A substantial layer of soil and stone (O74) was also dumped in front of the curtain wall (O24), on top of foundations (O110 and O124), forming a crude courtyard surface (Figure 4.66).

In the eastern half of Courtyard O, Phase 3a dumps were followed by more coherent surfaces (Figure 4.64). Towards the centre, loose cobbles (O70, O120 and O129) were laid, whilst in the south a larger spread of loose cobbles (O155) was present. In the north-east corner, a number of small mortar deposits (O209 and O223–225) overlay gravel (O222) and cobbles

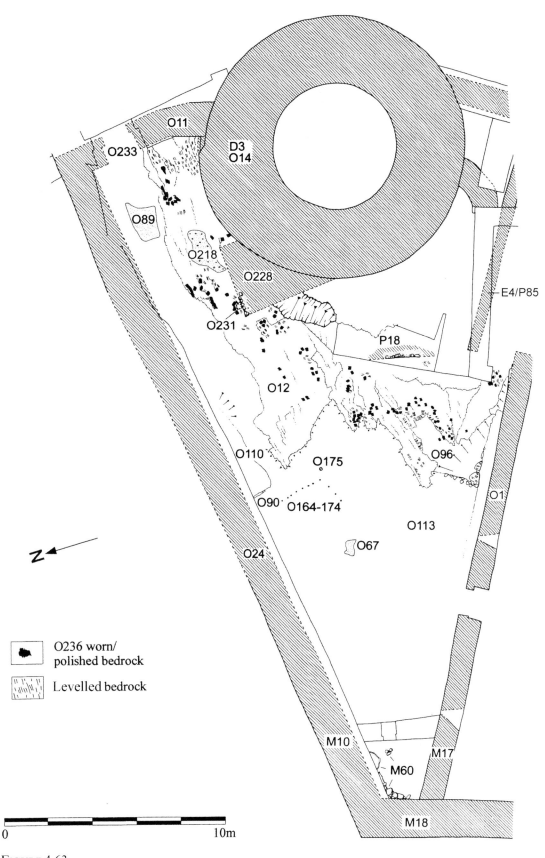

O236 worn/
polished bedrock

Levelled bedrock

FIGURE 4.63

Areas M, O and P: Phases 1–2. For a general location see Figure 2.5

127

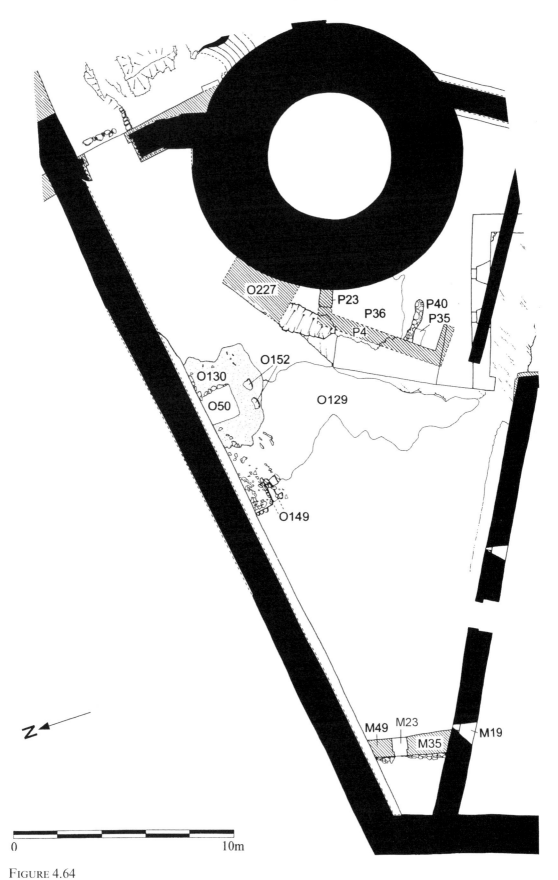

FIGURE 4.64

Areas M, O and P: Phases 2–3. For a general location see Figure 2.8

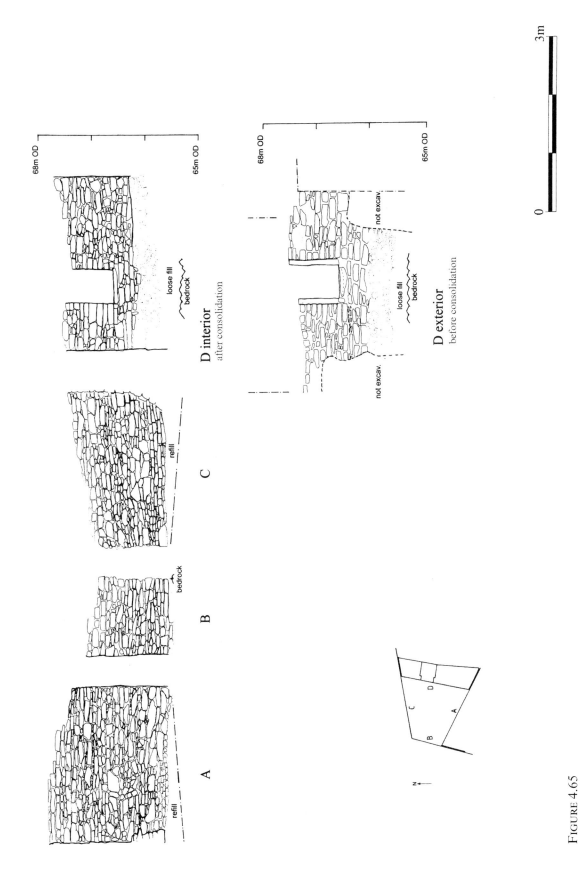

FIGURE 4.65

Elevations of the interior walls of the Prison M and the external east wall (M35)

South   North

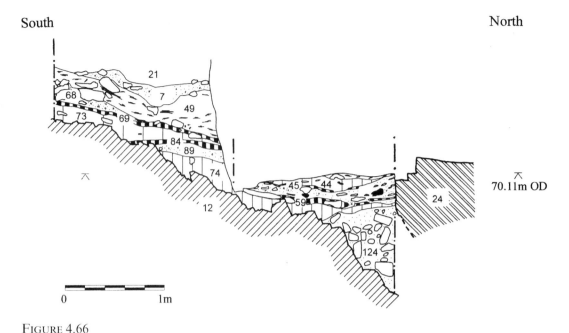

70.11m OD

0   1m

FIGURE 4.66

Section O1, through the castle rubble collapse, the surfaces and foundations of the Courtyard O

(O226). To the north of Round Tower D, a new buttress (O227) replaced the existing buttress (O228): at only 1.6m wide, it was somewhat narrower than its predecessor.

In Phase 3b, a midden (O131) developed at the western end of Courtyard O (Figure 4.67), whilst towards the centre, adjacent to the curtain wall (O24), a latrine pit (O50) was dug through the cobbles (O226) into the loose stone foundation (O110) beneath. The location chosen was one of the very few in the early castle where a pit could be dug without having to quarry away bedrock. Lined with mortar (O117 and O130), a possible overflow (O149) was created for the

latrine pit (O50) through the foundation wall (O90), emptying into the midden (O131) to the west. Two padstones (O152) seated within the mortar (O130) suggest that a post-built timber privy was constructed against the curtain wall (O24). Within the latrine pit (O50), waste deposits (O50, O77, O81, O114–115, O147–148, O151 and O235) included pottery sherds and a macehead [**W102**], although it is probable that these mostly date from the final period of the latrine's use, since it would have been regularly cleaned out before then.

Later in Phase 3b, a fire on the bedrock in the centre of Courtyard O not only scorched the bedrock itself,

South   North

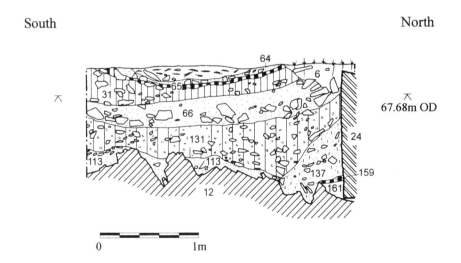

67.68m OD

0   1m

FIGURE 4.67

Section O2, through the midden (O66) and soil and rubble fill beneath the Phase 4a mortar courtyard surface (O65)

130

but also resulted in ash being deposited here (O79) and over the midden (O131) to the west (O109 and O119). Charcoal from this fire then spilt down into the now-disused latrine pit (O50) to form layer (O81). A coin ([C4], Section 9.3) found within the ash deposit (O79) produced a date of 1210–17.

Within the Prison M, a large pit dug through the cobbled surface (M60), probably during the period of construction in Phase 2c, was backfilled (M57 and M58) in Phase 3b and topped by a hearth deposit (M83). The ground level within the building was then raised by dumps of earth rich in organic material (M53), followed by shale (M55) and some further ephemeral deposits (M41) (Figure 4.68).

Phase 4

Phase 4a saw several important changes in Courtyard O (Figure 4.69). On the southern side, a flight of stone steps (O132) was built descending from the level of the eastern half of the Courtyard down into the undercroft of Great Hall K/L. These steps replaced any earlier means of access here, but it is not known what form this may have taken because of the need to preserve the existing steps (O132) *in situ*.

Also in Phase 4a, two revetment walls (O134 and O181) were built, running east and west from the base of the steps (O132), parallel with the north wall (M17/O1) of Great Hall K/L. Wall (O134) extended as far as the L-shaped wall (O96), whilst wall (O181) butted onto the east wall (M35/O178) of Prison M. These walls held back courtyard material dug out from a 0.4m-wide trench (O185) between them and wall (M17/O1), which functioned as a gutter. This was designed to catch rainwater from Courtyard O and the roof of Great Hall K/L and funnel it out through a drain (L12) which ran under the floor of the undercroft

(Section 4.3). It is likely that a gutter, perhaps the trench (O185), had existed here since Phase 2a, when Great Hall K/L was built, since the internal undercroft drain was part of the original building. The revetment walls (O134 and O181), however, were only constructed in Phase 4a and they were clearly in place before the castle siege of 1287, when a large trebuchet ball became securely wedged between walls (M17/O1 and O181) (Section 7.4).

Following this building work, the steps (O132) and revetment walls (O134 and O181) were now at a higher level than the surrounding courtyard area. In order to rectify this situation, deposits (O31, O36, O66, O75–76, O80, O95, O123, O180 and O188) were dumped in Phase 4a in the west of Courtyard O. These dumps were capped by mortar layers (O59, O65 and O67) (Figure 4.67) and there seems to have been a concerted effort to create a durable surface across the remainder of Courtyard O at this time (O59, O101 and O107). Three large stones (O100, O122 and O238) were evidently still needed to act as stepping-stones across a muddy patch in front of the Inner Ward gateway (O233).

On the south side of Courtyard O, a substantial mortar surface (O97) was overlain by rubble dumps (O127–128 and O133) and a further, more extensive mortar surface (O237). These layers were deposited in Phase 4a in an effort to raise the level of the courtyard surface and so counter the sinking of material dumped around the steps (O132). In order to contain the rubble dumps, further courses of masonry (O144) were added to the revetment wall (O134) and to the side-wall of the steps (O132). On top of the mortar surface (O237), a stone ridge (O27), constructed from single stones laid side-by-side in a line, was built running north from the revetment wall (O134). This may have been conceived to help drain rainwater from Courtyard O into the gutter (O185). Alternatively, it is possible to interpret

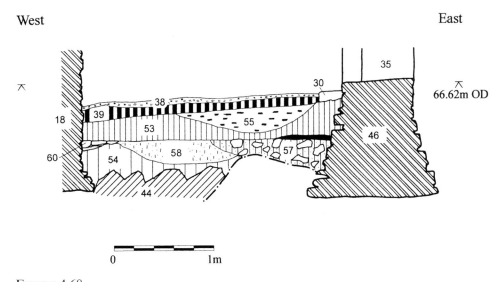

West   East

0   1m

FIGURE 4.68

Section M1, through the flooring levels of Prison M

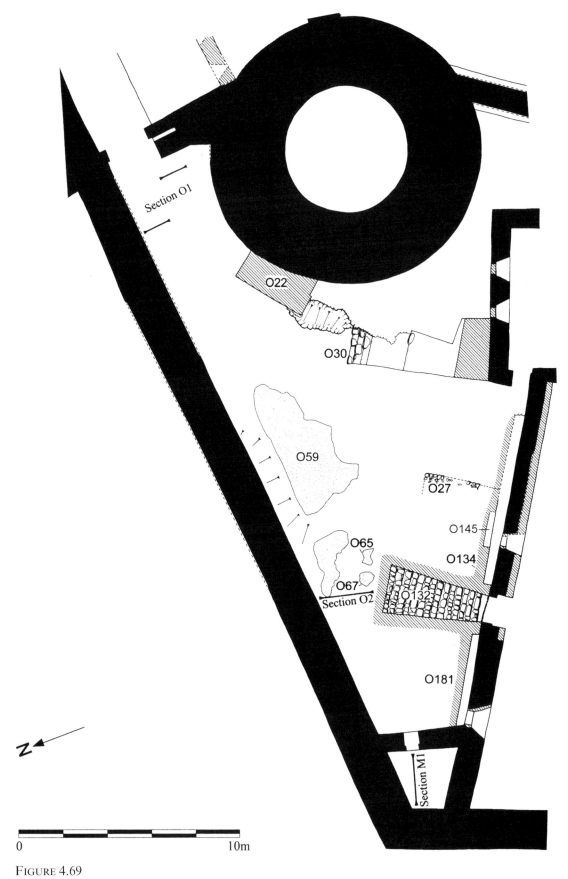

Section O1

O22

O30

O59

O27

O145

O65

O134

O67

Section O2

O132

O181

Section M1

0   10m

FIGURE 4.69

Areas M, O and P: Phase 4. For a general location see Figure 2.9

this feature (O27) as the eastern side of a raised platform, which gave access into the first floor of Great Hall K/L: if so, then the earlier first-floor doorway at the eastern end of wall (M17/O1) must by now have been superseded by a replacement entrance, located further to the west (Section 4.3).

Phase 4a saw the construction of the third and final buttress (O22) abutting Round Tower D. This measured 3.2 by 1.5m and was built of poor-quality shale for the lowest 2–3m with limestone higher up and a rendered finish. Small slots (O110), measuring 0.12 by 0.4m, which were visible at ground level in the north-east and south-west faces, did not lead to any drain and there was no central gully or downpipe that would suggest its interpretation as a garderobe chute. Instead, it is more likely that this buttress, just like its two predecessors, supported a flight of wooden steps connecting the first-floor entrance of Round Tower D with Area P below. A substantial fragment of masonry (O20) recovered from the Phase 6d castle rubble was a section of this buttress (O22) from a higher level. It contained two vertical slots, measuring 0.4m and 0.5m deep, which would have housed wooden posts connected with the superstructure of the steps (Figure 4.2).

Also in Phase 4a, the ground surface of Prison M, which was now slightly below the level of adjacent Courtyard O, was given a mortar floor (M39). Before this, however, a stone step (M30) was placed in front of the doorway (M23) in order to assist with entry down into the building: this step was 0.25m deep and had been worn flat with repeated use. There then followed the deposition of a series of lenses of material associated with the occupation of Prison M during Phase 4b, the most prominent of which was a charcoal layer (M38).

Further building works took place in Courtyard O during Phase 4c. Within the revetment wall (O134 and O144) a light well (O145) for a small window, formed in Phase 4a from a pre-existing arrowloop in the undercroft of Great Hall K/L, was constructed in hard white mortar. This same mortar was also used in the masonry of a passageway (O10), which was driven through the wall (O14) of Round Tower D, giving direct access at ground-floor level into the Round Tower basement. The passageway (O10) climbed steeply over an inclined mortar floor (O215 and O217) and rough bedrock slope. Access was not easy and it is likely that it was used primarily for moving heavy provisions in and out of the Round Tower basement, rather than as a means of reaching the higher-status accommodation above (Section 4.1).

Phase 4d activity in Courtyard O was marked by a series of soil and rubble dumps, in the south (O104–105), centre (O52, O61, O64 and O198), north-east (O84, O88–89 and O102) and east (O150, O208, O220 and O229) of this area. These were followed with an extensive, yet thin and ephemeral, surface, which was composed of crushed shale and slate (O58 and O99).

In the centre of Courtyard O, this surface was covered by a deposit of brown earth (O51).

Phase 5

In Phase 5a, Courtyard O was given a new surface of hard white mortar (O45, O54 and O63). In the centre of the courtyard, this surface was in good condition, possibly due to its preservation under a shelter or within a building. In the north-east corner, however, the mortar (O68, O72–73, O85–87 and O142) had been broken up, first by wear and then by the effects of the castle's demolition in Phase 6d (Figure 4.66). At the western end of Courtyard O, to the west of the steps (O132), there was no trace of either this mortar layer (O45) or those preceding (O59) and succeeding (O33) it. This was due to the extensive erosion which this, the steepest part of the courtyard, suffered during the later phases of the castle's occupation.

Over the course of Phase 5a, the floor of Prison M was resurfaced several times. Since these surfaces were each worn away through use, however, the exact sequence of deposits is difficult to establish. Layers of pink mortar (M31), clay and charcoal (M34) and an aggregate of mortared stone (M26) were all present. Use of the stone step (M30) continued throughout the lifetime of these floor surfaces. The last trace of occupation within Prison M was a charcoal layer (M29), which was deposited on the latest floor surfaces in Phase 5b. Within this layer were five fragments of window glass, which may derive from leaded glass windows elsewhere in the castle at this time, perhaps in Great Hall K/L or Great Chamber G (Section 6.7).

In Phase 5b, various dumps of material were made on top of the mortar surface (O45) in Courtyard O. In the centre of the area, these took the form of a black earth (O44, O53, O61 and O103) and a mixture of rubble and earth (O46–47, O71 and O108). In the south, a brown earth (O26) was recovered, whilst mortar fills (O62, O69 and O140) were present in the north-east corner. Above these layers was a slate deposit (O25), which was concentrated in the centre of Courtyard O and contained a number of nails and complete slates. This is interpreted as a dump of roofing materials, which may represent either a demolition deposit or possibly an improvised surface. Overlying this slate deposit (O25) were several mortar layers — (O33 and O43) in the central area, (O37) in the east and (O98) in the south (Figure 4.70). These were added in Phase 5c and represent a further resurfacing of Courtyard O.

Patching of the surface of Courtyard O took place in Phase 5d, when small deposits of clay, cobbles, earth and mortar (O34–35, O42, O55–56 and O205–206) were made. These patches were overlain in turn by a thin layer of crushed slate and shale (O28 and O41), which was the final surface seen in Courtyard O. In many places, it lay directly underneath slate-rich

FIGURE 4.70

Courtyard mortar surface (O33), looking north

destruction deposits, which made it difficult to determine the original extent of this last surface.

Phases 6 and 7

The successive decommissioning, looting, burning and demolition of the castle in Phase 6 left only faint traces in the Prison M and Courtyard O. An iron drain cover, whose presence is indicated by iron staining (O197) in the gutter (O185) at the base of the steps (O132), appears to have been looted in Phase 6b, prior to the fire.

Traces of the fire that engulfed the castle in Phase 6c are few, suggesting not only that Prison M contained little flammable material, but also that there were no major structures or buildings standing in Courtyard O at this time. A small patch of burnt material (O40) recovered in the very south-east corner of the courtyard was probably associated with the destruction by fire of Great Chamber G. Roofing slates from this building and also Great Hall K/L were found in heaps (O38, O49, O199 and O211) along the south side of Courtyard O, where they had spilled down from the burning roof structures.

A period of abandonment may have occurred following the fire, since there appears to have been a short period of soil formation, marked by layers (O32, O82, O135 and O203). This may have only lasted for a matter of weeks or months before all the buildings of the castle were demolished in Phase 6d, filling Areas O and M with rubble (M9, M13, O7, O9, O15–16, O176–177, O182, O187 and O189). Several large pieces of masonry (O19–21) (Figure 4.71) caused considerable

damage to the surfaces and structures onto which they fell. This was particularly true of Round Tower D, which collapsed northwards onto the curtain wall (O24) in Courtyard O, causing the wall to curve outwards with a maximum displacement from linear of 0.65m. This in turn caused fissuring and collapse of the deposits in Courtyard O to the north of this building. Finally topsoil (M1 and O6) formed over the rubble in Areas O and M in Phases 7b and 7c.

Courtyard

In Phases 1 and 2, Area O was an area of open hillside with a path along its eastern side providing access from Gateway Area B to Great Hall K/L, Round Tower D and the timber buildings in Area G. Stake alignments suggest the presence of animal pens. In Phase 3, the construction of Great Chamber G restricted space in the Inner Ward and, perhaps as a consequence, a midden, lean-to latrine and prison were all established in Areas O and M. Only in Phase 4a was Area O clearly established as Courtyard O, when the first in a series of surfaces was laid. These usually took the form of stone and earth dumps or mortar spreads and frequent patching indicates a high level of use. The stratigraphy and dates for the coins make it possible to ascribe the remodelling of Courtyard O to either of the major building phases 3a or 4a. However, it is ascribed to Phase 4a, since it contains features such as the impressive stepped entrance to the Great Hall undercroft and a courtyard surface large enough to turn wheeled vehicles.

FIGURE 4.71

Fragment (O21) of the Round Tower D displaced during the castle's destruction, looking south-east. The exterior surface has been rendered and given coats of lime wash

Good light and shelter from the wind in Courtyard O encouraged a wide range of practical and craft activities, one of which, leatherworking, is indicated by finds of two leather creasers [**F13** and **F14**]. Courtyard O also acted as a light well for Great Hall K/L; the light streaming in through the cinquefoil ogee windows would no doubt have impressed visitors to the castle. No attempt was made to give the courtyard a permanent stone surface. This is almost certainly because mortar was readily available for patching, so removing the necessity for a more durable, yet expensive, surface.

Prison

The presence of a door that opens from the exterior is frequently used to identify a prison, strong-room or storeroom, as in the case of the basement room in the keep at Dolforwyn (Powys) (Butler and Knight 2004, 27; Butler 1990, 87–88) and the rooms in the basement of the gatehouse towers at Kidwelly (Carmarthenshire) (Kenyon 2002, 26). The use of castles for holding prisoners is attested by the documented imprisonment of Maredudd ap Rhys by Llywelyn ap Iowerth in Criccieth Castle (Gwynedd) in 1259 (Section 2.1), whilst possible archaeological evidence for the detention of prisoners at Dryslwyn is provided by the fragment of iron shackle arm from a barrel padlock [**F96**] found in Area P in Phase 4a (Section 9.4). Some '20 iron shackles and 5 locks for these shackles', owned by Robert de Tibetot, justiciar for

West Wales 1281–98, are also recorded as being in the castle's stores in 1300–01 (Section 3.1), further suggesting that prisoners were kept in Dryslwyn Castle at this time. Given the availability of storage space within the undercroft of Great Hall K/L and the basement of Round Tower D, it is unlikely that Prison M was required for this purpose. Far more likely, in light of the building's sunken floor, is that it functioned as strong-room or prison. At present, Prison M has no direct comparison amongst Welsh castle architecture, but the small room in the base of the keep at Dolforwyn (Powys), which was formed by the insertion of a secondary wall and the basements of the towers at Dolwyddelan (Conwy) and Dolbadarn (Gwynedd), which are only accessible through trap doors (Avent 1994a, 25, 30), may well have served a similar purpose.

Latrines and garderobes

Apart from the possible identification of a drain outlet (D25) on the north side of Round Tower D, the earliest evidence for latrines in the castle occurs in Phase 3b, when a latrine pit (O50) was dug on the northern side of Courtyard O beside the curtain wall. This was probably enclosed within a wooden post-built structure supported on padstones. At the same time, in Area F, a square pit (F23) was dug and lined with woven wattles: this too probably had a wooden superstructure. In both cases the superstructure and, in the case of pit (F23), the upper levels of the deposit were removed by later building activity, so the exact form of these latrines is far from clear. Both pits were dug in the only two places in the Inner Ward that did not require the occupants to dig through bedrock and they probably served the occupants of Great Hall K/L, Great Chamber G and Round Tower D. In removing the need to walk outside the castle walls, they represented both a 'convenience' and an appreciable improvement to the castle accommodation. However, they were also very public and far more sophisticated toilet arrangements can be found in the castles at Criccieth (Gwynedd), Dolforwyn (Powys) and Dolwyddelan (Conwy), all of which have garderobe chutes built into Welsh castle masonry dating from the period 1230–80. This raises the possibility that these latrine deposits derive from a siege or period of conflict when access was restricted.

Given the sophistication and privacy of accommodation in Great Chamber G, Great Hall K/L and Apartments I/J in Phase 4a, it is almost certain that there would have been provision for garderobes. Fragmentary remains of a garderobe chute in the south wall (H60) of Chapel H (Figure 4.60) perhaps suggest that they were located in the angle between Apartments I/J and Chapel H. Unfortunately, the addition of garderobe chutes would have created a significant weakness in the southern façade of the Inner Ward at this point, perhaps explaining why, when the castle was demolished in the 15th century, almost all of this wall section was lost downhill. As a result, we can only speculate on the probable number of garderobes once present here, but it is likely that there were several, serving the occupants of all the private apartments in the Inner Ward.

The reconstruction of the curtain wall (F2) in Area E in Phase 4c, as part of the repairs following the siege of 1287, incorporated a garderobe with twin seats and twin chutes. This may have replaced earlier facilities here, as this location certainly provided easy access, via Area P, between Great Chamber G and Round Tower D. It was not unusual for garderobes (or privy chambers leading to garderobes) to be positioned between the lord's private accommodation and guest apartments, reflecting the increased level of planning that went into domestic arrangements in castles by the second half of the 13th century (Kenyon 1990, 135). It was certainly normal at this time for garderobes to be built into the thickness of walls and towers, for example at Beaumaris Castle (Anglesey) (Taylor 1985). In both Areas E and H at Dryslwyn, it would also have been possible to channel rainwater from the roofs of adjacent buildings through the garderobe chutes, thus helping to flush them out. This practice has been observed at Caernarfon Castle (Gwynedd) and Denbigh Castle (Denbighshire) (Wood 1983, 387), the waste from the garderobes spilling downhill to gradually compost or be washed away by rain.

MIDDLE AND OUTER WARDS: EXCAVATION EVIDENCE

5.1 AREAS A, X, Y AND XR: MIDDLE WARD

Areas A, X, Y and XR form a large proportion of the Middle Ward of Dryslwyn Castle, which was added to the existing Inner Ward in Phase 3a (Figures 1.3 and 5.1). Area A is located in the south-west corner and is characterised by a ridge of bedrock, which also extends under the neighbouring Gateway Area B and Area C. Its Phase 1 and 2 development has already been considered in Section 4.2 and will not be discussed further here. Areas X and Y together form the bulk of the north-west quarter of the Middle Ward. From Phase 3c, Area X contained a long rectangular building, referred to as Guest Hall X. Area Y saw the construction of two successive buildings, Buildings Ya and Yb, in Phases 3d and 4a. Area XR comprises a number of separate excavated and recorded features in the Middle Ward that were either above the surface or immediately below the turf (Figure 5.1).

Phase 3

Phase 3a saw the construction of the polygonal Middle Ward wall (Figures 5.1 and 5.2). The north and west sides (X7, X13, XR3 and Y2) were built on top of a bank of clay and stone, whilst the south and east sides (A3) were seated on the bedrock, perched above the steep natural hillside. Foundations (A17 and Y35) were identified in Areas A and Y. The Middle Ward wall (X7) was roughly 2m thick on its western side, broadening out to 4m immediately to the east of Area Y (XR3). This increase in thickness can be explained in several ways, from a conscious strengthening of the wall to the presence of a masonry building or perhaps adjacent stone steps. The absence of any observed internal faces within the wall (XR3), however, suggests that this 4m thickness was original to the initial wall construction, rather than a later addition.

The external face of the Phase 3a Middle Ward wall was located at various points in Area XR, including the junctions with the later, Phase 4a, Outer Ward wall (R2) and the buttress (R1). Here, the wall (XR3) was poorly preserved, due to extensive robbing of the stonework. In places, only a single course of masonry remained, seated above the clay and stone bank. Immediately to the west of the Outer Ward wall (R2), however, part of a sloping wall face (XR9) was uncovered. This is interpreted as either an external buttress to the Middle Ward wall (XR3) or, more probably, a stone facing constructed in front of the steep natural hill slope. The partial robbing or demolition of this facing and the clay and stone bank may account for the poor survival of much of the external face of the Middle Ward wall.

In the far south-east corner of the Middle Ward wall circuit was a gateway (XR12). This faced east, just above the precipitous slope of the south-eastern side of the hill, and it would have formed the outer entrance to the castle for a brief period in the third quarter of the 13th century, prior to the addition of the Outer Ward in Phase 4a (Section 5.2). Only one side of the gateway was uncovered by excavation, but it is clear that it took a simple form. There was a reveal for a single-leafed gate, but no evidence of either a portcullis slot or an enclosed passageway that would indicate the presence of a gatehouse.

Phase 3a may also have seen the construction of a thin wall (X14) that ran for a short distance west from the north-west corner of the Middle Ward wall circuit. The dating and purpose of this wall, which was crudely keyed into a hole battered into the exterior of the Middle Ward wall (X7), is unclear. It may be an additional protective wall added in a later phase, which was subsequently demolished. More probably, however, it was conceived as a Phase 3a afterthought, providing the beginnings of a defensive barrier along

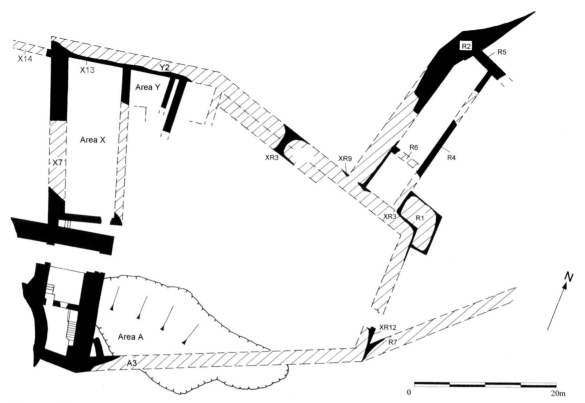

FIGURE 5.1

Principal features of the Middle Ward

the northern edge of a terrace in the hillside to the north-west, in a corner formed by the Middle and Inner Wards (Figure 3.1). The bank of clay and stones, on which the Middle Ward wall sat, certainly continued along this course.

In Phase 3c, the easternmost angle of the Middle Ward wall (XR3) gained a substantial masonry buttress (R1) against its external face, the construction of which is discussed below (Section 5.2). At the same time in Area X, a large building measuring approximately 20 by 3m was erected against the Middle Ward wall (X7 and X13). Guest Hall X, as it is known, is provisionally interpreted as additional accommodation for guests to the castle, based on its size, location and fine decoration, which included painted wall plaster (Section 6.4). The primary evidence for this structure comes from two partially excavated walls (X20 and Y3), which were aligned parallel to the western Middle Ward wall (X7) and appeared together to represent the east wall of a rectangular building. The south end of the building was not built directly against Gateway Area B, but a short passageway was inserted along the northern side of the curtain wall (B11/X11 and B15/X15) in order to give access up to the wall-walk of the Middle Ward wall (X7). The north side of this passageway and the south wall of Guest Hall X was formed by a new wall (X9), whilst steps (X10) were placed at the end of the passageway, leading up to the wall-walk. The Middle Ward wall (X7) was heightened (X8) here for the safety of those emerging onto the wall-walk from the steps (X10).

Later in Phase 3c, the eastern wall (X20) of Guest Hall X was heightened (X19) and it is probable that a wooden first floor, if not already present, was inserted into the building: there was evidence of sockets and corbel stones to support beams. An entrance (X22), constructed through the south wall (X9), gave access from this wooden first floor into the passageway. Construction of the passageway itself had clearly involved lowering the ground level beside the outer face of the curtain wall (B11/X11 and B15/X15) and this necessitated crude repairs to the base of the wall (B11/X11). The finished passageway was given a mortar floor (X17).

Phase 3d saw the construction of a further building in Area Y, butted up against the Middle Ward wall (Y2) (Figure 5.2). The full extent of this building, Building Ya, was not revealed in excavation, but its west wall (Y5) was found to be partially demolished. It had been built over a sequence of mortar surfaces (Y15, Y16 and Y20), beneath which were traces of an occupation layer (Y17 and Y23) containing sherds of pottery, a mortar fillet (Y18) and building rubble (Y19) (Figure 5.4). These deposits represent the early layers associated with the use of the Middle Ward wall (Y2) and the construction and occupation of Guest Hall X. Above the mortar surfaces (Y15, Y16 and Y20) were several occupation layers (Y9, Y28, Y32 and Y33). These had built up in Building Ya during its lifetime and were topped by a final layer of crushed shale (Y14) (Figure 5.3). The mortar surfaces (Y15, Y16 and Y20)

138

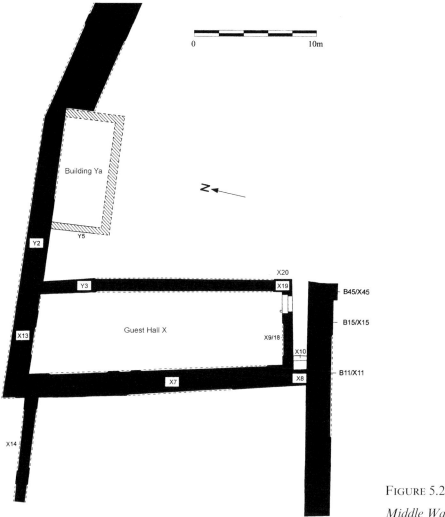

FIGURE 5.2

Middle Ward: Phase 3d

pre-date Building Ya, but had clearly been re-used as its floor.

Phases 4 and 5

In Phase 4a, Area A saw extensive remodelling (Figures 4.17 and 4.18). The Phase 2a rock-cut ditch (A19) was cleaned out and a large foundation of loose stones (A18) was laid in the south-western half of the ditch. Soil and loose stones (A11 and A16) were used to fill the north-eastern half of the ditch and a substantial stone wall (A2/B3/C6) was then built onto the loose stone foundation, projecting north from the Middle Ward wall (A3) and forming part of a new imposing Inner Ward gateway in the adjacent Gateway Area B and Area C. A fillet of mortar waste (A15) from the construction of the new wall (A2/B3/C6) was found partially overlying the loose ditch fill (A16).

Also present in the layer (A16) in Area A were traces of a partly demolished drystone wall (A5) made up of well-faced and well-laid stones, which were similar in form and dimensions to those of the houses in the township (Figure 4.18) (Section 8.2). This wall

represents the only surviving evidence of a temporary building, possibly a workman's hut in use during the construction of the gateway wall (A2). Although it survived to a height of three courses in a few places, notably on its north-eastern side, the south-west face of the wall (A5) had been extensively robbed and it was probably never more than a dwarf wall supporting a wooden superstructure.

Phase 4a also saw the construction of a second building, Building Yb, in Area Y (Figure 5.5). This replaced the earlier Building Ya, although its west wall (Y4) was situated 0.5m to the east of the now demolished wall (Y5). Only the lowest two courses of the wall (Y5) were retained as a revetment for the soil layers on which the new wall (Y4) was built, as this new wall had no foundations. To the south-west of Building Yb was a subterranean feature interpreted as either a cellar or the upper part of a well: safety concerns did not permit its full excavation. What is known is that construction of this feature in Phase 4a resulted in the removal of earlier occupation and ground layers across a substantial part of Area Y. A large pit was dug and two walls (Y29 and Y30) were set at right angles to one another to a depth of 0.5m

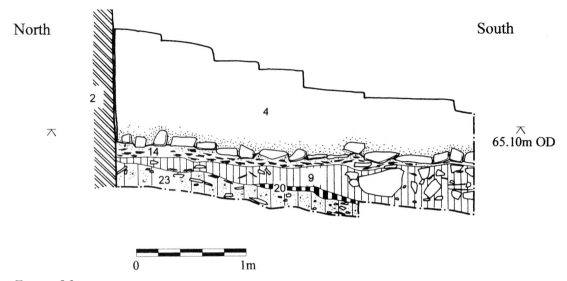

FIGURE 5.3

Section Y1, through the flooring deposits beneath wall (Y4)

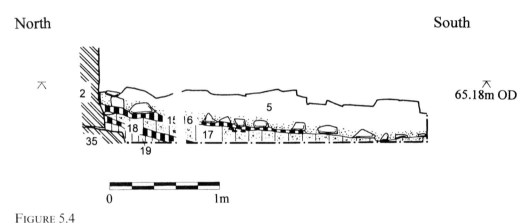

FIGURE 5.4

Section Y2, through the flooring deposits beneath wall (Y5)

below the surrounding ground level. During the Phase 6d demolition of the castle, collapsing masonry rendered extensive damage to these walls (Y29 and Y30) and this caused the fill of the pit behind to become exposed. This fill comprised rubble layers (Y11, Y21 and Y22).

In Phase 4d or Phase 5, following the completion of the cellar/well in Area Y, the area between it and the Middle Ward wall (Y2) received numerous dumps of building material. Above the pit fills (Y11, Y21 and Y22) were spreads of slate (Y6 and Y12), which were both concentrated in the corner between walls (Y2 and Y3). Between these slate layers (Y6 and Y12) was a more extensive deposit of mortar, slate, soil and rubble (Y7), which was probably the product of building demolition elsewhere in the castle. The absence of nails in the slate layers (Y6 and Y12) argues against the origin of this material as a collapsed building or shelter *in situ* in Area Y.

In Area A, charcoal and soil deposits (A6, A9 and A10) accumulated in Phase 4d in the gap between the drystone wall (A5) and the bedrock (A8) to its northeast. By this time, the temporary building associated with this wall (A5) had clearly been dismantled, since much of the walling stone had been robbed out and the remains of the wall (A5) itself were now partly covered by earthen deposits (A12 and A14). These incorporated a second mortar fillet (A13), which appears to have resulted either from spillage occurring during the rendering of the substantial wall (A2/B3/C6) or from the subsequent decay of this render.

Phases 6 and 7

The limited excavation evidence suggest that Middle Ward as a whole seems to have been relatively unaffected by the devastating fire that swept through

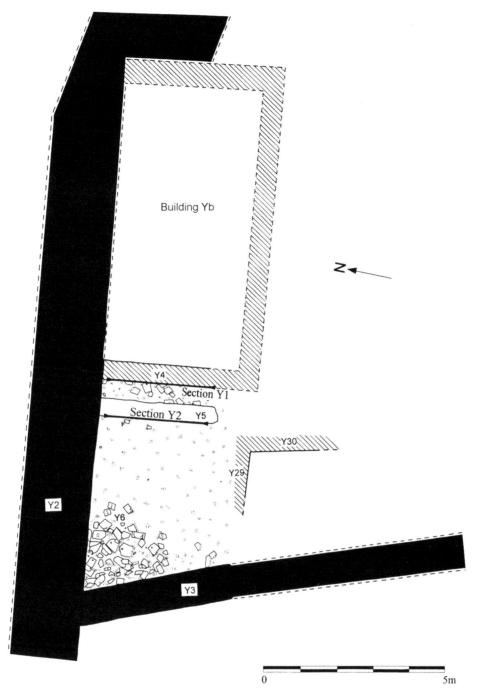

FIGURE 5.5

Middle Ward: Phase 4. For a general location see Figure 2.9

the Inner Ward in Phase 6c. In Phase 6d, however, the structures of the Middle Ward were demolished, along with those in the rest of the castle. This resulted in layers of stone rubble (A4, A7, X2, X6, X38, Y8, Y10, Y26–27 and Y34), which covered much of Areas A, X and Y. Underneath the rubble on the steps (X10) in Area X was a dump of clay (X21) and broken slate layers (X5 and X16). These probably derived from the collapsed roof of Guest Hall X. Within the cellar/well in Area Y was rubble both from this feature and also nearby Guest Hall X, including several voussoirs

and stones with fine rendered surfaces. A large piece of mortared stonework up to 1.5m thick was also recovered from Area Y. This was too substantial to have come from either the cellar/well or Guest Hall X and it had probably fallen instead from the Middle Ward wall (Y2), or perhaps even Gateway Area B.

During Phase 7b, topsoil (X1 and Y1) accumulated in Areas X and Y. In Area A, the stripping of this area by machine in 1992 prior to excavation led to modern contamination of the rubble layer (A4), in addition to the topsoil (A1).

Wells and cisterns

There is no well in the Inner Ward and no evidence of a cistern was recovered. It would appear, therefore, that the earliest castle relied on the nearby River Tywi for its water, a requirement that explains the existence and location of the postern gate in Area H. Other early Welsh castles, including Dolwyddelan (Conwy), also appear to have relied on river water for their supply, but some, such as Castell-y-Bere (Gwynedd) and Ewloe (Flintshire), have wells, whilst the castles at Criccieth (Gwynedd) and Dinas Emrys (Gwynedd) have cisterns.

Limited excavations in the Middle and Outer Wards of the castle and the town have failed to uncovered definitive evidence of either wells or cisterns, although the subterranean feature to the south-west of Building Yb in Area Y is interpreted as a possible well (see above). The presence of a well in either the castle or town during the English occupation is implied by a documentary reference of 1306 (Section 3.1), but the blocking of the postern gate during Phase 4a construction work may suggest that an internal water supply was already available to castle occupants by the 1280s. Water was certainly not scarce within the castle during the late 13th century, since rainwater from the roofs of Great Chamber G and Great Hall K/L was not collected, but carefully diverted into a drain and allowed to flow away. Since Dryslwyn hill consists mainly of limestone, any well sunk would need to have been deep in order to penetrate the water table.

5.2 AREAS R, W, WA AND WB: OUTER WARD AND CASTLE GATEWAY

Areas R, W, WA and WB together form a body of features identified and excavated in the Outer Ward of Dryslwyn Castle, which was added on to the existing Middle Ward in Phase 4a (Figure 1.3). Area W constitutes the Outer Ward gatehouse, Castle Gatehouse W, situated in the north-east corner of the Outer Ward. Area R comprises a number of separate features located in the south and west of the Outer Ward. Area WA is a section excavated through the Outer Ward wall and clay bank beneath, located approximately 7–9m west of Castle Gatehouse W. Area WB is a small sample excavation down to the top of archaeological deposits, conducted only 2m south of Area WA.

Phase 3

Against the north-eastern corner of the Middle Ward wall (XR3) in Area R was a substantial masonry spur buttress (R1) constructed of well-mortared and squared limestone blocks, the outer face of which had once been rendered (Figure 5.6). This structure was most likely added in Phase 3c, prior to the building of the Outer Ward, in order to give better protection to an otherwise vulnerable angle in the Middle Ward wall circuit (Section 5.1). It may even have formed part of a square tower.

FIGURE 5.6

Buttress (R1) constructed to protect the projecting angle of the Middle Ward wall

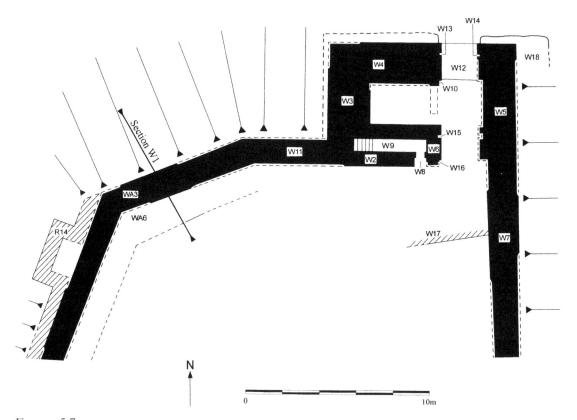

FIGURE 5.7

Outer Ward, Castle Gatehouse W: Phase 4c

Phase 4

Phase 4a saw the construction of the Outer Ward wall (R2, R7, W7, W11 and WA3), which enclosed and defined the Outer Ward (Figures 5.1 and 5.7). On the western side, in Area R, the only remaining substantial fragment of this wall (R2) currently stands over 3m high and is approximately 1.7–1.8m wide at its base (Figure 5.8). Its exterior face is battered 14% off vertical; in other words, it reduces 0.14m in thickness for every 1m in height. Given that the present ground surface is 0.3–0.4m above that of the 13th century, the Outer Ward wall here probably rose to an original height of around 3.5m, topped by a wall-walk and parapet.

On the southern side of the Outer Ward, traces of the eastern section (R7) of the Outer Ward wall were recovered, butting up against the existing Middle Ward wall (XR12). The width of this wall (R7) could not be ascertained; much of it had been lost downhill. It is likely, however, that it was in the region of 1.7m high, similar to the other sections of the Outer Ward wall investigated, suggesting that the whole of the Outer Ward wall circuit was constructed at the same time in Phase 4a. At the base of the exterior of the Outer Ward wall section (R7) were extensive traces of limewash (R10). The layers of limewash formed a deposit 100mm thick and were probably the result of spillage and dripping from higher up the wall. The clear implication is that the Outer Ward wall, like

FIGURE 5.8

The only remaining substantial fragment of the Outer Ward wall (R2), looking west

much of the rest of the castle, was whitewashed and, therefore, must have formed a striking spectacle when viewed from the surrounding countryside. Furthermore, the layered nature of the deposit (R10) suggests that limewash was re-applied at regular intervals during the life of the wall (R7), thus maintaining the effect.

In Area WA, to the west of Castle Gatehouse W, the Outer Ward wall (WA3) survived to a height of three courses and was 1.6–1.8m wide, constructed of mortared stone inner and outer faces with a clay-bonded core. The wall (WA3) was seated on an orange clay bank (WA10) (Figure 5.9). This may represent the remains of an earlier defence, perhaps constructed in Phase 3c and associated with a palisade. Alternatively, however, it may be merely the foundation for wall (WA3), put in place in Phase 4a. The upper surface of this bank contained a thin scatter of domestic refuse, derived from the Phase 3 occupation, pressed into its surface, including oyster shells, bone fragments and potsherds. This was overlain by a hard mortar mixed with stone (WA9), which was probably deposited during the construction of the Outer Ward wall (WA3). A similar mortar fillet (W18) was present on the east side of the gatehouse.

In Area W, parts of the eastern and northern sections of the Phase 4a Outer Ward wall were recovered as walls (W7 and W11). In between, however, stood Castle Gatehouse W. This was also constructed in Phase 4a and consisted primarily of a two-storey rectangular tower, built from dressed limestone blocks bonded with a high-quality white mortar. It measured 10.5 by 6.8m with north (W4), west (W3) and south (W2) walls, each 2.3m thick. A passageway, 2.15m wide, ran north–south through the gatehouse and its east wall (W5), which was also the east wall of the gatehouse itself, was an extension of the Outer Ward wall (W7). On the ground floor of the tower was a guard chamber, which only had access to the passageway. Situated above this, and extending over the passageway at first-floor level, was a second room that was filled with rubble derived from the collapsed inner face of the north wall (W4). From here, two portcullises (see below) could be operated.

Within the south wall (W2) of Castle Gatehouse W was a narrow east–west corridor (W9), barely 0.9m wide. This contained a flight of steps at its western end that gave access up to the first-floor room and possibly also to the wall-walk of the Outer Ward wall (W11). At its eastern end, the corridor (W9) turned south and opened into the Outer Ward via a small arched doorway (W8). The presence of a wooden door here was attested by a masonry rebate, designed to protect the hinge. The corridor (W9) had a vaulted stone roof that bore imprints in its mortar of an initial supporting wooden structure that had been removed once the mortar had hardened. Similar imprints of wooden shuttering have been found on large pieces of fallen masonry from Round Tower D in the Inner Ward (Section 4.1).

The main entrance to the castle through the passageway of Castle Gatehouse W was spanned on its north side by an archway (W10) which connected the north wall (W4) with the east wall (W5). This extension (W5) of the Outer Ward wall measured 2.1m in thickness, whilst the Outer Ward wall proper (W7) to its south was only 1.66m thick. The north end of the gatehouse passageway, beneath the arch (W10), was guarded by a portcullis: portcullis slots (W13 and W14) were observed, one on either side. 1.3m to the south of this portcullis was a rebate in the stonework of the arch (W10), indicating the presence of a gate, almost certainly double-leafed. Further measures to control access into the castle were present towards the southern end of the passageway, leading into the Outer Ward. Here, another archway (W16) spanned the gap between walls (W5 and W6). A second portcullis was evidenced by a portcullis slot (W15), which was recovered in wall (W6), whilst a rebate existed in the arch (W16) for yet another gate, again almost certainly double-leafed, which would have stood in line with the southern façade of the gatehouse.

In addition to the four lines of defence that the gatehouse passageway presented, it is likely that Castle Gatehouse W was entered over a narrow and potentially removable wooden bridge. No evidence of a drawbridge was recovered from the badly damaged gatehouse. The medieval roadway that accessed the town and castle of Dryslwyn from the east (Figure 8.11) passed beneath this bridge or drawbridge and snaked past the west and north sides of the Outer Ward before looping back over itself into the castle. Once inside the Outer Ward, the route that this roadway then took towards the Middle Ward entrance is uncertain.

In Phase 4c, following the initial construction of the Outer Ward wall and Castle Gatehouse W, Area R witnessed the construction of a revetment wall (R14) in the form of a shallow bastion, which protruded 1.25m from the base of the earthen bank beneath the Outer Ward wall fragment (R2). This may have been a turret overlooking the eastern roadway leading into the town, but the lack of any associated features prevents its firm interpretation. The revetment wall (R14) itself was composed of regular squared limestone blocks bonded with strong white mortar, a form of construction that is strongly associated with English occupation of the castle in Phase 4c (Section 6.1). It is most likely, then, that this feature (R14) was intended as a strengthening of the castle defences in response to the weaknesses exposed during the siege of 1287.

In Phase 4d, the stone and mortar cap (WA9) to the clay bank (WA10) in Area WA gained a layer of brown soil (WA8) above it. This contained domestic refuse that had been thrown over the Outer Ward wall (WA3) to lie on its northern (exterior) side (Figure 5.9). On the south side of the Outer Ward wall (WA3), within the Outer Ward itself, a surface (WA4) was recovered, which may also date to Phase 4d. This surface equates with the brown soil (WB8) containing bone and

144

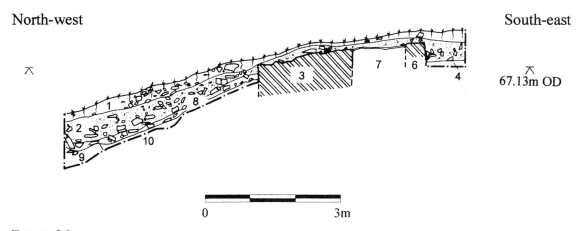

North-west

South-east

67.13m OD

0   3m

FIGURE 5.9

Section W1, through the Outer Ward wall

potsherds, which was found at a depth of 0.4m in Area WB to the south.

Phase 5

Seated on the Phase 4d surface (WA4) was a mortared wall (WA6), which was probably constructed in Phase 5a approximately 1–2m south of the Outer Ward wall (WA3) (Figure 5.7). Between these two walls was a compacted stony deposit of orange clay (WA7), which was in turn surmounted by a dark clay and earth layer (WA5) containing fragments of slate (Figure 5.9). The lack of a north face on the new wall (WA6) suggests that it acted as a retaining wall for the raised deposits (WA5 and WA7). The function of the resulting 1.4m-wide platform next to the Outer Ward wall (WA3) is far from clear: it appears too low for a wall-walk and too narrow for a building.

Phase 5a also saw the construction of a rectangular building, with approximate internal dimensions of 12 by 3.5m, which was identified butted up against the eastern side of the Outer Ward wall fragment (R2) in Area R. The north (R5), east (R4) and south (R6) walls were all roughly 0.75m thick, probably rising to the height of the eaves. Inside, split sandstone roof tiles were recovered. This roofing material is unique within the castle though it is used elsewhere in the region as for example at Carmarthen Greyfriars (James 1997). This building was probably originally constructed with other Outer Ward buildings in Phases 4 or 5, but its distinctive roofing material, coupled with the unusually complete form of the building, suggest that it was re-roofed and re-used, probably as a barn in Phase 7 (late and post-medieval activity) for housing animals grazing on the site.

Phases 6 and 7

In Phase 6a, many of the doorways within Dryslwyn Castle were blocked up when the castle was decommissioned. The northern entrance to the passageway through Castle Gatehouse W was no exception: this was blocked by a wall (W12), more than 1.5m thick, which was constructed from mortared masonry (Figure 5.10). This blocking wall (W12) filled the portcullis slots (W13 and W14) and must, therefore, have necessitated the prior removal of the northern portcullis. At a point approximately 4m to the south of the gatehouse, however, a wall (W17) (Figure 5.7) was discovered, projecting east from the eastern Outer Ward wall (W7). This appears to be one side of a building of uncertain date that was erected against the Outer Ward wall. If it was constructed in Phase 5, it would have forced traffic entering the castle to veer sharply right

FIGURE 5.10

Mortared stone blocking (W12) of the arched gateway entrance (W10) to the Castle Gatehouse W, looking south

in order to avoid it, consequently it may have been a short lived construction of Phases 6a and b. There then followed a period of robbing in Phase 6b, when all the carved freestone and squared, faced stone was removed from the walls of Castle Gatehouse W. In Phase 6d, Castle Gatehouse W and the other structures of the Outer Ward were partially demolished, leaving substantial rubble deposits (R8, W19, WA2, WB4 and WB6) over much of Areas R, W, WA and WB.

In Phase 7b, topsoil (WA1) formed in Area WA. Topsoil (W1) in Area W, can be dated to Phase 7c, as it contained sherds of 18th- and 19th-century pottery, presumably left by visitors to this scenic beauty spot. In Area WB, modern Phase 7d wheel ruts (WB2 and WB3) cut into the soil and rubble layer (WB4) were filled with compacted stones and earth (WB5 and WB7). These were in turn covered by a layer of topsoil and turf (WB1).

Middle and Outer Wards

The construction of the Middle Ward virtually doubled the size of the castle at Dryslwyn. Since it has only been partially excavated, however, the extent of and reasons for the enhancement of the defences and accommodation are not fully understood. Nevertheless, it is clear from Buildings Ya and Yb and Guest Hall X, the last containing painted wall plaster (Section 6.4), that the provision of high-status accommodation was one of its principal functions. The incorporation of a possible well (Y29 and Y30) (see above) within the castle may also have added both to the quality of life and defensive capability of the castle, although there is no evidence to suggest that the Middle Ward entrance was strengthened. It remained a simple gateway with a single- or double-leafed door and no portcullis, gatehouse or flanking towers, although it was sited above the precipitous south-eastern slope of the hill, thus preventing any attacking force charging directly at the entrance. The form of the buttress (Figure 5.6) is similar to the large spur buttresses at sites such as Goodrich (Herefordshire), Kidwelly (Carmarthenshire) and Martens Tower at Chepstow (Monmouthshire) in the period c1280–1300 and represents added protection for the protruding east corner. Though currently considered part of the Phase 3 development of the Middle Ward, given the squared stone construction and later parallels, this buttress could be a later Phase 4c post siege repair/enhancement of the castle defences. Constructed after the initial castle and several phases of alteration to the initial entrance, but before the late 13th-century Outer Ward and Castle Gatehouse W, the Middle Ward is most likely to have been added by Maredudd ap Rhys during the third quarter of the 13th century, a date that fits well with the ceramic evidence (Section 9.2).

The subsequent addition of an Outer Ward to the castle at Dryslwyn created a three-ward arrangement, as yet unparalleled at any other Welsh castle. Most Welsh castles are single-ward structures, for example Dinas Bran (Denbighshire), Dolbadarn (Gwynedd), Dolforwyn (Powys) and Dolwyddelan (Conwy). Expansion at these castles may have been limited by the topography of the hilltop location, or perhaps a lack of desire or resources to add on extra wards. Alternatively, it is possible that time and money was invested into the construction of additional towers or buildings within the one existing ward. Some Welsh castles did develop two wards, for example at Criccieth (Gwynedd) and Ewloe (Flintshire), although this is often attributed to expansion by Llywelyn ap Gruffudd, following the original construction of Llywelyn ap Iowerth (Avent 1983, 38; 1989, 14). The growth of a castle through the ribbon-like addition of wards is a phenomenon normally associated with large English or Marcher baronial castles, such as Chepstow (Monmouthshire) (Turner 2002a, 5–18), where building activity is linked to ownership by powerful and wealthy lords, a succession of such owners leading to multiple wards. By analogy, the growth of Dryslwyn Castle derives from successive periods of increased wealth and power for the lords of Dryslwyn (Section 2.1).

The limited excavations conducted in the Outer Ward afford us only a partial understanding of its origins and development. The presence of a clay bank beneath the Outer Ward wall, in addition to the flat topography of the ground just outside the early castle, makes it possible that some form of defended settlement originally occupied this area; although it could simply have been open ground between the town and castle (Figure 8.6). The construction of the Outer Ward increased the area of the castle by approximately 28%. The late 13th-century form of the gatehouse, coupled with the later addition of a revetment and bastion (R14) in the squared masonry characteristic of post-siege construction work, indicates that the Outer Ward must be the work of either Rhys ap Maredudd or King Edward I. However, there is neither record of expenditure nor good reason to attribute the addition of an Outer Ward and gatehouse to an English Crown that, with its vassals, already held a string of substantial castles in Carmarthenshire, at Carreg Cennan, Carmarthen, Dinefwr and Llandovery. There was no obvious reason to add further expensive defences to a castle that had successfully withstood siege for several weeks and was only a short distance from Dinefwr. Turning to Rhys ap Maredudd, he was the most powerful surviving direct descendant of the Lord Rhys after 1283, but he had been made to publicly quitclaim Dinefwr, the family seat of the lords of Deheubarth. After his marriage to Ada de Hastings, he was receiving income from lands roughly equivalent to the size of modern Carmarthenshire. Given his wealth and status, it would be surprising if he had not sought to expand and develop his castle of Dryslwyn into a residence fit for the court of a Welsh lord or prince.

Castle Gatehouse W

This gatehouse was constructed as an integral part of the Outer Ward, its east wall forming a continuation of the curtain wall. The gatehouse had an outer and inner portcullis and double-leafed gate, separated by a gate passage with a guard chamber on its west side. This provided a high level of security, as visitors could be admitted through the initial portcullis and doors, which were then closed prior to admission through the inner portcullis and doors. This ensured that the gateway could not be blocked and the castle entrance rushed. Well-defended gatehouses with an outer portcullis and gate and an inner gate, like that in Gateway Area B, could already be found at castles such as Montgomery (Powys) and Beeston (Cheshire), both constructed in the 1220s (Ellis 1993, 211). The Main Gatehouse at Chepstow had an outer portcullis and gate and inner portcullis as early as *c*1190 (Turner 2002a, 95). By the mid to late 13th century, gatehouses had developed into substantial buildings with long gate passages equipped with double or even triple sets of portcullises and doubled-leafed gates: examples include Caerphilly (Caerphilly) (1268) and Harlech (Gwynedd) (1283–89). The only substantial gatehouses in Welsh castles are at Dinas Bran (Denbighshire), where an asymmetric gatehouse of fine stonework construction is defended only by a single gate, and Criccieth (Gwynedd), which, although modelled on Beeston (Cheshire), has only a single portcullis and double-leafed gate. At Criccieth there is barely 2m between the portcullis and gate, consequently the portcullises must have been raised and the doors opened to admit wheeled vehicles, thereby negating the defensive advantages of having a double set of gates and or portcullises. If constructed in the period 1230–40 by Llywelyn ap Iowerth (Avent 1989, 11), this may suggest, like the stepped entrances to Welsh castles, that wheeled vehicles were not generally admitted to Welsh castles or that the principles of controlled entry through a gatehouse with front and rear gates or portcullis were not appreciated or considered necessary in early 13th-century Wales. Dryslwyn, therefore, is the only Welsh castle to have an effective functioning double-gate and portcullis gatehouse.

The gate passage in Castle Gatehouse W is off-centre. There are a number of mid to late 13th century gatehouses with off-centre gate passages such as Dinas Bran (Denbighshire), Laugharne (Carmarthenshire) and the larger examples at Goodrich (Herefordshire) (Renn 1993, 8) and the West Gate Tower at Trim (Meath). There are earlier examples such as the original form of Perveril's Gate at Dover Castle *c*1200 (Jane Goodall pers comm) also later examples such as the 14th–15th century bridge gate at the Warkworth (Hodgson 1899; Grundy *et al* 1992). However, no exact parallel for the Dryslwyn Castle Gatehouse W has yet been discovered. It is an extremely small and efficiently functional gatehouse, similar in some respects to the earlier gate towers of the late 12th century at Exeter (Devon) and Ludlow (Shropshire), and very different to the larger Edwardian gatehouses, such as Caernarfon (Gwynedd) and Harlech (Gwynedd), which were built as much for display as function.

CASTLE CONSTRUCTION

6.1 BUILDING METHODS AND MATERIALS
by Chris Caple, Ray Caple and Ian Betts

'Welsh' masonry construction

Prior to the use of mortared masonry, castles in Wales and the Marches were made of earth and timber, for example at Hen Domen (Powys) (Higham and Barker 2000), or drystone walling, as at Carn Fadryn (Gwynedd) (Avent 1983, 7). Mortared masonry construction was used for 11th- and 12th-century Norman castles, such as Chepstow (Monmouthshire) and Cardiff, and almost all castles constructed in Wales from the 13th century onwards. By the late 12th century, it was being used by Welsh princes and lords; in 1171, 'the Lord Rhys had built with stone and mortar the castle of Cardigan' (*BT* 155). Analysis of the material holding together the walls in Phases 1 and 2 of Dryslwyn Castle indicates that it had a low lime content (<36%) and was thus a lime-rich earth, rather than a mortar (Section 6.3).

Other evidence for earth-, lime-earth- or clay-bonded stone walling used in early Welsh castles includes, firstly, 12th-century Welsh castle sites with exposed walling, such as Nevern (Pembrokeshire), which appear to have a poor-quality brown sandy mortar or limey earth bonding the stones together. Secondly, the Welsh (Phases 1 and 2) construction at Dolforwyn (Powys) is described by Butler (1997, 142) as bonded with a brown sandy material. He suggests that 'no lime was used in the native Welsh construction work' (Butler 1997, 199); in other words, that the walls were earth- or clay-bonded. Thirdly, the walls of the 13th-century *llys* of Rhosyr (Anglesey) are described as being 'clay-bonded' (Johnstone 1999, 274–275). Finally, sites such as Penmaen (Swansea) have been identified as having drystone walling in their Welsh construction phases (Alcock 1966, 184). Several present-day Welsh castle ruins, including Cardochan

(Gwynedd) and Carn Fadryn (Gwynedd), also appear to have drystone walls. All these sites may originally have been bonded with earth, clay or poor-quality earth mortar, but this material has subsequently weathered away.

Many Welsh castles, such as Castell-y-Bere (Gwynedd), Dolbadarn (Gwynedd), Dolwyddelan (Conwy) and Ewloe (Flintshire), were uncovered and 'conserved' during the 19th and early to mid 20th centuries. This has meant that their remains are now consolidated with modern mortar and it is no longer possible to be certain about the nature of the original material binding their stone construction. Only the two most recently excavated Welsh castles, Dryslwyn and Dolforwyn, which have had their remains protected beneath the soil, have revealed an earth, clay or weak (sandy) earth mortar bonding the stonework and it is now seems likely that the masonry of many Welsh castles constructed in the late 12th and early 13th centuries was similarly bonded.

This type of construction is made more permanent and weatherproof if water is prevented from running through the wall. This may be achieved using a turf capping (as exhibited in present-day 'Pembrokeshire' banks), a stone capping and/or whitewashed exterior. It is probable that the early Welsh castle walls had some or all of these features. It also appears likely that this form of native Welsh stone wall construction evolved from traditional construction techniques used for field boundaries and smaller buildings, but copied Norman masonry castles in form. The arrival of the Continental European monastic orders undoubtedly transformed church construction, as did the increasing construction of masonry castles throughout Wales in the in the 13th century. Good-quality lime-rich mortar (>36% lime) was in use at Dryslwyn by Phase 3, in the mid to late 13th century.

In many instances, it is likely that walls bonded with the poor-quality earth mortar were subsequently repointed in the 14th century with good-quality lime mortar. This may well have occurred at Dryslwyn to the Phase 2 walls of Great Hall K/L, especially in the Phase 4a alterations.

Some of the external walls of the original Phase 1a construction, (H41, H42 and J29) for example, have an 8–10° batter at the base. Other stretches of this Phase 1a curtain wall, such as (O24), are either damaged or facing does not remain to a sufficient height to be certain. Nevertheless, it appears likely that this batter was present on the whole of the original castle wall. Some later walls, such as those of Chapel H (H60 and H63), also have evidence of a batter above slopes or difficult ground, but are vertical in more stable situations, for example (A2/B3). It would appear that this battered wall form, though not exclusively Welsh, was extensively used by the Welsh masons and probably also derives from the traditional method of securing stability for drystone or earth-bonded walls with a sloped or battered base. Battered bases are also seen on the northern wall of the square keep and the southern curtain wall at Dolforwyn (Powys) (Butler 1990, fig 5; 1997, 161). Battered bases to round towers are a widespread phenomenon seen on towers in France and Ireland, as well as on round towers in Welsh castles, such as Dinefwr (Carmarthenshire), Dolbadarn (Gwynedd) and Dryslwyn.

'The freemen of Llanegwad carried the timber and built and wattled the lord's houses at their own cost, but if stone buildings or buildings roofed with shingles, contrary to the Welsh method, were erected, then the tenants were free of all charge' (Rees 1924, 77). This passage from the *Black Book of St David's* would suggest that, in the 13th and early 14th centuries, the Welsh freemen of the Tywi valley normally used timber-framed construction with wattle and daub infill panels, roofed with thatch, for their houses. Masonry construction was clearly known, but considered a non-traditional method undertaken by specialist craftsmen. The need for such masonry skills was one of the driving mechanisms that led Welsh lords to place their 'renders and services on a more regular basis' (Davies 1987, 137). They consolidated a variety of feast and food renders and services into quarterly *gwestfa* payment, or its equivalent (Rees 1924, 223–224). This effectively created a regular rent or taxation system for the lord. Payment, which was increasingly by coin, provided the resources required for castle construction by specialists, such as masons.

Typically, the masonry on Welsh castles is naturally split stone, in a variety of sizes, roughly faced and coursed. The Edwardian castles, such as Beaumaris (Anglesey), Caernarfon (Gwynedd), Conwy (Conwy) and Harlech (Gwynedd), have well-coursed squared or rectangular block masonry. At Beaumaris, regular-sized limestone blocks were readily created and used, but, at Harlech and Conwy, considerable effort was required to dress the stone and a variation in stone size was accepted. Whilst not a definitive 'Welsh' and 'English' style of masonry, the varying amount of

resources expended on preparing the stone does effectively represent different building traditions, as noted by O'Neil (1944–45, 12, 14, 18) at Criccieth Castle (Gwynedd). At Caergwrle (Flintshire), Manley (1994, 91) detected six styles of masonry construction. He observed that the high-quality regular squared or rectangular stone-block masonry was present on the exterior face of the towers and curtain wall, whilst irregular and variable-sized masonry was used mainly on the internal wall faces. The regular block masonry form would suggest the use of English masons, whom Manley suggests (1994, 127–128) were employed at Caergwrle. The arguments advanced in the preceding paragraphs would suggest that a good-quality lime mortar was also used at Caergwrle. The masonry used at Dryslwyn is formed of faced, naturally split limestone, some patches containing regular-sized stone, some roughly squared-off, other areas have a range of stone sizes with small stones present between larger stones (snecking or pelleting). Thin stones are often inserted to alter the stonework levels. This style of stonework construction appears to be the normal native Welsh work from Phase 1a to Phase 6a, with the exception of the squared stone-block work seen in Phase 4c.

In Phase 4c, the masonry walls were constructed of squared stone blocks, examples of which include the upper parts of wall (E2/F2), the steps (E5), the garderobes (E9 and E17), the area around the south-facing windows (J86–87 and J92–99) in wall (J7), the buttress to wall (J7), wall (B3) and the bastion (R14). The lower part of wall (F2) is made of naturally split stone and the upper part is of squared stone blocks (Figure 6.1), indicating that the wall was rebuilt. This repair correlates well with the type of damage inflicted by a trebuchet (Section 7.2), almost certainly the one used in the 1287 siege. Masons and other craftsmen employed in the construction of the Edwardian castles of north Wales formed part of the besieging forces in the 1287 siege (Taylor 1976). Consequently, when the 'English' army were required to repair the siege-damaged castle of Dryslwyn, they probably used the squared stone blocks with which they were familiar. If, as appears likely, the squared stone-block masonry can be correlated with post-siege repairs, its use around the windows in wall (J4) and in the area around the Inner Ward gateway in wall (B3) attests that siege damage also occurred there. The squared stone western buttress to wall (J7) partially obscured a window in the earlier Phase 4a wall (J7) (Figure 4.36).

The English Crown spent £129 4s 10d on repairs to Dryslwyn in 1287–88, of which £109 3s 8d was on building a new mill and £21 19s was spent on repairs in 1288–89. Such sums would correlate well with the minor repairs described above. These sums are little different to those spent on the repair of other Welsh castles: £262 5s 11d on Castell-y-Bere (Gwynedd) (Brown *et al* 1963, 367–369), a minimum of £310 7s 10d (though this may be actually nearer £500) on

FIGURE 6.1

Wall (F2) with square stone block masonry above the earlier naturally split limestone construction

Criccieth (Gwynedd) (Brown *et al* 1963, 365–367) and 'a little under £300 which was spent on the refurbishment' of Caergwrle (Flintshire) (Manley 1994, 88). These are small sums compared to the £27,000 spent to construct Caernarfon Castle (Gwynedd) and demonstrate both the limited amount of damage caused by the sieges and Edward's lack of interest in altering or amending Welsh castles. They were clearly considered serviceable as they were, after appropriate repair.

Whilst the castle was primarily constructed of faced limestone quarried from the hill on which it sat, freestone used for architectural stonework was imported to the site (Section 6.2). An Old Red Sandstone, probably obtained from a local quarry in the commote of Is Cennan, was the most widely used freestone in Dryslwyn Castle during the reconstruction of Phase 4a and for subsequent repairs. It appears similar to the freestone used to construct Carmarthen Greyfriars (Carmarthenshire) in the 1250s (James 1997, 183) and was almost certainly also the freestone extensively utilised in the repair and construction work at the Carmarthenshire castles of Dinefwr and Carreg Cennan in the 14th century. Earlier freestones used at Dryslwyn, such as the fine-grained sandstones and

the travertine (also seen at Dinefwr), were probably obtained locally, but have yet to be provenanced. Oolitic limestone, used for the window or door surrounds of Round Tower D, was probably imported from Somerset and provide evidence of a trade in freestone up the Bristol Channel. Although fragments were recovered of the tracery of an ogee cinquefoil window (from the 1338 repairs to Great Hall K/L), almost all other carved stonework had been looted from the castle. Consequently, we are unable to see any of the carved stonework, fragments of which have been recovered from Castell-y-Bere (Gwynedd) (Butler 1974; Lord 2003, 131) and Deganwy (Conwy) (Alcock 1967, 196–197) and which undoubtedly originally decorated the halls and apartments of Dryslwyn Castle.

The construction of the masonry castle of Dryslwyn was undertaken between Phases 1a and 4a (*c*1220–87) by the Welsh lords of Dryslwyn. Archaeological evidence indicates that there was little or no new masonry construction in Phase 5, when most of the building work was either repairs or timber-framed construction. After 1287, the presence of written records (*NLW Add MS 455D*), which have been analysed by Webster (1987), reveals that local materials were primarily used for construction. Building stone and lime were obtained from the base of Dryslwyn hill, although it cost twice as much to bring them up the hill to the castle as was paid for the materials themselves. Lime was burnt using wood from forests of Glyncothi and Is Cennan and slates were obtained from 'a Carmarthen' quarry. The quantities of materials used led Webster (1987, 93) to suggest that the buildings constructed in the castle were built as lean-to structures against the castle wall. This corresponds exactly with the archaeological evidence.

No stones with masons' marks were recovered from Dryslwyn, nor have any been highlighted in the reports from Dolforwyn (Powys) or any other Welsh castle. They are, however, certainly present at Edwardian castles, such as Flint (Flintshire), where it has been suggested that these marks represent the use of piecework, payment of each mason based on the number of pieces of masonry each has produced (Manley 1994, 86–89). This system of payment can drive up the speed and down the cost of production when there is a surfeit of skilled labour. It is a development of the taskwork system, payment upon the completion of a specific task, which was used together with the daily rate payment system by the royal exchequer for funding the construction of castles and other buildings from the royal purse (Brown *et al* 1963). The lack of written records for the construction work at Dryslwyn Castle and other Welsh castles means that employment/payment systems for construction at Dryslwyn are unknown, but taskwork or daily payment is likely, whilst the absence of masons' marks suggests that piecework is not.

Ironwork

The ironwork recovered from the destruction deposits derives from the full span of the castle's occupation (Section 6.5). The presence of slags and furnace lining from smithing hearths (Section 9.10) attests the presence of smiths at Dryslwyn Castle forging nails, hinges, tools, cramps and other ironwork used during periods of castle construction. Building accounts of the 13th century record the presence of smiths forging ironwork on all major royal construction projects, such as Dover Castle (Kent) (Colvin 1971, 37) and Flint Castle (Flintshire) (Brown *et al* 1963, 37, 316). Iron objects, such as nails and hinges, were also purchased ready-made for castle construction. There was a high level of correspondence between the ironwork listed in the building records and that recovered from the excavation (Section 6.5).

Limewash

The walls of castles were frequently rendered and covered with limewash (often referred to as whitewash), to protect them against water damage; 'so that the wall of the said tower which has been newly whitewashed, may be in no wise injured, by the dropping of rain water, nor be easily weakened' (Wood 1983, 394). The technique of limewashing buildings was certainly understood by the Welsh. Gruffudd ap Cynon, a 12th-century prince of Gwynedd, is recorded by his biographer as having limewashed churches: 'Gwynedd glittered then with limewashed churches, like the firmament with stars' (Turvey 2002, 171).

Traces of limewash were recovered from the rectangular tower at Dolforwyn (Powys) (Butler 1990, 87) and a harling coat (render) was present on the round tower (Butler 1997, 200). Mid 14th-century building records refer to the need for a coat of render on Newcastle Emlyn Castle (Carmarthenshire) (Walker 1992, 39), whilst 13th-century records of royal expenditure indicate that whitewash was applied to the keep at Rochester (Kent), the walls of Corfe Castle (Dorset) (Wood 1983, 394) and the walls of Aberystwyth Castle (Ceredigion). References to processes such as 'daubing the walls of Conwy castle' also refer to limewashing (Brown *et al* 1963, 346). Limewash, however, has rarely been found to survive on castle walls because it wears away over a number of years under the constant assault of the weather. In the case of Dryslwyn, clear traces of limewash were preserved on sections of Round Tower D (O19–21), whilst the exterior footings of the Outer Ward wall (R7) produced a 100mm-thick deposit of limewash (R10). These deposits make it clear that the exterior of Dryslwyn Castle was limewashed, certainly in the 14th century, and this coating was maintained until just before demolition. The presence of fresh render on Round Tower D, protected beneath buttress (O22), revealed that the buttress had been erected after a new coat of render had been applied, but before the first coat of limewash. Since the buttress had been replaced at least three times (and was almost certainly rendered itself due to the use of the poor quality shale stone), it would suggest that the external render was replaced as well as coated regularly with limewash. The limewash coating was certainly functional, both reducing water penetration, so helping to preserve the masonry, and making the castle walls highly visible, thus ensuring that visitors could find the castle and the ford beneath even on the darkest nights. It was also symbolic, however, serving to highlight the largest man-made structure in the valley and so provide a bold statement of the power of the lords of Dryslwyn.

Limewash was also used internally, both as a coating for the wall surface and in order to reflect light around dimly lit rooms. Traces of limewash on render were recovered from the archaeological deposits inside Great Chamber G and fragments remained still adhering to the walls of Gateway Area B and the undercroft of Great Hall K/L. The historic records indicate that the walls of the undercroft were whitewashed during the repair work of 1313 (*NLW Add MS 455D*; Webster 1987, 94). Traces of plaster and limewash were present on many of the fragments of architectural stonework (Section 6.2), suggesting its widespread use throughout the castle. Lime was needed both for mortar and limewash and, as at Carreg Cennen (Carmarthenshire), Ogmore (Vale of Glamorgan) and several other 13th- and 14th-century castles (Kenyon 1990, 165–167), it is likely that limekilns were located close to Dryslwyn Castle itself, possibly near the base of the hill.

Excavation recovered several fragments of painted wall-plaster, indicating that wall-paintings decorated the rooms in Round Tower D and Guest Hall X (Section 6.4). Analysis of pigments revealed that minerals such as azure, orpiment and vermilion, which were imported from the Continent, were used to create these paintings. Wall-painting fragments have been recovered from a number of castles in Wales, including Dolforwyn (Powys), suggesting that, by the late 13th century, private apartments would have been decorated in both Welsh and Marcher castles.

Timber framing

As the earlier passage from the *Black Book of St David's* (Rees 1924, 77) suggests, traditional building in the Tywi valley comprised timber framing, of either post or sill form, with panels of wattle and daub filling the areas between the frames. These panels were usually composed of hazel withies (although briar stems or other long, strong and flexible branches or stems were also used), plastered with daub (limey soil, clay or earth), which were often covered with whitewash to make them waterproof. The wall structures were further protected from the rain by the construction of thatched roofs with overhanging eaves. Timber framing using sill beams was common at Dryslwyn. Impressions of sill beams were seen in the Phase 2 clay-floored buildings in Area G (Section 4.4). Sill beams were also seated on low stone walls in order to lift the wooden frame off the ground away from the damp and subsequent decay. This technique was almost certainly used in the construction of houses in Dryslwyn township (Section 8.2).

In Phase 5c, a timber-framed building was erected in Gatehouse Area B, as it provided a cheaper and quicker form of construction than masonry. The fact that it was less strong and fireproof than masonry was no longer crucial. It indicates the lack of perceived military threat in Wales in the 14th century and the importance of cost. Evidence for timber framing is present in the charred remains of the beams (Figure 4.23) and fragments of clay daub that would have covered panels of woven timber laths. This form of construction was also used internally. Evidence of internal walling occurs in the form of postholes in the mortar floor of Great Chamber G (Figure 4.54) and fragments of burnt daub with a smooth outer face and impressions of roundwood or split timber laths on the rear, which were recovered from Gateway Area B, Round Tower D, Great Hall K/L and Apartments I/J (Figure 6.2). Such internal walls would probably have been whitewashed, which was seen on a couple of small fragments from Great Hall K/L.

Flooring

A flagstone floor (D11) was present in the base of the wall of Round Tower D and formed a substantial part of this Phase 1a construction. The expense and effort involved in creating such a floor may suggest that the basement was used as a prison rather than merely a storeroom, as has been suggested for Bronllys (Powys) (Smith and Knight 1981, 15). Other Phase 1 and 2 surfaces are worn bedrock or trampled earth and stone. Expensive flagstone floors were used again for the Phase 4a ground-floor levels of Apartments I/J, where traces of broken flagstones were present in the base of wall (J7). Broken flagstones are also present in wall (F2), indicating that, in the post-siege period (Phase 4c), the middens of Area F were sealed under a substantial flagstone floor. These could be re-used flagstones from Round Tower D that were removed in this phase when the ground-floor access (D10) was created. Flagstones are an expensive flooring material used where a good-quality and hard-wearing floor is required. They were installed in Phases 1a, 4a and 4c, when substantial masonry building work was being undertaken.

Examples of crushed shale flooring come from Phase 2b (F59/F75/F101/F105), Phase 4d (O58/O99) and Phase 5b (K18). The shale was derived from seams (Diconograptus shales?) occurring in the Bala series limestones (Strahan *et al* 1909, 44–58) which form the bedrock of the north side of Dryslwyn hill and was thus available locally at low cost, providing a cheap flooring material that could be quickly deposited during occupation phases.

During Phase 3, in addition to well-trampled earth and stone surfaces, good-quality mortar floors were also in use. In Great Chamber G, there is a substantial sequence of mortar floor layers (G57) indicating that it was renewed several times, eventually forming a deposit up to 200mm deep in places. The use of mortar as an internal floor and external surface material continued in Phases 4 and 5, especially in Courtyard O and the undercroft of Great Hall K/L. Mortar surfaces were particularly prone to wear, with multi-layered repair indicating the most heavily used routes during the castle's occupation. For example, a series of separate replacement mortar layers (P19, P24, P29, P33, P38/P47 and P42/P48) built up as a result of repairs to the worn access across Area P to the garderobe in Phases 4 and 5. Similarly, the mortar layer (O33) in Courtyard O had six identifiable layers of replacement. The earlier suggestion that good-quality and hard-wearing lime mortar only became available in Welsh castles from the third quarter of the 13th century (Phase 3 at Dryslwyn) appears to be supported by its appearance and subsequent frequent use as a flooring material from this period.

Clay was used to form the substantial ground-level floors (G166 and G194) of the Phase 2c timber buildings to the east of Great Hall K/L (Section 4.4). It is a smooth, hard-wearing flooring material for interior use, which performs well when dry. A far cruder and less smooth clay flooring was also used for the houses excavated in Drylswyn township (Section 8.2). Clay flooring was frequently used to form ground-floor surfaces within timber-framed buildings.

Evidence for wooden plank flooring supported on substantial wooden cross beams is present in the form of sockets to support the cross beams within the walls of flared-based round towers, such as those at Bronllys (Powys) (Smith and Knight 1981, 19) and Cilgerran (Pembrokeshire) (Hilling 2000, 19; McNeill 2003). The walls of Round Tower D at Dryslwyn did not survive to sufficient height to preserve such evidence: however, it seems highly probable that all internal floors within the building were wooden from Phases 1a to 6a. A document of 1313 refers to a carpenter, who was paid for four days to repair the planks of the middle storey of the 'high tower' (Round Tower) (Webster 1987, 94). In Phase 4a, Great Hall K/L preserved ledges along the north and south walls, as well as a socket and corbel in the east wall and the corbel in the central stone pier, to support three substantial timber beams, on which would have lain a wooden plank floor at first-floor level. It is likely that any second storey would also have had a wooden plank floor. In Phase 5a, the

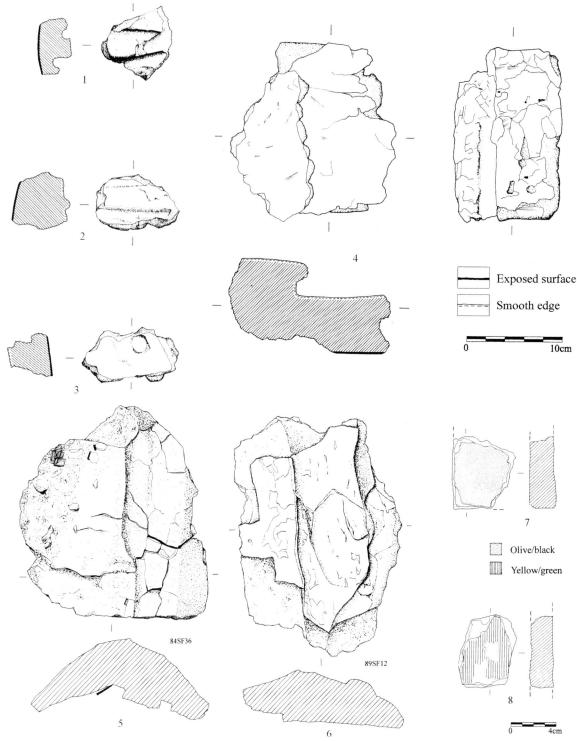

Exposed surface

Smooth edge

0   10cm

Olive/black

Yellow/green

0   4cm

84SF36

89SF12

FIGURE 6.2

Mortar roof apex, pieces of clay daub and glazed floor tiles

wooden first-floor level of Great Hall K/L was supported by a wooden pillar, whose padstone (WS17) (Figure 6.4) was recovered *in situ*. The north elevation of the south wall (J7) of Apartments I/J (Figures 4.36 and 4.39) indicates that there was insufficient depth to permit the arched masonry construction necessary to support a first-floor level of stone. Consequently, the upper floor level of Apartments I/J was also of wooden beam and plank construction. The presence of a substantial central posthole in Phase 4a and later (Phase 5c) postholes along the walls of Great Chamber G suggests that this too had a wooden plank floor at first-floor level. All the upper storeys of the buildings in the Inner Ward had plank floors.

The extensive deposits of clay recovered from the destruction debris of the timber-framed building in Gateway Area B (B16 and B31), Round Tower D (D5) and Great Hall K/L (K12) included fragments of flat sheets, 30–78mm thick, with timber impressions on one side and a crudely flattened surface on the other. These are the remains of a clay floor surface placed over the wooden plank floor, which created fireproof and soundproof flooring for the upper storeys of these buildings. The use of clay or rammed-earth floors applied over the floorboards of upper storeys, as well as on ground-floor levels, is widely attested (Wood 1983, 389). They were used in the towers of Dover Castle (Kent) in 1227: 'for 100 loads of earth called argil (clay) bought from the land of a certain poor woman, to place on the towers between the planks' (Colvin 1971, 71). The natural yellow glacial clay found above the bedrock of the hill would have provided the raw material for this flooring, although occasional organic impressions in the clay indicate that plant stems (probably straw or hay) were mixed in to improve its cohesiveness. Clay surfaces may have been present on all the plank floors of the Inner Ward buildings. The lack of such flooring material in Great Chamber G, together with destruction debris in the postholes, suggests that the wooden first-floor level had been removed prior to the destruction of the building (Section 4.4).

Two fragments of floor tile were recovered (Figure 6.2), one from the topsoil layer (J1/K1) and the other from rubble deposits (J47/K6) in Great Hall K/L. Both are 19–22mm thick and one has a black glaze, whilst the other has a light and dark green glaze over a white slip and a buff body fabric. Neither example shows any evidence of wear, suggesting that they were not part of the general flooring of the first-floor hall, but probably decorated one of the floors of the upper rooms of Great Hall K/L or Apartments I/J. They have the uneven surface characteristic of Lewis's Floor Tile Group 16 (Lewis 1999), which is also found in Carmarthenshire at Carmarthen Priory and further west at Whitland Abbey, and the laminated and irregular-shaped inclusions of Group 18 from Carmarthen Greyfriars (James 1997). Both date to the mid 14th century. The Dryslwyn glazed tiles, therefore, were probably laid as part of the 1338/39 refurbishment of Great Hall K/L.

Roofing

The occurrence of small fragments of slate in almost all soil and building debris deposits indicates that slate was used for roofing the castle buildings from Phase 2a onwards. Slate roofs were clearly preferable in castles to the cheaper thatch or wooden shingle roofing due to their longevity and inflammability. The presence of extensive deposits of broken slate in Phase 6c and 6d

levels indicates that, by the 14th century, the major buildings of Great Hall K/L, Great Chamber G and timber-framed guardhouse in Gateway Area B were all roofed in slate. This is also indicated by the nail types recovered from these areas (Section 6.6). It is probable that Apartments I/J and Chapel H were also roofed in slate.

Samples of complete roofing slates recovered from the collapsed roofing material in Areas B, G, K/L, H, O and Y were measured and features noted (Eastaugh 1994). Complete slates were 110–410mm in length and 75–300mm in width and typically 11mm thick. Graphic analysis indicates two size groups of slates: 330–430mm × 200–260mm and 180–300mm × 80–200mm. This suggests that the practice of using larger slates for the lower parts of the roof and smaller slates on the higher parts of the roof, to keep the bulk of the weight of the roof near the supporting walls, was in use by the 14th century. A similar grading technique was noted by James (1997, 179) at Carmarthen Greyfriars. The slates were secured through one or two holes, at the top of the slate, depending on the size of the slate, to wooden laths using broad-headed nails (Section 6.6). Present on many of the slates were traces of adhering mortar, which indicates that mortar torching was applied between the slates in order to make them weatherproof and prevent them from lifting in high winds. Reference to the expenditure in 1306 of '2s 2d for lime for the roof of the granary and bakehouse' (Webster 1987, 92) probably refers to torching for this slate-roofed building in order to keep it watertight and spark-proof. Two near complete examples of a mortar formed apex were recovered from Areas H and L (Figure 6.2) and fragments were also recovered from Courtyard O. Since no ceramic ridge tiles or lead ridge crests were found, the archaeological evidence indicates that both Great Hall K/L and Great Chamber G had mortar apexes running along the length of their roofs. This is a technique that was probably in widespread use during this period, but one that has left little archaeological trace (Innocent 1916, 183). The consistent use of good-quality slate roofing for all the major buildings in Dryslwyn Castle contrasts with the mixture of poor-quality shale, thin split sandstone and Pembrokeshire phyllite used to roof Carmarthen Greyfriars (James 1997, 178–183).

There are several locations in Deheubarth, such as the area around Cilgerran (Pembrokeshire) (Thomas 1961, 69), where good-quality roofing slate can be obtained. Confusingly, the records for the building of the granary and bakehouse in 1306 refer to slates obtained from a 'Carmarthen quarry' (Webster 1987, 92), although no source of good roofing slate is present in the vicinity of the town of Carmarthen. It probably refers to the fact that the slates were either obtained from the county of Carmarthenshire or imported through the port of Carmarthen.

The accounts for the construction of the Edwardian castles of north Wales record the purchase of lead for roofing not only for towers, but also for other buildings, including the kitchen and halls in Harlech Castle (Gwynedd) (Brown *et al* 1963, 363). Lead was bought as ingots, cast as sheets on site and attached with nails to the wooden roof framework, which rested on a bed of sand in order to avoid underside condensation, resultant lead corrosion and timber rotting (Colvin 1971, 71). Purchases of tin were made to solder together the edges of the lead sheets (Colvin 1971, 37), presumably to make them watertight. Despite the abundance of natural slate in north Wales, lead was the material of choice for Edwardian royal castle construction, as it had been for many earlier castles, such as Beeston (Cheshire) (Ellis 1993, 96). The recovery of lead sheet from over 40 contexts at Dolforwyn Castle (Powys) (Butler 1997, 194) indicates that the towers here were also roofed in lead. At Dryslwyn, the presence of offcuts of sheet lead throughout the site (Eastaugh 1994) suggests that lead was also used as roofing material within the castle. In particular, the lack of slate and the distribution of nails associated with lead work in Round Tower D (Section 6.6) indicate that this building was roofed in lead. Whilst slate was used to roof most of the buildings of the Inner Ward, the presence of solidified pools of lead recovered from Phase 6c and 6d destruction deposits in Areas D, G, K, L and O suggests that that lead was used for guttering, roof valleys, flashing, ridge crests and downpipes on Great Chamber G and Great Hall K/L. The accounts for 1300/01 and 1303/04 and 1305 record that William the plumber and a boy were paid to survey and repair the roofs of the royal castles in west Wales, which would have included Dryslwyn (Rhys 1936, 221, 325, 395). This work probably included repair of gutters and downpipes, as well as sheet lead roofing and flashing. The 1338/39 account records roofing repairs, including repairs to guttering and involving melting and recasting lead (Webster 1987, 96).

Reference to 'shingles of wood' in the building repairs to Dryslwyn Castle of 1313 (*NLW Add MS 455D*) indicate that this material was used for roofing at least some of the buildings of the castle. This form of roofing, which is referred to in the *Black Book of St David's* and was also used on Newcastle Emlyn Castle (Carmarthenshire) (Walker 1992, 39), was probably widespread in Wales, although it leaves no archaeological trace. It was not merely an insubstantial rural roofing material, as 10,000 wooden shingles were used for roofing domestic buildings at the palace of Westminster, London, in 1254 (Colvin 1971, 359). It is likely that where cost was a significant factor, such as in the houses of the township of Dryslwyn, thatch was used instead. Certainly, the absence of slate in Area T would suggest that the one townhouse investigated was roofed in thatch or wooden shingle.

In Phase 7a, tilestones (thin split sandstone that could be used to tile a roof and which were available locally from Trapp) were recovered from a late or post-medieval building located in the Outer Ward (Section 5.2).

Windows

Many castles, such as Dover (Kent), which was constructed in the 1220s, are only recorded as having glass in the windows of the chapel (Brown *et al* 1963, 137), but, by the late 13th century, glass was increasingly being used in non-royal castles (Kenyon 1990, 170) and other secular contexts. The presence of a number of fragments of window glass in the destruction deposits from Dryslwyn (Section 6.7) indicates the presence of glazed windows by the 15th century. It is likely that they were present much earlier and may well have been incorporated into the Phase 4a refurbishment of the castle by Rhys ap Maredudd. Fragments of window glass have come from other Welsh castles, including Castell-y-Bere (Gwynedd) (Butler 1974, 137) and Dolforwyn (Powys) (Butler 1997, 195). The presence of mortices in some of the dressed stonework (Section 6.2, WS27 and WS28) suggests iron bars or grills across at least some of the windows, similar to the example found at Caergwrle (Flintshire) (Manley 1994, 121, 123). It is uncertain if this was intended to prevent access in or out of the window.

6.2 ARCHITECTURAL STONEWORK
by R F Caple

Dryslwyn Castle is almost entirely constructed from the hard, dark grey crystalline limestone of the Llandeilo and Bala series limestones, which make up the south side of the hill on which the castle sits (Strahan *et al* 1909). The limestone is a stable building stone, used as the primary construction material in every building phase of the castle's construction, from the flagstones of the original (Phase 1) floor of Round Tower D to the voussoirs in the archways above the windows in the Phase 4 south wall of Apartments I/J. Thin beds of friable shale also occur interbedded with the local limestone. This was a poor-quality building stone used only for building foundations, such as those of walls (I5 and J21), which subdivided Apartments I/J from Phase 5a. It was also used to construct the platform (O22) which supported the wooden steps up to Round Tower D. This platform was not load-bearing and was almost certainly rendered to protect and hide the inferior shale.

The limestone from the hill could not be used as a freestone to produce cut mouldings for doors and windows and, consequently, all the architectural stonework of the site has been fashioned from stone imported to the site. Only six of the 87 examples of moulded freestone recovered were still bonded into the walls of the castle, so their original location and date is a matter of interpretation. Each piece of architectural freestone recovered during the excavation was given a unique WS number, geologically identified, described, drawn, photographed and catalogued (Figure 6.3). All this stonework, save the ogee cinquefoil window tracery, was buried in Prison M at the end of the excavation. All stones were examined and geologically identified in hand specimen, whilst petrological thin sections were made for the red sandstone.

Red sandstone

This stone (WS6, WS16–25, WS43, WS44, WS50–68, WS70–78 and WS85–88) ranges from a coarse conglomerate to a fine-grained texture and from purple, through reds, to orange in colour. The Carmarthenshire castles of Dinefwr and Carreg Cennen also contain substantial quantities of carved freestone of identical red sandstone type. Professor J R L Allen commented on the thin sections of this stone and found that it compares closely in texture and composition to facies of the Brownstones, the topmost formation of the Lower Old Red Sandstone (Siluro-Devonian) which outcrops a few kilometres to the south of Dryslwyn Castle (Strahan *et al* 1909, 63–75).

At Dryslwyn, coarse stone was usually used for corbels and flat faced stone, whilst both coarse and medium-grained stone was used for the blocks of stone with simple chamfered edges that probably formed the edging for a doorway or window. Almost all the stones from Dryslwyn had profiles unique to the site and unlike those seen at Dinefwr and Carreg Cennan. Finer-grained red sandstone was normally used for the finer carved work, such as that seen on the window mouldings. A group of pieces of this fine-grained red sandstone was recognised as fragments of a window head and window frame, which could be fitted together to form a complete twin-headed cinquefoil window with 280mm-wide openings, a matching stone mullion with rebates and twin arris. Scraps of a window sill were also recovered. The occurrence of numerous pieces of this stonework from the gap between Courtyard O and Great Hall K/L indicates that it almost certainly derived from the northern front of the Great Hall.

A second recognisable architectural form was made from conjoined fragments of a fine-grained sandstone, almost orange in colour, and another piece matched to it by profile (WS64, WS65, WS67 and WS73) (Figure 6.4). These suggest part of the head of a fireplace hood, which has similarities to another from the Old Deanery, Lincoln (Lincolnshire) (Wood 1983, 264). The hood showed no trace of re-use and the fragments had clean edges and traces of lime putty or whitewash as a straight line across the edge of the main dressed face. All fragments of the hood were found in Great Hall K/L, suggesting the presence of a fine fireplace in this building.

Three fragments of red sandstone (WS85–87) remain *in situ*, built into the southern wall (J7) of Apartments I/J, suggesting that all windows in the Phase 4a Great Hall/Apartment complex had red sandstone mouldings. These could have been original to the building's construction or inserted during the repair of the castle in Phase 4c, although it is perhaps more likely that good freestone would be quarried for the initial construction work in the 1280s.

The padstone (WS17) for a wooden pillar that supported the Phase 5a first floor in Great Hall K/L has been identified as a re-used damaged red sandstone corbel. Documentary references to work at this period (Webster 1987, 95; Section 3.1) indicate that new windows and a new doorway were introduced into the 'King's Hall' during this renovation. Traditionally, the cinquefoil ogee window form is regarded as a mid-14th-century and later feature, for example in the south range at Llawhaden (Pembrokeshire) which is dated between 1380 and 1400 (Turner 2000b). They were also in widespread use both in castles and ecclesiastical buildings in Ireland in the 15th century (Mark Samuel pers comm). Comparisons can be made, however, with a number of foliated arch windows of double ogee pointed cinquefoil type present in the early 14th century: for example, the Treasurer's House in Martock, Somerset (1330); Meare Manor, Somerset (1322–35); Brinsop Court, Herefordshire (1340); and with the single-pointed form in the Bishop's Palace at St David's, Pembrokeshire (1340s) (Turner 2000a). Indeed the cinquefoil form may occur at Wells (Somerset) as early as the 1290s and at Broughton Castle (Oxfordshire) by the early 14th century (Wood 1983, 250, 241). The ogee window form was being inserted into earlier structures by the early 14th century, as in the case of the ogee window inserted into the flared-based round tower at Bronllys Castle (Powys) (Smith and Knight 1981, 19). Consequently, it appears very likely that the Dryslwyn Castle ogee cinquefoil window derives from the 1338 renovation.

Red sandstone was used for this ogee window and, since the historic record indicates that the stone used for the 1338 renovation was derived from a quarry *upud Iskennen*, it would appear that this was the source for the red sandstone. As this stone is visually identical to the sandstone freestone used at the nearby Carmarthenshire castles of Carreg Cennen and Dinefwr, it is probable that all three castles were supplied from the same quarry. Carreg Cennen was constructed in the early to mid 14th century, a date which corresponds with the use of this stone at Dryslwyn, whilst red sandstone corbels were used in the rectangular tower, dated to the late 14th or early 15th century, at Dinefwr (Rees and Caple 1999). The likely presence of fragments of this red sandstone (WS85–87) in Phase 4a construction at Dryslwyn suggests that this quarry was active by the 1280s. It continued to supply freestone throughout the Tywi valley during the 14th century.

	Context	Phase	Architectural form	Curve/straight	Mortices	Geology	
WS1	B7	6d	Q/M4	St	M	micaceous sandstone	
WS2	B7	6d	Q/M4	C	M	micaceous sandstone	
WS3	O7	6d	Q/M1	St		micaceous sandstone	
WS4	O7	6d	Q/M1	St		micaceous sandstone	
WS5	O7	6d	Q/M1	St		micaceous sandstone	
WS6	O7	6d	Q/M1	St		red sandstone, coarse grained	
WS7	O7	6d	Q/M1	St		fine grained sandstone, grey	
WS8	O7	6d	Step stone			grey limestone	
WS9	O7	6d	Q/M1	C		fine grained sandstone, grey	
WS10	P7	6d	Q/M1	C		fine grained sandstone, grey	
WS11	O7	6d	Q/M1	C		fine grained sandstone, grey	
WS12	O7	6d	Q/M1	C		fine grained sandstone, grey	
WS13	O7	6d	Q/M1	C		fine grained sandstone, grey	
WS14	u/s	–	Millstone			red sandstone conglomerate	
WS15	u/s	–	Millstone			red sandstone conglomerate	
WS16	K1	7c	Corbel			red sandstone conglomerate	
WS17	L22	5a	Corbel		M	red sandstone, coarse grained	
WS18	O7	6d	Corbel			red sandstone conglomerate	
WS19	K7	7b	Corbel			red sandstone, coarse grained	
WS20	O182	6d	Tracery	C		red sandstone, fine grained	
WS21	K7	7b	Q/M2	St	M	red sandstone, fine grained	
WS22	O7	6d	u/c			red sandstone conglomerate	
WS23	O7	6d	Tracery	St		red sandstone conglomerate	
WS24	O182	6d	Q/M2	St		red sandstone, coarse grained	
WS25	O182	6d	Q/M2	St		red sandstone, coarse grained	
WS26	O7	6d	Tracery	St		oolitic limestone, gold	
WS27	O27	6d	Q/M3	St		oolitic limestone, gold	
WS28	O7	6d	Q/M3	St	M	oolitic limestone, gold	
WS29	P7	6d	Q/M1	St		oolitic limestone, gold	
WS30	P7	6d	Q/M3	St	M	oolitic limestone, gold	
WS31	P7	6d	Q/M1	St	M	oolitic limestone, gold	
WS32	O7	6d	Q/M1	St		oolitic limestone, white	
WS33	O7	6d	Q/M1	St		oolitic limestone, white	
WS34	O7	6d	Q/M1	St		travertine	
WS35	u/s	–	u/c			travertine	
WS36	u/s	–	u/c			travertine	
WS37	u/s	–	u/c			travertine	
WS38	I5	5a	Millstone			fine grained sandstone, grey	
WS39	O7	6d	Q/M1	St		micaceous sandstone	
WS40	O7	6d	Q/M1	St		micaceous sandstone	
WS41	O7	6d	Q/M1	C		fine grained sandstone, grey	
WS42	O7	6d	Q/M2	C		travertine	
WS43	u/s	–	u/c			red sandstone conglomerate	
WS44	A1	7d	Voussoirs			red sandstone conglomerate	
WS45	A1	7d	Voussoirs			grey limestone	
WS46	u/s	–	u/c	St		fine grained sandstone, grey	
WS47	B1	6d	Decorative moulding			micaceous sandstone	
WS48	O66	4a	Decorative moulding			grey limestone (not local)	
WS49	D4	6d	Millstone			red sandstone conglomerate	
WS50	O182	6d	Tracery			red sandstone, coarse grained	
WS51	O182	6d	Tracery			red sandstone, coarse grained	
WS52	O182	6d	Tracery			red sandstone conglomerate	
WS53	L1	6d	u/c			red sandstone conglomerate	
WS54	O7	6d	O/M2	St		red sandstone, fine grained	
WS55	O182	6d	O/M2	St		red sandstone, fine grained	
WS56	O182	6d	Tracery			red sandstone, fine grained	
WS57	O182	6d	Tracery			red sandstone, fine grained	
WS58	O182	6d	Tracery			red sandtsone, fine grained	
WS59	O182	6d	Tracery			red sandstone, fine grained	
WS60	O182	6d	Tracery			red sandstone, fine grained	
WS61	O182	6d	Tracery			red sandstone, fine grained	
WS62	K6	6d	Tracery			red sandstonefine grained	
WS63	L47	6d	Tracery			red sandstone, fine grained	
WS64	K4	6c	Tracery			red sandstone, fine grained	
WS65	K4	6c	Tracery			red sandstone, fine grained	
WS66	K10	6c	Tracery			red sandstone, fine grained	
WS67	K10	6c	Tracery			red sandstone, fine grained	
WS68	K10	6c	Tracery			red sandstone, fine grained	
WS69			Not used				
WS70	O7	6d	Tracery			red sandstone, fine grained	
WS71	O7	6d	Tracery			red sandstone, fine grained	
WS72	O182	6d	Tracery			red sandstone, fine grained	
WS73	K4	6c	Tracery			red sandstone, fine grained	
WS74	O6	7b	Q/M2			red sandstone, fine grained	
WS75	u/s		Tracery			red sandstone, fine grained	
WS76	D4	6d	Flagstone paving			red sandstone, coarse grained	
WS77	O7	6d	Tracery			red sandstone, fine grained	
WS78	u/s		Tracery			red sandstone, fine grained	
WS79	O 7	6d	Q/M1			sandstone, fine grain & mica	
WS80	u/s	–	Q/M5			oolitic limestone, white	
WS81	u/s	–	Millstone			red sandstone conglomerate	
WS82	B4	4a/c	Q/M3		M	sandstone	
WS83	B45	4a/c	Q/M3		M	sandstone	
WS84	B3	4a/c	Q/M3		M	sandstone	
WS85	J7	4a/c	Q/M2			red sandstone	
WS86	J7	4a/c	Q/M2			red sandstone	
WS87	J7	4a/c	Q/M2			red sandstone	
WS88	E49	4c	Q/M3		M	red sandstone	

Moulding profiles:

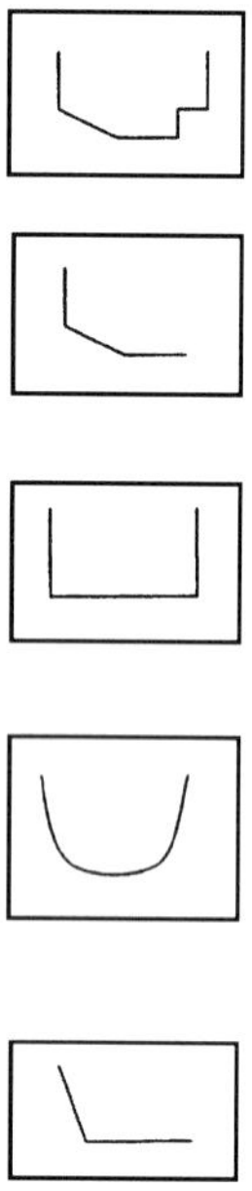

Q/M1

Q/M2

Q/M3

Q/M4

Q/M5

FIGURE 6.3

Architectural stone summary. Features noted on the stone may include: curved form (C), straight form (St), a mortice, hole or recess cut into the stone, usually to retain an iron bar (M)

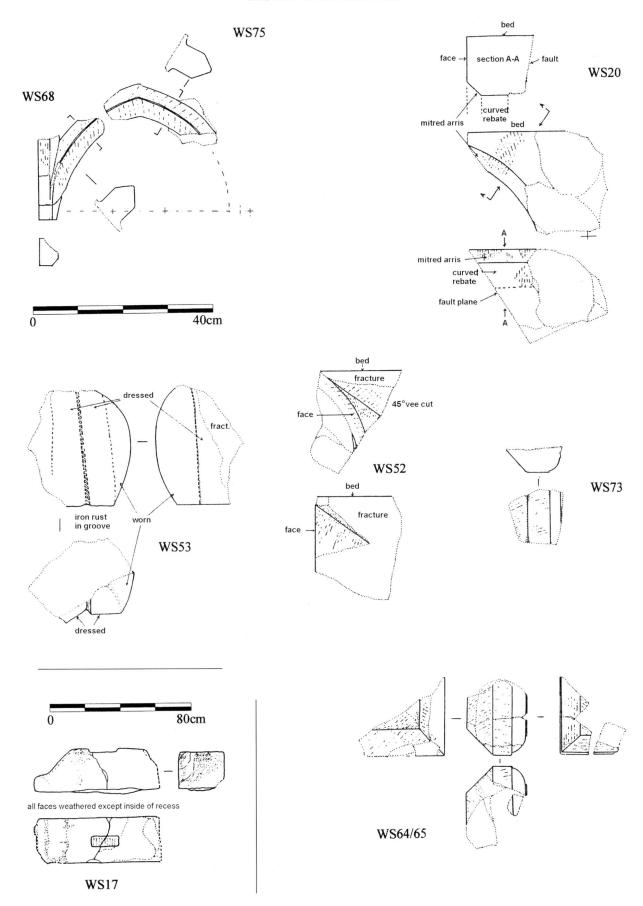

FIGURE 6.4

Red sandstone tracery and other decorative mouldings

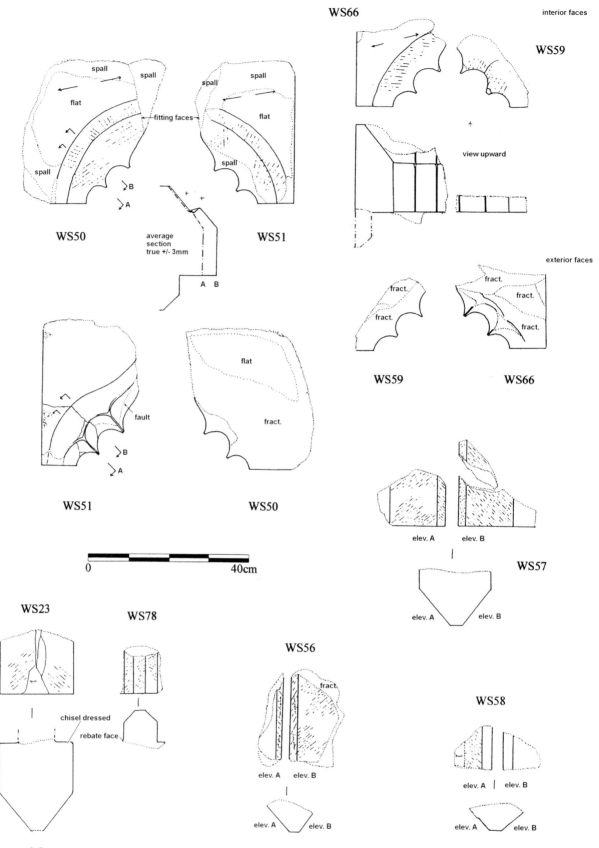

FIGURE 6.5

Red sandstone window tracery

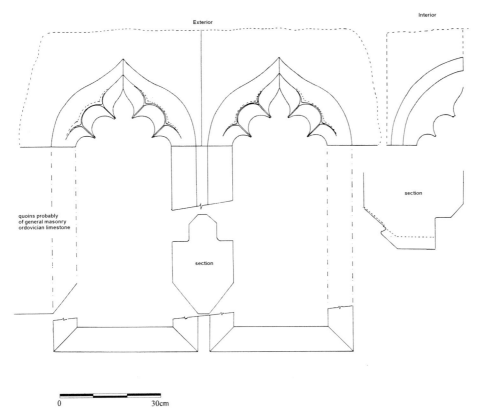

FIGURE 6.6

Reconstruction of the red sandstone cinquefoil ogee window

Fine-grained micaceous sandstone

All the fragments of this stone (WS1–5, WS39, WS40, WS47 and WS79) were recovered from Gateway Area B and Courtyard O and derive from a chamfered-edged rebated doorway or window jamb originally located in Round Tower D. Although probably a freestone from a Carmarthenshire source, the exact provenance of this stone has not yet been located. Its presence in Phase 1 construction would suggest that it was used in the early to mid 13th century.

Fine-grained sandstone

Most of the fragments of this stone (WS7, WS9–13, WS41 and WS46) were recovered from Round Tower D and Area P and once formed a chamfered-edged rebated doorway or window jamb located in Round Tower D. Although probably a freestone from a Carmarthenshire source, the exact provenance of this stone has not yet been located. Its presence in Phase 1 construction would suggest that it was used in the early to mid 13th century.

Oolitic limestone

This stone occurs in golden (WS26–31) and white variants (WS32, WS33 and WS80). All are re-used at least

twice, share the same markings for original cutting and have rough re-shaping, which would suggest that these pieces (particularly WS33) formed the surround to a wooden window frame bedded in mortar and protected by an iron grill. Their recovery from Courtyard O and Area P implies that they were part of a window facing the Courtyard in Round Tower D that was violently removed in Phase 6b. Oolitic limestone is a high-quality freestone, although the nearest sources to Dryslwyn are in south-west England or northern France. Using sea and river transportation, the importation of stone to Dryslwyn, especially from south-west England via Bristol and Carmarthen, would not have presented any great difficulties. Two different types of oolitic limestone imported from the Bristol Channel area were used in the construction of Carmarthen Greyfriars (James 1997, 183), thus confirming the existence of a 13th-century trade in this stone to west Wales.

Travertine

Three weathered pieces of this tufaceous limestone were recovered, probably from exterior decoration, in addition to two fragments from doorway surrounds (WS34–37 and WS42). Primarily excavated from Courtyard O, this stone was probably originally used in Great Hall K/L or Round Tower D. This unusual stone is found as a 130mm-thick stringcourse in the round tower in Dinefwr Castle (Carmarthenshire). Its use in two adjacent castles of the same period suggests the exploitation of a local source of travertine. Part of the original build of the Dinefwr flared-based round tower in c1220–40, this stone was almost certainly being used at Dryslwyn in the early 13th century during Phase 1 construction.

Discussion

Phases 1–3

Initially, architectural mouldings were carved from a number of different freestones: fine-grained sandstones, travertine and oolitic limestone. The travertine is almost certainly from a local source, whilst the oolitic limestone was imported from south-west England. This demonstrates that Welsh lords, such as those of Dryslwyn, could and would import high-quality building stones from English-controlled areas. Arguments that castles, such as Morgraig (Caerphilly), are constructed by 'English' baronial interests because they contain Sutton Stone, which was derived from the English-controlled Vale of Glamorgan, clearly fall a long way short of proof of 'English' baronial construction (RCAHMW 2000, 199).

Phase 4

At this time, Old Red Sandstone from a local source started to be used for architectural mouldings, possibly prompted by the rebuilding work at Dryslwyn. This stone was subsequently used throughout the region during the 14th century, for example in the construction work undertaken at the Carmarthenshire castles of Carreg Cennan and Dinefwr, as well as the 1338 repairs at Dryslwyn.

Phase 6b

The presence of only three pieces of architectural freestone *in situ* indicates the extent to which it was robbed out prior to the destruction of the castle. One good example of stonework almost certainly looted from Dryslwyn Castle is a complete pointed ogee-arched window at 'Court Henry', a substantial house in Dryslwyn village constructed in the late 15th century (Solomon 1982, 102). The rest of the stone may have been used in buildings in Llandeilo, Carmarthen, or remain undetected in local farmhouses.

Selected finds

WS17 Original corbel with ovolo mould and lip, approx. $700 \times 245 \times 260$mm deep. No original dressed faces visible. Very weathered (eroded) possibly by groundwater. Secondary mortice cut into lower face $54 \times 125 \times 15$mm deep. Found (mortice uppermost) on bedrock of Great Hall central between main walls; probably re-used as padstone for timber column. Red sandstone, Old Red Sandstone? Dark purple; sand to fine gravel (no pebble), up to 5mm. Context L 22. (Phase 5a) (Figure 6.4).

WS20 Very irregular shape; overall dimensions $210 \times 220 \times 330$mm. Probably piece of carved window head. Two tooled faces at right angles with traces of curved arris opposite one; these two faces considered main in/out and normal face considered bed. This accepted, the two 'ends' are clean parallel breaks along fault plains, creating trapezoid bed 250mm long with broken parallel faces 125mm apart. Face has 30×30mm arris on angle opposite bed/face and this is curved with inside radius of approximately 245mm for length of 130mm. Inside return is curved for c140mm at depth 65mm. Bed tooled at 70/85° to angle bed and face ridges 8mm apart. Face tooled at 60° to angle bed/face very fine. Arris and return face tooled; arris normal to arris, but only very small area visible. Only 130–140mm of curved dressed face. Probably from window approximately 0.5m wide if semi-circular and not pointed. Purple/red sandstone, fine grain but with pronounced bedding planes. Context O182 (Phase 6d) (Figure 6.4).

WS23 Fragment of window mullion. Width 170mm between dressed side faces, depth in excess of 200mm. Rear axial termination broken. Height (depth of bedding) 160mm between one broken end and flat bed. Symmetrical chamfers at approximately 52° probably meeting at point (now broken). No 20×20 arris (see **WS57**). Rear shows two 45mm rebates with 80mm rib (broken) between. Arrises weathered, probably exterior. One rebate shows vertical (i.e. normal) to bedding, tooling: fine parallel ridges. Bed shows tooling at 45° with traces of white mortar. Purple red sandstone conglomerate, showing level bedding with gravel pebbles in sand up to 8mm in diameter. Context O7 (Phase 6d) (Figure 6.5).

WS50 Dimensions: 350mm high, 340mm max width to front. Large piece of worked freestone 297mm between front and rear faces. Recessed 80mm to a 250mm radius with 40×40mm chamfered arris to curve (inside). Block cut to form ogival arch containing cinquefoil head with spandrels defined by fillets. The foils are struck from a centre 35mm to the soffit. The cestral foil is pointed, depth of foil 120mm. Exterior face badly spalled (medium grain bed) and weathered, probably part demolition. Only one recessed face retaining evidence of tooling: parallel fine ridges normal to face on interior curve of foils and at 45° to face on return and face of recess. Most of curved faces show traces of grinding after cutting. Originally one piece with **WS51**, but broken when found. Purple/red sandstone; generally of fine grain but with clear beds of medium grain with boundaries, which can form planes of breakage. Context O182 (Phase 6d) (Figure 6.5).

WS51 Dimensions: 360mm high, 240mm width max to front. Large piece of worked freestone 295–300mm between front and rear faces. Recessed 80mm deep to a 240–250mm radius curve with 40×40mm chamfered arris to curve (interior). Block cut to form ogival arch containing cinquefoil head with spandrels defined by fillets. The foils are struck from a centre 35mm to the soffit. The cestral foil is pointed. Carving deep cut. Three loose fragments found to complete the two foil spandrels. Good beds and base, side and top. Only recessed faces retain evidence of tooling. Parallel fine ridges normal to face on interior of foils and at 45° to face on interior return rebate and face of recess. Some faint traces of fine tooling at 45° to horizontal on internal face (both ways) and also one way on upper bed. All curved work shows trace of grinding/polishing after cutting. Pair with **WS50**. Purple red sandstone, as **WS50**. Context O182 (Phase 6d) (Figure 6.5).

WS52 Probable fragment of window tracery. Overall 230 × 180 × 180mm with one curved feature. A recessed curved sunk spandrel 45° in section and to a slight curve. Curving is 30mm deep (42mm on face) but this is incomplete. Carving cuts into possible bed with traces of mortar but spalled edges and abrasion make original form difficult to determine. Fine parallel tooling evident on inside faces of sunk spandrel. This fragment probably derives from a trefoil window head with heavily sunk spandrels. Purple/red sandstone conglomerate showing level bedding but with gravel pebbles in sand up to 8mm diameter. Context O182 (Phase 6d) (Figure 6.4).

WS53 A very abraded 'melon'-shaped lump of stone overall 240 × 210 × 260mm with one small flat face. Two rounded faces show pecked grooves up to 20mm deep. The 'rounding' is 300–500mm, giving an ovoid appearance. One groove has imbedded iron rust tight into groove suggesting iron banding. Two other once-rounded faces are very broken and spalled with signs of burning. Possibly iron banded counter weight or decorative moulding. Coarse grey sandstone (gritstone) with pebbles up to 7mm both quartz and hard limestone. Context L1 (Phase 6d) (Figure 6.4).

WS56 Piece of window mullion with two dressed faces at 80° but with 45° chamfer at angle, 24mm wide. Dressed faces end at fractures 110 × 50mm from arris. Length 220mm between fractured ends. One dressed face appears to show front also at a return of splay. Intersection angle at 55° to plane of face (50° to normal). Larger surface shows faint trace of broad chisel at 45° to arris. Arris surface shows old vertical scars possibly early vandalism. Purple red sandstone of fine grain with a few fragments of clear quartz up to 3mm. Context O182 (Phase 6d) (Figure 6.5).

WS57 A piece of mullion in two pieces. Two dressed faces at 80° with 45° chamfer at angle, 24mm on face. Dressed faces 110 and 112mm wide, to parallel faces at second arris of 40 and 48mm, ending in broken edges. One end/bed dressed at right angles to all faces of section. Length 112mm but with matching fragment apparently joining length is 210mm. End/bed hammer pecked and traces white mortar. Broad chisel tool marks at 45° to arris on all dressed faces (probably least weathered fragment recovered). Both fragments show some tooling. Purple sandstone of fine grain with few fragments of clear quartz up to 3mm. Bedding shows a discontinuity of deposition with paler sand laid at 30° to original bed, evident in both fragments. Context O182 (Phase 6d) (Figure 6.5).

WS58 Fragment of mullion or transom with two dressed faces at 90° with 45° chamfer at angle, 28mm wide. One face extends 40mm to raised angle where front occurs but 40mm wide face is clear. Second face is 70mm wide to fracture. All other faces fractured. 40mm wide face shows faint tooling at 45° to arris. Some traces of white mortar on dressed face opposite but probably from contact in burial. If **WS78** might reasonably be assumed as the inner mould of the mullion, then **WS58** would be the unmould of the transom with the longer splay. Purple red sandstone, fine grain. No visible inclusions. Context O182 (Phase 6d) (Figure 6.5).

WS59 Two fragments conjoining of cinquefoil window head, comprising three foils and two cusps. Identical to **WS50–51** but not of it. 140 × 80mm overall and 35 to 40mm thick, part of larger curved face. One edge corresponds to bed 35 × 40mm. Traces of tooling on bed. Front? face slightly weathered. Both faces have heavy soot deposit. Purple red sandstone. Fine grain curved bedding planes have manganese staining. Context O182 (Phase 6d) (Figure 6.5).

WS64 Two joined fragments which form the corner of feature appearing as dressed flat face with two adjacent arrises meeting at right angle. Arris in excess of 80mm wide and dressed at obtuse angle to face (135°) to create external chamfer. Overall 180 × 120 × 110mm in three conjoined pieces from two contexts. All three faces show similar dressing with broad chisel 1mm deep grooves at 4mm average apart. Traces of very white lime on all dressed faces. No signs of weathering. Conjoins with **WS65**. Orange red sandstone, fine grain with fragments up to 5mm of orange brown mudstone. Context K10, Context K4 (Phase 6c) (Figure 6.4).

WS65 Piece of carved projection, an external angle. Section consists of recessed quadrant mould 37mm radius, recessed 3mm adjacent to a 45mm face adjacent to an arris at an angle of 134°. Arris at least 50mm wide. Found in three separate conjoining pieces from two contexts, plus a fourth piece of quadrant section but of different geology (later matched to **WS67**). Traces of very white lime on arris face. Flat faces show identical dressing to that on **WS64**. No signs of weathering. **WS65** conjoins with **WS64** to give total arris width of 120mm and section with an external angle. This is a cornice or string, possibly the lower mould (string course) of a fireplace hood, with a chamfered surface above a flat band overhanging an ovolo separated from the band by a short straight piece. The white lime is from the fine plaster or whitewash of the wall above. Orange red sandstone, fine grain of identical geology to **WS64**. Context K10 (1 piece), context K4 (3 pieces) (Phase 6c) (Figure 6.4).

WS66 Large fragment of carved cinquefoil window head mirrored but identical to **WS50–51**. Overall size 250mm deep to fracture 200mm high bed to fracture and 205mm wide, front face to fracture. Block cut to form ogival arch containing cinquefoil head with spandrels defined by fillets. The foils are struck from a centre 35mm to the soffit. The cestral foil is pointed, foils 120mm deep. Traces of internal rebate. Rebate and curved arris to front above cusps. One horizontal lower bed, front half. Interior of foils dressed normal to face. Fine chisel dressing to arris, cusps, and rebate; weathered to all faces except inside of foils and rebate. The 'mirrored' bed fitting with **WS50–51**. The evident section of mullion found would indicate these pieces all formed a double ogee cinquefoil window. Purple red sandstone, fine grain. No visible inclusions. Context K10 (Phase 6c) (Figure 6.5).

WS68 Fragment of curved and straight window tracery. In two pieces, separate contexts, conjoined. One end shows? lower bed at right angles to straight? vertical member. Height vertical 155mm. Max size to end curve 180mm. Thickness maximum (front face to rear fracture) 85mm. Vertical member 46mm wide. Curved member to curve of 216mm, internal face has width of approx 60mm. Curve has external chamfering of approx 30 × 30mm with 5mm between and vertical has one 30 × 30mm chamfer. Front surfaces particularly subject to much soot giving brown/black patina. Fine parallel broad chisel marks at 45° to front flat face on arrises and suggestion of rubbing or grinding of high spots. Trace of white mortar in bed (see match with **WS75**). Orange red sandstone, uniform fine grain. No visible inclusions. Context K10 (2 pieces) (Phase 6c) (Figure 6.4).

WS73 Fragments of dressed stone of cross section comprising two dressed faces at obtuse angle of 135° for length of 120mm. One face 70mm wide to fracture. One face 50mm wide to parallel arris of rebate 3mm deep adjacent to part of quarter round of 37mm radius. Small fragment of identical geology and with identical quarter round mould and rebate (matched after photography but seen on **WS65**). Trace of white lime on edge of 70mm wide face. The very flat surface with pebbles ground to half section suggest this moulding was ground and rubbed after cutting. This is a cornice or string, possibly the lower mould (string course) of a fireplace hood, with a chamfered surface above a flat band overhanging an ovolo separated from the band by a short straight

163

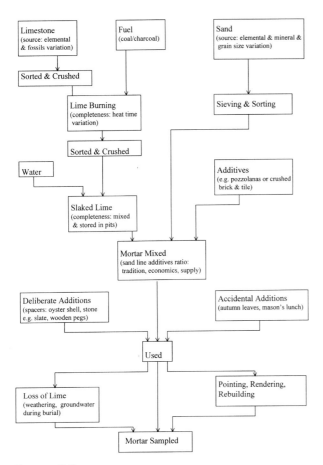

FIGURE 6.7

The creation of a sample of archaeological mortar

piece. The white lime is from the fine plaster or whitewash of the wall above. An exact match to section **WS65**, but slightly different in grain and colour. Purple red sandstone, fine grain with inclusions of red/brown mudstone pebbles up to 15mm long. Unstratified (×1) and from context K4 (Phase 6c) (Figure 6.4).

WS75 Fragment of tracery 240mm long showing curve of 400–500mm to inside face (uneven curve) with trace of meeting curve or straight at approx 130° at joint of tangents. Section 85mm wide and 50mm deep with double chamfered arris on front face to leave 5mm between (arris slightly uneven). To rear fractured but with suggestion of shoulders at least 15mm wide. Both faces of arris show traces of grooves from chisel, upper face at 45° to tangent of curve, but face later ground. At knee or apex evidence of attempt to even the irregular angle of chamfer. Some uneven cross chisel grooves to body of tracery. Purple red sandstone, fine grain. Unstratified (Figure 6.4).

WS78 Piece of mullion showing cross section and 115mm long. Section is 85mm wide between parallel faces and with two arrises 30×39mm leaving 25mm free between. Total depth face to rear fracture approx 40mm and there are very definite traces of rebate at fracture. Arrises both show traces of fine parallel ridge at 45° to angle and slight trace of similar dressing to 25mm face between arrises. The reveals show very slight trace of similar dressing but have been ground flat after dressing. This fragment fits to the rear of **WS23** or **WS57** to create complete cross-section of mullion to match that required to seat the sectional bed of **WS51** and **WS52**. Purple-red sandstone, fine to medium grained. Unstratified (Figure 6.5).

6.3 MORTAR
by Chris Caple

Mortar was used extensively in the construction of Dryslwyn Castle. Samples were extracted from the walls, foundations, floors, renders and mortared structures, such as drains, and subjected to analysis (Haynes 1993; Spencer Gregson 1990; Wade 1990).

Mortar analysis has traditionally been undertaken in order to characterise its composition and, through compositional similarity, relate the mortar of a wall or floor to a specific building phase. The underlying theory presumes that the sand and lime of which the mortar is composed (Figure 6.7) were obtained from different sources: the sand from riverine, marine or aeolian sources; the lime, obtained by burning limestone, from various limestone outcrops. The sand and lime could also be mixed in different ratios, depending on the required qualities of the mortar and/or the construction tradition of the builder. Since sources of the sand and limestone, in addition to the ratio of mixing, are likely to be consistent during one phase of building, the mortar of any one phase should have similar ratios of lime to sand, similar types of sand (particle size and chemistry) and similar limestone chemistry. It is possible to determine the sand to lime ratio, usually through the acid digestion of the lime component, and to calculate the distribution of the particle sizes of the sand component determined by sieving with decreasing mesh size. This has enabled researchers to characterise the mortar of specific building phases or periods and so match walls of uncertain period to particular building phases (Evans 1977; 1984; Mellor 1981).

It is also possible to use elemental analysis to characterise mortar samples. Elements such as magnesium (Mg) and strontium (Sr) frequently occur as impurities in the limestone, whilst elements such as potassium (K), sodium (Na), aluminium (Al), silicon (Si), iron (Fe), titanium (Ti) and manganese (Mn) are found in the feldspar minerals of which sand is composed. The level of phosphorous (P) will vary depending on the organic material added to the mortar or adsorbed from the environment. The fuel used in the burning of lime was originally charcoal but, by the post-medieval period, coal rich in sulphur (S) was being used. Weathering and/or burial of the mortar can lead to chemical changes, such as the dissolution of calcium carbonate and the deposition of iron minerals.

Although samples from Dryslwyn had their sand and lime content and particle size distribution determined, the largest and most useful data was obtained through elemental analysis. Sub-samples of 0.4g dried powdered mortar were pressed into 8mm diameter discs, which were analysed using an Energy Dispersive X-ray Fluorescence (EDXRF) System (Link Systems XR200 X-Ray Fluorescence Spectrometer). This system determines the concentrations of all elements of atomic weight greater than 11 (elements above sodium in the periodic table) (Pollard and Heron 1996, 41–49). The software within the computer of the EDXRF Spectrometer converts the analysed intensity of these elements as oxide weight percentages. To compare these results with standards and published sources, for example sand and lime content determined by dissolution, these results are normalised (total 100%). Analyses of known composition standards indicate that calcium oxide contents are accurately determined to within 4% of the analysed figure. Silicon, aluminium, iron and potassium were determined to within 30% of the analysed figure. Magnesium, titanium, strontium and phosphorous were correctly identified as present or absent, although quantification was inaccurate at low concentrations. Multiple sampling of a single wall revealed that the analytical variation was minimal compared to the natural variation seen within a wall due to the differential effects of weathering as well as poor mixing of the sand and lime components.

The results from the analyses undertaken by Wade (1990) and Spencer Gregson (1990) are given in Figure 6.8. Two samples had high phosphate levels, both of which were patches of lime, presumed to be the burning of limestone, recovered from the early phases of construction of Great Hall K/L, layers (K49) and (J12). The phosphate is probably urine/faecal contamination of this surface, which subsequently acted as an animal pen or waste dumping area. Another sample that stands out, with a medium phosphate level (1.6 wt %), is from wall (F4), which was immediately beside the latrine of Area F, clearly demonstrating that high phosphate contents can be derived from associated faecal or urine-rich deposits.

When the normalised calcium oxide weight percentage is graphed against phase (Figure 6.9), all the mortar samples of Phases 1 and 2, with the exception of the two phosphate-rich samples, have less than 53% calcium oxide and, in all but one case, less than 46%. With only a couple of exceptions, which come from the mortared blocking of an arrowloop, all mortared construction from Phases 3–5 and beyond has a minimum of 45% calcium oxide. This would suggest that a sand- or earth-rich mortar is used in the initial phases of the castle's construction, switching to a calcium-rich mortar later in the century, although still within the 'Welsh' occupation of the castle.

Generally low sulphate levels are seen in the mortars from Dryslwyn, but they are a little higher in the later samples, perhaps representing a general rise in the level of coal use and consequent dust or gas pollution during the later centuries of the occupation of the castle.

Discussion

The mortar of Phase 1 and 2 construction was of very poor quality, physically weak and crumbly to the touch. Analysis shows that it had a low lime content, effectively a lime-rich earth, which had probably been poorly fired. It contains very little calcium hydroxide and consequently would have had very limited strength once set. It would, however, have been sufficient to give some form of adhesion to allow the construction of the earliest stone buildings and defences of the castle. This soil-rich mortar may be an intermediate constructional technique between the earlier drystone walling and the substantial well-mortared stone masonry of later Welsh castle construction. The walls from which these samples were removed have suffered erosion and some dissolution of their mortar material is possible, even likely. However, the consistency of the analyses of these early mortars from Dryslwyn would suggest that the compositions obtained are typical of the construction technology of the period.

A good-quality, strong and lime-rich mortar is present from Phase 3a onwards and the composition of mortar becomes consistently lime-rich by the 1280s. Thereafter, there was little variation in the lime/sand composition. It would appear that mortar technology had advanced by the third quarter of the 13th century in Wales, perhaps as a result of the great number of castles being constructed in the early to mid 13th century by both the English Crown and Marcher lords.

No correlation was detected between composition and use of mortar. This would indicate that mortar of identical composition was used for floors and walls. A general increase in sulphur levels in samples of the later periods suggests that coal started to be used for lime-burning in the late 13th or early 14th century. Occasional flecks of coal were seen in the mortar samples, although this is not consistently detected in analysis. Coal-based pollution problems have been recorded historically in urban centres, such as York, by the 14th and 15th centuries (Brimblecombe 1989, 41).

6.4 PAINTED WALL-PLASTER
by Chris Caple and Phil Clogg

Some 23 small fragments of painted wall-plaster were recovered. The friable nature of painted plaster resulted in only small fragments surviving and these were difficult to recover during the excavation as they were buried amongst hundreds of tons of rubble. Many 13th-century sites, including Greyfriars in Carmarthen (Carmarthenshire), which may well have originally contained some painted plaster decoration, have not reported any fragments from their excavations (James 1997), whilst others, such as Clarendon Palace (Wiltshire), have recorded only a fraction of what we might have expected from historical sources (James and Robinson 1988, 250–258). Consequently, even a small number of painted plaster fragments probably represents evidence of extensive internal décor.

Context	Phase	Sample No.	Analyst	Visual	Ca oxides	Si oxides	Al oxides	Fe oxides	Ti oxides	Mn oxides	Mg oxides	Sr oxides	sulphate	Na oxide	K oxide	phosphate	Ca norm	Si+Al+Fe norm
D3	1a	1	FSG/39	Round Tower wall, outer	17.4	6.7	1.6	7.4	0.7	0.2	tr	tr	0.2	tr	1.1	0.7	52.6	47.4
D3	1a	2	FSG/44	Round Tower wall, inner	5.7	10.2	2.4	9.2	0.9	0.2	0.1	tr	tr	tr	1.7	0.3	20.7	79.3
D3	1a	3	FSG/41	Round Tower wall, outer	13.9	8.6	1.6	7.7	0.7	0.3	0.2	tr	0.5	tr	1.1	0.4	43.7	56.3
J29	1a	4	FSG/23	Original ward wall, west	8.5	9.4	2.3	8.6	0.9	0.2	0.1	tr	tr	tr	1.7	0.9	29.5	70.5
J10	1a	5	FSG/22	Original ward wall, south	14.6	8.1	1.7	7.3	0.7	0.2	0.2	tr	0.2	tr	1.3	0.6	46.1	53.9
O24	1a	6	FSG/6	Original ward wall, west	9.4	8.3	2.1	9.0	0.8	0.2	0.1	tr	tr	tr	1.5	0.6	32.6	67.4
O24	1a	7	FSG/4	Original ward wall, north	12.1	8.0	2.0	8.6	0.9	0.2	0.2	tr	tr	tr	1.4	0.5	39.4	60.6
K60	1a	8	FSG/K25	Hall K/L west wall & warc wall	10.3	8.2	1.9	8.3	0.8	0.2	0.2	tr	0.1	tr	1.4	0.6	35.9	64.1
F12	1a	9	FSG/36	Original ward wall	5.6	11.0	2.7	9.6	0.9	0.3	0.1	tr	tr	tr	1.9	0.5	19.4	80.6
J12	1b	10	FSG/J12	burnt lime from Hall construction	30.0	2.5	0.4	2.1	0.3	0.4	0.5	0.2	tr	tr	0.9	4.7	85.7	14.3
K49	2a	11	FSG/21	burnt lime from Hall construction	23.5	5.1	0.9	5.6	0.6	0.4	0.3	0.1	tr	tr	1.6	4.4	67.0	33.0
K59	2a	12	FSG/5	Hall K/L north wall	13.6	8.6	1.9	7.5	0.8	0.2	0.1	tr	0.1	tr	1.2	0.4	43.0	57.0
K66	2a	13	FSG/K7	Hall K/L south wall	11.1	9.3	2.0	8.4	0.8	0.4	0.2	tr	0.1	tr	1.6	0.9	36.0	64.0
K55	2a	14	FSG/18	Hall K/L original central plinth	12.5	7.4	1.3	8.1	0.7	0.4	0.2	tr	0.2	nd	1.1	0.4	42.7	57.3
K66	2a	15	FSG/28	Hall K/L south wall	6.7	10.5	2.4	9.6	0.9	0.4	0.1	tr	0.9	tr	1.9	0.9	22.9	77.1
F4	2a	16	FSG/34	EP/FG cross wall	12.9	8.3	1.9	8.1	0.9	0.2	0.1	tr	tr	nd	1.4	1.6	41.3	58.7
M49	2c	17	FSG/13	wall of prison	5.4	11.0	2.7	9.2	1.0	0.2	0.2	tr	tr	tr	1.8	0.7	19.1	80.9
I2	3a	18	FSG/51	I/H wall, east face	14.5	7.7	1.7	7.9	0.8	0.3	0.2	tr	0.2	tr	1.3	0.6	45.6	54.4
G2	3a	19	FSG/45	Hall G, west wall	16.0	7.3	1.6	7.5	0.7	0.3	0.1	tr	0.2	tr	1.1	0.4	49.4	50.6
F1	3a	20	FSG/32	Hall G, east wall	19.4	6.3	1.3	7.3	0.6	0.2	tr	tr	0.1	nd	1	0.4	56.6	43.4
G4	3a	21	FSG/46	Hall G, north wall	19.9	6.6	1.2	5.7	0.5	0.2	0.1	tr	tr	nd	0.8	0.5	59.6	40.4
I171	4a	22	FSG/50	I/H wall, west face	24.6	4.8	0.9	4.4	0.5	0.1	0.1	tr	0.2	tr	0.8	0.2	70.9	29.1
J7	4a	23	FSG/25	Apartment block south wal.	23.5	5.4	0.7	3.2	0.4	tr	0.1	tr	1.6	tr	0.5	0.2	71.6	28.4
J7	4a	24	FSG/24	Appartments south wall bu ress	15.0	8.8	1.4	7.0	0.7	0.2	0.2	tr	0.3	tr	1.1	0.5	46.6	53.4
K56	4a	25	FSG/17	Hall K/L addition to plinth	15.6	6.5	1.5	7.3	0.8	0.4	0.1	tr	0.1	tr	1.3	0.5	50.5	49.5
L53	4a	26	FSG/27	Hall K/L arrowslit blocking	4.8	10.9	2.5	9.2	0.9	0.2	0.2	tr	tr	nd	1.8	0.4	17.5	82.5
H60	4a	27	FSG/35	Chapel wall	20.7	7.6	0.9	4.8	0.8	0.1	0.2	tr	0.2	tr	0.5	0.4	60.9	39.1
O134	4a	28	FSG/14	reveting wall east of steps	22.0	7.4	0.9	4.4	0.4	tr	0.2	tr	0.3	nd	0.5	0.3	63.4	36.6
O132	4a	29	FSG/12	steps & reveting walls to cellar	14.5	8.4	1.6	7.3	0.7	0.2	0.2	tr	tr	tr	1	0.7	45.6	54.4
O132	4a	30	FSG/7	steps and reveting wall to cellar	8.8	9.7	1.7	8.1	0.7	0.2	0.2	tr	tr	tr	1.2	0.4	31.1	68.9
O132	4a	31	FSG/8	steps and reveting wall to cellar	17.1	7.8	1.5	6.8	0.6	0.2	0.2	tr	0.9	tr	1.1	0.9	51.5	48.5
O181	4a	32	FSG/2	reveting wall west of steps	13.0	8.3	1.3	6.5	0.7	0.2	0.2	tr	0.1	tr	0.7	0.3	44.7	55.3
D10	4c	33	FSG/42	Passageway into Round Torver	18.8	6.2	1.2	6.3	0.6	0.2	0.2	tr	0.2	tr	0.7	0.2	57.8	42.2
D10	4c	34	FSG/43	Passageway into Round Torver	18.9	7.4	1.1	5.4	0.5	0.2	0.1	tr	0.6	tr	0.6	0.7	57.6	42.4
F3	4c	35	FSG/31	Foundation Inner Ward wa.l. later	14.5	8.4	1.4	6.5	0.6	0.2	0.4	tr	0.3	tr	1.1	0.7	47.1	52.9
E12	4c	36	FSG/37	Garderobe Inner Ward wall.later	16.2	8.3	1.5	6.4	0.7	0.2	0.1	tr	0.1	tr	0.9	0.3	50.0	50.0
E5	4c	37	FSG/33	Steps to the wall walk	17.4	7.5	1.4	5.9	0.7	0.2	0.2	tr	0.2	tr	1.1	0.2	54.0	46.0
F2	4c	38	FSG/30	Inner Ward Wall, later	19.5	6.7	1.1	4.9	0.5	0.1	1.1	tr	0.4	tr	0.8	0.6	60.6	39.4
O63	5a	39	FSG/49	Courtyard, mortar surface	12.6	8.4	1.9	7.9	0.8	0.2	0.2	tr	tr	tr	1.2	0.8	40.9	59.1
E8	5a	40	FSG/54	Mortar floor, latest	20.3	6.4	1.0	5.4	0.6	0.2	0.1	tr	0.6	nd	0.7	0.3	61.3	38.7
K58	5a	41	FSG/K23	Hall K/L south wall rebuild	20.5	5.7	1.1	5.7	0.6	0.1	0.1	tr	0.5	tr	0.7	0.8	62.1	37.9
J3	5c	42	FSG/26	Plinth beside Hall wall	19.0	6.8	1.2	5.9	0.6	0.1	0.1	tr	0.3	tr	1.1	0.3	57.8	42.2
J3	5c	43	FSG/J3	Plinth beside Hall wall	14.8	6.9	1.4	7.2	0.7	0.2	0.2	tr	0.4	nd	1.2	0.9	48.8	51.2
O33	5c	44	FSG/48	Courtyard, mortar surface	20.6	7.0	1.1	5.8	0.6	0.1	0.2	tr	tr	tr	0.5	0.4	59.7	40.3
E13	5c	45	FSG/38	Step between P & E	22.4	4.2	1.0	5.9	0.6	0.2	tr	tr	tr	tr	0.7	0.3	66.9	33.1
K54	5c	46	FSG/15	Hall K/L cross wall, north, beside north wall	21.1	4.4	0.9	5.5	0.5	0.1	0.1	tr	0.3	nd	0.8	0.3	66.1	33.9
K29	5c	47	FSG/20	mortared top over drain	16.6	6.7	1.4	7.2	0.7	0.2	0.2	tr	0.1	tr	1.2	0.4	52.0	48.0
K53	5c	48	FSG/16	Hall K/L cross wall, north, beside plinth	24.2	4.7	0.9	4.9	0.5	0.1	tr	tr	tr	tr	0.8	0.3	69.7	30.3
K54	5c	49	FSG/19	Hall K/L cross wall, south	19.8	6.2	1.2	6.3	0.6	0.2	0.2	tr	0.3	tr	1.1	0.4	59.1	40.9
G21	5d	50	FSG/47	Hall G, mortar floor, latest	18.5	6.3	1.5	6.5	0.7	0.2	tr	tr	0.1	tr	1.1	0.6	56.4	43.6
—	7d	51	FSG/58	modern mortar	21.2	3.4	0.2	2.1	0.2	tr	tr	tr	0.3	tr	0.2	0.1	78.8	21.2

FIGURE 6.8

Mortar analysis (Spencer-Gregson 1990; Wade 1990)

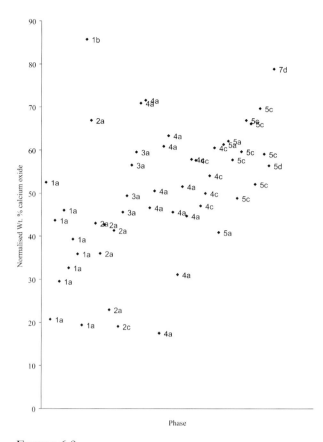

FIGURE 6.9

Normalised calcium oxide levels by phase
(Spencer-Gregson 1990; Wade 1990)

All fragments were measured and drawn (Figure 6.10) and the painted areas analysed using an Energy Dispersive X-Ray Fluorescence (EDXRF) Spectrometer (Link Systems XR200), which detects the presence of all elements with atomic numbers greater than 11. Given the limited number of pigments available in the medieval period (Howard 2003), this allowed the mineral pigments used to be identified (Figure 6.11). Elements present from the plaster itself, such as calcium, were excluded from the results and, where only small quantities of an element were detected, they are indicated in trace (tr) amounts.

Wall-paintings in 13th-century Britain were not normally executed in true (*buon*) fresco, as in southern Europe, but in *fresco secco*, in which the dry plaster was painted with pigments that were dissolved in lime-water, possibly with an additional skimmed milk binder (*secco*) (Caiger-Smith 1963). This technique held the pigments in a partially lime-cemented layer on the surface. Occasionally, pigments were applied in other (*tempera*) media, such as egg or oil, as in the wall-paintings of the Byward Tower, Tower of London (Caiger-Smith 1963), St Stephen's Chapel, Palace of Westminster (London) (Van Geersdaele and Goldsworthy 1978) and the Feretory of St Albans Cathedral (Hertfordshire) (Howard 1993). *Tempera* media were often used to apply valuable pigments,

such as ultramarine (lapis lazuli), or unstable pigments, including lakes (inorganic materials, such as powdered chalk, which had been dyed), which could discolour in direct contact with the alkaline environment of the plaster (Caiger-Smith 1963). Wall-paintings were normally executed by journeyman painters, who travelled from one building project to another applying paint to the walls of recently constructed and plastered buildings (Babington *et al* 1999, 15).

All the wall-paintings from Dryslwyn have a base plaster layer containing numerous very small dark-coloured pebbles, surmounted by a thin layer of smooth, hard white plaster, which is virtually devoid of sand, gravel or other filler material. No evidence was found for the use of an underdrawing (*sinopia*) beneath the painted design.

The red and orange pigments, both based on iron compounds and on vermilion (cinnabar), were well adhered on and into the top of the plaster layer. These appear to have been applied in limewater, possibly with a dilute protein binder solution such as skimmed milk (Rouse 1991). No tests were conducted to determine the nature, if any, of any binding medium. The blue pigment was poorly adhered to the surface and had clearly been applied as a separate layer; thus it was probably originally applied in an oil or egg tempera medium, which has now degraded.

Lead white was used, both as a white pigment for specific areas, as in the mid 14th-century wall-paintings in St Stephen's Chapel in the Palace of Westminster (London) (Van Geersdaele and Goldsworthy 1978), and as a general base coat or priming layer, as seen in the wall-painting of an Archbishop Saint in the Feretory of St Albans Cathedral (Hertfordshire) (Howard 1993, sample 9). It appears to have been used in both ways at Dryslwyn, since it is detected in the white areas of plaster and in many of the pigmented areas. The deliberate addition of lead white to whiten the surface of the plaster was employed to intensify the colours of the wall-painting and it suggests that money was readily available to achieve subtle effects in the wall-paintings at Dryslwyn Castle.

Vermilion or cinnabar (mercury sulphide) was frequently used at Dryslwyn to create bright, strong red and orange pigmentation. Vermilion was used on many of the high-status wall-paintings of the later medieval period and it is often extended by the addition of red lead (minium); for example, in the wall-paintings of St Gabriel's Chapel, Canterbury Cathedral (Kent) (Howard 1997, 44), as well as Dryslwyn Castle. Cinnabar was, at this time, normally imported from Spain, where the mineral was mined (Gettens and Stout 1966), and was probably imported through Bristol up to Dryslwyn. Traces of cinnabar have also been detected on a 14th- or 15th-century terracotta statue recovered from Greyfriars Friary, Carmarthen (Carmarthenshire) (Hunter 1987, 995).

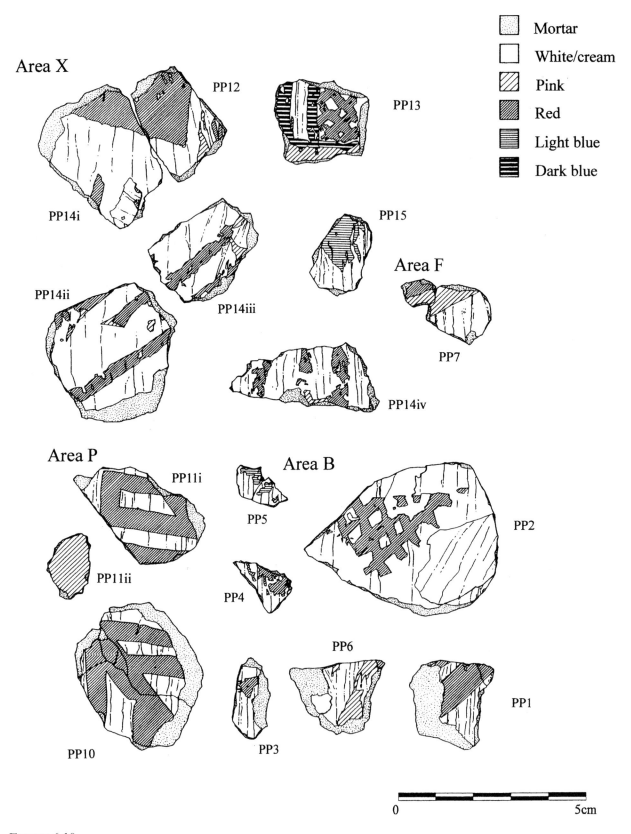

Area X

PP12

PP13

PP14i

PP15

Area F

PP14ii

PP14iii

PP7

PP14iv

Mortar

White/cream

Pink

Red

Light blue

Dark blue

Area P

PP11i

Area B

PP5

PP2

PP11ii

PP4

PP6

PP1

PP10

PP3

0   5cm

FIGURE 6.10

Painted wall-plaster fragments

Catalogue No.	Context	Phase	Size (mm)	Colours	Elements	Pigments
PP1	B43	4d	23 × 21	dark red	Fe	iron oxides
PP2	B43	4d	51 × 39	red	Fe, Pb (tr)	ochre/hematite and minium
PP3	B47	3b	21 × 10	orangy red	Hg, Pb	vermillion & minium
PP4	B72	4d	17 × 10	scarlet red	Hg	vermilion
PP5 i	B72	4d	9 × 7	blue	Cu, As, Ba (tr)	azurite
PP5 ii	B72	4d	8 × 9	blue	Cu, As, Ba (tr)	azurite
PP6	B87	4b	21 × 25	dark red	Fe, Pb (tr)	ochre/hematite & minium
				white	Pb	lead white
PP7 i	F31	3b	16 × 17	orangy red	Hg, Fe, Pb	vermilion, ochre & minium
PP7 ii	F31	3b	9 × 6	orangy red	Hg, Fe, Pb	vermilion, ochre & minium
PP8 i	L31	5a	45 × 36	grey brown	Fe, Ti (tr), Mn (tr)	umber
PP8 ii	L1	5a	25 × 16	grey brown	Fe, Mn (tr), Ti (tr)	umber
PP9	L9	6c	80 × 60	grey brown	Fe, Mn (tr), Ti (tr)	umber
PP10 i	P1/P6	6b	30 × 12	dark red	Fe	ochre/hematite
PP10 ii	P1/P6	6b	30 × 12	dark red	Fe	ochre/hematite
PP11 i	P2/P6	6b	35 × 20	dark red	Fe	ochre/hematite
PP11 ii	P2/P6	6b	18 × 11	dark red	Fe	ochre/hematite
PP12	X16	6d	25 × 18	red	Hg, Pb (tr), As (tr), Fe (tr)	vermillion & minium
				orange	Pb, Hg (tr)	minium & vermillion
				white	Pb, As (tr)	lead white
PP13	X16	6d	20 × 23	scarlet red	Hg, Pb (tr)	vermillion & minium
				blue	Cu, As, Pb (tr), Fe (tr), S (tr)	azurite
				white	As, Pb (tr)	degraded orpiment? & lead white
				pink	Pb, Fe, S	lead white & ochre/haematite
PP14 i	X16	6d	35 × 22	red	Hg, Pb (tr)	vermillion & minium
				white	Pb, As (tr)	lead white & degraded orpiment?
PP14 ii	X16	6d	33 × 35	red	Hg, Pb (tr)	vermillion & minium
				white	Pb, As (tr)	lead white & degraded orpiment?
PP14 iii	X16	6d	28 × 23	red	Hg, Pb (tr)	vermillion & minium
				white	Pb, As (tr)	lead white & degraded orpiment?
PP14 iv	X16	6d	38 × 17	red	Hg, Pb (tr)	vermillion & minium
				white	Pb, As (tr)	lead white & degraded orpiment?
PP15	X16	6d	20 × 14	blue	Cu, As (tr), Ba (tr), Fe (tr)	azurite

FIGURE 6.11

Mineral pigments used in the painted wall plaster (tr: trace)

Although 'ultramarine was the mineral blue normally employed in Romanesque wall-paintings' (Howard 1997, 49), azurite was the mineral pigment used at Dryslwyn to achieve a clear, strong blue colour. Azurite (basic copper carbonate) was first used in Britain in the mid 12th-century wall-paintings at Kempley (Gloucestershire) (Babington *et al* 1999), but was also used on high-status wall-paintings, such as the early 14th-century saint images in the Feretory of St Albans Cathedral (Hertfordshire) (Howard 1993, 38) and the mid to late 14th-century wall-paintings in the Chapel of Our Lady Undercroft, Canterbury Cathedral (Kent) (Howard 1997, 48). It was increasingly used in Britain during the later medieval and post-medieval periods and was probably mined and imported from countries in Central and Eastern Europe. It was certainly mined in Hungary by the 16th century (Gettens and Stout 1966) and was often imported through Germany; hence, it was often known as German azure (Babington *et al* 1999). Azurite is found more commonly as a pigment in Continental, rather than British, wall-paintings (Caiger-Smith 1963). It was usually coarsely ground and concentrated through sieving and flotation to give bright blue

particles, which gave the pigment a coarse 'sandy' texture when applied (Gettens and Stout 1966). This coarse texture is seen in the traces of blue pigment in the Dryslwyn samples.

Though arsenic may be present as an impurity in the blue azurite, the presence of arsenic in white areas of wall-painting suggests either the use of an arsenic oxide as a pigment (though this seems unlikely due to the ready availability of calcium carbonate and lead white) or, more probably, the use of the yellow pigment orpiment (As_2S_3). This was available from Spain and is often found in the same deposits as cinnabar (Eastaugh *et al* 2004, 285). It is used in English wall-paintings from the early 13th century (Howard 2003, 155), however, it has been noted that orpiment is not always stable and can degrade to white arsenic oxides (Colinart 2001; Howard 2003, 159).

Only a few secular 13th- or 14th-century wall-paintings still exist. Where these have been recognised (Tristram 1950; 1955), it is usually because of the datable nature of the figurative forms depicted. Patterning, borders, solid colour areas or imitation architectural detail are always difficult to date.

Wall-paintings in 13th- and 14th-century secular contexts come from private apartments in bishop's palaces, such as those at Exeter (Devon) and Lichfield (Staffordshire), royal residences, including Clarendon Palace (Wiltshire), and manorial halls or apartments, for example at Longthorpe (Peterborough), Luddesdown Court (Kent) (Tristram 1955, 15) and Stokesay (Shropshire) (Babington *et al* 1999). In addition to the religious figures, which so dominated the wall-painting schemes in ecclesiastic buildings, there were secular figures — for example, the kings and queens at Clarendon Palace (Wiltshire) that are attested by documentary evidence (Wood 1983, 397) — as well as images of animals — for example, the eagle depicted at Winchester Castle (Hampshire) (Wood 1983, 397) — and objects — for example, the ship at Longthorpe (Peterborough) (Tristram 1955, 15). Amongst the most prevalent images used were non-figurative decorative schemes, such as the scrollwork and plants at Stokesay (Shropshire) (Babington *et al* 1999), the starry sky images — deeply coloured backgrounds with a few gold stars — at Winchester Castle (Hampshire), Geddington (Northamptonshire) and Guildford (Surrey) (Wood 1983, 397), and the simple geometric patterns at Hadleigh Castle in Essex (Kenyon 1990). Most commonly seen were the red lines of false ashlar blocking, which adorned Marten's Tower, Chepstow Castle (Monmouthshire) (Turner and Johnson 2006, 163), the hall and chapel at Oakhampton Castle (Devon) (Kenyon 1990) and several rooms at Ludgershall Castle (Wiltshire) (Ellis 2000), amongst numerous other buildings.

The painted fragments available from Dryslwyn do not allow any decorative scheme to be clearly established. They show no evidence of drapery, animal or figurative forms, but evidence of patterning — something considerably more colourful and complex than the red-line, ashlar block style — is clearly visible. Fragments of wall-paintings are rare in Welsh medieval secular contexts, with just a few (as yet unpublished) fragments of plaster with red and black painted designs recovered from a pit in Dolforwyn Castle (Powys) (Butler 1994) to set beside the material from Dryslwyn.

It can be suggested that the primary purpose for wall-paintings in secular buildings was not, as at ecclesiastical sites, to support religious ideals through reproducing scenes from the Bible or allegorical tales, but for visual interest; the enjoyment of colours, shapes and the ideas and emotions it generated. However, wall-paintings also served as a sign of wealth and sophistication. The fact that only churches and lordly private apartments were decorated in this manner at this period clearly marks them out as important places, where the affluence of their owner was displayed. The wealth and sophistication of the Dryslwyn Castle wall-paintings was enhanced by the use of strong, bright colours, such as vermilion and azurite, which were expensive to procure. These visual displays of wealth are similar in purpose to extravagant architecture: thus, the creation of the wall-paintings would appear motivated by the same desires as led to the rebuilding of much of the castle in Phase 4a. Whilst many of the wall-paintings may date from that era, the occurrence of wall-painting fragments in Phase 3b clearly indicates that this method of decoration and display of wealth was not confined to one phase of construction, but was also prevalent in the earlier castle.

The occurrence of many of the fragments in Area X indicates that Guest Hall X, at the southern end of the Middle Ward, was highly decorated, probably used for visitors who would be impressed by such a display. The bulk of the other fragments come from Areas B and P. It is unlikely that Gateway Area B was itself painted. However, since the rubble from Round Tower D was deposited primarily in Areas B and P, it appears likely that there were apartments decorated with painted plaster in Round Tower D. Since almost all other examples of painted plaster come from private apartments, it appears likely that the rooms in the upper part of the Round Tower may have acted as apartments for the Lord of the Dryslwyn and his family. The only evidence recovered from Great Hall K/L for wall-painting was the dark brown 'paint' layer on mortar fragments recovered from context (L31), the high iron and manganese content suggesting that the pigment umber was used, although this would have made any room very dark. Virtually no rubble and associated internal plaster surface was recovered from Apartments I/J, since it was lost down the hillside when the castle was demolished. It is likely, however, that a number of these rooms and apartments originally had wall-paintings, although no evidence survives.

6.5 STRUCTURAL IRONWORK
by I H Goodall

The catalogue numbers (preceded by M, and bold if illustrated) refer to the complete catalogue of the ironwork for the whole site (I Goodall 2001).

Constructural ironwork

Iron was used extensively in the construction and fitting out of buildings and a wide range of objects has survived from Dryslwyn Castle. The items of structural ironwork include cramps, timber dogs, staples, wallhooks, hooks and wall anchors.

Cramps [M39–40] were used to secure stones in walls, particularly those that projected or were set at an angle and might slip. They were set into grooves cut between stones, the down-turned ends serving to lock them together, and they were sometimes further secured by being run-in with molten lead. Timber dogs had a variety of uses and the two complete examples, which are unusual in having arms pointing in opposing directions [**M41–43**], must have been used to join or strengthen woodwork. The U-shaped and rectangular staples [M44–45, **M46**, M47–48, **M49–50**] were versatile fittings, the former capable of holding chains and hasps in place, in addition to supporting rings and handles, whilst the latter were particularly suitable for joining timbers together. The wallhooks, either with hooks rising from the end of the shank [**M51–58**] or inset hooks [**M59–60**], were all-purpose hooks whose shanks were driven into joints in masonry or into timber. The hooks that were slighter in form [M61 and **M62**] had angled shanks indicating that they functioned by being driven into wood. Wall anchors [M63 and **M64**] held timber posts or boards against walls through their nailed terminals, whilst wedges [**M65**] could be used to strengthen weak points. The function of the long spike [**M66**] is uncertain, although it might have been embedded in masonry to deter access.

M39   Cramp with down-turned end and incomplete back, the latter retaining much lead caulking. Length 122mm. (86SF15). Context G7 (Phase 6d).

M40   Cramp with down-turned end and incomplete back. Length 155mm. (86SF17). Context G7 (Phase 6d).

M41–43   Timber dogs, all with two opposed arms (Figure 6.12).
M41: Length 60mm. (91SF24). Context G184 (Phase 2d).
M42: Length 125mm. (81SF4). Context K4 (Phase 6c).
M43: Length 112mm. (80SF27). Context K60 (Phase 6d).

M44   U-shaped staple, both arms broken. Length 34mm, Width 30mm. (91SF91). Context G193 (Phase 2c).

M45   U-shaped staple, both arms broken. Length 62mm, Width 25mm. (93SF81). Context A10 (Phase 4d).

M46   U-shaped staple, distorted, one arm broken. Length 110mm. (92SF61). Context B31 (Phase 6c) (Figure 6.12).

M47   Rectangular staple, arm tips out-turned. Length 98mm, Width 62mm. (80SF25). Context K9 (Phase 6c).

M48   Rectangular staple, one arm distorted. Length 108mm, Width 59mm. (84SF18). Context L9 (Phase 6c).

M49   Rectangular staple, one arm broken. Length 115mm. (84SF12). Context L9 (Phase 6c) (Figure 6.12).

M50   Rectangular staple. Length 120mm. (92SF17). Context B16 (Phase 6c) (Figure 6.12).

M51   Wallhook, shank tip lost. Length 114mm. (92SF53). Context B31 (Phase 6c) (Figure 6.12).

M52   Wallhook, complete. Hook distorted. Length 125mm. (92SF35). Context B50 (Phase 6c) (Figure 6.12).

M53   Wallhook, hook and shank broken. Length 112mm. (92SF55). Context B31 (Phase 6c) (Figure 6.12).

M54   Wallhook, shank distorted. Length 144mm. (80SF26). Context K9 (Phase 6c) (Figure 6.12).

M55   Wallhook, complete. Length 191mm. (89SF22). Context O6 (Phase 7).

M56   Wallhook, hook lost. Length 112mm. (81SF6). Context K3 (Phase 7b) (Figure 6.12).

M57   Wallhook, shank distorted, hook tip lost. Length 177mm. (91SF43). Context B6 (Phase 7b) (Figure 6.12).

M58   Wallhook, hook and shank broken. Length 179mm. (84SF92). Unstratified (Figure 6.12).

M59   Wallhook, hook and shank broken. Length 135mm. (92SF64). Context B31 (Phase 6c) (Figure 6.12).

M60   Wallhook, hook and shank broken. Length 121mm. (82SF19). Context M13 (Phase 7a) (Figure 6.12).

M61   Hook with angled shank, hook tip lost. Height 34mm. (85SF56). Context F23 (Phase 3b).

M62   Hook with angled shank, tip lost. Height 48mm. (86SF8). Context I7 (Phase 4a) (Figure 6.12).

M63   Wall anchor, head and shank tip broken. Length 81mm. (92SF81). Context B31 (Phase 6c).

M64   Wall anchor with nailed head. Length 182mm. (82SF11). Context M13 (Phase 7a) (Figure 6.12).

M65   Wedge, burred head. Length 67mm. (83SF35). Context J15 (Phase 4a) (Figure 6.12).

M66   Spike. Length 450mm. (84SF16). Context L9 (Phase 6c) (Figure 6.15).

Hinges and hinge pivots

The hinge pivots are of two basic types, namely those made specifically for setting in masonry and those driven into wood. Their wide variation in size and scantling reflects the range of gates and door hinges they carried. The hinge pivots that were set in masonry [**M67–68**] have parallel-sided shanks with upturned ends, a variant on the usual types of masonry pivot that, with greater utility, more commonly had down-turned or bifurcated ends (I Goodall 1990a, 330, fig 82, nos 558–559; 2000, 148, fig 6.21, nos 62–63). The more numerous hinge pivots, which were driven into wood, all have tapering shanks [M69, **M70–73**, M74, **M75**, M76–77], 4 with clenched tips [M68–71], 3 straight [M72–74] and 3 broken [M75–77]. The clenched tips may have been hammered round door-frames, or have been distorted when they encountered masonry during their installation. None of the shanks shows significant signs of wear from turning hinges, but the height of the guide arms varies considerably, usually in inverse ratio to the bulk of the hinge pivot. The majority of the strap hinges, on the evidence of their size and form, probably come from doors, gates or window shutters, but a few could be from trapdoors or from items of furniture. The hinges that are most likely to have come from these fittings are those with supporting eyes, which are either looped [**M78–88**] or are of a nailed U-shape [**M89–90**]. They are mostly reasonably large, and **M79** retains its hinge pivot. **M91** is unusual, since, although it has a nailed strap, it clearly pivoted rather than swung, a function appropriate to a trapdoor or small cover. Many of these hinges come from Phase 6c contexts and their generally incomplete, as well as occasionally distorted, form suggests damage during the looting of the castle.

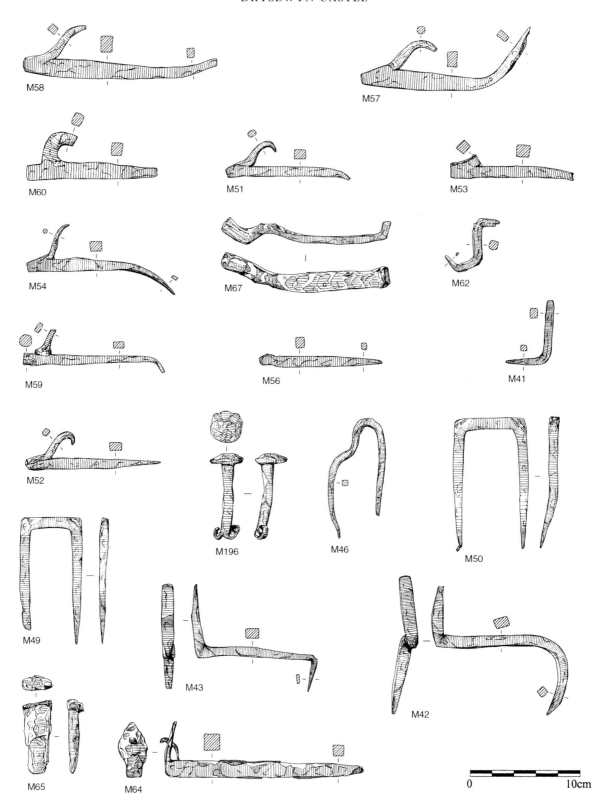

FIGURE 6.12

Structural ironwork

M67   Hinge pivot with distorted shank and up-turned end. Length 155mm. (86SF5). Context G7 (Phase 6d) (Figure 6.12).

M68   Hinge pivot with shank with upturned end. Complete. Length 207mm. (80SF41). Unstratified (Figure 6.13).

M69   Hinge pivot with tapering shank with clenched tip. Complete. Length 148mm. (89SF54). Context B31 (Phase 6c).

M70   Hinge pivot with tapering shank with clenched tip. Complete. Length 201mm. (81SF9). Context K10 (Phase 6c) (Figure 6.14).

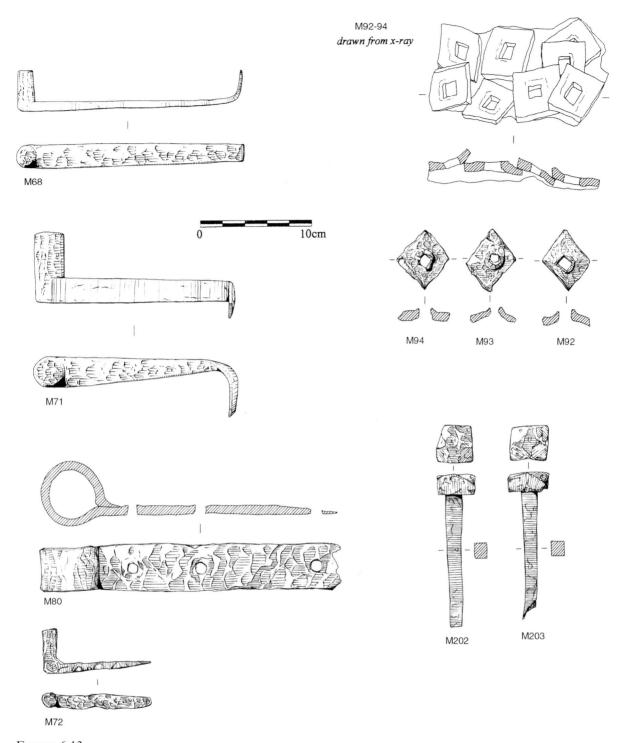

FIGURE 6.13

Structural ironwork

M71 Hinge pivot with tapering shank with clenched tip. Complete. Length 210mm. (92SF80). Context B16 (Phase 6c) (Figure 6.13).

M72 Hinge pivot with tapering shank. Complete. Length 69mm. (85SF32). Context F19 (Phase 3b) (Figure 6.13).

M73 Hinge pivot with tapering shank. Complete. Length 208mm. (80SF19). Context K9 (Phase 6c) (Figure 6.14).

M74 Hinge pivot with tapering shank. Complete. Length 222mm. (80SF20). Context K1 (Phase 7c).

M75 Hinge pivot. Guide-arm distorted, tapering shank broken. Length 122mm. (84SF11). Context L9 (Phase 6c) (Figure 6.14).

M76 Hinge pivot with broken tapering shank. Length 145mm. (84SF13). Context L9 (Phase 6c).

M77 Hinge pivot with broken tapering shank. Length 187mm. (80SF16). Context K9 (Phase 6c).

M78 Hinge. Looped eye, strap broken across shaped terminal. Length 199mm. (84SF21). Context L9 (Phase 6c) (Figure 6.14).

173

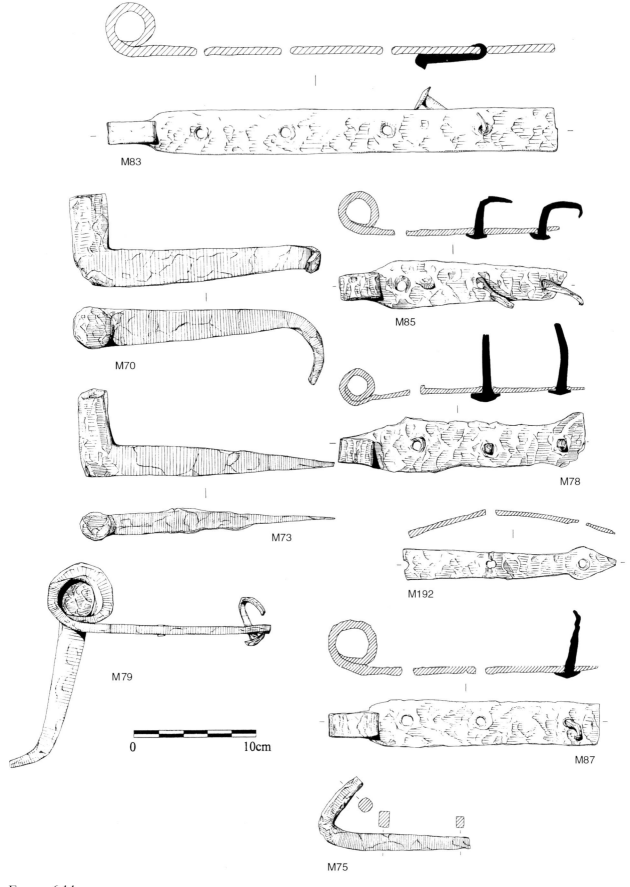

FIGURE 6.14

Structural ironwork: door hinges and hinge pillars

M79 Hinge with looped eye and broken strap, hinge pivot with broken tapering shank. Hinge Length 184mm. (91SF62). Context B16 (Phase 6c) (Figure 6.14).

M80 Hinge. Loped eye, broken strap. Length 271mm. (81SF14). Context K11 (Phase 6c) (Figure 6.13).

M81 Hinge. Looped eye, broken gently tapering strap. Length 361mm. (80SF22). Context K9 (Phase 6c) (Figure 6.15).

M82 Hinge. Looped eye, broken strap. Length 362mm. (92SF42). Context B16 (Phase 6c) (Figure 6.15).

M83 Hinge. Looped eye, broken strap. Length 364mm. (92SF49). Context B31 (Phase 6c) (Figure 6.14).

M84 Hinge. Looped eye, broken strap. Length 179mm. (92SF28). Context B16 (Phase 6c) (Figure 6.16).

M85 Hinge. Looped eye, broken gently tapering strap. Length 182mm. (84SF6). Context L1 (Phase 6d) (Figure 6.14).

M86 Hinge. Looped eye, broken and distorted strap. Length 362mm. (83SF76). Context D1 (Phase 7b) (Figure 6.15).

M87 Hinge. Looped eye, broken strap. Length 219mm. (80SF29). Unstratified (Figure 6.14).

M88 Hinge. Looped eye and gently tapering strap, both broken. Length 621mm. (82SF13). Unstratified (Figure 6.16).

M89 Hinge. Nailed U-shaped eye, broken gently tapering strap. Length 756mm (80SF34). Context K9 (Phase 6c) (Figure 6.16).

M90 Hinge. Nailed U-shaped eye, gently tapering strap with shaped terminal. Length 1077mm. (80SF17). Context K9 (Phase 6c) (Figure 6.16).

M91 Pivoting strap hinge, complete. Length 402mm. (81SF31). Context K12 (Phase 6c) (Figure 6.15).

M190 Hinge, broken strap. Length 360mm. (92SF32). Context B16 (Phase 6c) (Figure 6.16).

M191 Hinge, broken strap. Length 565mm. (92SF31). Context B16 (Phase 6c) (Figure 6.16).

M192 Decorative terminal end from broken strap hinge. Length 360mm. (83SF45). Context B16 (Phase 7b) (Figure 6.14).

Clench bolts and roves

Medieval doors and gates, as well as other fixtures that had to be opened, including window shutters, trapdoors and well covers, had three component parts, namely timber boards, a rear timber frame, and iron fittings. Several of the strap hinges from Dryslwyn Castle retain the nails that held them in place and, in several instances, their shank tips have been bent round or clenched to secure them firmly to the rear frame, whether that was merely a series of individual ledges or a more complex structure (Geddes 1999, 19–30). An alternative method of attachment, used on more substantial doors and gates, but also on well covers and boats, were clench bolts. These are nails with tips clenched over roves, which are, themselves,

small perforated iron plates that served to prevent the nails pulling through the wood. The size and shape of the rove varied according to need and fashion. Long, clasping, claw-like ones were used on rounded ledges in the 11th and 12th centuries, whilst simpler square or lozenge-shaped ones, such as those from Dryslwyn Castle, were used subsequently (Geddes 1999, 28, fig 2.17; Addyman and Goodall 1979, 89–90, figs 9 and 22; Goodall and Geddes 1980, 165, fig 17). The large square-headed bolts [**M202** and **203**] were used for securing substantial structural timbers and ironwork in the 14th-century wooden gatehouse of Gateway Area B.

M92–94 Roves. Ten from a total of 68 flat, lozenge-shaped roves found in a corroded mass. (84SF15, 84SF93, 84SF94). Context D15 (Phase 5d) (Figure 6.13).

M95 Rove. Flat, lozenge-shaped. (84SF1). Context D2 (Phase 6d) (Figure 6.13).

M196 Nail with split point, whose ends are curled back, probably a clench bolt. Length 178mm. (84SF9). Context L1 (Phase 6d) (Figure 6.12).

M202 Large square-headed bolt, broken end. Length 134mm. (92SF83). Context B31 (Phase 6c) (Figure 6.13).

M203 Large square-headed bolt, broken end. Length 125mm. (92SF82). Context B31 (Phase 6c) (Figure 6.13).

Twelve unillustrated roves, all flat and lozenge-shaped, were excavated:

— (86SF50), context J25 (Phase 2d),
— (93SF50), context B100 (Phase 3a),
— (83SF75), context D12 (Phase 4c),
— (84SF31, 84SF32, 84SF47, 84SF48, 84SF49, 84SF75, 84SF76), context D5 (Phase 6c).

6.6 NAILS
by Alice Thompson

Between 1980 and 1993, 6218 nails were excavated from the Inner Ward of Dryslwyn Castle. Most were recovered from the burnt deposits of Phase 6c, from Great Hall K/L and Great Chamber G. They indicate the presence of substantial wooden structures, containing large numbers of nails, still present in Phases 5d–6b, although they derive from construction undertaken in Phases 4 and 5. The overall number of nails recovered by excavation must represent a tiny fraction of the original number: for example, in 1338–39 alone, 20,000 nails were recorded as being used in major castle repairs (Webster 1987, 95; *NLW Add MSS 455D*). As iron was expensive in the Middle Ages — around ten times more expensive than it is today (Steane 1985, 218) — it was used as sparingly as possible. Nails would have been re-used wherever possible and were probably salvaged from ruins, hence the low recovery rate at Dryslwyn and other medieval sites.

Only one widely used typology is available for medieval nails (Figure 6.17), compiled from large

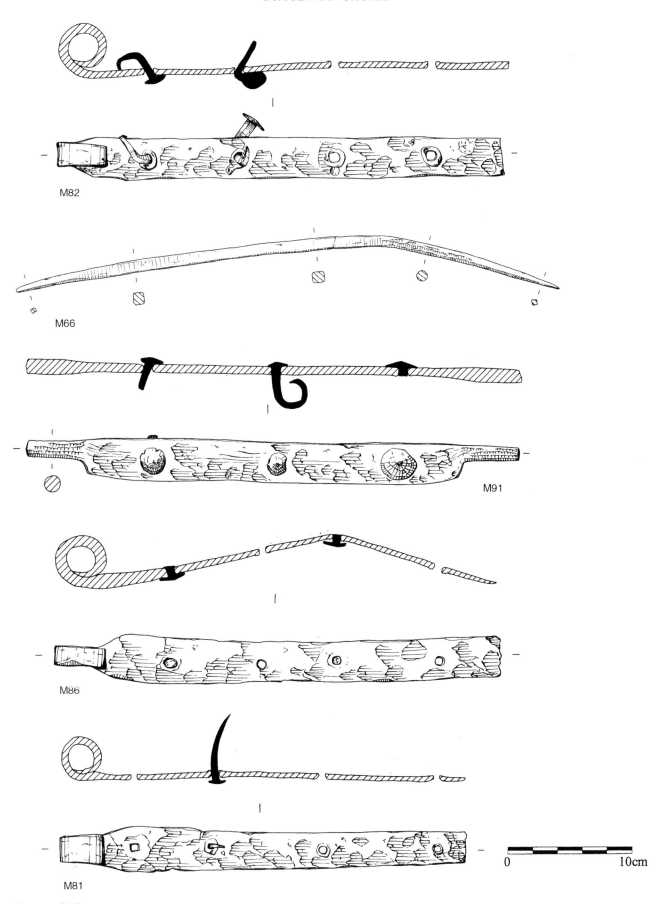

FIGURE 6.15

Structural ironwork: door hinges

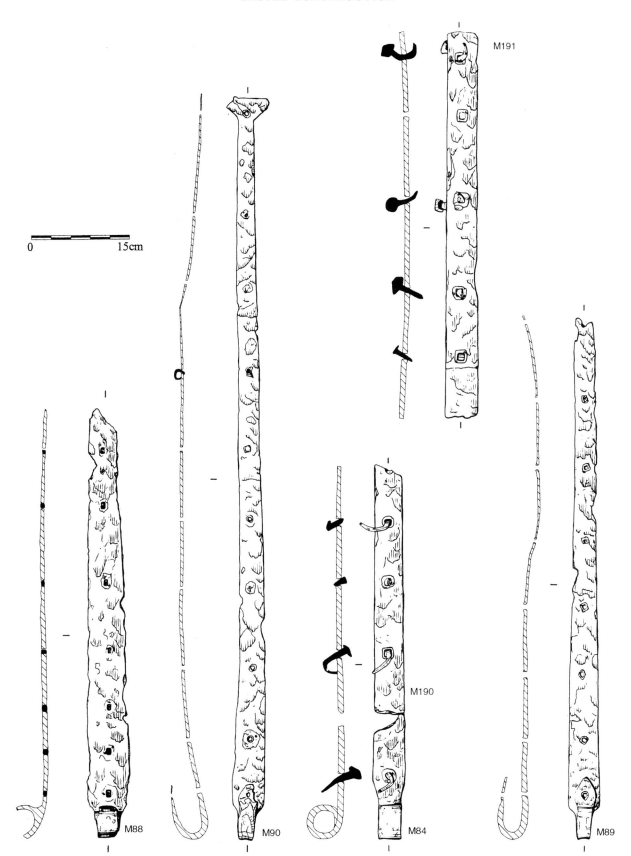

0   15cm

M191

M190

M88

M90

M84

M89

FIGURE 6.16

Structural ironwork: door hinges

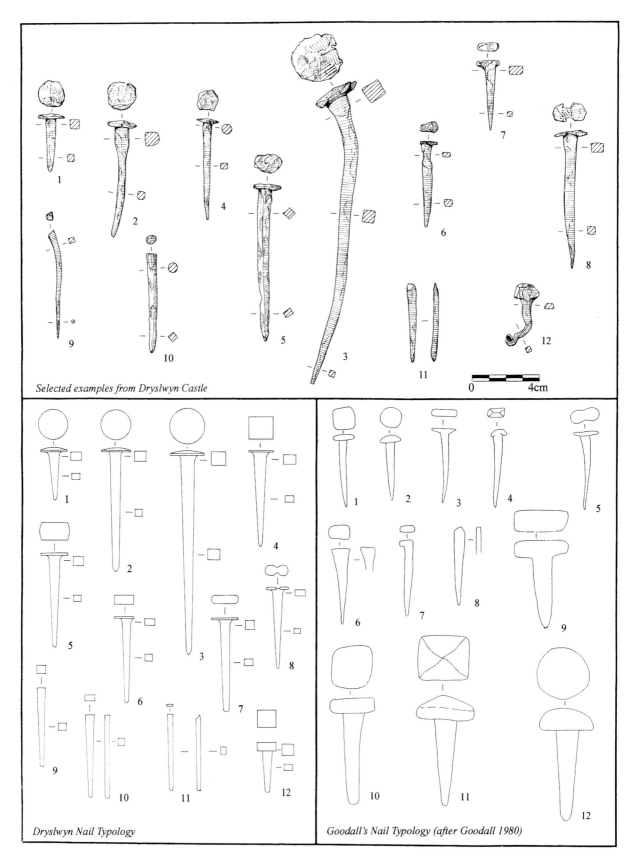

Selected examples from Dryslwyn Castle

0   4cm

Dryslwyn Nail Typology

Goodall's Nail Typology (after Goodall 1980)

FIGURE 6.17

Medieval nail typologies

assemblages at Waltham Abbey (Essex) and Ospringe and Stonar (Kent) (I Goodall 1980). The large number of nails from Dryslwyn cover a relatively short time span, from around 1220 to 1420. Consequently, there is little scope for variation in shape brought about by changes in the technology of nail-making or building and the large variation in head types at Dryslwyn is likely to be a reflection of different functions. A sample of 4468 nails retrieved from the castle were metrically and typologically analysed, in order to define different nail types and to try to identify their various uses. 13 different parameters — context, storage, location, completeness, straightness, corrosion, length, head type, head diameter, head thickness, shank thickness (at top), shank thickness (mid-point) and associated material — were measured or determined. Using multivariate methods (principal components, discriminant and cluster analysis) these nails were separated into 12 main groups (Thompson 1990; 1994) and their generic type illustrated along with Goodall's typology (Figure 6.17). The Dryslwyn typology was formed using a different set of data and parameters from Goodall's, but produces a similar set of head types, indicating both the robustness of the nail type classifications and the meaningful nature of the Dryslwyn Castle nail categories.

Dryslwyn Castle Nail Types

Type 1

Flat, round-headed nails with a large head in relation to shank length (Goodall Type 2). Short shank (less than 40mm, but typically around 15mm) with rather blunt tip (Figure 6.17). Shank is almost square in section and never bent. These nails were never associated with slate, but some had mineralised wood preserved on their shanks. Since the shanks are so short, however, these nails cannot have joined large structural timbers. It is most likely that the head was ornamental and that they are door studs. This type does not occur in large numbers on contemporary sites, presumably because doors were salvaged before the site was destroyed or fell into disuse. When they are found, the head can either be flat or domed. The drawn example from Sandal Castle is 32mm long, with a head diameter of 16mm (Mayes and Butler 1983, 279–280); these are typical dimensions for a Dryslwyn Type 1 nail. It is described as a 'tack nail', typically having a diameter greater than half the length of the shank, and used for fastening battens or window casements. Other examples with flat heads have been found at King's Lynn (Norfolk) (Clarke and Carter 1977, 297–298), St Catherine's Hill, Winchester (Hampshire) (Hawkes *et al* 1930, 245–247) and St Peter's Street, Northampton (Northamptonshire) (Williams 1979, 65–66), but were not associated with any particular building operation. Examples from Carmarthen

Greyfriars (Carmarthenshire) (Brennan's Type A1) were used for building and coffin construction (Brennan 1997). They are 18–40mm long, with heads between 14 and 18mm in diameter. Domed examples are known from Bramber Castle (West Sussex) (Barton and Holden 1978, 65–66) and Ospringe (Kent) (Smith 1979, 148–152), where they are found in relatively small numbers. As the head seems ornamental, it is probable they were also decoration for doors.

Type 2

Flat round or nearly square head, with a shank of medium length (40–99mm) (Figure 6.17). The tip has a sharper point than Type 1. Perhaps known as 'clouts', 'strakes', 'fixed nails', 'middelspyking', 'bragges', 'gaddes', 'mops', and 'bellows'. When the head is pyramidal, it is known as a 'rose nail'. The shorter nails in this group may be boardnails. These nails are never directly attached to slate, but have been found with wood impressions. According to Salzman (1952), 'clout' nails are one of the commonest all-purpose nails. Boardnails were used for the roofs of the granary and bakehouse at the castle, and also for the granary walls, which were wooden. It seems very likely that one use for the Type 2 nail was in roofing, for nailing battens to rafters. Since one Type 2 nail was found attached to lead, probably from the roof of Round Tower D, a further use for Type 2 nails may be attaching lead roofing sheets.

Many Type 2 nails were also used on doors, as they are commonly clenched and their lengths suggest that the doors were at least 55mm thick. It is likely that they are the 'fixed nails' mentioned in building records for the granary and bakehouse (Webster 1987, 92). The term 'fixed nail' probably refers to the fact that they were normally clenched. Some of these nails would have passed through the straps of hinges, in addition to the two layers of the door. They are not only clenched at one end, but also have a characteristic curved shank. Examples may be seen in Figures 6.14–6.16.

The granary built at Dryslwyn in 1306 used 200 'spikenails' for the doors. These are probably longer Type 2 nails, which may often have been used clenched in association with roves. Just one rove was found associated with a Type 2 nail, but a cluster of roves was found in Round Tower D, where they had probably been stored in a bag. Other uses for spikenails are given in repairs of 1338–39, when '200 nails called spykynges' were bought 'for fastening the aforesaid gutters and large posts and joists' (*NLW Add MSS 455D*). It seems, therefore, that the Dryslwyn Type 2 is an all-purpose nail, commonly used in roofing, doors and guttering, function depending on size.

Type 2 nails seem to be the most common at contemporary sites. Clenched nails, probably from doors, were found at King's Lynn (Norfolk) measuring 40–60mm long (Clarke and Carter 1977, 297–298); a stud from Sandal Castle (South Yorkshire), 80mm long with a head diameter of 36mm, was said to have come from a door (Mayes and Butler 1983, 279–280); a door stud from Bordersley Abbey (Worcestershire) was 76mm long (Rahtz and Hirst 1976, 191–198); from Basing House (Hampshire) came a door stud that was 96mm long with a 44mm diameter head; whilst an identical nail, called a 'strake' and used for cartwheels, was found at Riplingham (East Yorkshire) (Moorhouse 1971, 49–51).

Type 3

Flat, round head with a long shank (100+mm) and pointed tip. Perhaps a 'great spyking'. 'Great spyk-ings' were used for fixing rafters at St. Paul's Cathedral (London) in 1454 (Salzman 1952, 305) and in the 1338–39 repairs at Dryslwyn, where 'spykynges' were used for joining large posts and joists (*NLW Add MSS 455D*). 'Spykings' were also used for nailing the feet of rafters to the eaves board. At Pleshey Castle (Essex), nails of this type (80–220mm long) were interpreted as gate nails (I Goodall 1977). This type of nail corre-sponds to Brennan's Type A nail from Carmarthen Greyfriars (Carmarthenshire) and was used for building and coffin construction (Brennan 1997). The *Oxford English Dictionary* defines a 'spike nail' as 70–100mm long, suggesting there is some overlap between Type 2 and Type 3 nails. It is nevertheless clear that, in general, 'spykings' were longer than boardnails and shorter than 'great spykings' or gate nails.

Type 4

Square or plano-convex head, medium length, pointed tip (Goodall Type 1). Longer examples may be 'clouts', but the use of these nails is uncertain. Type 4 nails from Dryslwyn seem to be unusual in being of medium length, with heads approximately 15 by 15mm. The other sites mentioned above tend to have either very long versions, with large, thick, or pyramidal heads (probably 'spike nails' for doors), or very short nails (tacks) with square heads. Only at St Peter's Street in Northampton (Northamptonshire) is this type found in comparable size, usually 50–60mm long, with heads longer than 10mm (Williams 1979, 65–66). It appears likely that this is an ornamental type of nail. To make a plano-convex head, it is necessary to forge the head in a heading iron with countersunk head shapes; this would be a deliberate shape, more regular than the usual circular heads, which appear to have been made by beating down the end of the shank onto a flat surface (the 'bore'), giving irregularly formed heads.

Type 5

Rectangular or elongated recto-oval head. Shank of medium length with pointed tip. One of the most corroded types of nail found at Dryslwyn. These nails

are rarely found elsewhere. Two from Sandal Castle (South Yorkshire), measuring 52mm and 72+mm, are described as general carpentry nails (Mayes and Butler 1983, 279–280). A range came from St Peter's Street in Northampton (Northamptonshire), although the most common type was 50–60mm long, with a head less than 10mm long (Williams 1979, 65–66). As with Type 4, the head shape seems deliberate and decorative, so possibly these nails were also used on doors.

Type 6

Rectangular head, attached to the shank to give an L-shaped profile. Medium length, with a pointed tip (Goodall Type 7). Use unknown. Very few compara-ble nails were found. One came from Bramber Castle (West Sussex), 80mm long with a head 12 × 8mm (Barton and Holden 1978, 65–66). This is much longer than the average Type 6, which is relatively uniform in length, with a small standard deviation. The other nail, from Ospringe (Kent), was described as a 'brad', whose head expanded in the same direction as the shank (Smith 1979, 148–152). However, most of the Drysl-wyn Type 6 nails seem to have a head that is wider than the top of the shank, and were probably used for a different purpose. These nails tended to be concen-trated in Great Hall K/L, in particular in Area K, where 116 (52% of the total) were found. This head shape would appear ideally suited to hanging objects, such as slates. The single side head projection makes it easier to hang and remove slates.

Type 7

Rectangular head, curved at ends (Goodall Type 3). Flat. Shank is medium length, rectangular in section all the way down. The tip is pointed. One of the rusti-est types at Dryslwyn. Only one example has been noted, from Basing House (Hampshire), which is 44mm long with a rather long head, measuring 28 by 12mm (Moorhouse 1971, 49–51). No nails of this sort are described in the literature on medieval nails. At Dryslwyn, this type was associated with slate and was probably used for hanging slates on laths. It is possible that this is a style unique to Wales.

Type 8

Flat, figure-of-eight head (Goodall Type 5). Medium length shank, rectangular in section at the top, becom-ing square mid-way down. The tip is pointed. Perhaps a 'thacknail', 'duble thacknail' or 'spondyngnail?'. At Dryslwyn, this type was found associated with slate, accounting for 38% of all nails attached to slate. It is not widely found at other medieval sites. A few isolated examples came from Waltham Abbey (Essex) (Goodall's Type 5), although only one length was given, of 45+mm for the shank. At Ospringe (Kent), 28 nails of this type were found from a total of 843, most of which were mixed with roof tiles and building ironwork; shank lengths were 29–56mm and head lengths 7–13mm (Smith 1979, 148–152), which would agree with the Dryslwyn type. Of the 450 nails from St Catherine's Hill, Winchester (Hampshire), 100 belonged to this type and were found associated with heaps of broken roofing slate; both short (36mm) and long (85mm) examples were present (Hawkes *et al* 1930, 245–247). At Dryslwyn, by contrast, most of these nails were around 46mm in length. This nail head type also corresponds with Brennan's Type B nails from Carmarthen Greyfriars (Carmarthenshire), which were recovered from building and grave contexts (Brennan 1997).

There is no doubt that Type 8 nails were used for hanging slate, and at Dryslwyn this was probably their sole function. However, it is difficult to tell what advantage a figure-of-eight head would have over a rectangular head of the same dimensions. It is perhaps just a reflection of the technology of nail-making, rather than forming a rectangular head in a counter-sunk die: the head may have been quickly formed by two swift blows to the top of the shank, giving this characteristic shape.

Types 9, 10 and 11

All these nails are headless, of medium length with pointed tips. Types 10 and 11 tend to be rectangular in section under the head, becoming squarer in section further down. Type 9 tends to be square in section all the way down and its length has a slightly higher standard. Type 10 (Goodall Type 6) has a rectangular top, often at an incline to the line of the shank, as if the top has been cut off at an angle to make the flat head. Sometimes the head can have small 'ears' or a lip to one side, probably due to deformation in use. Type 11 is characterised by a pinched head; it corresponds to Goodall's Type 8.

They are probably all lathnails; the slight differences in shape are probably due to different methods of manufacture. They are also known as 'brodd', 'prig', 'sprig', or 'brads'. Since these nails had only to attach the thin laths to the battens, they would not have to be very strong, so heads would be unnecessary. Also, if the laths were covered by large-headed nails, it would be more awkward to nail down slates to the laths. Six lathnails, from the burnt castle destruction deposits in Gateway Area B, were found with very well preserved wood covering the upper half of the nail. On all six, the wood was consistently 15mm thick, suggesting that the laths attached to the battens were around the same thickness. As the lathnails were all around 46mm long, this suggests that the battens on the roof were at least 30mm thick. Another two lathnails were found side-by-side in the same piece of wood, only 10mm apart.

The majority of lathnails from Dryslwyn are straight, but some are consistently bent at the same angle, suggesting that they were nailed through the lath at an angle into the rafter and bent flat. At Austin Friars, Leicester (Leicestershire), wedge-shaped headless nails (which must be lathnails) were found in association with laths (Mellor and Pearce 1981). Similar nails came from St Peter's Street in Northampton (Northamptonshire), described as 'minimal' and having a shaft less then 3mm broad, which were used for panelling (Williams 1979, 65–66). Most of these nails were 3–5mm broad, like the Dryslwyn nails, and were distributed evenly between the houses. In addition to nailing laths, this type of nail was almost certainly used to nail planks onto flooring joists. The elongated head form made the nail capable of being hammered into the wood grain, so lying flat with the surface of the plank.

According to Salzman (1952, 310), 'of the various nails connected with roofing, lathnails were the commonest, occurring in the majority of accounts'. As early as 1208, 21,000 'nails for laths' were bought for repairs at Farnham (Surrey) (Salzman 1952, 310). This is comparable with the granary built at Dryslwyn in 1306, where 4000 lathnails and 860 boardnails were used for the roof (Webster 1987, 92–94). In this entry in the Pipe Rolls, lathnails were not listed for any other purpose. The granary built at this time also had lathnails in the roof, outnumbering the boardnails.

'Brodd' were by far the most numerous type of nail bought for repairs to York Castle in 1327, while of the 40,000 nails bought for Canterbury Cathedral in 1273, 30,000 were 'prig' or lathnails (Salzman 1952, 304). Despite the large numbers of lathnails recorded and used, they are rarely recovered in quantity from sites and are seldom the most common type; this was consistently found to be a round-headed type, such as Type 2. No lathnails were found at St Catherine's Hill in Winchester, despite the fact that 450 nails were found associated with roofing, and the only nail that could have been used in place of lathnails was a round-headed variety of medium length, which formed the prevalent class (Hawkes *et al* 1930, 245–247). The relative absence of lathnails cannot be easily explained by variations in the type of roofing material, as laths were always used for supporting thatch, tiles, shingles, slate or lead. They may not have been retained and reported by some excavators, who could easily have assumed them to be broken nail shanks. Without a head, they are difficult to retrieve from wooden rafters and reuse.

Type 12

These miscellaneous nails vary considerably in length and include a small number with a dice-shaped head ('knopnayls'), which may have been used for nailing tapestry rails. It is also possible, however, that some of the nails identified as 'knopnayls' were really horseshoe nails. They were around the same length as Goodall's Type B horseshoe nail, which had a similar head and was in use in the 13th and 14th centuries.

Perhaps surprisingly, few decorative nail heads were found: only one chamfered nail and one possible rose nail were recovered. Other site reports show that nails with tinned heads and pyramidal or faceted heads were relatively common, but none have been found at Dryslwyn. Tinned heads were also used on doors, but not, it seems, at Dryslwyn. This may have been a late medieval fashion and little 14th- or 15th-century material was recovered from the castle.

Discussion

The distribution of nail types by site area is recorded in Figure 6.18. The large number of nails deposited in the burning destruction Phase 6c suggests that Great Hall K/L, Great Chamber G and Chapel H were most probably roofed in slate, whilst most other areas were open in the final phase of castle occupation. The roofed areas have a similar distribution of nail types; lathnails (Type 10) are consistently the most common, accompanied by relatively large numbers of Types 6, 7 and 8 ('slate' nails). Round Tower D had far fewer 'slate' nails (Types 6, 7 and 8) than the slate-roofed Great Hall K/L and Great Chamber G. If Type 2 nails are, as suggested, 'clouts', then one of their uses was to fasten lead roofing to laths (Salzman 1952, 311). The presence of large numbers of Type 2 nails in Round Tower D and the presence of some examples of Type 2 nails embedded in lead would appear to indicate that the Round Tower was roofed in lead, whilst finds of some Type 10 lathnails and some Type 7 and 8 'slate' nails, especially in Gateway Area B, suggests that the Phase 5c timber-framed guardhouse had a slate roof.

Numbers of the large Type 3 nails ('great spykings') in Round Tower D and Great Hall K/L indicate the presence of substantial timberwork, probably associated with the presence of several wooden floors and roofing timbers. The paucity of this nail type from Great Chamber G suggests that the wooden first floor had almost certainly been removed before burning. An attempt to use a 3D plot of nail positions in the burnt deposits of Great Hall K/L to indicate the presence and pattern of any timber-framing — a technique also used at Caergwrle (Flintshire) (Manley 1994, 117–118) — failed to reveal any distributions that could be related to the form of any structural timber (Caple 1981).

Almost all of the Drylswyn nails were formed from two standard sizes of iron bar (the raw material for nail manufacture): most are 5 by 4mm in cross-section (before alteration, such as the flattening of the upper half of Type 10), whilst larger nails, such as 'great spykings', are typically 7 by 5mm in section. The existence of a series of standardised nail forms and standard dimensions of iron bar suggests either local manufacture to a well-known set of standards, or more organised manufacture by specialist nailsmiths, possibly regulated by guilds, working in towns or production centres, such as the Forest of Dean (Gloucestershire). The absence of tinned or faceted heads may be indicative of a relatively functional series of buildings.

	Area A	Area B	Area C	Area D	Area E	Area F	Area G	Area H	Area I	Area J	Area K	Area L	Area M	Area O	Area P	Area X	Area Y	Area Z	Total
Numbers																			
Type 1	2	56	2	7		10	43	24		4	59	53	52	139	24	11	2	1	489
Type 2		32	4	66	1	1	45	19	2	3	72	94	20	40	7		4		410
Type 3			1	5			1			1	1	11	2						22
Type 4		6	4	7		14	22	7		7	43	27	21	10		1			169
Type 5		7	4	1		4	9	5		1	33	7	8	5					84
Type 6		10	3	2		1	32	7			116	22	11	16	1		2		223
Type 7		34	4	18		9	123	44		4	106	104	19	51	7	2	6		531
Type 8		45	4	14		9	153	49	2	6	261	75	29	51	2	1	7	1	709
Type 9		12	5	8		5	98	4		10	52	30	6	41	6	2	5		284
Type 10		48	8	9	1	6	313	103	4	6	306	180	32	77	6	4	5	1	1109
Type 11		5		1			10	9		2	33	27	2	4					93
Type 12		3					1	1			3	1		5	1				15
Other		2	1		1		7	2			14	8	1	15	2				53
Total	2	260	40	138	3	59	857	274	8	44	1099	639	203	454	56	21	31	3	4191

	Area A	Area B	Area C	Area D	Area E	Area F	Area G	Area H	Area I	Area J	Area K	Area L	Area M	Area O	Area P	Area X	Area Y	Area Z	Total
Percentages																			
Type 1	100	22	5	5	0	17	5	9		9	5	8	26	31	43	52	6	33	12
Type 2		12	10	48	33	2	5	7	25	7	7	15	10	9	13		13		10
Type 3			3	4			0			2	0	2	1						1
Type 4		2	10	5		24	3	3		16	4	4	10	2		5			4
Type 5		3	10	1		7	1	2		2	3	1	4	1					2
Type 6		4	8	1		2	4	3			11	3	5	4	2		6		5
Type 7		13	10	13		15	14	16		9	10	16	9	11	13	10	19		13
Type 8		17	10	10		15	18	18	25	14	24	12	14	11	4	5	23	33	17
Type 9		5	13	6		8	11	1		23	5	5	3	9	11	10	16		7
Type 10		18	20	7	33	10	37	38	50	14	28	28	16	17	11	19	16	33	26
Type 11		2		1			1	3		5	3	4	1	1					2
Type 12		1					0	0			0	0		1	2				0
Other		1	3		33		1	1		1	1	1	0	3	4				1
Total	100	100	100	100	100	100	100	100	100	100	100	100	100	100	100	100	100	100	100

FIGURE 6.18

Distribution of nails by type and area

6.7 WINDOW GLASS
by Rachel Tyson

Five fragments of window glass were found in Prison M, next to Great Hall K/L (G3–7), whilst another burnt piece was found in Round Tower D (G2). Secular buildings were glazed from the late 12th or early 13th century onwards. One of the earliest examples is glass from the fill of the round tower at Ascot Doilly Castle (Oxfordshire), which was demolished around 1200 (Charleston 1984, 39). The large stained glass heraldic window recovered from Carmarthen Greyfriars (Carmarthenshire), dated stylistically to 1250–80 (James 1997; Hunter 1987), indicates that substantial stained glass windows were being commissioned and installed by the mid 13th century in the Tywi valley. The presence of two fragments of window glass from Castell-y-Bere (Gwynedd) (Butler 1974, 91) may suggest that there was some glazing in a few Welsh castles by the mid–late 13th century, although the insertion of the glass during the brief English Garrison period of occupation (1287–1294) cannot be discounted.

Although the window glass found at Dryslwyn Castle was recovered from Phase 6 and 7 contexts, it almost certainly derives from windows of 13th- or 14th-century date, which were dismantled during the looting and destruction of the castle. The occurrence of the glass in two locations implies that glazed windows once existed in Round Tower D and on the north side of Great Hall K/L. Given the large sums of money spent in Phase 4a to redevelop the castle, it seems likely that there was also glass in the lancet windows of Chapel H, the windows along the south side of Apartments I/J and possibly also the north side of Great Chamber G by the late 13th century.

G2   Possible fragment of burnt window glass. Layers of greenish glass visible in the centre. Surfaces covered by opaque reddish-beige weathering / burning. Original thickness c3–4mm. Maximum length 35mm, maximum width 27mm. Context D20 (Phase 6d). Not illustrated.

G3–7 Five fragments of flat window glass. Colourless glass with a greenish tinge. Thick opaque grey pitted weathering layers, unstable and crumbly. Thickness 3mm. Grozed edges. From a decorated leaded window with different shaped quarries. Context M13 (Phase 7a). Not illustrated.
3: Grozed along two edges at an angle less than 90°. Maximum length 35mm, maximum width 23mm.
4: Possibly grozed along a circular edge. Maximum length 28mm, maximum width 28mm.
5: Grozed along one straight edge. Maximum length 47mm, maximum width 22mm.
6: Grozed along one, or possibly two edges at an angle greater than 90°. Maximum length 34mm, maximum width 25mm.

7

SIEGE AND WARFARE

The excavation of Dryslwyn Castle produced physical evidence of a specific historic event, the siege of 1287. This is an event for which there is also considerable detailed documentary evidence. We have taken the opportunity afforded by this publication to draw together the various strands of evidence into a single chapter. This provides a uniquely detailed account of the longest siege of any Welsh castle, and marked the point at which Dryslwyn ceased to be the castle of a Welsh lord and became a garrison of the English Crown.

7.1 HISTORY OF THE REVOLT AND SIEGE (1287–97)
by Chris Phillpotts and Chris Caple

The siege of Dryslwyn Castle in 1287 is a richly documented and discrete series of events. Historical source material for the siege falls into two main categories: financial accounts of the English government relating to payments for the campaign of 1287, held at the Public Record Office, and contemporary chronicle entries (Phillpotts 2001a). From a combination of these sources, a sequence of events at the siege can be established (Phillpotts 2001b).

The revolt of Rhys ap Maredudd and the siege of Dryslwyn received the attention of several historians of Wales in the last century. Morris (1901) wrote a military account of the campaign, whilst Evans provided a narrative in the local context of Carmarthenshire (Lloyd 1935–39, i 203–207). Smith (1965, 151–163), meanwhile, investigated the origins of the revolt, whilst Griffiths (1966, 121–143; reprinted as Griffiths 1994, 67–83) reviewed its course and significance, and Taylor (1976) identified one of the more important leaders of the Anglo-Welsh army, the Savoyard Jean de Bevillard. Other historians have given briefer accounts, among them Powicke (1962, 438–440) and Warner (1968, 157), who concentrated

on the use of the siege engine. None, however, made full use of the documentation available to construct a detailed narrative of the siege and, of course, none had the benefit of accompanying archaeological evidence.

The revolt begins (8–14 June 1287)

Several chroniclers drew attention to the immediate cause of the revolt, the quarrel between Rhys and Robert de Tibetot, Edward I's justiciar of west Wales, over English and Welsh jurisdictions. After a series of legal actions (Section 2.1), Rhys refused to appear in the shire court at Carmarthen and Tibetot began the procedure to outlaw him. In response, Rhys sent a letter to King Edward, who was at Bordeaux, detailing his complaints about Tibetot. Edward replied on 15 April, ordering a suspension of the case for two months whilst its process was investigated (Lloyd 1935, i 204; Smith 1965, 157–159, 162–163; Griffiths 1966, 127–128; Edwards 1935, 167; *AC*, 109; *Dunstable Annals*, 338; *HC*, f32; *HAC*, f46v; *Worcester Annals*, 493; *Wroxham Continuation*, 306). Edward's cousin Edmund, Earl of Cornwall, who was regent in Edward's absence, sent three justices to Carmarthen to make inquiries; they were Ralph de Hengham, John de Cobham and Roger de Burghill (Edwards 1935). Tibetot subsequently informed Earl Edmund early in May that he would travel to London to discuss the case with him and the Bishop of Ely (Edwards 1935, 166–167; *CCRV*, 306). The three justices attended the Carmarthen County Court on 5 May, but again Rhys did not appear, nor was any error in Tibetot's legal processes uncovered (Smith 1965).

Rhys did not await the outcome of these inquiries and discussions. On 8 June 1287, Rhys ap Maredudd began open war against the English Crown. Taking the Carmarthenshire castles of Dinefwr, Carreg Cennen and Llandovery, which were held by the Crown, he slaughtered their garrisons and raided as far as Swansea, the commote of Ystlwyf, Llanbadarn and over the border into the lordship of Brecon, burning the suburbs of Carmarthen (Morris 1901, 206; Lloyd 1935, i 204–205; Griffiths 1966, 129; *AC*, 109; *Worcester Annals*, 493; *St Albans Chronicle*, 43). The bloody violence of his activities was deplored by the English chroniclers (*Waverley Annals*, 404; *Wykes*, 310; *FH*, 66; *HAC*, f46v), causing considerable alarm amongst the Marcher lords, English authorities and both urban and rural populations of west Wales. There is, however, no evidence of any great rising of the native Welsh population to follow Rhys.

There is little record of any armed conflict during July. Marcher lords and Crown officers may have moved to improve the defences of castles and towns against possible attack by Rhys: certainly, repairs are recorded at Llanbadarn (Ceredigion) and Castell-y-Bere (Gwynedd) (Griffiths 1966). Morris (1901, 207–208) suggested that Robert de Tibetot successfully organised the defence of Cardiganshire against any further incursions, whilst John Giffard is recorded as defending Builth and local forces began to patrol areas such as the Aeron valley and South Cardiganshire to suppress local support (Griffiths 1994). Alternatively, Rhys may have ceased his warlike activity, perhaps because he now held the whole of Cantref Mawr and Cantref Bychan, which he controlled from the family seat at Dinefwr Castle. This may have been the limited aim of his revolt.

In the campaign that followed, none of the ground gained by Rhys was held. The three castles appear to have been retaken by the Anglo-Welsh forces without difficulty, although Wykes' account implies that a formal siege was laid to Dinefwr, where Rhys' wife (and perhaps his family) may have been staying (Morris 1901, 212; *AC*, 110; *Wykes*, 310). The zone of Rhys' operations was quickly contained, and the chroniclers portray him as retreating to the woods. Rhys' only clearly recorded resistance was at his castle of Dryslwyn.

Gathering the Anglo-Welsh army (14 June–8 August 1287)

Edmund, Earl of Cornwall, responded to the news of the revolt with swift containment measures and, as soon as practicable, with overwhelming force. Presumably, he wished to avoid the rebellion spreading across Wales in a repeat of the events of 1282. Should the revolt get out of hand, he feared the wrath of Edward more than the actions of Rhys ap Maredudd.

On 24 and 25 June, Edmund issued orders to assemble the levies of Cheshire, Derbyshire, Gloucestershire, Herefordshire, Nottinghamshire, Shropshire and Staffordshire, 2600 men in all, to go to Wales. He also attempted to cut off supplies to the west Welsh

rebels by closing the markets of the Marches and border counties to trade with Wales. Orders were issued to confiscate the lands of Rhys ap Maredudd and all the territory he had seized and, on 5 July, a price of £100 was put on his head (*CCRV*, 306–307). These were but merely preliminary measures, however. On 14 June, Edmund had summoned the leading earls and barons of England to join him with arms and horses in an armed council at Gloucester. Here, on 16 July, and again at Hereford, on 23 July, orders were issued for the assembly of forces to proceed to Wales to combat Rhys and his rebels (Morris 1901, 206–207; Griffiths 1966, 130; Taylor 1985a, 211; *CCRV*, 307–308, 311–314).

Earl Edmund funded the expedition through several companies of Italian bankers based in London, who made loans to the Crown and advanced money against the collection of forthcoming revenues, including a hundred marks from the farm of London and £500 from the tallage of the Jews, the amounts totalling more than £7000. The bankers continued to be fully involved in the payments made to the expedition. They transported money to Wales and delivered it to the paymasters of the component parts of the Anglo-Welsh army. The loans appear to have been repaid to the Italians from wool customs within two years (*CCRV*, 309–311, 316; PRO C62/64 m4; E101/4/15, 16, 17; E372/132 m1-1d). This practice of funding the army directly or indirectly from the royal purse continued that followed by Edward in the wars of 1276–77 and 1282–83 against Llywelyn ap Gruffudd. The use of paid troops, who would stay and fight for the whole campaign, as opposed to using the feudal levy, who left after their statutory period of service, had proved successful before (Morris 1901) and marks the first emergence of a professional 'British' army.

The majority of the troops for the expedition were drawn from different districts of Wales. A substantial force came from Gwynedd, under the command of Jean de Bevillard; 2000 foot-soldiers and 20 horsemen were summoned here. Robert de Tibetot brought the men of Cardiganshire (400) and assembled 1000 foot-soldiers from the commotes of Carmarthenshire. The leaders of these men included former followers of Rhys ap Maredudd, such as Goronwy Goch, who had once been steward of Dryslwyn Castle. 1000 more came from Powys; 500 from Cynllaith, Nanheudwy and Radnor; 810 from Cemaes and Emlyn; 200 from Gwidigada; 100 from Elfed; 60 from Amgoed and Peuliniog; and 200 from Dyffryn Clwyd, Bromfield, Maelor Saesneg, Rhos and Rhufoniog, Tegeingl and Yale. Other troops came from the Marcher lordships of south and east Wales, including Caus (200), Ellesmere (240), Llanstephan (140), Montgomery (200) and the Strange and Fitzwarin lordships (200), in addition to Ewyas Lacy, Monmouth, St Briavels and Three Castles. The border counties produced contingents from Cheshire (1200); Herefordshire (1280), Stafford-shire and Shropshire (600). A body of 1000 troops was summoned from Derbyshire and Nottingham-shire, of which only 340 arrived. Specialist support was added by groups of crossbowmen from Bristol (26) and London (20) (Morris 1901, 208–209; Smith 1965, 161; Griffiths 1966, 132; Taylor 1985a, 211; *CCRV*, 312–314; PRO C62/64 m4; E101/4/15, 16 m1, 17m1, 19m2; E372/132 m1d).

The mounted element of the army was formed of the earls, barons and their followers and the mounted leaders of the troops of foot-soldiers, who were issued with letters of protection at Gloucester, Hereford and Westminster to cover the period of their service. Roughly 230 individuals can be identified or counted (*CPR 1281–92*, 271–275) and the total number of the horsemen is estimated at about 600, based on the payments made for them (Morris 1901, 210, 212; *CCRV*, 271–275). The total number of troops who arrived to besiege Dryslwyn Castle has been estimated at 10,600; but this, in fact, is a slight under-estimate as, accepting the figure of 600 for the mounted troops, there were about 11,400 men paid at Dryslwyn on 16 and 17 August. The vast majority of these men came from the Welsh Marches and would probably have spoken Welsh as their mother tongue. Thereafter, the total number fluctuated, but generally declined during the course of the siege.

These contingents of troops advanced into south Wales along a number of converging routes. Earl Edmund assembled his forces at Hereford on 24 July and marched to Carmarthen, via Usk, Newport, Cowbridge and Glamorgan, arriving on 8 August (Morris 1901, 208; Griffiths 1966, 131–132; PRO E101/4/17 mm1, 2). Reginald de Grey started from Chester on 3 August and marched via Montgomery and Llanbadarn, reaching Carmarthen on 14 August (Morris 1901, 209; Griffiths 1966, 131; PRO E101/4/15, 16 mm1, 2). Bevillard brought the north Welsh group to Llanbadarn by 9 August, reaching Carmarthen on the 15th (Morris 1901, 209; Griffiths 1966, 131; PRO E101/4/16 m4). The Earl of Gloucester gathered a large force, 12,500 strong. This did not join the other contingents at Carmarthen, but marched from Morlais through the lordship of Brecon, cutting roads through the forests and pacifying the country (Griffiths 1966, 132; PRO E101/4/18). The Earl of Hereford also appears to have had a force of his own tenants and been engaged in fighting the forces of Rhys, or guarding against them, in the area of Llandovery and Carreg Cennan. The lack of documentation for his force limits our knowledge of the immediate local military response to Rhys' rebellion, since the Earl of Hereford's force may have been active throughout June and July. The *Dunstable Annals* (338–339) name the Bishop of Ely, the Prior of the English Hospitallers and the Earl of Gloucester as the leaders of the English army. In reality, Edmund, Earl of Cornwall, commanded the army: his presence is attested at

Dryslwyn by unpublished correspondence (unrelated to Wales), which was issued by the Earl of Cornwall at Dryslwyn on 26 and 29 August 1287 (PRO SC1/25/52, 67 and 68). The granting of the mill (and manor) of Cilsan to Madoc ap Arauder by Earl Edmund (Griffiths 1966; Phillpotts 2001c), presum-ably for services rendered during the siege or revolt, occurred at this time. The Bishop of Ely, Treasurer of England, was also present, indicating that, for much of August, the besiegers' encampment before Dryslwyn Castle was the temporary seat of government business. The chronicle accounts suggest that Rhys and his followers avoided confrontation with the advancing armies and withdrew into the woods and hills (*Waverley Annals*, 404–405; *FH* iii, 66).

Amongst those summoned for the campaign, the sheriff of Shropshire was ordered to provide 200 carpenters and 200 diggers, Reginald de Grey to bring 200 woodcutters and 200 diggers from Cheshire for the Earl of Cornwall's force, the bailiff of St Briavels to send 400 woodcutters, and the counties of Shropshire and Staffordshire to supply a further 2000 wood-cutters and diggers for the Earl of Gloucester's force at Brecon (*CCRV*, 312–313). In practice, only a proportion of these specialist troops materialised. A substantial body of woodcutters, up to 609 strong, facilitated the Earl of Gloucester's advance through Brecon (PRO E101/4/18 mm1-3). Reginald de Grey brought 21 woodcutters with his army from Chester to Dryslwyn (PRO E101/4/15 and 16 mm1-3). Carpen-ters, masons, smiths and quarrymen in larger numbers came with the north Welsh contingents (Morris 1901, 209; PRO E101/4/16 m4).

From Carmarthen, Earl Edmund issued orders for the advance to Dryslwyn by his own troops and those of Tibetot, informing Reginald de Grey and the Bishop of Ely at Llanbadarn of his intended movements on 9 August, so that they might join him on 12th. The Anglo-Welsh army approached the castle through Pont-ar-Gothi, Llanegwad and Felindre, on the north side of the River Tywi (Griffiths 1966, 133; Edwards 1935, 46–47; E101/4/19 m3).

Establishing the siege (12–21 August 1287)

The first payment of the Earl of Cornwall's troops was made before Dryslwyn Castle on Wednesday 13 August, but this included the wages for the previous day, when they probably arrived (PRO E101/4/17 m2). The contingents of Tibetot, Grey and Bevillard arrived on Friday 15 and Saturday 16 August (PRO E101/4/16 mm2, 4; /19 m2). Reinforcements were still arriving from some of the Welsh districts on 17 August (PRO E101/4/17 m3). These troops presumably established an encampment at some unknown location nearby and took preliminary actions against the castle. Troops from Cemaes and Llanstephan may already have departed on detachment, perhaps to take Dinefwr Castle (PRO E101/4/19 m2).

The arrival of approximately 11,400 men to besiege Dryslwyn Castle created problems of logistics, as they all had to be fed and equipped. On 17 July, Earl Edmund ordered the counties of Gloucestershire, Herefordshire, Shropshire, Warwickshire and Worcestershire to sell the necessary food and equipment to the army at Brecon and Hereford, and the traders of Somerset to sell at Bridgewater and Bristol. A London poulterer was granted letters of safe-conduct on 23 July to supply the army in Wales with victuals and other supplies. These extended supply lines and the manipulation of the market did not operate successfully at first and Earl Edmund's forces suffered from a lack of food supplies. On 5 August, further orders were sent to the sheriffs of Herefordshire, Shropshire and Worcestershire to send victuals by horses and carts. This time, the orders were reinforced both by threats and by the assistance of royal clerks to organise the supply lines (*CCRV*, 308, 312, 314–315; cf. Prestwich 1996, chapter 10).

In advance of the troops' arrival at Carmarthen, purchases of corn were made by Robert de Tibetot through the burgesses of Carmarthen, Hereford and St David's (PRO E101/4/19 m3; E372/132 m1). Payments were also made to bring corn from Ireland (Taylor 1985a, 221). The constable of Bristol Castle sent wine, flour, hand-mills and millstones. He also organised a supply of arms, consisting of 8 single-foot crossbows and 1 with two feet, 12 baldricks and 21,400 quarrels. This was followed by another consignment of 20 crossbows, 20 baldricks and 6000 quarrels packed in a barrel, taken to Carmarthen by water (PRO C62/64 m4).

These resources, however, cannot have supplied all the needs of such a large body of troops. Presumably, raids were made into the local countryside to requisition livestock and agricultural produce. These raids would also have helped to induce the tenantry of Rhys ap Maredudd to submission. The reduced levels of rents derived from the commotes of Cantref Mawr in the years following the siege (Rhys 1936) testify to the damage, looting and destruction caused by the besieging army. There were several reductions in the numbers of men mustered in the various contingents at Dryslwyn; these may have been detachments sent into the country to forage, rather than casualties of combat or losses through desertion. One such detachment may have been the 140 foot-soldiers of Bromfield, who left the siege on 29 August to serve with the Earl of Warwick (PRO E101/4/16 m3).

The purchase of materials for the construction of a siege engine and other siege equipment and the manufacture of the tools for the undermining of the castle walls both appear to have taken place at Carmarthen before the main body of the Anglo-Welsh army even reached the area. Iron and steel were bought at Carmarthen on Monday 28 July to make 16 axes and 21 pick-axes, and another 5 axes and 2 pick-axes were purchased. These tools were subsequently taken to the siege via Pont-ar-Gothi (PRO E101/4/19 m3; E372/132 m1). Diggers had been part of the army contingents since the initial summons and we can safely assume that the siege of Dryslwyn Castle was an identifiable objective from the first.

The construction of the siege engine required large amounts of timber, cut locally in the woods and brought to the castle. Ox-hides and horse-hides, ropes of thick and thin grades, pulleys, nails, steel, many pieces of iron, 3 fotmels (99kg) — or perhaps 3 fothers (3 tons) if mis-transcribed — of lead and even an anchor were bought at Carmarthen. The iron, lead, ropes and some ammunition stones were transported to Dryslwyn by oxen, horses and small boats, where they were united with the locally cut timber (PRO E101/4/16 m4 and attached slips; E101/4/19 m3 and attached slip; E372/132 m1). The construction of the siege engine was under the direction of Master Richard the Engineer from Chester, who probably arrived at Carmarthen with the troops from Cheshire on 14 August. The engine was almost certainly a trebuchet, a counter-weighted catapult, in which the large throwing arm, revolving on a supported axle, was activated by a large falling counterweight (Section 7.4). The total recorded cost of building the machine has been calculated as at least £17 3s 9d (Phillpotts 2001b), rather than the £14 suggested by Morris (1901, 213). There were, however, many unrecorded costs; for example, items transported for which no purchase cost was recorded, as well as the use of local materials, such as timber, and costs of men to build and operate the engine (these were not separately recorded).

Engineering an assault (22–30 August 1287)

During this second period of the siege, several of the troop contingents were reduced in size. On Monday 25 August, there were roughly 9100 foot-soldiers at Dryslwyn. On 29 August, however, this total was further reduced to 8400 (PRO E101/4/17 m3; /19 m3). Some of these reductions may have resulted from casualties in the assault on the castle. Morris (1901, 213) speculated that the besiegers lost more than 850 men in attacking a breached wall, but this seems unlikely. More likely, the missing troops were sent out on detachment, either foraging or dealing with resistance from Rhys ap Maredudd's followers in other places. Some more irregular losses from 29 August onwards may have resulted from combat deaths in armed attacks on the castle (PRO E101/4/17 m2; /19 mm2, 3).

Master Adam, a mason, his associate and 18 labourers were paid from 16 August to make stones for the siege engine at a quarry. The masons continued work until 29 August, by which time they had created sufficient stone ammunition for Master Richard's engine. Four carters were employed to transport the stone balls created at the quarry to the trebuchet, indicating that the quarry was at some distance from the castle and presumably not beside the river, otherwise they would have used boats rather than carts for moving the stone balls. The carters were paid to move stone balls from the quarry to the trebuchet from 22 August until 8 September (PRO E101/4/19), during which time the siege engine was probably operating. Quantities of fat, grease and tallow to lubricate the sling trough and axle, as well as a series of replacement ropes and timbers, were purchased to keep the machine working. The dates of most of these purchases are not known, but horses were transporting materials from Carmarthen on 27 and 31 August, small boats were hired on 3 September and some boards, timbers and nails were bought on 4 September (PRO E101/4/16 mm4 and 5, and attached slips; E101/4/19 m3; E372/132 m1).

At the same time, attempts were made to undermine the castle walls in order to bring them down. A troop of 26 specialist diggers arrived at Dryslwyn and, from Monday 25 to Thursday 28 August, they are recorded as being paid to bring down the wall of the chapel by removing stones and mortar (*ad removendum lapides et mortar ad capellam et ad prosternendum murum capelle*) (PRO E101/4/16 m3). There is, however, no evidence to equate the undermining with the breach now visible to the west of Chapel H. Taylor's belief (1985a) that this breach must be that of 1287 is clearly incorrect, since no castle would have functioned as Dryslwyn did for at least another 120 years with such a yawning gap in its defences.

Several of the chronicle accounts describe the mining operations as underground passages (*vias subterraneas*), but these all appear to derive their terminology from the *Waverley Annals*, an early but confused account (*Waverley Annals*, 405; *FH* iii, 66; *London Annals*, 96). Wykes wrote rather of trimming (*putare*) the walls in a pit or trench (*fovea*), in addition to an underground cavern (*specus subterraneus*), its roof supported by inadequate props (*Wykes*, 310). In one account, tools were delivered to Master Richard to cut a trench and throw down the walls (*ad passus amputandum et muros prosternandum*) (PRO E372/132 m1). The *Hagnaby Chronicle* (HC, f32) speaks graphically of Robert de Tibetot trying to tear the castle up by the roots, whilst *Bartholomew Cotton* (168) and *St Albans Chronicle* (43) describe William de Monchensey and his followers digging out (*effodere*) the wall. The hard limestone rock on which the walls of the Inner Ward are founded would have made it very difficult indeed to dig passages or mines into the bedrock of the southern and eastern sides of the castle. Therefore, the balance of evidence suggests that the miners either sapped the walls — in other words, dug out the base of the wall above the bedrock — or, most probably, dug trenches into the earth and stone banks on which the walls of the town, Outer and Middle Wards (the northern and western sides of the castle) were founded. In undertaking this work, the miners/diggers would have been protected by mobile screens, known as 'sows' or 'cats', constructed on site (Bradbury 1992, 271).

When a group of leading knights from the Anglo-Welsh army rashly entered the 'mine' to inspect the work, the props gave way and both the ground and wall above suddenly collapsed onto them, crushing them to death. The known casualties were William de Monchensey, Gerard de L'Isle and Nicholas, Baron de Stafford (*AC*, 109; *Waverley Annals*, 405; *Dunstable Annals*, 339; *Lanercost Chronicle*, 51; *Wykes*, 310; *HC*, f32; *BC*, 168; *HAC*, f46v; *William Rishanger*, 117; *FH* iii, 66; *Worcester Annals*, 494; *Nicholas Trevet*, 315; *London Annals*, 96; *Wroxham Continuation*, 307; *St Albans Chronicle*, 43; *Thomas Walsingham* i, 30). All three were veterans of the Welsh wars of the late 1270s and early 1280s, whilst Monchensey and L'Isle had both fought in the Barons' War of the 1260s against King Henry III (*Cokayne* 1998, viii 48; ix 422–424; xii (1) 172). This was regarded as a tragic accident on the English side, but it was Monchensey's name that really had an impact on contemporaries and chroniclers, either because of his chivalrous reputation, or because of his wealth. He is called *Willelmus de Monchenessi le Riche* in the Hailes Abbey account of the incident, and Wykes mentions his many possessions (he was misidentified in Morris 1901, 213; see Taylor 1985a, 217 n4). Another casualty may have been Jean de Bevillard. The Welsh chronicles state that 'John Pennard' was drowned at the siege, but this may be better interpreted as 'crushed and/or suffocated' (Taylor 1985a, 217–218).

The exact date of the wall collapse is not known. Taylor (1985a, 218) suggests that the evidence of payments to Jean de Bevillard's clerk indicates a date before 30 August. Definite news of Monchensey's death had reached Westminster by 16 September, when the administration of his goods south of the Trent was granted to his executors (*CFR* i, 240). The diggers remained on the payroll at Dryslwyn, but their numbers were reduced from 26 to 14 on 3 September. Perhaps the other 12 diggers died in the collapse with the knights at about this date. The number of woodcutters was reduced from 21 to 10 on 6 September (PRO E101/4/16 m3). According to one early account, the besiegers took the castle as a result of undermining the walls (*AC*, 109).

Capitulation (31 August–8 September 1287)

At the end of August, there were still roughly 8200 foot-soldiers besieging Dryslwyn Castle and, presumably, still approximately 600 mounted troops. Over the next week, the total of infantry was progressively reduced to 2300, although a few small contingents continued to join the siege (PRO E101/4/19 m3). Some irregular reductions until 4 September suggest that there may have been combat losses in assaults upon the castle (PRO E101/4/17 m3), but whilst some men were undoubtedly lost as a result of injuries and disease, the bulk of these troops had probably left to return home and bring the harvest in. There is no indication that they had deserted the army and it was probably considered safe to let them depart. Some troops may perhaps have been detached to pacify the surrounding countryside, or to pursue Rhys ap Maredudd (PRO E101/4/16 m3).

Rhys escaped from the castle with his family and his household and concealed himself in the wooded hill country around: his fellow rebels, meanwhile, submitted to the English Crown (*AC*, 110; *Brut-y-Tywysogyon*, 121; *Brenhinedd-y-Saesson*, 261; *Dunstable Annals*, 339; *HC*, f32; *HAC*, f46v). Wykes pictures him as leaving at night with his wife and followers by a secret postern gate, undetected by the besiegers. He relates this to Dinefwr, the first castle besieged, but the details may well have been confused with events at Dryslwyn (*Wykes*, 310). It is not known when he left, but the severe reductions in besieging troops on 5 September from 8000 to 6700 infantry, and on 7 September from 6600 to 2300 infantry, suggest departing troops setting off to corner Rhys in the hills.

Whilst some writers have stated that the castle surrendered on 5 September (Morris 1901, 213; Edwards 1935, 166), carts continued to bring prepared stones from the quarry to the siege engine until Monday 8 September, suggesting that the trebuchet was still in operation, propelling stones to breach the castle walls. A likely possibility is that the town and Outer Ward were captured between 5 and 7 September and, consequently, the fall of the castle was now considered inevitable, leading to a reduction in the number of besiegers, whilst the remaining forces and the trebuchet continued their efforts to breach the Inner Ward.

In point of fact, Dryslwyn Castle probably did not finally surrender until 8 September, on which date Alan de Plucknet was appointed as constable and given the control of Rhys ap Maredudd's six commotes of Caio, Cethiniog, Maen-Ordeilo, Mallaen Iscoed, Mabelfyw and Mabudrud in Cantref Mawr. Plucknet and his garrison were installed in the castle, the troops drawn from the besieging army. Plucknet's accounts relating to the period when he took over the castle for the English Crown begin on 8 September 1287 (Morris 1901, 214; Griffiths 1966, 134 and n67, 140; *CCRV*, 311; C62/66 m5; E101/4/20, E101/4/23 and E372/134 m1, printed in Rhys 1936, 37–55, 454–466). The siege had, therefore, lasted for 28 days, from August 12th, three days before the Assumption of the Virgin Mary, until the day of her Nativity (8 September).

The contingents of the army now prepared to return home. The foot-soldiers of Cardiganshire returned to their county after 7 September (PRO E101/4/19 m3). On 9 September, 2300 troops now remained, although most of them probably departed on this day, since only 150 or so were still present on 10th. The returning soldiers congregated in Carmarthen on Saturday 13 September (PRO E101/4/16 mm4, 5; /17 m3). Where the local Welsh troops from Carmarthenshire were discharged, contingents from north Wales, the Marches and England received another week's pay to cover their march home (Morris 1901, 213).

News of the success of the siege was sent to King Edward I at Bordeaux, a report on the campaign being delivered to the king there on 7 December, probably by John Havering, who wrote to the Bishop of Ely in England that the king had listened eagerly to the news of the siege, but was particularly saddened by the untimely death of William de Monchensey and his companions. Within a short time, however, Edward was receiving reports of the renewed activities of Rhys ap Maredudd, his capture of the castle of Newcastle Emlyn and the slaughter of the garrison (Griffiths 1966, 134; Taylor 1985a, 217, 218n1; Edwards 1935, 174–175; *CCRV*, 311).

Final resistance (September 1287–January 1297)

Following the capture of Dryslwyn Castle, the Earl of Gloucester suggested at Michaelmas (29 September) that a truce or amnesty be offered to Rhys ap Maredudd (Griffiths 1994, 74). This perhaps betrays the fact that several Marcher lords were related to Rhys, although they may have already perceived that, without an active Welsh presence, the need for Marcher lordships, with their special status and privileges, could evaporate. In the years following 1287, whilst Edward I did not actively seek to reduce the powers and privileges of the Marcher lords, when the situation arose, he took the opportunity to reduce them and impose royal authority (Prestwich 1988, 351). The Crown did not offer terms to Rhys for his surrender, but, considering the effort and cost of the campaign, little effort was made to catch him (Griffiths 1994, 74). This is in marked contrast to the efforts made to track down Dafydd ap Llywelyn following the rebellion of the princes of Gwynedd in 1282–83.

On the night of 2 November, Rhys ap Maredudd renewed his revolt, capturing the castle of Newcastle Emlyn. He was reported to have kept the constable Roger Mortimer hostage, but slaughtered the garrison. Prior to 1287, Rhys had owned Newcastle Emlyn and surrounding lands. It is probable that the castle was initially taken by English forces as part of the suppression of Rhys' rebellion in the mid-summer of 1287. Had he lost it earlier, it would undoubtedly have been a target for Rhys in the early days of his revolt and its capture would have been recorded in the chronicles of the period. It is perhaps not surprising that Rhys was able to capture the castle 'by surprise' as he would have known the castle well, since his father built it, and would have spent much time there in his youth. Following the capture of Newcastle Emlyn and its castle and the re-ignition of Rhys' rebellion, the lords of the March remained defending their own lands and castles. Llandovery was sacked by the men of Caio and Mabelfyw on 4 November and Rhys, supported by Gruffyn Goch (beadle of Cethiniog) and others (Phillpotts 2001c), tried and failed to capture Dinefwr Castle by surprise, subsequently attempting to lay siege to it (Griffiths 1994, 75). In response, on 29 November, Goronwy Goch led 160 men from Elfed and Gwidigada to Dinefwr, presumably to relieve it. On 2 December, following the arrival of these troops, together with reinforcements led by Robert de Tibetot, the siege at Dinefwr was raised. In the days that followed, Tibetot's troops subdued the area of Is Cennen, which had also risen for Rhys. Goronwy Goch's forces scoured the Tywi valley up to Brechfa in search of Rhys, but failed to capture him (Griffiths 1994, 75).

Robert de Tibetot and his forces laid siege to the castle of Newcastle Emlyn on 28 December. The trebuchet made for the siege of Dryslwyn was brought here via St Clears and Cilgerran using a team of 40 oxen and 4 wagons. It reached Newcastle Emlyn on 10 January 1288. Stones were brought from the beach below Cardigan for the trebuchet to throw and bridges and hurdles were made ready for an assault (Griffiths 1994, 76). The trebuchet created at Dryslwyn would have been both jointed and nailed together — 20s was paid to Walter of Huntercombe for nails for the engine (PRO 372/132) — and it would have been partially disassembled to bring it to Newcastle Emlyn. After it had been reassembled, the trebuchet spent six days bombarding the castle with stones and, on 20 January, the castle surrendered. It is suggested (*AC*, 110) that many of Rhys' supporters were killed or captured, though he himself escaped. Tibetot made active attempts to apprehend Rhys, who made a further attempt to recapture Dryslwyn Castle by 'treachery' (Edwards 1935, 166).

Efforts continued throughout the following years to capture Rhys whilst rumours of a renewed revolt continued. In 1290, Edward I pardoned Rhys' supporters in Cantref Mawr and Cantref Bychan, a move calculated to encourage them to renounce their loyalty to him. From January 1288 until April 1292, Rhys dropped out of sight. Reports that he was aided by various Marcher lords and that he went to Ireland (Bridgeman 1876, 197) were merely contemporary rumour and subsequent speculation, as he was eventually captured in the woods of Mallaen on 2 April 1292, betrayed by four of his own men. He was tried for treason in front of the king in York on 2 June and found guilty of murder, arson, theft and destruction of royal castles. He was drawn and hanged on the Knavesmire at York later that same day (Griffiths 1994, 77). Following his death, Ada, Rhys' wife, is recorded as being allowed to retain the lands she held in her own right (Griffiths 1994, 77; Edwards 1935,

139). At first, Rhys' son, also called Rhys, probably remained with his mother. However, in 1297, when he had barely reached his teenage years, he was arrested and taken as a prisoner to Bristol Castle. Although there is record of his transfer to Windsor in 1300 (Fryde 1974, xv), he was principally incarcerated in Norwich Castle, surviving as a prisoner until at least 1340 (Griffiths 1994, 77). His capture and confinement in 1297 followed, and may have been triggered by, the revolt of Madog ap Llywelyn in 1295–96. The only surviving member of the Deheubarth dynasty, Rhys ap Rhys ap Maredudd, would have been a potential figurehead for future rebellion and warranted continued confinement far from Wales.

7.2 ARCHAEOLOGICAL EVIDENCE OF SIEGE AND WARFARE
by Chris Caple, Oliver Jessop, R F Caple and Chris Phillpotts

During times of trouble the principal function of the 13th-century castle was defence, however, actual conflict, whilst frequently attested in historical sources, rarely leaves any obvious archaeological trace. Castles such as Limerick (Limerick) (Wiggins 2001) and St Andrews (Fife) (Cruden 1982) are unusual in having produced archaeological evidence of siege. Excavations at a number of castle sites have produced weapons, including arrowheads at Criccieth (Gwynedd) (O'Neil 1944–45) and trebuchet balls at Caerlaverock (Dumfries and Galloway), although these are only rarely linked to specific historical events due to problems of dating and stratigraphy.

The excavations at Dryslwyn Castle unearthed an unusually large number of weapons: 92 arrrowheads, 6 crossbow bolts, 3 spearheads and a macehead (Section 7.3). They also produced physical evidence of a siege in the form of trebuchet balls (Section 7.4) and the resulting repairs to the castle walls (Section 6.1). Much of this evidence can be correlated with the unusually detailed historic accounts of the 1287 siege (Section 7.1). Dryslwyn has also produced evidence of a range of smaller lithic projectiles (Section 7.4). These were assiduously collected throughout the excavation and, although not previously studied, were undoubtedly a significant weapon for either attack or defence during most sieges. Much of the physical evidence for the siege was recovered from specific deposits (G45, G51, G53, G55, G59, H35, H50 and H59), which formed a layer of debris covering much of the floor of Great Chamber G. The prevalence of chain mail links, lithic projectiles and armour-piecing arrowheads, all extremely difficult to identify without specific recovery strategies, X-ray and conservation facilities, suggests that it is unlikely that the full range of weapons or personal protective equipment has been identified and recovered from previous excavations elsewhere.

The soldiers present in Dryslwyn Castle during the Welsh Lordship Period would have comprised, firstly, the *teulu* (a small band of warriors who formed part of the lord's household; Davies 2004, 14–49) and, secondly, the *llu* (the freemen who lived and worked in and around the castle and town and could have been summoned to form an army or defend the castle and land of their lord). The number of men that made up the *teulu* may well have fluctuated with the fortunes of the lord of Dryslwyn in the period 1230–71 but, by 1287, it had grown to full strength as Rhys was a powerful and wealthy lord. Its warriors were financially supported by the lord, as well as from raiding and looting. By the mid 13th century, the *teulu* would have been well armed and mounted and probably formed much of the force that captured castles and sacked towns in the initial days of Rhys' revolt. The freemen, on the other hand, were poorly equipped with either a spear or a bow and would have manned the walls of the castle during the siege.

The accounts (Section 3.1) indicate that, throughout the English garrison period, a small retinue of professional soldiers garrisoned the castle, typically 12 to 24 in number. They primarily utilised crossbows and would have been reasonably well armed and used to conflict. After 1287 the castle contained an armoury with a large number of crossbows and quarrels, as well as pieces of armour. This was maintained to support additional men who boosted the garrison during times of conflict.

Weaponry

The collections of arrowheads and lithic projectiles from Dryslwyn are amongst the largest and most precisely dated from a British excavation, whilst the macehead is only the second starhead mace recovered from an archaeological context.

The macehead derives from a Phase 3b (mid 13th-century) deposit (O151) and is almost certainly a weapon from a member of the *teulu*. There was no evidence for the swords, axes, armour, shields and other accoutrements of personal combat, but, given the value of such weaponry, even a single find is rare. The starhead form of leaded bronze macehead would originally have had a wooden shaft, 0.4–0.75m long, of which traces remained in the socket. The weapon itself would have been used by a mounted warrior to inflict impact injuries on the heads and limbs of foot-soldiers, an effective weapon, and since maces were also symbols of military authority in the medieval period (Halpin 1988, 174), may have been the property of a senior member of the *teulu*. The form of the macehead is paralleled by English, Welsh, Scottish and Irish examples, but Halpin (1988, 173) has suggested that its distribution correlates with Anglo-Norman activity. The fact that the Dryslwyn example was deliberately hidden in the base of a latrine pit

suggests a symbolic, as well as functional, role: indeed, there are similarities with the deposition of the York Anglian helmet (Tweddle 1992) and the Winchester Reliquary (Hinton *et al* 1981).

Two of the spearhead forms (from Phases 2d and 4c) are small and may be from light throwing spears. The larger spearhead (from Phase 4a) would have been mounted on a long pole and kept in hand as a thrusting weapon. Giraldus Cambrensis claimed the men of north Wales were 'very skilful with their long spears' (Thorpe 1978, 231), but Davies (2004, 149) notes that it was a widely used weapon and many of the men who would have come to serve either under Maredudd ap Rhys or Rhys ap Maredudd would have been experienced spearmen.

Despite the proximity of Dryslwyn to large tracts of forest in the 13th and 14th centuries, only one true barbed arrowhead [**W1**], the type specifically used for hunting, was recovered from the excavation. 16 multi-purpose arrowhead forms with narrow blades and restricted barbs that could have both military and hunting uses were also recovered. Large quantities of deer bones (Section 10.2) indicate that hunting was a far more frequent activity than the arrowhead numbers suggest. The remaining arrowheads were all narrow armour-piercing forms, specifically for use in warfare against armoured or mailed opponents (Jessop 1996). The presence of these highly adapted armour-piercing arrowheads from mid and late 13th-century contexts in a number of castles in Wales, including Caergwrle (Flintshire), Castell-y-Bere (Gwynedd), Flint (Flintshire), Loughor (Swansea), Montgomery (Powys) and Rumney (Cardiff), and in large numbers from Criccieth (Gwynedd) (118) and Dryslwyn (92), indicates the widespread use of the bow as a weapon in the late 13th-century wars in Wales. Giraldus Cambrensis refers to the prowess of the Welsh bowmen: 'those of the south, especially Gwent, use the bow to great effect' (Thorpe 1978, 231). Bowmen from Wales were often present in the English armies in Scotland and France in the 14th century (Davies 2004, 151–153) and many of the men fighting both for and against Rhys ap Maredudd in the siege of 1287 would have been bowmen. The size of bow generally used at this time is not known. The armour-piercing arrowheads from Dryslwyn are too long and too heavy to have been used with the short bows mentioned by Giraldus Cambrensis and they may have been much closer to a full-length longbow, which appears to have been in use by Welsh bowmen by the early 14th century (Hardy 1992, 41–50). It is possible that the almost-continuous armed conflict of the 13th century in Wales, in which bowmen were key protagonists, provided the competitive 'arms race' for a longer shooting range, which led to the development of the full longbow; it certainly produced extensive use of armour-piercing arrowheads.

Only six crossbow bolts were recovered from unstratified deposits within the castle. Crossbowmen from London and Bristol were part of the besieging forces in 1287 and at least 27,400 quarrels (crossbow bolts) and 20 crossbows are recorded as having been delivered to them during the siege (Section 7.1). Not one single crossbow bolt, however, was recovered from Phase 4c siege deposits, suggesting that they were salvaged, repaired and re-hafted: references in the year following the siege year to expenditure on 'thread, feathers and glue for repairing crossbows and quarrels' (Rhys 1936, 43) lend credence to this interpretation. Following the capture of Dryslwyn Castle and the installation of a garrison, there is no record of expenditure on bows or arrows, only on crossbows and bolts. Purchases of crossbows and quarrels were recorded in 1304/5 (Rhys 1936, 407) and in both 1303/4 and 1304/5, when the castle was visited by Roger the crossbowman, who surveyed and repaired the crossbows in Dryslwyn Castle, as well as the other royal castles of west Wales (Rhys 1936, 395) (Section 3.1). There was clearly a perception by the Crown that the crossbow was a superior weapon for castle defence, probably because they were easier to shoot from behind parapets and on wall-walks and did not expose the crossbowman in the way that firing a longbow might. The slower shooting rate of a crossbow was not a crucial factor when protected by a stone wall. This preference was expressed in terms of differential rates of pay; between 1289 and 1290, the castle garrison comprised 20 crossbowmen (paid 4d a day) and 29 archers (paid 2d a day) (Rhys 1936, 61). There appears a significant shift from bowmen who came with their own bows in the service of the Welsh lords of Dryslwyn prior to 1287, to the provision of crossbows owned and maintained by the castle authorities, which the men of the garrison used after 1287. Centralised authority had become responsible for weaponry and the creation of an armoury. The presence of armour-piercing arrowheads in deposits from Phases 5–7 may indicate either the continued presence of personal bows used by men of the garrison, or, more probably, that these arrowheads were redeposited from earlier deposits.

Lithic projectiles are rarely recorded from archaeological sites, since they can be difficult to distinguish from the natural stone of the site. They are also so commonplace that they go unrecorded by chroniclers of the period. However, they are a widely available and potentially effective weapon, as contemporary illustrations (Figure 7.1; Bradbury 1992, 111, 200,

FIGURE 7.1

15th-century illustration of handstones (Class 2 stones) being thrown at besiegers, from BL Cott. Nero EII, pt2, fi (By courtesy of the British Library)

245, 269, 271, 272) and the examples recovered from Dryslwyn amply demonstrate. Stones were selected to be lithic projectiles on the basis of their size, shape and weight for the appropriate method of propulsion (Section 7.4). They were almost all smooth and rounded and many were made of sandstone, in stark contrast to the naturally split limestone of the Dryslwyn hillside. Smaller stones (Class 1, Section 7.4) were thrown by slingers, such as 'William the slinger', who was recorded as a member of the castle's garrison in 1289/90 (Phillpotts 2001c). Similar slingstones have been recovered from Dolforwyn Castle (Powys) (Butler 1990, 94; 1997, 195). Slightly larger stones (Class 2, Section 7.4) could be thrown by hand from the castle walls or similar vantage-points, whilst larger stones (Class 4, Section 7.4) were normally thrown by engines, such as the mangonal, balista or perrier (catapults). Both Kenyon (1996) and Davies (2004, 207–217) cite references to Welsh forces using engines, such as catapults, in the 12th and 13th centuries. The largest stones (Class 6, Section 7.4) were only thrown by the largest of engines, the trebuchet, and are normally only seen during sieges. There is no evidence that the Welsh ever constructed or used trebuchets. They were invariably constructed by the forces of the English Crown, since they alone had access to suitably skilled engineers.

Only limited evidence of personal protection from weapons, in the form of links from mail, was unearthed at Dryslwyn. Illustrations indicate that mail was frequently used during this period. Due to its corrodability, however, it is rarely found in excavation, although some fragments have been recovered from Castell-y-Bere (Gwynedd) (Butler 1974, 95–97). The occurrence of links at Dryslwyn in Phase 3 and 4 contexts indicates the use of mail during the period 1250–87. By the late 13th century, whilst the lord of Dryslwyn may have possessed some plate armour, most warriors had mail protection over leather garments, as well as steel helmets (Davies 2004, 146–147). The later English garrison is recorded as having armour in its stores (Section 3.1), an armourer requiring four weeks to burnish and clean the (plate) armour in Dryslwyn and Dinefwr Castles (Rhys 1936, 407), but mail links were not recovered from either Phase 5 or 6 contexts, suggesting limited military activity or use of mail after 1287.

Siege

Welsh masonry castles of the 13th century were functional defensive structures (Section 2.3), as well as being symbols of power and wealth. They were constructed with the intention of withstanding short sieges with battering rams, scaling ladders and small-scale siege machines, such as catapults, which are recorded in the 12th and early 13th centuries (Kenyon 1996; Davies 2004, 207–217). It was expected that they would hold out for a short period until larger forces arrived to relieve them, which is why they were normally only constructed by princes and lords, such as Llywelyn ap Iowerth, Llywelyn ap Gruffudd and the Lord Rhys, who could muster such relief forces. They were ill equipped and had no experience of holding out against a large and well-prepared English army. Almost all were abandoned when English forces approached: only Dolforwyn (Powys), which held out for 9 days in 1277 (Butler 2000, 26), Castell-y-Bere (Gwynedd), which held out for 10 days in 1283, Newcastle Emlyn (Carmarthenshire), which held out for 23 days in 1288, and Dryslwyn, which held out 28 days in 1287, put up any significant resistance.

The siege of Dryslwyn Castle is notable for its use of the trebuchet, which figures significantly in the financial accounts, although it made no impression on the chroniclers of the time. So effective was this engine in prosecuting a siege that considerable efforts were made a few months later to remove it from Dryslwyn to besiege the castle at Newcastle Emlyn (Carmarthenshire). The cost and nature of the materials used in the construction of this siege engine, and the fact that it threw stone balls weighing some 50kg (Section 7.4), indicate that the engine used at Dryslwyn must have been a counterweight trebuchet. The events of the 1287 siege, therefore, take their place in the history of trebuchet use in 13th-century siege warfare, ranging from Château Gailliard in Normandy (France) in 1204, Rochester (Kent) in 1215 and Bedford (Bedfordshire) in 1224, to Caerlaverock (Dumfries and Galloway) in 1300 and Stirling (Stirling) in 1304 (Warner 1968, 132–133, 136–137, 145–147; Bradbury 1992, 132–133, 139–144, 256–258; Prestwich 1996, 284–285, 289–291, 297, 300; Keen 1999, 109–111, 174–175).

The purchase of materials for this engine prior to August 1287, and the presence of Richard the Engineer and other craftsmen in the initial days of the siege, indicate that the construction of a trebuchet was planned before the army arrived at Dryslwyn. An appreciation of the size of the engine can be gained from the measures taken to transport it to the siege of Newcastle Emlyn a few months later: it was hauled to Cardigan by 40 oxen and 4 wains, escorted by about 500 soldiers, whereupon 60 oxen transported it on to Newcastle Emlyn (Morris 1901, 216; Griffiths 1966, 136–137). Only a few master engineers had the knowledge and skills to construct a trebuchet. Richard the Engineer, responsible for the construction of the trebuchet at Dryslwyn, may also have been known as Richard of Paris, who was a pupil of Master James of St George.

Trials of modern replica trebuchets at Fasters Minden in Denmark and Caerphilly (Caerphilly) in 1992 (Hansen 1992; Humphries 1996) demonstrate that it is a remarkably accurate weapon for line of shot. When the machine is laid true and level, the trigger release is identical for every shot and, if the size and weight of the missiles are identical, then a spread of shot of 6m at 120m range can be achieved. This accuracy would allow repeated impacts on the same area of masonry walling. The need for uniformity of missiles was identified as important by King (1982) and Hansen (1992, 205). It was also acknowledged by Engineer Gerard, who was responsible for the king's works at Carlisle and Northumberland in 1244, where it is recorded that he had stones cut for his engines to a form and mould supplied by him (Harvey 1954). This need for uniformity is not mentioned in any historical accounts, but explains the need to employ two masons and 18 labourers to work for 13 days to produce stone balls for the trebuchet (Section 7.1). The fact that similar-sized trebuchet balls have been retrieved from Caerphilly (Caerphilly), Dolforwyn (Powys) and Dryslwyn suggests that a standard size of trebuchet was being constructed by the master engineers working for the English Crown in Wales during the period 1275–1300.

There is a documentary reference to payment for transporting stones from the river to the engine (PRO E101/4/16). This suggests that some stones, though not those shaped at the quarry, which were transported in carts, were being brought to the castle by boat. These could have come from the bed of the river itself, or been transported up from the coast, or down from the higher reaches of the river. Most likely, these stones were naturally formed boulders, rounded through wave or water action. At the siege of Newcastle Emlyn in January 1288, 'men were employed to pick up 480 stones on the beach below Cardigan and transport them by boat to Llechryd on the river and thence to carry them on 120 pack horses to the camp' (Morris 1901, 216). This description tallies with the large number of water-worn and shaped stones of 4–10kg size recovered from deposits associated with the 1287 siege at Dryslwyn (Section 7.4). Since the large, carefully shaped stone balls were used for accurate demolition of standing stone walls, it raises the question of what the 4–10kg water-worn boulders were used for. Perhaps these were smaller siege engines, such as perriers or mangonals, used to propel smaller stones at the castle (Bradbury 1992, 252).

Alternatively, the trebuchet may have thrown groups of these smaller stones, loosely held in some form of container, such as a barrel, or wrapped in a hide. This 'grouped' shot of rounded boulders would have been very damaging to those defending the castle, the stones being of sufficient size to kill and maim defenders, as well as to damage internal buildings. It may have been possible to propel many such small stones together from the trebuchet, possibly from missiles called 'beehives'. These are not skeps for bees, as is sometimes suggested (Bradbury 1992, 251, 280), but 'small stones fired into clay balls that scattered their content on impact' (Hansen 1992, 203). A single stone thrown by an unspecified machine at the siege of Tortona in Italy in 1155 fragmented, killing three knights (Bradbury 1992, 259), and major casualties in

19th-century naval warfare were principally from the effects of splinters created by cannon balls. The use of 'beehive' missiles at Dryslwyn, therefore, would have showered the castle with stones, crashing through roofs and killing defenders, and the hail of missiles could be kept up day and night, as it was at Rouen in France in 1174 (Bradbury 1992, 257). Such an unceasing lethal bombardment was undoubtedly intended to induce the defenders to surrender the castle. This was the most desirable outcome for any besieging army, since it captured the castle, but left it intact and available for immediate re-use, without great need for costly repairs. It also avoided sacrificing the lives of the besieging soldiers, who would otherwise have had to fight their way into the castle through a narrow breach in the walls.

It is traditionally thought that the trebuchet was placed far enough away from the castle so that its operation could not be halted by arrows shot from the castle walls. Given the range of the longbow, especially when positioned in an elevated position, this would suggest that a distance of at least 100–200m needed to be maintained. From the information gained from experiments firing a replica trebuchet (Hansen 1992), in addition to the likely size of the trebuchet at Dryslwyn and the fact that it projected a stone ball of 50kg, the maximum range of the trebuchet at Dryslwyn was in the range 160–200m on flat ground. If the trebuchet were positioned on the valley floor, it would need to raise the stone ball a vertical distance of 50–60m to land it in the Inner Ward of the castle. Given the trajectory of flight (Figure 7.2), the trebuchet would need to be sited approximately 100m from the castle to achieve such a shot. These locations are well within longbow range and, thus, the trebuchet and its operators would have needed firstly camouflage from the archers and, secondly, protection from a potential hail of arrows. Both were probably gained from hurdles, which the besiegers of Dryslwyn are known to have made (PRO E101/4/19).

Modern experiments show that impacts from trebuchet balls generally demolish the upper two thirds of a wall, whilst attack with battering rams or sapping damages the lower parts of the wall sufficiently to lead to total wall collapse. Archaeologically, therefore, repair of walls damaged by trebuchet missiles tends to show up as rebuilding of the upper courses of masonry, a feature noted by Butler (2000, 25) at Dolforwyn (Powys), which suffered trebuchet attack in 1277. At Dryslwyn, the squared masonry forming the middle and upper half of the curtain wall (F2) on the eastern side of the Inner Ward (Section 6.1) is almost certainly that built by Edwardian masons following the siege. It is interesting to note that, following the redevelopment of the south side of the Inner Ward in the early 1280s, the wall (F2) was the thinnest section of the curtain wall circuit and, therefore, the most vulnerable to attack. It is possible, then, that the besieging forces had local knowledge of the weak points of the castle. From the position of the

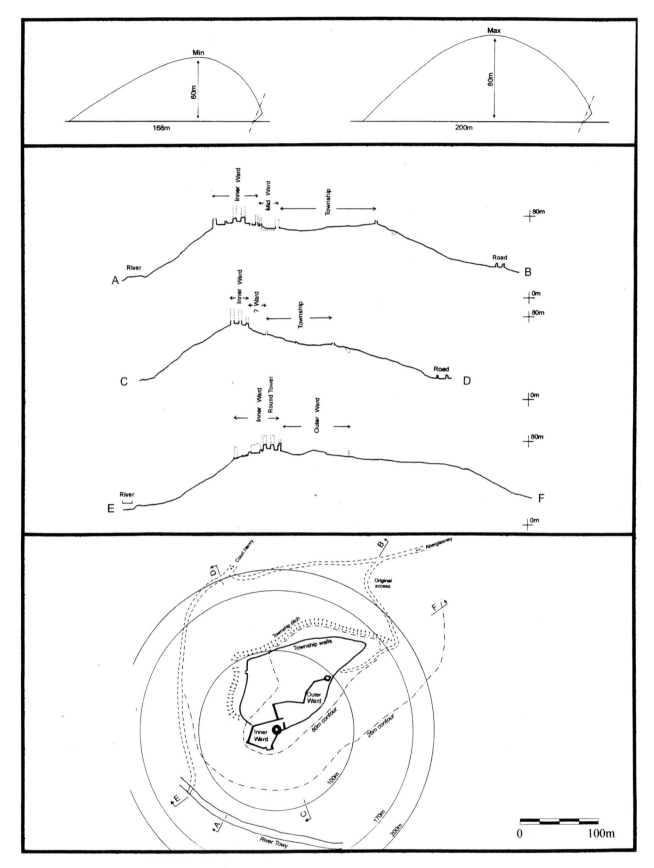

FIGURE 7.2

Trebuchet trajectories in relation to Dryslwyn Castle and hill

trebuchet balls recovered during the excavations — between the revetting wall of Courtyard O and Great Hall K/L and the midden in Area F — in addition to the location of the damaged wall (F2), we may deduce that the trebuchet was positioned to the east of the castle, firing up at the Inner Ward from the valley floor below.

Richard the Engineer would have been responsible for both the sapping of the castle walls and the construction of the siege engine. Diggers were paid to 'cut a trench and throw down the walls' (PRO 372/132), so undermining the castle walls and eventually leading to the capture of the castle itself. Records of the collapse of the 'mine', killing a number of inspecting English nobles, and possibly 12 miners, suggest that part of the castle wall above also collapsed, although there is no evidence of collapsed walling at foundation level at any point in the Inner Ward and it is as a result of Phase 6d demolition of the castle in the 15th century that a 7m length of the curtain wall west of Chapel H does not survive today. Instead, the undermining efforts were almost certainly effective in breaching the earthen banks supporting the walls of the town and Middle and Outer Ward defences, rather than the hard, crystalline limestone bedrock underlying the walls of the south and east sides of the Inner Ward. Excavation of the Outer Ward defences in Area R revealed the base of a bastion, constructed of squared and well-mortared masonry, in front of the Outer Ward bank. This was almost certainly the result of post-siege building works to repair the damage caused by undermining this section of the castle's defences.

7.3 WEAPONS
by Oliver Jessop

The assemblage of weapons recovered from the excavations at Dryslwyn Castle consists of 101 artefacts: a mixture of arrowheads, crossbow bolts, spearheads and a macehead. The majority of the weapons appear to be for military use and are similar to assemblages excavated at other Welsh castles, such as Caergwrle (Flintshire) (Courtney 1994), Caerleon (Newport) (unpublished), Caernarfon (Gwynedd) (unpublished), Criccieth (Gwynedd) (O'Neil 1944–45), Harlech (Gwynedd) (unpublished), Loughor (Swansea) (Lewis 1994), Montgomery (Powys) (Knight 1994), Rhuddlan (Denbighshire) (I Goodall 1994) and Rumney (Cardiff) (Lloyd-Fern and Sell 1992). Each type of weapon is discussed and catalogued in turn below and, unless otherwise stated, the type or classification of the arrowheads is based upon the generic typology advanced by Jessop (1996).

Arrowheads

In total, 92 iron arrowheads were recovered (Figures 7.3–7.7). They represent an important group,

as there are few well-dated collections of this size. The forms represented fall within three groups: hunting (1%), multipurpose (17%) and military (82%). This dominance of military types is not an uncommon occurrence in Welsh castles; for example, Caernarfon (Gwynedd), Castell-y-Bere (Gwynedd) (Butler 1974, 95), Criccieth (Gwynedd) (O'Neil 1944–45, 40) and Harlech (Gwynedd) all have assemblages with military forms of over 70% representation.

The group of hunting or multipurpose arrowheads consists of both centrally socketed examples (Type MP8) and the narrower winged varieties (Types MP4 and MP6), forms which may have played a role in the early military operations. The arrowheads [W6–16] (Type MP8) largely come from Areas G, H, I, J and O and from 13th-century contexts, although a couple come from the initial phase of occupation (Phase 1b) and are thus clearly associated with the Welsh period of occupation. Parallels have been found at the castles of Clough (Down) (Waterman 1954, 141) and Seafin (Ulster) (Waterman 1955, 94) in Ireland. The deposition of two of these arrowheads in Courtyard O is logical, as it would have been the focus of all activity within the inner part of the castle. Three of the arrowheads were recovered from the siege material dumped in Great Chamber G and Chapel H following the 1287 siege and suggest that this arrowhead form was still in use in the late 13th century.

Only one arrowhead [W1] was designed solely for hunting purposes. It is damaged, but is still a fine example of a small swallowtail head with long slender barbs that would be suitable for killing both deer and other forms of game. It dates to the 14th century and it is unusual to find only one example of this type by this date.

The number of arrowheads from Dryslwyn designed for piercing armour is substantial, amounting to 82% of the whole assemblage. They span the whole history of the site, from the early 13th to the early 15th century, and emphasise the military nature of the castle. Almost one fifth of the group [W22–37] is represented by the concoidal form (Type M6). This is unusual, although Brandon Castle (Warwickshire) (Chatwin 1955, 81) and Castle Acre (Norfolk) (I Goodall 1982, 235) have comparable percentages. They appear to be concentrated within the 13th-century layers (Phases 1–4) of Dryslwyn and the presence of examples of this arrowhead type from Phase 1 and 2 deposits suggests that it may represent an early form already in use by the early 13th century. They are possibly contemporary with the long narrow head M7 [W38–41], which is ascribed to the 11th century at Castle Acre (Norfolk) (I Goodall 1982, 235) and Goltho (Lincolnshire) (I Goodall 1987, 185). These two simple forms later developed into the larger and stronger armour-piercing Types M8, M9 and M10, which dominate the Dryslwyn assemblage.

W no.	Jessop Type		L	W	Diam	SF	Context	Phase	Fig
1	H3	Small and slender swallow tailed arrowhead. Socket and one barb missing, with diamond cross section	58	11	–	83SF47	O63	5a	7.4
2	MP4	Socketed small flat leaf shaped blade	50	9	8	93SF65	O94	u/p	7.4
3	MP4	Socketed with flat angular leaf shaped blade and damaged socket	58	14	12	92SF174	P43	4a	7.4
4	MP4	Broad angular leaf shaped blade with short socket, tiny shoulder at base of blade	66	22	10	80SF43	K9	6c	7.4
5	MP6	Small barbed head with damaged socket, wood traces and flat tip	37	13	8	92SF73	O52	4d	7.4
6	MP8	Tapering socket with slender rounded barbs, rolled socket with copper brazing and rivet	50	12	10	84SF40	Z16	4d	7.4
7	MP8	Narrow tapering socket with applied triangular barbs, socket missing with slightly curved profile	42	17	5	87SF73	J1	7b	7.4
8	MP8	Narrow tapering socket to square sectioned point, with narrow rounded barbs and copper brazing	65	14	9	90SF134	H59	4c	7.4
9	MP8	Tapering socket with applied rounded barbs, one third of blade and tip missing	42	17	9	92SF175	G456	1b	7.4
10	MP8	Tapering socket with applied angular barbs, two thirds of blade and tip missing	40	15	9	95SF21	VA4	7b	7.4
11	MP8	Tapering socket with unsymmetrical applied angular barbs, tip and socket missing	36	18	7	93SF96	O123	4a	7.4
12	MP8	Tapering socket with applied barbs, one third of blade and socket missing	22	16	10	82SF51	J72	1b	7.4
13	MP8	Narrow rolled tapering socket with applied angular barbs, tip missing	58	15	8	91SF80	O44	5b	7.4
14	MP8	Folded socket with flat unsymmetrical angular barbs, base of socket upturned and distorted	67	23	10	87SF95	G59	4c	7.4
15	MP8	Applied barbs for socketed arrowhead, socket missing and heavily corroded	32	22		91SF27	G190	2d	7.4
16	MP8	Tapering socket with small barbed head with diamond cross section. Wood traces in socket, tip and barbs damaged	58	10	11	87SF97	G59	4c	7.4
17	M3	Socketed with short angular barbs applied, diamond cross section. Rivet in socket and one barb missing	51	12	11	93SF47	A7	6d	7.4
18	MP9	Short socketed bullet point	30		9	85SF64	F19	3b	7.4
19	M5	Short socketed point with tapering diamond cross-sectioned blade	34	9	8	89SF5	H15	4a	7.4
20	M5	Short socketed point with tapering diamond cross-sectioned blade	38	12	10	95SF50	G27	4c	7.4
21	M5?	Short socketed point with tapering diamond cross section, very corroded and split	33	13	10	97SF98	G48	4c	7.4
22	M6	Socket tapering to concoidal point, tip missing	38		10	83SF30	F45	3b	7.4
23	M6	Socket tapering to concoidal point, tip missing	38		9	91SF2	P36	2d	7.4
24	M6	Rolled socket tapering to concoidal point, tip missing	45		10	91SF85	G193	2c	7.4
25	M6	Rolled socket tapering to concoidal point, tip missing and base of socket burred upwards	38		12	91SF95	O44	5b	7.4
26	M6	Socket tapering to concoidal point, tip missing	43		8	91SF102	O44	5b	7.4
27	M6	Socket tapering to concoidal point, wood traces and tip missing	43		10	92SF24	O52	4d	7.4
28	M6	Narrow folded socket tapering to concoidal point, corroded with tip missing	33		9	90SF82	H59	4c	7.4
29	M6	Socket tapering to concoidal point, corroded with wood traces and tip missing	36		9	91SF46	P42	4a	7.4
30	M6	Socket tapering to concoidal point, wood traces and half of blade/tip missing	36		9	85SF76	J18	1b	7.4
31	M6	Rolled and squashed socket tapering to concoidal point, tip missing	34		9	92SF41	O52	4d	7.4
32	M6	Socket tapering to concoidal point, tip missing	28		8	90SF137	H59	4c	7.4
33	M6	Socket tapering to concoidal point, tip missing and base of socket burred upwards	46		10	85SF78	F25	3b	7.4

FIGURE 7.3

Arrowheads and crossbow bolts (quarrels)

W no.	Jessop Type		L	W	Diam	SF	Context	Phase	Fig
34	M6	Socket tapering to concoidal point, half of blade and tip missing	40		9	85SF75	u/s		7.4
35	M6	Socket tapering to concoidal point, tip and back of socket missing. Wood traces and rolled tip	46		10	91SF108	G211	2d	7.4
36	M6	Large socket tapering to concoidal point, tip missing	62		10	85SF73	u/s		7.4
37	M6	Large square socket tapering to concoidal point, wood traces and tip missing	78		9	93SF103	O130	3b	7.4
38	M7	Long narrow blade of diamond cross section, with short socket. Wood traces and tip missing	160	7	8	92SF159	O68	5a	7.5
39	M7	Narrow blade of a distorted diamond cross section, tip missing and socket missing	59	7	5	95SF13	VD3	5d	7.5
40	M7	Long narrow blade of diamond cross section, with short socket. Half of blade and base of socket missing	88	5	6	93SF134	O77	3b	7.5
41	M7	Long narrow blade of diamond cross section, with short socket and tip missing	108	5	7	93SF64	O77	3b	7.5
42	M8	Long narrow tapering blade with diamond cross section, socket joins blade with prominent shoulder, majority of socket missing	88	9	7	91SF81	O44	5b	7.5
43	M8	Long narrow tapering blade with diamond cross section, tip and socket missing	75	9		95SF16	R8	6d	7.5
44	M8	Long narrow blade with thickening towards tip, diamond cross section. Majority of socket missing although joins blade smoothly, tip flat	83						7.5
45	M8	Fragment of narrow tapering blade with diamond cross section	53	10		83SF31	F45	3b	7.5
46	M8	Long narrow tapering blade with diamond cross section, socket joins blade with prominent shoulder, socket missing but stub twisted	80	8	8	90SF62	H59	4c	7.5
47	M8	Long narrow tapering blade with diamond cross section, socket joins blade smoothly. Tip twisted and socket missing	95	8	5	93SF55	O99	4d	7.5
48	M8	Long narrow bent tapering blade with diamond cross section, socket joins blade smoothly. Base of socket and tip missing	82	6	7	95SF18	VD3	5d	7.5
49	M8	Long narrow tapering blade with diamond cross section, socket joins blade with prominent shoulder. Tip and socket missing	70	8	5	88SF15	I82	2b	7.5
50	M8	Long tapering blade with diamond cross section, socket joins blade with prominent shoulder, socket missing	68	11	8	92SF23	O52	4d	7.5
51	M8	Fragment of long narrow tapering blade with diamond cross section, majority of socket missing but joins blade with prominent shoulder	48	9	5	90SF39	H59	4c	7.5
52	M8	Long narrow tapering blade with diamond cross section, very corroded and socket missing	70	10	9	90SF122	O25	5b	–
53	M8	Fragment of long narrow tapering blade with diamond cross section. Wood traces, but very corroded and fragmented	90	7	8	93SF97	O151	3b	–
54	M8	Long narrow tapering blade with diamond cross-section, rolled socket joins blade smoothly, half of blade missing	72	9	10	81SF45	K12	6c	7.5
55	M8	Long narrow tapering blade with diamond cross section, folded socket joins blade with prominent shoulder. Third of blade missing and base of socket burred upwards	85	9	10	91SF65	O25	5b	7.5
56	M8	Long narrow tapering blade with diamond cross section, socket joins blade smoothly. Very corroded with tip missing	83	10	11	83SF36	F19	3b	7.5
57	M8	Narrow tapering blade with diamond cross section, long socket joins blade smoothly. Very corroded with half of blade missing	70	8	10	92SF132	O31	4a	7.5

FIGURE 7.3

Continued

199

W no.	Jessop Type		L	W	Diam	SF	Context	Phase	Fig
58	M8	Long narrow twisted tapering blade with diamond cross section, folded socket joins blade smoothly. Very corroded with half of blade and base of socket missing	72	10	12	87SF99	G48	4c	7.5
59	M8	Long narrow tapering blade with diamond cross section, folded socket joins blade with slight shoulder. Wood traces and tip missing	115	7	8	90SF4	H35	4c	7.5
60	M8	Long narrow bent tapering blade with diamond cross section, socket joins blade with prominent shoulder. Two pieces, tip missing	133	8	8	82SF47	M41	3b	7.5
61	M8	Long narrow tapering blade with diamond cross section, folded socket joins blade with prominent shoulder. Wood traces and tip missing	135	11	11	91SF90	O44	5b	7.5
62	M8	Long narrow tapering blade with diamond cross section, folded socket joins blade smoothly. Wood traces and tip missing	126	10	11	92SF160	O66	4a	7.5
63	M8	Long narrow tapering blade with diamond cross section, folded socket joins blade with prominent shoulder. Tip missing	160	8	8	93SF110	O66	4a	7.5
64	M8	Corroded fragment of tapering blade with diamond cross section	56	11	9	86SF37	G12	6c	7.6
65	M8	Socket and tapering blade fragment, socket joins blade with prominent shoulder. Wood traces with two thirds of blade missing	58	10	12	83SF80	F45	3b	7.6
66	M8	Long narrow tapering blade with diamond cross section, socket joins blade with prominent swelling. Wood traces, tip missing and fragmented in two pieces	65/45	8	11	87SF73	G59	4c	7.6
67	M8	Long narrow tapering blade with diamond cross section, folded socket joins blade with prominent shoulder. Wood traces and third of blade missing	112	9	10	87SF72	G59	4c	7.6
68	M8	Long narrow tapering blade with diamond cross section, folded socket joins blade with prominent shoulder. Fragmented in two pieces, tip missing	131	9	10	92SF162	O66	4a	7.6
69	M8	Long narrow tapering blade with diamond cross section, folded socket joins blade with prominent shoulder. Rivet in socket, tip missing and blade buckled	110	11	10	91SF34	B7	6d	7.6
70	M8	Long narrow tapering blade with diamond cross section, socket joins blade smoothly. Very corroded, socket missing and blade in two pieces	115	9	10	87SF47	G45	4c	7.6
71	M8	Long narrow tapering blade with diamond cross section, socket joins blade with prominent shoulder. Wood traces and socket burred upwards	104	9	9	93SF22	B87	4b	7.6
72	M8	Long narrow tapering blade with diamond cross section, socket joins blade smoothly. Tip missing and bent	98	8	10	93SF41	B86	3a	7.6
73	M8	Long narrow tapering blade with diamond cross section, socket joins blade with shoulder. Base of socket damaged and tip buckled	95	9	9	93SF102	X16	6d	7.6
74	M9	Thick tapering blade with diamond cross-section, and large socket swelling from blade	124	11	14	93SF82	O140	5b	7.6
75	M9	Thick tapering blade with diamond cross section, and stub of socket. Blade swells towards tip	100	11	9	89SF14	P7	6d	7.6
76	M9	Fragment of thick tapering blade with diamond cross section, socket missing and tip bent	66	11		92SF67	O52	4d	7.6
77	M9	Fragment of thick tapering blade with diamond cross section, socket missing and blade cut diagonally	62	13		85SF42	F16	4b	7.6
78	M9	Large socket and base of blade. Very corroded with wood traces	76	13	13	92SF68	O52	4d	7.6
79	M9	Complete thick tapering blade with diamond cross section, and large folded socket. Wood traces	125	13	13	81SF44	K12	6c	7.6

FIGURE 7.3

Continued

W no.	Jessop Type		L	W	Diam	SF	Context	Phase	Fig
80	M9	Complete thick tapering blade with diamond cross section, and large folded socket. Wood traces and rivet	128	13	13	82SF17	F13	5b	7.6
81	M9	Complete thick tapering blade with diamond cross section, and large folded socket. Heavy	134	13	13	92SF136	B47	3b	7.6
82	M9	Fragment of thick tapering blade with diamond cross section, and large socket. Very corroded and half of blade missing, wood traces	100	14	14	83SF23	G48	4c	7.6
83	M10	Short thin blade with diamond cross section and damaged socket	65	8	10	85SF77	I1	7d	7.7
84	M10	Complete short thin blade with diamond cross section and socket. Wood traces	60	8	10	91SF25	H53	4a	7.7
85	M10	Short thin buckled blade with diamond cross section and socket. Tip missing and slightly swelled socket	65	10	10	91SF12	O29	u/p	7.7
86	M10	Short thin blade with diamond cross section and squashed socket. Tip missing	78	9	10	85SF30	F19	3b	7.7
87	M10	Short thin tapering blade with diamond cross section and short socket. Wood traces and tip bent	85	8	12	85SF16	F11	4a	7.7
88	M10	Complete short thin bent blade with diamond cross section and long folded socket	81	8	12	89SF20	O7	6d	7.7
89	M10	Short thin blade with diamond cross section and rolled socket. Wood traces and slightly damaged blade	73	11	11	87SF16	G23	5c	7.7
90	M10	Short thin blade with diamond cross section and damaged socket. Tip bent and blade damaged	78	9	9	80SF42	K9	6c	7.7
91	M10	Short thin blade with diamond cross section and rolled socket. Wood traces and tip missing	78	9	9	90SF127	O26	4d	7.7
92	M10	Complete short thin blade with diamond cross section and slightly damaged socket	95	10	10	84SF69	L31	5a	7.7
Crossbow Bolts / Quarrels									
	Ward Perkins Type								
93	11	Tapering conical socket with expanded triangular sectioned point, wood traces in socket	61		11	85SF68	u/s		7.7
94	11	Tapering rolled conical socket with expanded triangular sectioned point, wood traces in socket	69		10	85SF69	u/s		7.7
95	11	Tapering folded conical socket with small triangular sectioned point	65		11	85SF70	u/s		7.7
96	11	Tapering conical socket with expanded triangular sectioned point, wood traces and tip missing	68		11	85SF71	u/s		7.7
97	11	Tapering folded conical socket with expanded triangular sectioned point, wood traces with tip missing	65		13	85SF72	u/s		7.7
98	11	Tapering conical socket with expanded triangular sectioned point, wood traces and tip missing	66		13	85SF74	u/s		7.7

FIGURE 7.3

Continued

Arrowheads [**W38–92**] fall under the category of 'bodkins' and are a selection of three specialised forms intended for military use (Jessop 1997, 3). Essentially iron points of differing weights and thickness with a diamond-shaped cross-section, these are standard military forms that were in widespread use throughout the British Isles. Parallels are found in mid 13th- and 14th-century contexts at the castles of Beeston (Cheshire) (Courtney 1993, 157), Brandon (Warwickshire) (Chatwin 1955, 81), Criccieth (Gwynedd) (O'Neil 1944–45, 40), Lewis (East Sussex) (Bennell 1992, 95), Montgomery (Powys) (Knight 1994, 228),

Rhuddlan (Denbighshire) (I Goodall 1994, 188), Rumney (Cardiff) (Lloyd-Fern and Sell 1992, 134) and Urquhart (Highland) (Samson 1982, 466).

Type M8 [**W42–73**] is characterised by its long slender blade and is frequently found at Welsh castles, such as Caergwrle (Flintshire) (Courtney 1994, 112), Montgomery (Powys) (Knight 1994, 226), Rhuddlan (Denbighshire) (I Goodall 1994, 188) and Rumney (Cardiff) (Lloyd-Fern and Sell 1992, 134). Its design would have been effective in piercing both chain mail and plate armour. At Dryslwyn, 71% of examples occur in mid to late 13th-century contexts, clustering

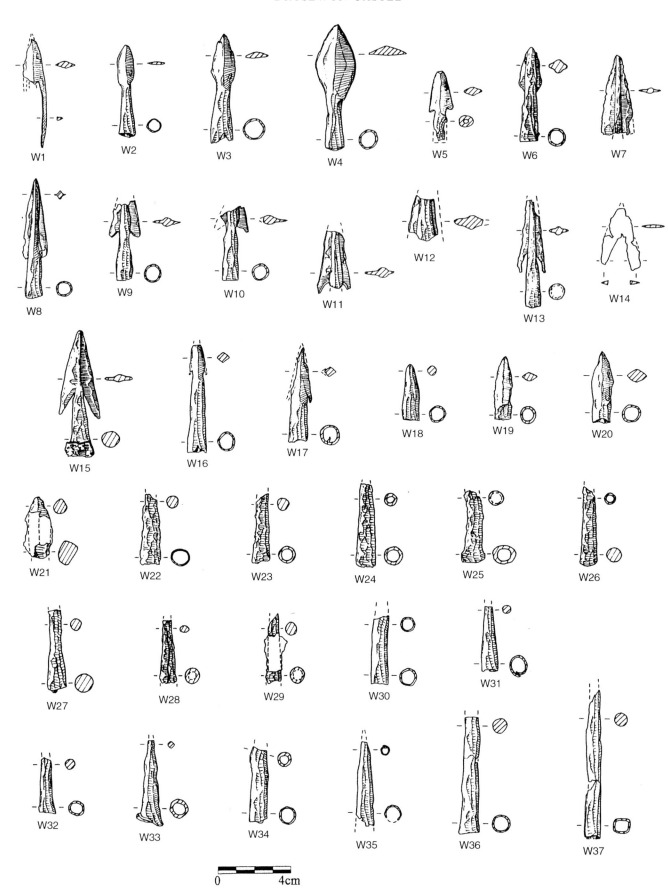

FIGURE 7.4

Arrowheads **W1–37**

202

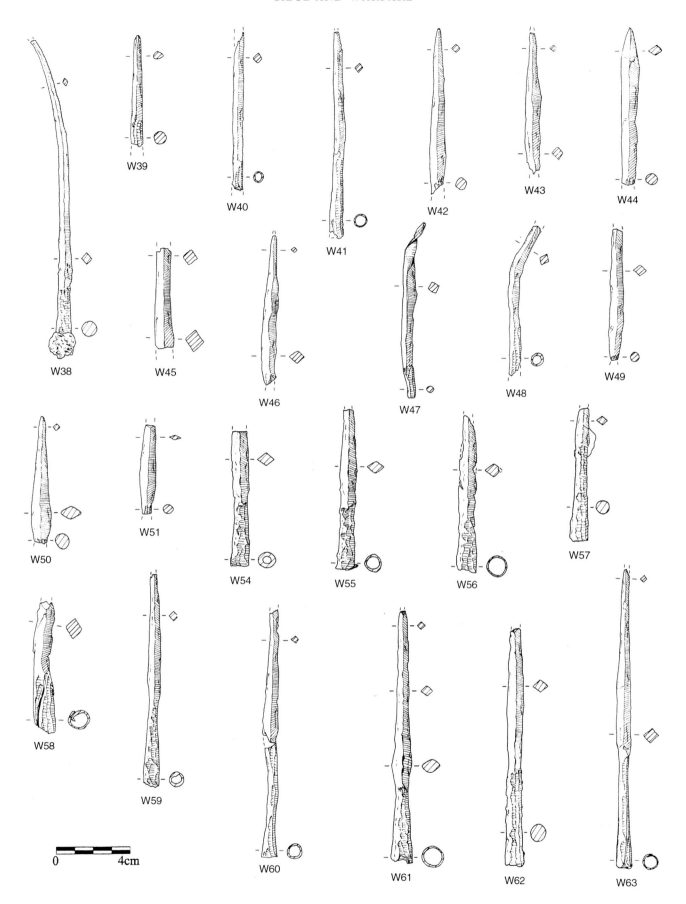

FIGURE 7.5

*Arrowheads **W38–63***

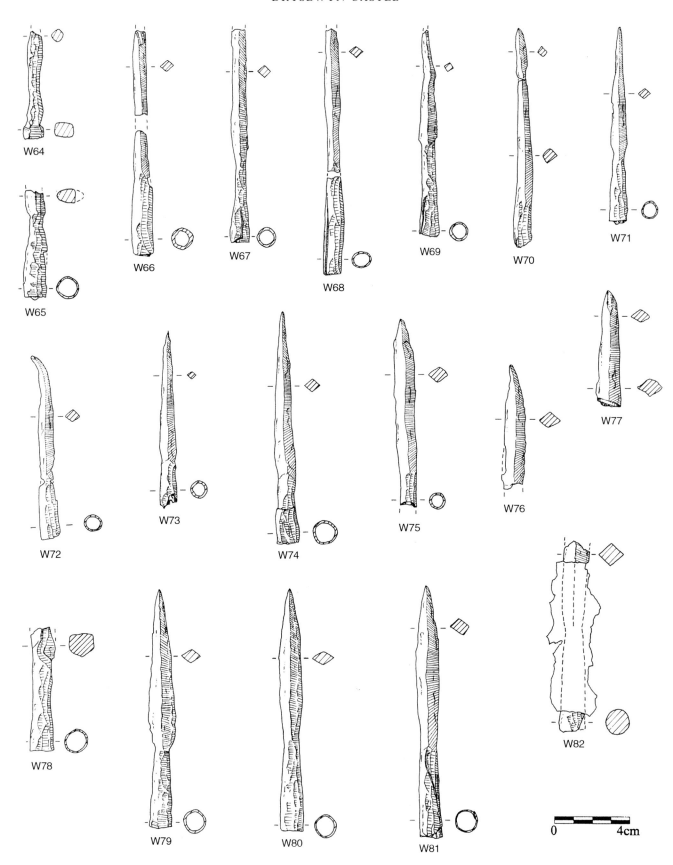

FIGURE 7.6

Arrowheads **W64–82**

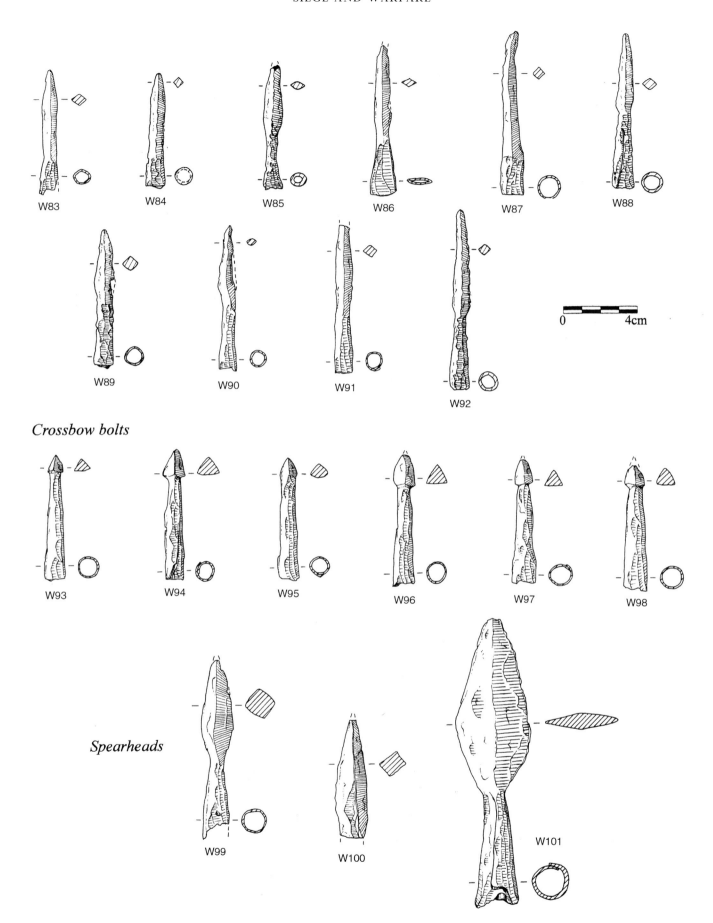

FIGURE 7.7

*Arrowheads **W83–92**, crossbow bolts and spearheads*

around the period 1280–87, and they were clearly favoured for use in the siege of 1287 (Morris 1901).

The group of nine thick armour-piercing forms [W74–82] (Type MP9) is interesting; the best parallels for these come from Criccieth Castle (Gwynedd) (O'Neil 1944–45, 40) and Urquhart Castle (Highland) (Samson 1982, 466). These are fairly widespread within the castle, having been recovered from Areas B, F, G, K, O and P, and span the period of its occupation from Phase 3b to Phase 6d. Consequently, little can be inferred from their distribution. Type MP10 [W83–92] is similar to Type MP9, having been recovered from a range of locations (Areas F, G, H, I, K and O) and from Phase 3b–6c deposits. Many of these arrowheads from later destruction deposits were probably redeposited. Elsewhere, these arrowheads have been mainly recovered from mid to late 13th-century locations, such as at Castell-y-Bere (Gwynedd) (Butler 1974, 95), Montgomery Castle (Powys) (Knight 1994, 226) and Urquhart Castle (Highland) (Samson 1982, 466).

Crossbow bolts/quarrels

Six crossbow bolts were recovered from the excavations (Figure 7.7). They were found as a discrete group corroded together in Area E. This part of the castle acted as a passageway to the latrines and up onto the wall-walk. It is possible, therefore, that they may represent a bundle of complete crossbow bolts kept in storage and lost during the destruction of the castle. The type classification is taken from the London Museum Medieval Catalogue (Ward Perkins 1940, 65). This form has parallels from similar 15th-century contexts at Bramber Castle (West Sussex) (Barton and Holden 1978, 61), Montgomery (Powys) (Knight 1994, 228), Urquhart Castle (Highland) (Samson 1982, 469) and within the collections at Salisbury Museum in Wiltshire (Borg 1991, 87).

Spearheads

Three spearheads of two differing types were recovered (Figure 7.7). All were socketed with diameters in the range 17–20mm. Ward Perkins (1940, 73) writes that hunting spearheads had projecting wings at the base of the blade, a feature lacking on the Dryslwyn examples. On this basis, it would appear that they are of a specific military design with narrow slender heads, similar to the design of arrowheads of the same period (Jessop 1996, Type M8). They may represent a response to the increasing use of plate armour during the 13th century, perhaps specifically to cause internal injury by punching a small hole in metal plating. The socket accounts for approximately half the length

of the weapon and parallels for nos. 99 and 100 can be found at Bishopsgate (London) (Ward Perkins 1940, 74, Type 2), Montgomery Castle (Powys) (Knight 1994, 228) and Sandal Castle (West Yorkshire) (Credland 1983, 265). However, these sites place this type of spearhead within the Tudor and post-medieval period and not the late 13th century, as at Dryslwyn. Other generally similar examples from Criccieth (Gwynedd) (O'Neil 1944–45, 41) and Rumney (Cardiff) (Lloyd-Fern and Sell 1992, 134) come from more certain 13th-century contexts.

The third spearhead (no. 101) is a less common type (Ward Perkins Type 3). The closest parallel comes from the River Thames, found in front of the Tower of London (Ward Perkins 1940, 74). This type has much longer cutting edges than Types 1–2 and may be earlier in date, perhaps even of Welsh origin. Examples of shorter (80mm) leaf-shaped X-section spearheads come form Loughor (Swansea) (Lewis 1993, 142) and several of the examples from Criccieth (Gwynedd) (O'Neil 1944–45, 41) are probably also of this type.

W99 Spearhead (Ward Perkins Type 2). Socketed with expanded square-sectioned blade, wood traces and rivet-hole in socket. Slight damage to socket and tip missing. Length 95mm, diameter 15mm, blade width 17mm. (87SF61). Context G48 (Phase 4c) (Figure 7.7).

W100 Spearhead (Ward Perkins Type 2). Expanded heavy square-sectioned blade, very corroded with socket and tip missing. Length 61mm, blade width 17mm. (86SF47). Context J25 (Phase 2d) (Figure 7.7).

W101 Spearhead (Ward Perkins Type 6). Socketed with leaf-shaped blade of diamond cross-section, with missing tip. Slightly squashed rolled socket with rivet. Length 152mm, diameter 20mm, blade width 40mm, blade diameter 7mm. (86SF11). Context I18 (Phase 4a) (Figure 7.7).

Macehead

A complete copper-alloy macehead [W102] was recovered from the northern edge of Courtyard O, found buried deep within the fill (O151) of a latrine pit (O50) that backed up against the curtain wall. This context was dated to 1250–60 and the macehead, therefore, would appear to have been in use in the early to mid 13th century. A Short Cross halfpenny [C5] retrieved from the same context was minted between 1205 and 1217 (Section 9.3). The weapon (Figure 7.8) was socketed with twelve barbs, knops or points forming a head. Maces are uncommon finds (Halpin 1988), but medieval illustrative sources (Caldwell 1981, 306) indicate that they were a favoured weapon of mounted troops throughout Europe from the 12th century onwards; parallels have been identified in Czechoslovakia and Hungary. Two examples of maceheads similar to the Dryslwyn example are illustrated in the Maciejowski Bible, which dates to c1250 (Cockerill 1969, f16r, f24v).

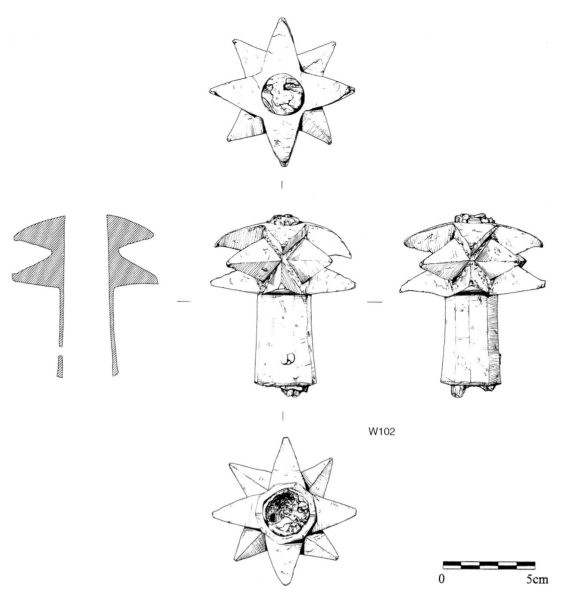

FIGURE 7.8

Mid 13th-century copper-alloy macehead

It has been suggested that maces were used as symbols of authority, even that they had ceremonial functions, as is the case today (Halpin 1988, 173). In total, 25 copper-alloy knopped maces have been recovered from Ireland and Scotland, although the only one with any archaeological context is from Perth (Perthshire) (Caldwell 1987, 125). To these should be added between 15 and 20 knopped copper-alloy maces that have been recorded from England, primarily as metal detector finds reported under the Portable Antiquities Scheme, although these too lack either context or dating. Three or four unprovenanced iron examples can be found in the collections of the British Museum and the Royal Armouries (Caldwell 1981, 306). Like the Dryslwyn mace, both Scottish maces have twelve points arranged in three rows attached to a cylindrical shaft. The Dryslwyn mace, however, has

a nine-faceted shaft that is, so far, unique. Its recovery from a latrine pit suggests that it was deliberately hidden, as it is not a place where it would normally be stored or accidentally lost. The reason for the concealment is unknown.

W102 Macehead, Group II (Halpin 1988). Socketed star-headed mace with tapering faceted shaft. There are nine facets on the shaft, each of which is approximately 48mm long, 10mm wide and 34mm in diameter at the base of the shaft. The internal diameter of the shaft is 27mm at the base and 23mm at the top of the head. There is a hole 10mm up from the base of one of the facets containing a copper-alloy rivet. The twelve projecting points forming the head are arranged in three layers, each offset by 45° from one another. The top and bottom set of barbs are triangular in cross-section, 20mm wide, 15mm in height and *c*27mm in length. The central layer consists of barbs that are four-sided and projecting *c*28mm. The lowest layer of points projects

5mm further than those at the top. All the barbs have lost their point tips, which are either pushed flat or curved downwards, suggesting that this macehead had seen considerable use. Surviving within the central socket are the preserved remains of the wooden shaft, which project slightly from top and bottom. Due to the decayed nature of the molecular cell structure of this material, it has not been possible to identify the species. It was noted during conservation (Williams 1993, 4) that two small fragments of an unidentified substance adhered to the underside of two of the barbs. Analysis has demonstrated that this has a similar cell structure to human skin, but no definitive conclusion as to its true nature can be drawn. EDXRF analysis of the artefact identified copper, tin and lead, indicating that it is made of leaded bronze. It has been cast, although there is no direct evidence for the precise technique that was employed, since the surfaces of the facets and barbs have been filed smooth at an angle of 45°, obscuring any evidence that might have survived from the casting process. Length 88mm, weight 523.5g. (93SF93). Context O151, (Phase 3b) (Figure 7.8).

Mail
by Ian Goodall

The mail found at Dryslwyn Castle was composed of interlinked circular rings arranged so that each one has four others linked through it. Many of the sufficiently complete rings were solid, some of them clearly with butted ends, but a number of others had the flattened, overlapping and riveted ends known from other medieval armour (Blair 1958, 20). F182–184 are corroded masses of rings, whilst F185–189 are a representative sample of individual rings. A further 18 rings were found, 2 from Phase 3, 5 from Phases 4a–b, 6 from Phases 4c–d and 5 from Phase 7a. Although no evidence of plate armour was recovered during the excavation, documentary evidence indicates that there was plate armour in the stores of Dryslwyn Castle for much of the late 13th and 14th centuries (Section 3.1). (Catalogue numbers relate to the Iron Catalogue and none of the mail rings is illustrated.)

F182–184   Mail. Corroded masses of rings.
F182. (87SF37). Context G53, (Phase 4c).
F183. (87SF26). Context G39, (Phase 4c).
F184. (87SF4). Context G25, (Phase 4d).

F185–187   Mail. Rings solid or with butted ends.
F185. Diameter 15mm. (82SF6). Context M13, (Phase 7a).
F186. Diameter 14mm. (82SF10). Context M13, (Phase 7a).
F187. Diameter 14mm. (81SF43). Context T2, (Phase 7b).

F188–189   Mail. Rings with overlapping pierced ends.
F188. Diameter 15mm. (89SF9). Context G158, (Phase 3a).
F189. Diameter 20mm. (88SF1). Unstratified.

7.4   LITHIC PROJECTILES
by R F Caple

Excavation uncovered a group of 65 stones that were unlike the Ordovician limestone that comprises the hill at Dryslwyn and almost all of the castle's masonry (Figure 7.9). A very high proportion of these stones were large, natural, water-worn ovoid pebbles that appear to have been deliberately selected and brought to the castle (Figure 7.10). It is highly likely, therefore, that these were lithic projectiles, which were collected either by the castle's defenders to be thrown out at potential attackers, or by its besiegers to be thrown into the castle from outside its walls. Analysis of the weights of 63 of the 65 lithic projectiles collected (Figure 7.11) do not form a random distribution and suggests that six distinct classes of projectile existed.

Class 1 (slingstones)

This class comprises 14 stones, each weighing less than 320g, seven of which can be regarded as very small pebbles of 60g or less (Figure 7.10). Whilst it is possible that these stones, especially those weighing less than 60g, could have functioned as gaming counters or children's toys, it is perhaps more likely that the majority are slingstones, which were placed in a sling and hurled at opponents with the intention of causing injury and perhaps even death. Slingers are recorded in the castle accounts of 1289/90, when 'William the slinger' was present (Phillpotts 2001c).

Class 2 (handstones)

This class consists of 20 stones, each weighing between 400g and 1.8kg. They show a wide variety in weight and shape and all but two are all well rounded and water-worn. These stones can readily be picked up and hurled (Figure 7.1), but they are unlikely to disable an opponent unless propelled with the force of a catapult or similar device.

A group of six of these lithic projectiles, ranging in weight between 822g and 1.408kg, was recovered from a single location in Gateway Area B, immediately beside the guardhouse. They may represent a pile of stones stacked here to be thrown down from the curtain wall to deter potential intruders. They would have made effective missiles cheaper than arrows and an effective non-lethal deterrent. It is also possible, although perhaps less likely, that they could have been 'balls' for playing a medieval equivalent of bowls or boules. These games were popular in the medieval period as the formation of the Southampton Town Bowling Club in 1299 demonstrates (Encyclopaedia Britannica 1978, 3:87). Security work undoubtedly had long periods of boredom, even in the medieval period.

Class 3

No stones occurred with weights between 1.8kg and 3.3kg, representing a hiatus in distribution. Stones of

LP no.	Class no.	Description	Dimensions (mm)			Weight (g) (as found)	Completeness (%)	Weight (complete)	SF No.	Context	Phase
1	4	Triangular pyramid, well rounded. Fine grain hard sandstone, grey colour, mainly quartz, some fine pebbles	160	190	110	4366	100		87SF83	G59	4c
2	4	Oblate, water rounded. Conglomerate sandstone, dark grey	100	120	220	3657	90	4063		u/s	
3	4	Oblong and slightly rounded. Limestone, hard, grey, crystalline	110	150	70	3770	55	6855	87SF84	G59	4c
4	4	Oblong head, square neck with rounded corners. Quartzite, grey, fine grain, hard	215	150	130	8845	100		87SF82	G59	4c
5	4	Triangular slab with rounded corners. Conglomerate sandstone, grey	170	160	100	3969	100		87SF80	G59	4c
6	4	Oblate and well rounded. Limestone nodule, hard, grey, some iron staining, natural pebble	140	180	220	7484	100		86SF9	I18	4a
7	4	Oblong with well rounded corners, split. Conglomerate sandstone, red/grey	170	180	110	5414	70	7735	87SF78	G59	4c
8		Oblong on bed, square in section, rounded corners. Conglomerate sandstone, grey	230	150	160	unknown	100		87SF79	G59	4c
9	4	Roughly chipped, rounded, split but 100%. Limestone, hard grey crystalline, local	180	210	220	8590	100		–	u/s	–
10	4	Oblong on bed square in section, well rounded. Conglomerate sandstone, grey	110	120	190	3940	100		87SF81	G59	4c
11	4	Trapezoid with well rounded corners. Conglomerate sandstone, grey	170	170	190	10,404	100		87SF74	G59	4c
12	4	Oblate and well rounded. Limestone, grey, hard and crystalline, natural pebble	220	160	100	5188	100		–	u/s	–
13	4	Irregular face, pyramid, well rounded. Conglomerate sandstone, grey	185	150	180	7229	100		87SF77	G59	4c
14	4	Oblate and well rounded. Conglomerate sandstone, grey, natural pebble	180	180	130	5925	100		87SF75	G59	4c
15	4	Oblate well rounded. Conglomerate sandstone, grey, natural pebble	220	190	130	6463	100		87SF76	G59	4c
16	4	Trapezoid and square with rounded corners. Conglomerate sandstone, grey, fine grain	230	170	140	8561	90	9513	–	O7	6d
17	4	Rounded with one square corner. Conglomerate sandstone, grey, fine grain	225	195	120	6463	100		90SF7	H35	4c
18	4	Oblate, rounded, part only. Limestone, grey, hard, crystalline	80	100	100	992	30	3307	90SF3	H35	4c
19	4	Oblong on bed, well rounded. Conglomerate sandstone, fine grain, mainly quartz	160	220	130	6378	100		90SF18	H35	4c
20	2	Oblate/Square, well rounded. Limestone, grey, hard crystalline	60	60	75	482	100		90SF19	H35	4c
21	4	Oblate, well rounded, natural pebble. Quartzite, white, face crystalline with iron staining, partially metamorphosed	220	135	175	5812	100		90SF20	H35	4c
22	4	Trapezoid on bed, triangular section, well rounded. Conglomerate sandstone, grey, coarse grain	190	160	105	3827	100		90SF21	H35	4c
23	4	Oblong on bed, well rounded, natural pebble. Quartzite, white with iron staining	230	180	125	7768	100		90SF22	H35	4c
24	2	Oblate and well rounded. Limestone, grey, crystalline, natural pebble	80	60	80	425	100		90SF35	H35	4c
25	4	Irregular cube with well rounded corners. Conglomerate sandstone, grey, coarse grain	185	195	200	8618	100		90SF25	H35	4c
26	4	Long ovoid, well rounded, natural. Sandstone, grey, fine grain with iron staining, very smooth	320	180	160	9188	99	9300	90SF26	H35	4c

FIGURE 7.9

Lithic projectiles

LP no.	Class no.	Description	Dimensions (mm)			Weight (g) (as found)	Completeness (%)	Weight (complete)	SF No.	Context	Phase
27	2	Oblate well rounded pebble. Limestone, grey, hard, crystalline	100	70	70	567	100		90SF27	H35	4c
28	4	Oblate and well rounded, now shattered. Limestone, grey, crystalline, very hard, smooth on unbroken surface				2523	30	9410	90SF86	u/s	–
29	2	Oblate well rounded, split. Limestone, grey, hard, crystalline, natural pebble	70	50	65	409	80	511	90SF101	H59	4c
30	2	Oblate and well rounded. Sandstone conglomerate, fine grain, red, natural pebble	130	100	110	1729	100		90SF124	O7	6d
31	6	Melon shaped, chipped and round. Sandstone, fine grain, grey with iron staining	310	320	250	42kg	90	46kg	91SF88	P47	4a (4c)
32	2	Ovoid and water rounded. Quartzite, fine grain with bedding/lines. Natural pebble, etched by weather/acid deposit	115	75	65	822	100		92SF44	B16	6c
33	2	Triangular pyramid, well rounded corners. Sandstone, fine grain, grey/yellow with black bedding, smooth surface	100	105	80	1105	100		92SF45	B16	6c
34	2	Triangular Pyramid, water rounded. Sandstone, fine grain, red with garnet inclusions	120	120	85	1408	100		92SF46	B16	6c
35	2	Trapezoid with well rounded corners. Fine grain sandstone, red with fine quartz, some garnet and bedding planes	90	100	75	921	100		92SF47	B16	6c
36	2	Trapezoid but well water rounded. Conglomerate sandstone of coarse grade, mainly quartz/quartzite	80	105	115	1233	100		92SF48	B16	6c
37	2	Trapezoidal and well water rounded. Sandstone, fine grain, red/purple with some quartzite	80	90	95	864	90	960	92SF113	B36	5d
38	4	Oblate and well rounded by water. Hard sandstone, grey/green fine grain with smooth surface	230	140	110	4763	100		–	O74	3a
39A	1	Oblate and water rounded. Hard sandstone, green, fine grain.	70	40	35	113	100		93SF67	O77	3b
39B	4	Oblate and well water rounded. Fractured. Limestone, grey and crystalline, fractured pebble	180	110	75	907	25	3628	91SF67	B6	6c
40	1	Oblate and water rounded. Quartzite, fine grain crystalline	80	60	45	311	100		93SF60	G468	1b
41	1	Oval, well rounded by water. Sandstone, fine grain, grey and hard	55	55	40	148	100		93SF66	O77	3b
42	1	Oval, water rounded. Sandstone, grey/green, hard with fine grain	40	35	25	57	100		–	B75	5a
43	1	Oblate and well water rounded. Yellow brown sandstone, medium grain	70	50	45	226	100		–	O131	3b
44	6	Cuboid, quarried and reshaped with three minor faces, all corners rounded. Sandstone, fine grey/yellow with dark brown iron streaks in bedding	350	340	340	52kg	100		83SF13	F19/21	3b (4c)
45	6	Ovoid. Quarried and chipped. Sandstone, fine grey/yellow with dark brown iron/manganese streaks in bedding.	260	330	350	42kg	85	49kg	83SF4	O182	6d
46	2	Rounded ball, water worn. Conglomerate sandstone, purple and red with coarse grain	90	90	90	907	90	1007	80SF21	K9	6c
47	2	Oblate and water worn. Red sandstone, fine grain	100	105	70	1106	100		80SF21?	K9	6c
48	2	Oblate nodule, natural. Limestone, hard grey and crystalline	105	80	75	964	100		83SF46	I30	5a

FIGURE 7.9

Continued

LP no.	Class no.	Description	Dimensions (mm)			Weight (g) (as found)	Completeness (%)	Weight (complete)	SF No.	Context	Phase
49	2	Oblate of uneven form, water worn, pebble. Quartzite, grey, half fine half coarse	115	95	80	1148	100		84SF27	L9	6c
50	2	Triangular, well rounded, water worn. Sandstone, red, fine grain	120	110	70	964	100		84SF28	L9	6c
51	2	Oblate and water worn. Sandstone, purple and red, very fine grain	115	95	75	1205	100		84SF29	L9	6c
52	2	Pyramidal, well rounded and water worn. Sandstone, purple/red, fine grain	120	105	80	1233	100		84SF30	L9	6c
53	2	Cuboid, well rounded, water worn and split. Sandstone, purple/grey, medium grain, semi-crystalline	100	80	130	1262	70	1800	93SF123	O131	3b
54	2	Oblate and water rounded, split. Sandstone, purple/red, medium grain	85	80	75	396	60	661	80SF32	L47	6d
55		Rounded, hand chipped. Sandstone, purple/red, medium grain	100	120		unknown			–	G12	6c
56	1	Oblate pebble, water worn. Hard Limestone, grey and crystalline	35	25	20	42	100		85SF33	F20	4a
57	1	Oblate. Surface fragile, not crystalline. Limestone, grey/brown nodule	20	10	50	29	100		84SF7	Z1	7b
58	1	Oval shaped pebble, water worn. Limestone, grey, hard, crystalline	70	50	50	255	100		87SF85	G59	4c
59	1	Round pebble, water worn. Quartzite, fine grain	30	25	25	43	100		89SF21	I59	1b
60	1	Oval and water worn. Sandstone, fine grey with brown stain	55	40	40	142	100		91SF105	G193	2c
61	1	Ovoid, water worn. Sandstone, grey and hard	40	25	30	56	100		85SF15	F18	4a
62	1	Ovoid and water worn. Limestone, grey and hard	30	25	25	43	100		81SF40	K12	6c
63	1	Irregular ovoid. Limestone, dark grey, hard	35	20	25	43	100		–	F19/21	3b
64	1	Ovoid, water worn. Sandstone, purple/red, fine grain	60	50	50	156	100		87SF90	G59	4c

FIGURE 7.9

Continued

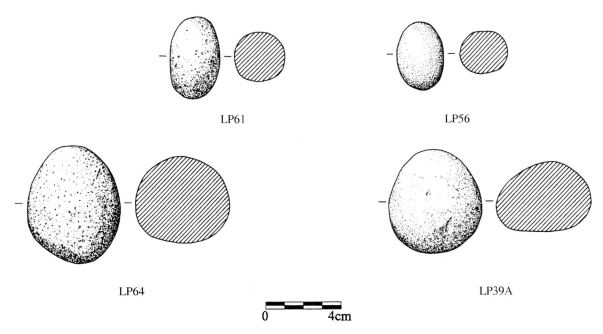

LP61   LP56

LP64   LP39A

0   4cm

FIGURE 7.10

Slingstones

211

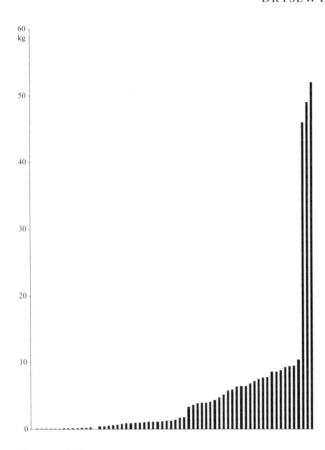

this size would be too heavy to be easily or accurately thrown by a man over any distance.

Class 4 (dropstones)

This class comprises 26 stones, each weighing between 3.3kg and 10.5kg. All but LP9, which has been carefully shaped by hand, are water-worn pebbles and are relatively evenly distributed throughout the weight range. When dropped from a height, such as a castle wall, or propelled using a siege engine, these stones are large enough to cause significant injury to the human body.

Class 5

No stones were found weighing between 10.5kg and 42kg, representing another hiatus in the distribution. Stones of this size are much too large to be easily thrown over any distance unaided by a man, but are too small to be worth throwing using a machine, since they would not cause serious structural damage to masonry buildings.

Class 6 (trebuchet balls)

This group consists of three stones [LP31, LP44 and LP45] of original weights 46kg, 52kg and 49kg. Each was shaped by hand (Figure 7.12). Their findspots

FIGURE 7.11

Lithic projectiles by weight, showing only complete specimens or estimated original weights for incomplete specimens

FIGURE 7.12

*Trebuchet balls **LP44** (83SF13) and **LP45** (83SF4)*

within the castle, as well as their size, make it highly likely that these stones were thrown at the castle by the trebuchet in the siege of 1287 (Figure 7.13). Given their similarity in both size and weight, it would appear that they were all designed to be approximately 330mm in diameter and 50kg in weight. These projectiles were of identical types of limestone and were probably quarried to a specified size and weight from the valley escarpment to the south, within 10km of the castle.

King (1982, 469) records spherical stone projectiles recovered from several castles of the mid 13th to 15th centuries where the trebuchet might have been used, or ammunition for a trebuchet might have been stored: these are Burg Stein (Germany) (430mm diameter), Caen (France) (490mm), Harlech (Gwynedd) (490mm), Lechenich (Germany) (430mm), Montrichard (France)

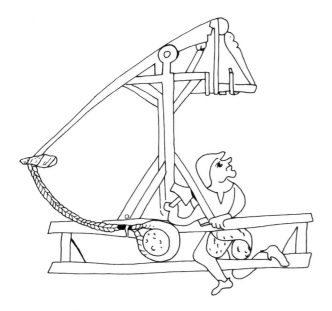

FIGURE 7.13

Illustration of a trebuchet drawn in 1316. Detail from a charter of Edward II depicting the Scots using a trebuchet at the seige of Carlisle in 1315. Note the rounded trebuchet ball hewn to shape (redrawn by Yvonne Beadnell) (Source: Charter Edward II, 12 May 1316 to Carlisle City Council)

(510mm), Newcastle (Tyne and Wear) (510mm), Norham (Northumberland) (470mm) and Pevensey (East Sussex) (430mm). Taking an average density between Bath Stone (oolitic limestone) and marble or granite, this would give a range of weights between 115kg and 185kg for these projectiles.

Other records or measurements made by the author of spherical stone projectiles include: stratified evidence of Malmstone balls, roughly 240mm in diameter, at Odiham Castle (Hampshire); stratified evidence of two balls, 250mm and 170mm in diameter and weighing 24kg and 7.7kg, at Kenilworth Castle (Warwickshire) (Rahtz 1966); four balls 330mm in diameter at Caerphilly Castle (Caerphilly); and three large stone balls, the largest measuring 356mm in diameter, which were recovered by excavation and almost certainly derive from the siege of 1277, from Dolforwyn Castle (Powys) (Lawrence Butler pers comm). From these records, it is clear that there was a range of different sizes of trebuchet throwing a range of sizes of missile. It should be noted, however, that the trebuchet stones known from Welsh castles (Caerphilly, Dolforwyn and Dryslwyn) are all 330–360mm in diameter, suggesting that there was a standard size of both trebuchet and trebuchet stone in use in Wales during the period 1270–1300.

The largest concentration (40%) of the lithic projectiles from Dryslwyn Castle comes from the very limited Phase 4c deposits, a relationship that clearly associates them with the siege activity of 1287. Of the 60 stratified examples, 17 (29%) come from the Phase 6c and Phase 6d destruction levels of the castle and probably represent stockpiled ammunition from the last phase of the castle's occupation. The only other concentration occurs in Phase 3b. Excluding one Class 6 stone (LP44), which crashed through higher deposits to come to rest in the Phase 3b deposits of the kitchen midden, there were five projectiles (8%) recovered from this phase which may suggest another period of conflict in the mid 13th century, possibly in 1245/6 when the castle was captured by the seneschal of Carmarthen for 'its rightful owner' (*AC* 86) (Section 2.1).

DRYSLWYN TOWNSHIP

8.1 HISTORY OF DRYSLWYN TOWNSHIP
by Chris Caple and Chris Phillpotts

The Welsh town

On 12 July 1281, Rhys ap Maredudd was granted a charter by Edward I to hold an annual four-day fair at Dryslwyn: 'one fair at his manor of Dryslwyn for four days duration, to wit on St Bartholomew's Day and the three days following unless the fair be to the damage of neighbouring fairs' (*CChR 1257–1300*, 253). This was probably the key event in the development of the native town, representing the consolidation of an established tradition of economic activity outside the castle wall. The permanence of this fair is indicated by the fact that, in 1287, a fence was put up around the fair ground and tolls were received (Rhys 1936, 41; PRO E101/4/20). Some form of permanent settlement was almost certainly present by this period and served as the basis of the fair. As the castle and its associated economic activity expanded, so this settlement grew into the town of Dryslwyn. Rhys ap Maredudd was certainly familiar with the advantages of the urban economy, as his borrowing of money from a burgess of Carmarthen indicates (Davies 1987, 168).

Following the siege of Dryslwyn Castle in 1287, a payment was made for cleaning out the town ditch, specified as *circa villam* (Section 3.1; Rhys 1936, 41). This indicates that there was already a substantial settlement outside the castle before the siege and that it was defended (Soulsby 1983, 133; Caple 1990b).

The English town

In a deed of 27 April 1294 (Webster 1987, 91; PRO Orig. R., 22 Edw. I, m 17), Edward I ratified the creation of 37 burgage plots in the town of Dryslwyn, which had been distributed by Robert de Tibetot. The burgages were probably laid out within the defensive ditch. Each of them had associated pieces of land, comprising in total 57¼ acres of demesne land, presumably carved out of Rhys ap Maredudd's lands of his *llys* of Dryslwyn, and 86¼ acres of 'Welsh' land, which had probably been appropriated from the free Welsh tenants of the district. The burgesses were therefore provided with enough land to support themselves in food and were not solely dependent on trade. Among the named burgesses whose holdings were confirmed were Robert le Porter, probably a janitor at the castle, Ralph le Blunt, who later became constable of Dryslwyn Castle, and Robert de Gower, later a burgess at Dinefwr and the store-keeper of the castle there. The new burgesses were not local men and only four were Welsh (*CFR 1272–1307*, 344–345; Griffiths 1966, 141; 1972, 242; Soulsby 1983, 133). This suggests that the existing settlement had been considerably expanded after the siege.

The accounts of Walter de Pederton, justiciar of west Wales, in 1298–1300 recorded the income from the commote of Cethiniog. The rents from the town of Dryslwyn were specifically noted. These record that there were then 43½ burgage plots, each yielding 2s per year rent. The total probably included plots inside the defences and outside the town walls along the road to the ford. Some fees were received from incoming burgesses, suggesting that the colonisation of the town was still in progress; Rhys suggested that these newcomers were to be identified with the later 'censers' (see below), but this seems unlikely. Other income from Dryslwyn town was drawn from two mills, one at Dryslwyn and one at Brechfa, each producing 26s rent *per annum*. The fair continued to thrive, producing an income of 31s 8d. An income was also derived from the 'pleas and perquisites' of the local court, comprising fees from land sales and court cases. A garden at Dryslwyn was also mentioned, which occasionally brought in rental income (Rhys 1936, 71, 89, 371).

In the accounting year 1300/01, the prior of Carmarthen, the chamberlain for west Wales, still recorded rents from 43½ burgage plots at Dryslwyn. Other sources of income were similar to previous years, deriving from the fair, the mills, and pleas and perquisites. Rents were also paid for the meadows, the park of Dryslwyn, the fishery and the garden. The garden functioned primarily as an orchard and, in the early 14th century, it was noted that 'nothing from the garden this year because there were no apples' (Solomon 1982, 52). A new millstone was also bought for the mill at Dryslwyn at a cost of 12s 6d, showing that the burdens of its repair and maintenance fell on the castle, rather than the lessees (Rhys 1936, 195, 217).

By comparison, there were at this time 30 burgage plots in Llanbadarn (Ceredigion), 32 at Dinefwr (Carmarthenshire) and 68 at Cardigan (Ceredigion); at the end of the 13th century, Dryslwyn's 43½ burgage plots probably formed the third largest town in Deheubarth after Carmarthen and Cardigan.

If it is assumed that there was one household for each burgage and that there were approximately four to five people in each household, Dryslwyn had a population of around 200 at this time. The total annual rental income from the rest of the commote of Cethiniog was £16 8s. If a similar ratio of rent to dwellings and people applied beyond the town, this would imply about 164 habitations and 700–800 people. In practice, it is likely that the rent levels in rural Cethiniog were lower than the burgage rents at Dryslwyn and, therefore, an estimate of roughly 1000 people is more probable. Some small settlements in the commote may have been granted as rewards to those who had aided the English cause during the siege of Dryslwyn and were therefore not included in its rental: these included the mill at Cilsan (PRO E101/4/23). By the period 1301–07, Goronwy Goch was holding a half-share in the mill at Brechfa at a rent of 6s 8d per annum (Griffiths 1972, 279).

Agricultural activities must have featured heavily in the economic basis of the Dryslwyn township. Not only did the inhabitants work their own lands, but the town probably also supplied goods and services to the surrounding area. The constable of the castle paid the townsmen 26s 3d annually for cutting and carrying the hay from 12 acres of meadow, presumably in the Tywi valley near Dryslwyn. Much of the £44 paid in wages to the constable and garrison of 24 men in the castle would have been spent in the local economy. Other officials, such as the seneschal of Cantref Mawr and the beadle and reeve of Cethiniog probably also spent much of their salaries locally. Additional sums were spent on purchasing food for the garrison locally, although after 1298 much of the garrison food was bought centrally at large market towns, such as Brecon, Carmarthen and Hereford, together with supplies for the other royal castles. The diminishing size of the garrison by 1300 meant that the castle's contribution to the local economy was probably not as significant as it had been in the 1280s.

In 1302, there were 34 named burgesses in the town of Dryslwyn, nearly corresponding with the 37 burgage plots owing rents in 1301/02 and 1303/04 and representing the approximate number of families in the town. The amount of land held by each burgess outside his burgage plot varied up to 12¼ acres. The total landholding for the burgesses was 119¼ acres, a reduction from the 143½ acres held in 1294. After an initial period of expansion, the borough seems to have remained static in its size, population and level of farming activity.

In 1301/02 and 1303/04, the accounts of William de Rogate, chamberlain for west Wales, noted 37 burgages within the town, each producing an annual rent of 12d, with a further 16s 6d rent paid from messuages and lands in *villa subtus castrum* (the vill below the castle). A distinction had therefore been made between the 37 burgage plots lying inside the defended town and 16½ parcels of land, many containing dwellings, situated outside the defences. The total of 53½ is exactly ten more than the previous total of 43½ burgages, which may suggest that there had been an accounting error. Later accounts repeat these figures without change.

For the first time, the accounts included payments by 'censers' (or 'chensars'), those non-burgesses resident in the borough, who did not hold burgage plots within the walls, but each paid an annual sum of 4s for the burgess privileges of buying and selling free of toll in the town. Other sources of income continued, such as the pleas and perquisites of the courts, the fair (its issues now farmed out to a burgess for 40s a year), rent from the town mill, and a hay crop from 4 acres of meadow. Part of the castle's hay crop was now being sold off, rather than being stored and used as winter feed for the castle animals. A new mill was constructed at Dryslwyn in the same year, at a cost of 71s 5½d (Lewis 1923–25, 73; Rhys 1936, 303–305, 327).

The Ministers' account for west Wales in 1304/05 repeats the figures of 37 burgage plots, producing an annual rent of 12d each, and a further 16s 6d rent from messuages and lands in the vill below the castle. The fair, the pleas and perquisites, the mill, and the hay crop from four acres of meadow all continued to yield an income, and the garden was again rented out (Rhys 1936, 371).

The changes in the total of burgages imply that the town changed its layout in around 1301, although the real changes may have been in status and accounting. If the number of burgage plots within the defences had really fallen from 43½ to 37, some may have been merged or lay unoccupied. Additional dwellings may have been established outside the town walls. Dryslwyn now consisted of 50–55 houses. Assuming that there were roughly five people per household, the population in and around the castle had now increased to *c*250–275. The distinction between the areas of settlement inside and outside the town walls indicates a two-tier society: those inside the walls had the rights and privileges of 'English' burgesses; those outside were not burgesses, lacked rights and privileges and were probably Welsh. They may have been the original inhabitants of the Welsh town, displaced and resettled outside the town's walls.

In 1307, the burgesses of Dryslwyn acquired further lands in Cethiniog, in particular in the demesne of Allt-y-gaer, where the lord settled his 'protection tenants'. Lands formerly held by native Welshman were granted to the new burgesses (Lloyd 1935, 319). This may indicate a further expansion of the landholding and economic wealth of the burgesses of Dryslwyn.

The military and mercantile aspects of the town were inextricably linked through overlapping personnel. As a burgess, Ralph le Blunt held a large area of the town lands, comprising 24 acres of demesne land and 6 acres of Welsh land. In 1298, he was appointed as constable of the castle (Griffiths 1966, 142). A leading role in the development of the town appears to have been played by Goronwy Goch, who had previously been Rhys ap Maredudd's constable of Dryslwyn Castle and had later led local men against Rhys during his revolt. After the English occupation of the castle, he remained prominent in Cantref Mawr, representing Dryslwyn as one of the assessors of the royal tax or tithe of December 1292 and being appointed steward of Cantref Mawr in 1299 (Griffiths 1972, 279). The families of Welshmen on the winning side continued to flourish in the area.

The inhabitants of Cantref Mawr made a complaint to the king in 1309 about the cost of bailiffs, both for the commote and for the cantref. They noted that they did not have to support these costs in the time of Rhys ap Maredudd (Rees 1975, 200). There appear to have been numerous complaints about these bailiffs at this time. The introduction of the forms of English rule into Wales in the 1280s had led to a considerable increase in the numbers of the posts of *rhaglaw* and *rhingyll*, equivalent to the English bailiff (Prestwich 1988, 207). On 9 December 1309, Roger Mortimer, acting as justiciar of west Wales, wrote to the Lord Chancellor to postpone the removal of Goronwy Goch from his post as steward of Cantref Mawr because it might endanger peace (Griffiths 1972, 279). Clearly, it was not a good time to remove a loyal and respected Welshman from his post when there was much local resentment against royal officials.

Prosperity, plague and decline

The presence of burgesses and burgage tenure implies that the town had been granted borough status after the Edwardian conquest. The burgesses were noted as holding their burgages and lands *per cartam Regis* (by royal charter) in the accounts of 1301/02 and 1303/04, but no formal record of the borough designation has ever been found. This creation of a new borough fits the pattern of Edward I's deliberate policy of urbanisation in Wales. The founding of towns of privileged status was an effective method of generating tax income by opening up Wales to trade. It also settled the land with bodies of new English tenants, who had an economic stake in the continuance of the occupation and, therefore, formed a potential pool of men loyal to the English Crown and ready to stifle any further attempts at Welsh revolt.

During his brief period of tenure of Dryslwyn, Hugh Despenser the Younger further promoted the trading capacity of the town. At his request, in 1324, a royal grant was made to the burgesses of Dryslwyn to permit them to hold a weekly market on Saturdays (*CChR 1300–26*, 461). This charter was confirmed in 1355 (*CPR 1354–58*, 172).

Welsh towns flourished and expanded their activities in the relatively peaceful period of the 14th century. The network of markets was now extended throughout Wales and was under the control of the towns. Their burgesses continued to insist on their privileged English status and sought to exclude the Welsh from within their walls, who nevertheless became assimilated into the urban population (Davies 1987, 413, 421).

In 1328, the castle's wood was referred to as *le parks* (*NLW Add MS 455D*). It may have been held together with the castle and the town by Richard Pembridge (Lewis 1998, 52). This enclosure had probably been formed as a deer park in the late 13th and early 14th century and later served more as a source of wood. Deer parks were normally divided from the landscape by a fence, wall or stockade, together with a ditch. Edward Morris was appointed as bailiff of Dryslwyn in 1343 (Griffiths 1972, 357).

In the accounting year 1356/7, John de Bokenhale was the reeve of Dryslwyn and was followed in the post by Walter le Yonge until 1360 (Griffiths 1972, 357). In the accounts for these years, the town walls of Dryslwyn were specifically mentioned as surrounding the borough. The remainder of the town's inhabitants lived beyond the walls on *Bruggestrete* (Bridge Street), the road on the west side of the castle that led to the ford 100m to the east of the modern bridge (*NLW Add MS 455D*). This suggests that the original ford across the River Tywi had now been replaced with a bridge and that the houses outside the walls were ranged along the road leading to it. The bridge at Dryslwyn was the only crossing of the Tywi between Llandeilo and Nantgaredig and might have been expected to increase the economic activity of the borough, but there is little evidence of this. An income of 13s from the park, 21d from the garden and 26s from the fishery of the River Tywi indicates that these parts of the estate continued to be profitable.

A total of 34 burgages was enumerated in the town, with a further 14 outside the town on Bridge Street. There was probably still a social distinction between the burgesses within the borough walls and those outside; the rents were certainly recorded separately (PRO SC6/1158/10 m7; *NLW Add MS 455D*, 186; Griffiths 1966, 142; Soulsby 1983, 133; Webster 1987, 96). This rent roll suggests that the town had contracted slightly and that some of the burgage plots and exterior messages had been amalgamated or were left unoccupied.

The town charters of 1324 and 1355 were confirmed in 1391, with additional letters patent giving the burgesses of Dryslwyn equal rights with those of English boroughs, such as Carmarthen. They were to be subject to the judgement only of 'English burgesses and true Englishmen' and not of Welshmen, a privilege that was not extended to the non-burgesses in the town (*CChR 1341–1417*, 328; *CPR 1391–96*, 7–8). This privilege reinforced social distinction in the borough and was intended to raise the status of the town and encourage men of substance to retain their habitations there.

The Black Death swept though the settlements of west Wales in 1349 and must have affected Dryslwyn. Trade and agriculture were both seriously disrupted throughout Wales. This may have reduced income from rents from the town, but this initial wave of plague did not have a significant long-term effect on its population (Lloyd 1935, 246; Lewis 1998, 54), as the only limited reduction in the number of burgesses in the town in 1356/57 attests. The plague returned to west Wales and the Tywi Valley in 1361 and 1369, again leading to disruption of agricultural activity and trade in the area and resulting in a drop in the rents and income from the town. The grant of privileges in 1391 suggests that the later outbreaks of plague had caused more substantial depopulation at Dryslwyn and that measures were necessary to encourage resettlement.

Dryslwyn town was presumably occupied by Owain Glyn Dŵr when the castle was surrendered to him in 1403. As it had not offered any resistance to the rebels, it probably escaped being burnt, unlike towns such as Haverfordwest (Pembrokeshire) and Cardiff. By the end of the revolt, a third of the burgage plots may have been vacated as a result of a combination of factors — the ravages of the plague, depopulation exacerbated by the conflicts of Glyn Dŵr's uprising and the anti-Welsh legislation that followed (Lewis 1998, 54).

On 15 February 1409, John Wodehouse was granted the farm of Dryslwyn town by Prince Henry of Wales for 20 years at a rent of £10 *per annum*. He probably also occupied the castle (Griffiths 1972, 137). The farmers of Dryslwyn, who held the town, lands and profits of Dryslwyn in return for an annual fixed rent, were still required to maintain the park and clean out its surrounding ditch in 1429. The charter of the town was again confirmed in 1444 (*CPR 1441–46*, 257), suggesting that it continued to survive at least until the middle of the 15th century.

Discussion

The original early 13th-century Welsh town of the lords of Dryslwyn was taken over and expanded by the occupying royal forces after the siege of 1287 and filled with English immigrants. In 1294, King Edward I confirmed the creation of the initial burgages and, by 1301/02, divisions in the settlement had been formalised into a split between the 'English' burgesses in the town and the Welsh 'chensars' outside the walls; a distinction that remained fundamental for the town for the rest of the 14th century. The number of burgage plots in the town was recorded as 43½ between 1298 and 1301, and as 37 burgages and 16½ messuages in 1301/02 and later accounts. This either indicates a significant change in the organisation of the town and its defences in 1302, such as the completion of the town wall of the expanded town, or merely two different standards of accounting.

During the 14th century, the inhabitants almost exclusively possessed English surnames (Lloyd 1935, 324). Either they formed an enclave of the descendants of English settlers, or, more probably, many Welshmen had adopted English surnames. This 'Englishness' was defended by the 1391 charter and was probably seen as a mark of wealth, rank and privilege, rather than as an accurate assessment of racial origin.

It is not certain if Dryslwyn was ever incorporated as a borough, since no royal charter or similar documentary evidence has been identified (Griffiths 1966, 142). It has been stated, however, that the men of Dryslwyn presented a petition to the king at Hereford for the establishment of a town, and that the king instructed his bailiff at Hereford to search the laws of the city for a model code so that towns such as Dryslwyn could be properly established (Lloyd 1935, 307, quoting Lipson). Others have also accepted that Dryslwyn must have obtained a full charter of incorporation, based on the customs of Hereford (Owen 1892, 339). Certainly, throughout the history of the town, the burgesses were accorded the privileges associated with a borough, including that of being judged by 'English burgesses and true Englishmen', granted in 1391. To all intents and purposes, therefore, Dryslwyn was a fully incorporated borough.

The reduction of the population in the second half of the 14th century after the Black Death and subsequent plagues resulted in a scarcity of men to farm the land and a consequent rise in the value of their services. This led to a marked reduction in the number of men of servile status as they sought freedom as the price for their labour (Davies 1987, 426–428). It also encouraged a move to the holding of land under the terms of English, rather than Welsh law, since this made it easier to buy and sell, and to pass on land through the female line. Another advantage was that land could be bequeathed as an undivided inheritance, instead of breaking it up into smaller parcels, as required by the Welsh custom of male partibility. These changes enabled Welshmen to expand landholdings over several generations, rather than to reduce them, thereby encouraging the accumulation of wealth. There was also an increase in the mobility of the population, since ties were loosened between families and particular parcels of land, and the lords of that land.

As a result, the power of the landowning class of the old Welsh kindreds was undermined. The laws passed by the English parliament in response to the Glyn Dŵr uprising not only prohibited intermarriage between English and Welsh, but also barred Welshmen from holding any significant public office or owning land in English boroughs. These measures hindered the transformation of Welsh society and did not encourage settlement in English boroughs, such as Dryslwyn.

Although it is unlikely that such laws were rigorously enforced at Dryslwyn, it may have been one of a number of factors that encouraged settlement in other locations: the steep and confined nature of the site was almost certainly other. With the mobility of the population increasing and its living standards rising, small towns that were adequate in the 14th century could no longer provide the range of goods and services required in the 15th century. Larger towns, such as Carmarthen, grew at the expense of smaller towns, like Dryslwyn, which contracted and declined. From the 15th to 17th centuries, the township of Dryslwyn continued to suffer depopulation until settlement had ceased altogether by the 18th century (Soulsby 1983, 134; Lewis 1998).

8.2 AREAS T AND S: TOWN HOUSE AND TOWN WALL

Due to site erosion within the township, there was often limited stratigraphy on sites excavated there. There was also a paucity of datable finds, making the resulting dating sequence and archaeological conclusions more tentative than those derived from the castle itself. Area T consists of a single trench, measuring 12 × 7m, which was dug to investigate part of the town wall and an adjoining rectangular depression surrounded by a raised grassy bank (Figure 1.2). Area S comprises a series of six trenches (denoted SA-SF), each typically measuring 0.5 × 2m, which were excavated to ascertain if any significant archaeological features would be affected by the construction of a pathway facilitating public access to the castle.

Phase 3

The earliest feature above the natural hillside (T79) was the town wall (T20 and T37). Only the back face and centre of this wall were recovered (Figure 8.1), the front face having been lost down the slope into the town ditch several metres below. There were some limited traces of the mortar originally used to hold the limestones of the back face of the wall together, but there was no trace of mortar in the earthy rubble core. Inside the wall, remains were found of a clay floor (T68 and T75) above a clay and stone sub-floor (T69 and T76). These would have formed part of a wooden building within the earliest township, similar in construction to those inside the castle in Areas G and H. The full extent of this clay-floored building was not recovered, since it lay beyond the limits of the excavated area and had suffered severe erosion due to later occupation. In the western half of the excavated area was a build-up of stone, clay and earth deposits (T59 and T62). Traces of an alignment of small stones (T81) suggest an ephemeral wall running south from the town wall, which may relate to a structure associated with the clay-floored building.

Phase 4

Phase 4 saw a number of improvements made to the town wall. Additional walls (T16, T19 and T36) were built inside the original town wall (Figure 8.1), so expanding its width and probably allowing for a wall-walk running around the inside of the town circuit. A break in the new thickening wall suggests that a feature, such as a flight of steps to gain access to the wall-walk, was positioned in this location, although no postholes or other evidence of a wooden structure were recovered. The presence of a paved area around the base of the putative steps is perhaps suggested by worn stones (T92), which are seemingly part of the Phase 4 construction, but do not conform to the alignment of the new wall face. A substantial pit (T38 and T65) and a small pit or quarry scoop (T74) may originally have been dug to obtain stone for this building work, before being backfilled (T67) (Figure 8.2).

Phase 5

During Phase 5, the putative flight of steps leading up to the wall-walk went out of use and was replaced in this location by a house, which butted up against the thickened town wall and had drystone walls (T13–15 and T34) (Figure 8.1). These walls were only 0.7m wide and probably represent dwarf stone walls,

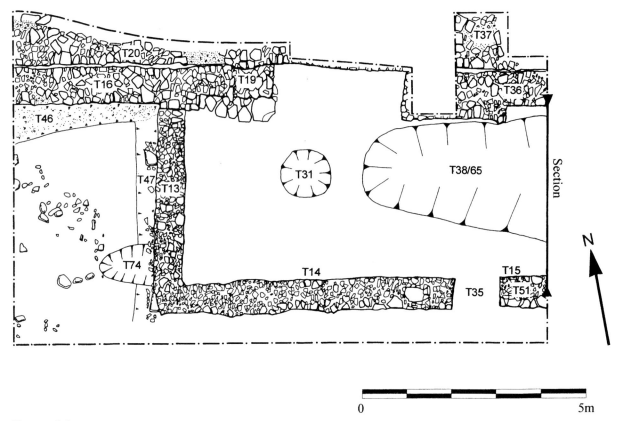

FIGURE 8.1

The house walls (T13–15) constructed adjoining the town wall (T19, 20)

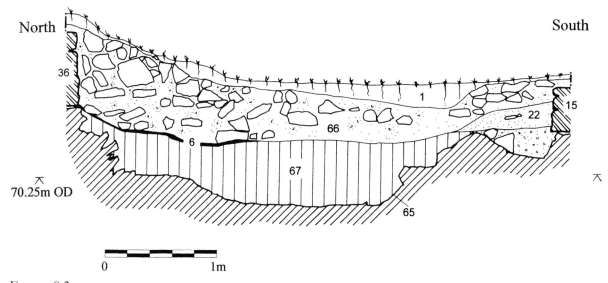

FIGURE 8.2

Section through the worn centre of the house (Area T)

originally 0.5–1m high, which would have supported a timber framework with wattle-and-daub panels. The lack of slate suggests that the building had a thatched or wooden shingle roof, whilst a doorway (T35) in the southern wall yielded a cluster of iron nails, indicating that there had once been a wooden door and frame here which had decayed *in situ*. Traces of stones running west from the west wall of the house, such as the offset (T34), may indicate that there were originally ephemeral stone lean-to buildings against this west side of the house. Traces were also recovered of buildings that may have replaced the earlier stone ones. The absence of a daub layer (T21, T71 and T72) in this area west of the house may indicate the positions of wooden beams (T23 and T47) against the west wall (T13) and also (T24 and T46) against the southern face of the town wall thickening (T16). This suggests that a wooden building with a daub floor (perhaps a byre) once butted onto the west end of the house.

At the same time, or just after the construction of the stone walls of the house, a clay floor (T17 and T32) was laid, which was later overlaid by further clay, stone and daub flooring (T9, T10, T22, T27, T28 and T55). Much of these flooring levels has been lost, since they were eroded away by subsequent activity within the house, thereby suggesting a lengthy period of occupation. They exist mainly as separate traces of clay and related materials around the edge of the house walls (Figure 8.2). A pit (T31) may also date to this period of occupation, since it is likely that the crushed shale (T18, T25 and T26) used as a flooring material inside the house came from the bedrock itself on which the building stood.

Excavation in Areas SA-SF indicates that a series of natural hillside terraces in the centre of the township (Figure 8.8) were probably enhanced to form house platforms in this period. Due to erosion, little or no stratigraphic deposits remained, but a thin scatter of domestic debris (fragments of clay, iron nails, mortar, lead droplets and naturally-glazed clay) attests occupation in this area.

Phase 7

Further evidence of activity was found at the house site in Area T in the form of burning, both in the recess in the wall thickening (T49 and T64) and in patches over the house floor (T6, T7 and T44). It is possible, then, that the house burnt down before being demolished (T90), which resulted in the deposition of a layer of stony rubble, for example (T3 and T66), over most of the site. This was overlain by a gradual accumulation of earth and stone, for example (T1), which had built up during the subsequent long period of abandonment.

8.3   AREA Z: TOWN WALL AND DITCH

Area Z (14 × 2m) was excavated across the town wall, town ditch and the counter-scarp bank beyond (Figure 1.2).

Phases 4c and 4d

The earliest feature in Area Z is the palisade trench (Z31), which was cut into the natural clay (Z4 and Z28) and weathered shale (Z17) above the bedrock (Z5) (Figures 8.3 and 8.4). The wooden palisade followed the contours of the hill beyond the town

ditch and was supported by piling excavated clay and turf (Z29 and Z30) on either side to form a bank (Figure 8.4). Since this palisade would have shielded attackers from the defenders on the town wall, it must predate the town wall, whilst it also runs so close to the town ditch as to be unstable once the ditch had been dug. This suggests, therefore, that it was constructed prior to the ditch as well, perhaps several years before both town wall and town ditch were added. Given its flimsy construction, however, the palisade would have represented a mere obstacle, rather than a barrier, to potential attackers and would perhaps have been used both to delimit the settlement and also retain stock. Alternatively, it is possible that the palisade was designed as a temporary defence to protect those involved in the construction of the town wall and town ditch behind, perhaps only preceding this major building episode by a few months. Whichever is the case, the wooden palisade was subsequently removed and the trench deliberately backfilled with the stone and soil (Z24). In this fill was a piece of red sandstone similar to the freestone used for window tracery in the Inner Ward of the castle, therefore suggesting that the palisade trench was backfilled in either Phase 4c or 4d.

Next, a ditch (Z34) was cut through the limestone and shale bedrock (Z5). This was a substantial defensive barrier, 7m wide and 2.4m deep, with a near vertical north face that would have been very hard to climb. The base of the ditch rose up the southern side gradually to form a bank 6.8 m high, rising at 45° to the base of the town wall (Figure 8.3). There is no evidence that this was a prehistoric ditch, perhaps part of a hillfort that has been suggested as originally occupying this site (Solomon 1982, 17): on the contrary, it appears to be a medieval excavation.

The town wall (Z22) was built of limestone on top of the southern bank inside the ditch. Only the lowest two courses of masonry survived intact and, whilst the inner face was recovered, the outer face had fallen into the ditch. There were no more than traces of mortar within the wall, which can, therefore, be interpreted as a very poorly mortared stone structure that seems to have been constructed in one phase. The wall itself was a minimum of 2.4m wide here and may thus have risen to a considerable height, perhaps also supporting a wall-walk.

The ditch contained a small amount of primary silt (Z19), mainly shale, washed down early in its period of use. Very shortly afterwards, a deliberate attempt was made (the reason for which is unclear) to fill the ditch by throwing in a large number of stones (Z11). Above the large, loose and voided stone were layers of large stone, shale and soil (Z16 and Z26), which contained charcoal and an arrowhead and appear to have functioned as a surface, perhaps providing access for attackers over the ditch to the town and its wall: if so, this represents military activity in the 14th century not previously recorded. The post-siege accounts (Rhys

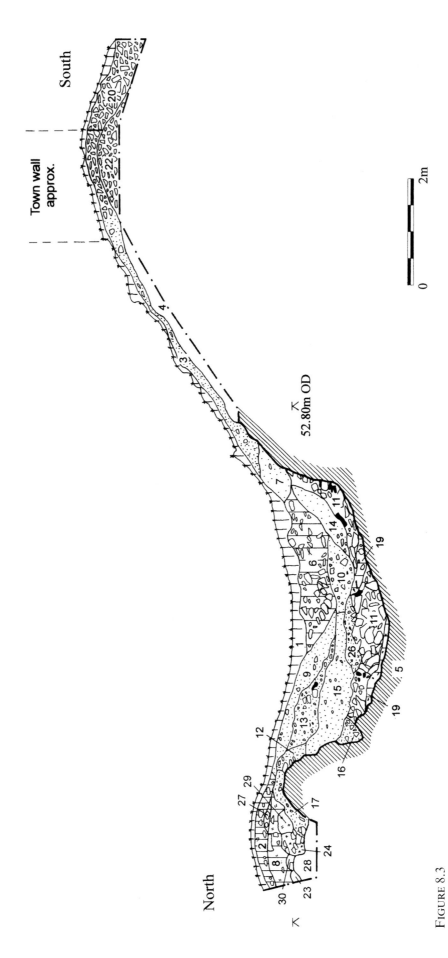

FIGURE 8.3

Section Z1, through the fill of the town ditch (Z34) on the north-western side of the town

South   North

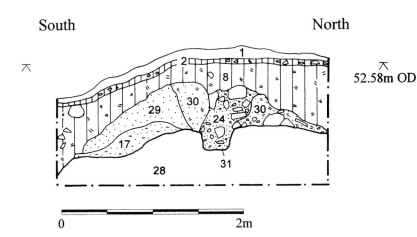

52.58m OD

FIGURE 8.4

Section Z2, through the palisade trench (Z31)

1936, 41) clearly indicate that the town ditch was cleaned out after the siege of 1287 and, consequently, any deliberate filling must have taken place after this date.

Phase 5

During Phase 5, brown soil deposits, for example (Z14), gradually accumulated within the ditch. The presence of medieval pottery sherds indicates that these soil layers formed when the town was still occupied in the 14th and 15th centuries. It is probable that the occupation surface (Z25) recovered adjacent to the inside face of the town wall also dates to this period.

Phase 6

Within the ditch and on the bank a later stony fill (Z13 and Z27) had been deposited, seemingly derived from a phase of either construction or demolition followed by a period of slow soil formation (Z9). The centre of the ditch was then filled again with stony material (Z6), which included traces of mortar identical to that present in the town wall. It would thus appear that the town wall was demolished (Z33) and its facing stone looted, before the rubble core was pushed into the ditch below. This event almost certainly marked the abandonment of the town as a defensive site, although there is no clear dating evidence to suggest when it occurred.

Phase 7

The final activity in this area was a gradual build-up of soil (Z3 and Z7), particularly at the base of the southern bank, followed by a more general soil accumulation (Z2) over the whole trench area. In the vicinity of the town wall, the soil layers (Z20 and Z21)

were associated with the demolished rubble from this structure.

8.4   AREAS U AND V: TOWN GATEHOUSE, TOWN DEFENCES AND ROADWAY

Area U (4 × 8m), lying in a hollow in the bank that surrounds the western side of the town (Figure 1.2), was excavated to a depth of approximately 1m in order to allow the construction of a flight of steps for visitor access. Area V, lying to the west of Area U (Figure 8.5), comprises four trenches (denoted VA-VD), which were excavated in advance of pathway construction to a depth of less than 1m across the town ditch and medieval roadway.

Phase 4c

The earliest feature identified was extensive traces of a very damaged mortared stone gatehouse (U6, U7, U12 and U13). Town Gatehouse U formed the western access into the town and, during much of the 14th century and later, it was the principal access into the town. Similar in plan to the asymmetric Castle Gatehouse W (Figures 5.7 and 8.5), its entrance passageway was 2m wide and its north wall (U6 and U12) was an extension of the town wall (Z22). The south side of Town Gatehouse U probably contained the guard chamber, although the walls (U7 and U13) were so badly damaged that it was difficult to determine their exact line.

On either side of the gatehouse passageway were portcullis slots (U15 and U19), which were located 0.35m in front of an offset in the masonry that would have protected the hinges of a double-leafed gate. The fact that a long passage stretches back from the front gate and portcullis suggests that this gateway, like that of Castle Gatehouse W, would originally have contained a double portcullis and gate arrangement, the second portcullis and gate located at the rear of the passage in an area not yet excavated.

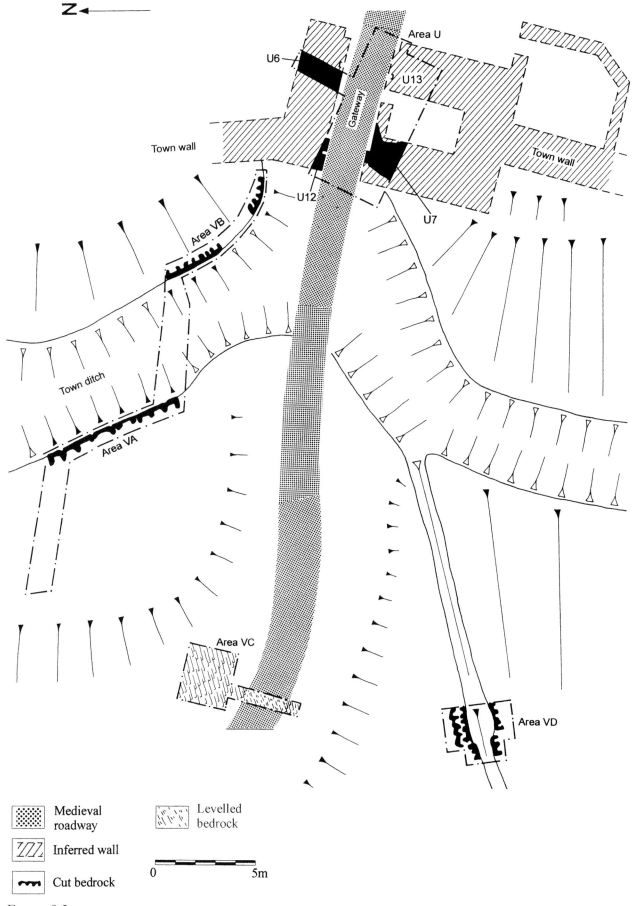

N

Area U

U6

U13

Town wall

U12

U7

Area VB

Town wall

Town ditch

Area VA

Gateway

Area VC

Area VD

Medieval
roadway

Levelled
bedrock

Inferred wall

Cut bedrock

0   5m

FIGURE 8.5

Areas U, VA, VB and VC: Phases 4 and 5. Town Gatehouse U

Beyond the gatehouse, the bedrock (VA2) had been excavated to create a 7m-wide ditch (VA6 and VB6) that curved around the hill in front of Town Gatehouse U, forming, in association with the town wall, an integrated defence system for the town (Figure 8.5). It is highly likely that a wooden bridge once spanned the town ditch in front of the gatehouse in order to provide access into the town. The ditch was cut with a near vertical outer face, so ensuring that it was very difficult to climb out of, whilst the bedrock beyond was levelled, possibly to provide building stone for the town wall and Town Gatehouse U.

In Area VC (Figure 8.5), part of the levelled bedrock surface had been worn smooth (VC4) by the passage of feet, hooves and wheels along what was once part of a medieval roadway leading to Town Gatehouse U. The roadway can still be followed as a shallow depression running down the hill slope, gradually curving north-west, although its route has been lost from the lower part of the hill where it has been quarried away. At some point, the roadway surface developed a pothole that was repaired with a fill of worn stones (VC5).

In Area VD (Figure 8.5), a shallow channel (VD7), 2m wide and 0.3m deep, had been cut and subsequently worn into the bedrock (VD5), natural clay (VD6) and clay and shale deposit (VD4). The base of the channel suggested that it was water-worn, perhaps acting as a drain for the town ditch. It is also possible that water exiting from the Great Hall drain (K16) could have run down into the south-western extent of the town ditch and finally drained down this channel.

Phase 5c

Only the upper part of the ditch fill was excavated. At the lower level, the excavated layers (VA9, VA12, VB9-12 and VB14) show that the ditch slowly filled with occupation material, as was also revealed by the similar ditch fills (Z10, Z12, Z14 and Z15) in the full excavated ditch section in Area Z. There was also a gradual accumulation of soil (VA10) beyond the ditch in an area that has produced occupation material in the form of a knife handle [B11].

In the soil and hillwash layers (VD2 and VD3) that filled the channel (VD7), ceramic sherds and two iron arrowheads [W48 and W39] were recovered. These finds appear to be occupation refuse from the town, perhaps discarded into the town ditch and then washed out.

Phases 6 and 7

Holes (U16 and U20) in the walls (U6 and U7) of Town Gatehouse U attest the removal of the iron hinges that once would have held the wooden gates in place. It is likely that these were wrenched from the walls during the looting of the castle in Phase 6b. This

was followed by the removal of the facing stone from the gatehouse walls (U6, U7, U12 and U13), leaving only the rubble core at the centre of the wall, which was buried in a series of rubble and soil deposits (U3 and U10). This contrasts with the pure rubble of the demolished castle and suggests that the destruction of the town walls appears to have happened more slowly, but with much more extensive looting of stone.

In the ditch, layers (VA7, VA8, VB7 and VB8) incorporated large quantities of stone. These were similar to layer (Z6) and can be interpreted as stone from the erosion, collapse or demolition of the town wall. Later, soil layers (VA3-5 and VB3-5) gradually accumulated across the whole of trenches VA and VB, culminating in the formation of turf (VA and VB1).

8.5 ARCHAEOLOGICAL EVIDENCE OF DRYSLWYN TOWNSHIP

Limited documentary documentary evidence indicates that a native Welsh township was already established outside the walls of Dryslwyn Castle before the period of the English occupation, perhaps as early as the 1220s or 1230s under the lordship of Maredudd ap Rhys. The term *tref*, indicating a settlement rather than a town, should perhaps be used for the initial period of Welsh settlement. However, given the role of Dryslwyn as the principle castle and centre of the lordship of Maredudd ap Rhys and as the commotal centre for Cethiniog by the 1230s, it may be more accurate to describe the settlement of Dryslwyn as a *maerdref* (Jones 2000; Rees 1924): the substantial agricultural settlement, normally associated with the *llys*, which provided 'sustenance to the court' (Jones 2000, 300). Since written records indicate that this settlement had acquired legal status for its annual fair by 1281 and had gained defences by 1287 (Rhys 1936, 41), it was clearly no longer solely dependant on agriculture and had a sense of separation from the surrounding land, through its defences: the term 'town' or 'township', therefore, can be applied with confidence to the settlement after 1280 (Grenville 1997). Dryslwyn is only the third example of a defended Welsh native settlement (Creighton and Higham 2005, 74).

Following its capture by the English Crown in 1287, the town of Dryslwyn was initially prosperous, but fell into a long decline in the later 14th and 15th centuries. Welsh towns, such as Dryslwyn, reflect a trend for new town foundations under seigniorial direction that took place across both England and Wales in the late 12th and 13th centuries. They were established as investments to increase the profits of lordship and, in the Welsh Marches, new towns were usually adjuncts to castles and had their own town walls (Davies 1987, 164–169; Soulsby 1983, 16–19).

The earlier (T20) of the two phases of town wall in Area T almost certainly relates to the initial Welsh town. Associated with this phase of walling was a clay-floored wooden house, similar to the clay-floored buildings in Area G of the Phase 2c castle occupation. The larger house forms, revealed by topographical survey (Webster 1981b; 1987), which are situated on a relatively flat surface at the north-eastern end of the hilltop, combined with the presence of an irregular ditch around the north-eastern edge of the hill and a possible turn of the ditch (now filled in) along the western slope of the hill, together suggest that the defended Welsh settlement occupied the northern end of the hilltop (Figures 8.6 and 8.7). It is unusual to find Welsh townships defended by a wall; they are normally open settlements, or merely defended with a ditch (Soulsby 1983, 166).

It is possible that much of the area now occupied by the Outer Ward was originally part of the town: alternatively, it may have served as open ground between the castle and the town, where fairs and markets were perhaps held. Whichever is the case, it was later built over and incorporated into the castle as the Outer Ward. Any existing town defences and the topography of the site will have influenced the development of the castle along the ridge. The road to the Welsh town appears to have entered from the north and east, the direction of Dinefwr, Llangathen, Llandeilo and other

centres of Welsh power and settlement. The lords of Dryslwyn, with their strong Marcher connections, would undoubtedly have appreciated the economic wealth to be gained from towns and it appears likely, given the defences of the town, that they deliberately established, or at least actively supported, the settlement of a town at Dryslwyn.

Since only a single phase of town wall was found in Area Z, in the lower part of the town, these defences appear to be a later addition. This wall enclosed the western half of the hilltop, forming an integrated series of defences with the castle. Contemporary with the town wall, a new entrance to the town was created with the construction of the west-facing Town Gatehouse U, which was of a single build with the town wall. This gatehouse had the double gate and portcullis entrance considered necessary by the end of the 13th century, but it also had an asymmetric form identical to that of Castle Gatehouse W (Figures 5.7 and 8.5). This has already been shown to be the work of Rhys ap Maredudd (Section 5.2) and was unlike the Edwardian gatehouses with a gate passage between double D-shaped towers that were employed in walled towns, such as Conwy (Conwy). In front of the gatehouse and the town wall was a 7m-wide ditch (VA6, VB6 and Z34) with an almost vertical outer face.

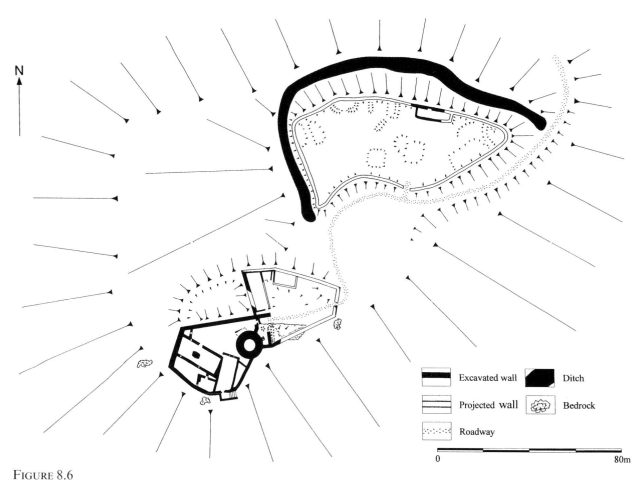

Excavated wall		Ditch
Projected wall		Bedrock
Roadway		

0   80m

FIGURE 8.6

The 'Welsh' town or settlement present in the third quarter of the 13th century

226

FIGURE 8.7

Aerial photograph of Dryslwyn township, looking east. Differences in the form of the town ditch can be attributed to at least two phases of construction (copyright RCAHMW)

The roadway (VC4), which was also constructed for this new lower town, faced west towards Carmarthen, the sea and the centres of English power and it appears likely that much of the town traffic would have switched to using this new westerly entrance. The earlier town defences were also enhanced, adding an additional wall (T16) to thicken the existing town wall (T20). The presence of a palisade (Z31) and bank beyond the ditch may suggest the need for protection of those undertaking this construction work, a technique utilised by Edward I (Morris 1901, 130).

There are two possible interpretations for the expansion of the town and the construction of these enhanced town defences. Firstly, the establishment of boroughs defended by walls and gatehouses in Wales in the late 13th and early 14th centuries is traditionally considered to be either directly or indirectly instigated by Edward I as part of his wider settlement policy for Wales (Davies 1987, 371–372). The construction of an expanded town with substantial defences could date from the years following 1287 as part of this Edwardian programme. The resemblance of Town Gatehouse U to Castle Gatehouse W could be due to the use of local masons, who simply copied the gatehouse they had previously constructed for Rhys ap Maredudd in the early 1280s. This work was completed by 1302, when the accounts indicate a clear division between

the 'English' burgesses within the walls and the Welsh 'chensars' residing outside the walls (Section 8.1). There is, however, no record of expenditure for this work, although the written records are neither complete nor so specific as to be certain that this work was not undertaken.

Secondly, if, as has already been suggested, Rhys ap Maredudd was seeking to establish a court, a centre of power and influence and a new principality of Deheubarth (Section 5.2), he may have had good reason to enlarge the township at Dryslwyn in the 1280s. Rhys was undoubtedly spending considerable sums expanding and remodelling his castle and he would have been well aware of the potential of towns to generate valuable extra income for Welsh (as well as Marcher) lords. The identical gatehouse forms of Town Gatehouse U and Castle Gatehouse W can best be explained as resulting from their construction in the same phase of building work; in other words, in Phase 4a, rather than 4c and is thus the building work of Rhys ap Maredudd.

Whichever of these two explanations is correct, there had been a substantial increase in the town size between 1280 and 1294, by which time the town contained 37 burgage plots (Figure 8.8). Inside the town defences, the terraces probably contained houses, although little archaeological evidence remains and an attempt to identify house sites by means of a geophysical resistivity survey proved unsuccessful (Keen 1992). The extent of the surface remains, surveyed by Webster (1982b; 1987), provide the current extent of archaeological evidence for the settlement of the township in the 14th century, from which the positions of the house sites can be estimated (Figure 8.9) and a reconstruction drawing of the 14th-century township created (Figure 8.10).

Comparisons can be drawn between Dryslwyn after 1287 and the Edwardian planted boroughs. New burgage plots could potentially be filled with English and Flemish immigrants, enticed to the expanding town by grants of land and administrative and economic privileges, which set it apart from the surrounding native community. This would have helped to establish an anglicised town that could service the royal castle and its garrison, support the regional administration and provide taxation income. The topography of the hilltop, however, prohibited any concept of a regular town plan, seen in other English boroughs. It was almost certainly laid out with respect to the contours of the hill and the best line of defence. The presence of Welshmen, such as Goronwy Goch, in the town indicates that it was loyalty to the English Crown, rather than racial origin, which was the key factor in becoming a burgess in this town. The appropriation of the homesteads of the existing Welsh inhabitants to make room for immigrants (Davies 1987, 372) almost certainly occurred at Dryslwyn.

The houses of the 14th-century township of Dryslwyn, such as those recovered during the excavation of Area T, were timber-framed, raised on dwarf stone walls (T13 and T14). They were probably of box-frame, rather than raised cruck, construction with wall panels of wattle and daub. There is a local tradition (observed by the author in the 19th-century barns present in the valley) of panels formed from woven briar stems, covered in mud or clay daub and coated with limewash. No evidence survives for the form of roofing, but the lack of roofing slate would suggest the use of either thatch or wooden shingles: a tradition of thatching survives today in the Tywi valley (William 1987), whilst the medieval use of wooden shingles at Dryslwyn is attested by documentary evidence. Given the plan of the house and the simple clay floor with no indication of sub-divisions or drainage gullies, it is unlikely that these structures were longhouses with animals stalled in the building, but were instead houses exclusively for human habitation. This would

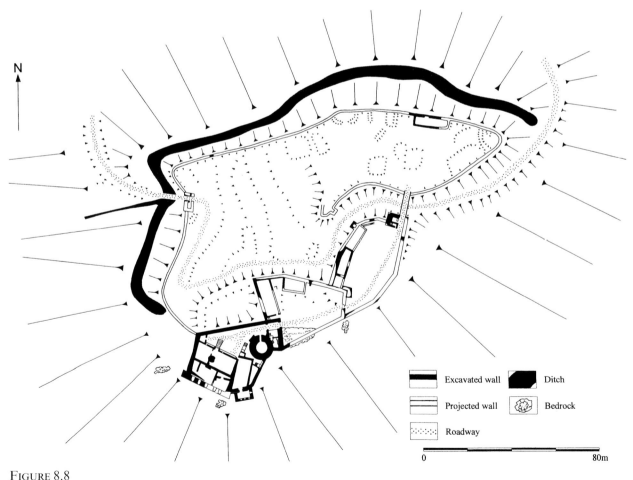

FIGURE 8.8

The 'English' borough of the early 14th century

228

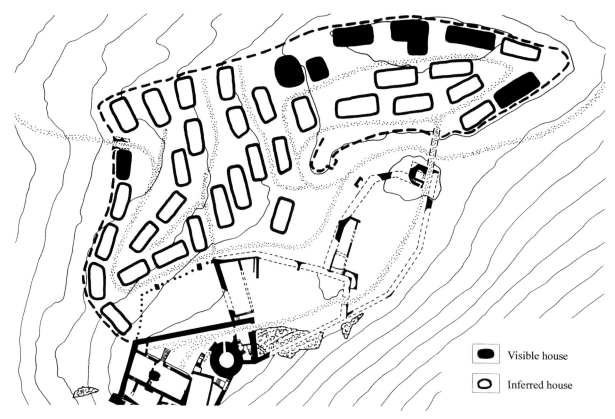

Visible house

Inferred house

FIGURE 8.9

Likely locations of house sites in the early 14th-century borough

suggest that the animals were accommodated in separate buildings or stock enclosures, probably outside the town.

The paucity of material remains from the town seems significant. As an illustration, only 11 out of the 207 iron objects (excluding weapons) recovered from the site derive from the town and its defences and none was related to a specific task or trade; although three honestones from Area T suggest the regular sharpening of knives or other blades. Four of the site's 98 arrowheads were from Areas VA-VD and Z indicating a defensive role for this area. The only coin recovered from the town was Roman [C1], probably kept as a token or memento and with no medieval monetary value. This lack of evidence of prosperity is also apparent in the ceramics (Section 9.2). Area T produced only 1.5% of the ceramics from the site as a whole, 3% of the utilitarian Dyfed gravel-tempered wares and just a few sherds of fineware (unglazed Saintonge pottery imported from Gascony). No copper-alloy, bone or glass objects were recovered from the town in the medieval phases, although an antler handle of a knife [B11] and two copper sheet fragments from Areas VA-VD suggest causal losses by travellers on the road to and from Dryslwyn. In contrast, the quantities of animal bones recovered from Areas T and Z suggest that the townsfolk were consuming more beef and far less pork than the occupants of the castle, whilst the presence of fish oils in the fabric of the two ceramic sherds tested from Area T indicates that the townsfolk were cooking and eating fish: it should be noted that the bones of both fish and birds do not survive well in the soil of the township (Sections 10.2 and 10.3). This limited material culture is similar to that seen at other small rural town and village sites in Wales from the 12th to the 15th centuries, including Llantrithyd (Vale of Glamorgan) (Cardiff Archaeology Society 1977), Newport (Pembrokeshire) (Murphy 1994), Radyr (Cardiff) (Webster and Caple 1980) and Wiston (Pembrokeshire) (Murphy 1997).

Although towns which grew up around castles in the late 13th and 14th centuries, such as Dryslwyn, served as local distribution centres, hosting weekly markets and annual fairs, they also supported trades such as smithing and were underpinned financially by their provision of agricultural produce and services to the castle garrison. For these reasons, the burgesses of each town held land outside the town; in Dryslwyn's case, roughly half a square mile surrounding the castle hill. In effect, these towns, whilst clearly identifiable as such in legal and administrative terms, functioned as little more than large villages. A walled town undoubtedly provided security for its inhabitants, but there was little room inside for animal husbandry or cultivation and we must therefore imagine that the barns and byres associated with such agricultural

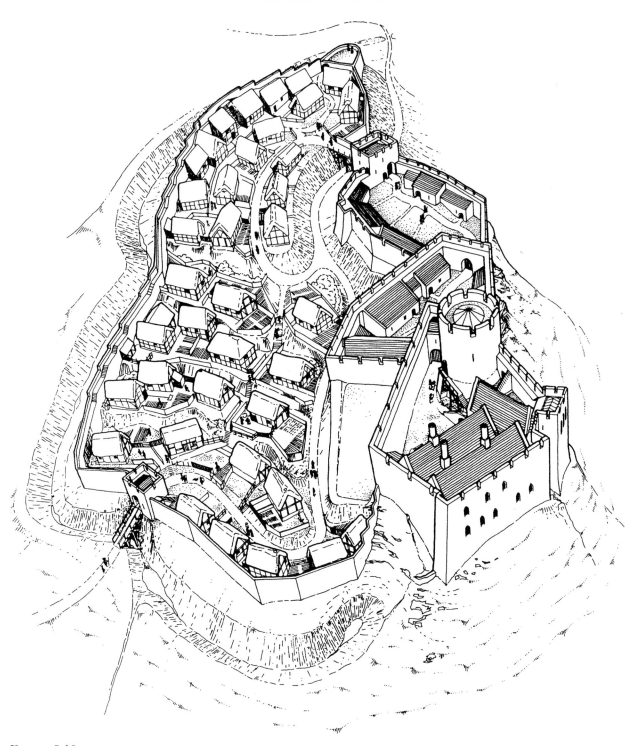

FIGURE 8.10

Reconstruction of Dryslwyn Castle and town c1300 (drawn by Chris Jones-Jenkins)

activities lay in the surrounding countryside, beyond the town walls. The difficulties in living in one place and working in another were balanced against the benefits that organising activities on a communal basis, especially defence, could bring. Eventually, such benefits were insufficient and the majority of the population would then have dispersed to live on their individual landholdings, together with their stock.

Maps, such as the parish tithe maps of roughly 1840 and 1851, in addition to the First Series Ordnance Survey maps of 1834, themselves derived from mapping of 1811–27, indicate the presence of a series of old cottages and ancient field boundaries, in particular those of crofts, which may be defined as small rectangular 'strip' fields containing traces of a house platform adjacent to a road (Figure 8.11). These lie beside the road running along the valley floor from Llanegwad, past the mill at Felindre to Dryslwyn Castle and then on, past Grongar and Aberglasney to the parish church at Llangathen. All field boundaries respect this original medieval road line, whilst all other roads cut the earlier field boundaries and were thus constructed at a later date. Behind the initial line of crofts associated with the road, the field boundaries have the sinuous curve of strip fields and the ridge and furrow indicative of medieval arable strip-farming practices. The current paucity of vegetation in many of these strip fields and the lack of later re-use of this land is suggestive of soil exhaustion, which may have occurred as a result of over-intensive medieval cultivation. The boundary between cultivated land and common land/meadow often formed the route for roads, along which interrupted row settlements often developed (Dyer 1994, 66). The strip field system may be that laid out, either for *tir cyfig*, the tenancy of bondland associated with the *maerdref* of Dryslwyn in the early to mid 13th century (Pierce 1972, 343), or for the burgesses of Dryslwyn in the period 1287–90. The fields to the north-east of Allt-y-gaer also have a remnant strip field form similar to that seen in the area around Dryslwyn. It is most likely that these were the medieval fields set out in the early 14th century and described as demesne land granted to the burgesses of Dryslwyn in 1307, though again they could drive from the earlier bondland associated with the *maerdref*. These field forms are different from the irregular mosaic of small fields present elsewhere in Cethiniog (SN550230, SN586260) which were probably created from the partible inheritance of Welsh freemen.

Fieldwalking conducted in a number of fields in the valley floor around Dryslwyn has only produced ceramics of 13th- to 20th-century date near a dwelling, marked as 'Castle House' on the mid 19th-century parish tithe maps, at the base of Dryslwyn Hill. The lack of sherds from the valley floor indicates that this land was not being manured and, thus, was probably not used for horticultural purposes during the medieval period. It is more likely, then, given the plant evidence regarding hay production and the documentary references that the valley floor was used as a water meadow for winter grazing and summer hay production (Section 10.5).

The proximity of the parish church of Llangathen to Dryslwyn, the absence of any historical reference to a church in the town and the 19th-century tradition of local people from the village of Dryslwyn walking to the church in Llangathen every Sunday would all suggest that there was no church in the medieval township of Dryslwyn. The route that was traditionally walked is indicated on Figure 8.11, running from the 11th- or 12th-century motte, parish church and settlement at Llanegwad, via Dryslwyn, where the road

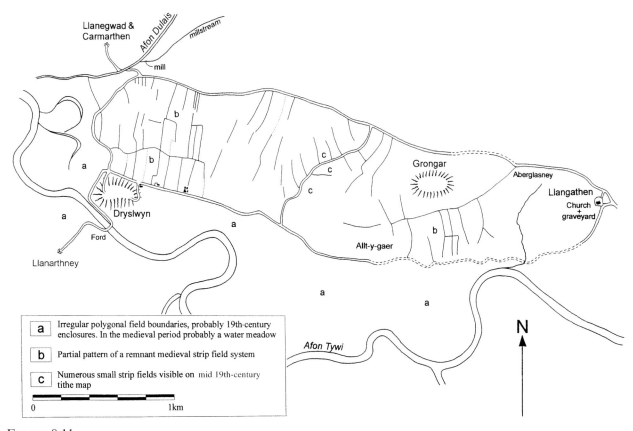

FIGURE 8.11

Features of the medieval landscape observable in the 19th and 20th centuries around Dryslwyn

parts to Llanarthney, and on to the 11th- or 12th-century parish church at Llangathen. The recovery of a coin of Edward I, minted between 1282 and 1289 and similar in date to those found at Dryslwyn, from the later gardens at Aberglasney may indicate activity along this Dryslwyn to Llangathen road in the 14th century (Blockley and Halfpenny 2002, 85). There is, however, no archaeological evidence to connect the later gardens at Aberglasney with the castle garden mentioned in the records.

After the increase in both population and personal wealth in the 13th century, the 14th century saw a marked reduction in the prosperity and population of Wales. The dreadful weather and poor harvest of 1315–18, combined with the increased taxation from 1337 to support the Hundred Years War (Davies 1987), the Black Death of 1349, which returned in 1361 and 1369, and the destruction following the rising of Owain Glyn Dŵr, all left the town short of inhabitants: indeed, by 1409, one third of the burgage plots of Dryslwyn lay unoccupied (Solomon 1982, 58). For those that did remain, however, the low price of land encouraged some burgesses to acquire land, leading to the establishment of larger landholdings. In addition, absentee English feudal lords gave stewarding posts to many prominent local 'Welsh' men during the 14th and 15th centuries and innovations in county administration saw the creation of new positions of power, giving rise to a nascent Welsh gentry by the 16th century (Smith 1975). Many members of this emerging social class built new houses on their farmed land, away from the confines of the boroughs and castles. The Sites and Monuments Record, Johns (1987) and Solomon (1982) all suggest that many of the earliest stone farm buildings seen in the Tywi valley are indeed of 15th-, 16th- and 17th-century date, the most prominent local example being Court Henry, which was probably a 15th-century hall in origin, to which additions were made in the 16th and later centuries (RCAHMW 1917). Evidence from layer (Z6) suggests that part or all of the Dryslwyn town wall was demolished and robbed of freestone, which was presumably recycled in the late and post-medieval farmhouses of the Tywi valley.

ARTEFACTUAL EVIDENCE

9.1 ARTEFACTS AND ACTIVITIES
by Chris Caple

Written history indicates that, prior to 1287, the castle was the centre of a lordship, which was never less than the commote of Cethiniog and, after Rhys ap Maredudd married Ada de Hastings in 1285, his landholding comprised 10 commotes: Amgoed, Caio, Cethiniog, Emlyn Uwch Cych, Mabelfyw, Mabwynion, Mallaen, Mabudrud, Peuliniog, Yststlwyf, possibly Gwynionydd, plus other lands associated with the barony of St Clears (Figure 2.2) (Section 2.1). This meant that Dryslwyn was the principal administrative centre for a dispersed lordship covering an area roughly the size of Carmarthenshire. It was also the principal residence of a major lord and his family, one descended from the Welsh princes of Deheubarth. Rhys would have maintained a court, similar to that described in the Welsh 'Laws of Court' (Charles-Edwards *et al* 2000; Turvey 2002, 117). It was also home to the retinue of servants and administrators who cared for the lord and his family and administered his lordships as well as to his fighting men (*teulu*), who protected the lord, his family, land and castle (Davies 2004). Thus, prior to 1287, the castle is most accurately described as the principal residence of a Welsh lord and his household. After 1287, the written records focus on the provisioning of a garrison of troops loyal to the English Crown. This garrison invariably comprised a constable, chaplain and keeper of the garnisture (stores) plus a variable number of men at arms. In 1289 there were nearly 70 men at arms: 13 horsemen, 20 crossbowmen, 30 archers, 3 gatekeepers (Phillpotts 2001c); by 1300 this had fallen to 24 men at arms and by 1385 there were only 12. There is no evidence that many of the castle's occupants after 1287 were born in England, merely that in the years after the 1287 siege the constable was appointed by and owed allegiance to the English Crown. After about 1290 the castle no longer acted as the principal administrative

centre of a lordship, but received rents from the adjacent town and was either accounted for, provisioned and maintained as one of a group of royal castles in west Wales, or was a minor holding in the control of a major English noble. In this period after 1290 the castle also formed an important political and economic element in supporting the town of Dryslwyn. The castle's demise in the early 15th century led to the eventual abandonment of the town.

The Welsh lord's household period

There is little or no written record to tell us of the activities and possessions of the household of a major Welsh lord. Consequently archaeological evidence provides much of our information and at Dryslwyn the majority of archaeological evidence relates to the lifestyle of the inhabitants of the Inner Ward of the castle between 1230 and 1287.

For lighting after sunset or in naturally dark corners, there is evidence for artificial lighting through the presence of iron candlesticks and candleholders [F114–117], ceramic candlesticks [P60] and rushlights or tapers [F118]. Evidence of beeswax, probably for candles, was recovered from ceramics (Section 10.9) and from traces spilt on a mortar floor in the Great Chamber G (Section 9.10).

Some of the internal walls, probably of the lord's private apartments in the Round Tower D and Guest Hall X in the Middle Ward which housed important guests, had wall paintings created with brightly coloured expensive pigments such as cinnabar and azurite (Section 6.4).

The rooms of Dryslwyn Castle were probably as sparsely furnished as those of English castles. The presence of small binding straps [F131], hasps [F128], handles [F124] and keys (e.g. [A39]) indicates that there were chests or similar pieces of lockable wooden furniture in some of the rooms. As at other Welsh castles there were few if any glass vessels on the tables (Section 9.6) though there were ceramic vessels, such as green glazed wares from Bristol and South Wales region and also plain and decorated glazed ceramics from Saintonge in France (Section 9.2). Saintonge ware appears to have been popular at Dryslwyn and has also occasionally been seen at other Welsh castle sites such as Castell-y-Bere (Gwynedd) (Butler 1974). The occurrence of polychrome Saintonge ware early in the Phase 3 deposits at Dryslwyn (1260s) is very early for the occurrence of this type of ceramic in the British Isles. However, a high status site such as Dryslwyn Castle, at the end of an active trade route through Bristol to south-western France, would probably have been one of the first sites to receive this colourful new ceramic product. Fine quality ceramic sherds are rare in the following 14th century period and it is probable that any such sherds are residual from this earlier phase.

Meals were cooked principally in Dyfed Gravel Tempered Ware, pottery derived from an earlier local ceramic tradition (Section 9.2) and in metal cauldrons [A51]. Examples of strainers [A44] and bakestones [S16] used in the cooking were recovered, as well as hand querns for grinding grain [S8–9] and millstones [WS14, WS15, WS49, WS81] probably used for making flour in the local watermills. The bones from the site indicate that the lord's family and immediate household would have eaten a large amount of meat; mainly prime beef, with smaller amounts of pork, mutton and venison. Feasting formed an important element of 13th-century Welsh aristocratic life and displaying wealth through food on such occasions would not only have led to the killing and eating of some young animals for example sucking pigs and unusual birds and animals such as white tailed sea eagle and seal, but would account for the wide range of birds (35 species) and fish (30 species). Fruits such as figs and raisins probably came from Spain or Gascony, from where wine was also probably imported.

The presence of silver coins [C4, C5] indicates the development of at least a partial cash-based economy in places in Wales such as Dryslwyn by the mid 13th century. The presence of large numbers of silver coins (Section 9.3) would suggest that the cash-based economy was becoming extensive in the Tywi valley by the late 13th century. It appears likely that food renders and services were increasingly being commuted to cash payments. This is hardly surprising given the presence of a settlement, a fair and the proximity to market towns such as Carmarthen, and the presence of a coastal trade importing foreign goods. The presence of a French denier turnois [C18] of the late 13th century probably represents trade or the presence of a French merchant or soldier in the late 13th or early 14th century, though the coin was redeposited from a later context.

In addition to the turnois, there is considerable evidence for a substantial trade network supplying artefacts and materials to Dryslwyn in the 13th century. Ivory was imported from Africa, probably through Bristol or London where the raw material was made into an object [B9]. Azurite pigment for the wall-paintings came from either Central Europe or the Mediterranean basin and cinnabar pigment for the same purpose came from Spain. Grapes, Saintonge ceramics and probably wine were imported from south-west France, cumin from Asia, figs and lentils from the Mediterranean and a grey schist honestone [S41] probably represents an import from Norway. This would confirm that Dryslwyn had access to goods from throughout Europe, probably imported through the ports of Bristol and Carmarthen, and argue for the high status of the Dryslwyn Castle site. There were also imports of materials and objects from elsewhere in the Britain such as oolitic limestone, Ham Green pottery and a rock crystal bead [V2] all of which come from the Bristol region. They indicate the importance of the trade network out of Bristol and out along the Bristol Channel to towns and castles of south and west Wales. Many objects and materials such as window glass and copper-alloy objects and sheet lead could also have arrived through this trade route. Local materials derived from the Carmarthenshire area are represented by a wide range of materials with specific desirable properties; coal, coarse ceramics, slate, old red sandstone and numerous types of fish and birds. Most other materials were local to the Dryslwyn area.

The presence of luxury objects such as ivory-handled knives [B9], the wearing of fashionable jewellery such as the silver gilt finger ring [A1] and buckles (e.g. [A6]) and the furs of squirrels, pine martins and other small animals, whose bones were recovered from the castle's middens, indicate the wealth displayed by the lords of Dryslwyn, his family, senior members of the household and guests. The single-sided antler comb [B20] suggests that grooming and appearance was also important. The household entertained themselves playing dice and other games, or playing music on bone whistles [B2] and other instruments. The bones of deer, wild boar and many smaller animals indicate that much of the lord's time was spent hunting, whilst the large number of bones of smaller birds may indicate that the Lords of Dryslwyn were enthusiastic falconers. The large number of winter migrants present in these bird bones would suggest that falconry was practised during the autumn and winter, the season during which the Lord of Dryslwyn was most likely to have resided at Dryslwyn.

The presence of horse bones and horseshoe nails from Phase 1 onwards attest the presence of horses, ridden by the lords of Dryslwyn and their retinue from the early 13th century onwards. An increase in numbers of horseshoes and horseshoe nails in Phase 4 suggests increased use of horses in the late 13th and

14th century. This may be related to the improved access for horse-drawn wheeled vehicles into the castle from Phase 4a on. Written sources such as legal documents and poetry suggest that horses were highly prized by the Welsh aristocracy (Davis and Jones 1997). Evidence from Dryslwyn of dog-gnawed horse bones, the cooking of horsemeat, and historic references to the curing of horsehides (Section 9.1), indicates that, in reality, a far more pragmatic approach to horses was taken in 13th-century Wales.

A probable book clasp [**A35**] and letters sent from Rhys ap Maredudd (Pryce 2005, 231–237) tell us that Rhys and/or his chaplain were literate. The extent of literacy in 13th-century Welsh society is unclear, but the use of personal letters by the princes of Gwynedd (Beverly Smith 1998), written records for legal and taxation purposes (Stephenson 1984) and the recording of annals such as the *Brut-y-Tywysogyon* in Welsh monasteries indicates that the senior members of the aristocracy, clergy and administrators both read and wrote.

The occurrence of tools and waste products indicates a number of practical crafts and trades were practised in the 13th-century castle. The presence of spindle whorls in bone [**B7**, **B8**] and stone [**S1–2**], the tooth from a woolcomb or flax heckle [**F6**], iron shears [**F10–11**], needles [F8–9] and loom weights from warp-weighted looms [**S6–7**] proves that all stages of textile manufacture, from combing the wool/flax fibres to weaving and sewing cloth, were all carried out at Dryslwyn. Though this was probably undertaken on wool from the sheep whose bones were recovered, the presence of flax seeds means that this evidence could equally well point to linen production, or both. That leather was also worked at Dryslwyn is shown by the leather creasers [**F13–14**], an awl [**F12**] and needles [F8–9] and it is likely that simple items, such as shoes or scabbards, were made in leather on this site. References to Grono ap Jevan who paid rent in 1287 in the form of six pairs of shoes (Phillpotts 2001c) suggests that Grono was a shoemaker (cordwainer) working in Cantref Mawr, whose products probably shod most of the residents of Dryslwyn Castle during this period.

Iron smithing was undertaken on the site in Phase 2, according to the volume of hearth bottom, smithing slag, fuel ash slag and vitrified hearth lining present (Section 9.10). This on-site smithing could have produced all the structural ironwork such as cramps, nails, roves and hinges necessary for large-scale building work such as the Great Hall K/L. The presence of much of this waste in Area J could suggest that a temporary smithy was set up beside the Great Hall K/L, though it is possible that the waste was created elsewhere around the castle and dumped in this area during or after this construction work. Smithing waste was also redeposited during Phase 4a, when another major phase of construction work would again have required the smithing of large volumes of ironwork.

A series of tools, which could have been used for smithing, such as a sledgehammer [**F1**], a cold chisel [**F2**], a punch [**F3**] and an incompletely forged knife [**F4**] also attest to smithing work occurring in and around the castle during its life. Repair of sheet metal copper-alloy vessels during this period is attested by the metal repair strips which have been recovered [**A54**, A52c] and lead strips indicate that repair of roofing or guttering was undertaken in almost all the phases of the castle's life. Since a splitting wedge and hammer were also recovered from Castell-y-Bere (Gwynedd) (Butler 1974, 97) and a cold chisel and punch from Criccieth (Gwynedd) (O'Neill 1944–45, 42) the tools and the crafts they represent must be considered as normally present in Welsh castles.

Some of the trades such as building work or carpentry have left no tools. Activities like shaping stone produced waste products such as the piles of stone chips which were recovered from layers such as (P52), (P67), (P68). Other trades such as carpentry whose waste has decayed or burnt, must be inferred from the presence of shaped and jointed wood, which in turn must be inferred from the presence of nails, hinges, corbels and other stone and metal supports and fittings. Tools which have been recovered, such as knives (e.g. F21), were used for many activities whilst honestones (e.g. [S32]) could be used to sharpen a wide variety of blades, including arrowheads and spearheads.

The working of antler is attested by the presence of waste pieces, particularly tine ends (e.g. [**B58**, **B62**]) during Phases 3 and 4 of the castle's occupation. Antler came from red and roe deer, probably hunted and killed, though shed antler could also have been collected and used. It is uncertain what types of object was manufactured. Knife handles [**B11**], toggles [**B17**], or the single sided antler combs [**B20**], which seem to have been popular in Wales during this period (Section 9.7), are all possibilities. There is also evidence, in the form of a number of partially made objects [**B28**, B33] for the manufacture of bone points or pins. These were concentrated around Phase 4c, the period of the 1287 siege. Given the presence of much of this bone and antler material in the Inner Ward, it appears likely that men at arms or household retainers were involved in these manufacturing processes. It is possible that they were supplementing their income with manufactured goods or craft services, which Dyer (1994, 168–189) suggests was a common activity for agrarian peasants.

The Welsh lordly household period was brought to an abrupt end by the siege of 1287.

The garrison period

There is a limited amount of archaeological evidence relating to the life and activities of the inhabitants of the Inner Ward of the castle in the period around

1287–1420s, evidence which is supplemented by intermittent written records for the income and expenditure of the garrison during some of the periods when it was under royal control after 1287.

The occurrence of decorative metalwork and jewellery, such as the annular brooch [A3], sexfoil mount [A22], and rock crystal bead [V2], which derive from the 14th-century occupation of the castle, indicate that, like the buildings, some elements of wealth and display were still active in the castle. The dearth of high-quality ceramics in this period is a clear indicator of the more functional nature of the castle's occupation, with far less emphasis on wealth display then the preceding period. The lack of coins dated post-1300 (Section 9.3), also suggests a far lower level of commercial activity and disposable wealth.

As at other sites in Wales the presence of dice [B6], counters [B4] and chessmen [B3] indicates the pastimes in which garrisons engaged. As the 14th century continued, coal slowly replaced wood as the principal fuel used for heating the rooms of the castle. As early as 1298–1300, some 200 bushels of sea coal are purchased from Haverford (west) (Pembrokeshire) by the Crown for its castles in west Wales including Dryslwyn (Rhys 1936, 177). Purchases continue throughout the 14th century, deposits of coal being recovered from layer (P5) in Phase 5b. The purchase of large amounts of parchment (Rhys 1936, 121), the recovery of a feather quill pen nib [V1], together with the written accounts from this period, indicates that the inscription of records occurred in the castle. The use of detailed written records suggests that the relevant individuals such as the constable, who was often a minor member of the Welsh gentry by the late 15th century (Section 3.1), as well as the chaplain and the keeper of the garnisture (stores) were presumably able to read and write.

The chapel remained an important place in the castle both before and after the siege. The presence of '1 pair of vestments with 2 chasubles and 2 silk copes, 2 consecrated towels for the altar and 1 consecrated portable altar' in the castle in 1300/01 plus the presence of a chaplain, recorded as part of the castles staff in the 14th century (Phillpotts 2001c) indicates that the castle's chapel was well endowed and functioned throughout this period.

Historic records (Rhys 1936) also indicate that sums of money were regularly spent on the provision and repair of crossbows and quarrels (crossbow bolts). Some crossbow bolt heads were also recovered [W93–98] from an unstratified context. Clearly the garrison were primarily expected to use crossbows to defend the castle since they could be fired easily and safely, if slowly, from behind battlements, parapets or arrowloops. They did not require the strength, practice and skill which was needed to accurately fire a longbow (Bradbury 1985) nor did they leave the archer so exposed to return fire. This contrasts with the extensive use of longbows in the previous period.

It is likely from the continued presence of longbow arrowheads in later deposits (e.g. [W48]) that the use of the longbow continued into the 14th century, though these were probably personal weapons and not purchased or maintained by the royal purse. The stack of lithic projectiles [LP32–37], demonstrates the defensive function of the castle gatehouse. It also reminds us that stones, from slingstones to trebuchet balls, could form an effective weapon when hurled with sufficient force.

Many of the trades and activities of the earlier period such as textile manufacture, bone- and antler-working appear to continue, but the effect of finds from earlier being redeposited in these later layers undoubtedly over-emphasises these activities in this later period. The men-at-arms present after 1287 are often recorded in the castle accounts as craftsmen, among them Mathew the Smith and Gruffyn the Smith (Rhys 1936; Phillpotts 2001c). The impression is one of minimal activity in the Inner Ward of Dryslwyn castle for much of this period.

9.2 POTTERY
by Peter Webster

The 1980–94 excavations at Dryslwyn Castle produced around 19kg of pottery, the vast majority of it medieval. In the light of the area excavated, the length of the occupation and the depth of some of the deposits, this must represent, however, only a small percentage of the pottery used and discarded on the site. This is shown by the small size of most sherds and the general absence of complete or nearly complete rims and profiles. Furthermore, the castle's hilltop location must be taken into consideration. It must always have been easy to discard rubbish down the slope of the hill, especially for the residents of the Inner Ward, which forms the bulk of the excavated area. As a result, the method of pottery analysis for Dryslwyn must be appropriate for an assemblage that is high in findspots but low in diagnostic rims. A report that concentrated only on surviving rims would be small indeed and unrepresentative of the material recovered. As an alternative, we have concentrated on fabric groups and on chronological and spatial distribution in an attempt to maximise the amount of information from a relatively small assemblage.

The method of quantification for such an assembly presents problems. The general absence of rims makes any form of vessel count difficult. This is compounded by the hand-made character and variable firing of many of the vessels, which makes it difficult to distinguish sherds from individual pots. However, the classes of vessel present are few (mainly jugs and cooking pots) and, with the sole exception of the Saintonge fineware vessels, they are likely to have been of broadly similar weight, whatever their fabric. In this situation, it would seem that a comparison of weights both between and within fabrics, groups and contexts would be meaningful and this is the method of recording adopted here. All pottery has been recorded by fabric, weight and context at archive level and a summary of this information is presented in Figures 9.1 and 9.2. Most rims recovered are listed in Figure 9.3 (Webster 2000, for a full catalogue) and illustrated in Figures 9.4–9.6.

Fabrics

The fabrics have been divided according to characteristics visible with the aid of a microscope. Fabric samples have been compared with examples in the Welsh National Fabric Collection housed in the National Museum and Gallery in Cardiff.

Fabric Group 1: Reduced hand-made cooking pots

This fabric is generally dark grey/brown to black in colour and contains frequent rounded grey stones (containing flecks of mica) with some iron-rich fragments and occasional quartz and limestone (Figure 9.4, **P1–13**). The matrix is coarse with plentiful sand and gravel. There is a slightly laminated appearance in the break, as if the clay was not well mixed. The interior surface shows finger marks running in several directions. The exterior is more smoothed, but still

shows signs of finger smoothing and possible rough burnishing. There is no sign of wheel-turning, except occasionally on the edge of the rim, where an evenness of line suggests rotation in finishing. The surfaces have sufficient mica to glisten in good light. Sooting is apparent, particularly on the exterior, and there seems little doubt that this fabric was used for vessels designed primarily for cooking over a fire. This likely use encouraged us to submit a range of samples of this fabric for residue analysis (Section 9.9). Although coarser than the vessels in Fabric Group 2, this fabric is likely to be of local origin and related to the Dyfed gravel-tempered ware tradition. Visually, it is closer to Loughor Fabric Group 9 (Lewis 1994, 137), although one would not describe the gravel within the Dryslwyn fabric as 'flat'. It is considered here to be an early variety of Dyfed gravel-tempered ware.

Fabric Group 1 makes up 23.5% by weight of all the medieval pottery recovered at Dryslwyn. Figure 9.2 clearly shows that it was distributed widely throughout the castle, although it was particularly concentrated in midden deposits (J37 and O77) in Areas J and O, perhaps suggesting that cooking facilities were to be found close by. If we discount post-occupation phases, the bulk of the material is from the period leading up to Phase 4a, giving a peak usage in the early and mid 13th century (Figure 9.1). It would seem, therefore, that this is the cooking ware of the Welsh lordly, rather than the English garrison, occupation of the castle.

Area	Fabric group 1	2.1	2.2	2.3	2.4	2.5	2.6	2.7	3	4.1	4.2	5	6.1	6.2	6.3	7.1	7.2	7.3	7.4	Total	%
1a	17	–	–	–	–	–	–	18	–	3	95	–	14	–	–	–	–	–	–	147	1
1b	233	–	–	–	–	–	7	11	–	354	28	–	–	5	–	–	21	1	–	660	3.5
2a	75	–	–	–	20	5	–	20	–	28	–	–	15	10	–	–	12	–	–	185	1
2b	60	18	41	–	–	–	–	225	14	581	36	–	26	–	–	–	1	–	–	1002	5.5
2c	33	11	8	–	–	9	–	1	–	45	37	–	–	–	–	–	5	–	–	149	1
2d	601	11	5	–	18	–	23	23	–	292	30	–	–	–	1	–	8	1	–	1013	5.5
3a	5	–	3	–	15	110	7	34	–	84	44	–	54	–	–	–	6	37	5	404	2
3b	867	46	12	–	152	196	19	47	16	109	44	92	9	–	–	5	30	9	–	1653	9
3c	–	–	–	–	–	–	–	–	–	–	–	–	–	–	–	–	–	–	–	–	–
3d	20	–	62	–	–	230	19	–	382	–	1	–	–	–	–	2	–	–	–	716	4
4a	1289	35	69	44	20	366	45	136	210	682	198	100	25	51	–	35	239	66	67	3677	19.5
4b	45	–	43	3	8	–	–	18	31	1	–	–	42	1	–	–	9	24	–	255	1
4c	15	74	23	13	18	686	19	322	–	171	362	–	2	18	–	8	69	18	–	1818	9.5
4d	152	23	66	–	–	64	–	10	164	–	–	–	32	18	–	–	48	24	–	601	3
5a	159	13	104	20	22	130	–	15	40	58	33	–	15	84	–	–	–	22	–	715	4
5b	9	9	20	14	25	28	34	114	7	27	–	–	4	18	45	–	33	–	–	387	2
5c	–	–	–	–	18	17	5	88	–	–	–	–	8	14	–	–	–	–	–	150	1
5d	12	20	55	282	14	29	30	309	33	21	5	–	13	–	–	–	1	–	–	824	4.5
6a	–	–	–	–	–	–	–	–	–	–	–	–	–	–	–	–	–	–	–	–	–
6b	–	14	18	–	–	–	–	–	–	–	–	–	–	–	–	–	–	–	–	32	–
6c	9	7	13	–	–	51	175	11	–	4	15	–	4	–	–	–	–	–	–	289	1.5
6d	92	3	120	178	124	12	15	108	5	68	110	–	3	–	–	23	8	48	–	917	5
7a	18	10	28	–	–	–	–	–	28	–	–	–	–	–	–	–	–	–	–	84	0.5
7b	503	40	59	9	–	40	–	56	18	161	22	–	3	45	–	–	50	35	–	1041	5.5
7c	–	–	–	–	11	–	–	–	–	65	14	–	–	–	–	24	–	–	–	114	0.5
7d	49	17	62	–	–	50	13	11	20	338	–	–	18	58	–	5	18	–	–	659	3.5
u/s	155	244	310	5	20	72	126	74	12	107	21	–	28	141	–	31	18	5	30	1399	7.5
Total	4418	595	1121	568	485	2095	537	1651	980	3199	1095	192	315	463	46	133	576	290	102	18861	101
%	23.5	3	6	3	2.5	11	3	9	5	17	6	1	1.5	2.5	–	0.5	3	1.5	0.5	99.5	

FIGURE 9.1

Weight of recovered pottery by phase and fabric group

Fabric group	Area A	B	C	D	E	F	G	H	I	J	K	L	M	N	O	P	T	X	Y	Z	u/s	Total	%
1	152	–	12	40	–	311	107	185	243	2156	87	22	22	–	962	–	70	–	–	13	36	4418	23.5
2.1	–	14	–	–	–	52	70	–	119	30	39	–	–	–	57	3	50	–	23	–	138	595	3
2.2	–	49	4	–	–	186	53	48	112	69	2	50	8	18	137	–	137	–	–	43	205	1121	6
2.3	–	–	–	–	–	3	13	–	–	9	20	28	28	–	490	–	–	–	–	–	5	568	3
2.4	–	–	16	–	–	192	29	–	8	–	–	30	15	–	128	18	14	15	–	–	20	485	2.5
2.5	–	78	3	2	5	235	138	856	79	20	143	1	1	–	253	–	9	–	233	20	20	2095	11
2.6	–	–	–	–	–	56	7	43	12	–	7	92	–	–	49	7	24	175	–	30	35	537	3
2.7	–	–	22	30	–	56	212	196	185	97	28	95	17	–	639	22	–	–	17	3	32	1651	9
3	–	–	33	–	–	59	–	–	117	–	–	11	–	–	219	–	–	–	541	–	–	980	5
4.1	–	–	3	3	15	81	177	133	1039	1240	48	32	7	–	358	30	–	–	–	23	10	3199	17
4.2	–	23	–	–	–	127	200	366	43	98	23	13	37	–	143	12	10	–	–	–	–	1095	6
5	–	–	–	–	–	–	–	–	–	90	–	–	50	–	52	–	–	–	–	–	–	192	1
6.1	–	4	–	–	–	63	8	–	33	62	–	43	–	–	94	–	–	–	–	8	–	315	1.5
6.2	–	–	–	–	–	59	32	–	–	73	–	90	–	58	131	–	–	–	–	20	–	463	2.5
6.3	–	–	–	–	–	–	1	–	–	–	–	–	–	–	45	–	–	–	–	–	–	46	–
7.1	–	–	–	–	–	5	–	32	5	5	–	24	–	–	30	–	2	–	–	–	30	133	0.5
7.2	1	–	–	–	–	33	66	70	50	96	–	12	–	–	243	2	–	–	–	–	3	576	3
7.3	37	–	–	–	–	34	34	5	30	–	–	22	–	–	97	8	–	–	23	–	–	290	1.5
7.4	–	–	–	–	–	–	–	–	–	5	–	–	–	–	67	–	–	–	–	–	30	102	0.5
Total	190	168	93	75	20	1552	1147	1934	2075	4050	234	699	185	76	4194	102	316	190	837	160	564	18861	99.5
%	1	1	0.5	0.5	–	8	6	10.5	11	21.5	1	0.5	1	0.5	22	0.5	1.5	1	4.5	1	3	99.5	

FIGURE 9.2

Weight of recovered pottery by area and fabric group

Fabric Group 2: Dyfed gravel-tempered ware

This is the largest fabric group represented at Dryslwyn, making up 37% by weight of all medieval pottery recovered. As a whole, the fabric is characterised by the use of water-worn gravel with considerable variation in gravel size and composition. Vessels made both with and without the use of a potters' wheel are present and all examples have been fired in an oxidising atmosphere. There is likely to be a connection to Fabric Group 1, but Group 2 vessels are more thinly potted and use finer gravels, resulting in a markedly less crude product. Other observers have suggested a range of sources for Group 2 pottery and, as a result, the group has been divided into a number of sub-groups in the hope of identifying the characteristics of individual producers. Two sherds in the catalogue [P33–34], however, could not be assigned to a particular sub-group within Fabric Group 2 (Figures 9.1 and 9.2).

Looking at the distribution and chronology of Group 2 pottery as a whole at Dryslwyn, significant amounts were recovered from Phase 2 and Phase 3 deposits, mainly concentrated in the south-eastern sector of the Inner Ward, with the midden in Area F particularly well represented. However, it clearly saw its major usage in Phases 4 and 5, both in contemporary occupation deposits, such as those in Area O dating from Phase 5d, and in areas where earlier occupation debris was used for later levelling; for example, the post-siege (Phase 4c) material in Area H. Overall, the chronological spread supports the suggestion already made above that Group 2 fabrics developed from Group 1 fabrics and follow them chronologically.

Fabric Group 2.1: Gravel-tempered, hand-made, unglazed

Where unsooted, the fabric is oxidised to a light red to pink-buff colour with a pimply surface, due to the presence of plentiful gravel in the fabric. Under the microscope, the filler appears as rounded gravel, some with a high iron content and with a tendency towards flatter elongated shapes, which can break giving some angular pieces. The matrix contains some sand, giving a noticeably rough break, but the overall appearance under the microscope is of gravels of varying size within a fairly smooth matrix. The matrix appears to contain grains of mica. Surfaces are smoother than in Group 1. Sooting externally is common, suggesting use for cooking. Sherds in this fabric were found across the site, but in too small a quantity to be sure that figures are meaningful. Higher percentages in Phases 3, 4 and 5 may be noted. It may be that the division between this and sub-group 2.2 is not significant. There were no rims suitable for illustration.

Fabric Group 2.2: Coarse grit-tempered, unglazed

The difference between this sub-group (Figure 9.4, P14–19) and 2.1 above is subtle, but the grit used appears to be slightly smaller. Whether this denotes a separate source for the gravel or simply variations within a single source must, of course, remain open to debate. Some examples have reduced cores. All or most of the vessels within this sub-group appear to have been made without the aid of a potters' wheel, despite their even finish. Some of the sherds will be from unglazed vessels, but many will probably be unglazed portions of glazed ware.

Number	Figure	Fabric group	Context	Phase
P1	10.4	1	J72	1b
P2	10.4	1	I88	2b
P3	10.4	1	F34	2d
P4	10.4	1	J28	1d
P5	10.4	1	O151	3b
P6	10.4	1	O151	3b
P7	10.4	1	J1	7b
P8	10.4	1	J31	2d
P9	10.4	1	G147	–
P10	10.4	1	F19	3b
P11	10.4	1	F22	3b
P12	10.4	1	T43	3d
P13	10.4	1	K12	6c
P14	10.4	2.2	u/s	–
P15	10.4	2.2	I82	2b
P16	10.4	2.2	J15	4a
P17	10.4	2.2	F16	4b
P18	10.4	2.2	O7	6d
P19	10.4	2.2	O7	6d
P20	10.4	2.4	G59	4c
P21	10.4	2.4	O178	6d
P22	10.4	2.5	L17	5a
P23	10.4	2.5	I1	7d
P24	10.4	2.5	H59	4c
P25	10.4	2.6	F23	3b
P26	10.4	2.6	X16	6d
P27	10.4	2.6	I3	4a
P28	10.4	2.6	Z12	5d
P29	10.5	2.7	F6	6d
P30	10.5	2.7	O7	5d
P31	10.5	2.7	H1	7d
P32	10.5	2.7	O74	3a
P33	10.5	2	I82, I95	2b
P34	10.5	2	L17	5a
P35	10.5	3	O31	4a
P36	10.5	3	Y7, Y9, Y12, Y33	3d, 4d
P37	10.5	3	I1, I6, I30, I41	4a, 5a, 7d
P38	10.5	4.1	I28	2b
P39	10.5	4.1	J1	7b
P40	10.5	4.2	J1	7b
P41	10.5	4.2	H43	4a
P42	10.5	4.2	J25	2d
P43	10.5	4.2	I95, J25	2b, 2d
P45	10.5	4.2	I65	2b
P47	10.5	7.2	O31	4a
P48	10.5	7.2	H53	4a
P50	10.6	7.3	I18, I42	3a, 4a
P51	10.6	7.3	G470	3a
P52	10.6	7.3	O31	4a
P53	10.6	7.3	O97	4a
P54	10.6	7.3	Y7, Y12	4d
P55	10.6	7.3	G346	–
P56	10.6	7.3	F44	3b
P57	10.6	7.3	P73	3a
P58	10.6	7.4	u/s	–
P60	10.6	7.4	O91	4a

FIGURE 9.3

Illustrated pottery details

Most noticeable is the poor representation of this sub-group in phases up to and including Phase 3c. The high proportion in later post-occupation levels is also noteworthy, but this may simply mean that disturbance is more likely to have occurred in upper occupation levels than lower ones. It may be suggested,

therefore, that this variety of Dyfed gravel-tempered ware is characteristic of Phase 3d occupation and later. It is tempting to see it as a refinement of Fabric Group 1 within the same industry or tradition and characteristic of the late Welsh and the English castle.

Fabric Group 2.3: Coarse grit-tempered, glazed

This is the glazed version of sub-group 2.2. The glaze tends to be a mottled olive-green and can seal the surface preventing oxidisation below it. There were no vessels suitable for illustration in this sub-group.

Fabric Group 2.4: Gravel-tempered with high ironstone content

The fabric is identical to sub-groups 2.2 and 2.3, with the exception that the gravel appears to have a higher content of iron-rich components (i.e. more than about 50%). Both glazed and unglazed examples are found (Figure 9.4, **P20–21**). Some have streaks of white within the fabric, suggesting that the clay matrix has not been mixed well. It is possible that this represents a different gravel source (and thus, perhaps, a different kiln), but variations within other sources is equally possible. As with other Group 2 fabrics, this sub-group was concentrated within Phases 3–6, but appears scattered both chronologically and spatially. Overall quantities are too small to tell if this is truly representative of a separate fabric or merely indicative of variations within Group 2 fabrics.

Fabric Group 2.5: Coarse grit in a smooth matrix

This sub-group appears to be formed without use of the potters' wheel (Figure 9.4, **P22–24**). However, there are signs of wheel throwing on some exteriors, suggesting use of a wheel or turntable in finishing. The fabric is distinguished from others by the large size of the rounded gravel used and the general absence of finer sand and small gravel. Some quartz is present. The finished fabric is, if anything, pimplier than sub-groups 2.1–2.4, but under the microscope the matrix appears visibly smoother. Glazed and unglazed sherds were noted. Reduced cores were also present, but not universal. The great majority of examples appear to be from Phases 3, 4 and 5a, perhaps suggesting a fairly short-lived source within the general gravel-tempered tradition. There is a marked concentration in Area H.

Fabric Group 2.6: Coarse grit/gravel, wheel-thrown and unglazed

This variant represents a wheel-thrown version of sub-group 2.2. The difference is one of technique rather than fabric (Figure 9.4, **P25–28**). As with other attempts to separate glazed and unglazed vessels, there will be some sherds that are from unglazed parts of glazed vessels. The material was separated in the

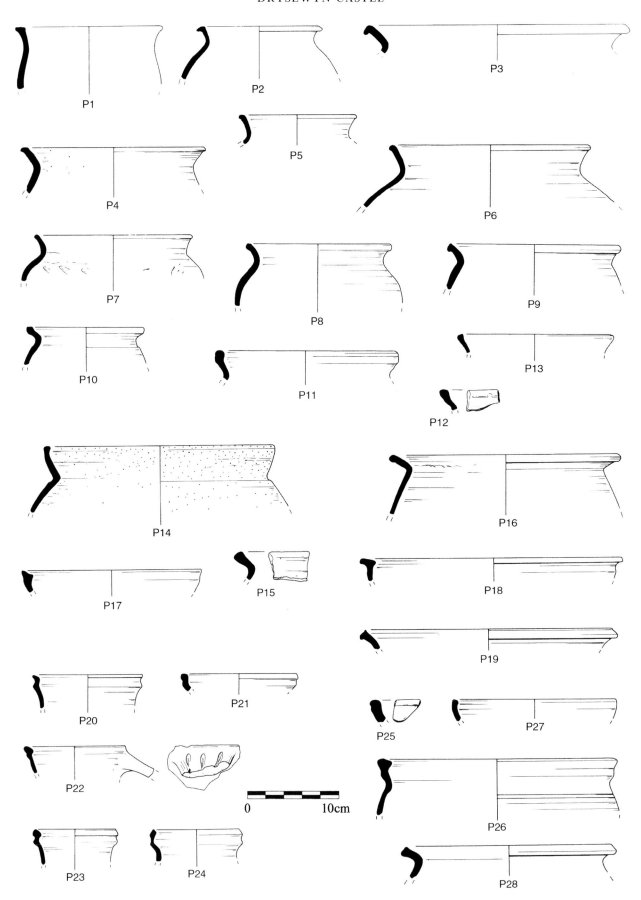

FIGURE 9.4

Pottery

hope that it might betray different chronological characteristics, but the quantities present are too small for meaningful comment.

Fabric Group 2.7: Coarse grit/gravel, wheel-thrown and glazed

This variant represents a wheel-thrown version of sub-group 2.3. As with sub-group 2.6, the difference is one of technique rather than fabric (Figure 9.5, **P29–32**). However, there appears to be more of this fabric than its unglazed counterpart. This sub-group appears to have been present throughout the period of occupation at Dryslwyn, with some evidence for a concentration of finds from Phase 2b up to and including Phase 5d.

Fabric Group 3: White grit-tempered

To the naked eye, this fabric differs in the break rather than on the surface from Group 2 and one may suspect a local source (Figure 9.5, **P35–37**). Surfaces show the pimply appearance characteristic of the presence of grit and tend to be light orange-buff in colour. Most examples of the fabric were made with the use of the potters' wheel. Grey cores, however, seem to be universal and this emphasises the distinguishing feature, which is the filler used. Some of the often iron-rich gravel, characteristic of Group 2, is present, but there is a high proportion of white, apparently calcitic, fragments, which give the ware a characteristic appearance in the break even without the use of a lens. The pattern of deposition is not unlike that for Group 2, but there appears to be a more distinct concentration from Phases 3d to 4d (Figure 9.1). Contrary to the norm for Dryslwyn, the figures mask substantial fragments of just a few vessels, rather than numerous small sherds.

Fabric Group 4: Ham Green and Bristol types

This fabric is common to the whole of the South Wales seaboard. The internal surface appears in colours from fawn to light orange-buff. The fabric may appear more grey in colour and contains a mixture of filler, including rounded gravel, fired clay and small red and black sand grains with some quartz. Where unglazed, the surface appears highly micaceous, especially under the microscope. Fabric Group 4 has been divided into two sub-groups, representing hand-made and wheel-thrown examples.

Chronologically, the Dryslwyn evidence fits well with the current dating of Ham Green Ware at Bristol, based partly on dendrochronology (Ponsford 1991). This would suggest a period of production for Ham Green B Ware lasting from *c*1175 to *c*1275. Thus, the presence of the ware at Dryslwyn from the start need occasion no surprise, whilst its marked decline in contexts later than the immediately post-siege period (Phase 4c) is in accordance with a mid–late 13th-century cessation of production.

Fabric Group 4.1: Ham Green type, hand-made

The internal surface of this fabric sub-group shows plentiful, if partial, fingerprints and is noticeably uneven (Figure 9.5, **P38–39**). The exterior is, however, much more even and finishing using a wheel or turntable seems likely. The fabric is widely distributed at Dryslwyn, but the pattern is markedly different to that for Group 2. Earlier phases are much better represented and there is a marked concentration only up to Phase 4c, suggesting, somewhat surprisingly in view of the likely English source, that this fabric was used primarily in the Welsh occupation of the castle. The high calcium content of the filler of Barton's Ham Green A Ware is absent (Barton 1963, 96–97) and this appears to correspond with his Ham Green B Ware. The glaze is characteristically a rich olive-green. Surface decoration does occur, although Dryslwyn does not have many pieces that suggest any of the more highly decorated Ham Green designs.

Fabric Group 4.2: Bristol ware type, wheel-thrown

The internal surface of this fabric sub-group shows clears signs of wheel-throwing (Figure 9.5, **P40–45**). This is, of course, largely obscured externally by the glaze. Horizontal grooves are sometimes present on the exterior, which can only be the result of use of a potters' wheel. At Dryslwyn, there seems to be less of the wheel-thrown Group 4 fabric in early occupation phases, but the scarcity after Phase 4c is again marked.

Fabric Group 5: White stone-tempered

A small number of sherds were present with a fabric characterised by a large amount of off-white, presumably calcitic, stone used as a temper. The fabric is pale buff and would appear to be formed without the use of a wheel. In the break, it can appear with pale streaks, as if the clay was not fully mixed. It includes some sandy temper as well as the large rounded stone lumps. The glaze is a speckled green, which can vary from an intense green in spots to pale orange-green at its thinnest. The fabric appears only in Phases 3b (Area O) and 4a (Areas J and O) and no sherds were suitable for illustration.

Fabric Group 6.1: Miscellaneous glazed (i), abundant quartz temper

Among fabrics represented by only a small number of sherds was a distinctive hard, light grey fabric with a sandy temper, which included abundant quartz of varying colour. It appeared to be wheel-thrown and, where glazed, this was a light olive-green. The

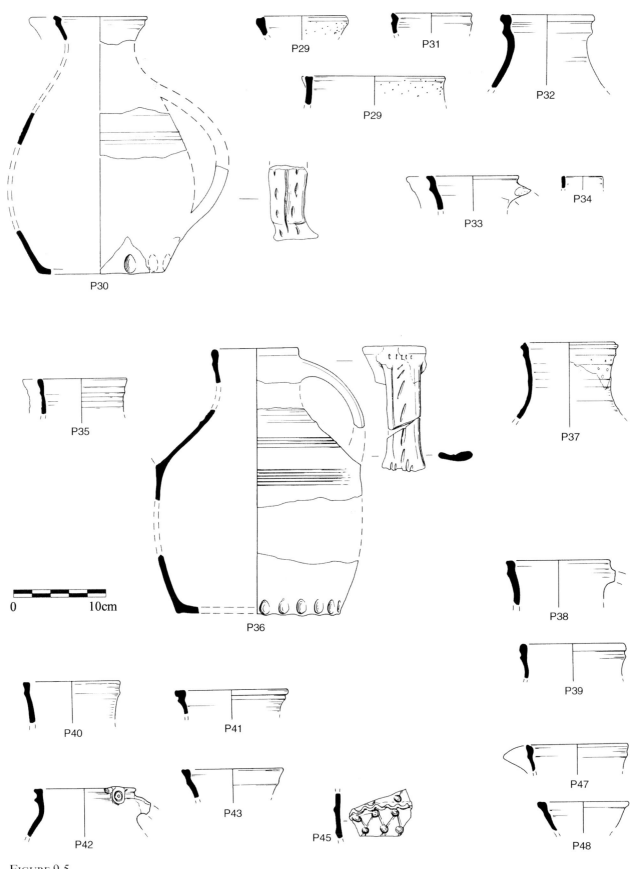

FIGURE 9.5

Pottery

242

total yield is too small to allow meaningful comment, although it should be noted that the bulk of the material was from earlier occupation deposits up to Phase 4. No sherds were suitable for illustration.

Fabric Group 6.2: Miscellaneous glazed (ii), pale fabrics

A collection of miscellaneous sherds have been grouped in this category. Most are characterised by a pale buff to off-white fabric. Several sources are suggested. The fabrics come from Phases 1, 5 and 7 and are scattered through several areas. No sherds were suitable for illustration.

Fabric Group 6.3: Miscellaneous (iii), red fabric

This distinctive fabric was present in only two contexts: (G178) (Phase 2d) and (O44) (Phase 5b). The fabric is red in colour and contains a fine sandy temper. The source is unknown. No sherds were suitable for illustration.

Fabric Group 7: Saintonge wares

The pottery of the Saintonge stands out among the Dryslwyn assemblage due to its fineness and, in some cases, its decoration. Three sub-groups have been created, dividing the fabric according to decoration (or lack of it). In all, the fabric is white or off-white and appears smooth to the naked eye. Under the microscope, small red and black flecks are visible along with fragments of mica. There is little difference between the appearance of the fabric in the break and on unglazed surfaces. Some examples, such as no. 50, included quartz and perhaps flint, which may suggest more than one source kiln. Vessels are wheel-thrown. In the main, jugs and the so-called pégaux (large wide-mouthed jugs) predominate. The presence of rare sgraffito vessels [P57] should be noted.

The distribution of Saintonge pottery in South Wales has been outlined by Papazian and Campbell (1992, 16–21, fig 4). In the main, it is coastal, making Dryslwyn one of the more inland of the findsites. It has always been assumed that the ware was a by-product of the Bordeaux wine trade and one might expect, therefore, that both the pottery and the wine would have entered western Britain via Bristol and then been shipped on to Wales by coastal vessels. Papazian and Campbell, however, have raised the possibility of direct trade into Haverfordwest and Carmarthen, and the large Carmarthen assemblage and relatively large Dryslwyn collection would seem to support this view. Transport onwards from the port of Carmarthen would probably have been by water on small river-craft. Papazian and Campbell suggest that the ware was not valuable enough to be traded very far inland. It may be, however, that the remarkable distribution is

due not to a lack of value, but to a restriction in supply. One thinks of the way in which Chinese porcelain was imported at a later date in the lower areas of the East Indiamen, where tea and silks would otherwise have been damaged by water. If comparable areas were smaller in the medieval wine traders, or if other more valuable cargoes could be fitted into them, the available amounts of pottery would be small and insufficient in quantity to penetrate very far beyond coastal markets.

Fabric Group 7.1: Saintonge ware, unglazed

Wherever possible, sherds from unglazed vessels have been separated from those unglazed sherds which are thought to have come from glazed vessels. Most unglazed Saintonge vessels at Dryslwyn appear to have been large pégaux. There were no examples suitable for illustration. This fabric sub-group was limited to Phase 3 and Phase 4 deposits, but, with such a small sample, this must be of doubtful significance, particularly in view of the wider chronological distribution of other Saintonge types.

Fabric Group 7.2: Saintonge ware, monochrome glazed

The category is restricted to sherds with the mottled green glaze characteristic of vessels (mainly jugs) glazed in a single colour (Figure 9.5, **P47–48**). Examples of this fabric are concentrated in Phases 1–4 and in post-castle disturbance. It seems likely that the period of importation of monochrome green-glazed jugs extended beyond the middle/late 13th century. Therefore, it is possible to suggest that the restricted Dryslwyn dating is a product of the castle's change of ownership after the siege of 1287. If so, then we are presumably looking at a by-product of the loss of a resident lord once the castle passed out of Welsh hands.

Fabric Group 7.3: Saintonge Ware, polychrome glazed

The best known and most exotic of the Saintonge products are those decorated in designs which use more than one colour (Figure 9.6, **P50–57**). The decoration on the polychrome jugs at Dryslwyn was in the main unexceptional, including heraldic shields and only one example of the common bird motif. Two pieces [**P56–57**] were more unusual, the first displaying a brown painted stripe and an impressed design, whilst the second showed clear evidence of sgraffito decoration.

The bulk of this material came from Phase 4 and Phase 5a deposits. Examples from phases earlier than Phase 3 are restricted to very small fragments, which are probably too small to make any significant comment on regarding chronology. Its appearance in Phase 3a, however, might suggest that this phase

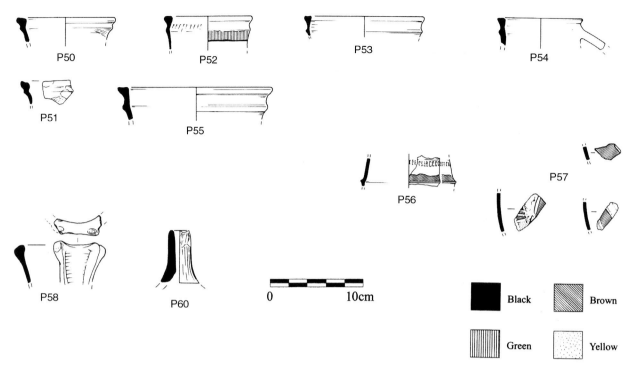

FIGURE 9.6

Pottery

should be given a slightly wider date range, as poly-chrome ware is generally thought to have appeared in around 1280. The ware probably did not continue to be imported after the early 14th century, as the gap in deposition after Phase 5a suggests. It may well be significant that 47.5% of all finds in this sub-group come from pre-siege levels and, if later redeposition in phases after 6a are ignored, this figure rises to 68%. This tends to confirm that Saintonge fineware is essentially a product of Welsh lordly occupation at Dryslwyn, as has already been suggested above.

Group 7.4: Saintonge ware, miscellaneous

These pieces have been separated, as they were not necessarily imported at the same time as the jugs and pégaux (Figure 9.6, **P58–60**). **P58** is a chafing dish, which was glazed externally in a pale apple-green glaze. **P59** is a handle with a thin greenish glaze that may have come from an aquamanile, whilst **P60** is a candlestick with external vertical burnishing and a partial mottled green glaze.

Discussion

An overview of the medieval pottery from Dryslwyn is best made in the context of Figures 9.1 and 9.2. Figure 9.1 shows that fabrics of Group 1 appear early, but are gradually replaced by those of Group 2. It is also interesting to contrast the pattern presented by the local Group 2 fabrics and those from Bristol (Group 4). The former appear in quantity later, but

predominate after the siege in 1287. The latter tail off markedly after Phase 4c. Taken as a whole, Figure 9.1 shows a clear division between pre- and post-1300 deposition. The 80 years or so of occupation leading up to 1300 (Phases 1–4c) produce 62.5% of the pottery and most of the imported wares. The 130 years from c1300 to c1430 (Phases 4d–6a), meanwhile, produce only 14.5% of the pottery and, even if we include the demolition and looting phases (Phases 6b–6d), this only adds a further 6.5%, the remainder coming from post-castle activities. Although this could represent a change in rubbish disposal methods, it seems more likely to reflect a change in the level of activity on the site, from periodic occupation by a local lord and his retinue to that by a constable and a small 'caretaker' garrison. Whilst the constable and his garrison seem to have relied almost totally on local supplies of pottery, the lord and his retinue appear to have bought in a much wider variety of pottery, including a number of items which can be regarded as exotic.

As for the spatial distribution on site, it is unlikely that such a small assemblage of pottery will provide conclusive proof for the use of particular areas within the castle. Nevertheless, a breakdown of pottery weights by fabric group and area is instructive. Both the size of individual areas and, to a lesser extent, the extent of excavation within them, will, of course, have varied. Not surprisingly, the Inner Ward produced most of the pottery, with Areas F and O particularly well represented. Areas G, H, I, J, K, and L yielded most of the cooking wares and also most of the finewares, although no clear patterns of usage emerged within these areas and the various castle buildings they represent. The paucity of pottery within the Round Tower D is perhaps surprising and might suggest that this structure played a largely defensive role, with the main business of living taking place elsewhere in the Inner Ward. However, the very limited depth of deposits derived from Area D and the presence of a flagstone floor prior to Phase 4c may go some way towards explaining the scarcity of sherds here.

In conclusion, the assemblage is much as one would expect for a site not occupied towards the very end of the Middle Ages. The pottery shows none of the diversification of that period. Instead, it is restricted almost entirely to jars (mainly or wholly cooking pots) and jugs. Its main interest lies in the light it may shed on the standard of living of a local Welsh lord in the period up to the final Edwardian conquest. It is clear that the English-Welsh division in the occupation produces a pattern contrary to that expected. The advent of an English garrison brings not an increase in the purchase of pottery from outside the region, but a marked diminution. In part, this is a reflection of the intensity of occupation, but it may also be an indicator of the social status of the inhabitants. It is clear that the presence of a lordly residence was sufficient to drawn in imported goods that would otherwise be restricted to coastal sites. If one were to place Dryslwyn on the distribution maps of either Ham Green or Saintonge pottery (Papazian and Campbell 1992, maps 3 and 13), it would be apparent how even a river as navigable as the Tywi does not normally result in the spread of these wares far from the coast. That they occur at Dryslwyn must surely be a reflection of the prestige of this site in the mid to late 13th century.

Roman pottery

Three contexts yielded sherds of Roman pottery. From Area H (H47) (Phase 4a) came a bodysherd of a late 3rd- or 4th-century Black Burnished jar. Area T also yielded a fragment of Black Burnished Ware, whilst a flanged bowl came from an unstratified context. The latter was from a bowl resembling the Samian form 38, but is more likely to be related to its colour-coated derivatives, which were current from the mid 3rd century. The 'assemblage' of Roman pottery, such that it is, would seem indicative of later 3rd- or 4th-century activity. Its minute size suggests that activity on the site was more likely to be agricultural, rather than related to habitation.

Post-medieval pottery

Post-medieval pottery was found in several contexts from Phases 6c to 7d. Much of it would appear to represent casual losses of the 19th and 20th centuries.

The earliest post-medieval sherd, from context (Y26) (Phase 6d), had a mottled brown glaze typical of the products of Bristol and Staffordshire in the later 17th and early 18th centuries. Of a similar date was a fragment of cream-glazed earthenware from context (L47) (Phase 6d), in addition to plates in white tin-glazed earthenware from contexts (D1) (Phase 7b) and (G12) (Phase 6c). Items of the 19th century seem mostly to date from the first half of the century and include banded creamware from contexts (J1) (Phase 7d) and (W1) (Phase 7c), various blue and black transfer-printed sherds from Areas K, O, P and W (Phases 6d, 7b–7d), a hand-painted pearlware saucer and plain pearlware bowl from context (W1) (Phase 7c), a 'sponged' blue cup from the same context and a plate with a blue 'feathered' edge from Area H (Phase 7d). The 20th century was represented by a near complete white cup with a stamp on the underside, which is probably that of the Salisbury Crown China Company of Longton, used in the late 1920s and 1930s (Godden 1964, no. 3443). The 19th- and 20th-century ceramics together seem to reflect use of the hill as a picnic spot with pleasing views of the surrounding countryside. They are all likely to derive from tea sets.

9.3   COINS
by Edward Besly

The coins found at Dryslwyn Castle are all of fairly common types and require little numismatic comment beyond that in the catalogue. Roman coins are found widely in south and west Wales, so the presence of a worn specimen of a common denarius of Vespasian [C1] need not be significant. The nummus of Diocletian [C2] is more unusual as a chance find, although such early tetrarchic issues are occasionally found in sizeable hoards. This example has clearly been pierced for use as a pendant (attested by signs of wear on the edges of the hole), although the date of this modification is not certain.

The earliest numismatic context for the castle itself is provided by a cut halfpenny of Short Cross Class 7b [C6], which was recovered from a deposit relating to the Phase 2a construction of the Great Hall K/L. A *terminus post quem* for this coin is provided by the appointment of the moneyer Richard de Neketon in 1230 (Brand 1994, 53), whilst the *terminus ante quem* is 1236, when production of Class 7b coins ceased (North 1988, 33). The coin may be worn, but was seen only in a cleaned condition. Two other Short Cross coins [C4 and C5], neither later than *c*1217 but both showing some signs of wear, were recovered from Phase 3b contexts in Courtyard O.

Evidence is beginning to emerge in Wales for the use of coinage in Welsh (as opposed to Anglo-Norman) contexts from the end of the 12th or early 13th centuries. This may to some extent simply reflect the greatly expanded availability of coinage in England from the end of the 12th century, exemplified by the Short Cross coinage of 1180–1247 (Rigold 1977; Besly 1995). The appearance of Short Cross and Long Cross pennies at Dryslwyn parallels the extensive Anglesey finds from the principality of Gwynedd at Llanfaes and, to a lesser extent, Rhosyr (Besly 1995, 55–56).

The interpretation of finds of Short Cross and the succeeding Long Cross coinages at Dryslwyn raises some problems. In principle, and to a large extent in practice, each type, the sole legal coinage of its time, was recalled and completely recoined as its successor when a change of design was decreed: the Short Cross coinage in 1247 and the Long Cross in 1279. To what extent the previous type survived and remained available in remoter areas, such as West Wales, after these recoinages is not certain. If the two Short Cross coins from the Courtyard O are regarded as losses from currency, there may be a case for a slightly earlier date, i.e. pre-1250, for the latrine pit in which they were deposited, although this is far from conclusive.

The most secure numismatic dating evidence at Dryslwyn appears to relate to Phase 4 activity. An unworn penny [C10] and a slightly worn penny [C11], both of 1280–81, came from occupation deposits dated to Phases 4b and 4d respectively. Thereafter, the complete absence of the common Class 10 pennies of the first decade of the 14th century, which account for nearly one third of chance finds of Edward I and II from Wales (writer's records), is noticeable, but the overall sample is small. Virtually all numismatic finds from Phase 5 contexts are from the Great Hall K/L and the Courtyard O. This clustering of coins and jettons indicates the areas receiving most use during this 14th-century occupation.

The French denier tournois [C18] is an unusual find from a British site, but by no means unparalleled. In Wales, a 13th-century example is recorded from Cowbridge in the Vale of Glamorgan. In England, Cook (1999) has recorded 16 finds of deniers tournois (13th–14th centuries) from southern England, ranging from Wiltshire to Norfolk. With a fineness typically of around 30% silver, these will have been incompatible with English currency.

Roman

C1 Vespasian, AD 69–79; denarius, probably as RIC 4 (Fortuna), 69–70. Much worn and incomplete. 81SF29. Context T9 (Phase 5a).

C2 Diocletian, AD 284–305; nummus, ?Trier mint *c*300–305. Much worn and holed at 12 o'clock (obv.). 92SF144. Context O66 (Phase 4a).

English and Irish medieval

C3 Short Cross penny, class 4b, London, moneyer Goldwine, *c*1194–1204. Somewhat worn and clipped. 90SF69. Context H43 (Phase 4c).

C4 Short Cross penny, class 6a, London, Ilger, *c*1210–17. Some wear (burnt?). 93SF25. Context O79 (Phase 3b).

C5 Short Cross cut halfpenny, class 5c–6c, London, Walter, *c*1205–17. Some wear. 93SF94. Context O151 (Phase 3b).

C6 Short Cross (Henry III) cut halfpenny, class 7b, London, Ricard, *c*1230–06. Some wear? (cleaned before examination). 82SF15. Context K35 (Phase 2a).

C7 Henry III, Long Cross penny, class 5b, London, Ricard, *c*1251 or later. Corroded, but not much worn. 91SF48. Context H53 (Phase 4a).

C8 Ireland, Henry III, Long Cross cut halfpenny, Dublin, Ricard, *c*1251–54. Some wear, clipped? 93SF39. Context O66 (Phase 4a).

Sterling

C9 Edward I penny, class 2a, London, *c*1280. Some corrosion, but not much worn. 93SF27. Context B93 (Phase 4a).

C10 Edward I penny, class 3c, London, *c*1280–81. Some pitting and weak striking, but unworn. 85SF3. Context F15 (Phase 4b).

C11 Edward I penny, class 3d, London, *c*1280–81. Slightly worn. 92SF20. Context O52 (Phase 4d).

C12 Edward I penny, class 3f, London, *c*1280–81. Corroded but not much worn. 84SF57. Context L31 (Phase 5a).

C13 Edward I penny, class 4a, Canterbury, *c*1282–89. Restruck, obv. on rev. Some wear. 82SF41. Context K18 (Phase 5b).

C14 Edward I penny, class 4d, London, *c*1282–89. Unworn. 86SF1. Context F1 (Phase 7b).

C15 Edward I penny, class 4d, London, *c*1282–89. Weakly struck, slight wear? 95SF9. Context O219 (Phase 5b).

C16 Edward II penny, class 11a1/3, London, *c*1310–14. Weakly struck, some wear. 93SF31. Context O77 (Phase 3b).

C17 Edward III halfpenny, 'Florin' coinage, London 1344–51, type 1, as SCBI 39, no. 1101. Not much worn. 82SF42. Context K30 (Phase 5b).

Foreign

C18 France, Philip III (1270–85) or Philip IV (1285–1314), denier tournois a l'Orond, *c*1280–90; Lafaurie (1951) 228, Duplessy (1988) 223. Not much worn (cleaned). 83SF12. Context O7 (Phase 6d).

Jettons

C19 English, early 14th century; sterling head/cross with pellets: cf. Berry (1974) type 1, pl 2, no. 5 (obv. same die?). Berry attributes to Edward II, resembling class 14 pennies (*c*1317–20). 82SF46. Context K31 (Phase 5a).

C20 English, early 14th century (fragment); cross moline both sides, as Berry (1974) pl 1, no. 5, rev.; time of Edward II? 82SF32. Context K18 (Phase 5b).

C21 French, crown/cross; legends PARAMOVRS SVIDONE[ST, rev.]. For reverse, cf. Barnard (1916) 67. A neat jetton, probably late 14th–early 15th century. The crown is a prominent feature of some French gold, silver and billon coins from Charles IV (1322–28) onwards. 86SF67. Unstratified.

C22 Dauphine, dolphin/cross; AVEMARIAGRACLGPL, obv. only: cf. Barnard (1916) 62, early 15th century. 81SF28. Context K12 (Phase 6c).

Modern

C23–24 Anglesey, Parys Mines Company, copper penny tokens, 1788. Both much worn. 80SF1. Context K1, 80SF2. Context K2 (Phase 7c).

C25 George V, halfpenny 1917. Worn. 89SF3. Context H10 (Phase 7c).

9.4 IRON ARTEFACTS
by Ian Goodall

The catalogue number (preceded by 'F') refers to the object sequence in the complete excavation ironwork catalogue (I Goodall 2001). Illustrated finds are in bold.

Tools

The tools from Dryslwyn, despite their limited number, hint at some of the activities undertaken on the castle site. Woodworking is not represented, but part of a sledgehammer, a cold chisel and a punch [**F1–3**] are blacksmith's tools, whilst a rectangular-sectioned blade [**F4**] is evidently an incompletely forged knife, which thus reflects this craft. The slender hammer [**F5**] could have been used to trim the edges of roof slates. The tooth from a woolcomb or flax heckle [**F6**], used in the preparation of fibres for spinning, is the sole example of its type from the site, but the needles and the delicate pair of shears [**F8–11**] reflect sewing and perhaps the repair of clothing. Leatherworking is represented by an awl [**F12**], which was used to pierce holes in leather, and by two creasers [**F13–14**]. Creasers are finishing tools with distinctive short blades, which were used to make lines on the surface of leather either as a guide for sewing or, more deeply, as decoration. A weedhook and part of a watering can [**F15–16**] could have contributed to maintaining the castle grounds. Tools such as an iron crowbar 'for breaking stones' are recorded as present in the castle's stores in 1300/01 (Section 3.1).

F1 Sledgehammer. Fragment of arm with burred face. Length 181mm. 90SF85. Context H44 (Phase 4c). Figure 9.7.

F2 Cold chisel with burred head, octagonal-sectioned body and broken blade. Length 124mm. 83SF72. Unstratified. Figure 9.7.

F3 Punch, rounded section becoming square before tapering. Length 107mm. 82SF26. Context M 13 (Phase 7a). Figure 9.7.

F4 Incompletely forged knife. Length 45mm. 90SF135. Context H59 (Phase 4c). Figure 9.9.

F5 Hammer. Slender, waisted body with small hole and one bevelled blade edge. Length 111mm. 87SF27. Context I55 (Phase 2b). Figure 9.7.

F6 Comb tooth, broken. Length 188mm. 84SF85. Context Z25 (Phase 5d). Figure 9.7.

F7 Needle. Eye complete, shank tip lost. Length 41mm. 88SF13. Context I82 (Phase 2b). Figure 9.7.

F8–9 Needles or pins, both retaining their tips but not their heads:
F8. Length 22mm, diameter 1.5mm. 85SF39. Context F25 (Phase 3b). Not illustrated.
F9. Length 22mm, diameter 1mm. 93SF132. Context O77 (Phase 3b). Not illustrated.

F10 Shears blade fragments. Length 44mm. 92SF117. Context B43 (Phase 4d). Figure 9.9.

F11 Shears with plain bow and blades. Length 63mm. 91SF52. Context O44 (Phase 5b). Figure 9.9.

F12 Awl with triangular-sectioned blade and remains of wood from handle on rectangular-sectioned tang. Length 95mm. 86SF65. Unstratified. Figure 9.9.

F13–14 Creasers with long tangs and short blades:
F13: Length 172mm. 92SF130. Context O31 (Phase 4a). Figure 9.7.
F14: Length 191mm. 92SF15. Context O52 (Phase 4d). Figure 9.7.

F15 Weedhook with broken blade. Length 59mm. 93SF88. Context B 116 (Phase 4a). Figure 9.9.

F16 Rose from watering can. Central hole surrounded by two concentric rings of holes. Diameter 42mm. 84SF65. Context L17 (Phase 5a). Figure 9.7.

F195 Projectile point or plumb bob with missing suspension loop. Length 58mm. 88SF30. Context J32 (Phase 2b). Figure 9.11.

Knives

The majority of knives have whittle tangs, which were inserted into handles, rather than scale tangs, which had riveted handles. The sufficiently complete examples of each of these types have been grouped together by blade shape. **F17–19** have backs and cutting edges that are parallel, before either the back angles down to the tip, or the back and cutting edge both converge to the tip. **F20–27** have blades that taper more or less evenly from tang to tip. This practical shape is the most numerous type represented at Dryslwyn Castle, as among British medieval knives in general. **F28–30** are too incomplete to classify, but **F31**, with its distinctive blade tip, is post-medieval in date. The scale-tang knife fragment [**F32**] is intrusive, since this type of tang was not introduced until the 13th or 14th century, but **F33** could be medieval. **F34–38** are the most distinctive knife blade fragments. The uses to which the knives were put can only be conjectured, but they must have been both domestic and industrial. The distinctive shape of **F17**, for example, suggests a craft use. None of the blades has decorative inlay and none has a cutler's mark.

F17–31 Whittle-tang knifes:
F17: Length 56mm. 90SF35. Context H59 (Phase 4c). Figure 9.10.
F18: Length 175mm. 88SF35. Context J42 (Phase 1b). Figure 9.10.

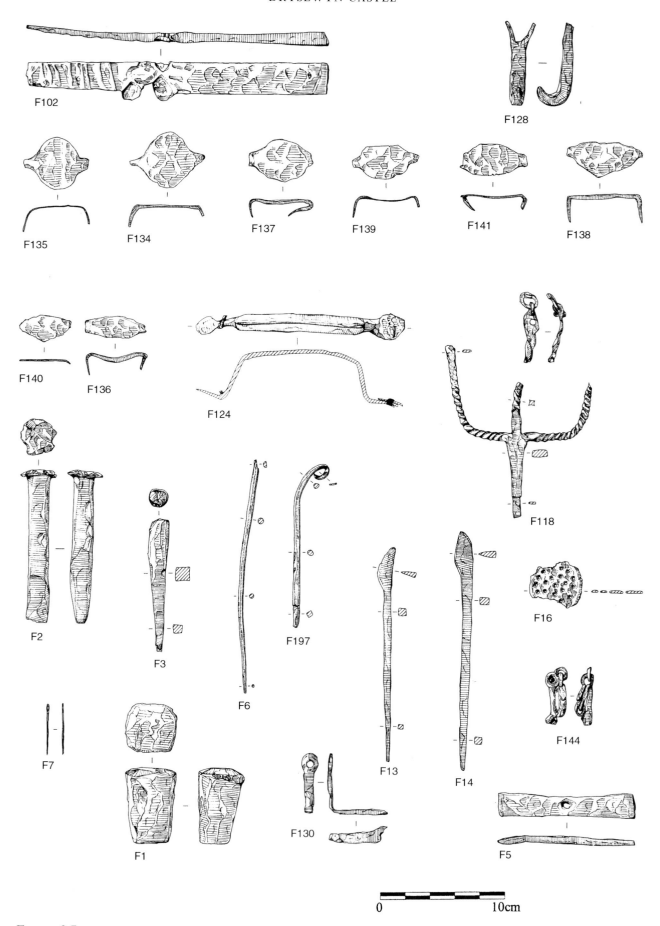

FIGURE 9.7

Ironwork: tools

F19: Length 114mm. 85SF12. Context F16 (Phase 4b). Figure 9.10.

F20: Length 171mm. 85SF8. Context F16 (Phase 4b). Figure 9.10.

F21: Length 78mm. 92SF37. Context G195 (Phase 2b). Figure 9.10.

F22: Length 103mm. 85SF35. Context F19 (Phase 3b). Figure 9.10.

F23: Length 121mm. 86SF10. Context F51 (Phase 3b). Figure 9.10.

F24: Length 130mm. 83SF6. Context M53 (Phase 3b). Figure 9.10.

F25: Length 85mm. 84SF64. Context L31 (Phase 5a). Figure 9.10.

F26: Length 175mm. 84SF83. Context Z25 (Phase 5d). Figure 9.10.

F27: Length 111mm. 85SF14. Context Y26 (Phase 6d). Figure 9.10.

F28: Length 78mm. 86SF19. Context I38 (Phase 4a). Figure 9.10.

F29: Length 108mm. 87SF68. Context J15 (Phase 4a). Figure 9.10.

F30: Length 87mm. 87SF63. Context G48 (Phase 4c). Not illustrated.

F31: Length 178mm. 81SF5. Context K32. (Unphased). Figure 9.10.

F32–33 Scale-tang knives:
F32: Length 46mm. 93SF43. Context G468 (Phase 1b) (intrusive). Figure 9.10.

F33: Length 71mm. 91SF20. Context O29. (Unphased). Figure 9.10.

F34–38 Knife blade fragments:
F34: 85SF36. Context F19 (Phase 3b). Figure 9.10.
F35: 83SF42. Context I7 (Phase 4a). Figure 9.10.
F36: 93SF52. Context G468 (Phase 1b). Figure 9.10.
F37: 84SF53. Context L17 (Phase 5a). Figure 9.10.
F38: 84SF58. Context L17 (Phase 5a). Figure 9.10.

Unillustrated knife blade fragments:
—84SF84. Context L40 (Phase 2a),
—93SF98. Context O151 (Phase 3b),
—92SF178. Context G350 (Phase 4a),
—92SF110. Context O31 (Phase 4a),
—84SF71. Context L17 (Phase 5a),
—95SF17. Context VC3 (Phase 7b).

Locks and keys

Padlocks, locks, keys and stapled hasps make up the furniture of a lock. Barrel padlocks of various types were in use during the medieval period (Ottaway and Rogers 2002, 2861–2879), but the fragmentary shackle arm [**F96**] is the only representative of these (apart from some padlock keys) at Dryslwyn Castle. Barrel padlocks with shackles were used to fetter human or animal limbs and this fragment is best understood in comparison with an example from Winchester, which is complete with a second limb shackle and a linking chain (I Goodall 1990b, 1001–03, 1011–12, figs 310, 314–316). The presence of '20 iron shackles and 5 locks for these shackles' owned by Robert de Tibetot, Justiciar for West Wales 1281–98, in the castle's stores in 1300/01 confirms the presence of shackles for restraining human prisoners in Dryslwyn at this period (Section 3.1).

Mounted or fixed locks, an alternative to padlocks on doors and cupboards, as well as on chests and caskets, were complicated objects, which are represented here not by complete examples, but by some of their component parts. Medieval locks were of two principal types, distinguished by the means in which their sliding bolts operated. **F97–101** come from locks where the bolt engaged in the staple of an external stapled hasp, whilst **F102** and **F103** come from examples in which the bolt passed outside the body of the lock. **F97** is part of a lockplate and an associated stapled hasp, whilst **F100** and **F101** are further stapled hasps. **F98** and **F99** are a mount and a tumbler from internal lock mechanisms. The manner in which these fragmentary remains functioned can be best understood in comparison with some near complete medieval locks from Winchester, which either have dished lockcases or flat lockplates (I Goodall 1990b, 1003–05, 1016–19, figs 319–321, nos 3687–88, 3691). These locks retain mounts, wards, tumblers and distinctive small, toothed lock bolts. The last of these in particular was absent from the finds from Dryslwyn Castle. The two lock bolts [**F102** and **F103**] are altogether larger and, although they come from locks whose mechanisms were not unlike those just described, their tips passed beyond the lockcase and out into an external doorframe. These bolts were held in place by staples within the lock, the turning bit of the key engaging one of the lower projecting teeth and either shooting the bolt out or withdrawing it. The upper nib on the bolt acted as a stop against which the tumbler rested, the turning key bit lifting the tumbler at the same time that it engaged one of the lower teeth, thereby withdrawing the bolt and opening the lock.

F104–107 are padlock keys, most with simple hooked terminals and laterally set bits that were drawn along the spring arms of padlock bolts. Their form is the most common and long-lived of padlock keys. The keys [**F108–113**] are of several types, most with solid stems. Those with symmetrically cut bits were for use in locks capable of being opened from both sides.

F96 Shackle arm from barrel padlock, broken. Length 115mm. 91SF36. Context P43 (Phase 4a). Figure 9.11.

F97 Lockplate fragment with keyhole and broken and distorted stapled hasp. Lockplate width 96mm, stapled hasp length 94mm. 81SF47. Context K12 (Phase 6c). Figure 9.9.

F98 Mount from lock with recessed side arms, one complete, the other repaired and broken. Main lozenge-shaped plate has keyhole flanked by stubs of two wards. Width 110mm. 84SF33. Context L9 (Phase 6c). Figure 9.9.

F99 Tumbler from lock. Length 132mm. 84SF23. Context L9 (Phase 6c). Figure 9.9.

F100 Stapled hasp with looped tip and shaped strap cranked at centre. U-shaped rear staple. Length 64mm. 92SF9. Context G350 (Phase 4a). Figure 9.10.

F101 Stapled hasp with looped eye and shaped strap with fingerhold at base. U-shaped rear staple. Length 123mm. 86SF31. Context G12 (Phase 6c). Figure 9.8.

F102–103 Lock bolts, similar in form:
F102: Length 246mm. 84SF17. Context L9 (Phase 6c). Figure 9.7.
F103: Length 268mm. 81SF3. Context K3 (Phase 7c). Figure 9.12.

F104–107 Padlock keys:
F104: Length 137mm. 93SF80. Context O77 (Phase 3b). Figure 9.9.
F105: Length 70mm. 93SF91. Context O123 (Phase 4a). Figure 9.9.
F106: Length 84mm. 87SF45. Context G48 (Phase 4c). Figure 9.9.
F107: Length 254mm. 80SF44. Context K9 (Phase 6c). Figure 9.9.

F108–113 Keys:
F108: Length 98mm. 93SF112. Context X16 (Phase 6d). Figure 9.9.
F109: Length 140mm. 82SF36. Context O28 (Phase 5d). Figure 9.9.
F110: Length 163mm. 82SF3. Context K4 (Phase 6c). Figure 9.9.
F111: Length 170mm. 84SF10. Context L9 (Phase 6c). Figure 9.9.
F112: Length 173mm. 81SF17. Context K12 (Phase 6c). Figure 9.9.
F113: Length 174mm. 84SF5. Context L1 (Phase 6d). Figure 9.9.

F197 Rod with a looped and flattened end, probably a key with looped terminal, bit missing. Length 135mm. 87SF86. Context G59 (Phase 4c). Figure 9.7.

Household fittings

Iron fittings were used extensively in and around buildings, some associated with lighting, others with furniture. Rushlights, tapers and candles were all used to light medieval interiors. Socketed candleholders [F114–117] were set in wooden blocks or driven into walls, as the different stem shapes of the most complete examples indicate. The decorative twisting of the stem of **F114** is repeated on **F118**, which is an elaborate but incomplete three-armed candlestick. This may have had socketed side arms, but the central upright, with its pierced terminal and loose end ring, was probably intended to support a rushlight. **F119** is part of a strike-a-light or steel, but it is probably residual, since its form is closer to some earlier forms (I Goodall 1990c, 981–983, fig 306, nos 3538–39).

The principal iron fittings associated with furniture (excluding locks) were hinges, handles and various types of hasp. Several hinges from Dryslwyn Castle seem more appropriate to furniture rather than doors, in particular those with end loops [F120–122]. The two with their intersecting loops could have secured the lid of a chest, one strap nailed to the back, the other across the lid. The spiked U-shaped eye of hinge **F123** could also have trapped the eye of an end-looped strap, which would thus have functioned much like the pairs just noted. The three rectangular-shaped handles might also be from furniture. **F124** is rigid and was secured in place through its terminals, whilst **F125–126** hung free in their pairs of fixing staples.

Fixed locks, as noted above, often worked in conjunction with stapled hasps, but figure-of-eight shaped hasps [F126–128] were used together with padlocks and could have fastened the lids of chests, or, with chains, have secured gates. Straps on chests were often wide and, when incomplete, resemble those from doors. Caskets, however, had smaller fittings and a near-complete corner binding [F130] and two lengths of binding strip with perforated circular terminals [F131–132] could come from caskets, as could the mid length fragment [F133], one of six pieces from Phase 3b–6d contexts. A reference to chests 'bound in iron' in the castle accounts of 1312–13 confirms the use of iron-bound caskets in Dryslwyn Castle at this time (Section 3.1). The function of the mounts [F134–141] is uncertain: all have flat, shaped backs and opposing side arms and could be decorative.

F142–157 are a miscellaneous group of fittings, comprising the lid of a vessel (probably of post-medieval date), a series of chain links, rings, collars, a swivel hook and three ferrules.

F114–116 Socketed candleholders:
F114: Height 191mm. 81SF36. Context K12 (Phase 6c). Figure 9.12.
F115: Height 87mm. 80SF23. Context K9 (Phase 6c). Figure 9.12.
F116: Height 107mm. 80SF24. Context K9 (Phase 6c). Figure 9.12.

F117 Socketed arm of a candleholder. Height 54mm. 82SF16. Context C18 (Phase 6d). Figure 9.11.

F118 Three-armed candlestick, incomplete. Height 175mm. 93SF53. Context O109 (Phase 3b). Figure 9.7.

F119 Strike-a-light. Length 40mm. 88SF33. Context J37 (Phase 1b). Figure 9.12.

F120 End-looped strap with down-turned end. Length 372mm. 88SF20. Context P7 (Phase 6d). Figure 9.12.

F121 Hinge. Pair of incomplete straps with intersecting end loops. Strap lengths 200 and 140mm. 81SF38. Separate strap probably from a second pair of straps with intersecting loop ends 81SF38i. Context K13 (Phase 5b). Figure 9.8.

F122 Hinge. Pair of straps, one complete, with intersecting end loops. Strap lengths 188 and 170mm. 81SF39. Context K13 (Phase 5b). Figure 9.8.

F123 Hinge. Spiked U-shaped eye, broken strap. Length 105mm. 83SF57. Context D6 (Phase 4c). Figure 9.9.

F124–126 Handles, rectangular in shape:
F124: Width 110mm. 93SF126. Context O77 (Phase 3b). Figure 9.7.
F125: Width 110mm. 81SF23. Context K12 (Phase 6c). Figure 9.8.
F126: Width 110mm. 81SF11. Context K10 (Phase 6c). Figure 9.8.

F127 Figure-of-eight hasp and U-shaped staple. Hasp length 128mm. 81SF8. Unstratified. Figure 9.8.

F128 Hooked base of figure-of-eight hasp. Length 68mm. 92SF167. Context O77 (Phase 3b). Figure 9.7.

F129 Tip of figure-of-eight hasp. Length 52mm. 86SF43. Context G14 (Phase 6d). Figure 9.10.

F130 Corner binding, one terminal broken. Length 48mm. 84SF2. Context L1 (Phase 6d). Figure 9.7.

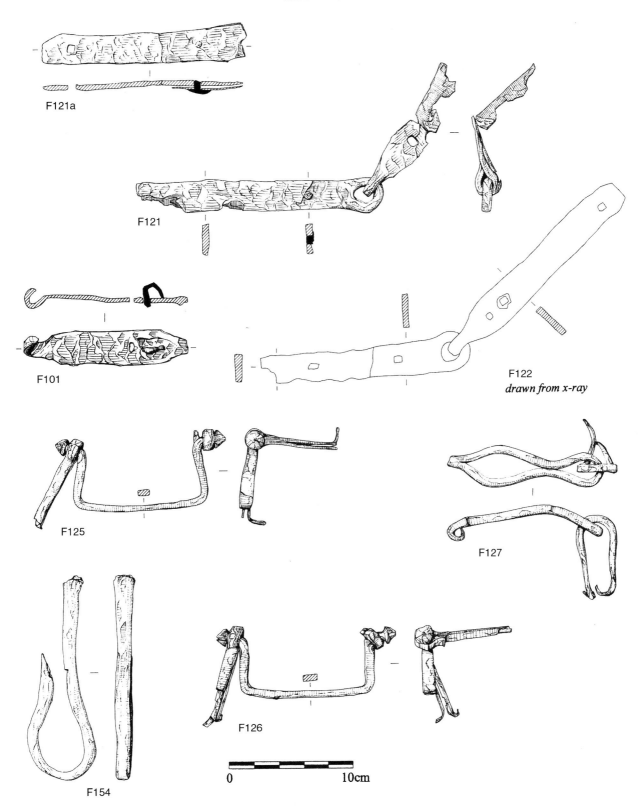

F121a

F121

F101

F122
drawn from x-ray

F125

F127

F154

F126

0   10cm

FIGURE 9.8

Ironwork

F131–132 Binding strip fragments with circular perforated terminals:
F131: Length 76mm, width 13mm. 82SF43. Context O192 (Phase 2b). Figure 9.12.
F132: Length 35mm, width 17mm. 84SF55. Context Z16 (Phase 4d). Not illustrated.

F133 Binding strip fragment. Length 67mm, width 13mm. 93SF92. Context O7 (Phase 6d). Not illustrated.

F134–141 Mounts with flat, rounded backs and opposed, tapering side arms, mostly broken:
F134: Width 62mm. 82SF38. Context T43 (Phase 3a). Figure 9.7.

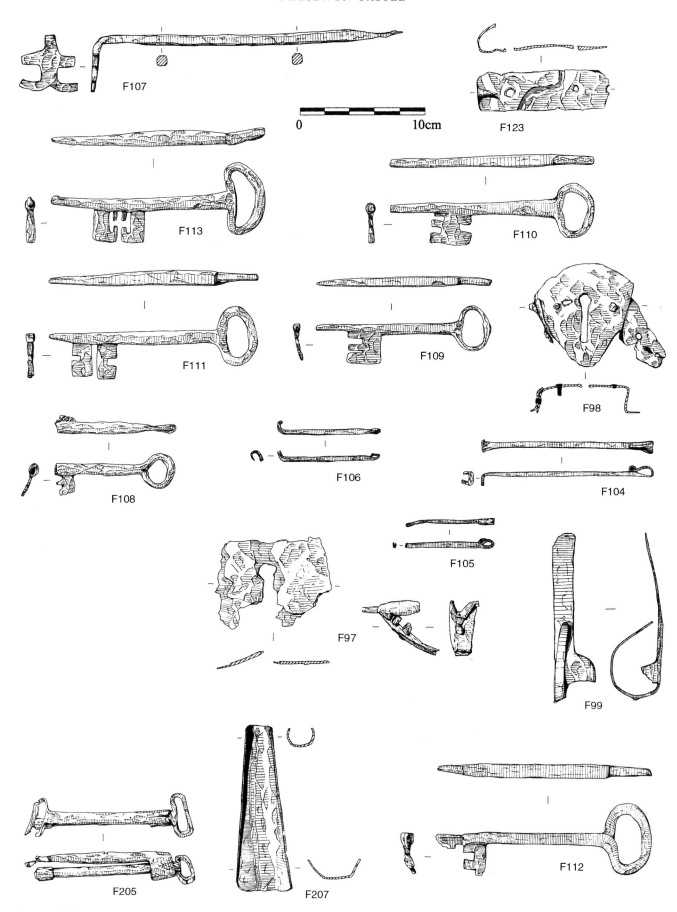

FIGURE 9.9

Ironwork: locks and keys

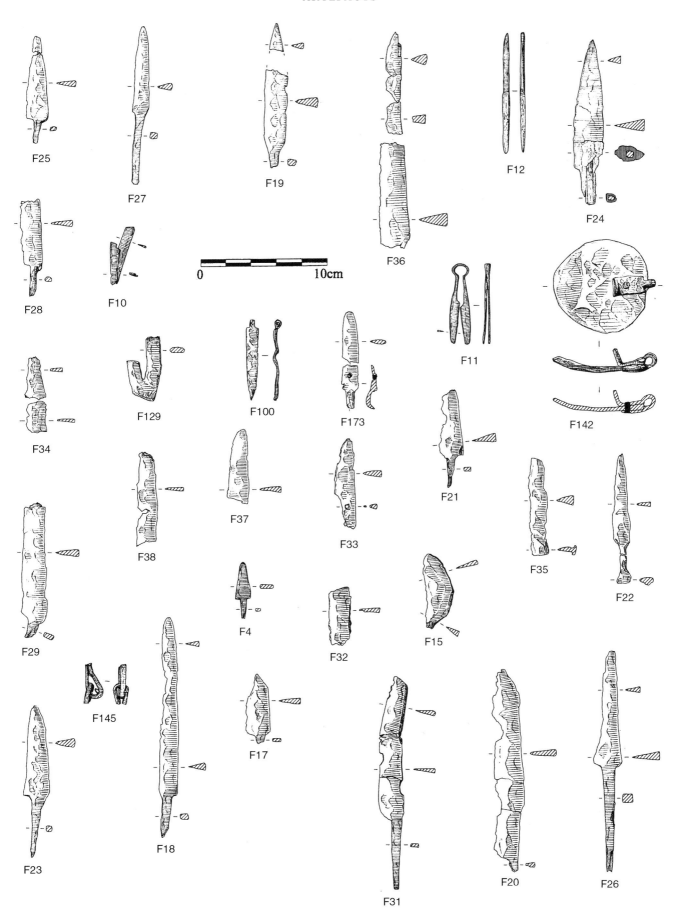

FIGURE 9.10

Ironwork: knives

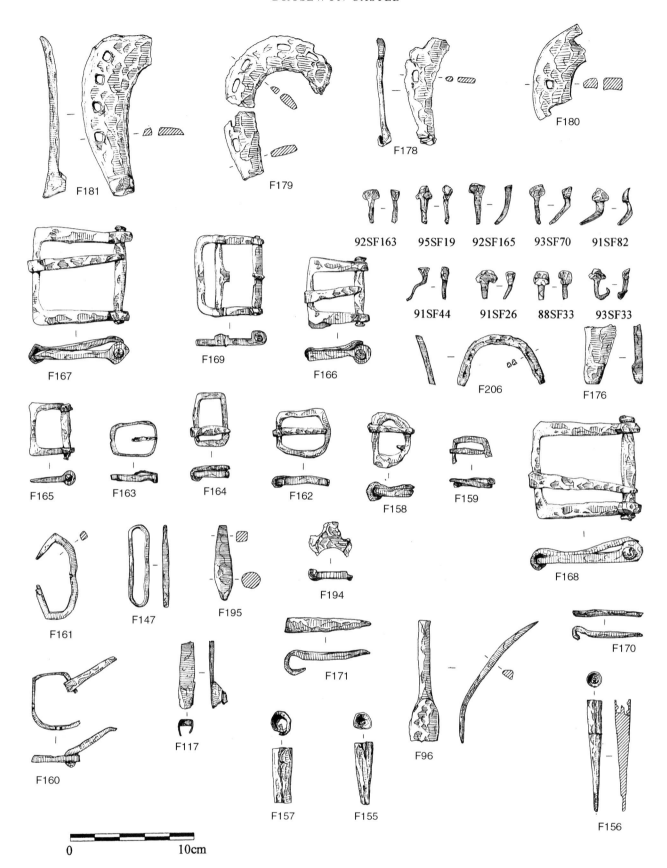

FIGURE 9.11

Ironwork: horseshoes and buckles

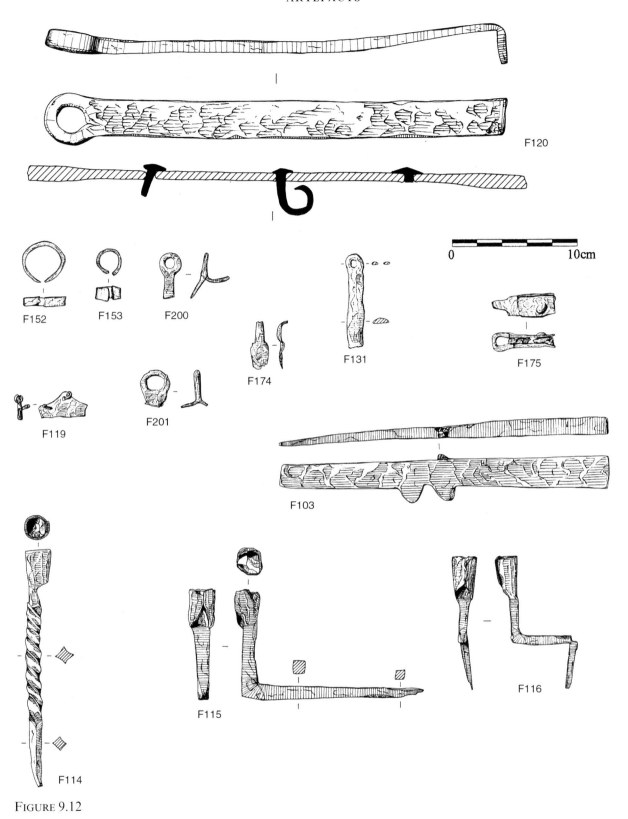

FIGURE 9.12

Ironwork

F135: Width 54mm. 81SF30. Context T10 (Phase 5a). Figure 9.7.

F136: Width.50mm. 84SF22. Context L9 (Phase 6c). Figure 9.7.

F137: Width 53mm. 81SF22. Context K12 (Phase 6c). Figure 9.7.

F138: Width 62mm. 84SF34. Context L9 (Phase 6c). Figure 9.7.

F139: Width 55mm. 81SF41. Context T11 (Phase 7a). Figure 9.7.

F140: Width 43mm. 87SF25. Context J1 (Phase 7b). Figure 9.7.

F141: Width 55mm. 81SF10. Context K3 (Phase 7b). Figure 9.7.

F142 Vessel lid with thumbhold. Width 74mm. 82SF2. Context J61 (Phase 7b). Figure 9.10.

(143 not used)

F144–147 Chains. Nos 144 and 145 are shorts lengths of chain. The remainder are individual links of identical shape:
F144: Length.46mm. 82SF28. Context M13 (Phase 7a) Figure 9.7.
F145: Length 24mm. 88SF28. Context J32 (Phase 2b). Figure 9.10.
F146: Length 61mm. 92SF20. Context O91 (Phase 4a). Not illustrated.
F147: Length 67mm. 84SF24. Context L9 (Phase 6c). Figure 9.11.

F148–151 Rings:
F148: Diameter 23mm. 83SF29. Context K33 (Phase 2a). Not illustrated.
F149: Diameter 25mm. 83SF60. Context K30 (Phase 5b). Not illustrated.
F150: Diameter 46mm. 81SF24. Context K12 (Phase 6c). Not illustrated.
F151: Diameter 44mm. 81SF12. Context K11 (Phase 6c). Not illustrated.

F152–153 Collars, both circular:
F152: Diameter 35mm. 91SF37. Context G211 (Phase 2d). Figure 9.12.
F153: Diameter 20mm. 88SF22. Context G116 (Phase 4c). Figure 9.12.

F154 Swivel hook. Expanded head damaged. Length 165mm. 86SF6. Context G7 (Phase 6d). Figure 9.8.

F155–157 Ferrules. Two with tapering sides, the third straight:
F155: Length 50mm. 83SF56. Context T71 (Phase 5a). Figure 9.11.
F156: Length 89mm. 81SF26. Context T1 (Phase 7b). Figure 9.11.
F157: Length 45mm. 80SF11. Context K5 (Phase 7a). Figure 9.11.

Buckles and belt fittings

The buckles [**F158–171**] are all plain and are likely to be from clothing and harness. D-shaped buckles and others with rectangular frames are the commonest, the latter including some with revolving pin bars, which eased the passage of belts, particularly on harness. The revolving T-shaped pin [**F169**] is an unusual variant, but one with medieval parallels (I Goodall 1990d, 526, 534, fig 140, no. 1322). Belts were commonly attached directly to buckles, but buckle plates [**F171**] were sometimes brought into use. The belt loops [**F173–175**] secured straps to rings, which served as strap distributors.

F158–162 Buckles with D-shaped frames:
F158: Width 44mm. 88SF18. Context J36 (Phase 1b). Figure 9.11.
F159: Width 22mm. 90SF117. Context P25 (Phase 5b). Figure 9.11.
F160: Width 38mm. 82SF35. Context O28 (Phase 5d). Figure 9.11.

F161: Width 70mm. 88SF19. Context P7 (Phase 6d). Figure 9.11.
F162: Width 40mm. 82SF22. Context M13 (Phase 7a). Figure 9.11.

F163 Buckle with sub-rectangular frame. Width 28mm. 83SF49. Context T73 (Phase 3d). Figure 9.11.

F164–168 Buckles with rectangular frame, 165–168 with revolving bars:
F164: Width 44mm. 81SF15. Context K11 (Phase 6c). Figure 9.11.
F165: Width 43mm. 81SF16. Context K11 (Phase 6c). Figure 9.11.
F166: Width 57mm. 81SF34. Context K12 (Phase 6c). Figure 9.11.
F167: Width 79mm. 81SF32. Context K12 (Phase 6c). Figure 9.11.
F168: Width.78mm. 81SF21. Context K12 (Phase 6c). Figure 9.11.

F169 Buckle with rectangular frame, revolving bar and internally-supported T-shaped pin. Width 65mm. 93SF46. Context O107 (Phase 4a). Figure 9.11.

F170–171 Buckle pins:
F170: Length 58mm. 91SF68. Context O44 (Phase 5b). Figure 9.11.
F171: Length 71mm. 83SF61. Context O32 (Phase 6d). Figure 9.11.

F172 Buckle plate. Tapering plate with single rivet hole, broken across paired arms, which wrapped around the pin bar of the buckle. Length 33mm, width 10mm. 90SF76. Context H59 (Phase 4c). Not illustrated.

F173–175 Belt loops:
F173: Length 35mm. 88SF31. Context J32 (Phase 2b). Figure 9.10.
F174: Length 39mm. 88SF5. Context J32 (Phase 2b). Figure 9.12.
F175: Length 52mm. 92SF89. Context O59 (Phase 4a). Figure 9.12.

Horseshoes

The horseshoes from Dryslwyn Castle are surprisingly few in number. Those with countersunk nail holes [**F176–179**] were superseded during the 13th and 14th centuries by examples with rectangular nail holes [**F180–181**] (Clark 1995, 91–97). Different types of horseshoe nail were used in these horseshoes. Fiddle-key nails, with heads no thicker than their shanks, were replaced during the 13th and 14th centuries by nails with eared heads, which expand in side view.

F176 Horseshoe. Arm tip with calkin, broken across countersunk nail hole. Length 51mm. 87SF67. Context J15 (Phase 4a). Figure 9.11.

F177 Horseshoe. Arm tip with calkin, broken across countersunk nail hole. Length 48mm. 82SF28. Context M13 (Phase 7a). Not illustrated.

F178 Horseshoe. Arm fragment with thickened tip and countersunk nail holes. Length 86mm. 86SF27. Context I18 (Phase 4a). Figure 9.11.

F179 Horseshoe. Toe and part of one arm with counter-sunk nail holes. Length 99mm. 85SF10&11. Context F16 (Phase 4b). Figure 9.11.

F180 Horseshoe. Toe and arm fragment with rectangular nail holes. Width 38mm. 90SF123. Context O25 (Phase 5b). Figure 9.11.

F181 Horseshoe. Arm with calkin and rectangular nail holes. Length 130mm. 86SF36. Context G12 (Phase 6c). Figure 9.11.
Horseshoe nails: 92SF163 (Phase 4a), 95SF19 (Phase 7a), 92SF165 (Phase 1a), 93SF70 (Phase 4a), 91SF82 (Phase 2c), 91SF44 (Phase 5c), 91SF26 (Phase 4a), 88SF33 (Phase 1b) and 93SF33 (Phase 4a). Figure 9.11.

Uncertain objects

It was not possible to identify all the iron objects from Dryslwyn, as some only survived in fragments, whilst others could only be assigned a general function.

F194 Three-arm fragment, probably from a cast iron grill or panel. Length 34mm. 83SF44. Context F6 (Phase 6d). Figure 9.11.

F200–201 Attachment rings with split bars.
F200: diameter 19mm. 91SF18. Unstratified. Figure 9.12.
F201: diameter 24mm. 87SF66. Context J15 (Phase 4a). Figure 9.12.

F205 Pair of oval bow-ended shafts that have loop ends, which grip each other's shaft, forming a sliding mechanism. Function unknown. Length 133mm. 84SF91. Unstratified. Figure 9.9.

F206 Toe iron. Width 69mm. 81SF20. Context T2 (Phase 7b). Figure 9.11.

F207 Curved iron sheet, sheathing or socket. Length 132mm. 81SF33. Context K12 (Phase 6c). Figure 9.9.

Fragments of sheet ironwork: 91SF100, 87SF48, 88SF7, 80SF31, 90SF74, 93SF92 (not illustrated).

Fragments of iron bar: 93SF20, 90SF99, 93SF104, 95SF51, 92SF153 (not illustrated).

9.5 COPPER-ALLOY AND LEAD ARTEFACTS
by Alison Goodall

Dress accessories and decoration

The high proportion of decorative objects from Dryslwyn, such as the filigree ornamented finger ring [A1], the inscribed annular brooch [A3] and the pendant attachment [A29], suggests a site of relatively high status. The pendant attachment would have supported a pendant possibly bearing a heraldic motif or badge and it may have been decorative or perhaps a retainer's badge. Mounts [A22–24] would have been attached to leather and were often used as decoration on belts. Most castle sites in Wales, including Castell-y-Bere (Gwynedd) (Butler 1974) and Loughor (Swansea) (Lewis 1993), have produced a range of buckles, decorative studs, belt and harness fittings similar to those seen at Dryslwyn.

A1 Large finger- or thumb-ring of silver gilt. It is made from plaited lengths of twisted wire set on a thin backing and with a border of twisted wire on both edges. Analysis shows traces of mercury from the gilding process. Diameter 23mm. 93SF95. Context X16 (Phase 4a). Figure 9.13.

A2 Crudely made finger- or thumb-ring, decorated with marginal grooves. Diameter 23mm. 81SF7. Context K10 (Phase 6b). Figure 9.13.

A3 Annular brooch. The frame and pin are cut from sheet. There is an area of cross-hatched decoration on the pin. The frame has incised marginal grooves and at one point there are compass-drawn incisions from the cutting out of another adjacent brooch. Within the grooves is a crudely incised inscription, reading 'X IHESVS NAZARENUS', with bands of rocked-tracer zigzag between the letters. The back of the frame is plain but the edges are down-turned as a result of scoring and cutting the sheet metal. The inscription may have had a talismanic or prophylactic significance. Diameter 29mm. 84SF46. Context L17 (Phase 5a). Figure 9.13.
This object was recovered from within the fill of the undercroft of the Great Hall K/L, deposited in the early to mid 14th century. The layer beneath the brooch produced a coin of 1280–81. This brooch is discussed by Mark Redknap in the context of other medieval brooches from Wales (Redknap 1994, 92–109). An annular brooch of silver gilt from Amesbury (Wiltshire) (Salisbury and South Wiltshire Museum 2001; museum accession no. 46/1981) has a very similar inscription, as does a silver brooch from London, dated to the second half of the 14th century (Egan and Pritchard 1991, 255, fig164.1337 and pl 6C). Joan Evans suggests that the legend 'Iesus Nazarenus Rex Iudeorum' was a prophylactic, offering protection against sudden death (Evans 1970, 47).

A4 Fragment from small buckle frame consisting of part of the recessed pin bar and the side bar. Length 10.5mm. 88SF9. Context I82 (Phase 2b). Not illustrated.

A5 Buckle and plate. The trapezium-shaped buckle frame has an ornamentally shaped front edge and the plate and pin are decorated with a fringe of small notches cut into the edges. Length 37mm. 85SF29. Context F19 (Phase 3b). Figure 9.13.

A6 Buckle frame with? iron pin. The frame is decorated with cross-hatching and is shaped to form two lobes with a possible pin-rest between them. Length 23mm. 93SF26. Context O95 (Phase 4a). Figure 9.13.
An almost identical example was found at Burton Dassett, Warwickshire (A Goodall forthcoming, SF1493).

A7 Stirrup-shaped buckle with simple undecorated plate. The front bar of the frame has a roller on it and the buckle pin is made from wire. Length 40mm. 92SF134. Context O31 (Phase 4a). Figure 9.13.

A8 Buckle frame with a broad pin rest on the front bar and a groove on either side of it. A fragment of the buckle plate survives; it is decorated with a traced border along the two long edges and has a hole for the buckle pin to swivel in. The pin does not survive. Length of plate 17mm. Height of buckle frame 14mm. 92SF96. Context O69 (Phase 5b). Figure 9.13.

A9 D-shaped buckle frame, undecorated but with gilding; the front is slightly pointed. Height 31.5mm. 87SF65. Context G59 (Phase 4c). Figure 9.15.

A10 Cast fragment with a flat back. The form resembles part of a buckle frame, but it is very crudely made and may be a waste fragment. Length 24mm. 82SF45. Context L42 (Phase 2a). Figure 9.15.
A rather more complete fragment, more closely resembling a buckle frame, was found at Burton Dassett (A Goodall forthcoming, SF512).

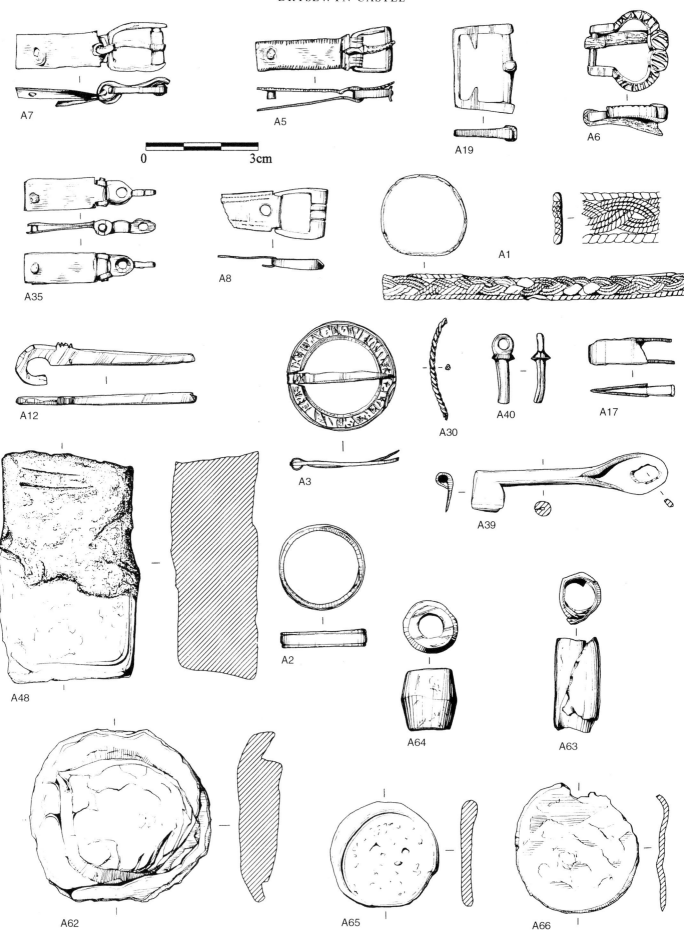

FIGURE 9.13

Copper-alloy and lead artefacts

A11 Slender pin, probably from a brooch, with the head rolled over to form a hinge. Length 22mm. 85SF40. Context J18 (Phase 1b). Figure 9.15.

A12 Pin from an annular buckle. It has a decorative moulding with transverse incisions and there are diagonal striations on the sides from finishing. Length 48mm. 82SF14. Context O7 (Phase 6d). Figure 9.13.

A13 Buckle pin, flattened and broader at the hooked end. Length 18mm. 91SF23. Context O32 (Phase 6d). Figure 9.15.

A14 Incomplete buckle plate with a single rivet hole and a slot for the pin. Length 17mm. 91SF4. Context G175 (unphased). Figure 9.15.

A15 Buckle plate decorated with white metal plating and with three rows of broad zigzag lines running longitudinally. There is a single rivet, possibly of iron. Length 29mm. 93SF32. Context O92 (Phase 4a). Figure 9.14.

A16 Fragment of strip with pin or rivet hole, possibly part of a strap-end or buckle plate. There is a hint of shaping at the narrower end for attachment of a buckle. One face has a smooth finish, the other is rougher. Length 17.5mm. 95SF11. Context VD2 (Phase 5d). Not illustrated.

A17 Small strap-end with a spacer or side pieces soldered or brazed in position. Fragmentary; surviving length 15mm. 90SF13. Context H59 (Phase 4c). Figure 9.13.

A18 Decorative fitting, possibly a strap-end, cut from sheet. Pointed at one end and with a repoussé boss. There is a pin hole at each end. Length 28mm. 91SF79. Context O44 (Phase 5b). Figure 9.15.

A19 Trapezoidal belt loop with internally projecting lugs. The front bar has decorative bosses at each end and one in the centre. Height 24mm. 86SF35. Context F34 (Phase 2d). Figure 9.13.

A20 Thin casting in a grey alloy, possibly an incomplete two- or three-lobed belt hanger for suspending a purse. Length 17mm. 93SF71. Context B70 (Phase 4a). Figure 9.15.

A21 Incomplete repoussé annular mount or eyelet, broken through the rivet holes. Decorated with a ring of impressed dots. Diameter 20mm. 86SF30. Context G13 (Phase 5d). Figure 9.15.

A22 Sexfoil mount, made from sheet. It is pointed in the centre and has two peripheral rivet holes, one retaining the rivet. Diameter 22mm. 81SF19. Context K12 (Phase 6c). Figure 9.15.

A23 Repoussé stud head with four projecting lobes and a central rivet. Width 13.5mm. 92SF88. Context B31 (Phase 6c). Figure 9.15.

A24 Plain domed stud head. There is no rivet hole but a shank may have been brazed onto the inside of the head. Diameter 13mm. 92SF122. Context B43 (Phase 4d). Figure 9.15.

A25 Plain round stud head with a central rivet hole. Diameter 13mm. 87SF8. Context G27 (Phase 4c). Figure 9.15.

A26 Large pin head or small button, bun-shaped with the remains of a shank projecting. Diameter 9mm. 92SF8. Context G195 (Phase 2b). Figure 9.15.

A27 Lace-end made from rolled sheet, tapering in profile, with rivet to secure it at the upper end. Length 25mm. 84SF42. Context L26 (Phase 5a). Figure 9.15.

A28 Slender, tapering lace-end made from rolled sheet with the edges butted. The upper end is damaged, but was probably not riveted. Length 31mm. 84SF8. Context D4 (Phase 6d). Figure 9.15.

A29 Gilded attachment for supporting a pendant, consisting of a bar with shaped pierced terminals. In the middle is a rectangular boss that is also pierced and is extended and folded back to form the hinge. The pivot was probably of iron. Length 74mm. 83SF1. Unstratified. Figure 9.15.
A pendant mount of similar form, though rather more crudely made, comes from Rattray Castle, Aberdeenshire, in a 14th- or 15th-century context (A Goodall 1993).

A30 Incomplete object made from three strands of wire twisted tightly and regularly together. Length 27mm. 87SF58. Context J15 (Phase 4a). Figure 9.13.

A31 Ten pins. Where the heads are present, they are made from coiled wire, but, except for one, they do not show evidence of having been stamped. Another pin with a coiled head shows traces of white metal plating on the shaft. The pins range in length from 32mm to 42mm. Figure 9.15:
A31a: 85SF1. Context F13 (Phase 4b);
A31b: 83SF15. Context F19 (Phase 3b);
A31c: 85SF19. Context J1 (Phase 7);
A31d: 92SF135. Context O26 (Phase 4d);
A31e: 92SF109. Context O31 (Phase 4a);
A31f: 91SF50. Context O44 (Phase 5b);
A31g: 91SF78. Context O44 (Phase 5b);
A31h: 92SF6. Context O51 (Phase 4d);
A31i: 92SF66. Context O52 (Phase 4d);
A31j: 81SF18. Context K12 (Phase 6c). Not illustrated.
Wound wire-headed pins of this form are used for pinning together clothing. Such pins are first seen in the 13th century at sites such as Winchester (Biddle and Barclay 1990) and Southampton (Harvey 1975) and are commonly recovered from castle and urban contexts of 14th- to 19th-century date. The numbers of wire pins rise as costume becomes more complex from the 14th century. As fabrics become finer and the technical abilities of wire manufacture and pin making increase, the pins become shorter and thinner (Caple 1992c). The presence of these wound wire-headed pins at Dryslwyn is early and suggests the presence of high-status clothing on the site, particularly in the late 13th century (Phase 4).

Military display

A few of the non-ferrous metal objects testify to the military nature of the site. Three riveted rings [**A34**], which almost certainly derive from chain mail or other mailed garments, were found. The scabbard chape [**A32**] is of a simple type and its small size suggests that it would have come from the sheath of a knife or dagger, rather than that of a sword.

A32 Small scabbard chape made from thin sheet with an overlapping seam at the back. The chape was secured by a rivet near the top edge, at the side. There is white metal plating on the outer surface. Fragments of wood were associated with the chape, but it is not certain that these formed part of the scabbard. Length 41mm. 82SF30. Context O178 (Phase 2c). Figure 9.14.

A33 Spur. It has neither prick nor rowel. The terminals are broken, but appear to have been simple loops or hooks. Length c100mm. Width between terminals 95mm. 85SF46. Context F23 (Phase 3b). Figure 9.14.

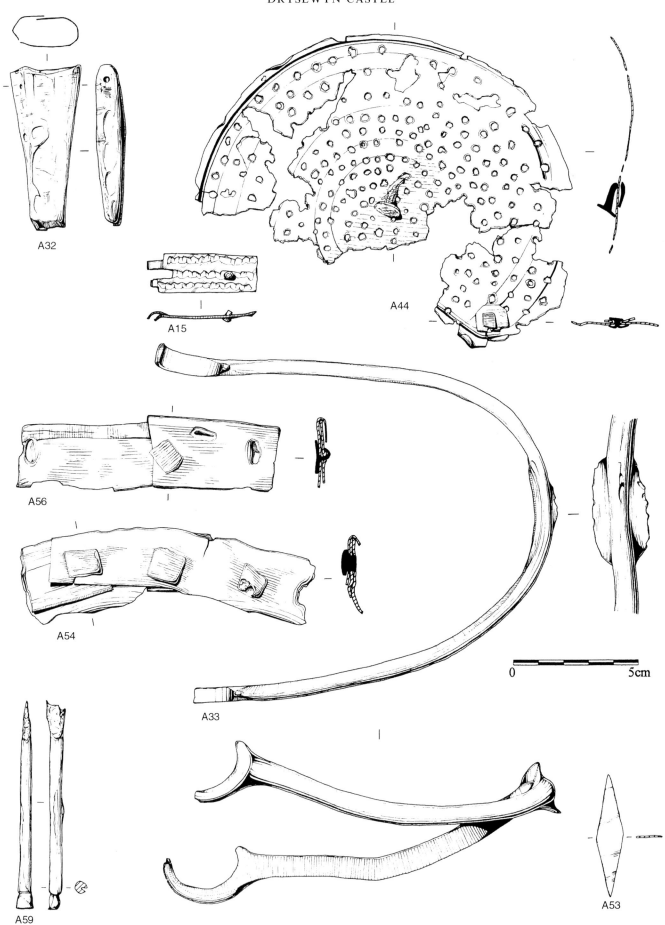

A32

A44

A15

A56

A54

A33

A59

A53

FIGURE 9.14

Copper-alloy artefacts

0   5cm

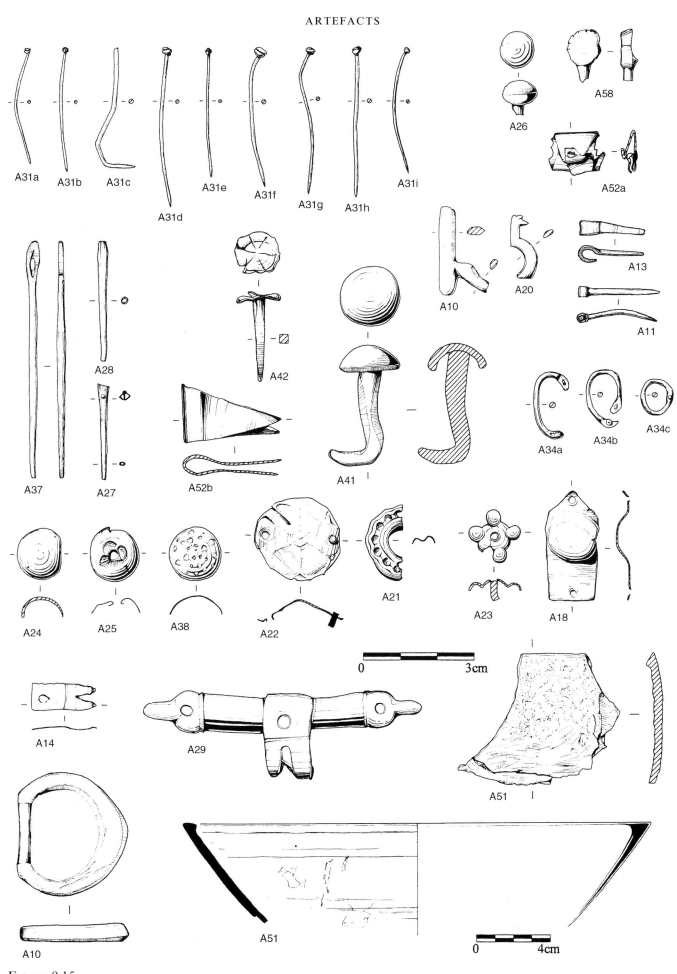

FIGURE 9.15

Copper-alloy artefacts

Blanche Ellis commented 'that the form of the spur is unusual having no obvious attachment for a prick or rowel, though this may be because any attachment has broken/corroded off. The terminals are of a simple ring form but proportionately larger than other 13th-century spurs. The sides of the spur have an unusually shallow curve for a dated 13th-century spur, in order to fit around the ankles of the wearer. There is a flange above and below the goad attachment area of the spur, which is not seen on other 13th-century spurs. This must raise the question of whether this is actually a spur' (Ellis 1995). However, the secure dating, the position in which it was recovered and all other aspects of its form leave little doubt that it is a spur, though of a highly unusual type.

A34 Three rings probably from chain mail, penannular with overlapping terminals, originally secured by a rivet, probably of iron. Diameter 9–10mm.
A34a: 83SF16. Context F45 (Phase 3b). Figure 9.15;
A34b: 90SF60. Context H39 (unphased). Figure 9.15;
A34c: 90SF5. Context H59 (Phase 4c). Figure 9.15.
Two of these rings come from deposits that contained large numbers of iron rings, chain mail links, and other debris associated with siege activity. Copper-alloy rings were often used to attach chain mail to leather or plate metal, as in the case of the Coppergate Helmet.

Functional

In addition to the dress accessories, another indicator of the status of the site is the strap-end with hinged terminal [**A35**]. This object may have been used as a fastening for a book cover and, if so, indicates the presence of books at the castle. Books in the 14th century were rare and expensive and fittings from the bindings are most commonly found on monastic or high-status sites. Other objects, such as the needle [**A37**] and key [**A39**], demonstrate the more mundane functions carried out at this site.

A35 Small strap-end or book fastening with hinged terminal, perforated in two planes, possibly to take a pendant. There is slight bevelling on the edges of the upper plate. Length 35mm. 91SF3. Context O25 (Phase 5b). Figure 9.13.
Strap-ends of this type are sometimes found on ecclesiastical or monastic sites, where other book fittings also occur. This makes the identification as a book fastening more attractive; however, the same form could just as well be used as a belt-end. Similar objects were found, for instance, at the Vicars Choral and Bedern Chapel sites at York, the former in a 14th-century context (Richards 2001).

A36 Rings of slightly irregular section and with diameters of 21–23mm. 92SF58 and 92SF60. Context B31; 92SF85. Context B32 (Phase 6c). Not illustrated.

A37 Needle with an approximately lozenge-shaped head and a rectangular eye set in a gutter. There is a very slight swelling in the shaft. The tip is missing. Length 62mm. 87SF28. Context J6 (Phase 4a). Figure 9.15.

A38 Small convex cap with a pattern of perforations; probably the top of a thimble. Diameter 14mm. 87SF35. Context J15, (Phase 4a). Figure 9.15.

A39 Key, crudely made from thick sheet, rolled to form the stem and left open to form the oval head. The bit is uncut. Length 53mm. 80SF8. Context J73 (Phase 5a). Figure 9.13.
This key was probably made for a simple lockable box or chest. A similar example was found at Beeston Castle, Cheshire (Courtney 1993, 150–151).

A40 Looped fitting, possibly for attaching a handle to a small chest or a drawer. Length 18mm. 83SF14. Context J14 (Phase 4a). Figure 9.13.

A41 Stud with traces of gilding on the head and a clenched shank, probably from furniture or a door. Length 30mm, head diameter 16mm. 87SF59. Context G59 (Phase 4c). Figure 9.15.

A42 Flat head tack. The head has three intersecting lines cut into it, forming a six-pointed star. Length 24mm, diameter of head 10–11mm. 82SF9. Context O7 (Phase 6d). Figure 9.15.

A43 Hinge, possibly incomplete since one end is curved and the other cut off straight. There are four rivets to secure the hinge plate, possibly originally of iron. Length 107mm. 92SF3. Unstratified. Not illustrated.

Household

The occurrence of fragments of metal cooking pots [**A49–51**] and other vessels [**A54–56**] shows that these were in use in the kitchens and at the dining tables of Dryslwyn Castle in the 13th and 14th centuries. There are also records of the purchase of such vessels '1 brass jar, one cooking pot, 1 cauldron' in the castle accounts of 1287 (Rhys 1936, 43) and the presence of 'one brass jar and two worn out pans' in the castle accounts of 1300/01 (PRO E101/8/29; Phillpotts 2001c). Metal vessels are not present, for instance, at the deserted settlement of Wharram Percy on the Yorkshire Wolds (Andrews and Milne 1979, 108–114). Since these vessels appear in wills and inventories, it would seem that they were highly valued. It is uncertain, however, whether they were simply not used at Wharram Percy because the villagers could not afford them, or whether they were handed on down the generations, rather than being discarded when broken. The fragments found at Dryslwyn show that both cast copper-alloy cooking pots and sheet metal bowls and dishes were being used in both the town and in the castle and that the fragments of broken vessels were being lost.

A44 Fragmentary bowl from a long-handled skimmer. The perforations appear to be arranged in random fashion. A rivet or clip made from folded sheet would probably have been part of the attachment for the socket of the handle. There is a trace of a decorative groove running round the circumference. Diameter c210mm. 84SF25. Context L9 (Phase 6c). Figure 9.14.
Skimmers with shallow perforated bowls mounted on long handles could be used for skimming cream for butter making or to remove fat during cooking. Fragments are found frequently on medieval sites: there are examples from Exeter (A Goodall 1984, 341, 345, fig 192.154–156), dated to the late 15th and late 16th centuries, and from Cuckoo Lane, Southampton, dated to 1375–1425 (Harvey 1975, 259).

A45 Sheet fragment, probably from the rim of a sheet metal vessel. Length 38mm. 91SF8. Context G176 (Phase 2d). Not illustrated.

A46 Probably a fragment from the rim of a sheet metal bowl or plate. There are chisel-like marks on the inside of the rim. Length 33mm. 83SF65. Context F16 (Phase 4b). Not illustrated.

A47   Fragment from the rim of a thin sheet metal bowl or plate. Length 38mm. 85SF17. Context F19 (Phase 3b). Not illustrated.

A48   Slightly irregular rectangular-sectioned foot from a cast cooking vessel, incomplete. Length 61mm. 86SF25. Context I39 (Phase 4a). Figure 9.13.
Analysis (EDXRF) indicated a composition of 84% copper, 3% tin and 12% lead, a typical high lead casting metal used for cauldrons at this period (Brownsword 2004, 94).

A49   Simple shaped foot from a cast cooking vessel with a strong, off-centre midrib. A number of indeterminate fragments were also associated. Length of foot 45mm. 83SF26. Context G7 (Phase 7b). Not illustrated.

A50   Small fragments from the body of a cast metal vessel. 84SF96. Length 30mm, width 19mm, thickness 3mm. Context L9 (Phase 6c); 86SF61. Length 30mm, width 21mm, thickness 4mm. Context G12 (Phase 6c). Not illustrated.

A51   Rim fragment from a cast cooking vessel. The rim is thickened on the inner edge. The inner surface of the vessel is smooth, while the outer face is rougher and striated. Length 85mm, width 65mm, thickness 4mm. 86SF2. Context I1 (Phase 7d). Figure 9.15.

A52   Rivets or clips made from folded sheet and used to secure a patching sheet or to mend a small crack in a sheet metal vessel.
A52a: Width 15mm. 92SF26. Context G350 (Phase 4a). Figure 9.15;
A52b: Length 26mm. 87SF64. Context G59 (Phase 4c). Figure 9.15;
A52c: Length 11mm. 86SF26. Context I15 (Phase 3a). Not illustrated.

A53   Elongated lozenge-shaped sheet, probably intended to be folded into a rivet, as above. Length 32mm. 91SF64. Context H53 (Phase 4a). Figure 9.14.

A54   Curved strip, probably part of the rim of a sheet metal vessel. Other strips have been attached to it using sheet rivets of the same type as above. These probably represent patching or reinforcing of the rim. Length 79mm. 85SF24. Context I6 (Phase 4a). Figure 9.14.
Similar repair patches on sheet metal vessels have been recovered from Southampton (Harvey 1975, 262) and Northampton (Williams 1979, 259).

A55   Rim fragment from a sheet metal vessel with a reinforcement strip riveted to it. One of the rivets survives and there are slots for a further six. Length 122mm. 95SF15. Context VA9 (Phase 5d) Not illustrated..

A56   Rim fragment from a sheet metal vessel with a reinforcement or patch riveted onto it. One rivet survives and there are slots for a further two. The patch is now folded over the edge of the rim; there are two further rivet holes that only pass through the patch and would have been useless in their current position. Length 77mm. 84SF39. Context Z15 (Phase 5d). Figure 9.14.

A57   Strip with slight curvature, possibly a rim fragment from a sheet metal vessel. Length 68mm. 81SF2. Context K6 (Phase 6d). Not illustrated.

Fragments and wires

Fragments of wire and sheet metal are recovered from most medieval sites, where mending damaged metal objects and vessels was a normal activity.

A58   Fragment with flattened spoon-like end. Length 14mm. 92SF123. Context B43 (Phase 4d). Figure 9.15.

A59   Rod or incomplete object made from thick sheet, which has been partially rolled. One end is flattened, whilst the other has been pinched to give a deliberate shaping, which may have been inserted into something. Length 55mm. 82SF7. Context K12 (Phase 6c). Figure 9.14.

A60   Small bundle of fine wires, probably looped over a ring and then bound tightly with fine wire. Overall length 33mm. 89SF16. Context H5 (Phase 7d). Not illustrated.

A61   Several lengths of fine wire, folded and partly twisted. Folded length 117mm. 89SF15. Context H26 (Phase 7c). Not illustrated.

Lead

Lead was used as a weight [**A63–64**] or as a cap [**A62**]. Circular discs of lead [**A65–66**] were found at Dryslwyn. Similar discs have come from Southampton (Harvey 1975, 269), Beeston Castle (Cheshire) (Courtney 1993, 152–153) and Castell-y-Bere (Gwynedd) (Butler 1974, 94–95). Although their function has not been formally recognised, it is possible that they acted as caps to containers, held in place with wax or a similar organic material. Biddle identifies circular lead disks from Winchester as pan weights (Biddle 1990, 918).

A62   Plug or cap of lead, approximately circular with a rebate on the underside. Diameter 45–49mm. 87SF7. Context G26 (Phase 5c). Figure 9.13.

A63   Cylinder made from rolled lead sheet, possibly a weight or net sinker. Length 26mm. 85SF48. Context J23 (Phase 1b). Figure 9.13.

A64   Weight or large bead, probably of lead. It is truncated biconical in profile with a wide perforation running through it. The outer faces have been smoothed. Length 16mm, maximum width 14mm. 93SF72. Context O77 (Phase 3b). Figure 9.13.

A65   Lead disc, possibly a weight. The upper face is irregularly concave. Diameter 28mm. 92SF19. Context O52 (Phase 4d). Figure 9.13.

A66   Thin irregular disc of lead alloy, possibly a weight. Diameter 32–34mm. 82SF39. Context M31 (Phase 5a). Figure 9.13.

9.6   VESSEL GLASS
by Rachel Tyson

Some 167 fragments of glass were excavated from Dryslwyn Castle. The majority were late 19th and early 20th century bottle fragments. Other glass included a fragment of a Roman jar, some medieval window glass, a medieval or post-medieval green glass base, and the rim of a 17th–18th century phial. The catalogue number refers to the object sequence in the complete excavation glass catalogue (Tyson 2002).

Medieval vessel glass

Only one possible medieval vessel fragment was found [G8]. This was a small fragment from the base of a flask or bottle, in very poor condition, and it is uncertain whether it is medieval or post-medieval, though its context indicates that it is late 13th century. Flasks and bottles were made of green 'forest' potash glass, with similar slightly kicked bases with pontil marks, up until the 18th century. They cannot be dated by the form of the base alone. Potash glass was made in England, using plant ashes as the flux, and is very unstable. It often disintegrates completely during burial. Medieval flasks of potash glass were common containers. Their use is specified in some medical, herbal, and alcoholic recipe preparations (Moorhouse 1993). It is likely that these are also the liquids that they stored. Though vessel glass is a common find on many castle sites in England (Tyson 2000), such as Ludgershall Castle in Wiltshire (Henderson 2000), or Knaresborough Castle in Yorkshire (Harden 1966, 606–607), it is rare on castle sites in Wales. Despite the presence of high quality imported ceramics, no medieval vessel glass is reported from excavations at Caergwrle (Flintshire), Rumney (Cardiff), Loughor (Swansea), Criccieth (Gwynedd), Castell-y-Bere (Gwynedd), and only from the later 16th and 17th century levels at Montgomery. Thus the presence of only a single fragment at Dryslwyn is not unusual. It is possible that if vessel glass was in use, tableware for drinking and serving drinks, or functional wares such as hanging lamps, flasks, urinals and distilling equipment, that they were disposed of elsewhere. The presence of fine French ceramics (Section 9.2) would suggest that delicate high-quality vessels were appreciated and used in mid–late 13th century Welsh aristocratic society. It is also possible that vessel glass was a luxury rather than an essential, and glass tableware may not have been fashionable in Wales.

G8 Fragment of the base of a flask or bottle, slightly pushed in, with a pontil scar on the underside. Greenish glass in the centre, covered by crystallization and silvery irides-cence, and a thick opaque brown weathering layer. Greatest width c. 30mm. Context F 16 (Phase 4b). Not illustrated.
This fragment is from a hand-blown flask or bottle, a tradition that began in the medieval period and carried on through to the moulded and machine made bottles. This type typical of the 15th to the 18th century (Charleston 1984, 142-S). However, closer dating is not possible from such a small fragment. The severe weathering is characteristic of the late medieval and post-medieval period. Drug jars of the post-medieval period made of green glass had similar kicked bases.

9.7 BONE, ANTLER AND IVORY ARTEFACTS
by Sonia O'Connor, Carol Spence and Chris Caple

The excavation yielded 60 bone, 20 antler and 2 ivory objects. The bulk of the bone objects were fabricated from the long bone shafts of a range of ungulates:

sheep, goat, pig, cattle and horse. Evidence of partially made objects and waste from manufacturing indicates both bone and antler objects were manufactured in Dryslwyn Castle. Bones were available at Dryslwyn as a by-product of butchery activity (Section 10.2). Antler from red, roe and fallow deer was available from freshly killed deer as well as shed antlers. The ivory finds are both derived from elephant tusk. Since there is no evidence for ivory working on the site, it is likely they entered the castle as finished objects. Marks on the surface of the objects attest the use of tools such as drawn blades, knives, saws, files, drills and lathes. Smoothing and polishing the finished objects, achieved using a range of abrasives, has removed the marks of manufacture.

Whistles

The two examples recovered from Dryslwyn Castle are fairly typical of other whistle fragments found in the medieval period (MacGregor 1985, 148–151). They were manufactured from the shaft section of a bone, with some shaping of the shaft by a knife then the holes were drilled and/or knife cut. Similar examples of bone whistles have come from medieval sites in Exeter (Megaw 1984) and Northampton (Oakley and Harman 1979, 318), and from Ludgershall Castle (Wiltshire) (MacGregor 2000, 163–167). Examples from Northampton and Ludgershall were, like one of the Dryslwyn examples, made from the bone of a goose. Though context (O94) was an unphased clear-ance level, the vast majority of finds from this context were of Phase 3 or 4 activity and thus both whistles are almost certainly mid/late 13th century in date.

B1 Whistle. Length 56mm, width 20mm, depth 18mm. Fragment of femur shaft with broken irregular ends. Two oval holes 5.5mm long by 5.0mm wide, have been cut by rotating knife tip. Material: pig bone, right femur. 93SF14. Context O94 (unphased). Figure 9.17.

B2 Whistle. Length 81mm, width 7mm, depth 6mm. A fragment of slender bone shaft broken with numerous longitudinal facets created using a knife. Three parallel-sided holes (2.5mm diameter) have been cut with a knife; a small dot marks an alternative position for the third hole. Material: large bird (probably goose) bone, tarsometatarsus shaft. 93SF56. Context O74 (Phase 3a). Figure 9.17.

Gaming pieces

Dice, counters and gaming figures have been recov-ered from many medieval sites. A high proportion come from castles: tablemen from Loughor Castle (Swansea) (Redknap 1993) and Hen Domen (Powys) (Higham and Rouillard 2000, 107), dice from Castell-y-Bere (Gwynedd) (Butler 1974, 92–93), Ludgershall Castle (Wiltshire) (MacGregor 2000, 163–164), Beeston Castle (Cheshire) (Courtney 1993, 152–155) and a chessman from Skenfrith (Monmouthshire) and Loughor (Swansea) Castles (Redknap 1993). This concentration of gaming finds may be related to the large number of men (English or Welsh) in castle garrisons who had little to do save in times of conflict. If, as appears likely, the chessman [**B3**] is redeposited, all of these gaming finds are derived from the late 13th and early 14th century, when the garrison was at its height.

B3 Knight from a chess set, length 17mm, diameter 9mm. A lathe turned, truncated conical piece with a single, angular projection at the narrow end. Examples of chessmen have come from urban sites such as Winchester (Brown 1990, 704) and Witchampton (MacGregor 1985, 137–138) and castles such as Skenfrith (Monmouthshire) and Loughor (Swansea) (Redknap 1993). Material: bone. 82SF5. Context O7 (Phase 6d). Figure 9.19.

B4 Counter, diameter 28mm, depth 3mm. A lathe turned disk decorated on both sides with five concentric rings about a central hole of 4mm diameter. Probably a gaming counter, similar to one from Exeter (Allan 1984, 350–351) and may possibly be a 'tableman' (used in the game of tables) or a piece from a draughts set. It is unusual, however, though not unique, in being decorated on both sides and is smaller than tablemen recovered from sites such as Winchester (Brown 1990, 702–703) and Loughor Castle (Swansea) (Redknap 1993). Material: bone scapula. 90SF28. Context H59 (Phase 4c). Figure 9.19.

B5 Die, length 8mm, width 8mm, depth 8mm. An approximately cubic die of conventional layout (scores on opposing sides adding up to 7), Brown's Type A, used from the Roman period to the present (Brown 1990, 692–694). The scores are represented by double ring and dot symbols. Material: longbone. 92SF133. Context O31 (Phase 4a). Figure 9.19.

B6 Die, length 19mm, width 10mm, depth 9mm. A lozenge shaped die with the conventional layout (scores on opposing faces add up to 7), the numbers 2 and 5 are on the diamond shaped faces. The scores are represented by drilled conical pits. This die is not readily paralleled, and a complex game where the numbers on the dice do not have an equal chance of being selected is suggested. Material: bone. 92SF59. Context O52 (Phase 4d). Figure 9.19.

Spindle whorls

Whorls were used with a spindle to twist fibres, usually wool, into thread. Many materials, such as ceramic, stone and metal, were used to make whorls. Both of the objects here have been manufactured from the femur caputs of cattle, a common occurrence from the Iron Age through to the 12th century. Usage appears to decline post 12th century. As one of these whorls [**B7**] is probably redeposited it is likely that both spindle whorls and hence textile production relate to the early period of the castle occupation c1220–50.

B7 Spindle whorl, length 38mm, width 36mm, depth 19mm. 10–12 mm diameter, knife-cut hole through the centre. Material: cattle bone femur caput. 86SF34. Context J1 (Phase 5a). Figure 9.17.

B8 Spindle whorl, length 35mm, width 30mm, depth 24mm. 8mm diameter central hole. Material: cattle bone, femur caput. 89SF7. Context J37 (Phase 1b). Figure 9.17.

Knife handles

Knives could be both a personal implement as well as a tool and were carried by all sections of society. Of the knife handles found at Dryslwyn, **B9** is worthy of special note. It was manufactured from elephant ivory and was probably brought to the site as a finished piece. The site phasing suggests a date of late 13th century for the context from which it was recovered. The extensive excavations in London during the 1970s and 1980s did not produce any examples of medieval ivory knife handles (Cowgill *et al* 1987) nor did the excavations in Winchester (Hinton 1990). This suggests ivory was a rare and thus high value material and indicates the status of Dryslwyn in attracting long distance trade items.

B9 Knife handle, length 76mm, width 14mm, depth 10mm. A longitudinal strip of ivory with a wedge shaped cross-section. It had a 3.5mm diameter, 40mm long, hole drilled for the tang. Material: ivory, elephant tusk. 85SF66. Context F16 (Phase 4b). Figure 9.17.

B10 Handle, length 54mm, width 9mm, depth 10mm. A square cross-section column tapering to approximately 8mm square. The natural oval cavity of the bone runs down the length of the object. Material: sheep tibia bone. 88SF25. Context J37 (Phase 1b). Figure 9.17.

B11 Knife handle fragment, length 48mm, width 14mm, depth 14mm. Part of antler tine produced for knife handle, possibly an unfinished piece. Shaft shows incised, slightly uneven cross hatching pattern, handcut by a knife, with an end band drawn around entire circumference of the shaft. 12mm deep hole drilled into the centre of the tine to receive the tang. A similar object was recovered from the Beeston Castle (Cheshire) excavations (Courtney 1993, 154). Material: deer antler tine. 95SF14. Context VA10 (Phase 5d). Figure 9.19.

Toggles

Of the seven toggles recovered, six were made from pig metapodials with central and axial perforations. Previous explanations for these bone toggles have included use in weaving or toggles for clothing (Oakley and Harman 1979, 313), though Lawson (Brown and Lawson 1990; Lawson 1995) suggests they were either a traditional musical instrument or a children's toy. Examples come from all periods of the Welsh lordly occupation (Phases 1–4).

B12 Toggle, length 53mm, width 16mm, depth 16mm. Incomplete pig metacarpal. 90SF31. Context H59 (Phase 4c). Not illustrated.

B13 Toggle, length 55mm, width 16mm, depth 15mm. Complete pig metacarpal. 90SF6. Context H9 (Phase 4c). Not illustrated.

B14 Toggle, length 59mm, width 15 mm, depth 16 mm. Complete pig metacarpal. 87SF88. Context G59 (Phase 4c). Not illustrated.

B15 Toggle, length 67mm, width 16mm, depth 15mm, wt. 7g. Complete pig metacarpal. 86SF60. Context I40 (Phase 3a). Not illustrated.

B16 Toggle, length 60mm, width 16 mm, depth 15mm, wt. 6g. Complete pig metatarsal. 87SF91. Context J28 (Phase 2d). Figure 9.16.

B17 Toggle, diameter 20mm, depth 7mm. Transverse section of roe deer antler beam, retaining the natural surface morphology, with a central perforation. 92SF146. Context B53 (Phase 4c). Figure 9.18.

B18 Toggle, length 68mm, width 19mm, depth 18mm. Complete pig metatarsal, only axial, no central perforation. 91SF97. Context G194 (Phase 2c). Figure 9.16.

Button

Though MacGregor (1985, 99–102) and Biddle (1990, 572–575) both provide examples of varying antiquity for bone buttons of disc form with four central perforations, this object was recovered from a topsoil layer and it is probably from post-medieval visitation of the castle.

B19 Button, dia.19.5mm, thickness 3mm max. A turned bone disc with a flat back and a slightly domed front, with a central, flat rebate and four drilled stitching holes. Material: bone from large ungulate longbone. 80SF12, Context K1 (Phase 7b). Figure 9.19.

Comb

This fragment is from a single sided antler comb. Galloway suggested that these combs are most commonly associated with the Late Saxon and Viking period, though they do continue into the 13th/14th century (Galloway 1990). However, since single sided antler/bone combs have been recovered from a number of castle sites in Wales, such as Loughor (Swansea) (Lewis 1994, 156–193), Montgomery (Powys) (Knight 1996, 150–151), Castell-y-Bere (Gwynedd) (Butler 1974, 93), Hen Domen (Powys) (Higham and Rouillard 2000, 107) and Flint (Flintshire) (Miles 1998, 128), and there is an absence of other comb forms, it is probable that single-sided antler/bone combs are the normal comb form in use in Wales throughout the 12th to 14th centuries.

B20 Comb side plate from a single-sided composite comb, length 55mm, width 16mm, depth 5mm. A longitudinally split tine with a smoothed 'D' cross-section, the lower edge has 16 irregularly spaced saw cuts from the cutting of the teeth and two 2.5mm diameter rivet holes. Ornamented with sawn lines forming 'V' shaped fields around each rivet hole and a vertical group of lines between the two fields. Material: antler tine. 91SF15. Context G178 (Phase 2d). Figure 9.19.

Bodkins

Two bone objects [**B21–22**] with blunt pointed shafts with expanded pierced ends are identified as bodkins. MacGregor (1985) suggests that in the medieval period bone bodkins had a function as dress pins and examples from Northampton (Oakley and Harmen

1979, 310) were described as pins. Large numbers of these bone objects occur at a wide range of sites from Southampton (Harvey 1975) and Exeter (Allan 1984, 350–351) to Goltho (Lincolnshire) (MacGregor 1987, 350–351). They are invariably too crude an object with which to perform convincingly the decorative function of a pin and are perhaps better identified by Keene as 'eyed weaving implements' (Keene 1990). In reality, they probably had a range of functions associated with weaving and sewing tough or large mesh materials such as leather or basketry.

B21 Bodkin/needle, unfinished, length 66mm, width 7mm, depth 4mm. A shallow groove is present at the rounded distal end. Material: pig fibula bone. 90SF48. Context H59 (Phase 4c). Figure 9.16.

B22 Bodkin/needle, length 95mm, width 9mm, depth 4mm. The proximal end has been trimmed with a knife and perforated by a 3.5mm hole. Material: pig fibula bone. 91SF86. Context O44 (Phase 5b). Figure 9.16.

B37 Bodkin/needle, length 92mm, width 12mm, depth 3mm. The distal end has been perforated medio-laterally with a 3mm diameter hole created by rotating the tip of a knife. Material: bone, pig fibula. 86SF58. Context J1 (Phase 7b). Figure 9.16.

B46 Bodkin/needle/pin fragment, length 35mm, width 6mm, depth 4mm. The shaft ends in a crescent shaped head and is pierced centrally with a 2.5mm diameter hole. Three horizontal lines scored with a knife may indicate where the hole should be cut. Material: pig bone fibula. 93SF38. Context O74 (Phase 3a). Figure 9.16.

Pricker

This bone object [**B23**] is a composite object comprising a bone handle with the remains of an iron point in its tip. It can be interpreted as a parchment pricker, which would have been used to lay out spacing on parchment sheets prior to the sheets being used. Knight (1996, 151–152) describes a similar object from Montgomery Castle (Powys) as a 'dry point stylus for ruling manuscripts'. A similar object from Beeston Castle (Cheshire) has been described as a pin or parchment pricker (Courtney 1993, 154).

B23 Parchment pricker/stylus/bobbin, length 80mm, diameter 7mm. Lathe turned and polished strip of longbone. It has an ovoid head that ends at a horizontal shoulder decorated with two narrow concentric incised lines. The hole in the narrow end contains the remains of an iron tip, now snapped off. Material: longbone. 85SF61. Context J2 (Phase 5c). Figure 9.16.

Pins

Bone pins have a shaft and a definable head. They may have been used for fastening clothing or hair, both as a practical and as a more decorative element. These examples have the smooth polished finish of a completed and used object. Though identified as pins they could have had uses as parchment prickers or styli.

266

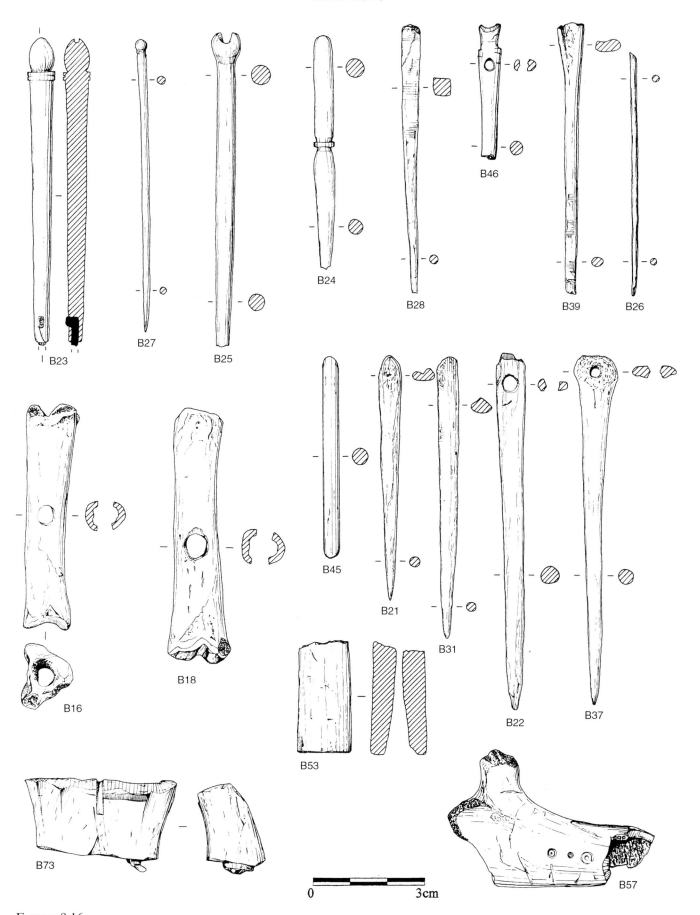

FIGURE 9.16

Bone, antler, ivory artefacts

B24 Pin, length 60mm, diameter 5.5mm. Lathe turned elongated head with collar, broken. 80SF3, Context K1 (Phase 7b). Figure 9.16.

B25 Pin, length 81mm, head diameter 7mm. Lathe turned spheroidal head with deep incised groove, broken. 83SF74. Context J13 (Phase 5a). Figure 9.16.

B26 Pin, length 65mm, diameter 1.5mm. Finely polished bone pin, broken at both ends. 95SF44. Context I18 (Phase 4a). Figure 9.16

B27 Pin, length 77mm, width 3.5mm. Hand-made with shallow spherical head, complete. 93SF76. Context A12 (Phase 5d). Figure 9.16.

Points or pin blanks

Points are shafts without a definable head or piercing. They may have had a basic pegging or non-decorative pinning function. Some polished examples with point and point, or point and chisel ends, from Winchester (Keene 1990) and Northampton (Oakley and Harman 1979, 110) have been identified as thread pickers or pin beaters utilised by the weaving industry. However, most examples from this assemblage at Dryslwyn are crudely shaped pieces of bone in the process of being made into pins or points. They were made from strips of large longbone shaped by knife, drawn blade and file, and then smoothed and polished. There are 13 blanks in various stages of preparation, one with the head marked out, another with an unfinished dragonesque head [**B48**] which suggests a possible pin as well as point or bodkin manufacture. At least one example had been polished [**B45**] suggesting that all stages of manufacture from roughing out to final polishing were carried out on this site. Examples come principally from Phase 1 and Phase 4 contexts so bone point manufacture was undertaken at both the start and the end of the Welsh lordly period of castle occupation.

B28 Point/pin blank, length 70mm, width 5mm, depth 5mm. 93SF78. Context A10 (Phase 4d). Figure 9.16.

B29 Hipped point or awl, length 86mm, width 11.5mm, depth 10mm. Material: cattle bone, left ulna. 92SF131. Context G367 (Phase 1b). Figure 9.17.

B30 Point/pin blank, length 78mm, width 12mm, depth 7mm. 83SF48. Context E24 (Phase 4c). Not illustrated.

B31 Point/pin or needle fragment, length 72mm, width 6mm, depth 4mm. Material: pig bone fibula. 85SF38. Context F25 (Phase 3b). Figure 9.16.

B32 Point/pin blank, length 72mm, width 9mm, depth 8mm. Context F47 (Phase 3b). Not illustrated.

B33 Point/pin blank, length 35mm, width 9mm, depth 9mm. 90SF32. Context H59 (Phase 4c). Not illustrated.

B34 Point/pin blank, length 114mm, width 12mm, depth 7mm. 90SF12. Context O7 (Phase 6d). Not illustrated.

B35 Pin blank, length 65mm, width 11mm, depth 6mm. A crude head form present. 90SF24. Context H35 (Phase 4c). Figure 9.17.

B36 Point/pin blank, length 122mm, width 14mm, depth 10mm. 88SF39. Context P6 (Phase 6c). Not illustrated.

B38 Point/pin blank, length 73mm, width 8mm, diameter 5mm. 95SF40. Context F47 (Phase 3b). Not illustrated.

B39 Point/pin, length 72mm, width 8mm, diameter 3mm. 95SF41. Context J1 (Phase 7b). Figure 9.16.

B40 Point/pin shaft, length 63mm, width 5mm, diameter 4mm. 95SF37. Context G456 (Phase 1b). Not illustrated.

B41 Point/pin blank, length 91mm, width 23mm. 95SF31. Context G59 (Phase 4c). Not illustrated.

B42 Point/pin blank, length 52mm, width 15mm, depth 8mm. 95SF32. Context H59 (Phase 4c). Not illustrated.

B43 Point/pin blank, length 202mm, width 13mm, depth 10mm. 95SF33. Context G59 (Phase 4c). Figure 9.18.

B44 Point/pin blank, length 52mm, width 7mm. 95SF34. Context G59 (Phase 4c). Not illustrated.

B45 Point/pin shaft, length 53mm, diameter 4.5mm. 93SF86, Context B107 (Phase 1b). Figure 9.16.

B47 Point/pin blank, length 113mm, width 13mm, depth 7mm. 90SF49. Context H59 (Phase 4c). Not illustrated.

B48 Unfinished head of a pin?, toy or decoration, length 20mm, width 12mm, depth 6mm. A rough-out of a dragonesque head with a sphere in its jaws carved from the metaphysis of a large longbone. This piece has been entirely worked with a knife and there is no evidence for subsequent smoothing or polishing. The neck end of the animal is snapped across and this damage may account for this item remaining unfinished. Material: longbone. 90SF73. Context H59 (Phase 4c). Figure 9.19.

B49 Working waste/?pin blank, length 46mm, width 20mm, depth 9mm. Knife cut. 95SF36. Context G350 (Phase 4a). Figure 9.18.

Objects of uncertain type

These are pieces of bone which have been shaped to form objects, though they have subsequently broken so that the exact form and function are not clearly identifiable.

B50 Fitting, length 14mm, width 8mm, depth 4mm, wt. <1g. A rectangle of bone worked to form a squared U-shaped fitting, the central gap. The front, sides and edges are decorated with a line of conical pits, approx. 1mm diameter. A pointed iron pin protrudes from the back of the fitting, which appears to hinge around a hidden pivot within the open end of the 'U' of bone. Material: longbone. 90SF9. Context H35 (Phase 4c). Figure 9.19.

B51 Decoration, length 134mm, width 10mm, depth 5mm. A loosely coiled, sinister, double helix cut from a single piece of bone. The two polished sinuous rods, approximately 4mm diameter, conjoined where they cross. 90SF38. Context H35 (Phase 4c). Figure 9.19.

B52 Handle blank, length 51mm, width 8.5mm, depth 8mm. A parallel sided square cross-section bar of bone. 85SF63. Context J2 (Phase 5c). Figure 9.17.

B55 Perforated plaque, length 15mm, width 10mm, depth 5mm. Rectangular fragment. Broken around a 2.5mm

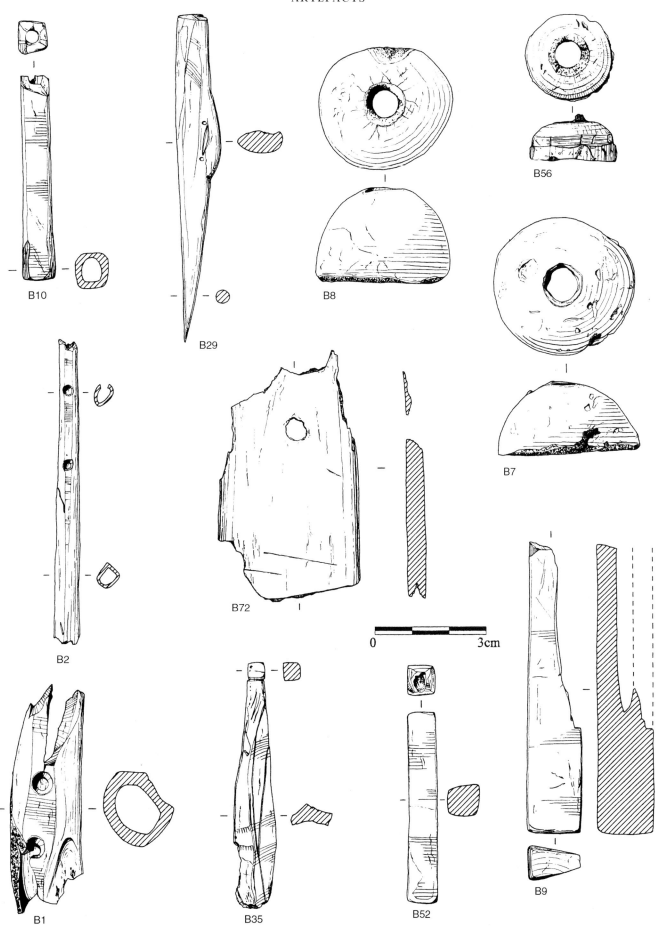

F<small>IGURE</small> 9.17

Bone, antler, ivory artefacts

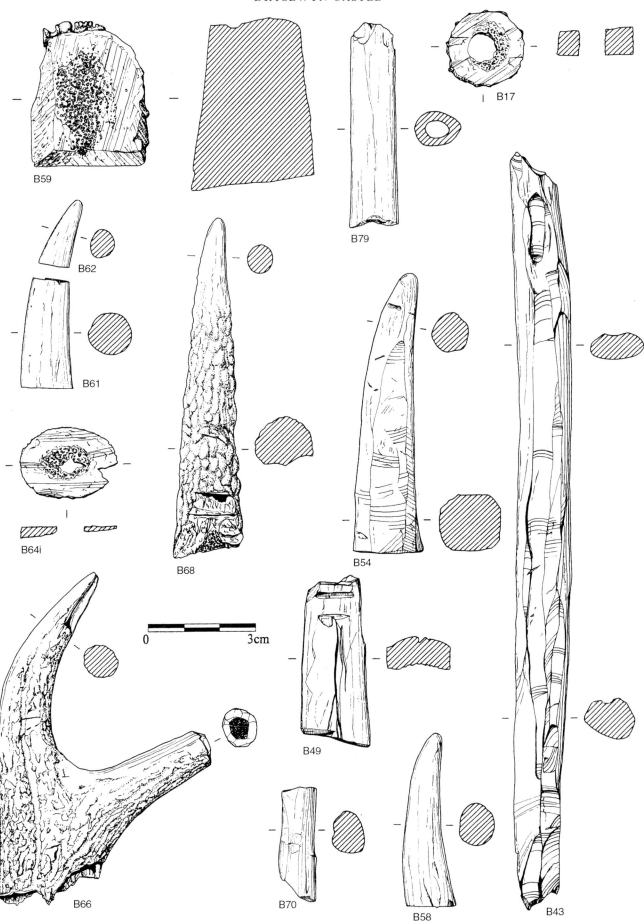

FIGURE 9.18

Bone, antler, ivory artefacts

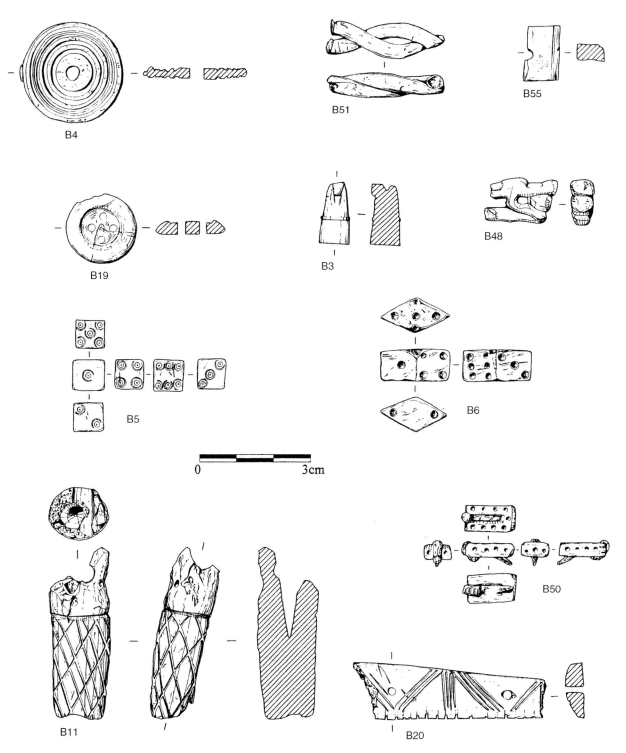

FIGURE 9.19

Bone, antler, ivory artefacts

diameter hole, which may have been for a rivet for securing the plaque. The front and moulded edge are highly polished. Material: elephant ivory. 92SF145. Context B52 (Phase 4c). Figure 9.19.

B57   Trial piece, length 55mm, width 41mm. Pig humerus with three ring-and-dot incisions approximately 5mm apart, centre to centre, in a line up the axis of the shaft. They are all cut using the same centre bit. 93SF128. Context O77 (Phase 3b). Figure 9.16.

Working waste

Pieces of bone and antler, which show evidence of working but have not been formed into objects are thought to be waste material from object manufacture. Almost all the pieces of antler recovered from the site have been interpreted as working waste. It has not been possible to be certain about the objects being fabricated, however the presence of a fragment of a composite antler comb side plate [**B20**] and an antler knife handle [**B11**], and the fact that antler combs and gaming pieces are the principal finds made of antler, make it highly likely that these were the objects being created. Since much of the antler-working waste comes from deposits of Phases 3 and 4 this would clearly suggest an antler working industry in the Welsh period of the mid to late 13th century. An unstratified piece of antler waste (no. 56) is derived from lathe turning and indicates a degree of mechanisation in the antler-working industry on this site. Similar evidence for antler working has come from a number of Anglo Scandinavian and Late Saxon sites such as York (Mac-Gregor 1978), Winchester (Biddle 1990) and St Peter's Street, Northampton (Oakley and Harman 1979, 318). Antler-working tends to be linked with a ready supply of antlers and this is almost certainly correlated with forest and woodland, the preferred habit of deer.

B56 Turning waste, diameter 24mm, depth 14mm. This section of beam retaining natural surface morphology is a waste end from a lathe-turned object. The top third to a half is turned and curved. The beam has been sawn off and drilled with a tapering hole (8mm to 7mm diameter) to mount it on a lathe. The turned item was made and then parted from this waste end, snapping the medulla. Material: roe deer antler beam. 91SF1. Unstratified. Figure 9.17.

Antler: pieces of antler tine, usually cut or sawn, from the tip to the complete tine:
B54 86SF29. Context I18 (Phase 4a). Figure 9.18.
B58 83SF19. Context F19 (Phase 3b). Figure 9.18.
B60 85SF2. Context F13 (Phase 4b). Not illustrated.
B61 85SF18. Context T18 (Phase 5d). Figure 9.18.
B62 85SF20. Unstratified. Figure 9.18. Not illustrated.
B64i 85SF25. Context F20 (Phase 4a). Figure 9.18.
B66 87SF70. Context G59 (Phase 4c). Figure 9.18.
B68 90SF2. Context H35 (Phase 4c). Figure 9.18.
B69 95SF35. Context G59 (Phase 4c). Not illustrated.
B71 95SF39. Context G20 (Phase 4a). Not illustrated.
B75 95SF52. Context O92 (Phase 4a). Not illustrated.
B78 Context O66 (Phase 4a). Not illustrated.

Antler: shaped pieces from the beam of the antler:
B53 85SF65. Context F19 (Phase 3b). Figure 9.16.
B59 83SF70. Context F19 (Phase 3b). Figure 9.18.
B67 89SF13. Context G157 (Phase 3a). Not illustrated.

Antler: thin sections cut or sawn through the antler beam:
B63 85SF22. Context F11 (Phase 4a). Not illustrated.
B64ii 85SF25. Context F20 (Phase 4a). Not illustrated.

Bone: pieces of bone showing marks of saws, knives and files:
B65 90SF33. Context H59 (Phase 4c). Not illustrated.
B70 95SF38. Context H59 (Phase 4c). Figure 9.18.
B72 95SF42. Context I1 (Phase 7d). Figure 9.17.
B73 95SF43. Context I17 (Phase 4a). Figure 9.16.
B76 95SF53. Context O77 (Phase 3b). Not illustrated.
B77 95SF54. Context O52 (Phase 4d). Not illustrated.

Bone: which bears evidence of cut and other marks associated with butchery activities such as jointing, skinning, de-fleshing and similar activities.
B79 80SF33. Context K20 (Phase 5a). Figure 9.18.
B80 80SF37. Context K20 (Phase 5a). Not illustrated.
B81 95SF47. Context I55 (Phase 2b). Not illustrated.
B82 90SF51. Context H59 (Phase 4c). Not illustrated.

9.8 STONE ARTEFACTS
by Hugh Willmott

A total of 65 medieval worked stone objects were recovered from Dryslwyn Castle. These were divided into four different functional categories associated with the utilitarian domestic activities undertaken on site.

Textile production

Seven artefacts associated with the hand spinning and weaving of textiles were recovered. Five are spindle whorls used to produce the thread that was subsequently woven. Two shapes occur at Dryslwyn, globular [**S1**] and disc [**S2–5**], with one example of the latter only being half-finished. Both were common forms throughout medieval Britain, similar examples occur in greater number at St. Peter's Street, Northampton, for example (Oakley and Hall 1979). They are hard to date typologically as similar whorls were used until the post-medieval period, despite the introduction of the spinning wheel in the 14th century (Postan and Rich 1952, 379).

The presence of two loom weight fragments is more unusual [**S6–7**]. Such weights are associated with the use of an upright loom to keep the warp (vertical) threads taut. This type of loom, whilst common throughout the early medieval period, had largely been replaced by the 12th century with the horizontal treadle loom, which required no weights (Geijer 1979, 30–32). One loom weight, which may be previously discarded hillwashed material [**S7**], comes from a poorly stratified deposit outside the town and castle site. The other [**S6**] comes from the early Phase 2 occupation and may represent the presence of an antiquated weaving practice. All the well stratified textile manufacturing objects come from pre-1287 siege levels, indicating that textile manufacture was practised during the Welsh occupation of the castle.

S1 A complete globular spindle whorl, 28mm diameter. 82SF12. Context C9. (Unphased). Figure 9.22.

S2 A complete disc spindle whorl, 32mm diameter. 85SF5. Context F16 (Phase 4b). Figure 9.22.

S3 A complete disc spindle whorl, 38mm diameter. 85SF55. Context F23 (Phase 3b). Figure 9.22.

S4 A complete disc spindle whorl, 33mm diameter. 82SF1. Unstratified. Figure 9.22.

S5 A half-finished disc spindle whorl, with the start of a bored hole on one side. 48mm diameter. 85SF51. Context I18 (Phase 4a). Figure 9.22.

S6 A fragment of loom weight. An irregular flat stone with curved edge. 90mm diameter. 91SF32. Context G208 (Phase 2d). Figure 9.22.

S7 A fragment of loom weight. A section of flattened stone with curved edge. 70mm diameter. 95SF12. Context V12 (Phase 5d). Not illustrated.

Food preparation

Nine artefacts concerned with food and other domestic preparation were recovered from the site. The most complete is the upper conical stone from a pot-quern [**S8**], very similar to a fragmented example from Hull (Watkin 1987, 190, no. 19). This stone rested partially inside a lower stone against which it rubbed not only on the bottom but also the sides. The second quern fragment [**S9**] is the upper rim from a lower stone, similar examples of which have been found in a 13th century context at Hadleigh Castle (Essex) (Buckley and Major 1983) and a 16th century context at Southampton (West and Anderson 1975, 311). Both the Dryslwyn fragments fit together exactly therefore it is likely that they originally operated together. A final small fragment [**S10**] may be part of a second upper stone from a pot-quern, although it is too fragmented for positive identification. It has been suggested that the pot-quern replaced the flat quern at the end of the first millennium on continental Europe (Buckley and Major 1983, 175), although flat querns still occur in Britain long after this date. Of fifty-four quern fragments published from excavations in Winchester only three can be positively identified as pot-querns (Biddle and Smith 1990, 881) and these range broadly date between the 12th and 16th centuries. However pot-querns were a ubiquitous form throughout the medieval period and have been identified at sites from the south coast of England to north Yorkshire (Dunning 1965, 62–63). Historic records indicate that in 1288 there was one quern and two small quernstones present in the castle's stores (Rhys 1936, 51). Thus the castle retained the capacity to grind its own flour despite the proximity of the mill at Dryslwyn. However, in the post-1287 period, since the castle purchased both whole grain and ready-ground meal (Rhys 1936) it may have not needed to grind its own flour. The quernstones and the stores of whole grain were presumably intended to allow the castle to feed itself during a long siege.

Five complete stone rubbers were also found, three being modified ovoid riverine pebbles [**S11–13**] and two fashioned from roughly squared granite blocks [**S14–15**]. Rubbers are often discarded on excavations, being misinterpreted as natural rocks. However they were originally used for a number of domestic purposes. Crushing and grinding of foodstuffs and other objects is evidenced by the wear patterns on the stones (particularly [**S11–12**]). Additionally round or oval rubbers were often heated and used as sleek stones to smooth linen or cloth.

Baking was indicated through the recovery of two fragments of a probable bakestone. The smooth flat stones were used in the oven to bake bread and other such items. Bakestones are traditionally used in Wales for baking flat breads or cakes over an open fire or in embers. Comparable examples of 13th century date have been recovered from Rhuddlan (Quinnell *et al* 1994, 173).

S8 A complete upper conical stone from a pot-quern. The top of the stone is tapered with a central funneled hole and vertical sides to fit into the lower stone. The top surface of the stone has three shallow holes for the insertion of turning rods. The central hole widens towards the base of the stone and has recessed notches for an iron cross bar (missing) to interlock with a vertical iron pivot on the lower stone. Both the base and lower sides have significant wear. A dark coarse-grained granite. Base diameter 230mm, lower hole 95mm, upper hole 60mm. 92SF168. Context G456 (Phase 1b). Figure 9.20.

S9 A fragment of rim from the lower stone of a pot-quern. The top edge is rounded and the interior worn smooth. The interior diameter fits the exterior measurement of no.8, both possibly belonging together. A dark coarse-grained granite. External diameter 240mm, internal diameter 230mm. 86SF66. Context G6 (Phase 6d). Figure 9.20.

S10 A small fragment, possibly from the upper stone of a pot-quern. Part of a convex smoothed outer surface. 93SF129. Context O71 (Phase 5b). Not illustrated.

S11 A complete ovoid rubber with a smoothed surface and linear scratch marks. 110 × 85 × 40mm. 93SF84. Context O131 (Phase 7b). Figure 9.20.

S12 A complete ovoid rubber with a smoothed surface and pounding wear at either end. 120 × 95 × 45mm. 89SF6. Context O6 (Phase 7b). Figure 9.20.

S13 A complete ovoid rubber. 87 × 67 × 40mm. 92SF112. Context G195 (Phase 2b). Not illustrated.

S14 A complete rectangular rubber. 75 × 70 × 60mm. 83SF22. Context F11 (Phase 4a). Figure 9.20.

S15 A complete rectangular rubber. 85 × 54 × 50mm. 83SF54. Context F16 (Phase 4b). Not illustrated.

S16 Two joining fragments of flat bakestone with smooth upper face. Two curved edges, Broken, presently 260 × 212 × 23mm. 87SF96. Context G59 (Phase 4c). Figure 9.20.

Honestones

All but one of the hones from Dryslwyn are made from local fine-grained hard sandstones or metamorphic rocks. The non-local stone example [**S41**] is of silver-grey schist, probably Norwegian 'Blautstein' Ragstone from the Eidsborg quarries (Moore 1978, 65), a type commonly traded throughout the Middle Ages.

The hones from Dryslwyn were classified by form into four categories, which are probably at least in part related to different functional tasks. Seven stones [**S24, S31, S43–46** and **S54**] of types B–D had secondary working (re-use) in the form of one or more deep 'v' shaped grooves either on the smooth faces or elsewhere on the stone. These were probably used for adding points to arrowheads or possibly nails or pins.

Two hones [**S26, S41**] have holes to enable the hones to be suspended. **S26** is a very finely made and unusually curved form, whilst the second **S41** is the imported Scandinavian schist stone. It is likely they were designed to be hung from the belt, as much for display as for use.

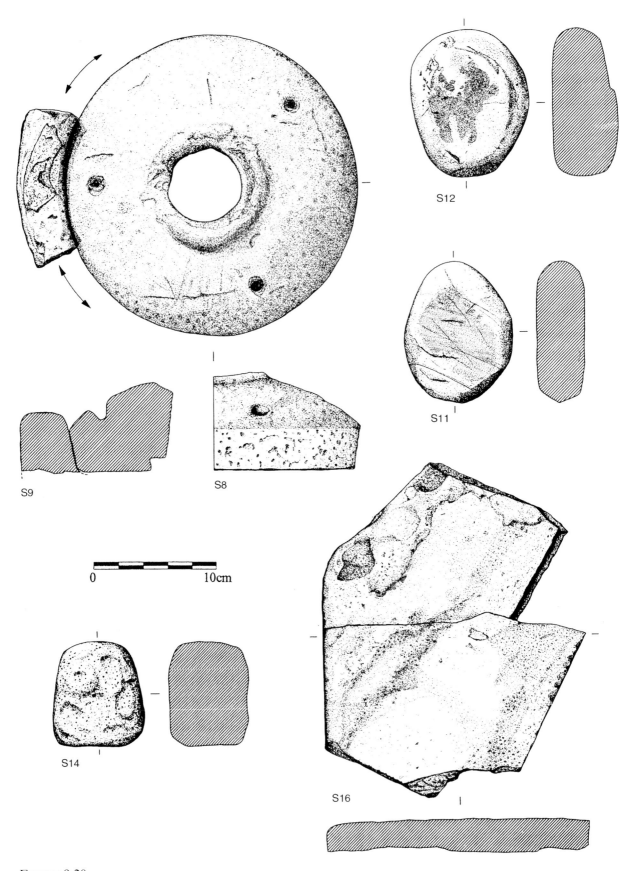

FIGURE 9.20

Stone artefacts used in food preparation

274

Type A, large flat stones

Large stones with one surface that is smoothed. In two out of the three examples from this assemblage only the centre of the stone was used. The size and shape of the stones suggests that they were held in a static position whilst a long or convex blade, such as a large knife, sword or even an axe was drawn against them. Few sharpening stones of this type have been identified from medieval excavations due the simplicity of their form. The closest parallels for this type of stone have been found at the Roman military sites of Leucarum (Loughor, Swansea) (Parkhouse 1997, 418–420) and Caerleon (Newport) (Parkhouse and Evans 1992, 192) consequently their primary use may have been for sharpening military equipment. Since S19 is redeposited and both S17 and **S18** come from context early in the castle's history this form of honestone was probably quickly superseded on this site.

Fragment from a large flat fine-grained stone with a smoothed area on one surface:

S17 86SF54. Context F70 (Phase 2d). Not illustrated.

S18 93SF115. Context O124 (Phase 1a). Figure 9.22.

S19 84SF50. Context Z15 (Phase 5d). Not illustrated.

Type B, sub-circular cross-sectioned stones

This type of hone stone is either sub-circular or 'D' shaped in cross-section. Most of the six examples in this category have a rough single flat face unsuited to sharpening. The wear patterns suggest that the rounded edge/side of the stone was rubbed along the blade. In some cases (e.g. [S22–23]) this resulted in a distinct longitudinal, rather than transverse, erosion of the stone. Such hones could only have been used on long straight blades, such as large knives and swords, or on concave blades, such as scythes. Though uncommon on medieval sites, similar types of hones have been found at Winchester (Ellis and Moore 1990, 871, no. 3061).

Sub-circular stone with one flat rough face:

S20 Fragment, 58mm (broken) × 27mm, curvature 68mm. 86SF48. Context F70 (Phase 2d). Not illustrated.

S21 Fragment, 105mm (broken) × 30mm, curvature 85mm. 90SF37. Context H59 (Phase 4c). Not illustrated.

S22 Complete, 170mm × 40mm, curvature 110mm. 93SF109. Context O151 (Phase 3b). Not illustrated.

S23 Complete, 170mm × 65mm, curvature 90mm. 92SF142. Context O31 (Phase 4a). Not illustrated.

S24 Fragment, 50mm (broken) × 54mm, curvature 85mm. 82SF49. Context O32 (Phase 6d). Figure 9.21.

S25 Fragment, 62mm (broken) × 55mm, curvature 135mm. 91SF104. Context P50 (Phase 2d). Not illustrated.

S26 Fragment from a small, curving sub-circular stone with an inner flat face. Tapers slightly to a perforated end. A light fine-grained stone. Length (broken) 53mm, width 38mm, curvature 30mm. 84SF37. Context Z13 (Phase 6d). Figure 9.21.

Type C, rectangular sectioned stones

Honestones with rectangular cross-sections. Of the 18 examples of this type most have one or two smoothed faces, usually on the broadest sides of the stones. However, in several examples (e.g. nos. 28, 30 and 35) the narrower side faces were those used for honing, suggesting their use for smaller blades. Most types of straight-sided blade could have been sharpened with these hones, depending upon the size of the stone. However the wear patterns, generally in the centre of the stones, suggests that they were predominantly used on knives. Rectangular hones were used throughout most periods in Britain and there is no way to typologically differentiate medieval examples from any other period.

Rectangular section stone

S27 Complete, 80 × 22 × 7mm. 92SF151. Context B43 (Phase 4d). Not illustrated.

S28 Complete, 92 × 25 × 11mm. 85SF59. Context F16 (Phase 4b). Not illustrated.

S29 Fragment, 98 (broken) × 30 × 20mm. 85SF52. Context F28 (Phase 3b). Not illustrated.

S30 Fragment, 47 (broken) × 30 × 16mm. 91SF55. Context G212 (Phase 2c). Not illustrated.

S31 Fragment, 123 (broken) × 45 × 20mm. 89SF8. Context H24 (Phase 7c). Not illustrated.

S32 Fragment, 112 (broken) × 50 × 22mm. 90SF129. Context H47 (Phase 4a). Figure 9.21.

S33 Complete, 121 × 34 × 24mm. 90SF70. Context H59 (Phase 4c). Not illustrated.

S34 Complete, 80 × 12 × 7mm. 87SF40. Context J1 (Phase 7b) Figure 9.21.

S35 Complete, 85 × 32 × 18mm. 85SF50. Context J2 (Phase 5c). Not illustrated.

S36 Fragment, 50 (broken) × 20 × 13mm. 88SF37. Context J37 (Phase 1b). Not illustrated.

S37 Fragment, 72 (broken) × 27 × 12mm (broken). 93SF124. Context O118 (Phase 4c). Not illustrated.

S38 Fragment, 55 (broken) × 38 × 8mm. 82SF31. Context O192 (Phase 2b). Not illustrated.

S39 Fragment, 49 (broken) × 14 × 7mm. 83SF78. Context O193 (Phase 2b). Figure 9.21.

S40 Fragment, 120 (broken) × 38 × 12mm. 82SF37. Context O28 (Phase 5d). Not illustrated.

S41 Fragment from a very small rectangular sectioned stone with two faces and a perforated hole at one end. A grey quite coarse-grained schist stone. Length (broken) 41mm, width 10mm, thickness 5mm. 92SF127. Context O31 (Phase 4a). Figure 9.21.

S42 Fragment, 35 (broken) × 28 × 17mm. 82SF50. Context T48 (Phase 3d). Not illustrated.

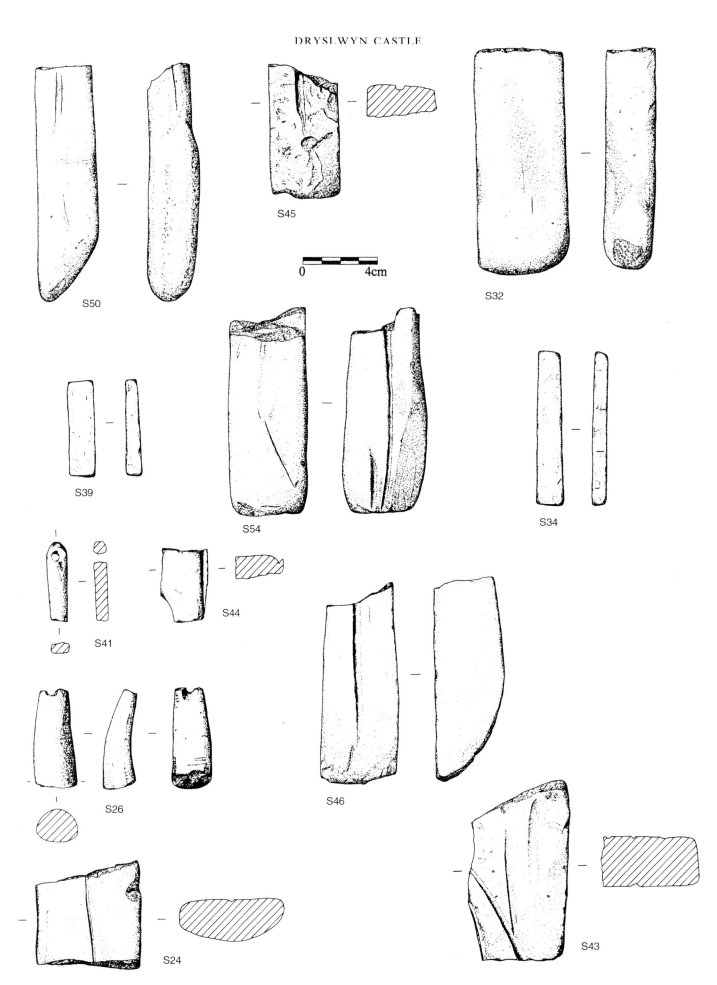

0   4cm

S50

S45

S32

S39

S54

S34

S41

S44

S26

S46

S24

S43

FIGURE 9.21

Honestones

S43 Fragment, 94 (broken) × 53 (broken) × 25mm. 87SF2. Unstratified. Figure 9.24.

S44 Fragment, 36 (broken) × 25 (broken) × 10mm (broken). 81SF25. Context T2 (Phase 7b). Figure 9.21.

Type D, square sectioned stones

Square sectioned hones, 14 examples. They were probably used for sharpening of small blades such as knives, probably smaller blades than the rectangular section hones. Ubiquitous in most periods throughout Britain.

Square Section stone:

S45 Fragment, 70 (broken) 36 (broken) × 18mm. 85SF60. Context F16 (Phase 4b). Figure 9.21.
S46 Fragment, 102 (broken) × 40 × 35mm. 86SF52. Context F34 (Phase 2a). Figure 9.21.
S47 Fragment, 76 (broken) × 20 × 15mm. 83SF37. Context F51 (Phase 3b). Not illustrated.
S48 Fragment, 55 (broken) × 17 × 14mm. 89SF1, Context H1 (Phase 7d). Not illustrated.
S49 Fragment, 85 (broken) × 25 × 23mm. 88SF6. Context J28 (Phase 2d). Not illustrated.
S50 Fragment, 122 (broken) × 30 × 25mm. 88SF36. Context J37 (Phase 1b). Figure 9.21.
S51 Complete, 77 × 20 × 17mm. 88SF21. Context J37 (Phase 1b). Not illustrated.
S52 Complete, 87mm, 12 × 12mm. 93SF79. Context O77 (Phase 3b). Not illustrated.
S53 Fragment, 38 (broken) × 20 × 15mm. 81SF42. Context T4 (Phase 7b). Not illustrated.
S54 Fragment, 107 (broken) × 45 × 40mm. 81SF13. Unstratified. Figure 9.21.
S55 Fragment, 27 (broken) × 19 × 9mm. 83SF53. Context E21 (Phase 5a). Not illustrated.
S56 Fragment, 64mm, width (broken), 17 × 9mm. 93SF137. Context O77 (Phase 3b). Not illustrated.

Grindstone

A single example of a very fine hard grey sandstone disc, probably Pennant stone, the stone type, shape and nature of the surface wear suggests that it was mounted on an axle, within a wooden frame and revolved by hand so that metal blades could be sharpened on its edge. It was found broken and built into a wall foundation (I5), which occurred in the 14th century occupation of the castle, discarded from an earlier phase of activity and re-used.

S57 Grindstone, circular disc of 290mm diameter and 60 to 65mm thickness pierced centrally with cut square hole 60 × 50mm approx. Approx. 75% of disc remains. WS38. Context I5 (Phase 5a). Not illustrated.

Millstones

Fragments derived from millstones made of a very coarse Old Red Sandstone were recovered from a number of unstratified contexts and from the base of the destruction deposits in the Round Tower D

(WS49). It would appear that these millstones were being stored in the castle presumably intended for subsequent use in a watermill. The accounts for Dryslwyn Castle show that in 1300 the castle authorities paid for a millstone for the mill at Dryslwyn (Rhys 1936, 217). Consequently it must be presumed that the castle owned or remained responsible for the mill at Dryslwyn hence the storage of millstones in the castle.

S58 Fragment of a circular millstone 412mm radius and 104mm thick. WS14. Unstratified. Not illustrated.

S59 Fragment of a hand millstone, domed disc 152mm radius and 50mm thick. WS15. Unstratified. Figure 9.24.

S60 Circular millstone (grindstone?) of 610mm diameter and 100mm thickness left in base of tower, subject to considerable fire damage and effects of demolition. Various fragments of identical geology from the same part of the same area which make up approx. 60% of circular slab of approx. 300mm radius, with central hole 90mm diameter approx. Slab is 110mm thick and ground level on both sides (grinding large quartz pebbles flat). The circular edge is fairly smooth but not as smooth as the disc faces. One half of edge is very burnt (discolouring inwards for some 50mm). Very coarse red sandstone with pebbles up to 40mm in size and uneven bedding. WS49. Context D4 (Phase 6d).

S61 Fragments of millstone/grindstone 200 × 190mm to broken edges, 110/130mm thick WS81. Unstratified. Not illustrated.

Other stone objects

S62 Fragment from a small tapering square sectioned siltstone, perforated end. 26 (broken) × 10 × 9mm. 83SF17. Context F120 (Phase 7c). Not illustrated.

S63 Fragment of smooth shale rod. 31 (broken) × 4 (diameter) mm. 92SF79. Context B 31 (Phase 6c). Not illustrated.

S64 Complete ovoid shale disc, evidence of wear. 52 × 42 × 7mm. 92SF111. Context O 51 (Phase 4d). Not illustrated.

S65 Complete circular mudstone disc. 56mm diameter. 86SF14. Context G 7 (Phase 6d). Not illustrated.

9.9 MISCELLANEOUS ARTEFACTS
by Chris Caple, Catherine Vinson and Hugh Willmott

Quill

A feather quill nib was recovered from the floor of the undercroft of the Great Hall K/L. This unique object was preserved through the presence of the surrounding charcoal and the de-oxygenation of the soil by the fire prior to the castle demolition. The feather quill, which almost certainly from a goose (Finlay 1990), has been cut to a shape that resembles a modern pen nib. It is likely that it performed this function, probably slotted into a wooden holder. The quill has traces of a black staining; either iron gall or carbon black ink (de Hamel

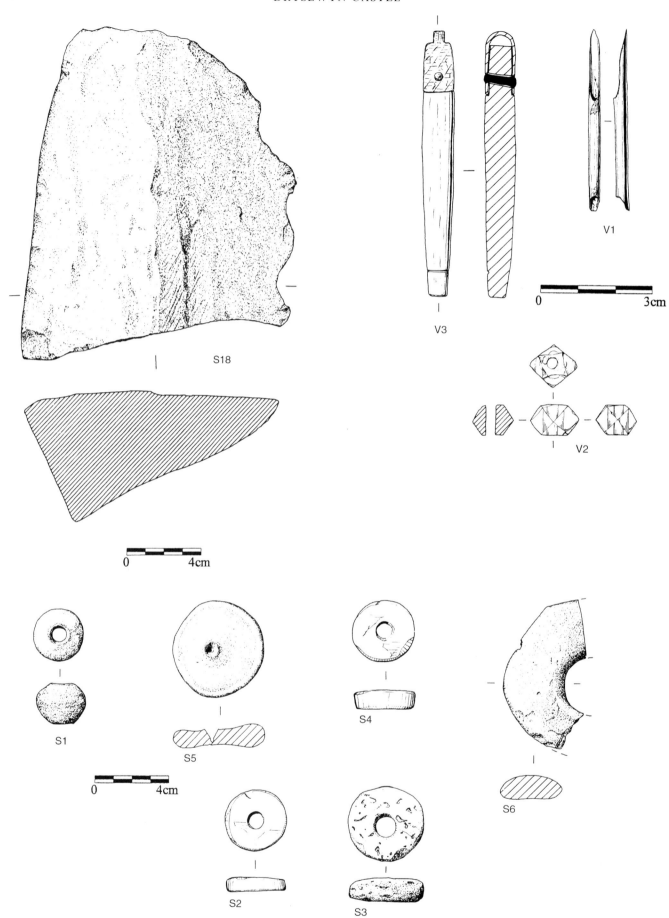

FIGURE 9.22

Stone and miscellaneous artefacts

FIGURE 9.23

Quernstone 92SF168

1992), present in its shaft. It is not split at the tip, unlike the copper alloy nib pens, which date from the 14th–15th century from Eltham Palace (Eltham, London) (Woods 1982). Rudimentary pens formed from goose radii have also been found in Norwich from contexts dating between the 14th and 16th century (Margeson 1993), but no comparative examples of quills survive. Writing activity at Dryslwyn in the 14th and 15th century is suggested by the existence of written accounts from 1287 onwards (Rhys 1936). Those same accounts also record that parchment was purchased, presumably for writing on, in 1288 (Rhys 1936, 47).

V1   Feather quill pen nib. The hollow shaft of a feather, cut to an elongated point at one end and a shallow rounded projection at the other. 48mm long, 4mm is diameter. Traces of black material in the shaft may be traces of ink. 82SF8. Context K11 (Phase 6c). Figure 9.22.

Bead

Beads were not a common form of jewellery in the later medieval period, but this facetted rock crystal bead comes from the 14th century occupation contexts on the mortar floors of the undercroft of the Great Hall (K/L). This bead is very similar, in both form and date, to an irregular rectangular bead with chamfered sides recovered from the North Enclosure of Ludgershall Castle (Wiltshire) and dated to the 14th–15th century (Ashworth 2000). It is suggested that the Ludgershall bead was made of rock crystal from the Bristol area. It appears likely that both beads derive from the same industry.

V2   A complete faceted rock crystal bead. Hand polished. Cuboid with a facet on every corner, creating a 14 sided form. 9 × 9mm and 8mm thick. Pieced by a straight sided 5mm diameter drilled hole. 82SF33. Context K13 (Phase 5c). Figure 9.22.

Plumb bob

A small tapering, square sectioned rod with an iron suspension loop, made of a stone so soft it was ineffective as whetstone. Almost certainly a plumb bob.

V3   Complete small square sectioned stone slightly tapering at either end. One end is capped with an iron suspension loop riveted to the stone. A fine-grained silt stone. Length 94mm, width 12 × 11mm. 86SF23. Context F33. Figure 9.22.

9.10   INDUSTRIAL RESIDUES

Metalworking
by David Dungworth

The principal types of slag encountered at Dryslwyn are smithing hearth bottoms (SHB), smithing slag

Type	Weight	%	Phase	Weight	%	Area	Weight	%
Smithing hearth bottoms	12240.4	75.2	1	8.8	0.1	F	68	0.4
Smithing slag lumps	28	0.2	2a–b	377	2.3	G	90	0.6
Vitrified hearth lining	786	4.8	2c–d	1478	9.1	I	64	0.4
Fuel ash slags	182	1.1	3a–b	121	0.7	J	12539	77
Uncertain	3038	18.7	3c–d		0	K	504	3.1
			4a–b	8960	55	L	1630	10
			4c–d	41	0.3	O	461	2.8
			5a–b	164	1	Y	1	0
			5c–d		0	?	919	5.6
			6		0			
			7	2129	13.1			
			u/s	2996	18.4			
Total	16276			16276			16276	

FIGURE 9.24

Distribution of metalworking residues by area, phase and type

lumps (SSL), fuel ash slag (FAS), vitrified hearth lining (VHL), and pieces too small or fragmented to allow classification (uncertain). The classification of slags in this way is explicitly tied to experimental reconstructions of iron making which suggest that the morphology of slags relates directly to the process which formed them (Crew 1991).

Smithing hearth bottoms (SHB) are lumps of slag, which accumulate in a blacksmith's hearth. They are plano-convex or concave-convex, are mostly black with some reddening of the upper surface and fracture surfaces show abundant but small-sized pores. Charcoal impressions on the upper and lower surfaces are common, as are attached fragments of fluxed lining. Most of the hearth bases from Dryslwyn are fragmentary (average weight 239g) and probably derive from regular clearing out of the 'clinker' from the hearth, something practised by many modern blacksmith's. The fragmentary nature of these remains makes it difficult to reconstruct the diameter of the hearths: the largest possible diameter reconstructable is 12.5 cm (and weighed 1079.4g). The nature of the iron smithing process generates far more SHB than any other type of residue (Figure 9.24).

Smithing slag lumps (SSL) are small pieces of slag that have smooth but flowing (occasionally contorted) original surfaces. Any fractures show little porosity and the slag is usually black. Smithing slag is assumed to be formed by expelling slag from iron during smithing operations.

Ash formed by the burning of fuel can vitrify at high temperatures to form a glassy product termed fuel ash slag (FAS). This is very variable in its morphology and colour but usually occurs as small lumps with low density. The examples from Dryslwyn are generally dark and highly vitrified with moderate to high vesicularity.

Metalworking hearths were normally lined with clay, which becomes fluxed or vitrified due to prolonged exposure to heat. Fragments of vitrified hearth lining (VHL) usually have one surface which is orange to red ceramic and one surface which is dark and glassy. The ceramic portions of the hearth lining fragments from Dryslwyn showed the presence of organic and sandy tempers.

Seven slag samples were examined under an SEM. These analyses and microstructure confirmed the identification of the iron working slag types (Dungworth 1999). The most common type of recognisable slag was hearth bases that make up 75% by weight of all the slag from the site. This clearly shows that some form of smithing was carried out at Dryslwyn rather than smelting. Conspicuous by its absence is any slag which could be associated with the smelting of iron, for example tap slag. This indicates that wrought iron or steel was imported to Dryslwyn and smithed to form objects on site. Other iron objects may have been imported ready made.

Iron smithing slag was recovered from many different phases of occupation at Dryslwyn (Figure 9.24), however, given the degree of building and disturbance of deposits over a long period of time much of the slag in later deposits is residual. The slag from Phases 1b and 2a was fragmentary and non-diagnostic; however, the slag concentration in Phase 2d deposits would indicate iron smithing activity in this phase. The slag from Phase 4a derives principally from a series of clay and cobble deposits that raised the floor level of Area J and were composed of redeposited material. Much of this material was the larger fragments such as smithing hearth bottoms which often become redistributed.

Slag was concentrated in two locations. The first concentration (919g of slag) was recovered from the 'Elsan' pits dug in the south-west corner of the town. Though this material was unstratified, its presence indicates that metalworking, primarily iron smithing, took place in the south-west corner of the town. The second concentration was in Area J of the Inner Ward, which produced 77% of the slag from the site with much of the rest coming from adjoining areas. Smithing slags and vitrified hearth linings, which tend to form in the vicinity of smithing activity, were only found in and around Area J.

It is possible that there was a relatively short period of ironworking in Phase 2d (e.g. contexts J25, J26, J28, J30, J31) taking place in Area J in-between the Great Hall K/L, the Kitchen I and the curtain wall. As no structures could be confidently identified as smithing hearths in this area during excavation it is possible that the iron smithing took place outside this area and the slag was dumped here or that hearths and other smithing structures were raised above ground level. Iron smithing residues are often found associated with castle building and construction phases, as at Caergwrle (Flintshire) (Courtney 1994). Where building record exist, as in the case of the royal castles and palaces, smiths are invariably recorded making appropriate iron fastenings, tools and re-sharpening tools (Brown, Colvin and Taylor 1963, 316). Similar activities are envisaged at Dryslwyn.

One piece of green and vesicular copper slag (84SF82) was recovered from the topsoil of the town ditch (Z2). Several fragments of cuprous casting waste were noted (Dungworth 1999), principally derived from Phase 4a redeposited contexts. No evidence of a specific copper-alloy metalworking location was recovered and it appears likely that some limited copper or bronze working occurred in Phases 2, 3 or 4, probably in the outer wards of the castle or in the town.

Wax
by Clare Pickin and Chris Caple

Two samples of translucent material which appeared from their colour and texture to be an organic material such as fat or wax were recovered from the mortar surface (G27) and the occupation material (G25) above it. These samples presumably related to the burning of candles or waterproofing materials, which had taken place in Phase 4d on a Phase 4c surface. Analysis of these samples and comparative compounds was undertaken using Fourier Transform Infra-Red Absorption Spectroscopy (FTIR) (Figure 9.25) (Pickin 2000).

The absorption bands in both samples correspond well with the absorbance bands in the known samples, confirming the identification as long chain organic compounds similar to wax or grease. The organic material in these samples will have undergone a certain amount of chemical degradation, such as hydrolysis, since the late 13th century. The resultant material of the samples contains absorption bands characteristic of both beeswax and beef tallow. Analysis of residues from putative 14th-century candle-holders and candlesticks from Fountains Abbey demonstrated the use of animal tallow, normally mixed beef and sheep fat, and beeswax (Frith *et al* 2004). Consequently it is likely that that these samples from Dryslwyn indicate the use of a mixture of beeswax and animal tallow for making candles which, given their context, were probably made in the Welsh lordly period and burnt in the period after the siege of 1287. Historic references suggest that beeswax candles, due to their higher price, sweeter smell and better flame were normally used in churches whilst pure tallow candles were associated with more domestic use (Frith *et al* 2004, 224–227). The analytical evidence from Dryslwyn and Fountains Abbey indicate that mixed beeswax and tallow candles were utilised on higher status monastic and castle sites.

Glazed stone
by Chris Caple

Four pieces of a fine grained igneous rock, probably a granite or diorite covered in a thick transparent green tinged glaze, came from contexts (F101), (G48), (H59) and (G14). The earliest of the these samples is from (F101) and comes from Phase 2b of the castle's occupation, indicating that some form of high temperature industrial activity must have taken place at this time in order to create this material, which was redeposited in subsequent phases.

This igneous fine grained stone is not local to west Wales and must have been imported to the site for example from Cornwall. The stone was probably chosen for its ability to withstand high temperatures. Analysis of the glaze using EDXRF revealed that the glaze had a composition similar to glass, rich in silica with small amounts of potassium, aluminium and calcium, with a reasonable quantity of iron giving the transparent glass/glaze a pale green tinge. This glass or glaze, though it could have formed naturally on the stones surrounding a hearth or fire, is more probably formed at a high temperature associated with glass manufacture or firing ceramics.

(G25)	(G27)	Beeswax	Tallow
3386.7			
2918.4	2923	2917.7	2922.7
2849.4	2850.8	2845.8	2851.4
2345.8	2361.2	2356.1	
	1737.7	1737	1743.1
			1634.4
1459.5	1459.5	1464.7	1463.9
1207.1			
		1171.1	1174.9
1084.6			1088.9
1006.1	1016.4		1014.4
	872.2		875.4
795			
		722.8	721.2
511.4			

FIGURE 9.25

Principal adsorption bands of waxy deposits and comparative samples

Abrasive
by Chris Caple

Two samples of a light porous material, possibly a stone such as pumice, were recovered from contexts (T78) and (G395). The sample (G395) is from Phase 2b activity in the castle and, given its smoothed side, appears to have been used as an abrasive: grinding, smoothing or polishing material in some form of trade or industrial activity. It was probably used for abrading or polishing either bone/antler, metal or wood in Phase 2 of the castle's occupation.

9.11 COAL
by Chris Caple

Coal was used as a fuel for industrial processes such as lime-burning from the late 13th century onwards. Evidence comes from fragments of coal in some of the mortar from Dryslwyn (Webster 1987, 95), supported by historic records which record the purchase of sea coals used in the building repairs of 1338/39 (*NLW Add MS 455D*), almost certainly for burning lime. There is similar record of extensive use of coal for lime burning for Edward I's castles in north Wales, for example 3114 tons of sea-coal purchased 1295–98 for lime burning in the construction of Beaumaris Castle (Anglesey) (Taylor 1987). Coal was also discovered in a 13th–14th century limekiln at Ogmore Castle (Swansea) on the Gower peninsula (Craster 1950–51).

Non-systematic collection of samples of coal from the excavated deposits of Dryslwyn Castle produced 105 samples, 5 from Phases 1a–3d, 100 from Phases 4a–7d. This indicates a significant increase in the use of coal as a fuel in Dryslwyn from the late 13th century onwards, as it has at other sites such as Rhuddlan (Quinnell *et al* 1994). In Phase 5d, there are far more extensive deposits of coal, especially layer (P9) which was composed largely of small pieces of coal and much coal dust, the type of deposit formed at the base of a coal store/bunker. Thus by the late 14th or early 15th, century coal is being stockpiled in the Inner Ward of the castle, which would suggest extensive use for domestic heating purposes. The occurrence of samples of coal from the house (Area T) and ditch (Area Z) of the town, suggests that by the late-medieval period coal was used as a fuel by every strata of medieval society in the Tywi valley.

One likely source of coal is the western exposures of the Lower and Middle coal measures of the South Wales coalfield which outcrop around Ammanford, Cross Hands and down the Gwendraeth valley. The Lower Pumpquart vein, a 1m vein of coal and one of the lowest coal seams in the coalfield, outcrops at Llandybie and at Bryngwyn north of Pen-y-groes

which is barely 6km from Dryslwyn, and at both locations it was reported in 1907 as having been worked in the past in pits or drifts (Strahan *et al* 1907, 119). Further south coal seams outcrop and were worked in drifts at Ponthenry, Pontyates and Pontyberem in the Gwendraeth valley (Strahan *et al* 1909).

The other likely source of coal is Pembrokeshire. In his accounts of the period 1298–1300 Walter de Pederton, the Justiciar of West Wales, records the purchase of 200 bushels of sea-coal from Haverford (Haverfordwest) (Pembrokeshire) (Rhys 1936, 177) which, though intended for all 'the castles' of the Crown in west Wales, namely Carmarthen, Carreg Cennan, Dinefwr, Dryslwyn and Llanbadarn, was stored as 'dead garnisture' at Llanbadarn Castle (Ceredigion) (Rhys 1936, 187). The term 'sea coal' and its supply from Haverford (Pembrokeshire) suggests that it was being obtained from the Pembrokeshire coalfield, perhaps from coastal exposures (hence sea-coal) and transported to Haverford (Pembrokeshire) and thence to Llanbadarn (Ceredigion) using boats; the most economic form of transport for such heavy, bulky cargo.

Since we would expect historical accounts to record large scale trade, whilst the small scale local trade and barter, especially between the town and surrounding area, goes unrecorded, it remains impossible to be certain which of these sources provided the bulk of the coal burnt during the 14th and 15th century at Dryslwyn.

The accounts also record that quantities of firewood were being purchased and stored at Dryslwyn (Rhys 1936, 219). In the case of Llanbadarn Castle (Ceredigion) peat was also purchased and stored (Rhys 1936, 167). Though some firewood is described as being used for drying corn (Rhys 1936, 167) and for drying meat (Rhys 1936, 219), this may suggest that coal was used for lime burning and even the heating of rooms, where its higher burn temperature would be beneficial. However, for cooking and smoking wood may have continued to be used, so that the coal did not taint the food.

Though it is likely, given the proximity of the forest to Dryslwyn, that prior to 1280 wood and charcoal were the dominant fuels used in the castle, after the 1280s coal usage increased. This may have initially been for industrial activities, but its use encouraged the development of the industry, and during the 14th century coal became increasingly used for domestic space heating. By the 15th century coal from south Wales was being shipped to England and France (Griffiths 1994, 12). Given the increasing amount of coal found in the late-14th/early-15th century levels at Dryslwyn, it is likely that coal had become the dominant fuel used by the end of the castle's life.

AGRICULTURAL AND DIETARY EVIDENCE

10.1 FOOD PRODUCTION AND CONSUMPTION IN WALES: 13TH TO 15TH CENTURIES
by Louisa Gidney and Chris Caple

Evidence for food production and consumption in Wales between 1220 and 1455 exists in a number of forms; each comes with its own limitations and biases.

Historic accounts exist for a number of English-controlled properties such as the castles of west Wales garrisoned by the English Crown in the early 14th century (Rhys 1936). As accounts, they focus on income and expenditure and so do not record barter or food production by the garrison and their families. They also only record the provisions of the castle, the 'dead garnisture' which comprised the non-perishable foodstuffs, such as bacon and salt. Fresh food (bread, fresh meat and vegetables) went unrecorded. There are also more general historic documents such as histories, poems and law books, which refer to aspects of Welsh life prior to English control. These mention renders, laws and events involving plants, animals and agricultural production (Rees 1924; Pryce 2005); they are, however, highly selective and do not provide a complete or coherent picture. Archaeological evidence of food production and consumption has come from a number of sites in Wales (Caseldine 1990). Unfortunately the dating of such deposits is often inexact, they are invariably limited in size and often contain residual material. Since acid soils dissolve bone whilst seeds only survive in waterlogged conditions or from burnt/charred deposits, evidence is biased by the soil conditions. Information also exists in written and archaeological form from sites throughout England, Scotland and Ireland, which may also be applicable to Welsh sites.

Early in the 13th century, the majority of the lord's income would have been rendered in kind, usually in food or services. In west Wales commutation of goods and services owed for cash payments had begun under the rule of the Lord Rhys (Davies 1987, 221), continued slowly throughout the 13th century, being actively fostered by English control (Davies 1987, 162–163), and escalated in the 14th century following the Black Death (Rees 1924, 253). The catchment area from which renders in kind would have been provided fluctuated dramatically during the 13th century, depending on the successes and reversals of the territorial and political ambitions of the lords of Dryslwyn. As this was not the only castle owned by its lord, it is probable that the lord and his household would not have been in continuous residence. Visiting the other castles in his territories would also have facilitated the exaction of food renders and billeting rights from the tenantry (Davies 1987, 145). During the 14th century, as a Crown garrison castle, Dryslwyn was supplied with food purchased at market and distributed through the English Crown properties of west Wales. This was no doubt supported with some local produce, which fails to appear in the accounts.

Dyer (1998) has suggested that medieval peasants living in the 13th and 14th centuries in southern and central England lived primarily on a subsistence-level, cereal-based diet of bread, ale and pottage (porridge of cereals and vegetables). Dyer's evidence of peasant diet comes principally from historical documents, such as the manorial records of food renders or agreements between older peasants surrendering their land to a younger generation in return for an annual maintenance (Dyer 1998, 55). Literary sources, such as Piers Ploughman, indicate that, during lean times, the late medieval peasant had a limited range of food in his house. 'In times of hunger', Piers had only two green (fresh) cheeses, curds of cream, oatcake, two loaves of beans and bran, parsley, potherbs and cabbage. Other poor people had beans, apples, cherries, chervils, small onions, green potherbs and peas, but they lacked the salt bacon of more plentiful times (Wells 1938, 86). Thus, in addition to the cereals and vegetables, the peasant diet also contained some dairy produce, some fruit when in season and, ideally, salt meat. White bread, fresh flesh, particularly pullets, geese and pork, and fish were the food of prosperous times, after the harvest (Wells 1938, 86–87). Archaeological evidence of animal bone recovered from medieval village sites, such as Wharram Percy (North Yorkshire), supports the suggestion that there was some meat in the peasant diet (Andrews and Milne 1979).

Describing agriculture in Wales in 1188, Giraldus Cambrensis wrote 'They plough the soil once in March and April for oats, a second time in summer, and then they turn it a third time while the grain is being threshed. In this way the whole population lives almost entirely on oats and the produce of their herds, milk, cheese and butter' (Thorpe 1978, 233). The tradition of cattle herding, *hendre-hafod* (summer and winter pasturing), may have led to higher levels of cheese and milk being made available to the Welsh peasant population than the peasants of southern and central England. In Wales, as well as the west and north of England, there was a 'predominance of oat cultivation' and the 14th-century records of Bolton Priory (North Yorkshire) indicate that it typically produced 80% oats, 12% wheat and 8% rye, barley and beans (Hammond 1993, 28).

Accounts of nobles victualling their troops provide a more holistic, although not complete, example of diet. In the case of Roger Bigod, Earl of Norfolk, victualling his troops in north Wales in 1283, 100 quarters of wheat, 200 quarters of oats, 77 beef cattle, 120 sheep, 57 pigs and 28 tuns of wine were obtained (Prestwich 1988, 199). When an historic account of the amount of food supplied is compared to the number of men, as in the case of the garrisons of the royal castles of England and Scotland *c*1300, it has been suggested that each man would have been supplied with 2lbs of flour, 1 gallon of ale, 1½lbs of fish, or 1lb of beef, 10ozs of pottage per day, plus some cheese, butter onions and garlic, providing a daily intake of around 5000 calories (Hammond 1993, 95). Even if this level of food is an overestimate and some food never made it to the troops for whom it was intended, or it was also intended to feed dependants (horse or camp follower), it may well have been slightly better than the food levels available to most peasants and, thus, an inducement to military service.

The land holding of each peasant controlled the amount they could grow and thus their wealth and their diet. Dyer (1998, 59) suggests that in purely arable terms, 30 acres of land provided a good living but less than 15 acres led to a struggle for existence. Hammond (1993, 5) quotes 20 acres as the 'usual peasant holding'. Most peasants grew vegetables in a plot around their house in order to supplement their diet and, in addition to their obligations to work demesne land, undertook tasks for their lord or other richer peasants, examples include gathering rushes, brewing ale or gathering the harvest for which they would receive payment, often in the form of food. The subsistence level and cereal basis of agriculture is emphasised by the failures of cereal harvests, especially in the period 1315–18 which led to famine and starvation of 10–15% of Britain's rural peasantry (Dyer 1998, 61). After the Black Death, however, and the resulting reduction of population, many individual peasant landholdings rose to a level that enabled a man to feed his family and generate a small surplus. The financial or food rewards for work also rose considerably; for example, a 15th-century Norfolk harvester could receive 1lb of meat, 6 pints of ale, and 2lbs of bread per day (Dyer 1994). Consequently the quantity of food and presumably the health of the peasants improved during the 15th century.

In Wales, the lands of freemen were divided amongst their male heirs. This created many small landholdings, though the kinship group (clan) acted communally to meet renders of food and service which were due to their lords on the original large landholding (*gwestfa*) (Rees 1924, 199–222; Davies 1987, 125–131). During the 13th century, these renders were increasingly commuted into cash payments (*gwestfa*). Pastoralism, principally based on cattle, the use of the *hendre-hafod* system, summer hill grazing, and pannage (autumn foraging by pigs in woodlands) were important elements in the Welsh agricultural economy. This social structure and these husbandry practices mean that individual landholdings often do not accurately convey the wealth of an individual nor the capacity to feed their dependants.

Surviving English household accounts suggest that the 13th- and 14th-century aristocracy ate a diet largely of bread, fish and meat. A few vegetables and some fruit were also consumed, as were dairy products and large quantities of ale and wine. These accounts primarily record purchases, overemphasising the presence of luxuries and spices in addition to purchased meat and game and underemphasising the fruit and vegetables from the castle garden which was traded or bartered from local producers. However, especially on feast days, the aristocracy did enjoy a wide range of meats and, on fast days, a range of fish. Christmastide epitomises the quantity and variety of foodstuffs available to the wealthy. Thus on 24 December 1289, a fast day, Richard de Swinfield, Bishop of Hereford, and his household dined on herrings, conger eels and codlings. The following day they dined on wild boar, beef, veal, venison, pork, fowl, partridge, geese, bread and cheese washed down with 40 gallons of wine. Spices, such as ginger, cloves, cinnamon, saffron, mustard and pepper, were imported from southern Europe and

Asia to flavour the bishop's food (Hammond 1993, 65). In contrast to the wide range of imported spices, the household of Richard de Swinfield ate only a few home grown vegetables: onions, leeks, peas, beans, salted and pickled greens (Hammond 1993, 71).

Considerable evidence of food production and consumption was recovered from Dryslwyn Castle in the form of substantial amounts of animal bone, as well as fish bone and plant remains present in water-logged deposits (middens, cesspits and occupation layers) and as charred remains, recovered due to an active on-site sieving and sampling programme. This enabled a large range of cereal grains, seeds, fish and bird bones as well as animal bones to be recovered and a uniquely detailed picture to be constructed of the food consumed in this castle, particularly for the Welsh lordship period of the late 13th century. In the period of the 1220s to 1287 the Inner Ward was home to the Welsh lord, his family and household (court, retainers, warriors and officials) plus visitors. In Phases 1 and 2 (early to mid 13th century) all castle activities took place in the Inner Ward, thus during the swine mote it resembled a farmyard rather than a castle. By Phase 4a (1280–87), Rhys ap Maredudd would, given his land-holdings, have had a substantial court accommodated in a substantial three ward castle. In the period of the English Garrison, Phase 4b–5d (1287–1405) there would normally have only been a constable, his family and their household resident in the Inner Ward, though Crown officials and occasionally the nominal English lord who was responsible for the castle, who probably came for the hunting, may have paid visits. Through-out all these phases, food would have been prepared in the Inner Ward to feed members of the household and family of the lord or constable, as well as great feasts for festive occasions and visitors. The majority of the environmental evidence related to Phases 3 and 4, when the Inner Ward would primarily have supported the immediate household and guests of the Welsh aristocracy.

Meat

The consumption of meat, represented by finds of animal bones, is the most obvious aspect of the medi-eval diet to have survived in the archaeological record. The greatest variety of meats would have been procured only for the lord and favoured members of his immediate household. Beef and bacon were staples for the whole household, with venison and mutton also available, but less abundant. The lower ranking, unfree, servants rarely had the opportunity to eat meat. Their basic staple diet was of maslin meal, oatmeal, peas and beans. Such servants explicitly had a feast of meat at Shrovetide, besides the feasts at Christmas and Easter (Rees 1924, 185).

Cattle

Cattle were an important element of the Welsh economy, as a source of meat, dairy produce and an exchangeable form of wealth. The skins were also prized for leather goods and clothing (Thomas 1975, 26). They were the basic unit of payment for a wide range of exactions: the death duty of unfree tenants was an ox (Davies 1987, 119). The *commorth* was a periodic tribute of cows rendered by the Welsh community (Rees 1924, 229). The *gwestfa* was a contribution of food for the local court, levied every winter and summer on all freemen. This included an ox in winter and a fat cow in summer (Rees 1924, 10–11).

In calculations of beasts, oxen are always enumer-ated separately, as they were of central importance to the agricultural economy. The owners of oxen were liable to services in kind on the demesne. Up to eight oxen would be yoked for ploughing, with several tenants contributing oxen to the plough team (Rees 1924, 159; Taylor 1975, 82; Rackham 1986, 167). These services in kind provided by the oxen were not merely agricultural duties, but also included haul-ing timber and building materials to the lord's castle (Rees 1924, 76). After the siege of Dryslwyn in 1287, 40 oxen were used to haul the trebuchet to Newcastle Emlyn (Carmarthenshire) (Griffiths 1994, 75).

The Welsh invested in cattle, rather than other livestock, when circumstances permitted. The confis-cation of the possessions of Llywelyn Bren in 1316 provides an indication of the relative numbers of beasts: 113 sheep, 71 goats, 84 pigs 469 cattle plus some oxen and a very few horses (Rees 1924, 218). Not only were cattle the principal animals present in the fields, hills and woodland margins of Wales in the 13th and 14th centuries, but there were large numbers of them. The Lord Rhys had access from the renders of his estates to 4000 cattle, which he gifted to the English king Henry II (Davies 1987, 156). If a beast was worth 3s 4d (Rees 1924, 80), this gift was the equivalent of 1000 marks or £666. It is unlikely that this action left Deheubarth depopulated of cattle, or the Lord Rhys impoverished.

Cattle could be brought to the castle from a wide range of places for a number of different reasons. In the Welsh Lordship period (1220s–87) they were present principally as a food render, although this could be from anywhere within the territories controlled by the lords of Dryslwyn. In the English Garrison period (1287–1405), cattle would have been purchased from market and could derive from anywhere in south and west Wales and the Marches. In a pastoral society with a long history of pillage and booty (Davies 1987, 157), cattle were an obvious source of movable wealth. In 1282 Rhys ap Maredudd drove off 3000 head of cattle when attempting to capture a rebel for Edward I and during his revolt in 1287, 200 head of cattle were plundered from Llandovery (Griffiths 1994, 69, 75).

Cattle bones were abundant in all phases of the castle's occupation (Section 10.2), emphasising the importance of cattle in the Welsh economy and beef in the diet of the castle's inhabitants. The preserved carcasses of beef found in the stores by the occupying English force may be indicated by the selective representation of body parts; there were comparatively few bones of the head, neck and feet as these had been removed and disposed of at the seasonal slaughter, salting and drying of the carcasses. The few head, neck and feet bones present probably derive from the small proportion of fresh beef cattle that had arrived on the hoof. Such fresh beef would have been appropriate when the full complement of the lord and his household was in residence, or the later constable was entertaining. Evidence for the importance of ruminant animals in the food prepared and consumed in the castle also comes from the pottery analysed for organic residues (Section 10.9). The most common finds were animal fats from sheep and deer, as well as cattle.

Some cattle would doubtless have been pastured all year round in the vicinity of Dryslwyn to provide fresh dairy produce for the inhabitants. The Welsh, unlike most contemporary societies, drank large quantities of fresh milk. The visit of Llywelyn ap Gruffudd and his Welsh retainers to the English court to pay homage to Edward I in 1277 stretched the capacity of the English victuallers to provide milk for them (Trow-Smith 1957, 103). The traces of milk fats found in a number of the potsherds, provides unambiguous evidence for dairying and the use of milk or secondary products such as cheese in the diet of the occupants of Dryslwyn Castle.

Local availability of cattle in the neighbourhood of Dryslwyn is likely to have varied seasonally due to the summer movement of livestock to hill pastures (*hafod*) from the valley farmstead (*hendre*) where they overwintered (Ryder 1983, 498). This system released the low land for hay meadow for winter fodder and, unwittingly, may have enhanced the fertility of the cows (Dahl and Hjort 1976, 34) and reduced mortality from parasite burdens. The fresh grass of the mountain pasture was converted into butter and cheese. This seasonality of mountain dairy cheese production continued into the 20th century (Minwel Tibbott 1995–96, 73). The cheese making season was from April to September in England (Trow-Smith 1957, 121). Dairy produce was demanded principally in the summer food renders; for example the summer *dawnbywd* was butter, cheese and bread (Rees 1924, 12). The rennet necessary for curdling the milk was obtained from a calf's stomach bag. Some calves would have to die to produce this necessary ingredient for cheesemaking. Whether calves were killed for this purpose or whether the natural infant mortality rate provided an adequate supply is unclear.

The high proportion of infant bones from calves indicates a high level of consumption of veal by the lord and his immediate entourage. Dryslwyn is not an isolated example of the presence of calf bones on Welsh sites. The broadly contemporary, but smaller, assemblage from Rhuddlan (Denbighshire) (Levitan 1994, 153), which lacks the quantity of high-status indicators seen at Dryslwyn, also has some evidence for young calves. This indicates that statements by historians such as Jenkins (2000, 268), 'calves were seldom slaughtered in medieval Wales', are simply inaccurate and demonstrate that normal animal husbandry practices were rarely recorded in texts. As Giraldus Cambrensis indicates (Thorpe 1978, 233) dairy produce was an important element in the diet at this time. The competing needs of calves and humans for a finite supply of milk would of itself suggest that a proportion of calves would need to be killed. A further necessity would have been the rennet for cheesemaking, obtained from the stomach bags of calves that had suckled but not eaten solid food.

Much of the beef consumed at Dryslwyn would have been in the form of salted beef. The account rolls of Alan de Plucknet, constable of Dryslwyn Castle (Rhys 1936, 37–63), give an insight into the provisions remaining in store when the castle was captured by the English and its subsequent victualling. These accounts concern the 'dead garnisture' or non-perishable foodstuffs kept in store. Amongst the goods in Dryslwyn which belonged to 'Res son of Mered' were 147 beasts and oxhides, which were subsequently sold by Alan de Plucknet and recorded in the account roll for 1287–89. A further 23 beasts 'from what was left of the stores of Res son of Mereduc' were sold and accounted for in the roll for 1289–90. These 'beasts' were in the stores, not on the hoof.

Pigs

Pigs thrive in woodland and both Welsh and Marcher lords held, directly or indirectly, a large number of pigs in order to exploit the resource of the extensive forests of Wales and the March. One Marcher lord is recorded as owning 1000 cattle, 2000 sheep and 'as many (swine) as they willed without number' (Davies 1978, 115). The pannage season, when the lord allowed tenants to loose their pigs into his forest to fatten them up on the acorns and beech mast, was generally confined to a period between September (at the earliest) and February (at the latest). The tenants pasturing swine in the forest of Glyncothi (Carmarthenshire) had to bring their pigs to the swine mote held at Dryslwyn Castle at the close of the pannage season. Here, a proportion of the swine was chosen by the lord's officials in payment for the pannage. This levy was usually proportional to the number of swine pastured per tenant. The pigs taken as pannage payment could be sold immediately or taken to market or killed for the castle larder (Rees 1924, 122–126). The accounts for Dryslwyn in 1289 record 'for 43 pigs , the proceeds of pannage, that were sold' (Rhys 1936, 45). The majority of the pork would have been salted or otherwise cured (Grigson 1970). Traditionally, only offal was consumed as fresh meat (Cobbett 1841), whilst rendered fat (white grease) was saved and used extensively for cooking and lubrication.

Whilst pigs could have been purchased throughout the year, some probably came in the form of renders at specific times; the *gwestfa,* and *dawnbwyds,* for example, could be paid in the form of three year old sows (Rees 1924, 11, 12). It is likely that a large proportion of the pork products consumed at Dryslwyn arrived on their own trotters via the swine mote. The transition from the Welsh system of renders in kind to the English system of payments in cash is clearly demonstrated in the surviving documents of the English administration. The first account roll of Alan de Plucknet (1287–89) records 'bacons. ... which belonged to the same Res, found and sold' and '43 pigs, the proceeds of the pannage, that were sold' (Rhys 1936, 39). In the second account roll of Alan de Plucknet, 1289–90, the record is only of '21s received for pannage' (Rhys 1936, 61). Walter de Pederton's accounts for 1298–1300 deal with the joint provisioning of Dryslwyn and Dinefwr (Carmarthenshire) Castles. In one year five pigs were still received from the pannage, but a further 41 were bought for the larder.

The high proportion of pig bones recovered from castle excavations probably reflects the bacon in the 'dead garnisture'. The large number of juveniles present at Dryslwyn and other sites indicates the popularity of spit roast piglet at this period, something which is also observable in the cookery books and illustrations of this period, such as the Luttrell Psalter.

Preserving meat

The preparation of beasts for the 'dead garnisture' is illuminated in the account of Walter de Pederton (Rhys 1936, 133): 46 pigs and 70 oxen and cows were bought for the larders of Dinefwr and Dryslwyn Castles and 2d a head for the cattle and ½d per pig was expended 'on the slaughtering and salting of the same animals and preparing them for the larder'. Further on (Rhys 1936, 149), Walter de Pederton's account records the purchase of firewood 'to dry the meat from the larder'. Later on the Prior of Carmarthen's account (Rhys 1936, 225) explicitly costs together the purchase of 41 oxen with 'the slaughtering, preparing and salting of the same in the larder, with the firewood bought to dry the aforesaid meat'. Still later, William de Rogate's account (Rhys 1936, 331) sums together '37 ox carcasses ... together with the salt and the pay of the butcher doing the larderwork this year'. From these accounts, the laying down of beef for the 'dead garnisture' was clearly an annual, seasonal event. Most

of the accounts are explicit that it is simultaneous with the slaughter of the pigs received from pannage, indicating a time in late autumn to early winter. The consistent recording together of the slaughtering and preparation for the larder of cattle and pigs, together with purchase of salt and firewood to dry the meat, suggests that both beef and pork were preserved in the same manner. Such events would also lead to distinct seasonality in the deposition of primary butchery debris, although no such deposits were detected at Dryslwyn.

Sheep and goats

In south Wales, under native rule, large-scale sheep farming appears to have been primarily a monastic enterprise (Rees 1924, 195). In 1212 the Crown gave a licence to the monks of Strata Florida (Ceredigion) to sell their wool overseas and by 1252 the monks of Margam (Neath Port Talbot) were selling their wool in London and Ghent (Turvey 2002, 187). Sheep do not thrive like cattle in the heavily wooded environment, which had been prevalent in much of Wales up to the 14th century (Davies 1987, 141). The ratio of sheep to cattle is illustrated by one late 13th-century tax return where the peasants had 1045 cattle but only 711 sheep (Davies 1987, 156). The wool from the indigenous sheep was not well regarded by merchants and was often exempt from export duties (Rees 1924, 197). The paucity and poor quality of the native wool is reflected in the garments worn: a thin cloak and shirt with bare legs and feet is described as the dress of both prince and pauper, with flea-infested blankets to sleep in (Davies 1987, 152). In contrast to the native Welsh, the lords of the March developed considerable sheep farming enterprises producing high-quality wool for the export market (Davies 1978, 116–117). During the 14th century, a combination of factors (for example, increased clearing of the waste, changes in demesne farming and manpower shortages after the plague) appear to have stimulated the growth of sheep farming.

Sheep were part of the food renders paid to the lords but were not demanded in the same number of head as cattle, reflecting the fewer numbers of sheep kept relative to cattle. The *gwestfa* specifies only one fat wether in summer, compared to an ox in winter and a fat cow in summer (Rees 1924, 11). Unlike sheep, goats thrive on browse. It is therefore somewhat surprising that there is infrequent mention of goats in the surviving sources. Goats are not as tolerant as sheep of wet weather and it is recognised that Wales was, and is, a region of high rainfall (Davies 1987, 142). The necessity to provide winter shelter may have been a limiting factor in the numbers of goats kept by peasants (Drury 1982, 23). The native Welsh certainly kept goats, as they feature in the heriot (death duty) payable to the lord (Rees 1924, 154). The Welsh lord Llywelyn Bren, had 71 goats compared to 113 sheep

(Rees 1924, 218) suggesting that dairy produce from the goats was valued. This may be a parallel with modern traditional pastoralists (Dahl and Hjort 1976, 200) who keep milking goats near the homestead when the milking cattle are on faraway pasture, such as the Welsh *hafod*. Small stock, such as goats, are also perceived by modern pastoralists as a means of rebuilding one's wealth (Dahl and Hjort 1976, 200). In native Welsh society, the possibility of losing one's cattle to a hostile raid was a very real fact of life.

The very fact that goats thrive on browse may be one reason for their comparative scarcity. Forest Law in England specifically excluded goats from the forest on the grounds that they drove the deer away (Drury 1982, 23). The constant trickle of people fined for infringing this Forest Law suggests that the products of the goat were worth the risks of being apprehended. Grazing of felled woodland by goats was identified as a significant factor in the retreat of the Welsh woodlands (Linnard 1982, 54).

Dryslwyn is unusual in having very good surviving evidence for the consumption of infant, milk-fed, lambs (Section 10.2). This is a clear indication of the occupation of the castle during the spring, when such young lambs would have been available. The association of spring lamb and the Easter feast is surely no coincidence. The mutton appears to have been mostly young and tender, from animals that had been wintered once, with only a few older mutton sheep represented. Prime quality meat appears to have been sourced for Dryslwyn rather than elderly culls from the wool flock. This may be seen as a further indication of the status of the lord of Dryslwyn and the role of foodstuffs in maintaining the prestige of the lord.

Sheep are conspicuously absent from the English account rolls for Dryslwyn. The only mention occurs in the first account roll of Alan De Plucknet, where a sum of money is recorded as received for 'the oats and lambs which used to be the fee of the constable' (Rhys 1936, 45). This would appear to be a native Welsh food render paid to the English and sold by them, the implication being that sheep meat was eaten as fresh, not preserved, meat and therefore would not appear in the accounts of the 'dead garnisture'. The establishment of Carmarthen as a staple town in 1326 (Owen 1989, 216) attests the increasing the increasing importance of wool and sheep rearing in Carmarthenshire in the 14th century.

Poultry

Eggs were used as a food resource in the medieval period and could be used to pay rent or other renders to the lord (Bennett 1937). However, the food allowances for the Sedgeford Harvesters in Norfolk included only 120 eggs in the large volume of food which supported 1443 man-days of harvesting work, suggesting that they were not commonly used as a food for the peasantry of the 13th century (Dyer 1994,

83) and therefore may have been more suitable for the lord's table.

Domestic poultry and eggs were the 'small change' of goods in kind paid as customary dues, although they appear not to have been used for this purpose in south and west Wales to the extent common in contemporary England (Rees 1924, 160–161). Hens and capons were most commonly requested; for example grazing dues in the forest of Cantref Selyf were paid in capons and hens (Linnard 1982, 41). Geese were of value also for their down and flight feathers, the latter being used for fletching arrows and quill pens (Section 9.9) (Heath 1971, 9). The first account roll (1287) of Alan de Plucknet explicitly records the purchase of 'thread, feathers and glue for repairing crossbows and quarrels' (Rhys 1936, 43). The fowls and geese of a person dying intestate were forfeited to the local officer, the *rhingyll* (Rees 1924, 9).

Rabbits

In the medieval period rabbits had yet to fully adapt to the wet British climate and needed cosseting in purpose-built warrens (Bailey 1988, 1). They were first introduced in the 12th and 13th centuries to the islands and coastal dunes of Wales. This coastal distribution was still prevalent into the 16th century in Glamorgan (Austin 1988b, 154). These coastal warrens, such as those at Pennard on the Gower, leave little archaeological trace, unlike the pillow mounds such as those at Bryn Cysegrfan which were in use by the 14th century and mark the start of the exploitation of the Welsh uplands for rabbits (Austin 1988b, 130–165) as well as sheep. The rabbit bones in the early phases of Dryslwyn may represent early coastal-reared rabbits, possibly a gift from the de Breos family on the Gower to Maredudd ap Rhys. Only later do rabbits become more commonly used for food, thus rabbit bones are only seen in deposits dated after 1300 at Oakhampton Castle (Devon) (Maltby 1982, 129).

Rabbit skins were valued as well as the meat. Capturing warren reared rabbits was not a pastime equivalent to hunting forest game; rather, it was a task that men with dogs and ferrets were hired to undertake (Rees 1924, 138–139). It is possible that rabbits became part of the 'small stock' which the treatise *Husbandry* indicates were the responsibility of the dairymaid (Oschinsky 1971, 425). Certainly, medieval illustrations, such as those in the Luttrell Psalter, depict women catching rabbits living in pillow mounds.

Horse

Literary sources suggest that a Welsh lord had both a stallion and a warhorse with individual grooms, all of whom were maintained by explicit customary dues (Rees 1924). These animals were one of the status symbols reinforcing the position of the lord. Horses were also working animals, although not usually yoked in the plough. The horse was the standard means of transport, whether of the warband or the traveller. In a region where topography and road conditions were unsuited to large wheeled vehicles, teams of packhorses, comprising between six and 30 animals, were reliable and efficient transporters of substantial volumes of goods, up to four hundredweights per animal (Moore-Colyer 1991, 126–127). An example from the English account roll of Walter de Pederton (1298–1300) records the hire of 36 horses at 2d each to convey 150 bushels of pilcorn from Carmarthen to Dryslwyn (Rhys 1936, 147). Horses were also used for draught; for example, the obligations of haulage of timber and building materials to the lord's castle could be undertaken by horses as well as, or instead of, oxen (Rees 1924, 76–77). Thomas (1968, 3) gives some numbers of livestock from rural north Wales which indicate that these communities had in the order of three horses (of all descriptions) to five oxen (excluding all other categories of cattle), the implication being that horses are directly comparable to oxen, being also beasts of burden, and that the bulk of heavy short-distance haulage was the remit of the ox, whilst the horse had a complementary, more wide-ranging, role.

There were many medieval names for kinds of horses (Hewitt 1983, 1), but such names are difficult to relate to the archaeological evidence. Faunal remains consistently show that medieval horses were small by modern standards with a withers height range of 12.2–15 hands (Rackham 1995, 22). The modern Welsh Section B and C ponies of up to 13.2 hands would be of comparable size to the general run of medieval horses. The animals at the 15 hands end of the range may be equated with the 'Great Horse' of the military and may not have been dissimilar to the modern Welsh cob of 14.2 hands (Clark 1995, 23–25). The Welsh lord's stallion and warhorse may have been of such a kind.

Horse bones are sparse finds on medieval sites. Horsemeat was not, in normal circumstances, a component of human diet. When a horse died, the hide could be salvaged and, possibly, the cannon bones removed for the manufacture of artefacts, but the carcass presented a problem in waste disposal (Rackham 1995, 20–21). Horse carcasses were sometimes fed to or scavenged by dogs, who are the most likely agents for the dispersal of horse bones on archaeological sites. Horse bones were rare at Dryslwyn, only seven bones in an assemblage of 7393 identified fragments. However, one bone had been chopped and two other bones had knife marks. These knife marks were probably associated with removing the lower hind leg in the hide, correlating with the record of the sale of hides from horses dead of the murrain (Section 10.2). Three bones had been gnawed by dogs. The organic residue found on sample D28 from a cooking pot has been determined to be the remains of horse fat (Section

10.9), although the Christian Church forbade the eating of horsemeat (Bonser 1963, 365; Simoons 1994) and there appears to be no literary evidence to support the consumption of horsemeat, other than as a famine or siege foodstuff. The balance of probability seems to suggest that horse bones, and possibly meat, probably stewed, were occasionally fed to the castle's dogs. This suggestion is enhanced by an entry in a medieval French hunting account (Cummins 2001, 257), which records the purchase of four carcasses of old, worn-out horses to feed several thin and ailing hounds. Other entries in the same account refer to broth and soup for the hounds. The preparation of cooked horsemeat for the dogs at Dryslwyn seems eminently feasible from both the animal bone and organic residue evidence, without invoking any human consumption of horsemeat, although human consumption remains entirely possible.

Game and fur animals

Hunting was a favourite pastime of both Welsh and English lords in Wales. One Welsh lord remarked that 'without the solace of hunting, it would be hard and tedious to stay at . . .' (Davies 1987, 145), whilst 'good hunting was one of the few reasons, short of war, which could persuade the English nobility to visit their lands in Wales' (Davies 1978, 120). For Welsh princes and lords the hunt also served a useful political purpose. The royal progress concurrent with the hunt facilitated the collection of the renders in kind owed to the court but, above all, the authority of the lord or prince was ensured, particularly in territories which had changed allegiance (Davies 1987, 63). The products of the chase were also seen as making a significant, if seasonal, contribution to the castle larder (Rees 1924, 110).

The free Welsh appear to have had hunting rights using traps and bows and arrows over the wastes, forests and commons. The Welsh laws indicate that the king and his retinue enjoyed a privileged period at the beginning of each hunting season, after which the community was free to enjoy the sport (Rees 1924, 109). There were a variety of further restrictions on hunting with hawk and hound, which varied depending on the type of land, the type of animal being hunted and the status of the hunter (Jenkins 2000).

In England, venison was particularly valued for household consumption at festivals or when guests were entertained, and was a gift whose importance should not be underestimated in a society where largess and patronage were crucial attributes of lordship (Birrell 1992, 113). This latter point is equally applicable to the native Welsh lords. Venison was not normally a commodity offered for sale, which also enhanced its status as a gift. The English hunting season was relatively short, from June to September for males and from November to February for females. Much venison was therefore salted to extend its availability and transported long distances, sometimes in barrels, to the current residence of the lord owning the deer: for example, venison from Cornwall was sent to the Duke of Cornwall in London in 1347 (Birrell 1992, 122). Conspicuous consumption of venison is also attested from a banquet given by the Bishop of Durham for King Richard II in London in 1387, where three tuns (barrels) of salt venison were procured in comparison with three fresh doe carcasses (Renfrow 1990, 335). The venison, in its medieval sense of 'vert and venison' (all game animals) (Linnard 1982, 30), brought to the larder at Dryslwyn could therefore have been provenanced from as wide an area as the cattle, and need not be representative of the game available in the immediate vicinity.

The Welsh laws also indicate that there were defined seasons for hunting specific game animals and in the value of skins from the fur-bearing animals (Thomas 1975, 25). The high values placed on some skins are a good indication of the extreme rarity of such animals as the beaver and marten whose pelts were worth 120 and 24 times the price of a sheep skin respectively (Veale 1966, 59). In comparison, it is worth noting that roebuck skins were of similar value to skins from domestic animals (Thomas 1975, 25). A necessary adjunct to both the hunter and the pastoralist were the tawyer and the tanner, working in furs and leathers. Fur and leather garments may have compensated for some of the deficiencies suggested for the indigenous woollen clothing, whilst also enhancing the status of the wearer (Veale 1966, 1–21). Fur was usually used to line woollen garments, although peasant women might own a leather jerkin lined with fur (Piponnier and Mane 1997, 24).

Thomas Charles-Edwards (2000, 336) has issued an informal challenge in his statement that 'since material wealth was relatively unimportant, an archaeology of the Welsh king's court would be in danger of missing almost everything of importance about it, unless it could find traces of *golwython*' and that 'inaccessible riches did not therefore prevent the household of a Welsh noble from imitating the courtliness of a royal *llys*'. *Golwyth* is glossed as a dish of food, often at the beginning of a feast, or translated as a portion of meat. It is closely associated with the term *anrheg*, a gift of food intended to honour the recipient, with the implication that it usually consisted of meat (Charles-Edwards *et al* 2000, 561–562, 566).

In this instance, the archaeology, in the shape of the bones of hunted game animals and birds, vividly illustrates the nature of the High Table dishes available to the lords of Dryslwyn. The quantity of venison and both quantity and diversity of game birds consumed at Dryslwyn (Section 10.2) are eloquent testimony to the richness of *golwython* available to the lords of Dryslwyn. Here is abundant and tangible evidence for the refuse derived from the courtly behaviour appropriate to the nobility of the period

and a significant manifestation of the honour of the lords of Dryslwyn and their perception of themselves as lords/princes of Deheubarth.

Dogs, as well as falcons and hawks, were essential for the procurement of both game animals and birds. The finds of dog faecal material (Section 10.7) are a reminder that the meat and bones at Dryslwyn were not obtained solely for human consumption. One dog bone exhibited knife marks indicative of dismembering (Section 10.2). Huntsmen were not sentimental about working dogs, the *Boke of St Albans* recommending for even the best hound that at nine years old 'have hym to the tanner'; such dog skins could then be made into jesses for the hawks (Cummins 2001, 29, 200).

Plant foods

Most peasants appear to have had small gardens in which they grew vegetables, herbs and fruits. The wealthy landowners had larger gardens, up to 2 acres in extent, with some nobles having 5–8 acre plots (Dyer 1994, 114), which invariably featured areas of orchard and even vineyard. Prices for a variety of crops in the late 13th century such as apples (4–8d per quarter), and beans (1s per quarter), compared to wheat (6s per quarter), show that cereals were the most valuable crop to grow (Dyer 1994, 127) and thus some peasants grew cereals and bought cheaper foods with the proceeds gained from selling part of their grain harvest, although there was probably considerable regional variation. Dried and stored vegetables are represented at Dryslwyn by the examples of pulses recovered from the charred and waterlogged seeds. The finds of undifferentiated peas/beans would have been a staple but more surprising and interesting were the finds of imported lentils in both Welsh and English phases.

Cereals

Of the range of cereals grown, wheat had the highest value, with rye and barley next and oats the lowest. Sometimes cereals were grown and harvested together, for example maslin (wheat and rye) and dredge (barley and oats) (Hammond 1993, 2). Large quantities of oats were grown, as these were used for feeding horses and cattle, as well as for human consumption. As a result, production levels do not reflect human diet. Wheat flour, which had been sieved, was used to bake the finest white bread, eaten by the richest. The brown or black breads (trencher bread) contained flour, often from a variety of cereals and even pulses, together with the bran, and were eaten by the peasants and household retainers. Oats and barley were also baked into flat cakes or used with vegetables, particularly peas and beans, to make pottages, broths and gruels. In addition to making bread, malted grain, especially barley, was used to brew ale. With a short shelf life, this was brewed fresh every week and formed the principal beverage for much of the population (Hammond 1993, 6). Other cereals could be used to brew ale although such brews are usually described as inferior. The monks of Bolton Priory (North Yorkshire) brewed their ale from oats (Hammond 1993, 28). Although there is evidence for growing different types of grain in every region of the British Isles, the drier weather conditions and lighter soils of the south and east favoured wheat production, the heavier soils, higher rainfall and shorter growing season of the north and west favoured growing oats.

Although modern descriptions of peasant diet frequently mention bread, it is clear from excavation evidence that few medieval peasant houses had ovens. Consequently bread may often have been a flat bread or cake baked on a stone or metal sheet, or baking may have been done communally, for example in the village oven at Corbridge (Northumberland).

Whilst the developing towns of Wales in the 13th and 14th century, such as Conwy and Cowbridge, have produced some limited botanical evidence of cereal cultivation (Caseldine 1990, 103) most of our ideas regarding cereal cultivation in medieval Wales derive from references in historic documents. Rees (1924, 216) suggests that 'oats were the main, and in many parts the only crop raised, although a little rye and even wheat are mentioned.' Mills are frequently mentioned and it appears that oats were grown extensively, even in upland areas, during this period. Welsh laws place specific importance on the kiln for drying oats, an essential step to allow their successful storage.

The importance of oats in the local economy was emphasised in the Tywi valley by the fact that the only tax or render, other than the *gwestfa*, was *dofraeth* (*hildovraeth*), an oat render, which all freemen were bound to pay to their lord as a measure of oats or oatmeal. This had evolved from the earlier renders to a lord for his horse and groom (serjeant rents or rent of extent). In the 14th century, the *dofraeth* for the commote of Is Cennen yielded 400 bushels of oats (Rees 1924, 227). Variants on this or similar dues or renders are seen over much of Wales. In the eastern March and elsewhere, oats and oatmeal were used, with coin and animals, as the forms of payment (Rees 1924, 228).

Oats were either the only or the principal cereal in almost all the deposits from Dryslwyn yielding plant remains (Section 10.5). Oats were principally ground into a meal from which oat cakes were made (*lagana* to Giraldus Cambrensis, although in more recent times known as *bara ceirch*). Traditionally, oatcakes were large and thin, baked on one side on a bakestone and then stood up to dry with the unbaked side towards the fire (Freeman 1981). This corresponds well with the 12th-century description by Giraldus Cambrensis 'Sometimes they serve the main dish on bread, rolled out large and thin, and baked fresh every day' (Thorpe

1978, 237). Freeman (1981) makes the point that the use of the word *bara* (bread) rather than *cacen* or *teisen* (cake), is indicative of the importance of oatcakes as a staple bread in Wales. Evidence of bakestones from Dryslwyn (Section 9.8) and Rhuddlan (Quinnell *et al* 1994, 173), provides corroborative archaeological evidence for this type of baking. The bakestones can be used directly for cooking or covered with an inverted metal or ceramic dish surrounded by hot ashes and used as an oven (Minwel Tibbott 1982, 23–26). This form of baking may explain the lack of evidence for ovens in the kitchen of the Inner Ward of Dryslwyn Castle.

Bread wheat was present from the earliest phase of the castle occupation, suggesting that wheaten bread was available for the lord and higher-ranking members of his entourage. Finds of barley were rare but slightly more common in the later deposits. There was no sign that any of the barley grains had germinated, so no evidence that the barley recovered had been malted and was thus intended for brewing, although this remains a possibility. Pearl barley is often used in soups and stews, such as Scotch broth, so the medieval pottage could also have included the hulled barley found. Alternatively, barley may have been made into bread in its own right, or mixed with other cereals for a mixed grain, or maslin, loaf. Barley bread was commonplace in Wales until the end of the 18th century, but, like the oatcakes, it was a flat, unleavened bread cooked on the bakestone. Freeman (1981) mentions in particular that these were used as plates for food, recalling the standard medieval use of bread trenchers. Rye grains were relatively common and, surprisingly, more abundant than those of barley. Whilst Wales may not have ideal conditions to grow rye, its use appears to have been widespread. Like barley, rye can be used either straight or as part of a maslin mix for breadmaking, where it has the property of keeping the bread from going stale (Brears 1998, 9–10).

Vegetables, fruits and herbs

All classes of society ate some vegetables; thus the king and his knights were expected to consume a meal including cauliflower and onions as part of the feudal dues of one family in Gascony (Prestwich 1988, 303). However, the volume of vegetables in the peasant diet, principally in the form of pottage, was much higher than that of the aristocracy. Principal vegetables grown were onions, peas, beans, leeks and cabbage, as well as some garlic and parsley. A 1390 recipe for a pottage of herbs indicates that numerous herbs, such as fennel, were also grown and used to flavour basic cereal and vegetable dishes (Hammond 1993, 43). Fruits, such apples, cherries, pears and a variety of berries, were also grown or collected from the wild. In the vicinity of large towns and cities, where there was a ready market for produce, a wider range of fruit, herbs and vegetables is recorded as being grown and offered for sale: these included basil, beet, borage, carrots, cucumber, fennel, grapes, hyssop, marjoram, medlars, mint, orach, plums, quinces, radishes, sage, sorrel, sweet chestnuts, turnips and walnuts (Dyer 1994, 125; Hammond 1993, 36 and 43). Seeds and pips derived principally from the archaeological excavation of cesspits indicate that parsnips and celery were also grown (Dyer 1994, 125) and fruits, such as bilberies, bramble fruits, damsons, gooseberries, hazelnuts, sloes, and strawberries, were also consumed (Hammond 1993, 101).

There is ample documentary evidence for the importation of spices into Britain by the 13th century. Household accounts of Edward I (Prestwich 1988, 159) record the use of ginger, pepper, galingale, saffron, caraway, cumin, as well as other imported luxuries, such as sugar, almonds, rice and fruit including oranges, lemons and pomegranates. These luxuries were imported into large ports such as London. Dried fruits including dates, figs and raisins were supplied by the royal fruiterer to the court of Edward I and archaeological occurrences of the seeds (stones) of such fruits from latrine deposits indicate that they were often eaten by the aristocracy. Other spices available by this date included cardamom, cumin and nutmeg (Hammond 1993, 11). Pepper was the most widespread and probably the cheapest spice used throughout the period of the 13th to 15th century, with a typical cost of 1s per pound. The level of trade was substantial, with ships coming into the port of London containing 2 tons of pepper, as part of mixed cargo, by the early 15th century (Hammond 1993, 11). Imported fruit was also becoming more readily available at this time. Even the monks at Winchester and the priests at Munden's Chantry (Hertfordshire) could eat dried figs and raisins.

Although the gardens of the aristocracy initially grew food for the lord's table and were worked as demesne lands in the 12th and 13th centuries, by the 15th century most had been rented out to tenants for income, whilst the lord bought his fruit and vegetables at the burgeoning urban markets. This enabled the lord to have access to a wider variety of fruit and vegetables. The extent to which the native Welsh cultivated fruit and vegetables remains unclear. The observation by Giraldus Cambrensis in 1188 that 'they do not have orchards or gardens, but if you give them fruit or garden produce, they are only too pleased to eat it' (Thorpe 1978, 252) may suggest a lack of cultivated vegetables and fruit in the diet, but the familiarity with vegetables and fruits is clearly present and probably indicates foraging and utilisation of wild vegetables, fruits and nuts. There is evidence from Usk (Monmouthshire) in the form of seeds of fruits such as apples and blackberries (Caseldine 1990, 103), to indicate that horticulture was supplying a variety of plant foods to the Welsh urban medieval population.

While most leafy vegetables are rarely represented in the archaeological record, documentary sources allude to the fundamental importance of these foods in the daily diet. Such foodstuffs are often associated with poverty and lean times; for example the discourse with Hunger in Langland's Piers Plowman (Wells 1938, 86–87). Organic residue analysis of pottery sherds from sites such as Raunds (Northamptonshire) has detected epicutical leaf waxes so providing evidence for the presence of leafy vegetables on other archaeological sites (Section 10.9). Members of the *Brassica* family were represented through seeds recovered from the Area F midden (Section 10.5). Radish was also represented in all the main Welsh phases. It was, therefore, surprising that none of the analysed sherds from Dryslwyn, from either the town or the castle, revealed any evidence to suggest the presence of leafy vegetables, such as cabbage and leeks (Section 10.9). The survival of other organic residues, including animals fats and fish oils, indicates that if leaf vegetables were cooked their epicuticle leaf waxes would have survived and been detected. Consequently, it appears either that few vegetables were present in the diet, or metal cauldrons were used for cooking many of the dishes, such as *cawl* (traditional Welsh leek and meat based stew/broth), which may have used vegetables.

The fruits from Dryslwyn fall into three broad categories. First are the fresh fruits available seasonally which need to be eaten fresh and do not keep well. Examples from Dryslwyn include sloe, probable cherry, plum or cherry, blackberry, elderberry, raspberry and crowberry. The second group comprises fresh fruit available seasonally that can be stored for a limited period, including apples, crab apples and pears. Lastly are the fruits that were generally imported as dried fruit and so might be consumed at any time but were often used in medieval cookery to ameliorate the meatless diet of fast days; examples include figs and grapes. Hazelnuts were common in Phases 1 and 2, early in the castle's Welsh occupation. Collected seasonally, they would have been stored and consumed throughout the year. The charcoal samples (Section 10.6) show that hazel was the second most common type of wood recovered from the site. Both as part of the forest and the local hedgerows, hazel was a well exploited natural resource.

Herbs were primarily grown in the small peasant gardens or collected from the wild. The waterlogged and carbonised samples from Dryslwyn preserved seeds from a number of different species. Ignoring a number of 'weed' herbs whose seeds were probably preserved as part of hay deposits, several specific examples of cultivated herbs and spices used for flavouring food were recovered. The seeds of mint and fennel were recovered from Phase 3 deposits whilst those of cumin were present in Phase 4 (Section 10.5). Cumin features in a Welsh poem of the 15th century, extolling the spices flavouring the food at Oswestry Castle (Shropshire) (Roberts 1982). It exemplifies the trade in spices from Asia to Welsh castles, such as Dryslwyn, in the mid 13th century.

Whilst herbs and spices were used for flavouring food, they also had medicinal uses, with mediciners often present in large households such as that of Rhys Gryg (Owen 2000, 117). The presence of hemlock, an example of a purely medicinal herb, as well as selfheal, hedge woundwort and marsh woundwort, whose vernacular names illustrate their past medical use, illustrates the presence of medicinal herbs within the castle.

Honey (and beeswax)

One commodity that is often considered invisible in the archaeological record, but is known from the documentary sources to have been highly prized, was wild honey, which was collected from the wastes and forests. This was indispensable for the production of mead. The honey and wax from wild bees was claimed as a prerogative of the lord, whilst tolls were exacted on the hives of the tenantry. The taking of wild honey could damage the timber to the extent that the practice was banned in the forest of Glyncothi (Rees 1924, 122).

Organic residue analysis detected beeswax residues in three of the 44 sherds analysed (Section 10.9). The beeswax could have been used to waterproof the containers, or may have been mixed with other animal fats to form candles. The mixture of beeswax and beef tallow seen in two samples from the Great Chamber G (Section 9.10) and in the pottery (Section 10.9) indicates an important non-culinary use of animal fat for lighting. The cheaper tallow appears to have augmented the more expensive beeswax. In one Welsh compensation payment a doctor was allowed 1d for tallow and 1d for a light every night (Owen 2000, 123). The beeswax may have been imported or recovered locally from wild bees' nests, which are normally found on the edges of woodlands. Since one sherd (D24), derives from a Phase 2d context, this activity dates from the second quarter of the 13th century.

The occurrence of beeswax in ceramics may derive from its separation from honey, the presence of which in the castle is attested by written references in 1289 (Rhys 1936, 51). Thus it appears likely that honey was the primary sweetening agent used in both the Welsh Lordship and English Garrison periods of occupation. It is also likely that if there was honey available, mead, the most valued and honorific beverage, may have been made and drunk (Charles-Edwards 2000, 328–333).

Drink

Although most of the urban and rural poor drank water, the quality depended on the source. Producing ale requires the boiling of the water, so killing the microbes and making ale safer to drink than water.

Records show that between 50 and 112 gallons of ale could be brewed from 2 quarters of barley, although around 90 gallons was normal. Estimates of 1 gallon of ale consumed per man per day in both aristocratic households and monasteries have been made (Hammond 1993, 72), though the Duke of Northumberland's accounts of 1512 suggest the more modest 3 pints. Although ale was a staple beverage, archaeological evidence for brewing on site was not found at Dryslwyn. The mentions of malt in the account rolls for the English occupation suggest that there was a brewhouse attached to the castle, but this has not yet been located.

Wine was produced in England, from at least the mid 11th century onwards, with substantial quantities generated by the 13th century; for example one vineyard at Ledbury (Herefordshire) produced 882 gallons of wine and 126 gallons of verjuice (sour grape juice) annually (Hammond 1993). Best ale cost 1½d per gallon in 1337 with sweet wine from Gascony at 6d per gallon in 1383 (Hammond 1993, 565), prices in 1419 rising from 3–4d for basic wine to 8d per gallon (Hammond 1993, 73). Whilst peasants drank ale and cider, further up the social scale wine consumption increased. During the mid 12th century, the amount of imported wine, especially from Gascony, rose considerably. By the 14th century, Hammond (1993, 14) suggests that records indicate that even the soldiers of the garrison of Dover Castle (Kent) were drinking up to 2 pints of wine per day, although this was probably consumed in a watered-down form.

Even in the absence of archaeological and historic evidence, it is likely that aristocratic households, such as that of Rhys ap Maredudd, would be drinking wine, probably imported from Gascony, throughout the late 13th century. There is a substantial amount of Saintonge pottery in the Welsh phases of occupation at Dryslwyn (Section 10.2), which is considered to be a by-product of the Bordeaux wine trade. The inference is that the tangible pottery reflects the intangible commodity of wine. It is likely that the lords of Dryslwyn imported and consumed wine from Gascony, probably via Bristol and Carmarthen, as did most of the castle-owning aristocracy of south and west Wales, a cultural habit undoubtedly influenced by their Anglo-Norman relatives and acquaintances. Wine was undoubtedly drunk by the constable and members of his household during the 14th century, where it is recorded in the 'dead garnisture'. It is first mentioned in the castle accounts of 1289, where the 11 casks recorded could derive either from the earlier Welsh Lordship or English Garrison period (Rhys 1936, 51).

Fish

Fish formed an important part of the diet, both as a principal food on fasting days (Fridays, Saturdays) and, in some households up to the 15th century, Wednesdays as well as during Lent (Hammond 1993, 18). It also had a significant role in feasting and display. Large specimens of fish such as pike, eels or bream often formed gifts; for example two bream and two tench given by the town of Hull to the officer in charge of the king's customs in 1464 (Dyer 1994, 109). Such fish were often consumed in large quantities during feasting. On 13 October 1257, Henry III celebrated St Edward's Day with a feast consuming 250 bream, 15,000 eels and 300 pike (Dyer 1994, 110). The importance of fish to feasting is evidenced by the fact that efforts were made to try to control the prices that fishmongers charged for pike, eels, salmon and lampreys during the celebrations at the coronation of Edward I (Prestwich 1988, 89).

Historical evidence of the availability and range of fish consumed in the 13th century is indicated by the siege of Rochester in 1264 where, since it occurred partially during Lent, the garrison is recorded as confined to eating mackerel, mullet, salmon and whiting. The range of fish available is further indicated by the species mentioned in the household accounts of Edward I: cod, eels, herring, lampreys, salmon and sturgeon (Prestwich 1988, 157). A similarly wide range of fish were served in aristocratic households of the 14th century: bream, eels, herrings, perch, pike, roach, salmon and tench, conger eel, hake, haddock, mackerel and saltfish (cod, hake, ling and whiting) (Dyer 1994, 106; Hammond 1993, 63). There was some regional variation in the supply of fresh fish; barbel, chub, dace, gudgeon, minnows, ruff and trout being consumed in households in the Chilterns; chub, dace, grayling and trout in Staffordshire (Dyer 1994, 106). There was also seasonal variation, the *Menagier de Paris* (1393) advising round sea fish in winter, flatfish in summer, mackerel in June, ray in September and October (Power 1928, 272–273).

If, as Dyer suggests, 1–2lbs of meat or fish was consumed every day by most members of aristocratic households of the 14th century (Dyer 1994, 102), there would have been a substantial and consistent demand for fish by this date. This demand helped to support a sizeable marine fishing industry and created a significant trade in fish which, in addition to fresh fish, supplied; smoked fish ('red' herrings), dried (stock) fish (usually cod), and salted fish (white fish such as herrings preserved by salting). The substantial level of demand led to importation of fish, presumably salted or dried, into London from the Baltic and into Bristol from Ireland and Iceland. Fresh marine and freshwater fish were available at inland markets, such as Coventry, Bicester, Oxford and Wantage since rapid transport systems had been established by the 14th century (Hammond 1993, 19).

Freshwater fish were primarily caught in rivers and streams using traps or weirs. Fishponds were created by monasteries, and later by aristocratic households of the 12th and 13th centuries, in order to ensure a

regular supply of fresh fish. Initially they contained a range of native species such as bream, perch or roach: carp, a species that did particularly well in fishponds was introduced in the 15th century. As markets supplying a wide variety of fresh fish had become widely established by the 15th century many aristocratic households moved away from self sufficiency, leasing fishponds to local entrepreneurs and purchasing their fish from local markets (Dyer 1994, 107).

Dyer (1994, 101) has suggested from documentary evidence that the price of fish was such that the aristocracy, town-dwellers and monasteries were the principal consumers of fish whilst the rural poor rarely ate it. This was particularly true for high-priced fish, such as tench and pike. However, the price of fish was very variable and, depending on the season and place, could be reasonably cheap; for example 6–9 herrings costing only 1d in London in 1382 (Hammond 1993, 27). Peasants, with access to a market, could consume modest amounts of cheap marine fish, such as salted herrings or dried cod. If they were catching or poaching fish from the local rivers, 'expensive' freshwater fish could occasionally be expected. Both would result in discarded fish bones characteristic of the type of fish consumed. This hypothesis has yet to be widely tested, since few medieval rural peasant sites with appropriate preservative deposits have yet been excavated.

Giraldus Cambrensis describes the Welsh in 1188 as fishing for salmon using lines from coracles (Thorpe 1978, 252). He identifies a number of different types of freshwater fish including eels, perch, pike, trout and tench, and a number of rivers such as the Teifi, Usk and the Wye which were regarded as rich in particular types of fish. This indicates that the 12th-century Welsh and Marcher populations utilised a range of readily-available fish from the rivers of Wales as part of their diet. The consumption of a range of fish is undoubtedly seen as a celebratory activity in 14th-century Wales, where the menu for a feast on St Stephen's Day in Usk included 460 herrings, 8 stockfish and 100 lampreys as well as salmon, tench, roach, eels and conger (Knight 1996 190).

Welsh law books indicate that the rights to fish were normally invested in the local lord; 'the king's villeins were not entitled to the fish of their streams and the king could legally make weirs on these streams to trap the fish' (Jenkins 2000, 255). Consequently, although freemen and villeins of Wales were familiar with fish and fishing, they would normally require permission or pay a toll for river fishing (Rees 1924, 198). This is further emphasised by specific records of dues received from fishing: in 1303–04 fishermen of Llechryd paying 16d for the right to fish with boats and nets in the River Teifi. In 1300–01 and 1356–57 Dryslwyn Castle derives income from the 'fishery', presumably the right to fish the River Twyi below the castle (Section 8.1). In contrast to the toll taken on freshwater fishing, the Welsh law books state that 'the fish of the sea were free for all to take' (Jenkins 2000, 255), which would indicate that there was no restriction upon marine fishing and presumably encouraged exploitation of this resource. The remains of fish traps, many dated by radiocarbon or dendrochronology to the 12th–13th centuries, have been recovered from the foreshores around Wales. In particular, evidence from Carmarthen Bay attests the presence of a substantial shoreline fishing industry in this period (Turner 2002b). From the textual and archaeological evidence, fishing in both freshwater and the sea appears to be an activity frequently undertaken in medieval Wales and thus fish was part of the native Welsh dietary tradition.

Dryslwyn produced one of the richest fish assemblages ever recorded for a medieval site in Britain (Section 10.3) with 35 different varieties of fish identified. The sieving of the exceptional deposits encountered in Area F contributed significantly both to the number of fish bones recovered and variety of species identified. It is apparent that freshwater, estuarine, inshore and deep-sea marine species were obtained.

Herring bones were the most numerous fish remains recovered. It is not possible to tell from the bones whether the herrings were fresh or preserved, since whole fish can be salted, pickled or smoked. However, it would be surprising if preserved herring did not form part of the stored provisions of the castle. Other fish present that may have been preserved by salting and drying are cod, haddock, hake and ling. These provisions are more likely to have been bought in and would have been suitable victuals for the more menial members of the household on fish days. The smaller quantities of bones from fish that are usually served fresh may, like the poultry and game bones, reflect provisions for the higher-ranking members of the household when the lord was in residence.

Shellfish

Shellfish, such as oysters, were extensively eaten in the medieval period, as indicated by the numerous shells recovered from many urban and aristocratic medieval sites, including Okehampton Castle (Devon) and Barnard Castle (Durham). Oysters and mussels were recorded as being available in many medieval fishmarkets and oysters, costing 4d per bushel in 1382, could be afforded by all but the peasantry (Hammond 1993, 47; Bond 1988). Commercial collection and trade in shellfish, such as cockles, mussels, oysters and winkles had begun at least as early as the 10th century (Hammond 1993, 22). Evidence of cultivation and harvesting of oysters has been derived from the oyster shells from Okehampton castle (Devon) (Higham *et al* 1982). The current lack of detailed evidence from other sites prevents us from knowing whether oysters were a widely farmed resource or if such regular harvesting was confined to the south-west of England. Other shellfish, such as cockles, mussels and whelks, although recovered from Kirkstall Abbey (Leeds), Castle Acre

Priory (Norfolk), Austin Friars, Leicester (Bond 1988), Barnard Castle (Durham) (Kenyon 1990, 180), Kings Langley (Hertfordshire) (Neal 1977), Lewes Castle (East Sussex) (Cartwright 1992a) and the town of Bedford (Steane and Foreman 1988), are less commonly noted on medieval sites. They were probably only eaten on a few occasions each year (Bond 1988). Many Welsh sites, including Valle Crucis Abbey (Denbighshire) and Criccieth Castle (Gwynedd), have not reported recovering any shells. Reasons include failure to report or recover shells in the excavation process, the use of shells for fertilizer and building work during the medieval period and the loss of shells due to poor preservation. In Wales oyster shells have been recovered from many medieval occupation sites such as Conwy and Hen Gwrt, Rhossili (Swansea). Loughor Castle (Swansea), like the English medieval sites, produced oyster plus a few cockle and mussel (Caseldine 1990, 108).

Oysters were the most numerous marine shells recovered. The oyster-fishing industry off the Gower at The Mumbles and Port Einon was productive into the mid 19th century (Freeman 1980, 33) and provides a possible source for the oysters found at Dryslwyn. While oyster shells were not numerous in the earlier phases of occupation, the largest shells were found in Phase 2, suggesting that commercial exploitation of oyster beds began in the second quarter of the 13th century. The other shellfish found at Dryslwyn, cockles, mussels and whelks, could also have been obtained from the same area, but, historically, the major cockle beds were in the sands of Carmarthen Bay at Laugharne (Carmarthenshire) and Llanstephan (Carmarthenshire) (Freeman 1980, 32).

10.2 ANIMAL AND BIRD BONES
by Louisa Gidney (based on data supplied by Patricia Collins)

This report presents a synopsis of the in-depth report by Gidney (2002) which contains the data on which the following discussion is based. A large assemblage of animal bone was collected by hand throughout the excavation process. The discovery of waterlogged deposits in Area F led to samples of these deposits being sieved, resulting in a diverse species count.

Previous work on aspects of this faunal assemblage include Gilchrist's (1987) report on waterlogged contexts from Area F, which formed the basis for the dietary evidence for the castle discussed by Caple (1990b, 52–54). Gidney (1994) reported on the whole assemblage from Area F, including the deposits already examined by Gilchrist. The bulk of the assemblage was studied by Collins (1995; 1996; 1997). The present work is not a summary of Collins', although this work is crucial and should be referred to by those interested in the analyses. Collins' data and the overall site phasing are used to discuss the trends apparent within the whole assemblage, particularly whether the evidence from the Welsh phases corresponds with the historical sources and whether the change to English administration is reflected in the faunal remains.

The historical sources mentioned in this section are fully discussed and referenced in Section 10.1 and so are not duplicated here. This discussion complements Section 10.1 by comparing the archaeological information with both site specific and general historical sources, and should be read in conjunction. The methodologies used by Gidney and Collins are complementary but not compatible, hence most of the analyses of the overall site phase assemblages have had to utilise the fragment counts of the fragments identified to species, excluding those assigned only to size category. Preservation of the animal bones was generally very good, with even bones from infant animals recovered in excellent condition. There was little evidence of post-depositional damage. The few rolled or weathered fragments seen were principally in topsoil contexts. The animal bones generally appear to have been deposited in fresh condition, with no sub-aerial weathering before burial.

Spatial distribution

In Phases 1 and 2, the whole castle household lived in the Inner Ward, with food preparation in the Kitchen I. Much culinary refuse would have been disposed of through the postern gate, although some was discarded in J. After the construction of the Great Chamber G, middens were created in O and F. Living quarters and food preparation were split between two wards. By Phase 4, accommodation included the Outer Ward, so the midden in F acquired waste solely generated by the residents of the Inner Ward: the lord, his family and guests.

The overall quantities of animal bones from each individual area are listed in Figure 10.1, irrespective of phase. This gives an impression of the diversity of species represented, as well as the crude numbers of identifiable bones. The richest areas for faunal remains are Areas G, H, I, J and O in the Inner Ward. The assemblages from the other wards, and the areas excavated in the township, were sparse. Data from these small areas are included in subsequent general analyses by phase from the whole site. Area F was not

													Area										
	A	B	C	D	E	G	H	I	J	K	L	M	O	P	T	U	VA	VB	WA	X	Y	Z
Cattle	5	49	6	13	21	787	732	519	816	190	265	114	2070	138	27	3	40	1	2	27	41	29
Sheep/Goat	3	32		3	13	428	250	279	457	124	175	36	652	79	11	4	1			12	18	11
Sheep	2	10	6	8	3	173	121	113	214	53	85	13	302	37	1	4			1	2	12	1
Goat							1	3	16	2	1		4									2
Pig	9	25	6	10	23	908	646	622	595	205	137	95	1231	181	5	1	7		1	14	14	6
Dog	3	1			1	5	9	1	8	4	5		5	2	2		4		1			4
Cat						18	2			4	1		3									
Horse						3	1				2	1	5	3	1						2	4
Red Deer				2		52	53	16	25	10	19		62	4						1		1
Roe Deer		1		2		111	46	70	7	16	12	3	80	11	1					2	2	2
Fallow Deer			1								1		3									
Deer						4	7	4	1		2	1	5	1							1	
Boar													1									
Hare		3				65	21	18	9	10	18		33	5			2				4	1
Rabbit		1	1			1	61	12	4	25	7		4	1	1			3	1		1	
Fox	1	1									2		19			1						
Badger							2						1									
Squirrel						1	2	1														
Pine Marten							1						2									
Polecat											1											
Ferret							2															
Stoat							1															
Hedgehog														1		1						
Seal													1									
C/RD		1	1	1	1	95	64	20	33	24	35	4	40	21	2					2	2	
H/C	1					42	40	1	5	8	13			2								
S/G/R	2	1	1		6	157	68	43	19	39	48	4	76	37					1			2
D/S/G/R		1			1	30	9	9	4	5	4		7	5								
Totals	26	126	22	35	73	2880	2139	1731	2213	719	833	271	4607	527	52	15	52	4	7	60	97	63

FIGURE 10.1

Bone fragment counts for the mammal species present by area (excluding Area F)

	Phase									
	1a	**1b**	**2b**	**2c**	**2d**	**3a**	**3b**	**4a**	**4b**	**4c**
Cattle	25	24	14	32	117	2	222	73	182	1
Sheep/Goat	71	6	10	25	70	1	119	20	41	1
Sheep	1			1	2					
Goat	1						1			
Pig	18	9	12	58	159	2	155	33	64	2
Dog		1		1			9	1	3	
Cat							2	2		
Horse								1		
Red Deer				1	3		19	2	8	
Roe Deer	1	1		2	36		51	10	20	1
Fallow Deer										
Deer							1			
Boar										
Hare				2	3		12	2	3	
Rabbit	1							1		
Fox									1	
Badger										
Squirrel										
Pine Marten										
Seal										
L. Ung.	6	5	5	13	12		25	15	10	
S. Ung.	36	1	1	7	6		22	8	7	1
Totals	160	47	43	141	408	5	638	168	339	6

FIGURE 10.2

Bone fragment counts for the mammal species present in Area F, by phase

recorded in a manner compatible to the rest of the site, so the results are presented separately in Figure 10.2.

Figure 10.3 uses the numbers of identified larger mammal bones as a rough guide to the concentrations of faunal detritus within the areas and phases of the Inner Ward. Some general trends are apparent. Little faunal debris was recovered from Areas B, C, D and E. Area F produced abundant identifiable fragments. These counts are not directly comparable with those for the other areas but do demonstrate peaks of deposition in Phases 1a, 2d, 3b and 4b. Area G accumulated faunal debris among the rubble of the levelling deposits beneath floors from Phases 1 to 4 of the Welsh occupation, with a substantial build up in Phase 4c, followed by reduced dumping in Phases 5 and 6 of the English occupation. The abnormal conditions during the siege may be reflected in the rich deposits of faunal remains from Areas G and H. The latter is certainly related to infilling of the tower, earlier deposits here had been removed in Phase 4a.

	PHASE																			
	1a	**1b**	**2a**	**2b**	**2c**	**2d**	**3a**	**3b**	**3c**	**4a**	**4b**	**4c**	**4d**	**5a**	**5b**	**5c**	**5d**	**6b**	**6c**	**6d**
AREA																				
B		8					21	9		19	1	9	34	2		1	4		8	9
C														1		8			1	13
D	2											1					2		1	28
E	1			10				12				14					4			3
F	160	47		43	141	408	5	638		168	339	6		4		8				1
G	10	266	15	228	122	232	194	2		167		1354	12			81	31		27	67
H	13									510		1487							19	
I		9		464	48	94	172			908				20						
J	67	420	1	166		310				776				123	223					83
K	1		202			63								33	77	1		2	197	61
L		75		16				36				12		353		63			134	141
M				206		4														
O	153			301			126	715		1385		92	331	10	505	9	175		5	603
P	5			14		71	87	38		203	37	4			32		16			12

FIGURE 10.3

Total numbers of identified larger mammal bone fragments, by phase and area

Bones were deposited in the kitchen and yard, Areas I and J, during the kitchen's use in Phase 2. During the redevelopment of this area in Phase 4a, bones indicate that kitchen midden debris, was used to raise the floor level. Apart from the construction Phase 2a, few bones were discarded in the Hall K/L until it was remodelled during the English Phase 5. Area M, interpreted as a prison, only produced animal bones in number in Phase 2c, suggesting the incorporation of midden material in the construction deposits. The Area O courtyard was possibly used for livestock lairage in Phase 2b. The peak of animal bones in this phase may reflect a combination of stable and kitchen middens in one place, while in Phase 3a this changed to dumps of builders' detritus and midden. Area O continued to be the repository of faunal debris in the English occupation Phases 5 and 6. The peak of bones in Area P was in Phase 4a, another association of building construction work and refuse dumping.

Cattle-size bones are indicative of obtrusive waste disposal. Bird bones are much smaller and may therefore be metaphorically 'swept under the carpet' in a way that is not possible with larger bones. The same general trends may be observed in Figure 10.4 for the bird bones as were described for the mammal bones in Figure 10.3. Bird bones, however, are remarkably abundant. While this obviously has implications for status and diet, it does also suggest that the smaller bird bones were less obtrusive and may have accumulated in proportionally greater numbers than the larger mammal bones.

Species: the exploitation of mammals

Fragment counts for all the species present are listed by phase in Figure 10.2 for Area F and Figure 10.5 for the remainder of the site. Bones of the domestic species (cattle, sheep/goat and pig) predominate.

Hunted animals (red deer, roe deer and hare) are consistently present, suggesting that these provided a lesser but regular food supply. Also present in small numbers are the domestic companion animals (dog, cat and horse) and a range of wild, mostly fur-bearing, animals. Figure 10.6 indicates the chronological variation in the proportions of the ungulate bones deposited. Cattle bones occur at a consistent level (39% or 40%) in all phases. This may suggest that the provision and consumption of beef remained at a constant level per capita throughout, and was not influenced by historic events.

The sheep/goat bones start with a peak of 32% in Phase 1, drop to 19% in Phases 3a–d and rise again to 33% in Phase 6a–d. The variation in the proportion of sheep/goat is directly mirrored by the pig bones. Pig fragments in Phase 1a/b contribute 26% of the ungulate bones, peak at 40%, equivalent to the cattle, in Phase 3a–d and decline to 24% in Phase 6a–d. Interestingly, the species proportions in Phase 1a–b, the earliest Welsh occupation, mirror the pattern in Phase 6a–d, the latest English occupation.

Red deer bones are regularly present as 1% of the ungulate bones in Phases 1a–b to 4a–b. There is a small increase to 3% in Phase 4c–d, the first period of the English occupation, with a decline to 1% in Phase 6a–d. Possibly the English constable enjoyed the pursuit, and consumption, of noble quarry as much, if not more, than his Welsh predecessors. Roe deer remains are marginally more abundant than those of red deer in Phases 2a–d, 4a–b and 6a–d.

Two contemporary sites are included in Figure 10.6 for comparison. Phase 6 for Launceston Castle in Cornwall is dated to the late 13th century (Albarella and Davies 1994; 2006). Launceston was built and occupied by Richard, Earl of Cornwall and younger brother of Henry III, until his death in 1272. Period V for Barnard Castle in Co. Durham is dated 1230–92,

									PHASE											
	1a	1b	2a	2b	2c	2d	3a	3b	3c	4a	4b	4c	4d	5a	5b	5c	5d	6b	6c	6d
AREA																				
B		2					6	14		12	2	18	18				6		32	2
C																10				20
D	10											2								56
E																				
F	1	3		1	9	20	9	225		16	150	50		53		3				4
G	2	66		40	164	122	48			30		386	8			62	10		96	80
H	2									92		290							18	
I		4		120	8	16	72			418				24						
J	8	48		34	40					76				28		28				56
K	2		44				30							62	92				88	16
L	2		22	2						10		2		228		50			124	74
M				20		2														
O	16			190		26	100			536		2	144	2	236	2	72		8	176
P				4	8	8	12			66	4	4			26	4				

FIGURE 10.4

Total numbers of identified bird bone fragments, by phase and area

PHASE

	1a	1b	Totals	2a	2b	2c	2d	Totals	3a	3b	3c	3d	Totals	4a	4b	4c	4d	Totals
Cattle	109	250	359	98	479	147	200	924	181	326		20	527	1423	14	987	212	2636
Sheep/Goat	35	172	207	26	170	59	118	373	77	84	1	6	168	627	6	380	74	1087
Sheep	4	73	77	13	91	33	44	181	36	52		1	89	287		158	26	471
Goat	2	1	3		5	1	3	9					0	8			1	9
Pig	80	148	228	90	331	111	247	779	257	275		3	535	1188	7	952	72	2219
Dog		2	2	1	3			4	4			1	5	6	1	8	4	19
Cat				4				4	4	1			5			2		2
Horse		1	1		2	1	2	5		1		2	3	2	1	2	2	7
Red Deer	4	5	9	4	8		8	20	4	6			10	49		89	11	149
Roe Deer	1	7	8	8	18	10	25	61	16	1		1	18	121	1	73	13	208
Fallow Deer								0					0	1				1
Deer		1	1		5	1		6					0	5		9	2	16
Boar								0					0	1				1
Hare	2	11	13	4	6	7	13	30	23	8		3	34	31		36	7	74
Rabbit	5		5	2	5		2	9			1		1	13		14		27
Fox					3	2		5	1				1				6	6
Badger								0					0	3				3
Squirrel					1		1	2					0			2		2
Pine Marten					1			1					0			1		1
Stoat																1		1
Polecat																		
Ferret																		
Hedgehog																		
Seal								0					0				1	1
C/RD	3	10	13	13	12	10	19	54	18	1		1	20	63	4	95	10	172
H/C		1	1	8	8	4	4	24	4	1			5	24		44		68
S/G/R	7	17	24	19	31	6	16	72	33	9	1		43	85	4	113	11	213
D/S/G/R		5	5	3	4		5	12	8	2			10	16		20		
Totals	252	704	956	293	1183	392	707	2575	666	767	3	38	1474	3953	38	2986	452	7393

PHASE

	5a	5b	5c	5d	Totals	6b	6c	6d	Totals	7a	7b	7c	7d	Totals
Cattle	191	216	138	122	667		117	424	541	12	21	26	8	108004
Sheep/Goat	101	157	52	57	367		54	238	292	6	12	20	8	74106
Sheep	37	66	17	25	145		29	124	153	4	8	6	4	35442
Goat			1	2	3		1	4	5					0
Pig	134	111	133	49	427	2	112	222	336	5	10	20	8	69273
Dog	5	1	2	6	14		1	5	6		1	1		3222
Cat	1		2	7	10		3	4	7					0
Horse				1	1		2	2	4	1				1611
Red Deer	14	10	5	4	33		3	10	13		1	1		3222
Roe Deer	4	15	8	2	29		7	26	33		1	2		4833
Fallow Deer		1	1	1	3				0					0
Deer	2				2				0			1		1611
Boar					0				0					0
Hare	6	4	2	2	14		13	5	18	2	1			4833
Rabbit	1			4	5		5	20	25	1	1	45	2	78939
Fox			6		6			3	3	1				1611
Badger					0				0					0
Squirrel					0				0					0
Pine Marten					0				0					0
Stoat														
Polecat					0			1	1					0
Ferret					0				0			2		3220
Hedgehog					0			1	1	1				1610
Seal					0				0					0
					0				0					0
C/RD	23	6	12	2	43		15	19	34			2		3220
H/C	4		1	1	6		5	3	8					0
S/G/R	27	20	18	7	72		25	35	60	1	2	4	1	12880
D/S/G/R	4	1	2		7			4	4					0
Totals	554	614	394	292	1854	2	392	1150	1544					

FIGURE 10.5

Bone fragment counts for the mammal species present by phase (excluding Area F)

	PHASE							Barnard Castle	Launceston Castle
	1a–b	2a–d	3a–d	4a–b	4c–d	5a–d	6a–d	Period V	Phase 6
Cattle	359	924	527	1437	1199	667	541	959	397
	40%	39%	39%	39%	39%	40%	39%	18%	29%
Sheep/Goat	287	563	257	928	639	515	450	302	500
	32%	24%	19%	25%	21%	31%	33%	6%	36%
Pig	228	779	535	1195	1024	427	336	2108	463
	26%	33%	40%	32%	34%	25%	24%	39%	33%
Red Deer	9	20	10	49	100	33	13	1600	16
	1%	1%	1%	1%	3%	2%	1%	30%	1%
Roe Deer	8	61	18	122	86	29	33	381	13
	1%	3%	1%	3%	3%	2%	2%	7%	1%
Totals	891	2347	1347	3731	3048	1671	1373	5350	1389

FIGURE 10.6

Proportion of ungulates from bone fragment counts by phase (excluding Area F)

when the castle was in the ownership of the Baliol family (Jones *et al* 1985). Both sites are therefore comparable in date and status to the floruit of Dryslwyn. Considerable differences are apparent. Neither of the English sites has the high proportion of cattle bones seen at Dryslwyn. Sheep are surprisingly scarce at Barnard Castle but are the most abundant remains at Launceston. Pig remains are the most commonly identified fragments from Barnard Castle and occur with virtually equal frequency to sheep at Launceston. Phase 3a–d at Dryslwyn has a comparable level of pig fragments to Period V at Barnard Castle, while Phases 2a–d and 4a–d at Dryslwyn have an equivalent proportion of pig to Phase 6 at Launceston. Red deer were strikingly abundant at Barnard Castle, being second only to the pig remains, while roe deer bones were more numerous than those of sheep. Launceston has the token 1% red deer and roe deer bones seen for most phases at Dryslwyn. It would appear that each castle exploited the faunal population most suited to its local environment.

Staple meat animals

Cattle

The abundance of cattle remains (Figures 10.5 and 10.6) contrasts with both Barnard Castle and Launceston Castle, and corroborates the documentary and historical sources for the importance of cattle to the Welsh economy. Horn cores and frontal bones were consistently under-represented in all phases, so it is impossible to assess whether primarily horned or polled types were utilised. Until the 18th century there were many local races of cattle in Wales, with those in the south of the country being of more dairy type (Hall and Clutton-Brock 1989, 38–40). The general type of medieval cattle at Dryslwyn may be envisaged from the herd of white park cattle at Dinefwr (Carmarthenshire), the senior residence of the Rhys family, reputed to have been there for over 700 years. Unlike other

herds of emparked white cattle in Britain, the Dinefwr herd was always domestic, supplying plough oxen until 1871 and milch cows until 1951 (Whitehead 1953, 84–91).

Phase 3b in Area O produced a grouping of bones from one 'neonatal' animal, with an age at death estimated from the toothwear by Collins of 1–8 months. There were knife marks on two of the bones and gnawing on a third, which suggests the discard of bones from a veal carcass, possibly cooked whole as a spit roast.

Only 11 complete metapodials were found. These give an estimated average withers height of 1.04m with a range of 0.99m to 1.10m, using the factors given by Zalkin (1960, 126) where the sex of the animal is not known. The cattle were therefore small by modern standards but similar in height to the range seen in the Dexter. The metapodials are sexually dimorphic in cattle. The distribution of the distal breadth measurements indicated a bimodal distribution with a preponderance of smaller females to larger males. This is to be expected if surplus male calves were consumed as veal.

Bones with pathological or other abnormalities were uncommon given the size of the assemblage. Most frequent was degeneration of the hip joint, with 20 acetabula affected and 18 proximal femora. Collins identified 11 of the acetabula as female. Regular articles in the modern farming press demonstrate that lameness is the most common reason for culling dairy cows.

Skeletal distribution

The bones from Phases 1a–b show very selective representation of the carcass with few fragments from the head, neck and extremities of the feet. However, metapodials occur at similar levels of frequency to the meat bearing limb bones. There are more fragments of humerus than any other element and bone fragments from the forequarter are more numerous than those of the hindquarter. This pattern is unlikely to result from purely taphonomic processes and suggests some preferential consumption, and subsequent disposal of, forequarters of beef compared to hindquarters. The sparse representation of the extremities could suggest the provision of ready-dressed carcasses, sides or quarters of beef. The relative abundance of the metapodials militates against this proposal and may rather indicate the usual disposal of the missing extremities outside the confines of the original castle.

Phases 2a–d also show a very selective pattern but, in contrast to Phase 1a–b, the most numerous element is the femur and there is better representation of the bones of the hindquarter rather than the forequarter. Bones of the head, neck and toes are again sparse. The metapodials are present but are less numerous than the meat bearing upper limb bones. This fundamental pattern is apparent for the remaining phases. There is no radical difference between the Welsh Phases 2a–d to 4a–b and the English Phases 4c–d to 6c–d. The consistent paucity of bones from the head, neck and toes does suggest that these parts were disposed of elsewhere, together with a proportion of the metapodials, which are consistently less well represented than the other limb bones. The surviving documentary evidence lists the supply of live cattle, which were butchered in the castle, and of dressed carcasses. The latter would arrive without head and lower leg/toe bones and therefore explain, in part, the poorer representation of these body parts. This suggests that the English garrison maintained the practices of their Welsh predecessors.

Differential disposal of cattle elements is documented for Barnard Castle. Horn cores contributed only 1% of the cattle bones from the Main Area, comparable to the Inner Ward at Dryslwyn. However the proportion of horn cores rose to 18% of the cattle bones from the Town Ward and 68% from the Ramparts. It is suggested that horn working activity was centred in the Town Ward, which received supplies from the beasts slaughtered in the Main Area and deposited its refuse over the ramparts (Jones *et al* 1985, 8–9). A similar scenario may be envisaged for Dryslwyn, with some of the poorly represented cattle elements deposited outside the castle area.

Analysis of age structure

Canid gnawing has almost certainly reduced the epiphysial evidence for younger animals. Nonetheless there was consistently high representation in the 'new-born' category in all phases. Collins defines 'new born' as animals dying within a few weeks of birth. In practice these could be deliberate culls rather than the normal proportion of neonatal deaths (Dahl and Hjort 1976, 38) and therefore not indicative of parturition on site. By the 19th century the taste for very young 'bobby' veal was remembered as a former epicurean delicacy but had gone from England and Scotland,

instead slaughter was at 8–10 weeks old (Beeton 1861, 402–404). Abnormally high levels of infant calf deaths are generally associated with dairy production. Given the known Welsh predilection for fresh milk and dairy produce (Section 10.1), this explanation seems reasonable. All phases have a few unfused bones from slightly older calves. An occasional fatted calf may have been prepared for special occasions. The major cull is apparent among the bones that fuse at less than four years old, where unfused diaphyses and epiphyses and fusing epiphyses far outnumber the fused ends in all phases. These bones represent prime beef carcasses. The males could possibly have worked one year in the yoke or the females calved once. This pattern does confirm the documentary evidence that the best animals were requisitioned for the provisioning of castles. Older animals are indicated by the fused epiphyses in the group fusing after four years old. Some cheaper beef from old milch cows or oxen may have been provided for more menial members of the household, or these may have been all that some of the peasantry could provide for their renders.

There are no obvious differences in the age structure of the cattle supplied during the English tenure of the castle, compared to the Welsh. This may in part reflect the known longevity of the beef in the 'dead garnisture' taken over by the English and continuity in the sources of supply. This abundance of infant calves is in stark contrast to the finds from Barnard Castle, where the epiphysial evidence suggested that the majority of the cattle were killed after the age of four years (Jones *et al* 1985, 13). This appears to be a further indication that the English garrison maintained the Welsh provender.

It proved impossible to reconcile the cattle tooth wear recording system used by Collins with Grant's (1982) system. For Area F only, the Mandibular Wear Stage (MWS) data show a striking peak of very young animals at MWS 0. These jaws had deciduous premolar 4 barely in wear and can derive from calves aged, at the most, weeks old at death. There are two jaws at MWS 18 and 29 which indicate animals with molar 2 and molar 3 coming into wear and therefore aged over one and over two years respectively. Three jaws at MWS 40–42 are from aged animals. Comparison with jaws of Dexter cows of known age in the author's reference collection suggests these were over 10 years old at death. These jaws indicate cull draught or breeding stock. Collins identified a further 72 mandibles from which comparable MWS could have been determined. A similar abundance of infant calves is apparent from the data for the rest of the site (Figure 10.7), although breakage has caused under-representation of mandibles with the full adult tooth row for MWS.

Calf's heads were not considered an inferior dish. A 15th-century illustration of a butcher's stall, reproduced by Redon (*et al* 1998), has only four calf's heads on the table. The dish retained its popularity into the 19th century (Beeton 1861). This initial cull of bobby

Teeth present	MWS equivalent	No. of jaws	% in category
Deciduous premolar 4 only	MWS 0–3	56	77%
Molar 1 only	MWS 6 onwards	4	6%
Molar 1 & Molar 2	MWS c13–20s	2	3%
Molar 1–Molar 3	MWS late 20s on	10	14%

FIGURE 10.7

Tooth wear data for cattle (excluding Area F)

veal calves would have liberated the dams for milking. Some indication of the potential milk yield from such cows is given by the last cow milked at Dinefwr, who gave 690 gallons over a single lactation period. The Dinefwr cows were reputed to have very high butter fat but were not a deep milking strain (Whitehead 1953, 90).

The tooth wear indicates a limited cull of immature beasts and a continuing cull of aged animals which were probably no longer suitable for draught or breeding. The last Dinefwr plough ox, killed in 1871, was aged about 14 years and an 'aged' cow was present in the herd in 1951 (Whitehead 1953, 86 and after 88). Such mature beef could be used for the highly spiced stewed beef dishes attested in medieval cookery, for example *The forme of cury* recipes 306 and 307 (Pegge 1780), consistent with the status of the Dryslwyn household.

The mandibles from Barnard Castle (Jones *et al* 1985, fig 11.1) have a few infants present at MWS 0 but the first major cull is apparent at MWS 31–38 with molar 3 in wear, from animals aged in excess of about two years old. However, the peak cull occurs at MWS 40–50, especially MWS 45 with 13 examples, and continues beyond MWS 50. By analogy with the author's own reference collection of Dexter cattle, the MWS above 40 are from cattle aged in their teens or older.

The tooth wear data corroborate the epiphysial evidence for a different pattern of cattle exploitation between Dryslwyn and Barnard Castle, with a striking emphasis on the consumption of calves in Wales. Not until the 15th-century deposits at Launceston Castle was an increase in veal age cattle observed, where it forms part of a nation-wide phenomenon (Albarella and Davis 1994, 24–25; 2006).

Sheep and goat

Collins demonstrated the presence of goat remains but in negligible numbers compared to those of sheep and the joint category sheep/goat. Indeed, goat is absent from Phases 3a–d. Goat was identified at Launceston Castle but was not separated from sheep/goat at Barnard Castle.

Complete bones were scarce, the whole site produced only five metacarpals, seven metatarsals, six radii and one tibia. Using the factors of Teichert

(Driesch and Boessneck 1974, 339), these indicate an average height of 52cm with a range of 49cm to 58cm. Six metacarpals from period 6 at Launceston Castle (Albarella and Davis 1994, table 25) indicate an average height of 55cm with a range of 49cm to 57cm. Similarly, 12 metapodials from Exeter for the period 1200–1300 (Maltby 1979, table 79) suggest an average height of 54cm with a range of 48cm to 57cm. The south-western English sheep and the Welsh sheep were of comparable stature. The small sample of nine metatarsals from Barnard Castle (Jones *et al* 1985, table 32) suggests, however, the northern English sheep were slightly larger, with an average height of 56cm and a range of 51cm to 65cm.

The distal tibia was chosen for metrical analysis as it is a robust element that survives well. The measurements of the distal end showed a very close distribution that is indicative of a single population. The distal tibia breadth has been used by Maltby (1979, 49) to demonstrate a gradual increase in size through time. At Exeter, 31% of the medieval sheep/goat tibiae had a distal breadth of 25mm or greater, in comparison Dryslwyn has 28%. Regional, rather than temporal, variation is demonstrated by the sheep from period 6 at Launceston Castle which were considerably more gracile with only 6% in this size range, while those from Phase V at Barnard Castle were most robust with 56%.

Within the Inner Ward, two partial sheep bodies were deposited in Phase 6d. That from Area L was almost complete with the feet absent, suggesting that the body had been skinned. The other, from Area J, was less complete, which is suggestive of a carcass dismembered for consumption, despite the absence of cut marks on the remaining elements. Whole spit roast carcasses would not exhibit any butchery marks of dismemberment and the majority of the meat could be sliced off leaving the main skeletal elements in articulation.

The demolition rubble of Phase 6d in Area Y attracted the burial of an adult female sheep together with an infant lamb, suggesting one of the inevitable casualties of lambing time. This suggests that some in-lamb ewes were brought here for lambing after the demolition of the castle. The topsoil in Area K produced the remains of three recent sheep bodies.

Congenital and pathological abnormalities were infrequent among the sheep bones. The most common conditions observed by Collins were oral, particularly ante-mortem loss of premolar 2. Six limb bones exhibited various exostoses. Today, oral problems and lameness are major reasons for culling sheep.

Skeletal distribution

Like the cattle, the representation of sheep/goat elements show consistently low proportions of horn cores, neck vertebrae and phalanges, indicative of removal for use elsewhere. The major limb bones, particularly tibia, radius and humerus, besides meta-podials and mandible, are well represented, in contrast to the neck vertebrae, tarsals and phalanges. This pattern may partly reflect patterns of survival and recovery, rather than initial deposition. The limb bones include the metapodials, the lower, meatless, leg bones. It would seem sensible for the sheep to have walked up the hill to the castle. The English Phases 5 and 6 show very similar patterns but the preponderance of particularly robust elements suggests a decline in survival and recovery compared to the earlier phases.

Sheep meat, whether lamb or mutton, is normally consumed fresh, not preserved by salting and drying like beef and bacon. The frequency of the sheep bones found may not be affected in the same way by seasonal episodes of slaughter for storage and consequent disposal of primary butchery waste, such as heads and feet. Nonetheless there is consistently low representation of these body parts. Given that cattle and pigs are known to have been slaughtered within the castle precincts, it seems likely that most, if not all, sheep meat was procured on the hoof and butchered to order. The interpretation of animal lairage in Phase 2a is of relevance to this concept. Medieval recipe books make it very clear that the cook also acted as slaughterman for poultry and smaller livestock, such as kid (Hieatt 1988, 94), and expected to be able to select the principal ingredient alive for guaranteed freshness. Toes and heads with horns may have left the Inner Ward attached to sheepskins for the fellmonger (Serjeantson 1989). The consistently greater frequency of mandible fragments, compared to other parts of the head and neck, may indicate that the tongue was removed attached to the mandibles. As previously noted, sheep's tongues were a delicacy fit for the lord's hawks.

Analysis of age structure

Like the cattle, the sheep/goat remains show consistently high representation in the 'new born' category in all phases. This suggests seasonality of consumption. Calves can be born at any time of year but sheep have a much more restricted period of reproduction in the spring, centring on April. It seems improbable that sheep were brought to the Inner Ward for lambing, so these bones are unlikely to indicate natural levels of mortality. Even if the 'new born' category encompasses animals several weeks old, such animals would not be available for about nine months of the year. Baby lamb was particularly associated with the feasting at Easter (Redon *et al* 1998, 6) after the rigours of the long Lenten fast. Such baby lamb survived as a luxury into the early years of the 20th century. The meat was white and the fat exceedingly delicate (Spry 1956, 553). A dish fit for the lords of Dryslwyn. Like the calves, the deliberate cull of infant lambs would liberate the dams for milking, as depicted in the Luttrell Psalter

(Backhouse 2000, 30). Older lambs are indicated in all phases by unfused or fusing epiphysial ends in the grouping that fuse by one year old but in no phase do they approach the number of bones in the 'new born' category.

If most surplus lambs were culled as infants, there would be few spare to kill at weaning as fat lambs off grass. A second substantial cull in all phases is attested by the unfused and fusing epiphysial ends in the group that fuse by two years. These bones probably indicate shearlings, overwintered once, shorn once and at maximum body weight for minimum input (Jewell *et al* 1974). This is widely recognised as the optimum time to slaughter sheep of primitive type. The third major cull is evidenced by the paucity of bones with fused epiphysial ends in the group fusing in the third and fourth years. Those bones with the ends in the process of fusing represent prime muttons, from which two or three wool clips would also have been obtained. The fused bones indicate that a very small proportion of the sheep supplied appear to have been adults in excess of 3 to 4 years old, probably culls from the breeding flock. The English administration is not reflected in any dislocation in the slaughter pattern of the sheep. Presumably the Welsh flockmasters continued their standard practices of flock management and the English received the proceeds thereof, a producer rather than consumer led system.

The MWS for Dryslwyn show very clear patterning that is complementary to the epiphysial data for preferred slaughter patterns. Three distinct peaks of almost equal numbers of mandibles were observed, suggesting culls in similar numbers of three preferred age groups. The first third of the cull is of lambs at MWS 0–11. The majority are new born infants at MWS 0–3 with little or no wear on deciduous premolar 4, although a small proportion at MWS 7–11 survived long enough for molar 1 to begin erupting at about three months of age. These would have been luxury milk fed lamb. The second peak cull is of animals with molar 2 erupting and coming into wear at MWS 15–25, at over a year old. These animals would have yielded one wool clip but are less likely to have bred. The third cull is of adult animals aged from two years old, with molar 3 erupting and wearing down at MWS 29–44. Besides two wool clips, any females in this category could have bred lambs at least once. There are few mandibles with extensive tooth wear in excess of MWS 36, only 12% of the total, indicating that prime, not aged, mutton was supplied. While the epiphysial and tooth data are in close agreement for the age structure of the cull population, the MWS data are more precise in suggesting that, overall, there was an almost equal division of supply between the three age groups identified.

There is a distinct contrast with Barnard Castle where the majority of sheep appear to have been killed aged over four years as culls from a wool oriented production system (Jones *et al* 1985, 13), with all the

303

16 sheep/goat jaws between MWS 30–40. Similarly, Launceston Castle lacked very young sheep and appeared to be largely supplied with mutton from animals aged about 2–6 years old (Albarella and Davis 1994, 25).

Pig

The abundance of pig bones is unusual by contemporary urban English standards, where 15% pig bones by fragment count is average (Gidney 1991, 23), although, as seen from Figure 10.6, other English castles also have a preponderance of pig remains. Albarella and Davies (1994, 15; 2006) discuss this phenomenon and show that 58% of the castles in their study have in excess of 20% pig bones. This may relate to the need for castles to have well provisioned stores for the victualling of the resident garrison, as well as the lord's household. As previously noted, beef and bacon formed the mainstay of the 'dead garnisture'.

Within Wales, an unusually high proportion of pig remains was also observed in the 5th–7th century occupation at Dinas Powys (Vale of Glamorgan) (Gilchrist 1988, 57). This may suggest either the suitability of the Welsh forests for pig raising or a regional taste for pork products. There was no indication of wild pig at Dinas Powys, rather the preferred slaughter of young animals was taken to indicate domestic stock.

Both Collins and Gidney assume that the pig bones derive from domestic specimens, Collins identified only one bone from Phase 4a as wild boar. The literary evidence indicates that the wild boar enjoyed the same status in the hunt as the red deer stag and hare (Rooney 1993, 3). The hunting of 'noble quarry' was an exhibition of status, however, not designed to fill the larder.

Foetal or neonatal piglets were the most commonly found partial skeletons, which is an interesting contrast to the general epiphysial evidence, discussed below, with least evidence for infant piglets compared to calves and lambs. Area I, Phase 2b, produced parts of two piglets, with further parts of two piglets in Phase 2d and at least three piglets in Phase 4a. The incomplete nature of these tiny bodies and their proximity to the kitchen hearth suggests these are culinary waste rather than natural mortalities. The Luttrell Psalter clearly depicts the roasting and portioning of sucking pig (Backhouse 2000, 12–14). Into the 19th century, sucking pig was recommended to be eaten at less than three weeks old (Beeton 1861, 397), which coincides with Collins definition of 'new born' as animals dying within a few weeks of birth. The adjacent Area J produced bones from at least five piglets in Phase 5a, suggesting the English occupants also relished sucking pig. One further piglet was recovered from Area L, Phase 6d.

Abnormal and diseased bones were infrequent with only five oral defects and 22 limb bones with various exostoses.

The life expectancy of the pigs was not great, hence comparatively few fused epiphysial ends and consequently few metrical data were recorded. The distal humerus is one of the first epiphyses to fuse. Measurements of the distal trochlea produced a disappointingly small sample with a narrow range of sizes. The two groupings that were observed may simply be a product of small sample size. Phases II–V at Barnard Castle produced a comparable number of bones covering a broadly similar size range to those from Dryslwyn but with a few smaller examples (Jones et al 1985, fig 15).

Skeletal distribution

The pig fragments for Phase 1a–b show an interesting peak of femur fragments. This element has late fusing epiphyses, so it is particularly vulnerable to canid gnawing and decay. The femur is the bone within the meatiest part of the ham and can be removed to facilitate the cure; if left in, the meat may taint near the bone (Grigson 1970, 184, 199). The excessive saltiness of bones from well salted and long stored hams and bacon may have deterred dogs from chewing them. The other meat bearing bones of the fore and hind limb are represented in similar proportions. As has been seen for both cattle and sheep, bones of the head, neck and extremities are also sparse for pig, with the exception of the mandible. A change in the pattern of representation is apparent for Phases 2a–d, where fragments of humerus equal those of femur. Metapodials are more abundant, suggesting the discard of trotters. Phases 3a–d show the same dual peak of humerus and femur fragments but much depressed frequencies for all other body parts compared to Phases 2a–d, suggesting a general decline in the proportion of bones per carcass deposited in the archaeological record. More probably the high numbers of humerus and femur fragments indicate the supply of salted joints containing only these bones, in addition to the whole carcasses indicated by the fairly even representation of all the other elements. The dual peak of humerus and femur is again seen in Phase 4a–b, with higher frequencies of the other major limb bones than was seen for Phase 3a–d. A change is apparent in Phase 4c–d, where peak representation is of tibia, followed by femur and humerus. Mandible fragments are relatively more abundant than in any earlier phase. A reversal of previous trends is seen for Phase 5a–d with a predominance of humerus fragments. The peak of tibia and femur fragments seen in Phase 4c–d is still visible but dwarfed by the abundance of humerus. This may suggest some change in carcass utilisation during the English occupation by a garrison of soldiers and no resident lord, together with his household, requiring the provision of the choicest viands. The final phase of English occupation (Phase 6c–d) shows a return to the dual peak of humerus and femur seen earlier for the Welsh Phases 2–4. All the meat bearing limb bones are comparatively well represented, and also the mandible and metapodials.

The patterns of skeletal element frequency for the pigs contrasts with that observed for the castle at Barnard Castle, where bones of the skull and mandible were most abundant (Jones *et al* 1985, 7). In part this may reflect differences in recording method, many more parts of the skull were identified for Barnard Castle than for Dryslwyn.

Analysis of age structure

The pig slaughter pattern is dissimilar to that described for cattle and sheep. Bones of 'new born' piglets are present but in proportionally far fewer numbers than the comparable calves and lambs. As Collins noted, this is in direct contrast to the fecundity of these species. Sucking pig would not appear to have received the same culinary treatment as sucking lamb and bobby veal. Unfused epiphyses from animals older than 'new born' are instead numerous, suggesting a significant cull of weaned first year animals as prime porkers with the later fusing epiphysial ends indicating that a small proportion of pigs survived into their second/third year. These may indicate cull breeding stock. Epiphysial evidence for older animals is absent or minimal in all phases. Given the documentary evidence for renders of three year old sows and the importance of bacon in the provisioning of the castle (Section 10.1), more evidence might have been expected of pigs carried to greater age and weight for bacon. The slaughter of bacon pigs at the close of the pannage season seems to be indicated by the fused elements from animals over about a year old, and the unfused elements from animals less than about two years old.

Some similarity with the slaughter pattern for the Barnard Castle pigs is apparent, where the majority had been killed aged less than about two and a half years old (Jones *et al* 1985, 14). The MWS tooth wear data are strikingly abundant, especially when compared to the equivalent data from Barnard Castle (Jones *et al* 1985, fig 11.3) where pig was the main food animal. The MWS show a clear emphasis on juvenile animals. Infant piglets at MWS 0–3 are more abundant than was suggested by the epiphysial data. This may reflect better recovery of the larger mandible than the tiny, delicate limb bones. Weaners with molar 1 coming into wear at about four to six months old are indicated by the peak of jaws at MWS 6–9, equivalent to the epiphysial evidence for young animals older than 'newborn'. Culling continued at a lower level at MWS 10–14 then peaks again with the emergence of molar 2 shown by the jaws at MWS 15–20, animals aged from the second half of their first year into their second year. Lesser, but still substantial, numbers of pig were killed from MWS 21–35. These have molar 3 coming into wear from animals aged from mid second year onwards. These jaws will include the three year old sows stipulated for renders, with the jaws at MWS 40 and 46 probably from even older animals.

The MWS data suggest that the Dryslwyn pigs were killed at rather younger ages, the majority up to MWS 20, compared to the Barnard Castle pigs where the peak cull begins at MWS 20.

Butchery

The butcher and cook had a significant impact on the fragmentation of the bones deposited. Standard instructions for dealing with meat in the *Forme of cury* (Warner 1791) are 'hewe hem to gobettes' or 'smyte hem to pecys', indicating a robust approach to the dismemberment of meat. This was necessary in a society without the fork, which therefore ate bite-sized chunks with the fingers from a communal dish, or mess (Henisch 1976, 175–176). The extraction of bone marrow and bone grease was probably also standard practice. The Anglo-Saxon method: 'beat the bones with an iron axe, and seethe and skim off the grease' (Cockayne 1866, 15) would result in severe bone fragmentation, compatible with that seen at Dryslwyn. Bone marrow was an essential ingredient of a wide range of medieval dishes and was also enjoyed in its own right by both humans and dogs (Henisch 1976, 126–127). The breaking of defleshed bones for marrow extraction has been a standard culinary practice, as distinct from chopping bones during the butchering of a carcass. For example shattering the pig jaw below the molars exposes the largest marrow content of the jaw, still used as an ingredient of Dutch pea soup (van Wijngaarden-Bakker 1990, 171). Similarly, ox cheek soup enjoyed long popularity in Britain with one recipe commencing 'first break the bones of an ox cheek' (Raffald 1782, 5).

Collins (1995; 1996; 1997) recorded that butchery marks were less frequent than those of gnawing but were sufficiently frequent, up to 22% in certain areas and periods, to be consistent with human butchery and domestic waste as being the principal source of the bone discarded in the Inner Ward. No obvious alternative explanation is apparent for the quantity of faunal remains recovered from the densely occupied but not easily accessible Inner Ward! Collins studied the butchery marks in detail, separating chop and knife marks, and comparing the results with Binford's (1981) observations between butchery for dismembering, filleting and skinning. Collins found virtually no marks indicative of Binford's criteria for skinning, although cut marks not matching Binford's observations were also recorded. Collins consistently found that on the pig, cow and sheep bones there were more marks indicative of dismembering than of filleting. Evidence for chopping was significantly higher on the cattle bones than on those of sheep and pig. The bones of the two latter species produced slightly more evidence of filleting than those of cattle. Collins suggests that these differences represent different approaches to preparing the carcasses in both primary and secondary butchery, based not only on the differing sizes of the species, but possibly in response to particular kitchen requirements. This latter point is particularly valid in the light of the extant account rolls which detail the number of salt beef and bacon carcasses held in store. Such salt meat will have been treated differently in its initial processes of preservation, known to have been undertaken within the castle precincts, and would require a different cooking method to fresh meat.

Companion animals

Dog

Dog bones were sparsely distributed. Phase 1b in Area J and Phase 4a in Area F produced groupings of dog bones that appear to derive from separate redeposited corpses. Both were juvenile animals with some unfused epiphyses. Only one of the dog bones, from Phase 4c, was sufficiently complete or mature to be measured, from which a height of 55cm is estimated using the factor of Harcourt (1974, 154). A single dog bone exhibited signs of butchery, identified by Collins as knife marks indicative of dismembering.

Dogs do not appear to have been eaten in Britain in historical times except in times of famine. Simoons (1994, 200–252) rehearses the evidence for and against the consumption of dogflesh. Deceased dogs could be fed to their kennel mates (Wilson and Edwards 1993), and dog fat has been utilised as a pomade for the hair (Gidney 1996, 8). The use of dog skins, particularly from natural mortalities, is well documented (Thomson 1981, 171).

The dog bones are not assumed to represent human food waste but indicate general redeposition during the complex phases of activity. The presence of dogs in all phases is abundantly demonstrated by the gnaw marks on bones of other species.

The scale of hunting suggested by the quantity of deer and hare bones would require a pack of hounds. By the 14th century there were specialised breeds for different aspects of the chase (Longrigg 1977, 27–30).

Dog bones were present in small numbers throughout the medieval occupation at Launceston Castle, where a large degree of variation in size was noted (Albarella and Davis 1994, 14), and also at Barnard Castle, where some particularly large bones were noted (Jones et al 1985, 4). Comparable evidence was not recovered from Dryslwyn.

Canid gnawing

Gnawing by dogs has been a major taphonomic process modifying this assemblage. Collins recorded levels of carnivore gnawing ranging from 25% to 54% of the identified fragments, depending on area and phase. The results from Area F are not directly comparable, but canid gnawing was consistently observed throughout the deposits. The proportion of identified fragments with gnaw marks severely underestimates the impact of dog gnawing, which had rendered large numbers of fragments unidentifiable. Area F produced many small elements, such as carpals of sheep/pig/roe deer size, which had passed through the canine gut. Their surfaces had been etched by the digestive acids and could no longer be identified to species. Collins noted that a significant proportion of the sheep/goat/roe deer astragali appeared to have been digested by dogs. Dogs were not only being fed on bones but defecating within the Inner Ward (Section 10.7). The impact of dogs on this assemblage is likely to have seriously distorted the representation of smaller species, for example birds, whose bones could be eaten whole. Only two fowl and one woodcock bones were seen with gnaw marks from Area F. A small, terrier- sized, dog can render pig bones unidentifiable in a short space of time (Stallibrass 1990, 157–159). Dogs also preferentially attack the unfused ends of bones, thereby destroying the evidence for immature animals.

Collins suggests that dogs were scavenging bones from the open middens but also comments that the loss of vulnerable softer and later fusing skeletal elements is not as great as anticipated given the high incidence of canid gnawing. An alternative explanation may be that dogs were kennelled, or otherwise confined, where they were given certain bones as part of their diet (Henisch 1976, 127). Surviving medieval illustrations often depict the presence of both the hound and the lap dog in the hall at meal times, for example the New Year feast of the Duc de Berry (Pognon 1979, 17), who doubtless cleaned up any unconsidered morsels. Chewed bones on the floor would eventually be swept up and deposited on the middens. The gnawed bones and faeces from kennelled hounds could also subsequently be deposited on the middens together with the kitchen and table waste, to which none of the dogs may have been given access. The absence of weathered bone is of relevance. If dogs had free access to the middens and were able to roam at will within the Inner Ward, more finds of weathered fragments which had been distributed by dogs and subsequently abandoned would be anticipated.

Cat

Cat bones were overall slightly less abundant than those of dog. Since the deposits were mainly receiving domestic food debris, it is not surprising that cat is not well represented. These bones could be redeposited from the disposal of cats used for their skins, suggested by the knife marks noted on two metatarsals by Collins, or kept as household animals for vermin control. There remains a possibility that some of these bones may derive from wild cats hunted for their skins. The wild cat did not become extinct in Wales until 1880 (Easterbee 1991, 434).

Domestic cat bones are common in urban deposits in Leicester from the 12th century onwards (Gidney

1991, 21), but are sparse throughout the occupation of both Launceston Castle and Barnard Castle. This may reflect the general status of castles, whose owners could afford to wear more prestigious furs than cat (Veale 1966, 4).

Horse

Horse bones are present in all phases but in extremely low numbers. Horse is extremely unlikely to have been part of the diet of the human inhabitants, given the known taboo (Simoons 1994). These few bones are, therefore, unlikely to be representative of the number and variety of horses known, from the historical sources, to have been utilised.

The small enclosed space of Area F produced only seven horse bones in total. The rational for the introduction of horse bones to the Inner Ward is indicated by three of these bones, which had been gnawed by dogs, while a further bone had repeated chop marks. Horse flesh on the bone may have been provender for dogs. From the enclosed position of Area F, it seems unlikely that these bones represent the scavenging by dogs of a buried horse carcass.

Phase 4a in Area J produced the articulated bones of two horse hind feet, with knife marks on the calcaneum and astragalus. Although discarded unused, these bones may have been procured for craft work. For example horse metapodials were frequently used for bone skates. One of these metatarsals was the only horse bone found from which an estimate of withers height could be made, using the factor given in Driesch and Boessneck (1974). This appears to have been quite a large animal, in the order of 1.5m or about 15 hands high. This is about the stature of a modern Welsh Cob and Clark's (1995, 23–24) interpretation of the size of medieval horse bred for military use.

A recent, probably 20th-century, horse burial was excavated in Area H.

The accounts of Alan de Plucknet in 1287 refer to the selling of 'hides of mares and foals of the stud dead of murrain' (Phillpotts 2001c). This indicates that horses were skinned, so giving rise to cutmarks on bones and disassociated foot bones. That such hides had a commercial value suggests that this was a common practice in 13th-century Wales. Although horses were often the prized possessions of Welsh nobility (Davies and Jones 1997), once dead they were a resource to be exploited whether for hides, as dog bones or, as the occurrence of horse fat could suggest (Section 10.9), for tallow and grease.

Game animals

Red deer

Too few red deer bones were present to analyse by phase. Both Collins and Gidney noted that the bones

of the hindquarter were generally better represented than those of the forequarter, also that the feet are well represented but not the head. The limited data from Area F suggested that the majority of the red deer were adult, with fused epiphysial ends.

The documentary evidence for salting venison, means that the presence of deer bones cannot be used as a reliable guide to the seasonality of the hunt. The red deer bones may indicate some gifts, probably of venison quarters, as well as whole hunted carcasses. The former option would still explain the good representation of metapodials, as on a deer carcass these may be left on the joint rather than removed with the skin. The condition of the hoof gives an indication of the age of the animal and therefore the best method of cooking the joint (Gore 1976, 143).

The hunting of red deer was a sport of the nobility which 'was a stylised and complex procedure which involved considerable outlay and must usually have cost much more to stage than the value of the meat it yielded' (Rooney 1993, 2).

Roe deer

Roe deer fragments were more numerous than those of red deer, but not approaching the abundance of the domestic species. Bones of both head and feet were consistently found, indicating that entire carcasses were brought to the castle, unlike the larger red deer. The extremities of roe deer are valued for culinary purposes in their own right, cooked similarly to a sheep's head (McNeill 1974, 184).

The majority of the roe deer bones from Area F were from adult animals with fused epiphyses and full adult dentition. Collins' examination of the tooth wear data from the remaining areas indicated a higher proportion of sub adults with an estimated age at death of between one and two and a half years. This pattern is consistent with exploitation of younger males, which, having been driven out of the adult male territories, congregate in more marginal and exposed areas where they are more vulnerable to predation (Legge and Rowley-Conwy 1988, 42).

Red deer stags were always hunted individually. Roe deer could be hunted in a deer drive: 'in this, as many deer as possible were flushed out from the forest and driven past hunters waiting at their appointed stations who used bows and arrows as well as hounds to bring down the deer' (Rooney 1993, 4). Such a difference in hunting technique could explain the greater abundance of roe deer bones compared to those of red deer.

Fallow Deer

Only four fallow deer bones were found in total, one from the late Welsh occupation in Phase 4a and the other three from the English occupation in Phase 5. These few bones seem more likely to represent gifts of venison.

Fallow deer are believed to have been a Norman introduction to England (Chapman and Chapman 1975), where they were emparked for the purposes of the chase. It is therefore not surprising that fallow deer is absent from the earlier Welsh phases. Written references to a park at Dryslwyn in the 14th century (Section 8.1) could refer to a deerpark that could have held fallow deer. Fallow deer bones were only found in number at Barnard Castle in the 14th century and later phases (Jones *et al* 1985, 3), while at Launceston Castle fallow deer bones outnumber those of both red and roe deer in the late 13th century Phase 6 (Albarella and Davies 1994; 2006).

Hare

Hare bones were present in all phases, making a small but consistent contribution to the table. Hare bones outnumber those of red deer in Phases 1–3 and 6, though of course the meat yield is far less. Hare was classified as 'noble quarry', having the same status to hunt as the red deer stag (Rooney 1993, 3).

Phase 2b in Area I produced the bones of a hare's left hind foot in articulation. This is most likely to be kitchen debris but a hare's left hind foot has traditionally been considered a good luck charm. A partial skeleton was recovered from a surface deposit in Area U, probably a recent natural mortality. Cut marks indicative of culinary use were seen on various elements by Collins. Very few limb bones with unfused epiphysial ends were seen. Older hares are more suitable for jugging than roasting, of relevance to the organic residues from such vessel types. The low proportion of immature animals suggests that human predation on the hare population was not severe (Tapper 1991, 160).

Rabbit

Rabbit bones were far less numerous than those of hare in Phases 1–5 but slightly outnumber hare in the English Phase 6. Rabbit bones were abundant in the surface deposits, including a virtually complete skeleton in Area K. Some rabbit bones are probably recent intrusions. A cut mark on a stratified bone does indicate genuine mediaeval culinary waste. Phase 6d in Area Y produced a mixture of bones from at least nine, mostly juvenile, rabbits. Knife marks on one bone indicate a human agency for this collection.

Lever (1977, 65–66) suggests that rabbits were introduced to Britain in the 12th century but did not become widespread until the mid 13th century. The early occurrence of rabbit in Phase 1 may indicate the procurement of a luxury food. When first introduced, the rabbit found the damp British climate inhospitable and required careful rearing inside specially created warrens (Bailey 1988, 1–2). Rabbit meat was a rare and highly prized foodstuff (Bailey 1988, 1)

commensurate with the status of the lords of Dryslwyn. Since rabbits were captured by employees in warrens, the meat did not have quite the same status as the wild hare hunted by the lord.

Fur-bearing animals

Fox

Fox bones are present in small numbers from Phase 2 onwards. Collins noted the presence of both gnaw marks and butchery marks indicative of skinning. Fox fur was generally worn by the middle social classes of medieval society (Piponnier and Mane 1997, 24). Fox hunting was not such a prestigious sport as deer and hare hunting but, into the 16th century, was resorted to when other game was not available (Longrigg 1977, 52–53). The presence of fox in the recent deposits of Phase 7 may suggest the presence of a fox earth after the site was abandoned. Collins observed that some of the fox bones could possibly be later intrusions.

Badger

Only three badger bones were recovered from the whole excavation, all from Phase 4a. The rarity of badger bones suggests this was not perceived as human food but may have been procured for its skin. Badger bristles have been used for specialised items, for example shaving brushes.

Squirrel

Two squirrel bones were present in each of Phases 2 and 4. These almost certainly represent pelts. Squirrel fur was highly prized for garments and had a range of technical names, such as vair and minever (Veale 1966). The greyer winter coat of the red squirrel was the most valued and the pelt was skinned down the back to leave the pale belly fur with a darker border, minever.

Pine marten

This species was represented by single bones from Phases 2b and 4c, both phases with abundant deposition of faunal waste, suggesting intensive human activity. Given the value placed on marten skins in the Welsh laws, it seems most likely that these bones were brought onto the site in a body for the pelt to be removed. The pine marten still exists in North Wales but was formerly widespread throughout mainland Britain, exploiting a wide variety of habitats (Velander 1991, 367–376).

Polecat and ferret

Only one polecat or ferret bone was found in a stratified context in Phase 6d. Two further bones were

308

recovered from surface deposits. Wild polecat rather than domestic ferret could be represented, as Wales is the last area of Britain where the wild polecat is still widely distributed (Blandford and Walton 1991, 400).

Stoat

A single stoat bone was found in Phase 4c. The winter pelage of the stoat is ermine, a fur highly prized during the medieval period for trimming garments (Piponnier and Mane 1997, 24).

Seal

A single seal bone, comparable with grey seal, was recovered from Phase 4d. This is a metatarsal with a knife mark probably indicative of skinning. Whether the meat arrived at the castle as well as the skin is unclear.

Bones of these wild, fur-bearing species are not numerous but are represented principally in the Welsh phases. Such wild animals are conspicuously rare at Barnard Castle, with only weasel and possibly fox present in Phase V, in contrast to the importance of wild, hunted venison. Fox and badger were present at Launceston Castle, but not the mustelids nor squirrel. There is also the possibility that some of the wild mammals from Phase 6d, such as rabbit, fox and polecat, may represent the remains of wild animals that burrowed into the loose rubble after the demolition of the castle.

Small mammals

Hedgehog was found in the English Phase 6d, where it could be intrusive, and in surface deposits.

Bones of small mammals, such as mice shrews and voles, were not abundant (Figure 10.8) and may well

	PHASE											
	2a	2b	3a	4a	4c	4d	5a	5b	5c	5d	6c	6d
Small mammals												
House mouse	2	1			4						2	2
Cf. Woodmouse					8				1		17	10
Field vole					9				1	24	14	
Bank vole					2						3	
Water vole									1			
Common shrew					13						26	8
Water shrew					2						9	2
Pygmy shrew										7		
Rat							1				1	
Mole			1									
Amphibians		1	2	46	74	2	16		2	8	31	33

FIGURE 10.8

Small mammal and amphibian bones by phase

be under-represented. Such small bones are difficult to retrieve by hand. The hand-recovered finds of small mammal mandibles show an interesting concentration with finds in nine contexts in Hall G, seven contexts in Hall K/L and only one further context in the postern gate, Area H. The majority of the identified small mammal mandibles occur in the English phases of occupation, when the human activity within the Inner Ward was at a lower level and the buildings were not well maintained.

Further evidence for the presence of small mammals within the confines of the Inner Ward is the small number of other animal bones, 34 mammal and 51 bird in total, with marks of rodent gnawing.

O'Connor (1987, 112) points out that small mammal species are often found in archaeological contexts which bear little relation to their present habitat preferences. Water vole is frequently found on sites far removed from water, mole and bank vole occur in medieval towns. Armitage (1985, 70) suggests that human activity on the outskirts of towns increased the variety of potential habitats and created conditions favouring species enrichment whereas the inner, built up, areas resulted in a wholly artificial environment with consequent impoverished small mammal fauna. The Dryslwyn evidence suggests that the earlier, Welsh, phases were as attractive to small mammals as inner urban areas while the later, less intensive, English occupation, like the outskirts of towns, provided more attractive conditions for small mammals.

Amphibians

No distinction was made between the bones of frog and toad. Like the small mammals, frog/toad bones are generally under-represented in hand collected assemblages due to their small size and fragility. The distribution of finds of frog/toad bones is similarly restricted with 12 contexts in Area G, 6 contexts in Area H, 4 contexts in Area L and one or two contexts in Areas E, J, K and I (Figure 9.8).

Again, like the small mammals, the majority of the frog/toad bones were retrieved from the English phases of occupation. Although this may reflect the importation of such small bones in earth brought in for make-up levels, it is more likely to be the result of the sparse occupation of the site creating a suitable environment for colonisation by small creatures.

The exploitation of birds

The bird species present are detailed by phase in Figure 10.9 for Area F and Figure 10.10 for the remainder of the site.

	PHASE											
	1a	1b	2b	2c	2d	3a	3b	4a	4b	4c	5a	5c
Domestic fowl	1	3	1	5	13	1	169	7	69	1	1	1
Domestic goose				1	1		35	3	21			
Duck				2	2		2		3			
Teal									1			
Pigeon							10		2			
Partridge							6	1	9			
Woodcock					1			1	10			
Snipe									4			
Thrush							1		9	1	3	1
Passerine									2			
Small passerine									3			
Rook/Crow									1			
Jackdaw					2							
Cf Jackdaw											4	
Magpie									1			
Rallidae							1					

FIGURE 10.9

Bone fragment counts for the bird species present by phase in Area F

Domestic birds

Domestic fowl bones were the most numerous bird bones recovered, with goose bones also relatively abundant. The goose bones are thought to be from domestic birds, although it is difficult to rule out the possibility that (wild) greylag geese are also present. A clear trend is apparent for a decline in the numbers of fowl bones and a proportional increase in those of geese. The later 13th century Phase 6 at Launceston Castle is remarkably similar in both numbers of bones and proportions of fowl to geese to Phase 2 at Dryslwyn. The roughly contemporary period V at Barnard Castle is more like the later, English, phases at Dryslwyn with relatively more goose bones. While the goose bones are outnumbered by those of fowl, they probably represent a greater resource in terms of meat and feathers.

The proportion of immature fowl bones present (Figure 10.11) suggests they were bred locally, and gives some idea of seasonality. There is little variation in the proportion of immature fowl present in the Welsh and English phases, with approximately a quarter of the fowl consumed being tender, young birds rather than boiling fowl.

The length measurements for the tarsometatarsi show two clear groupings, a large spread up to 71mm, probably of females and younger males, and a small spread over 75mm probably of mature males. These size ranges compare closely with those from medieval Exeter (Maltby 1979, 70), Launceston Castle (Albarella and Davis 1994, fig 22) and Barnard Castle

(Jones *et al* 1985, fig 25) suggesting little variation in the type of fowl available.

There was only one find, from Area L, Phase 6d, of articulated fowl limb bones, from a juvenile bird. The most common pathological conditions seen by Collins were a range of exostoses, affecting some 14 bones in total. Some of these growths were the result of healed fractures caused by natural fighting activity. In contrast to the fowl, bones of immature domestic geese were scarce in all phases. Metrical data are equally sparse with only four complete measurable carpometacarpi from the entire excavation. This bone is normally an abundant find, so its comparative absence suggests that this part of the wing, which bears the primary flight feathers, was detached for use elsewhere. These feathers have been used for arrow flights, quill pens, basting and hearth brushes. Exceptional finds of concentrations of this bone in features at Leicester (Gidney 1993, 9) and Beverley (Scott 1992, 239) indicate it was traded for commercial use.

Wild birds

A wide range of wild bird species were exploited but, like the game mammals, the sport would have been of greater significance than the quantity of meat provided. Some of the less common but highly prized species may have provided only a single mess for the high table. It is apparent from Figure 10.10 that the large assemblages from Phase 2b and 4a have particularly diverse collections of wild birds. The relatively low numbers of bird bones from Phases 3b and 4b for the site in general are partly offset by the assemblage from Area F (Figure 10.9) although exact comparisons of identified fragments are not valid.

Wild bird species form about a quarter of the identified bird bones from all phases, though an increase in the proportion of wild birds, to over a third, is apparent for the later English Phase 6. This is almost certainly due to colonisation of the increasingly derelict site by wild species rather than deliberate human exploitation. The paucity of bird species from the recent, Phase 7, deposits is consistent with the evolution of the castle into an open hillside that offered a limited range of habitats. Wild species form considerably smaller proportions of the bird assemblages from both Launceston Castle and Barnard Castle. Crane is the only high status table bird that is absent from Dryslwyn but present at both the other sites.

Some of the wild species give indications of the seasonality of deposition as they are either summer or winter migrants, or resident species that move seasonally. The Tywi valley is today an important wildfowl wintering ground. Wild birds were also exploited from a variety of habitats, the local farmland as well as the wetlands.

Duck bones and mallard bones were found throughout the occupation but appear to have been relatively more popular, compared to goose, in the earlier Welsh

| | **PHASE** | | | | | | | | | | | | | | | | | | | | | | |
	1a	1b	2a	2b	2c	2d	3a	3b	3d	4a	4b	4c	4d	5a	5b	5c	5d	6c	6d	7a	7b	7c	7d
Domestic fowl	24	82	38	210	178	148	126	78	2	718	4	452	94	220	188	84	44	194	240	2	10	22	4
Domestic goose	4	6	10	20	8	18	28	14		164	2	76	26	44	64	16	16	50	70		10	6	
Goose				2								2											
Duck		12		12	2	8	8	6		38		22	8	6	8		2	2	20				
Cf Duck						2																	
Mallard				6	2	4	6	2	2	12				2	2		2		2				
Teal			2	6						26					2				4				
Pigeon	2	2	2	62				12	2	6		10	2	22	26	8	4	22	54				
Cf Pigeon												2		2		6		2					
Partridge	2	2	2	6		2				38		2	4	10	4		2	6	8				
Cf Partridge												2						2					
Quail	2														2				2				
Swan														2									
Heron				2						2				2	2	2		2					
Coot										2													
Woodcock		4	6	4		2	6			64		18	4	10	12		2	2	8				
Cf Woodcock				2		2				14		2			2			2					
Snipe						2				20		2	2				2		2				
Cf Jack Snipe										2									2				
Golden Plover										8								2	2				
Cf Golden Plover														2									
Wader		10								16		14	2	2	4	6	2	8	10			4	
Cf Grey Phalarope				2																			
Cf Turnstone										4			4										
Thrush				4		2	2			6		32	2	10		10	8	34	42			2	
Cf Song Thrush										4									6				
Blackbird														2									
Cf Blackbird					2					4								2					
Cf Redwing	2																		6				
Cf Fieldfare						2																	
Cf Starling			2							2					2				2				
Skylark																		2	2				
Swallow																			2				
Passerine	4		4	22		2	6	8		62		48	8	12	8	8	4	28	22				
Crow			10		2			2	2	6		10	16		8		2	4	6	8	2	2	
Rook/Crow			2							2			2				2		6	6			
Jackdaw			8		2					8		4	8	14			6	4	16	12	6	2	
Cf Jackdaw			4				2					8		6			2						
Magpie										4									2				
Cf Jay	2									2		2	2						2			2	
Raven																			2				
Buzzard			2							2													
Cf Buzzard																			2				
Cf White tailed sea eagle					2					4													
Tawny Owl										2													
Kittiwake																2							

FIGURE 10.10

Bone fragment counts for the bird species present by phase (excluding Area F)

Phases 1b and 2b. It is unclear whether the mallard size duck bones derive from domestic or wild birds. The generally low numbers of duck bones relative to those of fowl and goose may suggest these were wild rather than domestic birds. Wild mallard were more prized than farmyard birds, as in the reign of Richard II the price of the best river mallard was fixed at 1d more than the best dunghill mallard (Mead 1931, 38).

The teal bones identified in Phases 2a–b, 4a, 5b and 6d certainly indicate the hunting of wild ducks. Teal is a resident bird, breeding on moorland and moving to lowland waters in winter. There is also a large influx of winter migrants (Reid-Henry and Harrison 1988, 59–60). The present shooting season is from October to February but Simon (1952, 603) suggests teal are at their culinary best before Christmas.

Pigeon bones were present throughout and in sufficient abundance in some phases to suggest that some, if not all, of these could derive from dovecote pigeons. For example, over a third of the pigeon bones from Phase 2b were from immature birds, suggesting the exploitation of dovecote squabs.

311

	PHASE					
	1	**2**	**3**	**4**	**5**	**6**
Number immature	28	120	48	378	150	110
Percentage immature	26%	21%	23%	30%	28%	25%

FIGURE 10.11

Proportions of immature fowl bones by phase

Partridge is represented by small numbers of bones in all phases. The partridge is a bird of temperate grassland, that has adapted to the pastures and growing crops of farmland (Reid-Henry and Harrison 1988, 95). Partridges have been highly prized in England for many centuries and were eaten at all times of the year (Simon 1952, 578).

In the Welsh occupation, quail is only present in the early phase 1a, but reappears in the English phases 5b and 6d. Quail is the only migratory gamebird, it is a summer visitor attracted to farmland, especially growing crops and open grassland. The numbers reaching north-west Europe vary greatly from year to year (Heinzel *et al* 1972), which may explain its absence from the rich assemblage of birds in Phase 4a.

Swan appears only in the English Phase 5a. Swan is regularly listed among the birds consumed at formal banquets (Mead 1931, 87). The Northumberland Household Book quoted by Mead (1931, 226) details that 20 swans were ordered in September for consumption over the Christmas festivities. Wild swans, Whooper and Bewick, are winter visitors. Swan was present only in Phase V at Barnard Castle and the early 13th century Phase 4 at Launceston Castle.

Heron bones were present in the Welsh Phases 2b and 4a, which have the most diverse range of bird species present. While not abundant, heron is more consistently present in the English Phases 5a, 5b, 5c and 6c. In contrast, heron was not present in the comparable phases at Launceston Castle and Barnard Castle where its place would seem to have been taken by crane. Medieval recipes for heron, for example Harleian MS.4016 (Renfrow 1990, 144), indicate that the birds were brought to the kitchen alive and killed as needed by the cook. Scully (1995, 72–73) makes the point that for a grand two day banquet the chef at the court of Savoy sent out orders two months in advance for the supply of game, including 'partridge, pheasants, small birds (whatever they can find of these, without number), doves, cranes, herons, any wildfowl'. These birds would have needed penning and feeding in the period between capture and consumption.

Coot is only represented in the rich assemblage from Phase 4a. The coot needs open water. Britain hosts a winter influx of continental birds (Reid-Henry and Harrison 1988, 99). Simon (1952, 546) states that the

bird is edible but is not nearly so much appreciated now as it was in the past. The coot would appear to come under the category of 'any wildfowl', mentioned above. Perhaps Rhys ap Maredudd held a particularly sumptuous banquet in Phase 4a which necessitated scouring the countryside, particularly the Tywi valley, for an impressive array of birds which did not normally grace his table.

Woodcock is a highly comestible bird whose bones are present in all phases. The woodcock, as its name suggests, is a woodland bird and was formerly widespread as a migrant winter visitor (Reid-Henry and Harrison 1988, 108). Woodcock was, and still is, greatly prized as food (Simon 1952, 612).

Snipe bones were absent from Phases 1 and 2. Jack snipe is probably present in Phase 4a. The snipe is a widespread resident bird, living in inland marshy places (Reid-Henry and Harrison 1988, 106–107). Simon (1952, 600) esteems snipe as one of the finest of all game birds, both for the sportsman and the gastronome. The current shooting season is from October to February, but snipe are better eating in the earlier part of the season.

Golden plover is surprisingly absent from the Welsh Phases 1–3, particularly the diverse assemblage of birds in Phase 2b, but bones are present in small numbers subsequently in the English Phases 5a, 5d and 6d. The golden plover is a moorland breeding bird which moves to lowland grass or ploughland in winter (Reid-Henry and Harrison 1988, 102).

Grey phalarope is probably represented in Phase 2b. This species is found only as a passing migrant during the spring or autumn. Turnstone is probably present in Phases 4a and 4d. Like the coot, these bones may represent opportunistic captures for a special event.

Bones of other unidentified wader species were also present in Phases 1b, 4, 5 and 6 but are conspicuously absent from Phases 2 and 3, particularly Phase 2b.

The various members of the thrush family and the passerines were probably caught for the table, as mentioned above, by size with little regard for particular species. The probable presence of redwing in Phases 1a and 6c and fieldfare in Phase 3a indicates some capture of winter migrants, while the swallow in Phase 6d fell victim in the summer.

There is a range of literary evidence to suggest that such small birds were regularly eaten: 'birds of all sizes — even those which scarcely made a mouthful — were limed and netted, and by the sporting gentry as well as by their labourers. The liming of small song birds was still regarded as good sport in the early 19th century' (Longrigg 1977, 30–31). *The forme of cury*, compiled by the master chefs of Richard II, includes a dish called Drepee which instructs 'take small bryddes (birds)' (Warner 1791, 7), a further recipe for Crustade begins 'take chekyns, and pejons, and smale briddes' (Warner 1791, 65). In the 17th century recipes for larks, sparrows and blackbirds are given by Murrell (1638, 21 and 37). Roast larks and sparrow dumplings still appear in the 18th century (Raffald 1782, 67 and 184).

The corvid bones, particularly the jackdaws, may derive from wild birds living around the castle. Normally only juvenile corvids are eaten. Two thirds of all the corvid bones from Phase 2b were from immature birds, all the corvid bones from Phase 3 and over half the corvid bones from Phase 4. If wild jackdaws, in particular, were living in the castle precincts, it might have been convenient to include a few young ones among the miscellaneous 'small birds'. The proportion of immature corvids declines in the English phases to a third in Phase 5 and a sixth in Phase 6. The decay of the site in Phase 6 may have encouraged increased colonisation by the crow family and an increase in natural mortalities of more mature birds. Very few birds are present in the recent and surface deposits of Phase 7, which enhances the interpretation of human exploitation for the wide range of wild bird species in the stratified phases. The presence of corvids may suggest some use of the site as a roost but not to any great extent. Raven is represented only in Phase 6d. The raven is a carrion eater which would have been attracted by the rubbish generated at the castle, at one time ravens were protected for their waste disposal services. The same suite of corvids was present at both Launceston Castle and Barnard Castle, further suggesting that these are commensals associated with any major settlement with refuse to scavenge. Explicit reference to the culinary use of corvids appears in the Ménagier de Paris, which lists jackdaw, magpie, jay and crow among the birds suitable for the table (Crossley-Holland 1996, 97).

Buzzard was present in the Welsh Phases 2a and 4a. This bird, like the corvids, will feed on carrion and may have been attracted to the castle as a scavenger. Such birds may have met an untimely end as Heath (1971, 10) mentions the use of buzzard feathers for fletching. A similar fate may have befallen the white-tailed sea eagles represented in the Welsh Phases 2c and 4a. The bones from Phase 4a appear to derive from one bird, three showed traces of butchery and one was burnt. Parker (1988, 201) notes that 'eagle wings have historically been used as brushes, and feathers (sometimes still attached to all or part of the carcass) have been transported, even over long distances, for quill pens or arrow flights'. The white-tailed sea eagle was formerly widespread in Britain with a traditional habitat of lakes and marshes flanked by tall stands of trees for eyries, such as the Tywi valley. Like the buzzard and raven, the sea eagle was attracted to the offal, carrion and poultry found in association with human habitations (Parker 1988, 217; O'Connor 1993).

Tawny owl was found only in Phase 4a. This is not normally eaten today but may have found its way into a dish of 'small birds', though perhaps not for the high table, likewise the kittiwake from Phase 5c. Long-eared owl certainly appears to have been eaten in Roman Holland (Parker 1988, 202), while

kittiwakes appear to have been traded as an article of food since the Iron Age (Coy 1987, 20).

Discussion

Any comparison of the provisioning of the castle between the Welsh and English phases of occupation is limited due to the comparatively sparse data from the English phases, which suggest that the Inner Ward was no longer the hub of the castle in terms of provisioning and waste disposal. The documentary evidence also makes it clear that there was a substantial carry over from the Welsh to the English occupation not only of the 'dead garnisture' but also of the food render supply mechanisms. The continuity in supply patterns noted in several analyses suggests that at this point in history the local economy was producer not consumer led. In such a case the English garrison would have had to accept what produce was on offer from the indigenous farmers rather than creating a market for new products (O'Connor 1989). What is clear is that the English occupation saw a decline in the quantity of faunal refuse disposal within the Inner Ward. The incoming constable would have neither the need nor the resources for the displays of lavish hospitality which would have been a necessary attribute of the status of a lord of Deheubarth. On a more modest scale consumption of luxury items appears to have been maintained, for example fallow deer and heron in Phase 5.

The apogee of the Welsh lords is suggested by the rich and diverse assemblages from Phase 2b, probably associated with Maredudd ap Rhys, and Phase 4a, presumed to be the period of his son Rhys ap Maredudd. The historical evidence for the central importance of cattle is reflected in the predominance of cattle bones in the archaeological finds. Together with the abundant pig bones, these corroborate that salt beef and bacon were the store room staples. Fresh meat is suggested, in particular, by the seasonal provision of milk fed lamb besides bobby veal and sucking pig. There is abundant evidence for the supply of a wide range of game animals and birds which would have reflected the status of the diners at the high table.

Comparison with two castles of equivalent status in England does suggest some regional differences in livestock exploitation, both in the proportions of the domestic livestock consumed in each castle and the preferred age of slaughter. Dryslwyn has much higher proportions of infant calves and lambs, which may be the archaeological evidence to corroborate the historical evidence for the importance of milk and dairy products in the Welsh diet. The English sheep appeared to have survived to greater ages, reflecting the importance of wool to the English economy.

The excavator has pointed out the similarities between the lists of provisions for the household of Edward I (Prestwich 1988, 157ff) and the archaeological and documentary evidence for Dryslwyn.

Scully (1995, 202–203) emphasises the international links between the aristocracy and royalty of Europe at this time and the common themes within the actual surviving compilations of recipes (Scully 1995, 212–217). A distinction was also made by contemporary authors between the foods suitable for the dainty (in its medieval sense, Scully 1995, 191–192) appetites and digestions of grandees: 'It is to be noted that some foods are appropriate for nobles and the wealthy who live sedentary lives, such foods as partridge and pheasant, pullets, capons, hares, deer and rabbits, each variously prepared according to its specific nature'. All of these foods, with the exception of pheasant, are recorded from the Welsh phases. In comparison other foods were perceived as more suitable for the coarser natures and digestions of the household: 'Some foods are appropriate for robust, working men, these foods being beef and goat, salt pork, stag, peas, beans, barley and wheat bread' (Scully 1995, 191). Again, the meats in this list are known to have been utilised at Dryslwyn.

The comparisons with the contemporary assemblages from Launceston and Barnard Castle indicate that the lords of Dryslwyn had access to the same suite of butcher's meat and game. Differences between the three sites may reflect both the local terrain and its suitability for stock raising and the personal tastes of the individual lordly households.

10.3 FISH BONES
by Alison Locker

Dryslwyn Castle was well placed for the consumption of a wide variety of fish throughout the year, close to the River Twyi and less than 25km from the coast. Fish bones were recovered from all phases of occupation and from most excavated areas in the Inner Ward. The majority of the bone was collected by hand, with sieving carried out on site on selected deposits from Areas F, I and O. Consequently the results are biased in favour of the larger fish and the absence of some species in certain areas cannot be regarded as significant.

In total, 2358 bones were identified to species or family level of which 56% were from Phase 3 and 38% from Phase 4, particularly Phases 3b and 4b in Area F with the exceptional organic preservation of rubbish deposits (Figure 10.12). Identification and quantification data of fish bone retrieved from sieving and hand collection from two midden and latrine contexts (F16), (F19) and (F23) by Gilchrist (1987) are presented alongside the data derived for those layers in this report in Figure 10.13.

Results

The following list shows all the species identified at the site. Figure 10.12 indicates the fish present in each phase in each area.

The species present comprise: Elasmobranch indet., rays (*Rajidae*), roker (*Raja clavata*), sturgeon (*Accipenser sturio*), eel (*Anguilla anguilla*), conger (*Conger conger*), herring (*Clupea harengus*), Salmonidae, pike (*Esox lucius*), smelt (*Osmerus eperlanus*), dace (*Leuciscus leuciscus*), chub (*Leuciscus cephalus*), minnow (*Phoxinus phoxinus*), Cyprinidae, cod (*Gadus morhua*), haddock (*Melanogrammus aeglefinus*), ling (*Molva molva*), hake (*Merluccius merluccius*), Gadidae, stickleback (*Gasterosteus aculeatus*), gurnard (*Triglidae*), bullhead (*Cottus gobio*), bass (*Dicentrarchus labrax*), perch (*Perca fluviatilis*), scad (*Trachurus trachurus*), red sea bream (*Pagellus bogaraveo*), sea bream (*Sparidae*), thin-lipped grey mullet (*Liza ramada*), grey mullet (*Mugilidae*), mackerel (*Scomber scombrus*), brill/turbot (*Scophthalmus rhombus/Scophthalmus maximus*), plaice/flounder (*Pleuronectes platessa/Platichthys flesus*) and flatfish indet. Wrasse (*Labrus sp.*) and spurdog (*Squalus acanthuias*) were also detected by Gilchrist (1987).

All of these species would have been eaten with the likely exception of stickleback and bullhead, discussed below, and show a thorough exploitation of freshwater, estuarine and marine environments, both inshore and in deeper water. The majority of the fish species were identified from a mixture of skull and vertebral fragments, rays were identified from dermal denticles and teeth, roker from the characteristic 'bucklers', sturgeon from a dermal scute, the cyprinids from pharyngeal bones and teeth, scad from scutes and vertebrae. The small amount of material identified from Phase 7 is almost entirely redeposited from earlier activity and has not been included in this report.

Dryslwyn Castle has produced some of the richest fish assemblages ever recorded for a medieval site in the UK. The majority were recovered from Area F, with a total of 2050 identifiable bones (Figure 10.13). An unusually large number of species were recovered from the kitchen middens (F16), (F19) and the latrine deposit (F23). Some bones from the latter showed evidence of deformation consistent with being eaten (Figure 10.14). There is not a simple correlation between sieving and an increase in the number of fish bones and species identified. In some areas where deposits were sieved, notably the Phase 5b deposits in Area O, only a single bone of a very small species, stickleback, was recovered. Consequently the Area F deposits must be regarded as accurately recording an unusually high variety of fish species consumed by the residents in the period 1250–80.

Fresh-water and estuarine fish

The true freshwater species include pike, all the cyprinids (dace, chub and minnow), stickleback (though it is also found in brackish and marine conditions), bullhead and perch. Pike and perch were few, but there were large numbers of small cyprinids, specifically identified from their distinctive pharyngeals. There is

	1a	1b	2a	2b	2c	2d	3a	3b	3c	3d	4a	4b	4c	4d	5a	5b	5c	5d	6a	6b	6c	6d	Total
																							Phase
Elasmobranch								4				1											5
Ray								16				2											18
Roker			3			2		1			1	3	1										11
Sturgeon								1															1
Pike				1																			1
Eel	1	4	1	20		1	1	224			8	91	1										352
Conger	1		2		1		1	27			20	5	6		3								66
Herring						1	5	562			44	425	3		6								1046
Salmonid				6		1	1	50			7	24	1		1	2			1				94
Smelt												2											2
Dace								56				13											69
Chub								3															3
Minnow								2															2
Cyprinidae								211				3											214
Cod		1	1	2			1	20			6	15											46
Haddock				1			1	11			4	9											26
Ling					2							3	3										8
Hake		1					1	6			7	46	2		2		1						66
Large Gadid	1		2	3	3		8	36			5	2	4		4								68
Stickleback								6				1				1							8
Gurnard				1		1	1	3			20	40											66
Bullhead								3				2											5
Bass		1			1			2			3		1										8
Perch								1				3											4
Scad								10															10
Red Sea Bream								1															1
Sea Bream																					1		1
T L G Mullet	1			1				1				1											4
Mullet				2							1												3
Scombrid								17				1											18
Turbot/Brill								6															6
Plaice/flounder				18	1	1	3	13			13	37	5	2	3						1		97
Flatfish		1		9		1	3	4			5	4	1		1								29
Spurdog	2	1	3	31	5	6	15	103			47	91	11	2	8	1					1	1	328
Total	4	5	7	64	8	13	26	1297			144	733	28	2	20	3	1		1		1	1	2358

FIGURE 10.12

Bone fragment counts for the fish species present in Phases 1a–6d

always the possibility that such small fish (less than 10cm) are the stomach contents of other larger carnivorous fish such as pike, or piscivorous birds such as the heron (Section 10.2). However, the large numbers here, particularly of dace, suggest that they are food remains from human consumption. There are contemporary medieval references for cooking stews of small fish and these small cyprinids together with stickleback and bullhead (not usually regarded as food fish) could have been netted in the river and cooked together. The bony scutes and spines of stickleback and the very small size of these and bullhead suggest both were an accidental inclusion.

Fish found seasonally in the river, but not true freshwater species, include eel, identified in many deposits, especially those sieved, and representing fish ranging from quite small individuals of less than 20cm in total length to over 50cm (after Libois *et al* 1987). The large eels are likely to be females, as males do not generally exceed 50cm (Wheeler 1978, 62). They may have been caught using a multi pronged spear or trapped in 'eel bucks', wicker traps stretched across the river.

Salmonid vertebrae were also identified from a number of contexts, apart from a few large vertebrae, most were small and may be from small salmon (*Salmo salar*) or trout (*Salmo trutta*). The coracle was used in the recent past for salmon fishing on the Tywi, with seine netting in the estuary (Freeman 1988, 3–4). Smelt, a relation of the salmonids, was tentatively identified from two vertebrae in (F15) and (F16) and is an inshore migratory species entering rivers in winter for spawning. Wheeler's (1978, 88) distribution map for this species suggests smelt are not currently found on the South Wales coastline.

The thin-lipped grey mullet is a summer visitor to southern British coastlines and is an adaptable species, essentially inshore marine, but can be found in estuarine and fully freshwater conditions. This species was identified in low numbers from Phases 2, 3 and 4 suggesting continuity in its availability, if not abundance.

The largest fish present, transitory between freshwater and marine conditions, is the sturgeon, which enters rivers in spring for spawning. The cartilaginous

PHASE:	3b	3b	3b	3b	3b	3b	4b	4b	4b	4b	4b
CONTEXT:	F23	F23	F23*	F19	F19	F19*	F15	F15	F16	F16	F16*
Processing:	h	s	s	h	s	s	h	s	h	s	s
Elasmobranch		4								1	
Ray		6	14		10	5				2	3
Roker						1			2	1	4
Sturgeon				1							
Eel		158	59		66	27		8		83	16
Conger				20	3	3			4	1	
Herring		70	167	1	491	171		7	2	416	108
Salmonid		33	1	4	9		1	4	5	14	6
Smelt								1		1	
Dace		52	4		4					13	
Chub		3	4								
Minnow		1	6		1	1					4
Cyprinidae		211						1		2	
Cod	2	10	24	5		1			15		14
Haddock				7	2	23			6	3	
Ling									2	1	
Hake		1		4	1		3	2	37	3	
Large Gadid	10		2	24		13	1	1			8
Stickleback		6				1				1	
Gurnard				2	1	1	1		18	21	9
Bullhead		1			2					2	
Bass		1			1	1					
Perch		1				4				3	4
Scad		4	1		6						
T L G Mullet				1					1		
Scombrid						17			1		
Turbot/Brill				6							
Plaice/flounder		3	2	3	6	5			8	29	26
Flatfish				4			1	2		1	
Spurdog			2								
Wrasse			1			1					
Pike						3					
Total	12	565		82	621		7	26	101	598	

* earlier sample sorted and identified by Gilchrist (1987)

FIGURE 10.13

Bone fragment counts for the fish species present in contexts (F23), (F19), (F15) and (F16) (h: hand-collected; s: sieved)

skeleton does not normally survive and it was identified from a single bony scute, found in rows along the body, from Phase 3b, Area F. This species is often regarded as representing high status and was served as a focal point at feasts or festive meals.

Marine fish

The inshore coastal waters around the Twyi estuary would have been ideal for catching flatfish either by trapping along the shoreline and up into the estuary or on lines in shallow water. Plaice and flounder seem to have been eaten in all phases while caudal vertebrae of brill/turbot were only identified from (F19) (Figure 10.13). Rays were regularly caught including the roker, as was conger eel, which hides in rocky coastlines and can be trapped or caught on a line.

Gurnards were also caught in coastal waters, the tub gurnard (*Trigla lucerna*) is the most common and the largest of the species available locally, but the red gurnard (*Aspitrigla cuculus*) and the grey gurnard (*Eutrigla gurnardus*) could also have been caught. It has not been possible to separate species on the fragmentary bones present. Bass is also common along the Welsh coastline, will swim up into estuaries (Wheeler 1978, 231), makes good eating and was identified from Phases 2, 3 and 4.

Scad, mackerel and red sea-bream are all schooling fish that could have been caught off the Welsh coastline. Both scad and mackerel are pelagic and are found in large numbers together.

The most numerous of all species in sieved deposits was the herring. This fish is seasonally found in great abundance and was the most important of all stored fish in the medieval period. As the fish are stored skeletally whole, whether salted, pickled or smoked there is no osteological evidence to suggest whether the remains represent stored or fresh herring. Herring,

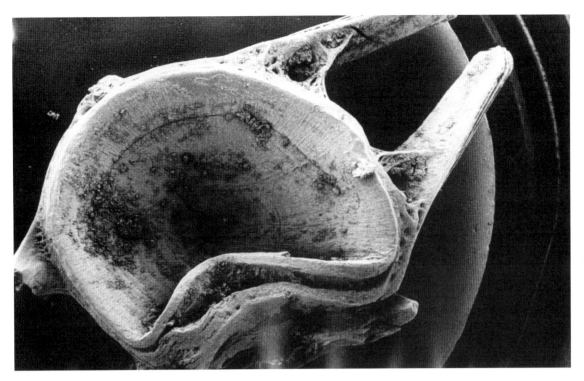

FIGURE 10.14

Scanning electron micrograph of a plaice vertebra from a latrine deposit distorted as a result of being bitten (f: fragments)

stored in many forms, was an important export from Ireland in the 16th century (Longfield 1929, 51) to the west coast of Britain and the castle may have bought in some supplies as well as eating fresh herring. Historically, herring fishing and curing were important occupations in Wales, with the coast described in the 17th century as 'enclosed in with a hedge of herrings' (Freeman 1988, 22).

The remaining species are all 'whitefish' with a low fat and high water content. These include cod, haddock, ling and hake and were stored by drying or salting. Whiting is conspicuously absent, even in the sieved material.

Despite the occasional larger specimen, the cod are not normally very large. Sizes calculated after Wheeler and Jones (1976) suggested fish of between 60 and 85cm (n = 10), with no discernible differences between phases. Possibly these indicate the product of a local inshore winter line fishery. Haddock included cleithra from two very large specimens of around 84cm (after Bereenhout 1994) and along this coastline could also have been part of a winter fishery. Ling is a deep water fish and suggests a more distant fishery than cod and haddock, as does hake, typically an important constituent of fish assemblages in the south-west along with conger, but could have been fished in shallow waters during the summer.

There is no evidence that any of the four species described above are from stored fish remains, since there are head elements present for all four and these are usually removed during preparation for salting or drying. There were 500 dried fish and 17 meases (approx. 8500) salt herrings recorded as stored at Llanbadarn Castle (Ceredigion) for consumption by garrisons of the royal castles of West Wales in 1300/01 (Rhys 1936; Phillpotts 2001c). Knight (1996) quotes a reference to the supply of 1800 'stockfish' to the garrison of Caerphilly Castle (Caerphilly) in 1328 and such supplies may have formed an important, though not necessarily large, part of the victuals of castle garrisons of this period.

That Dryslwyn produced 35 different species of fish indicates the variety of fish resources that could be exploited. In comparison, Barnard Castle (Durham) produced only 12 (herring, cod, ling, haddock, pike, conger eel, eels, trout, whiting, gurnard, carp family, ray/dogfish and flat fish) (Donaldson *et al* 1980). A similar range of fish was also recovered from the 13th–16th century contexts of a substantial medieval house (merchant or minor nobility) at Langport in Somerset (Grant 1988). This unusually large range of fish species from Dryslwyn Castle indicates both the ready access to a range of different aquatic environments and the high status enjoyed by this castle's occupants.

The lack of appropriate preservative conditions and sieving of samples of excavated deposits have resulted in very few collections of fish bone data from medieval sites in the UK. Those collected are invariably the larger bones which do not require preservative (anoxic) conditions to survive and so are comparable with the hand collected material from Dryslwyn. High medieval sites such as Valle Crucis (Denbighshire) (Butler 1976), Southampton (Wheeler 1975), Montgomery Castle (Powys) (Knight 1996), Lewes Castle (East Sussex) (Drewett 1992), Clough Castle (Down) (Jope 1954) and Rhuddlan (Levitan 1994), have all produced bones from cod as well as smaller numbers of bones from the other large fish such as: conger, rays, roker and Salmonidae. Where sieving has taken place, the bones of smaller fish such as herring and bass have been recovered as they were from the cesspit of the 16th century merchant's house, Tenby (Caseldine 1990). At both Barnard Castle and Langport there were few, if any, freshwater fish eaten, save for eels, despite the proximity of a river to both sites. Clearly marine fish accounted for the vast majority of fish eaten in practice. Similarly, in south Wales, despite their positions beside rivers, marine fish such as cod and flatfish (turbot, halibut and skate) were the principal fish recovered from the 13th century deposits at Rumney Castle (Cardiff) (Jones 1992) and Loughor Castle (Swansea) (Wheeler 1993). These sites complement Dryslwyn in indicating that there was exploitation of coastal waters by a well established fishing industry whose products supplied castles and other sites with good coastal access. The remains of fish traps, dated by radiocarbon and dendrochronology to the 12th–13th century, recovered on Welsh foreshores, especially in the Severn estuary, indicate one of the approaches to coastal fishing (Turner 2002b). The presence of ling and hake bones at Dryslwyn suggests fishing in deeper waters (Gilchrist 1987) and thus the presence of a deep sea fishing industry in the 13th century, probably fishing in the Irish Sea, can be considered to have existed. Fish bones from ling, recovered from the 14th-century palace of King's Langley, Hertfordshire (Wheeler 1977) and hake and ling from 13th–16th century contexts at Langport (Grant 1988), provide further evidence for the existence of deep sea fishing at this date. The fact that inland sites such as Valle Crucis Abbey (Butler 1976) and Montgomery Castle (Powys) (Knight 1996) have produced cod bones from early 13th-century deposits indicates that there was a trade in marine fish from the Welsh coast inland, probably as dried, smoked or salted fish, by this date. This trade was, as historic references show, clearly well established by the early 14th century (Knight 1996).

Conclusions

The richest deposits are typically associated with the kitchen midden in Phases 3b and 4b, and here retrieval has been maximised with sieving. However the overall assemblage shows that the diet of the occupants of Dryslwyn Castle in the mid to late 13th century contained a rich and varied fish component. Freshwater species would have been caught in the River Twyi, there is no evidence of fish ponds to suggest management of freshwater fish as a food resource. The river estuary and marine conditions from shallow coastal waters to the open sea were a rich source of marine fish.

The only species specifically associated with high status is sturgeon, identified from a single scute. The remainder are common food fish, though good sized specimens of bass and thin lipped grey mullet could have served as an attractive centre piece to a fish course.

There is no evidence from the assemblage for the consumption of stored fish and the proximity of the coast made the transport of fresh fish comparatively easy, though some stored herring and large gadids may have been bought in as long term provisions.

10.4 SHELLFISH
by Jacqui Huntley

Methodology

Marine mollusc shells were collected routinely during excavation and were grouped according to species after washing. The analyses identified the species of shell fish that were consumed during the different periods of occupation. The available shell data were analysed by phase due to the limited numbers of shells from any one context (Figure 10.15). Specific attributes were recorded for whelks and oysters: the length and breadth of the shell for whelks and for oysters whether the valve was upper or lower, the size (categories 1-small to 15-large) and 'damage' (1–7 category). Damage referred to the position and degree of breakage during the opening of the shell, not to natural abrasion either pre- or post-deposition. Such changes in size and damage to the shells may reflect changes in the exploitation and use of these shellfish.

Results

Oysters were the most common shellfish recovered, forming more than 80% of the assemblage (Figure 10.15). Whelks and cockles, although scattered throughout most of the phases, were most common during Phases 4a and 4b, the latter part of the Welsh occupation. Mussels were rare with no sign of any concentration in the extant finds. However, large numbers of fragile, highly comminuted mussel shell fragments were seen from the 'waterlogged' deposits in Area F but these have not survived. The 'other species' noted were clams and scallops, although never more than a few fragments of individuals per context (denoted f in Figure 10.15). A few of these species occurred in most contexts. Of note is the absence of

318

		Phases																										
		1a	1b	2a	2b	2c	2d	3a	3b	3c	3d	4a	4b	4c	4d	5a	5b	5c	5d	6a	6b	6c	6d	7a	7b	7c	7d	Total
Mussels	*Mytilus edulis* L.		3		1	1	2					4	6		3	19	6	7	6			5	37	2	2			104
Whelks	*Buccinum undatum* L.		1		1	1	4					8	116	15	4	4	5	2	1			1	8	1	2	2		176
Cockles	*Cerastoderma edule* L.											148	3		1	8	1	1	4			3	13	3	3			188
Oysters	*Ostrea edulis* L.	1	3	38	17	5	3	12	45			218	157	20	148	444	242	88	46	1		113	179	72	3	31		1918
Clam	*Lutraria sp*		f		f	f	f	f				f		f	f	f		f				f			f	f		
Scallop												f					f	f	f									

FIGURE 10.15

Mollusc shells recovered from stratified contexts, by phase

limpets or periwinkles, both of which would almost certainly have been found in the Twyi estuary. Had these shells been present, they would have been recovered either during excavation or sieving. Their absence indicates that they were not procured among the shellfish consumed at the castle.

Oysters

Over 1900 oyster shells were recovered, with most from Phases 4 and 5 (Figure 10.15). Overall, 403 lower, more concave, valves and 496 upper, flatter, valves were counted, suggesting that these represent complete oysters. Hence these shells were probably deposited in the contexts where found immediately after use, i.e. there is no specific bias for upper or lower valves: they were opened, eaten and the shells disposed of. A similar pattern has been observed on material from Okehampton Castle in Devon (Higham *et al* 1982, 138).

The size distribution across the phases is presented in Figure 10.16, where there are suggestions that more, larger shells were recovered from Phase 2. This might be interpreted as older animals or might simply mean animals grown in a more favourable environment. However, it most probably reflects an oyster population just starting to be exploited in the early 13th century. Subsequent collections in the later 13th and 14th century may have been at intervals precluding time for the bigger shells to develop. Such a scenario would suggest regular activity at a limited number of oyster beds.

The shapes of the size frequency plots approximate to a skewed normal distribution, particularly in those phases with reasonable totals (n > 100). There are no strong biases towards smaller or larger animals. It therefore seems reasonable to suggest that these shells represent the whole of a collection from one population, whether wild or cultured, with no preferential sorting.

Of the 81 layers with oyster shells, only six produced more than 100 shells (Figure 10.17), The others contained generally only up to around 20 each and are of little interpretative value by themselves. Not surprisingly, these rich layers were either kitchen middens (F16) or dumped earth and stone deposits containing occupation debris (O44), (L17), (O52) and (O31). Two of these deposits are dated to the Welsh occupation and four to the English phases of control, suggesting that both Welsh lords and English constables enjoyed oysters on occasion. As the vast majority of excavated deposits and evidence relates to the 'Welsh' occupation, it is clear, however, that a disproportionately high level of oysters come from the otherwise poorly represented later 'English' occupation phases. This would suggest that although the Welsh lords and their household ate oysters as part of their diet, oysters were a more popular food during the later period. The consumption of oysters at Dryslwyn Castle would appear to be comparable to that seen at other 13th century castles such as Barnard Castle (Durham) (Donaldson *et al* 1980) and Okehampton Castle (Devon) (Higham *et al* 1982).

In terms of the damage to the shells, i.e. the methods of opening, Phase 2 again stands out as slightly different in that damage classes 1 and 2 are the most commonly recorded whereas class 7 is more or less as important as 1 and 2 in all other phases. These three classes seem to be representative of leverage across the shell using a long bladed instrument rather than probing and twisting with the tip of a knife or other implement. There is no significant difference between Welsh and English habits of opening the shells.

Whelks, cockles, mussels

The majority of whelk shells were recovered from a limited number of contexts in Phase 4b, immediately predating the siege. This may reflect a single population of animals from one area of the shore. The whelks were large, mostly 50–90mm in length. This is not a normal population distribution where a few larger and many small individuals would be expected. This suggests that there was deliberate harvesting of whelks; regular collection preventing any growing too large, whilst the smaller ones were deliberately left to develop further. On average each shell produced 30–40g meat, with a total of 1800–2400g represented overall. Therefore whelks did not contribute significantly to the diet, probably being an occasional delicacy.

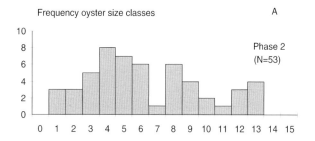

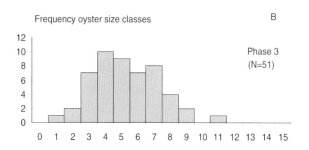

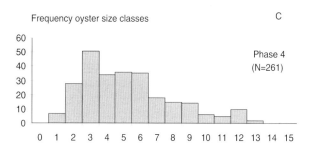

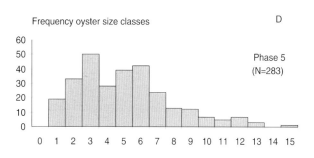

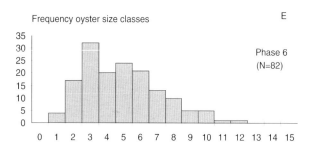

Size	1	2	3	4	5	6	7	8	9	10	11	12	13
Diameter (mm)	37	42	47	52	57	62	66	70	74	78	81	84	87

FIGURE 10.16

Frequency of oyster shell size by phase

Context	Phase	No. of shells
O7	6d	109
O44	5b	177
L17	5a	321
O52	4d	117
F16	4b	100
O31	4a	165

FIGURE 10.17

Contexts with significant numbers of oyster shells

Cockles were relatively abundant in Phase 4a with 148 valves recovered although, again, these do not necessarily represent much meat. Cockles occur constantly, although in small numbers, throughout the later Welsh and all of the English phases. This would indicate that they were considered a desirable food. Other medieval sites such as Barnard Castle (Durham) (Donaldson *et al* 1980), Loughor Castle (Swansea) (Lewis 1994) and Kirkstall Abbey (Leeds) (Bond 1988) show a similar pattern of deposition of small quantities of cockles, whelks and mussels. Consumption of these particular shellfish, in preference to others, was clearly a widespread tradition, possibly of a deliberately sourced delicacy for fast days. Historically, the major cockle beds were in the sands of Carmarthen Bay (Freeman 1980, 32) with a year round fishery in the Twyi estuary (Jenkins 1984, 1).

The disintegrated finds of mussel shell complement the other finds of shellfish from the deposits in Area F. In contrast, the surviving mussels, although never common, were more plentiful in the later phases and thus may have been preferred by the English garrison. As the majority of any of these shells is found only in a few contexts, an aspect of perhaps merely one or two specific meals may be represented. Although mussels would have been abundant in the Tywi estuary, historically mussel beds were not harvested between April and October, unlike cockles which were gathered throughout the year without a break (Jenkins 1984, 3). Both taphonomic factors and seasonality may have influenced the representation of mussel shells.

While none of these shellfish appears to have formed an important dietary component, the supply of shellfish may have been influenced by several factors. The rapid fluctuations in the territory controlled by the lords of Dryslwyn may have resulted in occasional food renders from coastal areas. Shellfish may have been eaten particularly during the fasts of the church year, such as Lent, and so may not have been obtained in quantity if the lord and his entourage were not in residence at these times. Conversely, shellfish are traditionally only eaten when there is an 'R' in the month, so a summer residence by the lord might not be reflected in the provision of shellfish.

Discussion

The fact that only specific edible species are present means that all the shells recovered were selected for food and consequently provide limited evidence regarding local coastal habitats. Shellfish do not keep well, restricting transportation distance. Historically, cockle women could walk 22.5km to market in bare feet with tubs of cockles balanced on their heads (Jenkins 1984, 20), the use of pack animals would extend this range. Oysters, however, were transported reasonable distances, as by the late 14th century fresh oysters could be obtained from the market in Coventry (Dyer 1994, 105).

The oysters were clearly enjoyed by both the Welsh lord and the English constable of the castle and, arguably, were obtained from a single population. The largest animals were recovered from Phase 2 and this suggests the initial exploitation of oyster beds in the early to mid 13th century. Subsequent decades saw more intensive exploitation and consequently slightly smaller oysters. Whelks and cockles were apparently favoured by the Welsh whilst the extant mussels were more prevalent in the English phases. However, relatively few concentrations of any of these shells were recorded, so only the penchant of one or two people, rather than a nationalistic trend, may be represented.

10.5 PLANT REMAINS
by Jacqui Huntley and John Daniell

No environmental sampling was initially envisaged at Dryslwyn Castle since it was considered unlikely that plant remains would be recovered from an exposed Welsh hillside with a thin limestone soil. The emergence of deposits with both carbonised and waterlogged plant material led to *ad hoc* on-site wet sieving and sorting of selected deposits and the retention of seven 'whole earth' samples for laboratory processing. Finds from both types of recovery were subsequently analysed in order to identify the plant remains and to discuss these in terms of diet and economy, as well as the local vegetation, and to compare the on-site recovered material with that processed in the laboratory, to determine the efficacy of these methods of recovering plant remains.

Since there is contemporary documentary evidence regarding victualling and provisions within the castle for the late 13th century (Rhys 1936) a third objective was to compare the archaeobotanical and documentary evidence.

Methodology

On-site: unrecorded weights of soil were wet sieved through a series of five sieves with mesh sizes from 7.1mm to 0.5mm. Discernible 'seeds' were picked out of the sieves with tweezers, by untrained personnel, without the aid of magnification. The seeds were subsequently examined in the laboratory by the authors, identified if possible and either counted if

numbers were low or scored if they were high. Given the inevitable bias resulting from the sorting strategy it was not considered cost effective to count everything.

The whole earth samples were processed by manual flotation in the laboratory with both flot and residue retained upon 500μ mesh. After drying, all of the flots and the >1mm fraction of the residues were sorted using a stereomicroscope at magnifications of up to ×50. Material, in all cases, was identified by the authors of this report by comparison with modern reference material held in the Biological Laboratory, Department of Archaeology, University of Durham. The <1mm residue fractions were scanned but nothing identifiable was seen.

The results from the on-site recovery are presented in Figures 10.18–10.22. The total numbers of seeds of each taxon present in each layer are presented with data for other layers in that phase. The results of an earlier report on seeds recovered from layer F23 (Gilchrist 1987) are presented as an additional column (F23*) in Figure 10.20. The data derived from the laboratory processing of the samples are presented in Figure 10.23. Unless otherwise stated all numbers are counts of seeds, 'SCORES' are based upon a 5-point abundance scale with 'one' = a few individuals to 'five' = dominant ('four' = some hundreds) and these values are written out in the tables to distinguish them from simple numerical counts. The single letter code in brackets which follows the taxon name reflects the mode of preservation: (c) charred, (w) waterlogged and (m) mineralised.

An additional group of samples of carbonised material recovered from 'destruction' deposits were

	Context	F144	J50	J37	G512
	Phase	1a	1b	1b	1a
Taxa	Deposit type	RH	SO	SO	SH
Corylus nut fragment (c)	hazelnut	3		2	
Corylus nut fragment (w)	hazelnut		4		
Triticum aestivum (c)	bread wheat			1	
Avena (c)	oats				2
Urtica dioica (w)	stinging nettle		1		
Sonchus asper (w)	sow thistle		3		

Deposit definitions	Preservation definitions
R: Redeposited	(c): charred
S: *In situ*	(w): waterlogged
H: Hearth	(m): mineralised
M: Midden	
O: Occupation layer	
F: Fill layer of soil and stone rubble	
C: Charred material	
L: Latrine deposit	
D: Drain fill	

FIGURE 10.18

Plant remains recovered from Phase 1 contexts

321

Taxa	Context	G370	G214	F35	G197	G161	F53
	Phase	2b	2c	2c	2d	2d	2d?
	Deposit type	RH	SO	SC	SC	RM/F	SO
Corylus nut fragment (c)	hazelnut	four	5	1	21	23	
Avena (c)	oats	four			3	18	
Prunus spinosa (c)	sloe				1	1	
Lens culinaris (c)	lentils	1					
Triticum aestivum (c)	bread wheat	4				2	
Rumex acetosella (c)	sheep's sorrel	2					
Carex lenticular (c)	sedges	1					
Plantago lanceolata (c)	ribwort plantain	1					
Prunus cf. *cerasus* (m)	?cherry						1

Deposit definitions

R: Redeposited
S: *In situ*
H: Hearth
M: Midden
O: Occupation layer
F: Fill layer of soil and stone rubble
C: Charred material
L: Latrine deposit
D: Drain fill

Preservation
definitions
(c): charred
(w): waterlogged
(m): mineralised

FIGURE 10.19

Plant remains recovered from Phase 2 contexts

also analysed in the laboratory, using the laboratory procedures outlined above, to determine the nature of the vegetation involved in these 'destruction' events.

Results 'on site'

Phase 1 (Figure 10.18): Plant remains were rare with the almost ubiquitous hazelnut shell fragments (both charred and uncharred) common throughout, although never in large numbers. Charred bread wheat (*Triticum aestivum*) and oats (*Avena spp.*) indicate some use of cereals, whilst the nettles (*Urtica dioica*) and sow thistles (*Sonchus asper*) reflect some disturbed ground which, nonetheless, had been present for some time in order to allow these biennials to have produced seeds. One layer (F114) also had a laboratory processed sample (Figure 10.24).

Phase 2 (Figure 10.19): This phase produced one very rich sample with some hundreds each of charred hazelnuts (*Corylus avellana*) and burnt oats. Lentils (*Lens culinaris*) indicate a traded commodity whilst the sloe (*Prunus spinosa*) and ?cherry (*Prunus* cf. *cerasus*) probably reflect locally gathered fruit.

Phase 3 (Figure 10.20): This was a very active period and well sampled with respect to the latrine pits and midden deposits. One layer (O109) contained vast numbers of charred oat grains with some bread wheat and straw fragments. Given the lack of other food plants, it seems most likely that this layer represents the disposal of domestic, burnt rubbish. (F23), on the other hand, contains huge numbers of fig pips (*Ficus*

carica), grape seeds (*Vitis vinifera*) and apple (*Malus sylvestris*) pips as well as small numbers of seeds from other fruits. Most of these are preserved through waterlogging and/or partial mineralisation. This layer comprises faecal material. The presence of the fennel (*Foeniculum vulgare*) seed would indicate the culinary use of fennel in the 13th century.

Phase 4 (Figure 10.21): This phase encompasses the period of the siege and take over by the English, although most of the plant remains relate to samples from the Welsh occupation. While food plants are infrequent, remains are scattered throughout, mostly oat grains with a little bread wheat, fig and elderberry (*Sambucus nigra*). More of the remains relate to cereal processing or arable weed communities and, since most are charred, may reflect remains of on-site processing of cereals.

Phases 5 and 6 (Figure 10.22): The later phases are not well represented by samples but lentils are abundant in one layer (B16) and barley (*Hordeum* sp.) plus oats are more common than elsewhere.

Overall, from these 'on site' processed samples, the most numerous and frequent remains are those of either cereals or fruits, reflecting aspects of the diet of the inhabitants. They are most common in the latrine deposit (F23). The figs, apple and grape remains are again sometimes partially mineralized, probably reflecting high phosphate levels in these deposits combined with minerals such as calcium hydroxide (lime), presumably added for hygienic reasons. The high score for lentils in Phase 6c is of interest and demonstrates a further aspect of the carbohydrate staple of the diet, as

Taxa	Context	B48	I66	O147	O109	O77	F23	F23*	F19
	Phase	3a	3a	3b	3b	3b	3b	3b	3b
	Deposit type	SO	SD	SH	RC	SM	SL	SL	SM
Corylus nut fragment (c)	hazel nut		1	1	6	4	1		
Corylus nut fragment (w)			17						
Prunus spinosa (c)	sloe			1					
Prunus sp.	plum/cherry							1	
Malus/Pyrus (w)	apple/pear						92		
Malus (w)	crab apple						4		
Vitis vinifera (w)	grape						4	3	
Ficus carica (w)	fig						5	4	
Rubus fruticosus (w)	blackberry						8	1	
Rumex sp. perianths (w)	docken						10		
cf.*Caltha palustris* (w)	?king cup						2		
Chenopodium album (w)	fat hen						5		
Galeopsis tetrahit (w)	hemp nettle						2		
Chenopodiacea cf. *Atriplex* (w)	orache						2		
Triticum (hexaploid) (c)	hexaploid wheat						1		
Lens culinaris (c)	lentil						1		
Gramineae >2mm (w)	grasses								1
Gramineae <2mm (w)									3
Sambucus nigra (w)	elderberry	1					1	1	
Compositae undiff. (w)	dandelion family				2		1		
Legume <4mm (c)	pea/bean				1		1		
Avena (c)	oats				4		1	1	
Triticum aestivum (c)	bread wheat				17				
Cerealia indet. (c)	indet. cereal				1				
Rumex sp (c)	docken				3				
Hordeum (c)	barley				4				
culm nodes (c)	straw				6				
Chrysanthemum segetum (c)	corn marigold				1				
Labiatae undiff. (c)					1				
Polygonum aviculare (c)	knotgrass				1				
Lithospermum arvense								1	
Rubus ideaeus	raspberry							1	
Foeniculum vulgare	fennel							1	

Deposit definitions	Preservation definitions
R: Redeposited	(c): charred
S: *In situ*	(w): waterlogged
H: Hearth	(m): mineralised
M: Midden	
O: Occupation layer	
F: Fill layer of soil and stone rubble	
C: Charred material	
L: Latrine deposit	
D: Drain fill	

* — An earlier sample sorted and identified by Gilchrist (1987)

FIGURE 10.20

Plant remains recovered from Phase 3 contexts

well as of a traded commodity. Oats and bread wheat were the favoured cereals and, as expected, these were all charred. Cereals generally do not survive well unless charred. Almost no chaff was recorded although such material is small and could easily have been missed. Equally, the nature of the site — high status, on top of a dry hillside — would suggest inappropriate conditions for cereal processing. Culm nodes, the more robust and distinct remains of straw, were present in deposits from Area O. The non food remains were limited in number and tend to be of the more robust and distinct seeds.

Results 'laboratory processed'

The data from the laboratory-processed whole earth samples are presented in Figure 10.23. In terms of the matrix components charcoal was dominant, not surprising in flotation samples, but small mammal, fish and comminuted mammal bones were also quite common. The small mammal material was largely non-specific vertebrae and long bone fragments and simply suggests that mice and vole size animals were present (Section 10.2). The fish and comminuted mammal remains are probably derived from faecal

Taxa	Context	H47	O31	F16	H43	B52	H59	B72
	Phase	4a	4a	4b	4c	4c	4c	4d
	Deposit type	RO	SO	SM	RO	RO	RC	SC
Avena (c)	oats	1	5	8	2		26	
Chrysanthemum segetum (c)	corn marigold		21					
culm nodes (c)	straw		5					
Rumex acetosella (c)	sheep's sorrel		2					
Anthemis cotula (c)	stinking mayweed		1					
Polygonum sp. (c)	bistort		1					
Brassica sp. (c)				4				
Cerealia indet. (c)				4				
Sambucus nigra (w)	elderberry			3				
Ficus carica (w)	fig			2				
Stellaria media (w)	chickweed			1				
Avena (m)	oats			1				
Hordeum (c)	barley					1		
Stachys cf. *Palustris* (w)						1		
Corylus nut fragment (c)	hazelnut						1	1
Triticum aestivum (c)	bread wheat						1	

Deposit definitions

R: Redeposited
S: *In situ*
H: Hearth
M: Midden
O: Occupation layer
F: Fill layer of soil and stone rubble
C: Charred material
L: Latrine deposit
D: Drain fill

Preservation definitions

(c): charred
(w): waterlogged
(m): mineralised

FIGURE 10.21

Plant remains recovered from Phase 4 contexts

material; certainly at least some of the fish vertebrae had the oval deformed shape characteristic of having passed through a digestive system. Fly puparia and insect remains were remarkably scarce. This could suggest that material was buried rapidly thus preventing much decay or that preservation is such that these items have not survived. However, it may be that the chemicals which led to the mineral replacement also had the effect of inhibiting colonisation by flies. The very low values of earthworm egg cases probably indicates that little in the way of soil has been added to these deposits.

Oats are the most common and abundant cereal grain recovered with several thousands present in (O109). One or two were noted as having germinated but this could easily reflect poor storage conditions or even late cutting and the occasional grain having started to germinate prior to harvest. Clearly this was not a major feature of the grain. Oat awns are common although the species diagnostic floret bases were not. However, the abundance of the grains infers that it is the cultivated oat that is present and not the wild oat. As such *Avena strigosa* is more likely since it has large numbers of awns whilst *A. sativa*, the common species of 20th-century Britain, does not. Rye (*Secale cereale*) grain and internodes were also common and

provide evidence of another cereal probably locally grown. Barley grains are surprisingly rare given that this species is tolerant of colder wetter climates than rye, for example, and is the typical cereal, along with bread wheat, of Wales today. This may suggest that some of these cereals may derive from animal fodder, as the treatise of Walter of Henley (Oschinsky 1971, 319) indicates that oats were fed to cattle in the sheaf.

The presence of the straw and chaff ('ear' fragments) suggests that at least some of the crops were being grown locally, since such bulky material may not have been transported far. Both straw and chaff would have been important commodities in their own right, being used for animal fodder and bedding. The main processing of the crops (threshing, winnowing, etc) may well have been carried out at either the producer farms or within the settlement below the castle. Whilst the chaff included remains of rye and bread wheat as well as cereal bases, indicating straw itself, the dominant item was oat awns, suggesting the use of chaff for fodder. Walter of Henley (Oschinsky 1971, 331) recommends mingling wheaten or oaten chaff with cattle feed but not barley chaff as this could hurt the mouths of the animals. When the proportions of cereal grain to cereal chaff to weed and ruderal taxa for each bulk sample with > 50 charred remains of these categories

	Context	B35	B16	B31
Taxa	Phase	5a	6c	6c
	Deposit type	SC	SC	RO
Lens culinaris (c)	lentil	1	4	
Labiatae undiff. (c)		1		
Centaurea cyanus (c)	cornflower		15	
Plantago sp. (c)	plantain		3	
Cerealia indet. (c)			2	
Triticum aestivum (c)	bread wheat		1	
Rumex sp (c)	dock		1	
Avena (c)	oats		1	31
Legume <4mm (c)	pea/bean		1	6
Hordeum (c)	barley			21
culm nodes (c)	straw			10
Corylus nut fragment (c)	hazel nut			3
Chrysanthemum segetum (c)	corn marigold			1
Prunus spinosa (c)	sloe			1

Deposit definitions	Preservation definitions
R: Redeposited	(c): charred
S: *In situ*	(w): waterlogged
H: Hearth	(m): mineralised
M: Midden	
O: Occupation layer	
F: Fill layer of soil and stone rubble	
C: Charred material	
L: Latrine deposit	
D: Drain fill	

FIGURE 10.22

Plant remains recovered from Phase 5 and 6 contexts

are considered, whilst grain is over 70% of the assemblages, it is equally clear that chaff and weeds are moderately important components and thus it could be argued that the grain was only partially processed. There is an over-emphasis on chaff in (O109) where the main component of this group is oat awns. This deposit may be the burnt remains of animal fodder waste. The weed seeds may have been brought in with this straw, corncockle (*Agrostemma githago*) and corn marigold (*Chrysanthemum segetum*) are the two most abundant weed seeds present. They are both characteristic of cereal fields, the former often being associated with wheat or rye and the latter oats. The weed seeds did include a few taxa characteristic of lighter soils but the majority were from plants of heavier and well manured soils. These taxa include the *Polygonaceae* and goosefoot (*Chenopodium* sp.) as well as chickweed (*Stellaria media*). Grass caryopses (*Gramineae*) were quite common and may have formed part of the weedy assemblage or represent grassland communities being grazed. There are no strong indications that hay was being used and discarded in these layers. Wet ground taxa such as sedges (*Carex* spp.) are rare. This suggests that low lying wet ground was not being used for cultivation, which is somewhat unusual when compared to medieval deposits elsewhere in Britain. It would, however, tie in with the

dominant cereal species recorded from these layers, rye and oats both preferring free draining soils. Bread wheat is more tolerant of heavier and wetter soils and it is not that common here. This corresponds with the landscape information (Section 8.5), which would suggest that arable cultivation, as represented by strip fields, occurred on the higher ground north of Dryslwyn, the valley floor was used as a water meadow for grazing and hay production.

The mineral replaced seeds are mostly present in (F23), the faecal deposit. A moderate selection is recorded although identification is often only at a low level. The seeds represent a variety of habitats similar to those of the charred assemblage. Waterlogged taxa are not especially abundant either although figs (*Ficus carica*) are dominant in (F23) and apple/pear (*Malus/Pyrus*) and blackberry (*Rubus fruticosus*) common. Most of the waterlogged taxa are either food plants or possible medicinal plants, such as hemlock (*Conium maculatum*). However, the latter also is a ruderal and the low numbers may simply reflect naturally occurring plants in the area.

In summary, the laboratory bulk processed samples have demonstrated that a wide variety of taxa found their way into these layers. Many were charred and represent cereal food and some processing debris or animal fodder. The relatively low numbers and variety of waterlogged taxa are indicative of the poor preservational conditions, with the deposits not being fully waterlogged and anoxic. In general the waterlogged taxa are those with more woody and resistant seeds. The latter were sampled only from very restricted context types but nonetheless provide important data relating to specific dietary components, notably fruits.

Processing comparison

Samples from five contexts were processed both on-site and in the laboratory. There were differences in the number of taxa recovered from each context (Figure 10.24). As expected the majority of the medium (1–2mm) and smaller seeds (<1mm) were only recovered from the laboratory and microscope-investigated material. However, the majority of taxa of the large (2–4mm) seeds were recovered by the 'on site' selection procedures. The larger volume of material which was able to be processed on site meant that several taxa were recovered, in every seed size, which were undetected by the laboratory processing. The detection of seed material on site ensured that the value of this site for producing evidence of medieval diet was appreciated and consequently samples were saved for laboratory processing and funding was available for the necessary specialist reporting. The value of on-site sampling and sieving programmes for indicating both the potential of a site to provide information on plant material and to indicate the

	Context		F114	J18	O77	O109	F19	F23	F16
	Phase		1a	1a	3b	3b	3b	3b	4a
	Deposit type		RH	SO	SM	RC	SM	SL	SM
	Vol. processed (litres)		5	10	9	9	14	6	12
	Charcoal fragments		4	4	4	4	5	3	4
	Coarse sand/gravel		1	2	1			2	2
	Earthworm egg cases			1					
	Fish bone		1	2			2	3	3
	Fly puparia			1				1	
	Insect fragments			1	1	1			
	Small mammal bone		1	1	2		2	2	3
	Calcined mammal bone					1			
Taxa	*Mammal bone*		2	1	2	1			2
Agrostemma githago	corncockle	(c)				8			
Anthemis cotula	mayweed	(c)		1					
Chenopodium album	fat hen	(c)	1			4			
Chrysanthemum segetum	corn marigold	(c)				8			
Polygonum persicaria		(c)				4			
Stellaria media	chickweed	(c)				4			
Avena grain	oat	(c)	44		51	1000s	8		129
Cerealia undiff.	other cereal	(c)			4	196			126
Hordeum indet.	barley	(c)				15			
Secale cereale grain	rye	(c)				60			5
Triticum aestivum grain	bread wheat	(c)				18			22
Lens culinaris	lentil	(c)				21			
Gramineae >4mm	grass	(c)	1						
Gramineae 2–4mm	grass	(c)	3		2	16			
Plantago lanceolata	ribwort-plantain	(c)				16			4
Triticum/Secale grain	wheat/rye	(c)				15			
Empetrum nigrum	crowberry	(c)				8			
Pteridium aquilinum frond frag.	bracken	(c)				4			
Galium aparine	goosegrass	(c)	2			8			
Lapsana communis	nipplewort	(c)	1			60			
Potentilla anserina	silverweed	(c)	1						
Raphanus raphanistrum pod frag.	radish	(c)	1			25			12
Rumex acetosella	sheeps sorrel	(c)	3		1	72			4
Rumex obtusifolius-type	docken	(c)	2		2	48			
Avena awn	oat chaff	(c)				148			4
Avena sp(p). fl. base	oat chaff	(c)	1						
Culm nodes	straw	(c)	1		1	96			
Secale rachis internode	rye chaff	(c)			3	76			
Triticum aestivum internode	bread wheat chaff	(c)							1
Corylus avellana nut frag.	hazel nut	(c)	89		8	8	6		
Rosa thorn	rose	(c)	5						
Rubus fruticosus	blackberry	(c)	1						
Carex (lenticular)	sedge	(c)			2	16			
Isolepis setaceus		(c)	1						
Juncus	rush	(c)		1					
Gramineae <2mm	grass	(c)	5			112			
Legume <4mm	pea/bean	(c)	1		2	4			2
Legume >4mm	pea/bean	(c)				1			
Polygonaceae undiff.		(c)	1	2	2	12	2		
Ranunculus repens-type	creeping buttercup	(c)							4
Rumex sp. perianth		(c)	2						
Avena grain	oat	(m)						2	
Prunella vulgaris	selfheal	(w)						2	
Compositae undiff.		(m)						2	
Galeopsis tetrahit	hemp nettle	(m)						2	
Lamium sp.	dead nettle	(m)		1					
Lapsana communis	nipplewort	(m)						1	
Rumex acetosella	sheeps sorrel	(w)						2	
Rumex obtusifolius-type	sorrel / dock	(w)						2	

FIGURE 10.23

Plant remains recovered in laboratory conditions from selected contexts

Context			F114	J18	O77	O109	F19	F23	F16
Phase			1a	1a	3b	3b	3b	3b	4a
Deposit type			RH	SO	SM	RC	SM	SL	SM
Rumex sp.	sorrel / dock	(w)		1					
Stachys sylvatica	hedge woundwort	(w)		1					
Umbelliferae undiff. (cf Cuminum)	cumin	(w)						1	
Stachys cf. palustris	marsh woundwort	(w)	1						
cf. Cirsium sp(p).	thistle	(w)			1				
Chenopodiaceae undiff.	goosefoot	(w)						2	
Ficus carica	fig	(w)		1				4	
Vitis vinifera	grape	(w)						1	
Gramineae 2–4mm	grass	(w)						1	
Conium maculatum	hemlock	(w)		1					
Urtica dioica	nettle	(w)		2					
Malus/Pyrus	apple / pear	(w)						2	
Rubus fruticosus	blackberry	(w)				1		2	
Sambucus nigra	elderberry	(w)				1			1
Carex (lenticular)	sedge	(w)						1	
Gramineae <2mm	grass	(w)		1					
Mentha-type	mint	(w)						1	

Preservation definitions
(c): charred
(w): waterlogged
(m): mineralised

FIGURE 10.23

Continued

	Context				
	F114	F109	F23	F16	F19
On site	1	12	17	2	7
Laboratory	21	30	16	3	12

FIGURE 10.24

Comparison of taxa recovered through on-site and laboratory processing

range and nature of the type of food plants utilised was highlighted by Caseldine (1990). The laboratory processing of samples provided both a wider range of taxa than on-site sorting and permitted objective quantification, essential for providing a more accurate and holistic appreciation of the floral record, than could be provided by the on-site samples.

Results 'destruction samples'

A group of small (20–100ml) 'charcoal' samples recovered from 'destruction' deposits was processed in the laboratory by wet sieving to 350µ and subsequent drying. The seeds and other diagnostic plant material were identified and quantified (Figure 10.25). Five of these samples, (F114), (G161), (G198), (O81), (B31), are similar to the charred grain and weed material seen elsewhere in the castle and reflect charred and burnt material derived largely from partially processed grain brought into the castle. The samples from (F114) show that cultivated and useful wild plant material (oat, thorn rose, mint) was present from the earliest phase (Phase 1a) of construction and occupation.

The samples from layer (B19), the burnt remains of the wooden gatehouse of the final phases of occupation in Area B, were very different and add a further dimension to the plant remains' story, that of hay. The bulk of the material consisted of fine grass stems with stems of rush (*Juncus* spp.) and the occasional triangular stem typical of sedges (*Carex*). Bracken frond fragments were also present as were some quantities of an angled ridge stem and what have been identified as the tendrils of *Vicia/Lathyrus*. The seed assemblage was dominated by seeds of hardheads or knapweed (*Centaurea nigra*), small legumes and a variety of grass caryopses although seeds and, indeed, fruits, of ribwort plantain (*Plantago lanceolata*) were also quite common. Whole heads and involucral bracts of hardheads were also present and it seems likely that the ridged stems belong to this species as well. The small legumes were of three obvious types: two spherical and one more roundly oblong. Both the spherical types ranged from just under 1mm to about 2.5mm in diameter. One had a short, broad hilum and 'dimpled' surface pattern, the other, much more common type, had a longer and wedge-shaped hilum and smooth, occasionally dimpled, surface. The third category included a few more oval, certainly longer than broad, legumes which had, mostly, lost their hila. From comparison with modern reference material it seems most likely that the more common wedge-shaped hilum type is probably common vetch (*Vicia sativa*). The other spherical category is more problematic: short, broad hila are typical of spring vetch (*Vicia lathyroides*) and grass vetchling (*Lathyrus nissolia*) although both have a rugose 'spotty' textured surface pattern. These may, of course, disappear when burnt. The latter species is most common in south and east England today although still only scattered occurrences and thus seems unlikely in west Wales. The former is characteristic of dry sandy soils scattered throughout Britain. The oblong category may have been something like meadow vetchling (*Lathyrus pratensis*) typical of a wide range of soils and in grassy places, an early flowering species however. Preservation was excellent and there is no obvious reason why the assemblage does anything than represent the original vegetation. This deposit can be compared to the 12th-century hay/animal bedding vegetation from Hen Domen Castle (Powys) (Greig *et al* 1982) which also provided information on the wide range of plant species present in river valley meadows associated with a castle. The location of (B19) indicates that this deposit of hay was stored, probably in the loft, of the wooden gatehouse in the final phase of occupation. The sample from layer (G13) also has grass and sedge seeds and no cereal and thus may also be interpreted as the partial remains of hay or straw, suggesting that the Great Chamber G could have been used as a barn or stable in the final phase of castle occupation.

Discussion of the plant remains

Seed survival has largely been through charring, with some mineral replacement and a little waterlogging (Figure 10.23). The deposits were not fully or permenantly anoxic and the more delicate seeds and tissue have decomposed through time leading to a further bias in the surviving assemblage. The charred remains largely reflect the cereals and their associated weeds and ear fragments. Most are cereal grains themselves with only limited evidence for discard of crop processing debris. As the deposits are from within a high status site it is not unexpected that the bulk of processing debris was not recovered. It is most likely that primary processing was undertaken in either the town below the castle or outlying farms where the concentrations of threshing and sieving debris might be found. Straw does seem to have been used and probably reflects discarded fodder or bedding material. The paucity of sedge/grass remains would suggest that floors were not strewn with this material although, as always, it may not have been discarded in these particular layers.

Oats are seen as either the only or the principal cereal in almost all deposits from which plant remains were recovered. They were especially prevalent in the early to late 13th-century deposits (Phases 1–4). The on-site processed deposits of Phase 6, the early 15th-century destruction of the castle, suggest that a larger proportion of lentils, barley, etc may be coming into use in the later period. It is also noticeable that where there were larger samples as in the case of layers (O109), (O77), (F16), small amounts of other grains; barley, rye and bread wheat are also present. This apparently dominant use of oats with other mixed grains appears so frequently that it appears to be the 'normal' form of grain deposits seen at Dryslwyn. This 'dominant oat with some other cereals' deposit is also seen on a number of other Welsh sites such as the urban sites of Rhuddlan (13th century) (Holden *et al* 1994) and Carmarthen Greyfriars (11th–13th century) (James 1997); the castle sites of Loughor (Swansea) (Carruthers 1993), where it was found as carbonised material associated with corn drying ovens, and Wiston (Pembrokeshire) (12th century) (Caseldine 1995). It also occurs at the 13th-century farmstead sites of Capel Maelog (Powys), Cefn Graenog (Gwynedd) and in the 15th-century farmstead site of Collfryn (Powys) (Caseldine 1990). The same range of weed seeds, corn marigold (*Chrysanthemum segetum*) in particular, was seen in deposits from Loughor, Rhuddlan, Wiston and other sites, as well as at Dryslwyn. The extensive occurrence of this weed rich, oat dominant mixed grain crop supports Hillman's suggestion that, as with modern day traditional societies, Welsh medieval societies harvested the grain crop before it was fully ripe, in order to minimize grain loss from ripe ears, from fields which contained a range of cereal weeds. The resultant grain was only coarse sieved and winnowed before it was dried in a corn drier oven. This created an oat grain rich product which contained husked grain and a large number of smaller, but heavy weed seeds (Hillman 1981; Holden *et al* 1994). The presence of this oat rich mixed cereal crop in the Inner Ward of Dryslwyn Castle, especially from the latrine deposit (F23) would suggest that was not used as animal feed but for human consumption. Oats and pilcorn (partially de-husked oats) were purchased at various markets and brought back to Dryslwyn, thus at least some of the archaeobotanical remains could be of this stock. *Dovraeth* oats are also mentioned as a render to the lord of the castle.

Oats were undoubtedly the favoured cereal in Wales and elsewhere in the north and west of the UK due to their tolerance of damp growing conditions. However, the climatic improvements of the 13th century could have led to conditions, even in west Wales, where wheat and rye might have been grown successfully. In later periods historic records indicate that cereals such as oats and barley were sometimes deliberately grown together and referred to as 'drage' (Holden *et al* 1994). Possible evidence of such a mixed crop, principally barley with a substantial number of oats, was recovered from the 1270–90 destruction deposits of the hall of Rumney Castle near Cardiff (Williams 1992) and similarly Prudhoe Castle (Tyne and Wear) produced a charred assemblage of bread wheat and oats (Vaughan 1983).

Wheat, principally bread or club wheat has been recovered from a number of 12th to 14th century sites in Wales both as relatively clean deposits of wheat from Rumney Castle (Cardiff) (Williams 1992), Conway and Cowbridge (Caseldine 1990) and Loughor Castle (Swansea) (Carruthers 1993) as well as in more mixed grain deposits from Rhuddlan (Holden *et al* 1994), Laugharne Castle (Carmarthenshire) (Caseldine 1990) and Dryslwyn. Even this small number of sites suggests a greater likelihood of wheat growing in the fertile south-east of Wales and on Anglesey, rather than extensively throughout Wales. The presence of rachis fragments of bread wheat most likely suggest some local production but it is also clear from contemporary documentary evidence (Rhys 1936) that once Dryslwyn was a garrisoned castle of the English Crown, wheat was brought in from markets at considerable distances from Dryslwyn, such as Brecon and Hereford.

Rye is perhaps unexpected given the geographical location of the castle but documentary records confirm the usage of this cereal and, indeed, of its local production (Rhys 1936). Maslin (rye and wheat grown together) was noted by Alan de Plucknet, the constable in 1287–89, although no other details are given. Rye, typically, is found in more continental climates, where it is well able to withstand the extremely cold but essentially dry winters. Rye was also recovered from 13th–14th century carbonised deposits associated with a corn drying oven at Rhuddlan (Holden *et al* 1994). There are no records of rye having been purchased and thus it could be argued that the rye represented in these samples is all a local product.

Barley, as noted earlier, is rare but tends to be more common in the later deposits. The grains are all hulled but it is not known whether the species was the 2-row or the 6-row. No chaff was recovered and none of the grains had germinated. The only reference to presumed barley in the documentary evidence is with the purchase of chief malt and curral malt although oat malt is also specifically mentioned. Clearly the surviving material is not malt or it should have shown signs of germination.

The presence of a rotary quern [S8] (Phase 1b) and reference to a 'hand quern' in the castle stores of 1300/01 (Rhys 1936; Phillpotts 2001c) indicates that grain could be ground within the castle. Consequently whole grain may well have been stored in the castle. However, the presence of a mill (Section 8.5), within half a mile of the site, which was operational during the 'Welsh' period, would suggest that ready ground flour was normally available in the castle. Indeed, both wheatmeal and oatmeal regularly appear in the Manor Rolls as considerable purchases (Rhys 1936).

The occurrence of >4mm legumes in the Dryslwyn samples corresponds with the recovery of peas (*Pisum sativum*) and/or field beans (*Vica faba*) from a number of 13th-century contexts such as Rhuddlan and Cefn Greanog (Powys) (Holden *et al* 1994) and Rumney Castle (Cardiff) (Williams 1992). The large number of field beans in a clean deposit at Rumney indicated the careful cultivation and cleaning of this crop, which had been preserved through accident. Pulses may have been a significant element in the 13th and 14th century Welsh diet but as they are dried naturally, without the use of fire, kilns, etc, they are less likely to be charred and hence survive. Beans were noted as being in the dead garnisture for 1304/05.

Lentils, preserved in the charred state, especially in layer (O109), would have been a traded commodity imported from the Mediterranean or further east. There are few comparative examples for lentils in the 13th century, though they were imported in the Roman period and have been found in locations such as Carlisle (Huntley 1989). As with the other legumes they will only be charred by chance or accident and therefore are likely to be under-represented in the archaeological record.

Numerous figs and grape seeds were recovered from the latrine deposit (F23) of Phase 3b, an affluent time in the castle's history (Section 2.1). It is presumed that these were imported fruits that provide evidence for trading perhaps via the port at Bristol. Grapes would probably have been imported from Spain or France and figs from the Mediterranean area generally. Grape and fig seeds were have also been recovered from the 16th-century latrine deposits of the Tudor merchants' house in Tenby (Caseldine 1990), and a grape pip was recovered from 13th-century carbonised deposits at Rumney Castle (Cardiff) (Williams 1992). These have invariably been interpreted as imported exotic fruits, though the presence of pollen from the grape vine (*Vitis vinifera*) from the latrine at Tenby (Caseldine 1990) is a reminder that grapes could have been grown in west Wales at this period. As both fig and grape dry well for transport, survival on a sea journey was not necessarily a problem. Fig seeds from medieval sites such as the Palace at Kings Langley (Hertfordshire) (Neal 1977) and Norwich (Murphy 1979) suggest that dried figs were traded throughout the UK by the 14th and 15th centuries. Fig and grape pips from 13th-century contexts in Oslo indicate that this medieval trade in fruits was increasingly extensive by this date (Griffin 1979). The presence of a fig seed in the Phase 1a occupation layer (J50) is a surprisingly early occurrence, which suggests that this trade in exotic fruit was already established by the early 13th century, perhaps supplying clients such as the Lord Rhys and Rhys Gryg at Dinefwr as early as the late 12th century.

The possible cumin seed also hints at trade from further afield, probably the Asian sub-continent. Two pounds (*c*900g) of cumin was procured from

Taxa	Context	F114	G161	G198	O81	G13	B31	B19 a	B19 b	B19 c
	Sample							a	b	c
	Phase	1a	2d	2d	3b	5d	6c	6c	6c	6c
Hordeum hulled			1				3			
Triticum aestivum			2							
Avena sp		1	1	8	19		7			1
Indet. cereal			1							
Triticum aestivum glume base				1			1			
Avena strigosa pedicel							2			
Avena awn							2			
Avena sativa floret base							6			
Culm nodes		1			10		8			1
<4mm legume			1		1					
Lapsana communis					1					
Rumex acetosella					1		1	1		8
Chenopodium sp.					1					
Cerastium sp.					1			4	4	
Trifolium type					11			4		
Anthemis cotula		1			3					1
Raphanus raphanistrum pod					1		1			
Polygonaceae undiff.		2			2					
Chrysanthemum leucanthemum					7					2
<2mm *Gramineae*						+		22		22
2-4mm *Gramineae*		1				+		17	20	29
Plantago lanceolata						++		28	40	16
<4mm legume				2				42	c400	
Vicia/Lathyrus pods+tendrils							2		++	c40
Centaurea nigra								2	260	6
Centaurea nigra bracts+heads								12	32	
Rhinanthus minor								4	4	
>4mm *Gramineae*								5		14
Carex (trigonous)						+				1
<2mm legumes						++				
>4mm legume		1								
Rosa thorn		4								
Mentha-type		1								
Corylus avellana nutshell				2						
Prunus spinosa				1						
Pteridium frond							+			
Spergula arvensis							1			
Chrysanthemum segetum							3			
Bromus sp.									12	
Rumex acetosa										1

FIGURE 10.25

Charred plant remains recovered from 'destruction' deposits

Carmarthen but nothing remained in the dead garnisture for 1298–1300. The cumin provides evidence for culinary or medicinal use as it was one of the more common culinary spices in the 13th and 14th centuries (Grieve 1931). Medicinally it was used against flatulence or a languid digestion, colic and headache.

Evidence for a further culinary or medicinal herb was found by Gilchrist (1987) in the shape of a fennel seed (Figure 10.26). It was used against witches and also eaten with salt fish. The presence of brassica seeds from the midden (F16) may suggest the use of cabbage or other leaf vegetables of the brassica family as a food source or, indeed, mustard type seeds as culinary/medicinal herbs. Hillman had proposed that green leaves found in the waterlogged deposits of the latrine at Usk could be from cultivated or gathered wild leaf vegetables used as food (Caseldine 1990). However, the lack of any leaf waxes in the organic residue analysis of the ceramics (Section 10.9) suggests that leaf vegetables were not cooked with the meats, fish and dairy products and thus may either not have formed part of the diet or they were eaten raw.

Native fruits such as pear, cherry, plum and raspberry were probably locally grown, perhaps in the castle garden (Section 8.5), whilst blackberry, elderberry, sloes and crab apple may either have been deliberately grown or gathered from the wild. A similar range of fruit pips and seeds were recovered from the medieval latrine at Usk (Caseldine 1990) and other

FIGURE 10.26

Scanning electron micrograph of a fennel seed

UK medieval sites have produced evidence of various fruits: elderberry seeds from early 15th century contexts at St Peters St, Northampton (Keepax *et al* 1979), elderberry and blackberry seeds from a cesspit in the Palace at Kings Langley in Hertfordshire (Neal 1977), numbers of cherry/sloe type kernels were excavated from Saxon monastic contexts in Hartlepool (Huntley 1988), apple pips, blackberry and elderberry seeds from Norwich (Murphy 1979), sloe and elderberry from Barnard Castle (Durham) (Donaldson *et al* 1980) and apple pips from mid 12th-century contexts at Castle Acre in Norfolk (Green 1982). It is clear from the preservation of these seeds from the latrine deposit (F23) that fruit formed an element of the diet and that the range of fruit eaten was as wide, or wider, than from other UK sites. The amount of fruit eaten and the exact proportions of the various fruits remains uncertain, but the sale of fruit recorded from the castle garden in the 14th century (Rhys 1936) would indicate that fruit was readily available in the castle and that any surplus was sold.

Hazelnuts survived well, even in partially waterlogged deposits. They were recovered from more than half of the analysed deposits in the castle, and were particularly prevalent in the early Phases (1–3) of occupation, where nuts are present in a high percentage of the deposits. Sites such as Rhuddlan (13th century) (Holden *et al* 1994) and Castle Acre (Norfolk) (12th century) (Green 1982) have also produced hazelnuts, which would have formed a useful element in the diet of either animals or humans. The proximity of the Glyncothi forest (Carmarthenshire), the most likely source of hazelnuts, may have led to

the greater exploitation of this food resource at Dryslwyn than at other sites. However, the quantities are not enormous and, given the high survivability of the shell, may well be over-represented in the surviving plant remains.

When using the surviving plant remains to obtain a picture of the local flora the assemblage which is largely preserved by charring produces a bias towards cereals. In this case, the weed and ruderal taxa represented indicate that a variety of soils were being cultivated and that manuring seems to have been undertaken too. There is little evidence for use of heavy clay soils, which are likely to have been within the river valley, for cultivation and thus it might be hypothesised that these areas were used primarily as grazing for livestock. There is no evidence for maritime communities and thus salt marsh is not likely to have been used to a great extent. There is little evidence for heathland. The few heathery remains may well represent roofing but clearly were not the main roofing material.

The small samples taken from 'destruction' contexts seem most likely to have been hay which had originated on damp neutral to slightly alkaline soils such as would typically be found in the river valleys locally. The assemblage consists predominately of grasses, knapweed, ribwort plantain and vetches/tares with a small amount of yellow rattle (*Rhinanthus minor*) and is a rather species-poor assemblage. The lack of other typical hay meadow species such as buttercups (*Ranunculus acris/bulbosus*) is interesting in that many of these plants produce robust seeds, which generally survive well. This may simply be the result of small samples or may reflect a late hay cut, since knapweed does not produce seeds until September and plantain can continue to do so until October whilst the buttercups are generally fruiting by July to August. The vetches and tares tend to have quite a long flowering, hence fruiting, season. Rhys (1936) quotes several instances of hay being procured from a variety of local meadows with the associated costs of cutting and carting back to one castle or another. She also notes that on several occasions it was of poor quality and in one instance 'lost through inundation', reflecting wet summers or late cutting, or both.

In overall summary, the material processed and recorded on site provided valuable information about the potential of the site as well as some indication of the range of species being used. The laboratory-processed material produced, as expected, a more objective dataset. Much of the plant material had been preserved through charring and thus related largely to the cereals, their chaff and associated weeds. Oats were the most commonly recovered cereal followed by bread wheat and rye with very little barley apparently being used. Whilst all of the three major cereals could and probably were locally grown and processed, in the 14th century a certain amount of oats and some wheat were also bought at markets, some from considerable distances away. The weed seeds suggest that a variety of local soils were being used and that these were being manured to improve yields. The cereals tie in well with other sites of a similar period and region. The limited evidence for hay is, nonetheless, valuable and demonstrates the probable use of the river valleys for more than just pasture.

The waterlogged/mineral replaced material likewise gives a biased suite of taxa principally as a result of the nature of the contexts: the latrine. They provide excellent evidence for a range of food plants. Whilst many of the seeds were from fruits which could have been growing wild or cultivated locally others gave indications of 12th–14th century trade. Lentils, figs, grapes and fennel probably came from the Mediterranean area whilst the cumin was probably from further east.

The documentary evidence

Following the capture of Dryslwyn Castle, in 1287, it was garrisoned by the Crown. During the period 1287–90 the constables of Dryslwyn Castle were required to submit annual accounts to the Royal Exchequer. Subsequently in the period 1298–1306 Dryslwyn was one of a number of castles that were overseen by the king's justiciar in West Wales who submitted accounts to the Royal Exchequer for garrisoning and provisioning of these castles. Details of some of these statements of account, which were preserved in the Public Record Office were translated by Rhys (1936) and they provide us with valuable

information regarding the plants and animals being bought, sold or consumed by the castle's garrison. The accounts of foodstuffs in storage (dead garnisture) provide information as to how long goods were kept and how commodities were moved between the castles.

It appears that for the initial years after its capture, Dryslwyn may have continued to act as a commotal centre. There are no records of expenditure on food, but the accounts show large surpluses of food, much of which was sold off. The garrison appear to have consumed food still present in the castle when it was captured and fresh produce brought in as part of the annual renders to the lord such as the 'dovraeth oats' (Section 10.1). It is also possible that crops and animals were still raised directly on the demesne land and thus came to the constable of the castle. Therefore, it is likely that the plants and animals sold or consumed by the castle's garrison were the produce of the commote of Cethiniog,

After a break in the records, the entries for 1298 and subsequent years indicate that only rents are received from the town of Dryslwyn and the rest of the commote. The mills, gardens and other assets of Dryslwyn castle have been 'farmed out', probably to the inhabitants of the town, who pay a rent for the facility. There is no evidence of food renders, all the food coming into the castle is paid for under the expenditure accounts. The food for the group of royal castles in West Wales: Dryslwyn, Dinefwr, Emlyn, Cardigan, Llanbadarn and Carmarthen is purchased centrally from towns such as Hereford, Haverford, Brecon and Carmarthen and then distributed to the individual castles in the group. The impression, gained from these accounts, is one of moving from an agricultural produce economy to a cash-based economy. Though the agricultural base of the economy remained, the royal accounts indicate that arrangements were sought that yielded rents in cash rather than produce. The purchase of foodstuffs was preferred, quite literally, at market prices.

Large volumes of wheat and oats were sold in 1287–89 suggesting that these were the principal grain crops of Cethiniog. Smaller quantities of malt and maslin were also sold indicating that rye and barley were also grown. Reference to 'poor wheat mixed with rye' (Phillpotts 2001c) present in the castle when first entered by the Crown forces in 1287, also indicates that rye and wheat were grown and/or stored together. References to apples and nuts (Rhys 1936, 41, 45) and to a garden suggest that there had been a garden, which was in large part an orchard, supplying apples and nuts to the castle. These facts correspond well with the recovered plant remains. Hay is mentioned in almost every year of the Dryslwyn accounts, with the castle continuing have up to 12 acres of field which was cut as hay and stored in the castle (Rhys 1936, 121). This hay meadow was most probably located on the valley floor, which was not divided into fields until the 19th century, (Section 8.5). Thus the plant remains from (B19) may describe the nature of the vegetation of the valley floor. Elsewhere at Llanbadarn Castle (Ceredigion) one meadow, at Dysfrynclaragh, which may also have been on the valley floor, seems to have been subject to inundation and to produce poor quality hay.

The mention of pigs from pannage and lambs derived from the constable's (lord's) fee which were sold in 1288/89 indicate some of the animals raised in Cethiniog at this time (Rhys 1936, 45). The fact that 1¾ tuns of salt was recorded as present in the castle stores (dead garnisture) when they were first entered by Crown forces in 1287 (Rhys 1936, 49) suggests that the salting of meat was commonly practiced by the Welsh at Dryslwyn. This practice continued after the siege with 24 quarters and 3 bushels of salt recorded as in store in the royal castles of West Wales in 1298/99. 86 oxen and 12 pigs were salted down in that same year (Rhys 1936, 175). In addition to purchasing animals and salt, firewood was purchased for Dryslwyn and other castles 'to dry the meat' (Rhys 1936, 149). This would suggest drying or smoking of meat was being undertaken as well as salting in order to preserve the food. There is also mention of using the firewood for drying corn (Rhys 1936, 149), which explains the presence of charred grain, especially oats on site. Both grain and meal (flour) are recorded as stored in the castle, one for use, the other for longer term storage. Stored grain could be ground in the mill at Dryslwyn, or in the hand querns within the castle (Section 10.8).

The importation of wine, by direct purchase or through 'prise', a royal tax on imported wine which was levied at Carmarthen and Cardigan in 1303/04 (Rhys 1936, 327), secured wine for royal castles (Rhys 1936, 175). Rents, recorded as paid to the Justiciar in pepper and cumin, confirms the trade and presence of these spices in Carmarthen by the end of the 13th century.

Though there are considerable quantities of animals and cereals bought for consumption in the 1298–1306 period, there is no evidence of vegetables, fruit, spices and or even fish (18 meazes of herrings are bought but subsequently sold) for the diet of the garrison of the castles. They may have been purchased locally and not been included in these accounts, but it indicates that the bulk of the diet for the royal garrisons remained one of bread, pottage, ale and meat. Some wine and honey was used to vary the diet (Rhys 1936, 147–149).

Figure 10.27 summarises the information regarding the types and quantities of plant products recorded in these Ministers Accounts for West Wales (Rhys 1936); 19 commodities are mentioned of which 14 relate to cereals. The others include beans, at almost 20,000 litres, in the stores in Dinefwr Castle (Carmarthenshire) in 1304/05. The 25,000 litres of honey purchased at least in part at Carmarthen seems to have been moved from Dryslwyn and Dinefwr Castles where

some was classed as 'old honey'; it was worth about 8½d a gallon then. The only mention of purchase of honey was in the 1298–1300 record when it cost 8d a gallon. Between 1304/05 32 stone (approx. 201kg) of hemp were purchased. It is presumed that the hemp was purchased as the raw fibre as there were also records of costs for men to beat and dress the hemp.

The cereals referred to are mainly oats and wheat. A very small amount of maslin (wheat and rye mixture) is mentioned. Of the oats and wheat, more than 50% of the volumes quoted relate to the whole grains with about 25% each to malts and meal. The malts either specifically refer to oat or just to generic malt. Today this would be barley malt and would be used in the brewery industry. Malt or 'chief' malt in the 13th–14th centuries would probably have been barley but there is no conclusive evidence. Curral malt refers to malted tail grain, the smaller grains of oats in this instance. Presumably the malted products were being used in brewing but could have been used to produce a naturally sweet porridge.

References in 1300/01 to the loss of grain because 'it was dried on the kiln so that it hardened too long' and wood in the stores 'used for drying corn' (Rhys 1936; Phillpotts 2001c) indicates that parching of grain was being practiced in or around the castle during the late 13th–early 14th century.

Meal refers to ground grains and, of the species, oatmeal is clearly the most important at 16% with wheatmeal and unspecified meal at 1 and 3% respectively. The oatmeal may well have been made into a porridge or into unleavened bread, the traditional Welsh oatcakes (Section 10.1). In terms of prices for oatmeal, they vary considerably and some are referring to 'old' oatmeal, presumably some that has been kept in store for some considerable time. Prices varied between 1298–1300 with 74 quarters being bought at Brecon for £22 4s (a rate of 9d a bushel) and some bought locally from Cilsan Mill (Carmarthenshire) at almost 5d a bushel although only 3d a bushel was paid for old oatmeal. This would suggest that these prices included transport costs given that the oatmeal purchased at Brecon was the most expensive. The wheatmeal, probably equivalent to modern day 'stone-ground wholemeal' flour may well reflect a fine quality product destined for the constable's and chaplain's tables in the form of leavened bread.

Wheat and oat grains were both quite commonly purchased products, with more wheat than oats. The wheat was bought in from Haverford, Brecon and Hereford ranging in price from 6d a bushel for old wheat, 11d and 12d at Hereford, 11d at Haverford and an extraordinary 6/8d a bushel at Brecon; this is undoubtedly a clerical error and should read 6–8d per bushel.

Between 1298 and 1306 oats were purchased at 'divers places' more often than at specific markets probably reflecting relatively local surpluses and more ad hoc supplies. Prices varied from 1d to 2d a bushel

Plants	Quantity	Cost	Notes
1287–89			
Oats			Alan Plukenet £8 5s 7½d including lambs; the two used to be constable's fee
Wheat, maslin (rye + wheat mix), malt, apples and herbage)			Alan Plukenet again, no other details
Poor wheat	0.5q	12d	Remains in store
Oatmeal	2.5 q	2/-	Remain in store
Wheatmeal	3q	24s 8d	
Chief malt	3q		Remain in store
Curral malt	6q		30/- with the chief malt. Curral (cursal) small or refuse corn
Meal	2 casks (8 q)	38s 2d	Remain
1289–90			
Wheat	60q		This & 3 below from dead garnisture from Mallaen
Wheatmeal	11q		
Maslin	0.5q		
Malt	9q		
Wheat	7 bushels		The issue from Henllys Mill & 2 below
Pilcorn	1q 5 bushels		Corn cleaned of husks; generally refers to hulled oats
Dovraeth oats	65q 5bushels		Oats used as tribute
Oatmeal	3q 3 bushels	11s 5½d	From Cilsan Mill
1298–1300			
Pepper	1 lb	12d	
Cummin	2 lbs	2d	
Pepper	1 lb	12d	Assessed rent for Carmarthen at a feast
Wheat	38 quarters	2/8 per q	Old wheat from garnisture
Oatmeal	580 bushels	£7-5s total	Old oatmeal, 3d per bushel
Oats	40q	26s8d	8d per quarter
Herring	18 meazes	2/- per meaze	
Hay		26s3d & 8s10d	For mowing, lifting and carrying hay from 12 acres meadows plus a further 8s10d for 3 acres of doing the same at Dinevor Castle
Wheat	34q	£13-12-0	Bought at Hereford; 8/1 per quarter
Oats	7q3.5bushels	9s11d	Bought at divers places16d per quarter
Chief malt	8.5q	£7 4s 6d	Bought at Hereford, carried to Llanbadarn 7/- per quarter
Oat malt	25.5q		Also bought Hereford, carried to Llanbadarn 3s4d per quarter
Hay		35/-	35/- for mowing, lifting and carrying to castle from 10 acres meadow
Firewood and peat		1-/-	
Hay		10/-	5 acres, mowing etc carrying to Cardigan Castle
Hay		5/-	2 acres Emlyn Castle
Wheat	138.5 b	£46 3s 4d	6s 8d/bushel, bought at Brecon carried to Dinevor and Dryslwyn
Oats	43q	57s4d	16d per quarter, bought Brecon for Dinevor and Dryslwyn
Oatmeal	592 bushels making 74q	£22 4s	6/- per quarter Brecon for Dinevor & Dryslwyn
Salt	33q3b	100s 1½d	3s per quarter for salting pigs & larder
Honey	168 gallons	112s	8d/gall bought at Carmarthen for Dinevor & Dryslwyn
Hay		28/-	12 acres meadows & lifting to Drys; 2s4d per acre
Hay			3 acres & lifting to Dinevor
Wheat	47.5q	£17 8s 4d	7/4d per quarter bought Hereford transported to Llanbadarn
Wheat	69.5q	£25 9s 8d	7s4d/q; bought at Haverford, transport by sea to Llanbadarn
Oats	22q 6b	30s4d	Bought at divers places and transported to Llanbadarn
Chief malt	35.5q	£12 13s 9d	19q6b @ 7s/q bought at Haverford and 15.5q 2b @ 7s4d at Hereford to Llanbadarn
Oat malt	99q 2b	£16 10s 10d	3s4d/q bought at Haverford taken to Llanbadarn
Pilcorn	300 bushels	£12 10s	10d/bushel for the dead garnisture of Dryslwyn & Dinevor from Carmarthen; 150 bushels transported by 36 horses at 2d a horse: 6s; other 150 bushels to Dinevor 36 horses, 4d/horse: 12s
Honey	2 casks	£22 13s 4d	10/- carriage for one cask to Dinevor, 6s8d the other to Drys
Firewood		2 × 10/-	Brought to the two castles for drying meat from the larder
Wheat	173q 3 bushels	£63 11s 5d	Haverford to Llanbadarn, 7s4d/quarter
Oats	64 q	£4 5s 4d	@16p/quarter Haverford to Llanbadarn
Oatmeal	439 bushels	£16 9s 3d	9d/bushel
Chief malt and oat malt	121q 3b	Var	Various prices for different batches - bought at Brecon and Hereford

FIGURE 10.27

Plant details from Ministers Accounts: royal income and expenditure related to the garrison at Dryslwyn Castle, from Rhys (1936)

Plants	Quantity	Cost	Notes
1298–1300			
Wheat	34q		1st June-27th September for Llanbadarn constable & 50 men
Oats	7q 3.5 bushels		Same period and numbers
Oats	7q 3.5b		1 horse fodder for 119 days
Chief malt	8.5 q		Same period/men
Oat malt	25.5 q		Ditto; they also ate 7½ ox carcases
Hay, firewood and peat			Dryslwyn, Dinevor, Llanbadarn, Cardigan and Emlyn castles
Pepper	1 lb		Rent at Carmarthen, nothing remians
Cummin	2 lbs		Rent at Carmarthen, nothing remains
Honey and wine	Umpteen caskets		
Sea coal	200 bushels		Purchased at Haverford
1300–1301			
Wheat, oats and oatmeal and salt (as well as wine and a carcase)			Being sold off since they were old - from Emlyn, Dryslwyn, Dinevor and Llanbadarn
Peat			Bought to burn at Llanbadarn
Firewood			Bought to dry meat in store at Drys and Dinevor
1303–04			
Hay		28s 8d	Meadow called Dysfrynclaragh at Llanbadarn 30 acres + a memo saying hay had been lost through inundation
1304–05			
Poor wheat	18q	36/-	Sold at end of 2nd year, left at Dinevor Castle
Beans	2q 7bushels	6s8.5d	2s 4d/bushel from the garnisture of Dinevor
Beans	61q 2 bushels	£7 2s 11d	2s 4d/bushel bought in the second year
Honey (old honey)	160+152 gallons	£10 9s	From garnisture of Drys and Dinevor
Hay		Nothing	Meadow called Dysfrynclaragh at Llanbadarn 30 acres, handed over to divers men of the welshery to mow etc. Half went to Llanbadarn and of small value before mowing
Hemp	32 stone		Presumably fibre/rope, raw since later account to pay 2 men for 4 days work to beat and dress hemp 2d/day each

Gallon = 4.5 litres
Bushel = 8 gallons = 36.4 litres
Quarter = 8 bushels = 291.2 litres; quarter also measure of weight = 28 pounds = 12.7 kg
Cask = 8 quarters = 2329.6 litres
Pound (weight) = 0.45 kg
Stone = 14 pounds
Money is pounds, shillings and pence

FIGURE 10.27

Continued

showing that oats were considerably cheaper than wheat even when bought at Brecon or Haverford. It is assumed that most of these oats remained in their husks thus requiring further processing before being used as human food. In comparison, pilcorn consists of oats which have been de-husked and their value demonstrates this in that they were worth 10d a bushel.

In terms of consumption the accounts for the dead garnistures are invaluable. One record for 1298–1300 notes that about 7.5 quarters (2166 litres) of oats '1 horse fodder for 119 days', i.e. 18 litres per day, For the same period, 50 men and a constable consumed the same amount of oats plus 34 quarters of wheat, 8.5 quarters of chief malt and 25.5 quarters of oat malt as well as 7.5 ox carcasses. Whilst this may not reflect a varied or particularly balanced diet it still provides adequate sustenance and it is quite likely that, in addition, some vegetables were available locally. Assuming that Dryslwyn oxen produced about 150kg meat each, about equivalent to modern Dexter cattle of a similar size to the medieval stock (Section 10.2), these stores suggest a daily diet for each man of about 0.2kg beef, 1.6 litres wheat, 0.35 litres oats and 1.6 litres malt. This represents 4oz of meat, nearly 4 kg wholemeal buns followed by almost 1kg of porridge washed down with a hefty 164 litres of ale. This volume of ale is unduly high so it is likely that the malt was also being used for other food purposes or that, whilst these stores were available per day, they were not used and actually included 'emergency rations' for those days when the castle was under siege or had unexpected guests. It must be remembered that the meat diet was probably supplemented by salted pork products (Rhys 1936, 183) and locally bought produce.

10.6 CHARCOAL

by Chris Caple, Jennifer Miller and Susan Ramsay
(additional identification by Jacqui Huntley)

There was no systematic recovery or sampling of the charcoal found during excavation, but 48 bags of charcoal samples were collected from deposits noted as rich in charcoal. The vast majority of these (70%) were recovered from the burnt destruction deposits found in the undercroft of the Hall K/L, deriving from the wood used in the construction of the upper floors and roof. Other samples were collected from occupation layers throughout the site that contained charcoal, probably derived from firewood.

A representative selection of charcoal fragments was identified from each of the 48 bags, with the remainder of each sample scanned for additional taxa. Charcoal identification was undertaken (JM and SR) using the reflected light of a Zenith metallurgical microscope at a magnification of ×200. Reference was made to pictures and descriptions in Schweing-ruber (1990). Vascular plant nomenclature follows Stace (1997). The results obtained are displayed in Figure 10.28 and included data on the weight of charcoal fragments identified and the taxa from which they derive. Also included is an estimation of the curvature of the growth rings, which provides a crude approximation of the size, and thus the role, of the piece of timber. This information was recorded togeth-er with the nature and phasing of the deposits which produced charcoal.

Large samples of charcoal, initially identified as beams, were recovered from the burnt destruction deposit (K12) in the undercroft of the Great Hall (K/L). Samples of 'beam' were fractured by hand in the laboratory and examined (JPH) at magnifications of up to x200 using a Leica DM/LM epiluminescent, bright field microscope. The characteristics of the sample were noted in the three planes of observation (transverse, longitudinal radial and tangential). Iden-tification was by the combination of specific charac-ters and by comparison with modern charred wood and slides of wood sections held in the Department of Archaeology, University of Durham, in conjunction with illustrations and descriptions in Schweingruber (1978) and Gale and Cutler (2000).

Results and discussion

The majority of the wood recovered from the destruc-tion deposits of the Great Hall K/L was oak (*Quercus*), and almost all of it had growth rings that appear almost straight in cross section indicating that the samples derive from substantial pieces of timber. The other species of timber recovered from these deposits, ash (*Fraxinus*), beech (*Fagus*) and hornbeam (*Carpi-nus*), also had straight or shallow curved growth rings indicating that they derived from large timbers. These

results clearly indicate the dominance of oak used in the Great Hall K/L, and medieval wooden buildings in general, because of its strength and durability (Edlin 1973). A similar predominance of oak was seen in other examples of 13th-century timber construction such as the refectory of Valle Crucis Abbey (Denbigh-shire) (Bartley 1976). Some of the timberwork used in the Great Hall K/L could derive (in its original posi-tion or reused) from the earliest phase of the early to mid 13th century, whilst timbers were probably added in the remodelling of the 1280s and the renovation of the 1330s. The fact that charred grain was recovered from charcoal sample 4 (K10), indicates that there was other material caught up in the fire which engulfed the Great Hall K/L in Phase 6c and samples did not exclusively represent structural woodwork.

Upon examination the large charcoal 'beam' samples proved to be composed of a number of pieces of charred wood. Analysis indicated that the material from (K12) represented the remains of an interior, probably non load-bearing wall, similar to the modern stud-partition walling (Figure 10.29). Ash and acer (maples; probably *Acer campestre*, field maple) (faced roundwood poles) formed vertical support struts to which was attached thin oak planking (radially split planking or laths from large slow grown trees), which was probably covered with mortar or daub on at least on one side (Section 6.1). In a few cases there is obviously a 'more' burnt side with the mortar being redder. The notes of the site supervisor who recovered these samples recorded 'a burnt beam with seemingly some attached planks (as previous examples) was found in the south corner of the excavation area on the mortar floor of the cellar. Several poorly preserved examples of regular strips of charcoal equating to planking were found during the excavation of these layers' (Day Diary Area K (02) 15 July 1981, Dryslwyn Archive).

The samples derived from layers (K24) and (K16) were from wooden features built in association with the drain, constructed in the undercroft of the Great Hall K/L. This feature is contemporary with the construction of the hall and the structural timber is again principally oak, confirming its use in the wooden structures of the early phases of the castle. Some roundwood was also recovered in these samples, indicating the presence of occupation material in these mixed construction and occupation deposits. The smaller branches (roundwood) present highly curved growth rings in cross section, indicating smaller material. Whilst this could be remains of firewood it could easily reflect the small diameter material typically used in wattle and daub structures.

The interpretation of the remaining charcoal samples taken from occupation deposits, as wood burnt as firewood, is supported by the high percentage of examples of round-wood recovered from these samples. Some larger timber, perhaps damaged, old or unused structural timber, was also being burnt. It is

336

Context	Phase	Type	Sample	Betula	Carpinus	Corylus	Fagus	Fraxinus	Quercus	Salix	Ulmus	Cinder	Unid.	Other
				Birch	Hornbeam	Hazel	Beech	Ash	Oak	Willow	Elm			
L 47	6d	D							5.4g (S)				0.5g	
K 6	6d	D							17.4g (S)				37.5g	
O 7	6d	D							10.3g (S)				2.8g	
K 12	6c	D	1						64.7g (C)				40.75g	
K 12	6c	D	2						9.2g (S)				8.55g	
K 12	6c	D	3						2.8g (S)				7.1g	
K 12	6c	D	4						65.7g (S)				303.8g	
K 12	6c	D	5				34.4g (S)		15.2g (S)				137.4g	
K 12	6c	D	6						10.0g (S)				3.8g	
K 12	6c	D	7						5.8g (S)				6.55g	
K 10	6c	D	1						12.0g (S)				27.3g	
K 10	6c	D	2						33.9g (S)				8.35g	
K 10	6c	D	3						6.7g (S)				0.2g	
K 10	6c	D	4		3.2g (C)				1.0g (S)				0.1g	grain*
K 10	6c	D	5						4.8g (S)				1.0g	
K 10	6c	D	6						27.9g (S)				9.4g	
K 11	6c	D	1						18.0g (S)				13.5g	
K 11	6c	D	2						13.1g (S)				7.45g	
K 11	6c	D	3						8.6g (C)				3.2g	
K 11	6c	D	4						10.7g (S)				1.15g	
K 11	6c	D	5		5.0g (?)				2.4g (S)				1.05g	
K 11	6c	D	6						0.5g (S)				0.9g	
K 4	6c	D							6.2g (S)				0.4g	
K 9	6c	D	1						22.9g (S)				14.0g	
K 9	6c	D	2				93.4g (C)						46.0g	
K 9	6c	D	3						56.7g (S)				32.95g	
K 9	6c	D	4						89.9g (S)				126.3g	
K 9	6c	D	5						6.1g (S)				2.55g	
L 9	6c	D							14.6g (S)				18.45g	
L 14	6c	D	1						19.5g (S)				13.8g	
L 14	6c	D	2						2.9g (S)				13.3g	
L 14	6c	D	3						2.1g (S)				10.7g	
H 12	6c	D	1						8.8g (S)				4.7g	
H 12	6c	D	2						1.0g (S)				0.4g	dicotolydon
K 24	2a	C/O	1						90.5g (S)				157.8g	
K 24	2a	C/O	2		8.5g (R)	0.7g (R)			69.3g (S)				116.6g	
K 24	2a	C/O	3						112.8g (S)				75.9g	
K 24	2a	C/O	4			5.4g (R)			45.5g (S)				81.6g	
K 16	2a	C/O				2.3g (R)			0.5g (S)	1.2g (S)			0.7g	
O 143	1a	O				2.2g (R)		1.9g (S)					5.6g	
K 33	2a	O	1			14.1g (R)		4.6g (R)	32.4g (S)				0.6g	
K 33	2a	O	2						20.0g (S)				2.35g	
K 35	2a	O							3.1g (S)				—	
K 14	3a	O							42.6g (S)				11.4g	
M 53	3b	O							16.5g (S)				0.3g	
F 50	3b	O		1.0g (?)		8.1g (R)	14.5g (S)		3.9g (S)	0.6g (S)			97.3g	grain **
O 109	3b	O		0.4g (S)		0.4g (R)			13.8g (S)				2.0g	
Y 7	4d	O							1.3g (S)			15.8g	0.2g	

*	3 *Avena*, 2 cf Avena, 1 *Avena* floret, 3 *Poaceae* culm frags (all carbonised)
**	30 *Avena*, 5 cf Avena, 1 *Avena* floret, 6 cereals indet., 24 *Poaceae* culm frags (all carbonised)

D	Destruction deposit
C/O	Construction and occupation deposit
O	Occupation deposit

(S)	Straight rings indicating large timber usually structural
(C)	Curved rings, substantial brach firewod or small constructional use
(R)	Roundwood, invariably firewood, very rarely a small object

FIGURE 10.28

Wood species present as charcoal, by context

337

Context	Sample	Charcoal characteristics
K12	1	Fragments 100mm across with remians of daub or mortar Angular pieces lacking edge bark strong curvature of rings indicates 200–300mm trunk, *Fraxinus* (ash) Roundwood stake, 80–100mm diameter with longitudinal slices to form a flat face, *Acer campestre* (field maple)
K12	2	Radially split planks, 50–100mm thick, narrow rings of a large slow grown tree, *Quercus* (oak) Many charcoal fragments attached to partially burnt daub and mortar, some between two mortar layers Flakes of charcoal, oak, 10mm wide, mortar on one side
K12	3	Thin charcoal, oak, flakes
K12	4	Fragments of radially split planks, oak, with narrow rings Deep red mortar adhearing to some charcoal fragments

FIGURE 10.29

Large 'beam' charcoal samples

Species	Sample	% by weight	% by occurrence
Quercus	(Oak)	83.6	70.8
Corylus	(Hazel)	2.7	10.8
Fraxinus	(Ash)	8.1	4.6
Fagus	(Beech)	4	3.1
Carpinus	(Hornbeam)	1.4	4.6
Betula	(Birch)	0.1	3.1
Ulmus	(Elm)	0.1	1.5
Salix	(Willow)	0.1	1.5

FIGURE 10.30

Percentages of the major wood species present as charcoal

noticeable that a much greater range of wood species was recovered as charcoal from the occupation layers suggesting that any form of wood was appropriate for firewood, compared to a more restricted group of species used for structural use.

Hornbeam and hazel (*Corylus*) were the principal finds of small diameter roundwood Hornbeam is a species of southeastern England and, though it may have reached the limestone lands of the Vale of Glamorgan, it is not normally considered a native of Wales (Condry 1981). Its presence at Dryslwyn may suggest that some timber was imported or that the range of this tree was somewhat greater in the warmer climate of the 13th century than previously suspected. Both hazel and hornbeam have been coppiced extensively in Britain to obtain rods for a multitude of purposes. Hornbeam is renowned for its hardness and has been used in the past for pegs and dowels, which is why it may have been imported to the site, and it is conceivable that the roundwood from these contexts may be pegs, used to join timbers during the building of the castle. Fast-growing wood species, such as hazel and willow, were coppiced or pollarded in order to encourage quick growth, producing a regular and managed supply of roundwood for fuel. A much larger sample would be required to demonstrate the use of deliberate techniques for managing woodland around Dryslwyn in the 13th century.

Though a large percentage of the charcoal cannot be identified and the selection of the charcoal from the site equates to a random process, the lack of any discernible bias may mean that the timber represented by the charcoal from Dryslwyn is not very dissimilar to the timber resources available in the forests around Dryslwyn and utilised in the 13th century (Figure 10.30). The smaller wood was used for fuel, the larger for structural timber.

The identification of charcoal fragments from other archaeological sites provides comparative evidence of the species utilised for firewood during the 13th and 14th centuries. It is clear that oak dominates with some use of hazel and birch (*Betula*); Loughor Castle (Swansea) (Carruthers 1993; Ling and Ling 1973), Valle Crucis Abbey (Denbighshire) (Bartley 1976), St Peters St, Northampton (Oakley 1979, 319), Rhuddlan (Morgan 1994) and Sandal Castle (Wakefield) (Smith *et al* 1983). This is a surprisingly consistent picture despite the different nature of the various sites and the wide range of locations. As time progressed, sites such as Sandal Castle and Lewes Castle (East Sussex) suggest that the use of oak declined slightly in favour of a wider range of species (Smith *et al* 1983; Cartwright 1992b). Collections of wooden objects such as those recovered from the well at Montgomery Castle (Powys) (Knight 1993) which span the medieval period also show a similar range of tree species being utilised for object manufacture.

The pollen diagrams from the pool at Dinas Emrys (Gwynedd) (Seddon 1960) and the moat from Sycharth (Powys) (Caseldine 1990) also indicate that substantial amounts of oak dominated the composition of the Welsh forests of the 12th–15th century with lesser amounts of hazel, birch and some pine (*Pinus*), alder (*Alnus*) and elm (*Ulmus*). The percentages of these lesser species varied with geography, soil drainage and underlying geology. The general consistency of such data would suggest that the charcoal samples from Dryslwyn give a surprisingly accurate picture of the composition of the surrounding woodland and its exploitation for timber for use within the castle.

10.7 COPROLITES
by John Daniell

The coprolites recovered come primarily from Phases 2c to 4a occupation (Figure 10.31). They occur largely as discrete stools usually incorporated into soil and

Context	Phase	Weight	Parasite egg No.	Coprolite form
F47	3b	7.8	0	
F70	2d	4.8	2	S
F86	2c	6.8	0	
I17	4a	13.3	0	B
I18	4a	7	2	S
F84	2c	5.1	0	N
F108	1b	4.6	2	S
F113	1a	3.2	0	
G59	4c	5.4	0	
P64	4a	5.7	0	
G159	3a	4.5	0	
O51	4d	4.6	0	
O66	4a	7.9	49	R

S: smooth coherent coprolite
B: coherent coprolite containing many bone fragments
N: natural acclomeration of soil, bone and other material

FIGURE 10.31

Coprolite samples, weight and intestinal parasite egg numbers

rubble material either naturally built up soil or deliberately deposited material for levelling ground. They are probably derived from the middens or dunghills and the presence of such material in these 13th-century deposits suggests that dungheaps or middens were present within the castle and contained human as well as animal excreta (Section 4.5). Much of this material was redistributed and buried around the castle during the rebuilding Phase 4a and, with the exception of a coprolite in the siege debris (G59), the lack of such material from later deposits suggests that habits were changing. From the 1280s onwards, it was no longer considered acceptable to have middens within the Inner Ward of the castle and human faecal material was consistently disposed of outside the castle walls, for example through the use of the garderobe chutes in Area E.

Upon examination, some of the possible coprolites contained large pieces of bone, suggesting that they may have been produced by dogs (Figure 10.32) though the possibility of many of the samples being merely aggregations of organic refuse cannot be ruled out. Some of the smoother and more coherent specimens (Figure 10.32) were examined for the presence of host-specific intestinal parasite eggs, in order to determine whether they were in fact coprolites, and if so, what animal had produced them. The details of the samples selected and whether eggs were found are given in Figure 10.31. A 16.4g sample of cesspit fill (F23) was also processed, yielding a large number of parasite eggs.

Methods

Using the extraction methodology of Jones (1983), the weighed dry sample of coprolite was disaggregated in 10% HCl. The residue was filtered through 180µ nylon mesh; the filtrate washed in distilled water and concentrated by centrifugation. Removal of denser mineral materials was attempted by centrifugation in a heavy liquid, ZnCl solution (Huntley and Allen, 1992), but both the resulting fractions contained parasite eggs. These were stained with aqueous safranin and sub-samples taken and mounted as slides in silicone oil. Each complete slide was scanned at × 100 under a compound microscope (Leitz Diaplan) and any parasite eggs found identified using Thienpont *et al* (1986). The length and diameter of trichurid eggs found were measured using an eyepiece graticule at × 400, and dimensions in microns calculated from these measurements.

Results

The following list shows details of the parasite eggs found in the different samples, Figure 10.33 illustrates the nature of the parasite eggs found (sample number in brackets, followed by parasite eggs recovered and interpretation).

— (F70) 2 *Trichuris* sp.
  Although rather small, this could be a coprolite of human origin both on the basis of its appearance and its trichurid egg dimensions.
— (I18) 1 *Ascaridia* cf. *galli* (bird), 1 *Trichuris* sp. (bird) = pigeon, goose, duck, chicken.
  From its appearance, this could also be of human origin, the bird parasite egg (*Ascaridia galli*) being a later accretion. However as only one egg of each species was found in this sample nothing can be said of its origin with any certainty.
  The bird parasite egg unfortunately tells us little. It may suggest the presence of poultry within the castle, but could equally well be the result of pigeon infestation as the parasite species represented utilises a variety of hosts (Thienpont *et al* 1986).
— (F108) 2 *Trichuris* sp.
  This contains two trichurid eggs that have different sizes. The balance of probability, given the egg dimensions and the appearance, is that this is a human coprolite.
— (O66) 1 *Capillaria* cf.. *caudinflata* (bird), 38 *Ascaris lumbricoides* (human), 10 *Trichuris* sp.
  This is rather different. Its general appearance of roughness, combined with the large protruding fragments of bone preclude its being purely a coprolite of human origin. Nevertheless a sub-sample was found to contain 10 trichurid eggs all lying within the range of *T. trichiura* sizes given by Beer (1976) and also 38 *Ascaris lumbricoides* eggs, again of probable human origin (Thienpont *et al* 1986) together with a bird parasite egg (*Capillaria* cf. *caudinflata*). Overall it seems likely

FIGURE 10.32

A human coprolite that was found to contain Trichuris sp. eggs and a dog coprolite containing large pieces of bone

that this sample represents an accumulation of rubbish with a high component of human faecal material.

— (F23) 132 *Trichuris* sp.

This fill of the latrine pit contained large numbers of trichurid eggs. These covered a wider range of sizes than the other samples, but their mean suggests that they are *T. trichiura*, consistent with the origin of the sample.

In addition to the present work, a sample of the fill of the latrine deposit (F23) had been examined in 1987 (Gilchrist 1987). Using similar methods to those employed here, eggs of both *Trichuris* and *Ascaris* were identified. The presence of *Ascaris* further confirms the human origin of the faecal waste in this feature. Also recovered from this deposit was a *Sphaerocerio* fly puparium (Figure 10.34). This fly is normally only found in association with human faeces providing further confirmation of the origin of this deposit.

Discussion

The different species of the host specific parasite *Trichuris sp.* are generally only determinable by measurement (Jones 1983; Beer 1976). The eggs of trichurids found in dog (*T. vulpis*), rat and mouse (*T. muris*) or ruminant (*T. ovis*) faeces are much larger than any of those found in these samples (Thienpont *et al* 1986). However, the species found in humans (*T. trichiura*) and pigs (*T. suis*) are of an appropriate size, but have partially overlapping size ranges. The difference in length of the eggs of the two species is diagnostic (Beer 1976) but this is largely a result of the differences in the nature of the polar plugs which are normally present in trichurid eggs.

Unfortunately these plugs were not preserved, leading to considerable overlap between the egg lengths of the two species. The width distribution of the eggs of the two species is more distinct, and in conjunction with the length provides some basis for the separation

340

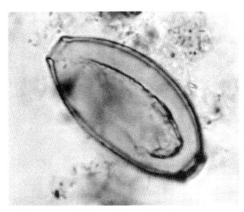

Trichuris trichiura **46.5 x 24.8** μ
O66

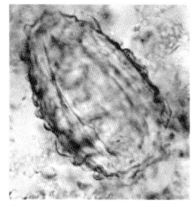

Ascaris lumbricoides **53 x 37** μ
O66

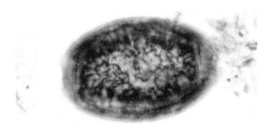

Capillaria cf *caudinflata* **43.4 x 27.9** μ
O66

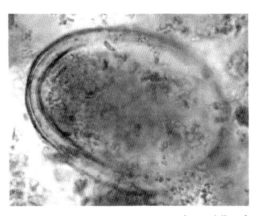

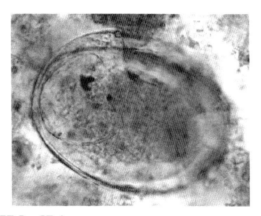

Ascaridia cf *galli* **77.5 x 57.4** μ
I18

FIGURE 10.33

Micrographs of types of parasite egg found in Dryslwyn Castle samples

of the two. Figure 10.35 shows the dimensions of all trichurid eggs found at Dryslwyn related to the size ranges (less plugs) of *T. suis* and *T. trichiura* (Beer 1976). This figure suggests that while most of the Dryslwyn samples lie in the *T. trichiura* range, at least one lies in the *T. suis* range and a number are smaller than either. The latter may have not have been lying parallel to the plane of the microscope slide and so measured shorter than in reality. Since many of the smaller eggs come from one context (O66), it is possible that something within the deposit caused shrinkage of the parasite eggs.

It is of note that, generally, the trichurid eggs recovered lie at, and in some cases beyond, the low end of the range of dimensions suggested by the literature. This may be a result of the conditions of preservation (mineralisation, etc) and techniques of processing and examination. Few studies have been carried out in this

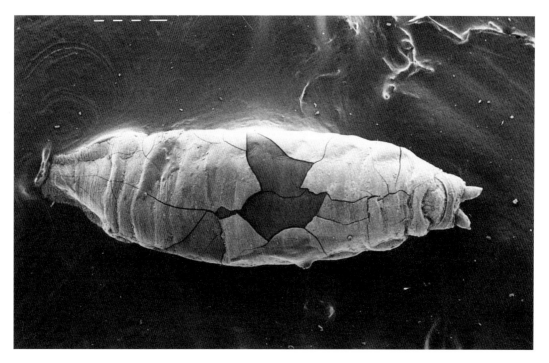

FIGURE 10.34

Scanning electron micrograph of a fly puparia from the latrine context (F23)

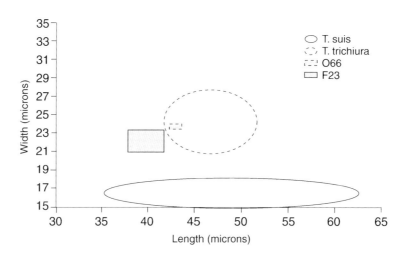

FIGURE 10.35

Dimensions of Tricurid sp. eggs from Dryslwyn Castle

field, even on fresh material, and the egg dimensions of these species may be more variable than presently suggested.

Conclusion

It seems likely that some of the material examined is of human origin, though the presence of pig parasite (*T. suis*) eggs cannot be ruled out. The small numbers of eggs in those coprolites most likely to be human suggest low rates of infestation (Jones 1983). The larger numbers found in the cesspit fill are probably the result of concentration, though individual hosts could not be assigned. Despite the presence of faecal type material containing bone fragments, thought to be of canid origin, no evidence for parasites specific to dog were recovered.

10.8 EGGSHELL
by Chris Caple and Louisa Gidney

Though eggs were used as a food resource in the medieval period, they had a greater role in the diet of the lord than the peasant (Section 10.1). The consumption of eggs in a lordly household is demonstrated by the surviving account roll of 1265 of Eleanor, Countess of Leicester, where 500 eggs were purchased on April 28th for 17½d and 700 eggs on April 29th, a meatless day. The purchase of several hundred eggs a day continues over the two weeks of the published fragment (Wade Labarge 1965, 194–195).

Eggs were probably only available seasonally. The treatise Husbandry, dated c1300, only expects a hen to lay 115 eggs annually (Oschinsky 1971, 425). A seasonal glut of eggs is also suggested by the surviving account roll of 1265 of Eleanor, Countess of Leicester, where 150 eggs were received from rents on April 26th but over the two weeks of the published fragment no further eggs were received (Wade Labarge 1965, 194–195).

To supply this demand, poultry keeping must have been widespread and/or large scale. Archaeological finds of poultry bones from urban sites, such as Exeter (Maltby 1979, 67–68, 130–132), attest to the ubiquity of domestic fowl. Though there are regular historic references to eggs, eggshell is rarely recovered from archaeological excavations due to its fragile nature. For example only a few eggshell fragments were recovered from refuse material from Hen Domen (Powys) (Greig et al 1982).

Samples of eggshell were recovered from two contexts at Dryslwyn castle:

— (B19) and (O49), from Phase 6c–d contexts, probably eggs from nesting birds caught up in the castle's destruction
— (F58) and (G161), from Phase 2c–d contexts, probably hen eggs from egg consumption within the castle.

Without artificial light, old fashioned hens moult in the autumn and thereafter do not lay over the winter months. Egg laying and chicken rearing are consequently concentrated in spring and summer. Eggs would have proved a welcome addition to the diet, especially the celebrated (Easter) eggs, the earliest eggs of the spring season. Poor survival of eggshell makes it impossible to assess the relative contribution of eggs to the diet.

10.9 ORGANIC RESIDUES
by Jeremy Reid, Stephanie Dudd, Mark Copley and Richard Evershed

Fats and waxes, entrapped as absorbed residues associated with ceramic vessels during the processing of organic materials in antiquity, are well protected from chemical decay and microbial attack (Heron and Evershed 1993). Modern analytical techniques enable even highly degraded remnants of natural commodities to be characterised and identified (Evershed et al 1990; 1994; 1997a; 1999). Often, data obtained from organic residue analysis provides the only evidence for the exploitation and processing of non skeletal animal commodities or leafy vegetables. The use of chemical analyses has enabled the identification of animal fats (Evershed et al 1992), beeswax (Charters and Evershed 1995; Needham and Evans 1987), birch bark tar (Charters et al 1993a) and the epicuticular waxes of leafy vegetables (Charters et al 1997; Evershed et al 1991).

Degraded animal fats (lipids) are by far the most commonly identified residues found in association with pottery vessels. They can be characterised by the distribution of one of their principal components triacylglycerols and their breakdown products; diacylglycerols, monoacylglycerols and free fatty acids (Evershed et al 1995). Triacylglycerols are polymers formed from glycerol (CH_2OH, $CHOH$ CH_2OH) and free fatty acids ($RCOOH$) in which R is a carbon chain typically of 16 or 18 atoms ($C16:0$ or $C18:0$), which through reaction with water (hydrolysis) or microbial reactions breaks down to its component parts (Evershed et al 2001, 334–335). To date, identification of animal fats have been made based primarily upon the distributions of free fatty acids present (Needham and Evans 1987; Rottlander 1990). However, new approaches such as stable isotope values can be used to make unambiguous distinctions between remnant fats derived from different animal species.

Stable isotopes are present in differing concentrations in biological material as a result of preferential selection of one isotope over another (fractionation) during physical and biological processes (Pollard and Wilson 2001; Sealey 2001). Thus materials from differing creation processes can have different stable isotopic ratios. Since different plants and animals have different food sources and different metabolic processes their stable carbon isotope ratio is potentially different. The $\delta^{13}C$ values (ratio of the carbon isotopes C12 to C13) have been determined for individual organic compounds derived from the solvent extracted residues from a pottery vessels from the Raunds area project in Northamptonshire (Evershed et al 1994). This confirmed that the lipids being investigated were formed from carbon from the metabolic processes of temperate zone vegetation (C3) origin. Further analysis revealed that the lipid compounds derived from Brassica species, such as cabbage. Utilising fundamental differences in the stable carbon isotope composition of the fatty acid component of the adipose (degraded animal) fat in the major domesticates, has permitted clear distinctions between remnant fats of different origins in archaeological ceramics to be achieved (Evershed et al 1997a; Dudd and Evershed 1998; Mottram et al 1999).

The absorbed organic residues from pottery from Dryslwyn Castle was analysed from sherds recovered from a variety of contexts and from a variety of vessel types in order to:

— determine the amount and likely origin of any lipid extracted from sherds

— determine whether there is any correlation between the amount and type of lipid recovered and the type of vessel, area of the site or phase of occupation from which it was derived,

— create a holistic understanding of the diet of 13th and 14th century castle inhabitants using organic residue information together with bone and seed data and written historical information.

Gas chromatography (GC) Analysis

The sample set consisted of 44 sherds chosen from a variety of excavated contexts. The bulk of the 13th–14th century ceramics recovered from the site consisted of jugs, jars and 'cooking' pots. Sherds from these vessel types have been investigated, as well as a possible bee-skep. Several of the sherds were found to be glazed on one side, and no visible carbonised surface residues were detected. A complete list of the organic samples taken, the sherd from which it derived, the vessel type, their context and their ceramic type is detailed in Figure 10.36.

Lipids were extracted using solvent (chloroform and methanol) from a powdered 20µg sample of cleaned potsherd (Evershed *et al* 1990; Charters *et al* 1993b). A sub sample of the lipid extract was chemically treated (trimethylsilylated), an internal standard (n-tetratriacontane) was added, then submitted directly to analysis by gas chromatography (GC). Quantification of the lipid extracted from potsherds was achieved by comparison of the peak area for the internal standard (n-tetratriacontane) with the summed lipid peak area in each of the GC traces (Figure 10.37). It was found that 20 (*c*45%) of the samples had a lipid content lower than 15µg g-l. (microgrammes of lipid per gramme of powdered ceramic). There appears to be a general correlation with vessel type and lipid concentration. The jars displayed the lowest mean lipid concentration with 76µg g-l; whereas the jugs had a mean lipid content of 115µg g-l; and the 'cooking' pots yielded the highest concentration of lipid, with a mean of 299µg g-1. There is clearly a significant difference between the lipid concentrations in the 'cooking' pots and the jugs/jars, which is probably associated with vessel use.

High temperature gas chromatography (HT-GC) and high temperature gas chromatography with mass spectrometry analysis (HT-GC/MS)

A further sub sample of the lipid from the sherds with >15µg g-l total lipid extract was chemically treated, then passed through high temperature-gas chromatography (HT-GC) and high temperature-gas chromatography/mass spectrometry (HT-GC/MS) to identify the lipids present.

Almost all samples contained lipid distributions characteristic of degraded animal fats (Figure 10.37, Sample D4) (intact triacylglycerols and their degradation products: diacylglycerols, monoacylglycerols and free fatty acids). Despite often advanced degradation, there are several chemical criteria that can be used to identify the species of animal from which the lipids originated.

Many of the samples (including D1, D3a, D3b, D4, D5) showed the presence of significant quantities of branched chain alkanoic acids (C15:0br and C17:0br components) and an abundance of odd carbon numbered straight chain components, signifying lipid from a ruminant (normally bovine or ovine) origin.

The chromatograms of several of the extracts showed the peaks corresponding to C18:1 fatty acids being resolved into two components, i.e. isomers (molecules of mirror image form). This is another indication of ruminant fats.

The heating of a mixture of C16:0 and C18:0 fatty acids in the presence of fired clay results in the formation of ketones, principally in the range of C31 to C35 (Raven *et al* 1997; Evershed *et al* 1999). The presence of these mid-chain ketones in four of the samples (D19, D23, D30, and D38) is direct evidence for the heating of fats in the pottery vessels. Interestingly, three of these vessels are described as cooking pots, the organic residue confirming their use and the vessel type confirming the organic residue interpretation.

Distributions of triacylglycerols have proved to be diagnostic in determining lipid origin. Ruminant adipose fats are characterised by distributions of triacylglycerols ranging between C46 to C54 with relatively high abundance of C48, C50 and C52 components. Ruminant dairy fats can readily be distinguished from adipose fats by a greater abundance of lower carbon number triacylglycerols present in the former. The distribution of triacylglycerols from a porcine source is distinguished by a distinctively narrow range with components C48 to C54, with the C52 component dominant and the C50 in slightly lower abundance. Dairy fats are characterised by broad triacylglycerol distributions, with higher abundance of C40 to C46 components.

Using these criteria, it is possible to distinguish between porcine adipose fats, ruminant adipose fats and ruminant dairy fats, though given the loss of smaller molecules this is far from a definitive form of identification (Dudd and Evershed 1998). Fifteen of the sherds from Dryslwyn Castle had intact triacylglycerols. From these, it can be seen that sample D4 displays a typically porcine triacylglycerol distribution. Eight other samples had distributions typical of ruminant adipose fats (D3a, D7, D13, D17, D20, D21, D25 and D37). The distribution of the triacyglycerols make it is possible to state that three of these fats (D3a, D7 and D13) are more likely to be from an ovine source and one sherd (D20) is more likely to contain fat from a bovine source. Samples D3b, D9 and D11

Sample No.	Context	Phase	Vessel type	Fabric	Lipid (ug/g)	Free Fatty Acids	Monoacylglycerols	Diacylglycerols	Triacylglycerols	Other	Description
D1	J1	7b	Cooking pot: base	1	41.6	14–18, 17br, 18:1	16, 18	32, 34, 36	48, 50, 52, 54		Degraded animal fat
D2	F22	3b	Cooking pot: rim	3	14.6	16, 18	16, 18				Degraded animal fat
D3a	J37	1b	Cooking pot: body	1	161.6	14–20, 15br, 17br, 18:1, 20:1	16, 18	32,34,36,42,44,46, 48,50,52,54,56	48, 50, 52, 54	Alk, Alc	Degraded animal fat
D3b	J37	1b	Cooking pot: body	1	1038.2	14–20, 18:1	16, 18	30, 32, 34, 36	42, 44, 46, 48, 50, 52, 54, 56		Degraded animal fat (dairy)
D4	F19	3b	Cooking pot: body	2.1	184.4	14–20, 17br, 18:1	16, 18	32, 34, 36	46, 48, 50, 52, 54		Degraded animal fat (pork)
D5	A10	4d	Cooking pot		276.7	14–20, 17br, 18:1	16, 18		46, 48, 50, 52, 54	Wx,Alc,Alk	Beeswax and degraded animal fat
D6	L16	5c	Jug: shoulder	2.5	6.7	16–18	Trace				Degraded animal fat
D7	J15	4a	Cooking pot: body	1	318.7	14–20, 15br, 17br, 18:1	14, 16, 18		46, 48, 50, 52, 54		Degraded animal fat
D8	O16	6d	Jug: shoulder	6.2	6.3						Trace lipid (pork)
D9	J72	1b	Cooking pot: shoulder	1	1111.7	14–20, 15br, 17br, 18:1	16, 18	32, 34, 36	44, 46, 48, 50, 52, 54, 56		Degraded animal fat (dairy)
D10a	O86	5a	Cooking pot: shoulder	1	31.4	14–20, 15br, 17br, 18:1			48, 50, 52, 54	Wx,Alc,Alk	Beeswax and degraded animal fat
D10b	O86	5a	Cooking pot: body	1	0						Trace lipid
D11	H53	4a	Bee skep: base	1	93	14–20, 15br, 17br, 18:1	16, 18	32, 34, 36	46, 48, 50, 52, 54		Degraded animal fat (dairy)
D12	F19	3b	Cooking pot: base	2.4	13						UCM (fish?)
D13	O151	3b	Cooking pot: shoulder	1	554.8	14–20, 15br, 17br, 18:1	16, 18	32, 34, 36	46, 48, 50, 52, 54		Degraded animal fat
D14	L17	5a	Jug: shoulder	2.5	14.9	14–20, 15br, 17br, 18:1	16, 18				Degraded animal fat
D15	G147	u/s	Cooking pot: body		0						Trace lipid
D16a	J18	1b	Jug: base	4.1	799.4	14–20, 15br, 17br, 18:1	16, 18	32, 34, 36	46, 48, 50, 52, 54		Degraded animal fat
D16b	J18	1b	Jug: base	4.1	0						Trace Lipid
D17	J17	2b	Jug: body	4.1	32.2	14–20, 15br, 17br, 18:1		32, 34, 36	46, 48, 50, 52, 54		Degraded animal fat
D18	J82	2b	Jug	4.1	39.8						UCM (fish?)
D19	F28	3b	Cooking pot: base	1	12.9	16, 18				MCK	Trace Lipid (heated)
D20	O6	7b	Cooking pot	1	673.9	14–20, 15br, 17br, 18:1	16, 18	32, 34, 36	48, 50, 52, 54		Degraded animal fat
D21	O178	2c	Cooking pot	1	561.3	14–20, 15br, 17br, 18:1	16, 18	32, 34, 36	48, 50, 52, 54		Degraded animal fat
D22	F16	4b	Cooking pot	1	113.3	14–20, 15br, 17br, 18:1	16, 18		48, 50, 52, 54		Degraded animal fat
D23	A6	4d	Cooking pot	1	623.8	14–20, 15br, 17br, 18:1				MCK	Degraded animal fat (heated)
D24	F35	2d		1	1594.7	14–20, 15br, 17br, 18:1			48, 50, 52, 54	Wx,Alc,Alk	Beeswax and degraded animal fat
D25	G147	u/s	Cooking pot	1	1615.3	14–20, 15br, 17br, 18:1	16, 18	32, 34, 36	46, 48, 50, 52, 54		Degraded animal fat
D26	H47	4a	Cooking pot	1	2.2						Trace lipid
D27	I18	4a	Cooking pot	1	3.2						Trace lipid
D28	J82	2b	Cooking pot	2.1	833.7	14–20, 15br, 17br, 18:1	Trace	Trace	Trace		Degraded animal fat (horse)
D29	J1	7b	Cooking pot: neck	1	25.5						Degraded animal fat
D30	J28	2d	Cooking pot	1	1.7	14–20, 15br, 17br, 18:1				MCK	Degraded animal fat (heated)
D31	T72	5c		2.7	872.8	14, 16, 18, 18:1					UCM (fish?)
D32	O53	5b	Cooking pot	2.3	2.2						Trace lipid
D33	X16	6d	Cooking pot	2.3	3.1						Trace lipid
D34	G59	4c	Jug, glazed	2.3	10.3						Trace lipid
D35	G59	6d	Jug: base	2.4	9.4	14, 16, 18:1					Degraded animal fat
D36	X16	6d	base	2.1	12.1						Trace lipid
D37	O52	4d	Jar	2.1	156.4	14–20, 15br, 17br, 18:1	16, 18	32, 34, 36	48, 50, 52, 54	MCK	Degraded animal fat
D38	F16	4b	Jar, glazed	2.7	47.5	14, 16, 18:1					Degraded animal fat (heated)
D39	T67	4c	Jar	2.5	57.3						UCM (fish?)
D40	F16	4b	Jar	2.1	323.4	14–20, 15br, 17br, 18:1	16, 18	Trace	Trace		Degraded animal fat
D41	G59	4c	Jar	2.2	47.1						UCM (fish?)
D42	Y7	4d	Jar	2.2	0.6						Trace lipid
D43	O66	4a	base	2.3	7.3						Trace lipid
D44	H59	4c	Jar, glazed	2.7	3.8						Trace lipid

FIGURE 10.36

Ceramic sherds used for organic residue analysis and their lipid content

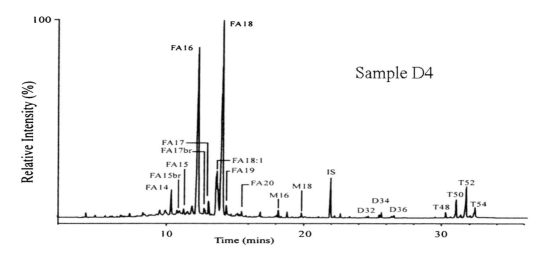

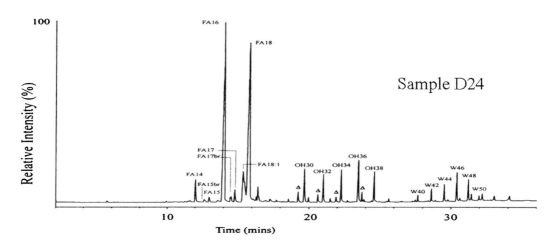

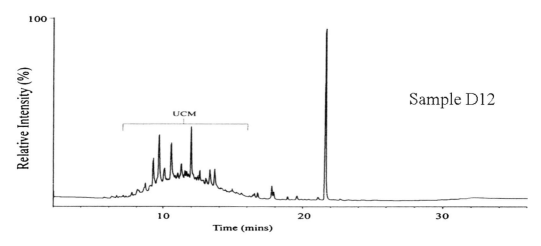

FIGURE 10.37

HT/GC Chromatograms of total lipid extract from samples D4, D24 and D12

exhibited broader distributions that are similar to that of degraded dairy fats. The remainder is indicative of mixtures of bovine and ovine adipose fats.

The chromatograms of three of the sherds (D5, D10a, and D24) revealed distributions that contained compounds not observed in any of the other extracts. HT-GC/MS analysis confirmed that these include the major components of beeswax (a homologous series of n-alkanes, palmitic wax esters and long-chain free alcohols) (Figure 10.37, Sample D24). Since all three samples also showed trace abundance of triacyl-glycerols, and high abundance of free fatty acids, a mixture of beeswax and animal fat is likely.

The chromatograms of the potsherds (D12, D18, D31, D39 and D41) contained examples of unresolvable complex mixtures (UCM), (Figure 10.37,

346

Sample D12), which it is thought arise from the hydrolysis and polymerisation of highly unsaturated fatty acids such as fish oils.

Gas chromatography-combustion-isotope ratio mass spectrometry analysis (GC-C-IRMS)

Samples of lipid with suitable quantities of hexadecanoic acid (C16:0) and octadecanoic acid (C18:0) were chemically treated then analysed by gas chromatography-combustion-isotope ratio mass spectrometry (GC-C-IRMS) to determine their $\delta^{13}C$ values (ratio of stable isotopes of carbon C13 to C12 calibrated against an international standard).

Thirty-four of the samples contained sufficient abundances of the C16:0 and C18:0 fatty acids for GC-C-IRMS analysis, and are plotted in Figure 10.38, together with values for fresh porcine and ruminant adipose fats, fish and dairy fats together with the theoretical mixing curves of those fats. The majority of the sherds plotted approximately in the region associated with ruminant fats, although few of the samples actually plotted directly in the areas that correspond to reference fats.

There is good agreement between the isotope data and analysis of the triacylglycerol distributions. For example, sample D4, which showed a typical porcine triacylglycerol distribution, had less depleted $\delta^{13}C$ values and plots near to the non-ruminant reference fats.

The samples that had ruminant-like triacylglycerol distributions plotted amongst the ruminant reference fats; for example sample D3a displayed an ovine distribution.

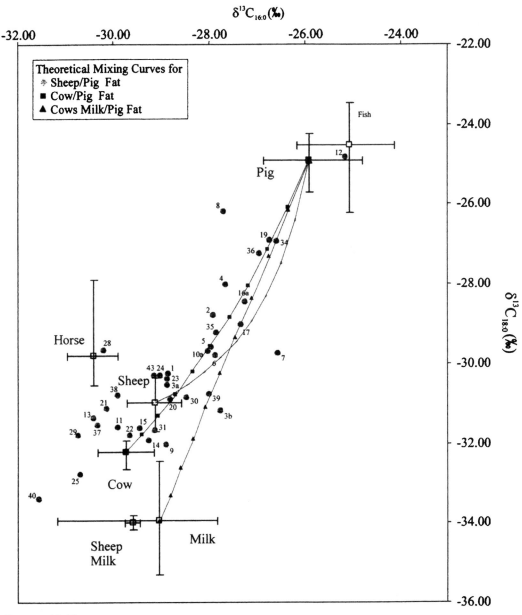

FIGURE 10.38

Plot of the $\delta^{13}C$ values of reference fats and Dryslwyn Castle samples

347

Samples D9 and D3b showed dairy-like distributions, and both had $\delta^{13}C$ data that plotted towards the milk reference values. However, none of the sherds plotted directly within the dairy fats region of the graph. A diagonal trend is observed, with the majority of the samples lying in the region of the ruminant/non-ruminant mixing curves. Several samples appear to plot along the cow's milk/pig adipose mixing curve.

The lipid extract of sample D12 that had revealed the presence of an unresolved complex mixture (UCM), had $\delta^{13}C$ values which plotted within the area associated with fish/pig. Other samples that had UCMs did not have sufficient abundances of the C16:0 and C18:0 fatty acid components for stable isotope analysis.

The three samples that contained beeswax all had similar $\delta^{13}C$ values for their fatty acids, and they plotted along the ruminant/non-ruminant mixing curve, near to the region associated with sheep reference fats.

The stable isotope data obtained for sample D28 plotted in the region associated with horse reference fats.

Conclusions

A correlation between lipid content and vessel type was detected; 'cooking pots' contained, on average, a greater concentration of lipid than the jugs. The glazed pottery did not appear to show any significant differences from the unglazed pottery in terms of lipids extracted. The lipid extracts comprised degraded animal fats; the majority of which were clearly of ruminant in origin, indicating the importance of sheep and cattle to the diet of those living in Dryslwyn Castle. This correlates well with the faunal evidence that has shown that the predominant species of animal found at the site is the bovid (Section 10.2). There is also support for the presence of non-ruminant fats in several samples (D4 for example), and the possible presence of horse fat in one of the vessels, is very unusual and may indicate the limited processing of horse meat or horse fats.

The occurrence of fish in the diet, as indicated by the unresolved complex mixtures in the chromatograms, corresponds well with the large numbers of fish bones recovered from the castle middens. The occurrence of two sherds with fish oil residues in the town site indicates that the consumption was widespread in medieval society (Section 10.1).

Beeswax was detected in three vessels, along with animal fats; there are several plausible explanations for the discovery of these two components in a single vessel. The beeswax could be present in the vessel as a result of a post-firing treatment applied in order to decrease permeability (Rice 1987) for storing liquids such as milk. The vessel may have been used for several culinary purposes including storing wax combs filled with honey or used for separating the wax from the honey with previous or subsequent use for cooking meat or dairy products. Alternatively, since beeswax was a valuable commodity, it may be that animal fats were added to the beeswax in order to eke it out; in candle making, for instance, cheaper animal fats were often used in combination with beeswax (Crane 1983). Deposits of a wax-like material were recovered from one of the floors in the Great Chamber G, (Section 10.10). Analysis showed the presence of both beeswax and animal fat. The use or manufacture of candles of beeswax and tallow appears to be the most likely origin of this material.

Stable isotope data indicate the presence of dairy produce at Dryslwyn, but the vessels used in such food preparation were also used for cooking with other animals fats, leading to the detection of mixed residues.

Significantly, none of the extracts revealed the presence of higher plant leaf waxes. Vegetables, such as cabbages, lettuce and leeks, would have been assumed to be an important part of the medieval diet. A previous study of medieval pottery from West Cotton (Suffolk) revealed plant lipids in 30% of the pottery vessels (Dudd 1999). Whilst it may be suggested this evidence did not survive burial, the survival of other organic compounds makes this unlikely. This means that either there were alternative methods of processing vegetables at Dryslwyn or else vegetables were not normally consumed in any quantity by the inhabitants of the Inner Ward of Dryslwyn Castle. This could indicate that a meat, bread and fruit based diet was the norm for the upper echelons of Welsh medieval society. This corresponds with the written historic evidence (Section 10.1).

11

CONCLUSIONS

Castles were normally used to symbolise and exercise control of territory and to safeguard their inhabitants. Anyone who has clambered up the hill at Dryslwyn to the castle at the top will recognise that this castle has been deliberately sited in a highly defensible and very visible location in order to perform these functions.

Rhys Gryg created the castle of Dryslwyn (Phase 1 and 2?) to safeguard his son Maredudd ap Rhys and his inheritance (the commotes of Cethiniog and Mabudrud possibly Mabelfyw and briefly Gwidigada), from the hostile intent of his older brother Rhys Mechyll. Dryslwyn was intended, like other castles, to resist attack for limited time, until a relief force was raised. In the early years of this castle's existence, this would have been mounted by Gilbert Marshall, Earl of Pembroke, and Maredudd's guardian until he came of age. Even when young Maredudd was resident in the household of his guardian, he retained his castle of Dryslwyn in Cethiniog, quite literally a foothold on power.

Like many other castles Dryslwyn was established at the crossing of routeways: where the road from Llangathen to Llanarthney crosses the River Tywi, by ford or bridge. This enabled it to control traffic on these routes and encouraged economic activity at the site. It was, by the mid 13th century, the commotal centre for Cethiniog and the Great Hall of the castle would have been the centre for the legal business of the commote, settling disputes and rendering dues. The castle was placed on the south end of the hill to make it visible from the whole of the valley floor and most of the surrounding hills, 'a permanent and visible symbol of authority' (Turvey 2002, 104). The walls were placed at the break of slope to make them as conspicuous and as effective a defence as possible. Welsh castles are, with the exception of Ewloe (Flintshire), all sited on top of small hills or the edges of scarps visible from the valley floor. The Round Tower D, which protected and housed the family of the lord, was placed on a ridge of rock occupying the very highest point on the hilltop. This created an obvious visible symbol of the lordship of Dryslwyn and Cethiniog, emphasising the rights of Maredudd ap Rhys as lord of these lands. The form of the early castle (Phase 1) was a polygonal wall enclosing a hall with a large flared base round tower in the wall. This was a castle form current in Wales and Ireland in the early 13th century.

By the 13th century Dryslwyn had, like other Welsh castles, superseded the *llys* as the lord's principal residence. The layout of buildings around the hall in a *llys*, as revealed by the excavations at Rhosyr (Anglesey) (Johnstone 1997; 1999), may to some extent be mirrored in the layout of the buildings around the Great Hall at Dryslwyn. Any associated settlement beside the castle would have effectively functioned as the *maerdref* (Jones 2000), though it is probably more accurately characterised, at least by the mid to late 13th century, as a town. The observation by Giraldus Cambrensis in 1188 that 'they [the Welsh] do not live in towns, villages or castles ... It is not their habit to build great palaces or vast towering structures of stone and cement' (Thorpe 1978, 251) is, by the mid 13th century, no longer true. The late 12th-century Welsh castle construction at Nevern (Pembrokeshire) and the early to mid 13th-century (Phase 1 and 2) construction at Dryslwyn are of masonry held together with poor quality earthy mortar. Mid to late 13th-century Welsh castles such as Caergwrle (Flintshire) and Phases 3 and 4 at Dryslwyn are built with strong white mortar. Towns and castles are developing across the Welsh landscape.

Maredudd ap Rhys was raised as Lord of Deheubarth. Part of Welsh-speaking Wales, the region was governed by Welsh laws and controlled by Welsh princes and lords (*pura Wallia*). He was descended from kings and considered himself the social equal of Llywelyn ap Gruffudd, Prince of Gwynedd, whom he helped to power in 1251. However, following Llywelyn's refusal to allow Maredudd to retain the lands of Ystrad Tywi, which he won at the battle of

Coed Llathen/Cymerau (Carmarthenshire) in 1257, Maredudd sought to keep his homage direct to the English king. He had considerable connections with the Marcher lords, who controlled the part of Anglo-Norman ruled Wales (*marchia Wallie*), particularly with the Marshal family; Gilbert Marshal was his guardian and he married Isabel, Gilbert's niece. Like his father Rhys Gryg, Maredudd was a castle builder, his construction of the castle at Newcastle Emlyn (Carmarthenshire) demonstrating his belief that the most effective way of retaining control of land and symbolising that control was to build a castle in it. Though there is no written reference to construction work by Maredudd at Dryslwyn, the archaeological evidence indicates the construction of a second ward to the castle and the addition buildings in the Inner Ward (Phase 2? and 3). This enabled him to bequeath what by 1271 was a substantial castle to his son Rhys. Maredudd's actions indicate he was driven by the ambition of recreating the original lordship of his father Rhys Gryg: Cantref Mawr and Cantref Bychan. When Maredudd died, he had held substantial amounts of territory twice, in 1241 when allied with Gilbert Marshal and again in 1257 when allied with Llywelyn ap Gruffudd. He had been promised the whole of Ystrad Tywi by the English Crown in 1257 in return for his homage. By virtue of the value of his fealty (5000 marks) Maredudd must be judged one of the most powerful lords in Wales. He had seen his ambition of a significant land holding, the ancestral 'lands of his fathers', dashed from his hands twice. At his death he passed to his son, Rhys, the inheritance of the castles of Dryslwyn and Newcastle Emlyn and a number of commotes, but he also passed on the dream of recreating the lordship of Rhys Gryg and the promises of an English king.

Wales in the 12th and 13th century was a land of legends, lineage and prophecy. Giraldus Cambrensis wrote that 'the Welsh value distinguished birth and noble descent more than anything else in the world ... They would rather marry into a noble family than a rich one. Even the common people know their family tree by heart and can readily recite from memory the list of their grandfathers, great grandfathers and great, great grandfathers back to the sixth or seventh generations' (Thorpe 1978, 251). Rhys ap Maredudd had the blood of princes running in his veins, his father was a hero from the battle of Coed Llathen/Cymerau (Carmarthenshire) and he had defied Llywelyn ap Gruffudd. In the conflict of 1276 and, alone of the Welsh lords, in the conflict of 1282/83 Rhys sided with the English king. Though no doubt driven by his family's antipathy to Llywelyn ap Gruffudd who had held both Rhys and his father hostage, this was his chance to recover Cantref Mawr and Cantref Bychan. After the English victory of 1283 he undoubtedly expected Edward I to live up to his father's promise to return to Rhys his ancestral lands and allow him to establish his court in the family seat of Dinefwr Castle (Carmarthenshire).

Despite the fact that he was granted many of the commotes of Cantref Mawr and Cantref Bychan, Rhys was made to quitclaim the castle of Dinefwr (Carmarthenshire) by Edward I, who retained the castle with a garrison of English troops. This was a bitter blow to Rhys, the discontent led him to rebuild Dryslwyn castle (Phase 4a). The occurrence of 7 of the 25 coins from the site minted in a period 1280–89, is a remarkable concentration. It leaves little doubt that there was a flurry of building work at Dryslwyn at this time as Rhys sought to create a substantial castle, comparable to the major Marcher castles of Wigmore (Herefordshire) and Pembroke (Pembrokeshire). His marriage in 1285 to Ada de Hastings, a ceremony attended by all the great Marcher lords, further signified Rhys's status and provided him with even greater wealth. Through his grandmother he was related to the de-Clares, the Lords of Glamorgan, and through his mother to the Marshal family, the Earls of Pembroke. As a Welsh Marcher lord he was answerable directly only to the English king and had as many connections with the Marcher lords as he did with Welsh nobility. After 1283, Rhys ap Maredudd of Deheubarth and Gruffudd ap Gwenwynwyn of Powys were the principal surviving members of the princely Welsh families. Though they had been referred to as lords since the mid 12th century (Pierce 1972, 28) and barons since the rise of Llywelyn ap Gruffudd (Moore 2005, 231), they had identities both as Marcher lords and Welsh lords. Their substantial castles at Dryslwyn and Powis (Powys) provided suitable venues at which to host a Welsh court.

The development of Dryslwyn castles in the 1280s sees the construction of a third ward, developing the castle in a linear form along the south-east ridge of the hill. This maximised the visibility of the castle, as well as maintaining its defensive character. Though artistically literate (Lord 2003) there is no evidence that the Welsh had a significant masonry architectural tradition. Consequently, unlike the initial Norman hall at Chepstow Castle (Monmouthshire) (Turner 2002a, 24; Turner and Johnson 2006, 26) there was limited visual symbolism employed in the construction of Dryslwyn. The rendered and limewashed exterior for Dryslwyn was certainly present by the late 13th century and may have been in place from the earliest castle phases. It undoubtedly gave the castle a distinctive white visual appearance. Siting atop the green hillside this image of a massive white walled, three-ward castle guarded by portcullised gatehouses with walled town nestling in its shadow, was identical to the popular French and English image of the castle by the 14th century, as depicted in books of hours, such as the castle of Rapaille, depicted in the image of 'Christ as a Man of Sorrows', *Tres Riches Heures* of John Duke of Berry (f75r; Harthan 1977, 63). This was not the original image of Dryslwyn, which started as a typical early 13th century Welsh castle, a towered masonry hilltop stronghold. As the 13th century progressed, however,

Rhys ap Maredudd in particular sought to change the identity of the castle, and perhaps by extension himself.

Turner (2006) has suggested that from the 1290s there was an increase in castle construction in South Wales Marches following the defeat of Llywelyn ap Gruffudd. Marcher families such as the Valences, de Clares, and Bigods were constructing or redeveloping castles or hunting lodges such as Goodrich (Gloucestershire), Castell Coch (Cardiff), Llangibby (Monmouthshire) and Cas Troggy (Monmouthshire) (Priestley and Turner 2003). Though functioning castles, these buildings were primarily competitive architectural displays as their wealthy lords vied with one another. The Phase 4a redevelopment and enlargement of Dryslwyn castle in the 1280s may also be seen in this regional Marcher context of competitive constructional aggrandisement.

The claim by Giraldus Cambrensis that 'the whole population [of Wales] lives almost entirely on oats and the produce of their herds, milk, cheese and butter. They eat plenty of meat, but little bread' (Thorpe 1978, 233) appears from the Dryslwyn evidence to still be an accurate summary of the Welsh diet in the 13th century. The variety of cereals and wide range of species of fish and bird indicates, however, that for those occupying the Inner Ward at Dryslwyn there was considerably greater variation in this diet than his comments suggest. The further claim that 'they [the Welsh] do not have orchards or gardens, but if you give them fruit or garden produce they are only too pleased to eat it' (Thorpe 1978, 252) has only limited resonance with the evidence of 13th-century diet of the inhabitants of Dryslwyn castle. Though no evidence of leaf vegetables in the diet was evident from the organic residue analysis, seed remains attest the consumption of a substantial range of fruit and herbs. There is also historic evidence for a castle garden.

With the exception of a few luxury imports (wine, dried fruit and glazed ceramics), Dryslwyn Castle and its occupants were fully supported by the goods, materials and services provided from the lands of the Lordship of Dryslwyn. It was largely a self-sufficient community.

The presence of the town provided both economic income to the castle, goods and services to the occupants and acted as a symbol of prestige. Welsh lords and princes had increasingly appreciated the benefits of urban development through the 13th century. The princes of Gwynedd supported the town of Llanfaes (Anglesey) and Gruffudd ap Gwenwynwyn had established the town of Welshpool (Powys) by the mid 13th century (Soulsby 1983, 166, 266). The Lord Rhys had supported the boroughs of Llandovery (Carmarthenshire) and Cardigan (Ceredigion) as early as the mid 12th century (Turvey 2002, 58). To date there has been little archaeological investigation for the presence of urban developments around Welsh castles, but like Dryslwyn, later settlements outside Dolforwyn

(Powys) and Castell-y-Bere (Gwynedd) castles almost certainly had Welsh precedents. Settlements may be present outside most Welsh castles.

As part of the Phase 4a Outer Ward construction a new compact gatehouse was constructed to control entry into the castle. An identical gatehouse, which controlled access into the town, may also have been constructed at this time. These gatehouses emphasised the power and control by the lords of Dryslwyn. The visitor passed beneath an outer portcullis, which dropped shut and the gate closed before the visitor was admitted passed the guardhouse and the inner gate opened and portcullis raised to admit the visitor into the town or castle. Though these gatehouses and other defences were effective for most occasions, they were unable to withstand a full siege.

Despite his wealth, his impressive castle and associated town, Rhys was being dragged through the shire courts under 'English' law by Robert de Tibetot, the king's justiciar in Carmarthen. Rhys, possibly due to his perceived status as a lord of Deheubarth, his recent role as an ally of the king or his belief that he was only answerable to the king under Welsh law, refused to engage with, or attend, the courts. Consequently he was about to be outlawed when he rose in revolt in June 1287. His revolt went unsupported by fellow Welshmen and was consequently unsuccessful, hardly surprising given his recent support of the Crown against Llywelyn ap Gruffudd (Smith 1965; Griffiths 1966). Rhys may have been expecting royal intervention, none came and he was besieged in Dryslwyn castle between 12 August and 8 September by an army of up to 11,400 men. Written accounts of the siege and the archaeological evidence of weaponry and subsequent rebuilding provide a detailed picture of the longest siege of any Welsh castle.

Following the capture of Dryslwyn in 1287 the castle was garrisoned by 'English' troops. These garrisoned castles of the Tywi valley (Carmarthenshire) (Carreg Cennan, Llandovery, Dinefwr, Dryslwyn, Carmarthen, Llansteffan) formed 'the handle' by which the English Crown securely grasped west Wales. During the 14th and 15th century Dryslwyn castle was part of a large complex 'state' supply system. The garrison was paid by the Crown, or English barons who held the lordship and received rents from the town, commote or wider area. Any surplus of rental income over garrison costs went to the Crown or English barons. Goods were bought centrally and supplied to the castle, which operated a cash economy. The garrison defended the castle with crossbows supplied from a central castle armoury rather than using traditional personal weapons such as 'long' bows.

Though the English Crown sought to keep firm grip on Wales during this period, expensive wars in France meant that it sought to do so at an increasingly reduced cost. There is, consequently, little sign of new masonry building activity in the castle (Phase 5).

Where later building does occur it is in wood, such as the guardhouse in Area B. The economic emphasis had largely switched to the town, and though the limited nature of excavation in the town means that a full picture is not yet available. The town had expanded to 43½ burgage plots, with perhaps as many as 200 inhabitants by the end of the 13th century, making it the second largest town in Carmarthenshire. The costs of maintaining a garrison, however, rose during the 14th century due to the depopulation effects of plague and increasing cost of labour. The rents recovered from the town and associated agricultural lands increasingly struggled to meet these costs and the garrison recorded in the early 14th century as 24 men had declined to 12 by 1385. Pounds (1990) suggestion 'The history of most castles is one of gradual decline, decay punctuated by short periods of fabric repair and rebuilding' is an accurate description of Dryslwyn Castle after 1287.

The population of *pura Wallia*, the area of geographic Wales controlled by the princes and lords of Wales during the mid 13th century (Rees 1951, plates 38–41), was increasing throughout the period 1100–1300 (Davies 1987, 147–150), a phenomenon which was noted by contemporary commentators (Thorpe 1978, 266). It can be expressed crudely in terms of what constituted an army. That raised by Gruffudd ap Cynan to capture North Wales in 1075 was around 1000 men (Davies 2004, 58–59). Stephen Bauzan marched an army of 3000 men up the Tywi valley in attempt to capture the lands of Ystrad Tywi in 1257 and by 1287 the Earl of Cornwall raised over 11,000 men to besiege Dryslwyn and put down the revolt of Rhys ap Maredudd. There was also a change in social structure and organisation with fewer bondmen and increasing numbers of freemen during the 12th and 13th centuries (Owen 1989). Together with the consolidation of the *gwestfa* in areas such as Gwynedd and Deheubarth, this would have resulted in a change from a wide range of small food renders and services commuted to a small number of payments, effectively taxation (Turvey 2002, 107). There is also evidence for the use of coinage both in terms of increased numbers of archaeologically recovered coins and in terms of tributes, which had been expressed in terms of cattle in the 12th century, but were expressed as cash amounts by the late 13th century (Turvey 2002, 130–131; Pierce 1972, 33). The increasing population and, through development of taxation and coinage, the ability to generate usable wealth, Wales became an increasingly valuable potential asset.

The literary sources which describe Welsh laws (Wade Evans 1909) and the rules of the Welsh court (Charles-Edwards *et al* 2000), though written as manuscripts in the 13th and 14th century, refer to the *llys* and the *maerdref* which were present in Wales in the 10th–12th centuries. There is little or no mention of the towns and castles which archaeological evidence increasingly attests as the dominant features of the 13th-century Welsh landscape. Despite this differential distribution of evidence, historians have recognised that 'Welsh society was changing rapidly, particularly from the mid 12th century onwards' (Davies 1987, 171; Pierce 1972, 20). The social changes of 13th-century Wales reduced the importance of kinship and traditional social structures, the increasingly money-based economy encouraged displays of wealth and power. Dryslwyn Castle is one such display of wealth and power and is part of the increasing use of masonry structures. It is also part of the increasingly substantial archaeological record of mid and late 13th century Wales, one which contrasts with the dearth of archaeological evidence from the 11th and 12th centuries.

Wales had never been an easy place to capture and control, a fact readily appreciated by contemporary commentators (Thorpe 1978, 267–273). During the 12th and 13th century English kings who sought to control Wales did so through the use of punitive expeditions. These were frequently unsuccessful and thus the English Crown was forced to utilise client rulers such as Rhys ap Gruffudd (the Lord Rhys) and Llywelyn ap Gruffudd. However, throughout the 13th century the structures of governance were greatly enhanced by the princes and lords of Wales (Pryce 2005; Charles-Edwards *et al* 2000; Stephenson 1984). The development of castles and towns in the 13th century led the people of *pura Wallia* to become used to more centralised authority which operated from fixed points in the landscape namely towns and castles. It is these fixed points which could be captured and held by an invading force. *Pura Wallia* had thus become a land capable of capture and evidence of its increasing wealth had made it worth the effort and cost of invasion. Though much attention has been lavished on the large Edwardian castles of North Wales, these massive and costly constructions, extravagant and excessive visual symbols of royal authority merely enabled a thin strip of land along the northern coast to be controlled. The vast territories of mid and west Wales were held by Edward I using the existing royal castles such as Builth, Cardigan, Carmarthen, Llanbadarn and the existing Welsh castles of Dolforwyn, Castell-y-Bere, Dinefwr and Dryslwyn. In these buildings, the Welsh had already constructed their own yoke.

BIBLIOGRAPHY

Abbreviations

AMLR: Ancient Monuments Laboratory Report

BAR: British Archaeological Reports (British Series unless otherwise stated), Oxford

CBA: Council for British Archaeology

RIC: Roman Imperial Coinage, Vol. 2 (Mattingly and Sydenham 1926)

SCBI: Sylloge of Coins of the British Isles (North 1989)

Primary sources

AC: Annales Cambriae (ed J Williams ab Ithel), Rolls Series 1860, London

BC: Bartholomaei de Cotton Historia Anglicana (ed H R Luard), Rolls Series 1859, London

BT: Brut y Tywysogyon (Chronicle of the Princes) Peniarth MS 20 Version (translated and with notes by T Jones), 1952, University of Wales Press, Cardiff

Brut y Tywysogyon (Chronicle of the Princes) Red Book of Hergest Version (translated and with notes by T Jones), 1955, University of Wales Press, Cardiff

Brenhinedd y Seasson (The Kings of the Saxons) BM Cotton MS Cleopatra B v & the Black book of Basingwerk NLW MS 7006 (translated and with notes by T Jones), 1971, University of Wales Press, Cardiff

Cal Inq Misc: Calendar of Inquisitions Miscellaneous, Chancery, London 1916

CCRV: Calendar of Chancery Rolls, Various 1277–1326, London 1912

CCR: Calendars of Close Rolls, London

CChR: Calendar of Charter Rolls, London, 1903–27

CFR: Calendar Fine Rolls 1327–37, London 1911–63

CPR: Calendar of Patent Rolls 1281–92, London

Dunstable Annals: Annales Monastici de Dunstaplia et Bermundeseia (ed H R Luard), Rolls Series 1866, London

FH: Flores Historiarum, per Matthaeum Westmonasteriensem collecti (ed H R Luard), Rolls Series 1890, London

HC: Hagnaby Chronicle (BL Cotton MS Vespasian B xi f32)

HAC: Hailes Abbey Chronicle (BL Cotton MS Cleopatra D iii f46v)

London Annals: Chronicles, Edward I and Edward II. Annales Londonienses de tempore Edwardi Primi (ed W Stubbs), Rolls Series 1882, London

LC: The Chronicle of Lanercost 1272–1346 (translated by H Maxwell), 1913

PRO: Public Record Office, Various Accounts (E101)

Register of Edward the Black Prince, Public Record Office, London, 1930–03

St Albans Chronicle: Chronica Monasterii Sancti Albani. Johannis de Trokelowe et Henrici de Blaneforde Chronica (ed H T Riley), Rolls Series 1865, London

Thomas Walsingham: Chronica Monasterii Sancti Albani. Thomae Walsingham Historia Anglicana (ed H T Riley), Rolls Series 1863, London

Nicholas Trevet: Nicolai Triveti Annales (ed T Hog), English Historical Society 1845, London

NLW Add MS 455D: National Library of Wales, Additional Manuscript Collection 455D. Collection of documents concerning the castle, township and lordship of Dryslwyn, compiled by E A Lewis, 1907

Walsingham: Chronica Monasterii Sancti Albani. Thomae Walsingham Historia Anglicana (ed H T Riley), Rolls Series 1863, London

Waverley Annals: Annales Monastici de Wintonia et Waverleia (ed H R Luard), Rolls Series 1865, London

William Rishanger: Chronica Monasterii Sancti Albani. Willelmi Rishanger Chronica et Annales (ed H T Riley), Rolls Series 1865, London

Worcester Annals: Annales Monastici de Oseneia, Chronicon Thomae Wykes, et de Wigornia (ed H R Luard), Rolls Series 1869, London

Wroxham Continuation: Le Livere de Reis de Brittanie e Le Livere de Engleterre (ed J Glover), Rolls Series 1865, London

Wykes: Annales Monastici de Oseneia, Chronicon Thomae Wykes, et de Wigornia (ed H R Luard), Rolls Series 1869, London

Secondary sources

Addyman, P V and Goodall, I H, 1979 'The Norman church and door at Stillingfleet, North Yorkshire', *Archaeologia* 106, 75–105

Albarella, U and Davies, S, 1994 *Medieval and post-medieval mammal and bird bones from Launceston Castle, Cornwall: 1961–1982*, AMLR 18/94

Albarella, U and Davies, S, 2006 'The mammal and bird bones: a brief revisit', in A Saunders, *Excavations at Launceston Castle, Cornwall*, Society for Medieval Archaeology Monograph 24, Leeds, 447–453

Alcock, L, 1966 'Castle Tower, Penmaen: a Norman ringwork in Glamorgan', *Antiquaries Journal* 46, 178–210

353

Alcock, L, 1967 'Excavations at Deganwy Castle, Caernarvonshire, 1961–6', *Archaeological Journal* 46, 178–210

Allan, J, 1984 *Medieval and post-medieval finds from Exeter, 1971–1980*, Exeter Archaeological Report 3, Exeter

Altschul, M, 1965 *A baronial family in medieval England. The Clares 1217–1314*, Baltimore

Andrews, D and Milne, G, 1979 'Domestic settlement 1: Areas 10 and 6', in J Hurst (ed), *Wharram: a study of settlement on the Yorkshire Wolds Vol. 1*, Society for Medieval Archaeology Monograph 8, London, 108–114

Apted, M R, 1963–64 'Excavations at Kildrummy Castle, Aberdeenshire 1952–62', *Proceedings of the Society of Antiquaries of Scotland* 96, 208–236

Armitage, E S, 1912 *The early Norman castles of the British Isles*, London

Armitage, P L, 1985 'Small mammal faunas in later mediaeval towns', *Biologist* 32 (2), 65–71

Ashworth, M, 2000 'Objects of stone', in P Ellis, *Ludgershall Castle, excavations by Peter Addyman 1964–1972*, Devizes, 177–180

Austin, D, 1988 *Barnard Castle*, London

Austin, D, 1988 'Excavation and survey at Bryn Cysegrfan, Llanfair Clydogau, Dyfed, 1979', *Medieval Archaeology* 32, 130–165

Avent, R, 1981 'Laugharne Castle 1976–80', in R Avent and P Webster, *Interim reports of excavations at Laugharne Castle Dyfed, 1976–80, and Dryslwyn Castle, Dyfed, 1980*, Cardiff, 1–33

Avent, R, 1983 *Castles of the Princes of Gwynedd*, Cardiff

Avent, R, 1989 *Criccieth Castle*, Cardiff

Avent, R, 1994a *Dolwyddelan Castle, Dolbadarn Castle*, Cardiff

Avent, R, 1994b 'Castles of the Welsh Princes', *Chateau Gaillard* 16, 11–16

Avent, R, 2006 'William Marshall's castle at Chepstow and its place in military architecture', in R Turner and A Johnson (eds), *Chepstow Castle: its history and buildings*, Logaston, 81–90

Babington, C, Manning, T and Stewart, S, 1999 *Our painted past*, London

Backhouse, J, 2000 *Medieval rural life in the Luttrell Psalter*, London

Bailey, M, 1988 'The rabbit and the medieval East Anglian economy', *Agricultural History Review* 36 (1), 1–20

Barker, P, 1979 *Techniques of archaeological excavation*, London

Barker, P A and Higham R A, 1988 *Hen Domen, Montgomery: a timber castle on the English Welsh Border, excavation 1960–1988, a summary report*, Exeter and Worcester

Barnard, F, 1916 *The casting-counter and the counting-board*, Oxford

Bartley, D D, 1976 'Valle Crucis: report on wood and charcoal', in L A S Butler, 'Valle Crucis Abbey: an excavation in 1970', *Archaeologia Cambrensis* 125, 116 (80–126)

Barton, K J and Holden, E W, 1978 'Excavations at Bramber Castle, Sussex, 1966–67', in D Parsons (ed), *Five castle excavations*, London, 11–79

Barton, K, 1963 'A medieval pottery kiln at Ham Green, Bristol', *Transactions of the Bristol and Gloucestershire Archaeological Society* 82, 95–126

Bartrum, P C, 1974 *Welsh genealogies AD 300–1400*, Cardiff

Beer, R J S, 1976 'The relationship between *Trichuris trichiura* (Linnaeus 1758) of man and *Trichuris suis* (Schrank 1788) of the pig', *Research in Veterinary Science* 20, 47–54

Beeton, I, 1861 *The book of household management*, London (1982 facsimile edition)

Bennell, M, 1992 'Non-structural metalwork', in P L Drewett, 'Excavations at Lewes Castle, East Sussex 1985–88, *Sussex Archaeological Collections* 130, 95–98 (68–106)

Bennett, H S, 1937 *Life on the English manor*, Cambridge

Bereenhout, B, 1994 'What conclusions can be drawn from mature haddock bones in a Neolithic site in the Netherlands?', *Archaeo-Ichthyological Studies*, 51, 341–347

Berry, G, 1974 *Medieval English jetons*, London

Besly, E, 1995 'Short cross and other medieval coins from Llanfaes, Anglesey', *British Numismatic Journal* 65, 46–82

Biddle, M (ed), 1990 *Object and economy in medieval Winchester*, Winchester Studies 7.ii, Oxford

Biddle, M and Barclay, K, 1990 'Sewing pins and wire', in M Biddle (ed), *Object and economy in medieval Winchester*, Winchester Studies 7.ii, Oxford, 560–570

Biddle, M and Smith, D, 1990 'Sharpening and grinding stones: ii. The querns', in M Biddle (ed), *Object and economy in medieval Winchester*, Winchester Studies 7.ii, Oxford, 881–890

Binford, L, 1981 *Bones: ancient men and modern myths*, New York

Birrell, J, 1992 'Deer and deer farming in medieval England', *Agricultural History Review* 40 (ii), 112–126

Black, A, 1864 *Black's picturesque guide to South Wales*, London

Blair, C, 1958 *European armour circa 1066 to circa 1700*, London

Blair, J, 1993 'Hall and chamber: English domestic planning 1000–1250', in G Meirion-Jones and M Jones (eds), *Manorial domestic buildings in England and northern France*, Society of Antiquaries Occasional Papers 15, London, 1–21

Blandford, P R S and Walton, K C, 1991 'Polecat', in G B Corbet and S Harris (eds), *The handbook of British mammals*, Oxford, 396–405

Blockley, K, and Halfpenny, I, 2002 *Aberglasney House and Gardens*, BAR 334

Bond, C J, 1988 'Monastic fisheries', in M Aston (ed), *Medieval fish, fisheries and fishponds*, BAR 182, 69–112

Bonser, W, 1963 *The medical background of Anglo-Saxon England*, London

Borg, A, 1991 'Arms and armour', in P Saunders and E Saunders (eds), *Salisbury Museum Medieval Catalogue 1*, Salisbury, 79–92

Bradbury, J, 1985 *The medieval archer*, Woodbridge

Bradbury, J, 1992 *The medieval siege*, Woodbridge

Brand, J, 1994 *The English coinage 1180–1247: money, mints and exchanges*, Stroud

Brears, P, 1988 *Ryedale recipes*, Beverley

Brennan, D, 1997 'Iron nails', in T James, 'Excavations at Carmarthen Greyfriars 1983–90', *Medieval Archaeology* 41, 186–187 (100–194)

Bridgeman, G T, 1876 *History of the Princes of South Wales*, Wigan

Briggs, C S, 1999 'Aberglasney: the theory, history and archaeology of a post-medieval landscape', *Post-Medieval Archaeology* 33, 242–284

Brimblecombe, P, 1989 'The history of air pollution in York and its effects on York Minster', *European Cultural Heritage Newsletter on Research* 3 (4), 41–43

Brown, D, 1990 'Dice, a games board and playing pieces', in M Biddle (ed), *Object and economy in medieval Winchester*, Winchester Studies 7.ii, Oxford, 692–705

Brown, D and Lawson, G, 1990 'Toggles', in M Biddle (ed), *Object and economy in medieval Winchester*, Winchester Studies 7.ii, Oxford, 589–596

Brown, R A, 1954 *English medieval castles*, London

Brown, R A, 1984 *The architecture of castles*, London

Brown, R A, Colvin, H M and Taylor, A J, 1963 *The history of the King's Works 1–2: the Middle Ages*, London

Brownsword, R, 2004 'Medieval metalworking: an analytical study of copper alloy objects', *Historical Metallurgy* 38 (2), 84–105

Buckley, D G and Major, H, 1983 'Medieval pot quern from Hadleigh Castle', *Essex Archaeology and History* 15, 175–176

Butler, L A S, 1974 'Medieval finds from Castell-y-Bere', *Archaeologia Cambrensis* 123, 78–111

Butler, L A S, 1976 'Valle Crucis Abbey: an excavation in 1970', *Archaeologia Cambrensis* 125, 80–126

Butler, L A S, 1990 'Dolforwyn Castle Montgomery, Powys. First report: the excavation 1981–1986', *Archaeologia Cambrensis* 138, 78–98

Butler, L A S, 1994 *Dolforwyn Castle, Powys. Interim report on excavation, July 3rd–30th, 1994*, unpublished report

Butler, L A S, 1997 'Dolforwyn Castle Montgomery, Powys. Second report: the excavation 1987–1994, *Archaeologia Cambrensis* 144, 133–203

Butler, L A S, 2000 'The siege of Dolforwyn Castle in 1277', *Chateau Gaillard 19*, 25–26

Butler, L A S, 2003 'Dolforwyn Castle: prospect and retrospect', in J R Kenyon and K O'Connor (eds), *The medieval castle in Ireland and Wales*, Dublin, 149–162

Butler, L A S and Knight, J K, 2004 *Dolforwyn Castle, Montgomery Castle*, Cadw, Cardiff

Caiger-Smith, A, 1963 *English medieval mural pPainting*, Oxford

Caldwell, D, 1981 *Scottish weapons and fortifications, 1100–1800*, Edinburgh

Caldwell, D, 1987 'Macehead', in P Holdsworth (ed), *Excavations in the medieval burgh of Perth 1979–1981*, Society of Antiquaries of Scotland Monograph 5, Edinburgh. 125

Caple, C, 1981 *Site notes for Area K, 1980–1982*, unpublished report, Dryslwyn Castle Excavation Archive

Caple, C, 1985a 'Dryslwyn Castle', *Medieval Archaeology* 29, 229

Caple, C, 1985b 'Dryslwyn, Dyfed', *CBA Newsletter and Calendar* 8 (1984–85), 138

Caple, C, 1990a 'Dryslwyn Castle Excavation 1989: interim report', *University of Durham & University of Newcastle upon Tyne Archaeological Reports 1989*, 55–60

Caple, C, 1990b 'The castle and lifestyle of a 13th century independent Welsh Lord: excavations at Dryslwyn Castle 1980–1988', *Chateau Gaillard 14*, 47–59

Caple, C, 1991 'Dryslwyn Castle excavation 1990: interim report', *University of Durham & University of Newcastle upon Tyne Archaeological Reports 1990*, 53–55

Caple, C, 1992a 'Dryslwyn Castle Excavation 1991: interim report', *University of Durham & University of Newcastle upon Tyne Archaeological Reports 1991*, 51–54

Caple, C, 1992b 'Dryslwyn Castle', *Medieval Archaeology* 36, 230

Caple, C, 1992c 'The detection and definition of an industry: the English medieval and post medieval pin industry', *Archaeological Journal* 148, 241–255

Caple, C, 1993a 'Dryslwyn Castle Excavation 1992: interim report', *University of Durham & University of Newcastle upon Tyne Archaeological Reports 1992*, 51–55

Caple, C, 1993b 'Dryslwyn Castle', *Medieval Archaeology* 37, 300

Caple, C, 1993c 'Dryslwyn Castle', *Archaeology in Wales* 32, 79–80

Caple, C, 1994a 'Dryslwyn Castle Excavation 1993: interim report', *University of Durham & University of Newcastle upon Tyne Archaeological Reports 1993*, 56–61

Caple, C, 1994b 'Dryslwyn Castle', *Medieval Archaeology* 40, 281–283

Caple, C, 1996a *An interim guide to Dryslwyn Castle and its excavation*, unpublished site report, Dryslwyn Castle Excavation Archive

Caple, C, 1996b 'Dryslwyn Castle Excavation 1995: interim report', *University of Durham & University of Newcastle upon Tyne Archaeological Reports 1995*, 69–75

Caple, C, 2002 *A Welsh lord's castle of the 13th century; Dryslwyn Castle excavations 1980–1995*, unpublished excavation report, Dryslwyn Castle Excavation Archive

Caple, C, (forthcoming) 'Nevern Castle: a reassessment'

Caple, C and Denison, S, 1994 'Rise and fall of Welsh power at Dryslwyn', *British Archaeological News* July 1994, 2

Caple, C and Jessop, O, 1996 'Dryslwyn Castle', *Archaeology in Wales* 36, 85–86

Caple, C and Jessop, O, 1997 *Dryslwyn Castle, Dyfed, data structure report for 1980–1995 archaeological excavations*, unpublished report, Dryslwyn Castle Excavation Archive

Caple, R F, 2000 *Lithic projectiles*, unpublished report, Dryslwyn Castle Excavation Archive

Cardiff Archaeology Society 1977 *Llantrithyd; a ringwork in South Glamorgan*, Cardiff

Carruthers, W, 1993 'Charred plant remains', in J M Lewis, 'Excavations at Loughor Castle, West Glamorgan 1969–1973', *Archaeologia Cambrensis* 142, 173–177 (99–180)

Cartwright, C, 1992 'Charcoal', in P Drewett, 'Excavations at Lewes Castle, East Sussex 1985–1988', *Sussex Archaeological Collections* 130, 102 (68–106)

Cartwright, C, 1992a 'Marine molluscs', in P Drewett, 'Excavations at Lewes Castle, East Sussex 1985–1988', *Sussex Archaeological Collections* 130, 100–102 (68–106)

Caseldine, A, 1990 *Environmental archaeology in Wales*, Lampeter

Caseldine, A, 1995 'The charred plant remains from layer 63, pit 49', in K Murphy, 'The castle and borough of Wiston, Pembrokeshire', *Archaeologia Cambrensis* 144, 86–88 (71–102)

Chapman, D, and Chapman, N, 1975 *Fallow deer*, Lovenham

Charles-Edwards, T M, Owen, M E and Russell, P, (eds) 2000 *The Welsh King and his Court*, Cardiff

Charles-Edwards, T M, 2000 'Food, drink and clothing in the laws of court', in T M Charles-Edwards, M E Owen and P Russell (eds), *The Welsh King and his Court*, Cardiff, 319–337

Charleston, R J, 1984 *English glass and the glass used in England 400–1940*, London

Charters, S and Evershed, R P, 1995 'Evidence for the mixing of fats and waxes in archaeological ceramics', *Archaeometry* 37, 113–127

Charters, S, Evershed, R P, Heron, C, Blinkhorn, P and Goad, L J, 1993a 'Identification of an adhesive used to repair a Roman Jar', *Archaeometry* 35, 91–101

Charters, S, Evershed, R P, Goad, L J, Blinkhorn, P W and Denham, V, 1993b 'Quantification and distribution of lipid in archaeological ceramics: implications for sampling potsherds for organic residue analysis', *Archaeometry* 35, 211–223

Charters, S, Evershed, R P, Quye, A, Blinkhorn, P W and Denham, V, 1997 'Simulation experiments for determining the use of ancient pottery vessels: the behavior of epicuticular leaf wax during boiling of a leafy vegetable', *Journal of Archaeological Science* 24, 1–7

Chatwin, P B, 1955 'Brandon Castle, Warwickshire', *Transactions of the Birmingham Archaeological Society* 73, 81–82

Clark, G T, 1884 *Medieval military architecture in England*, London

Clark, J, 1995 *The medieval horse and its equipment c1150–c1450*, Medieval Finds from Excavations in London 5, London

Clarke, H and Carter, A, 1977 *Excavations in King's Lynn 1963–1970*, London

Cobbett, W, 1841 *Cottage economy*, Oxford (1979 facsimile edition)

Cockayne, O, 1866 *Leechdoms, Wortcunning and Starcraft of Early England*, vol III, London

Cockerill, S C, 1969 *Old Testament miniatures*, London

Colinart, S, 2001 'Analysis of inorganic yellow colour in ancient Egyptian painting', in W V Davies (ed), *Colour and painting in Ancient Egypt*, London, 1–4

Collins, P, 1995 *Dryslwyn Castle: the animal bones from Areas G, H, K and L*, ARCUS 198, unpublished report, Dryslwyn Castle Excavation Archive

Collins, P, 1996 *Dryslwyn Castle: the animal bones from Areas A, D, E, I, J and P (with some K and L)*, ARCUS 198, unpublished report, Dryslwyn Castle Excavation Archive

Collins, P, 1997 *Dryslwyn Castle: the animal bones from Areas B, C, M, O, T, U, V, W, X, Y and Z*, ARCUS 198, unpublished report, Dryslwyn Castle Excavation Archive

Colvin, H M, 1971 *Building accounts of King Henry III*, Oxford

Condry, W, 1981 *The natural history of Wales*, The New Naturalist 66, London

Cook, B, 1999 'Foreign coins in medieval England', in L L Travaini (ed), *Moneta straniera: Italia ed Europa XI–XV secolo, the Second Cambridge Numismatic Symposium*, Milan

Coulson, C, 2003 *Castles in medieval society*, Oxford

Courtney, P, 1993 'The medieval and post-medieval objects', in P Ellis (ed), *Beeston Castle, Cheshire. A report on the excavations by Laurence Keen and Peter Hough*, Historic Buildings and Monuments Commission for England Report 23, London, 134–161

Courtney, P, 1994 'Ironwork', in J Manley, 'Excavations at Caergwrle Castle, Clwyd, N Wales 1988–1990', *Medieval Archaeology* 38, 112–114 (83–133)

Cowgill, J, de Neergaard, M and Griffths, N, 1987 *Knives and scabbards*, Medieval finds from excavations in London, London

Coy, J, 1987 'Non-domestic faunal resources in the South West', in N D Balaam, B Levitan and V Straker (eds), *Studies in palaeoeconomy and environment in South West England*, BAR 181, 9–30

Crane, E, 1983 *The archaeology of beekeeping*, London

Craster, O E, 1950–51 'A medieval limekiln at Ogmore Castle, Glamorgan', *Archaeologia Cambrensis* 101, 72–76

Credland, A G, 1983 'Military finds', in P Mayes and L Butler, *Sandal Castle excavations, 1964–1973: a detailed archaeological report*, Wakefield, 265–266

Creighton, O and Higham, R, 2005 *Medieval town walls*, Stroud

Crew, P, 1991 'The experimental production of prehistoric bar iron', *Historical Metallurgy* 25, 21–36

Crossley-Holland, N, 1996 *Living and dining in medieval Paris*, Cardiff

Cruden, S, 1982 *St Andrews Castle*, Edinburgh (2nd ed)

Cummins, J, 2001, *The hound and the hawk*, London

Dahl, G and Hjort, A, 1976 *Having herds, pastoral herd growth and household economy*, Stockholm

Daniel-Tyssen, J R, 1878 *Royal charters and historical documents relating to the town and county of Carmarthen*, Carmarthen

Davies, R R, 1978 *Lordship and society in the March of Wales 1282–1400*, Oxford

Davies, R R, 1987 *Conquest, coexistence and change: Wales 1063–1415*, Oxford (republished 1991 as *The Age of Conquest. Wales 1063–1415*)

Davies, R R, 1995 *The revolt of Owain Glyn Dwr*, Oxford

Davies, S, 2004 *Welsh military institutions 633–1283*, Cardiff

Davies, S and Jones, N A, 1997 *The horse in Celtic culture*, Cardiff

Davies, J C, 1940 *The Welsh assize roll 1277–1284*, Cardiff

Davis, P R, 1988 *Castles of the Welsh Princes*, Swansea

de Hamel, C, 1992 *Medieval craftsmen: scribes and illuminators*, London

Donaldson, A M, Jones, A K G and Rackham, D J, 1980 'Barnard Castle, Co Durham. A dinner in the Great Hall: report on the contents of a fifteenth-century drain', *Journal of the British Archaeological Association* 133, 86–96

Drewett, P L, 1992 'Excavations at Lewes Castle, East Sussex 1985–8', *Sussex Archaeological Collections* 130, 69–106

Driesch, A von den and Boessneck, J, 1974 'Kritische Anmerkungen zur Widerristhohenberechnung aus Langenmassen vor- und fruhgeschichtlicher Tierknochen', *Saugetierkundliche Mitteilungen* 22, 325–348

Drury, J L, 1982 'Early goat-keeping in upper Weardale, Co. Durham', *Transactions of the Architectural and Archaeological Society of Durham and Northumberland* (new series) 6, 23–25

Dudd, S N and Evershed, R P, 1998 'Direct demonstration of milk as an element of archaeological economies', *Science* 282, 1478–81

Dudd, S N, 1999 *Molecular and isotopic characterisation of animal fats in archaeological pottery*, unpublished PhD thesis, University of Bristol

Dungworth, D, 1999 *Dryslwyn Castle slag report*, unpublished report, Dryslwyn Castle Excavation Archive

Dunning, G C, 1965 'Heraldic metalwork and other finds from Rievaulx Abbey, Yorkshire', *The Archaeological Journal* 45, 53–63

Duplessy, J, 1988 *Les monnaies francaises royales vol. I*, Paris and Mastricht

Dyer, C, 1994 *Everyday life in medieval England*, London

Dyer, C, 1998 'Did the peasants really starve in medieval England?', in M Carlin and J T Rosenthal (eds), *Food and eating in Medieval Europe*, London, 53–72

Eastaugh, N, Walsh, V, Chaplin, T and Siddall, R, 2004 *The pigment compendium*, Amsterdam

Eastaugh, N, 1994 *Preliminary investigation into the lead and slate archive from Dryslwyn Castle Excavation 1980–1993*, unpublished report, Dryslwyn Castle Excavation Archive

Easterbee, N, 1991 'Wildcat', in G B Corbet and S Harris (eds), *The handbook of British mammals*, Oxford, 431–437

Edlin, H L, 1973 *Woodland crafts in Britain*, Devon

Edwards, J G, 1935 *Calendar of ancient correspondence concerning Wales*, Cardiff

Edwards, J G (ed), 1940 *Littere Wallie*, Cardiff

Egan, G and Pritchard, F, 1991 *Dress accessories c.1150–c.1450*, Medieval Finds from Excavations in London 3, London

Ellis, B M A, 1995 'Spurs and spur fittings', in J Clark (ed), *The medieval horse and its equipment c1150–1450*, Woodbridge, 124–156

Ellis, P, 1993 *Beeston Castle, Cheshire. A report on the excavations by Laurence Keen and Peter Hough*, Historic Buildings and Monuments Commission for England Report 23, London

Ellis, P, 2000 *Ludgershall Castle, Wiltshire. A report on the excavations by Peter Addyman, 1964–1972*, Devizes

Ellis, S E and Moore, D T, 1990 'Sharpening and grinding stones: i. The hones', in M Biddle (ed), *Object and economy in medieval Winchester*, Winchester Studies 7.ii, Oxford, 868–881

Encyclopedia Britannica, 1978 'Bowling', 3, 86–91 (15th ed)

Evans, J, 1970 *A history of jewellery 1100–1870*, London (2nd ed)

Evans, J, 1977 'Analysis of mortar samples from the sub-vault', in G Black (ed), 'The redevelopment of 20 Dean's Yard, Westminster 1975–77', *Transactions of the London and Middlesex Archaeological Society* 28, 204–209 (190–210)

Evans, J, 1984 'The mortars', in M Audouy (ed), 'Excavations at the Church of All Saints Brixworth, Northamptonshire 1981–2', *Journal of the British Archaeological Association* 137, 16–23 (1–44)

Evershed, R P, Heron, C and Goad, L J, 1990 'Analysis of organic residues of archaeological origin by high-temperature gas chromatography and gas chromatography-mass spectrometry', *Analyst* 119, 1339–42

Evershed, R P, Heron, C and Goad, L J, 1991 'Epicuticular wax components preserved in potsherds as chemical indicators of leafy vegetables in ancient diets', *Antiquity* 65, 540–544

Evershed, R P, Heron, C, Charters, S and Goad, L J, 1992 'The survival of food residues: new methods of analysis, interpretation and application', *Proceedings of the British Academy* 77, 187–208

Evershed, R P, Arnot, K I, Collister, J, Eglinton, G, and Charters, S, 1994 'Applications of isotope ratio monitoring gas chromatography-mass spectrometry to the analysis of organic residues of archaeological origin', *Analyst.* 119, 909–914

Evershed, R P, Charters, S and Quye, A, 1995 'Interpreting lipid residues in archaeological ceramics: preliminary results from laboratory simulations of vessel use and burial', *Materials Issues in Art and Archaeology IV, Materials Research Society Symposium Proceedings* 352, 85–95

Evershed, R P, Vaughan S J, Dudd, S N and Soles, J S, 1997 'Fuel for thought? Beeswax in lamps and conical cups from Late Minoan Crete', *Antiquity* 71, 979–985

Evershed, R P, Dudd, S N, Mottram, H R, Charters, S, Stott, A W, Lawrence, G J, Gibson, A M, Conner, A, Blinkhorn, P W and Reeves, V, 1997a 'New criteria for the identification of animal fats preserved in archaeological pottery', *Naturwissenschaften* 84, 1–6

Evershed, R P, Dudd, S N, Charters, S, Mottram, H, Stott, A W, Raven, A, van Bergen, P F and Bland, H A, 1999 'Lipids as carriers of anthropogenic signals from prehistory', *Philosophical Transactions of the Royal Society of London Series B* 354, 19–31

Evershed, R P, Dudd, M J, Lockheart, M J and Jim, S, 2001 'Lipids in archaeology', in D R Brothwell and A M Pollard (eds), *Handbook of Archaeological Science*, Chichester, 331–349

Faulkner, P A, 1958 'Domestic planning from the twelfth to the fourteenth centuries', *The Archaeological Journal* 115, 150–183

Fawcett, R, 1990 *The Abbey and Palace of Dunfermline*, Edinburgh

Finlay, M, 1990 *Western writing implements in the age of the quill pen*, Carlisle

Forde-Johnston, J, 1979 *Great medieval castles of Britain*, London

Freeman, B, 1988 *A book of Welsh fish cookery*, Talybont

Freeman, B, 1980 *First catch your peacock: a book of Welsh food*, Griffithstown

Freeman, B, 1981 *A book of Welsh bread*, Cardigan

Frith, J, Appleby, R, Stacey, R and Heron C, 2004 'Sweetness and light: chemical evidence of beeswax and tallow candles at Fountains Abbey, North Yorkshire', *Medieval Archaeology* 48, 220–227

Fryde, N, 1974 *List of Welsh entries in the Memoranda Rolls 1282–1343*, Cardiff

Gale, R and Cutler, D, 2000 *Plants in Archaeology*, Otley

Galloway, P, 1990 'Combs of bone, antler and ivory', in M Biddle (ed), *Object and economy in medieval Winchester*, Winchester Studies 7.ii, Oxford, 665–676

Gastineau, H, 1830 *Wales illustrated*, London

Geddes, J, 1999 *Medieval decorative ironwork in England*, London

Geijer, A, 1979 *A history of textile art*, London

Gettens, R J, and Stout, G L, 1966 *Painting materials*, New York.

Gidney, L J, 1991 *Leicester, The Shires 1988 Excavations. The animal bones from the medieval deposits at Little Lane*, AMLR 57/91

Gidney, L J, 1993 *Leicester, The Shires 1988 Excavations: further identifications of small mammal and bird bones*, AMLR 92/93

Gidney, L J, 1994 *The animal bones from Area F, Dryslwyn Castle. Durham Environmental Archaeology Report*, unpublished report, Dryslwyn Castle Excavation Archive

Gidney, L J, 1996 'The cosmetic and quasi-medicinal use of dog fat', *ORGAN* 11, 8–9

Gidney, L G, 2002 'Dryslwyn Castle: animal and bird bones' in C Caple, *A Welsh lord's Castle of the 13th century; Dryslwyn Castle excavations 1980–1995*, unpublished excavation report

Gilchrist, R, 1987 *Environmental evidence from Dryslwyn Castle, Area F. Archive Report*, EAU York, unpublished report, Dryslwyn Castle Excavation Archive

Gilchrist, R, 1988 'A reappraisal of Dinas Powys: local exchange and specialised livestock production in 5th- to 7th-century Wales', *Medieval Archaeology* 32, 50–62

Glenn, T A, 1915 'Prehistoric and historic remains at Dyserth Castle', *Archaeologia Cambrensis* 15, 47–86, 249–252

Godden, G, 1964 *Encyclopaedia of British pottery and porcelain marks*, London

Goodall, A, 1984 'Objects of non-ferrous metal', in J Allan, *Medieval and post-medieval finds from Exeter, 1971–1980*, Exeter Archaeological Report 3, 337–348

Goodall, A, 1993 'Copper alloy objects', in H Murray and J Murray, 'Excavations at Rattray, Aberdeenshire. A Scottish deserted burgh', *Medieval Archaeology* 37, 188–195 (109–218)

Goodall, A, 2002 *Dryslwyn Castle, Dyfed: non-ferrous metal objects' (revised)*, an unpublished report, Dryslwyn Castle Excavation Archive

Goodall, A, forthcoming, 'Non ferrous metalwork', in Palmer (ed) 'Excavations at Burton Dasset'

Goodall, I H, 1977 'Timber nails', in F Williams (ed), *Excavations at Pleshey Castle (XII–XVI century): excavations in the Bailey 1959–1963*, BAR 42, 182–183

Goodall, I H, 1980 *Ironwork in medieval Britain: an archaeological study*, unpublished PhD thesis

Goodall, I H, 1982 'Iron objects', in J G Coad and A D F Streeten, 'Excavations at Castle Acre Castle, Norfolk, 1972–77', *Archaeological Journal* 139, 227–235 (138–301)

Goodall, I H, 1987 'Weapons', in G Beresford, *Goltho, the development of an early medieval manor c.850–1150*, English Heritage Archaeological Report 4, London, 185–186

Goodall, I H, 1990a 'Building ironwork', in M Biddle (ed), *Object and economy in medieval Winchester*, Winchester Studies 7.ii, Oxford, 328–349

Goodall, I H, 1990b 'Locks and keys', in M Biddle (ed), *Object and economy in medieval Winchester*, Winchester Studies 7.ii, Oxford, 1001–1036

Goodall, I H, 1990a 'Iron fittings for lights', in M Biddle (ed), *Object and economy in medieval Winchester*, Winchester Studies 7.ii, Oxford, 981–983

Goodall, I H, 1990d 'Iron buckles and belt fittings', in M Biddle (ed), *Object and economy in medieval Winchester*, Winchester Studies 7.ii, Oxford, 526–537

Goodall, I H, 1994 'Arrowheads', in H Quinnell, M Blockley and P Berridge, *Excavations at Rhuddlan, Clwyd 1969–75, Mesolithic to medieval*, CBA Research Report 95, London, 188–189

Goodall, I H, 2000 'Iron objects', in P Ellis, *Ludgershall Castle, Wiltshire. A report on the excavations by Peter Addyman, 1964–1972*, Devizes, 143–156

Goodall, I H, 2001 *Dryslwyn Castle: iron objects*, unpublished report, Dryslwyn Castle Excavation Archive

Goodall, I H, and Geddes, J, 1980 'Iron objects', in A D Saunders 'Lydford Castle, Devon', *Medieval Archaeology* 24, 165–167 (123–186)

Gore, L, 1976 *Game cooking*, Harmondsworth

Grant, A, 1982 'The use of tooth wear as a guide to the age of domestic ungulates', in B Wilson, C Grigson and S Payne (eds), *Ageing and sexing animal bones from archaeological sites*, BAR 109, 91–108

Grant, E, 1988 'Marine and river fishing in medieval Somerset: fishbone evidence from Langport', in M Aston (ed), *Medieval fish, fisheries and fishponds*, BAR 182, 409–416

Green, F, 1982 'Plant remains', in J Coad, and A D F Streeten (eds), 'Excavations at Castle Acre Castle, Norfolk 1972–7', *Archaeological Journal* 139, 273–275 (138–301)

Greig, J R A, Girling, M A and Skidmore, P, 1982 'The plant and insect remains', in P Barker and R Higham, *Hen Domen, a timber castle on the English-Welsh border*, London, 60–71

Grenville, J, 1997 *Medieval housing*, London

Grieve, M, 1931 *A modern herbal*, London

Griffin, K O, 1979 'Fossil records of fig, grape and walnut in Norway from medieval time', in U Korber Grohne (ed), *Festschrift Maria Hopf*, Archaeo-Physika 8, 57–68

Griffiths, R A, 1966 'The revolt of Rhys ap Maredudd, 1287–88', *Welsh History Review* 3, 121–143

Griffiths, R A, 1972 *The Principality of Wales in the later Middle Ages: the structure and personnel of government I. South Wales 1277–1536*, Cardiff

Griffiths, R A, 1994 *Conquerors and conquered in medieval Wales*, Stroud

Grigson, J, 1970 *Charcuterie and French pork cookery*, Harmmondsworth

Grundy, J, McCrombie, G, Ryder, P, Welfare, H and Pevsner, N, 1992 *The buildings of England: Northumberland*, London

Hague, D B and Warhurst, C, 1966 'Excavations at Sycharth Castle, Denbighshire', *Archaeologia Cambrensis* 115, 108–128

Hall, S J G and Clutton-Brock, J, 1989 *Two hundred years of British farm livestock*, London

Halpin, A, 1988 'Irish medieval bronze maceheads', in G Mac Niocaill and P F Wallace (eds), *Keimelia. Studies in medieval archaeology and history in memory of Tom Delaney*, Galway, 168–192

Hammond, P W, 1993 *Food and feast in medieval England*, Stroud

Hansen, P V, 1992 'Experimental reconstruction of a medieval trebuchet', *Acta Archaeologia* 63, 189–208

Harcourt, R A, 1974 'The dog in prehistoric and early historic Britain', *Journal of Archaeological Science* 1, 151–175

Harden, D B, 1966 'Glass', in H E J le Patourel, 'Knaresborough Castle', *Yorkshire Archaeological Journal* 164, 607 (591–607)

Hardy, R, 1992 *Longbow: a social and military history*, Yeovil (3rd ed)

Harthan, J, 1977 *Books of hours and their owners*, London

357

Harvey, J H, 1954 *English medieval architects*, London

Harvey, Y, 1975 'Catalogue', in C Platt and R Coleman-Smith (eds), *Excavation in medieval Southampton 1953–69. Volume 2: the finds*, Leicester, 254–295

Hawkes, C F F, Myres, J N L and Stevens, G G, 1930 *Saint Catherine's Hill, Winchester*, Winchester

Haynes, J, 1993 *A study of mortar from Dryslwyn Castle, Dyfed*, unpublished BSc dissertation, University of Durham

Heath, E G, 1971 *The grey goose wing*, Reading

Heinzel, H, Fitter, R and Parslow, J, 1972 *The birds of Britain and Europe*, London

Hemp, J W and Gresham, C, 1943 'Park Llanfrothen and the Unit System', *Archaeologia Cambrensis* 97, 98–112

Henderson, J, 2000 'The vessel glass', in P Ellis (ed), *Ludgershall Castle Excavations by Peter Addyman 1964–72*, Devizes, 168–177

Henisch, B A, 1976 *Fast and feast: food in medieval society*, Pennsylvania

Heron, C and Evershed, R P, 1993 'The analysis of organic residues and the study of pottery use', *Archaeological Method and Theory* 5, Arizona, 247–284

Hewitt, H J, 1983 *The horse in medieval England*, London

Hieatt, C B, 1988 *An ordinance of pottage*, London

Higham, R and Barker, P, 2000 *Hen Domen, Montgomery: a timber castle on the English Welsh Border. A final report*, Exeter

Higham, R and Rouillard, M, 2000 'Metalwork and other material from the bailey', in R Higham and P Barker, *Hen Domen Montgomery, a timber castle on the English-Welsh border*, Exeter, 98–110

Higham, R A, Allan, J P and Blaylock, S R, 1982 'Excavations at Okehampton Castle, Devon. Part 2: the bailey', *Proceedings of the Devon Archaeological Society* 40, 19–151

Hilling, J B, 1975 *The historic architecture of Wales*, Cardiff

Hilling, J B, 2000 *Cilgerran Castle, St Dogmaels Abbey*, Cardiff

Hillman, G, 1981 'Crop husbandry: evidence from macroscopic remains', in I G Simmons and M J Tooley (eds), *The environment in British Prehistory*, London, 183–191

Hinton, D, 1990 'Handles', in M Biddle (ed), *Object and economy in medieval Winchester*, Oxford, 560–571

Hinton, D A, Keene, S and Qualmann, K, 1981 'The Winchester reliquary', *Medieval Archaeology* 25, 45–75

Hodgson, J C, 1899 *The parish of Warkworth, with the chapelry of Chevington: Shilbottle; the chapelry or extra parochial place of Brainshaug*, The History of Northumberland 5, Newcastle upon Tyne

Holden, T G, Morgan, G, Hillman, G and Moore, P, 1994 'Botanical Remains', in H Quinnell, M Blockley and P Berridge, (eds), *Excavations at Rhuddlan, Clwyd 1969–1973. Mesolithic to medieval*, CBA Research Report 95, York, 160–163

Howard, H, 1993 'Workshop practices and identification of hands: Gothic wall paintings at St Albans', *The Conservator* 17, 34–45

Howard, H, 1997 'Scientific examination of medieval wall paintings', in ICCROM (ed) *Western medieval wall painting studies and conservation experience*, Rome, 43–50

Howard, H, 2003 *Pigments of English medieval wall painting*, London

Howarth, J, 1991 Lower Brockhampton, Herefordshire, unpublished leaflet issued by the National Trust

Humphries, P, 1996 'Destruction Engines', *Heritage in Wales*, Winter 1996

Hunter, K, 1987 'The Friars Park Window: excavation, conservation and preservation of a 13th century window', in ICOM Committee for Conservation (eds), *The ICOM Committee for Conservation 8th Triennial Meeting, Sydney, Australia, 6–11th September 1987*, Los Angeles, 989–997

Huntley, B and Allen, J R M, 1992 *Standard methodology for obtaining, preparing and counting pollen analytical samples*, unpublished report, University of Durham

Huntley, J, 1988 'The botanical remains', in R Daniels (ed), 'The Anglo-Saxon monastery at Church Close, Hartlepool, Cleveland', *The Archaeological Journal*, 145, 201–202 (158–210)

Huntley, J, 1989 *Plant remains from Annetwell Street, Carlisle: a synthesis*, AMLR 107/89

Hurst, J G, 1961 'The kitchen area of Northolt Manor, Middlesex', *Medieval Archaeology* 5, 211–299

Huws, D, 2000 *Medieval Welsh manuscripts*, Aberystwyth

Innocent, G F, 1916 *The development of English building construction*, Cambridge (1971 reprint)

James, T, 1997 'Excavations at Carmarthen Greyfriars 1983–90', *Medieval Archaeology* 41, 100–194

James, T B and Robinson, A M, 1988 *Clarendon Palace: The History and Archaeology of a Medieval Palace and Hunting Lodge near Salisbury, Wiltshire*, Report of the Research Committee of the Society of Antiquaries of London 45, London

Jenkins, D, 2000 'Hawk and hound: hunting in the Laws of Court', in T M Charles-Edwards, M E Owen and P Russell (eds), *The Welsh King and his Court*, Cardiff, 255–280

Jenkins, J G, 1984 *Cockles and mussels: aspects of shellfish-gathering in Wales*, Cardiff

Jessop, O M, 1996 'A new artefact typology for the study of medieval arrowheads', *Medieval Archaeology* 40, 192–205

Jessop, O M, 1997 'Medieval arrowheads', *Medieval Finds Research Group 700–1700 Datasheet 22*

Jewell, P A, Milner, C and Morton Boyd, J, 1974 *Island survivors: the ecology of the Soay sheep of St Kilda*, London

Johns, C N, 1970 *Criccieth Castle*, Cardiff

Johns, F, 1987 *Historic Carmarthenshire homes and their families*, Carmarthen

Johnson, M, 2002 *Behind the castle gate: from medieval to Renaissance*, London

Johnson, S, 1989 *Conisbrough Castle*, London

Johnstone, N, 1997 'An investigation into the locations of the Royal Courts of thirteenth century Gwynedd', in N Edwards (ed), *Landscape and settlement in medieval Wales*, Oxford, 55–69

Johnstone, N, 1999 'Cae Llys, Rhosyr: a court of the Princes of Gwynedd', *Studia Celtica* 33, 251–295

Jones, A K G, 1983 'A coprolite from 6–8 Pavement', in A R Hall, H K Kenward, D Williams and J R A Greig (eds), *Environment and living conditions at two Anglo-Scandinavian sites*, The Archaeology of York 14/4, York, 225–229

Jones, A K G, 1992 'Fish', in K Lightfoot, 'Rumney: a ringwork and manorial centre in South Glamorgan', *Medieval Archaeology* 36, 154 (96–163)

Jones, G and Jones, T, 1949 *The Mabinogion*, London

Jones, G R J, 2000 'Llys and Maerdref', in T M Charles-Edwards, M E Owen and P Russel (eds), *The Welsh King and his Court*, Cardiff, 296–318

Jones, R T, Sly J, Simpson, D, Rackham, D and Locker, A, 1985 *The terrestrial vertebrate remains from the Castle, Barnard Castle*, AMLR 7/85

Jope, M, 1954 'Animal remains from Clough Castle', in D M Waterman, 'Excavations at Clough Castle, Co. Down', *Ulster Journal of Archaeology* 17, 150–153 (101–163)

Keen, H J, 1992 *An electrical resistivity survey of the abandoned town of Dryslwyn*, unpublished BA dissertation, University of Durham.

Keen, M (ed), 1999 *Medieval warfare: a history*, Oxford

Keene, S, 1990 'Eyed weaving implements', in M Biddle (ed), *Object and economy in medieval Winchester*, Winchester Studies 7.1, Oxford, 232–234

Keepax, C A, Girling, M A, Jones, R T, Arthur, J R B, Paradine, P J and Keeley, H, 1979 'The environmental analysis', in J H Williams, *St Peter's Street Northampton, Excavations 1973–6*, Northampton, 337

Kenyon, J, 1990 *Medieval fortifications*, Leicester

Kenyon, J, 2002 *Kidwelly Castle*, Cardiff

Kenyon, J R, 1996 'Fluctuating frontiers: Norman Welsh Castle warfare 1075–1240', *Chateau Gaillard* 17, 119–126

King, D J C, 1988 *The castle in England and Wales: an interpretive history*, London

King, D J C, 1982 'The trebuchet and other siege machines', *Chateau Gaillard* 9–10, 457–470

King, D J C, 1983 *Castellarium Anglicanum*, New York

King, D J C, 1974 'Two castles in Northern Powys: Dinas Brân and Caergwrle', *Archaeologia Cambrensis* 123, 113–139

Knight, J K, 1980 *Grosmont Castle*, Cardiff

Knight, J K, 1993 'Excavations at Montgomery Castle, Part I. The documentary evidence, structures and excavated features', *Archaeologia Cambrensis* 141, 97–181

Knight, J K, 1994 'Excavations at Montgomery Castle, Part II. The finds: metalwork', *Archaeologia Cambrensis* 142, 226–228

Knight, J K, 1996 'Excavations at Montgomery Castle, Part III. The finds: other than the metalwork', *Archaeologia Cambrensis* 143, 139–203

Lafaurie, J, 1951 *Les monnaies des rois de France: Hugues Capet a Louis XII*, Paris

Lawson, G, 1995 'Pig metapodial "toggles" and buzz discs, traditional musical instruments', *Finds Research Group 700–1700 Datasheet 18*

Legge, A J and Rowley-Conwy, P A, 1988 *Star Carr revisited*, London

Lever, C, 1977 *The naturalised animals of the British Isles*, London

Levitan, B, 1994 'The vertebrate remains', in H Quinnell, M Blockley and P Berridge, (eds), *Excavations at Rhuddlan, Clwyd 1969–1973. Mesolithic to medieval*, CBA Research Report 95, York, 147–159

Lewis, A, 1998 *The last siege of Dryslwyn Castle*, Carmarthen. (private publication; see Solomon)

Lewis, E A, 1923–25 'The account roll of the Chamberlain of West Wales from Michelmas 1301 to Michelmas 1302' *Bulletin of the Board of Celtic Studies* II, 49–86

Lewis, J M, 1994 'Excavations at Loughor Castle, West Glamorgan 1969–73', *Archaeologia Cambrensis* 142, 99–180

Lewis, J M, 1999 *The medieval tiles of Wales*, Cardiff

Libois, R M, Hallet-Libois, C and Rosoux, R, 1987 'Elements pour l'identification des restes craniens des poissons delcaqui-coles de Belgique et du Nord de la France', *1. Anguilliformes, Gasterosteiformes, Cyprinodontiforms et Perciformes, Fiches d'osteologie animale pour l'archaeologie*, series A; Poissons. No 3, Centre de Recherches Archeologiques du CRNS

Liddiard, R, 2005 *Castles in context: power, symbolism and landscape, 1066–1500*, Macclesfield

Lightfoot, K, 1992 'Rumney Castle: a ringwork and manorial centre in South Glamorgan', *Medieval Archaeology* 36, 96–163

Ling, R and Ling, L A, 1973 'Excavations at Loughor, Glamorgan: the north-east and south-east angles of the Roman Fort', *Archaeologia Cambrensis* 122, 99–146

Linnard, W, 1982 *Welsh woodlands and forests: history and utilization*, Cardiff

Lloyd, J E, 1912 *A history of Wales, from the earliest times to the Edwardian conquest*, London

Lloyd, Sir J E, 1935 *A history of Carmarthenshire*, Cardiff and London

Lloyd-Fern, S, and Sell, S H, 1992 'Objects of iron, bronze and bone', in K Lightfoot, 'Rumney Castle, a ringwork and manorial centre in South Glamorgan', *Medieval Archaeology* 36, 134–144 (96–163)

Longfield, A K, 1929 *Anglo-Irish trade in the 16th century*, London

Longley, D, 1996 'Rhosyr', *Current Archaeology* 150, 204–208

Longrigg, R, 1977 *The English squire and his sport*, London

Lord, P, 2003 *The visual culture of Wales: medieval vision*, Cardiff

MacGregor, A, 1985 *Bone, antler, ivory and horn: the technology of skeletal materials since the Roman period*, London

MacGregor, A, 1987 'Objects of bone and antler', in G Beresford, *Goltho, The development of an early medieval manor c 850–1150*, London, 188–193

MacGregor, A, 1978 'Industry and commerce in Anglo-Scandinavian York', in R A Hall (ed), *Viking Age York and the North*, CBA Research Report 27, London, 37–57

MacGregor, A, 2000 'Objects of bone, antler and ivory', in P Ellis (ed), *Ludgershall Castle, Excavations by Peter Addyman 1964–1972*, Devizes, 160–168

Maltby, M, 1979 *Faunal studies on urban sites: the animal bones from Exeter 1971–75*, Exeter Archaeological Reports 2, Sheffield

Maltby, M, 1982 'Animal and bird bones', in R A Higham, J P Allan, and S R Blaylock, 'Excavations at Okehampton Castle, Devon. Part 2: the bailey', *Proceedings of the Devon Archaeological Society* 40, 114–135 (19–151)

Manley, J, 1994 'Excavations at Caergwrle Castle, Clwyd, North Wales 1988–90', *Medieval Archaeology* 38, 83–133

Margeson, S, 1993 *Norwich households: the medieval and post-medieval finds from Norwich survey excavations 1971–1978*, Norwich

Marshall, P, 2002 'The Great Tower as residence in the territories of the Norman and Angevin kings of England', in G Meirion-Jones, E Impey and M Jones (eds), *The seigneurial residence in western Europe AD c800–1600*, BAR International Series 1088, Oxford, 27–45

Mattingly, H, and Sydenham, E, 1926 *Roman imperial coinage vol 2*, London

Mayes, P and Butler, L, 1983 *Sandal Castle excavations 1964–1973: a detailed archaeological report*, Wakefield

McNeill, F M, 1974 *The Scots kitchen*, St Albans

McNeill, T, 1997 *Castles in Ireland: feudal power in a Gaelic world*, London

McNeill, T, 2003 'Squaring circles: flooring round towers in Wales and Ireland', in J R Kenyon and K O'Connor (eds), *The medieval castle in Ireland and Wales*, Dublin, 96–106

Mead, W, 1931 *The English medieval feast*, London

Megaw, V, 1984 'Bone musical instruments from medieval Exeter', in J P Allan, *Medieval and post-medieval finds from Exeter, 1971–1980*, Exeter, 349–351

Mellor, J, 1981 'The mortar analyses', in J E Mellor and T Pearce, *The Austin Friars, Leicester*, CBA Research Report 35, York, 78–80

Mellor, J E and Pearce, T, 1981 *The Austin Friars, Leicester*, CBA Research Report 35, York

Miles, T J, 1998 'Flint: excavations at the castle and on the town defences 1971–1974', *Archaeologia Cambrensis* 145, 67–151

Minwel Tibbott, S, 1982 *Cooking on the open hearth*, Cardiff

Minwel Tibbott, S, 1995–96 'Cheese-making in Glamorgan', *Folk Life* 34, 64–79

Moore, D, 2005 *The Welsh wars of independence*, Stroud

Moore, D T, 1978 'The petrography and archaeology of English honestones', *Journal of Archaeological Science* 5, 61–73

Moore-Colyer, R J, 1991 'Horses and equine improvement in the economy of modern Wales', *Agricultural History Review* 39 (II), 126–142

Moorhouse, S A, 1971 'Finds from Basing House, Hampshire (c. 1540–1645): part II, *Post-Medieval Archaeology* 5, 35–76

Moorhouse, S A, 1993 'Pottery and glass in the medieval monastery', in R Gilchrist and H Mytum (eds), *Advances in monastic archaeology*, BAR 227, 127–148

Morgan, G, 1994 'Charcoal', in H Quinnell, M Blockley & P Berridge (eds), *Excavations at Rhuddlan, Clwyd 1969–1973. Mesolithic to medieval*, CBA Research Report 95, York, 162–163

Morris, J E, 1901 *The Welsh wars of Edward I*, Oxford

Mottram, H R, Dudd, S N, Lawrence, G J, Stott, A W and Evershed, R P, 1999 'New chromotographic, mass spectrometric and stable isotope approaches to the classification of degraded animal fats preserved in archaeological pottery', *Journal of Chromatography A* 833 (2), 209–221

Munby, J, 1993 *Stokesay Castle*, London

Murphy, K, 1994 'Excavations in three medieval burgage plots in the medieval town of Newport, Dyfed, 1991', *Medieval Archaeology* 38, 55–82

Murphy, K, 1997 'Small boroughs in south-west Wales: their planning, early development and defences', in N Edwards (ed), *Landscape and settlement in Medieval Wales*, Oxford, 139–156

Murphy, P, 1979 *Macroscopic plant remains from the Norwich Survey excavations*, AMLR 2952

Murrell, J, 1638 *Two books of cookery and carving*, Ilkley (1985 facsimile edition)

Neal, D S, 1977 'Excavations at the Palace of King's Langley, Hertfordshire 1974–1976', *Medieval Archaeology* 21, 124–165

Needham, S and Evans, J, 1987 'Honey and dripping: Neolithic food residues from Runnymede Bridge,' *Oxford Journal of Archaeology* 6 (1), 21–28

North, J, 1988 'A re-examination of class 7 and 8 of the Short Cross coinage', *British Numismatic Journal* 58, 25–39

North, J, 1989 *Sylloge of coins of the British Isles 39: the J J North Collection*, Oxford

O' Connor, T, 1987 'Why bother looking at archaeological wild mammal assemblages?', *Circaea* 4 (2), 107–114

O'Connor, T, 1989 'What shall we have for dinner? Food remains from urban sites', in D Serjeantson and T Waldron (eds), *Diet and crafts in Towns*, BAR 199, 13–23

O'Connor, T, 1993 'Bird bones', in P J Casey, J L Davies and J Evans (eds), *Excavations at Segontium (Caernarfon) Roman Fort, 1975–1979*, CBA Research Report 90, York, 119

O'Neil, B H St J, 1944–55 'Criccieth Castle, Caernarvonshire', *Archaeologia Cambrensis* 98, 1–51

Oakley G E and Harman, M, 1979 'The worked bone', in J H Williams, *St Peter's Street Northampton Excavations 1965–1976*, Northampton, 308–318

Oakley, G E, 1979 'Charcoal and Wood Remains', in J H Williams, *St Peter's Street Northampton, Excavations 1973–76*, Northampton, 319

Oakley, G E and Hall, A D, 1979 'The spindle whorls', in J H Williams, *St Peter's Street Northampton. Excavations 1973–76*, Northampton, 286–289

Oschinsky, O, 1971 *Walter of Henley and other treatises on estate management and accounting*, Oxford

Oswald, A, 1962–63 'Excavation of a thirteenth century wooden building at Weoley Castle, Birmingham 1960–1. An interim report', *Medieval Archaeology* 6–7, 109–134

Ottaway, P and Rogers, P, 2002 *Craft industry and everyday life: finds from medieval York*, The Archaeology of York: The Small Finds 17/15

Owen, D H, 1989 'The Middle Ages', in D H Owen (ed), *Settlement and society in Wales*, Cardiff, 199–223

Owen, E, 1892 'Reviews and notices of books', *Archaeologia Cambrensis* (5th series) 9, 335–339

Owen, M E, 2000 'Royal propaganda: stories from the law-texts', in T M Charles-Edwards, M E Owen and P Russell (eds) *The Welsh King and his Court*, Cardiff , 224–254

Papazian, C and Campbell, E, 1992 'Medieval pottery and roof tiles in Wales AD 1100–1600', *Medieval and Later Pottery in Wales* 13, 1–107

Parker, A J, 1988 'The birds of Roman Britain', *Oxford Journal of Archaeology* 7 (2), 197–226

Parkhouse, J, 1997 'Stone objects', in A G Marvell and H S Owen-John, *Leucarumn, Excavations at the Roman auxiliary fort at Loughor*, Britannia Monograph Series 12, 418–425

Parkhouse, J and Evans, D R, 1992 'Objects of stone', in D R Evans and V M Metcalf, *Roman Gates Caerleon*, Oxbow Monograph 15, Oxford, 191–193

Parry, C, 1987 'Survey and excavation at Newcastle Emlyn Castle', *The Carmarthenshire Antiquary* 23, 11–27

Pegge, S (ed), 1780 *The forme of cury, a roll of ancient English cookery, compiled in 1390 by the Master–Cooks of King Richard II*, London

Pennant, T, 1773 *A tour in Wales*, London

Phillpotts, C, 2001a *Siege of Dryslwyn Castle 1287: historical research contract, Stage One Report: source material*, unpublished report, Dryslwyn Castle Excavation Archive

Phillpotts, C, 2001b *Siege of Dryslwyn Castle 1287: historical research contract, Stage Two Report: siege article*, unpublished report, Dryslwyn Castle Excavation Archive

Phillpotts, C, 2001c *Siege of Dryslwyn Castle 1287: historical research contract, Stage Three Report: accounts translations*, unpublished report, Dryslwyn Castle Excavation Archive

Phillpotts, C, 2003 *Dryslwyn Castle history*, unpublished report, Dryslwyn Castle Excavation Archive

Pickin, C, 2000 *Identification of wax like samples from Dryslwyn Castle, South Wales*, unpublished report, Dryslwyn Castle Excavation Archive

Pierce, T J, 1972 *Medieval Welsh society*, Cardiff

Piponnier, F and Mane, P, 1997 *Dress in the Middle Ages*, London

Platt, C and Coleman Smith, R, 1975 *Excavation in Medieval Southampton 1953–69. Volume 2: the finds*, Leicester

Pognon, E, 1979 *Les Tres Riches Heures du Duc de Berry*, Geneva

Pollard, A M and Wilson, L, 2001 'Global geochemical cycles and isotope systematics: how the world works', in D R Brothwell and A M Pollard (eds), *Handbook of archaeological science*, London, 191–201

Pollard, A M and Heron C, 1996 *Archaeological chemistry*, Cambridge

Ponsford, M, 1991 'Dendrochronological dates from Dundas Wharf, Bristol, and the dating of Ham Green and other medieval pottery', in E Lewis (ed), *Custom and ceramics: essays presented to Kenneth Barton*, Wickham, 81–103

Postan, M M and Rich, E E, (eds) 1952 *Trade and industry in the Middle Ages*, Cambridge Economic History of Europe II, Cambridge

Pounds, N J G, 1990 *The medieval castle in England and Wales*, Cambridge

Power, E, 1928 *The Goodman of Paris c. 1393*, London

Powicke, Sir M, 1962 *The thirteenth century*, Oxford (2nd ed)

Prestwich, M, 1988 *Edward I*, London

Prestwich, M, 1996 *Armies and warfare in the Middle Ages: the English experience*, New Haven and London

Priestley, S G and Turner, R, 2003 'Three castles of the Clare family in Monmouthshire during the thirteenth and fourteenth centuries', *Archaeologia Cambrensis* 152, 9–52

Pryce, H, 2005 *The acts of Welsh rulers 1120–1283*, Cardiff

Quinnell, H, Blockley, M and Berridge, P, 1994 *Excavations at Rhuddlan, Clwyd 1969–1973. Mesolithic to medieval*, CBA Research Report 95, York

Raby, F J F. and Reynolds, P K B, 1987 *Framlingham Castle*, London

Rackham, D J, 1995 'Skeletal evidence of medieval horses from London sites', in J Clark, *The medieval horse and its equipment c. 1150–c. 1450*, London, 169–174

Rackham, O, 1986 *The history of the countryside*, London

Radford, C A R, 1986 *Restormel Castle*, London

Raffald, E, 1782 *The experienced English housekeeper*, London (1970 facsimile edition)

Rahtz, P, 1966 *Kenilworth Castle*, Oxford

Rahtz, P and Hirst, S, 1976 *Bordersley Abbey, Redditch. Hereford-Worcestershire. First report on excavations 1969–1973*, BAR 23

Raven, A M, van Bergan, P F, Stott, A W, Dudd, S N, Evershed, R P, 1997 'Formation of long-chain ketones in archaeological pottery vessels by pyrolysis of acyl lipids', *Journal of Analytical and Applied Pyrolysis* 40–41, 267–285

RCAHMW 1917: Royal Commission on Ancient and Historical Monuments and Constructions in Wales and Monmouthshire, 1917 *An inventory of the ancient monuments in Wales and Monmouthshire V. County of Carmarthen*, London

RCAHMW 2000: Royal Commission on the Ancient and Historical Monuments of Wales, 2000 *An inventory of the ancient monuments in Glamorgan Volume III-Part1b: medieval secular monuments, the later castles, from 1217 to present*, Aberystwyth

Redknap, M, 1993 'The bone gaming pieces', in J M Lewis, 'Excavations at Loughor Castle, West Glamorgan 1969–73', *Archaeologia Cambrensis* 142, 150–156 (99–180)

Redknap, M, 1994 'Some medieval brooches, pendants and moulds from Wales: a short survey', *Archaeologia Cambrensis* 143, 92–138

Redon, O, Sabban, F and Serventi, S, 1998 *The medieval hitchen*, Chicago

Rees, S and Caple, C, 1999 *Dinefwr Castle, Dryslwyn Castle*, Cardiff

Rees, W, 1924 *South Wales and the March 1284–1415. A social and agrarian study*, Oxford

Rees, W, 1951 *An historical atlas of Wales: from early to modern times*, London

Rees, W, 1975 *Calendar of ancient petitions relating to Wales*, Cardiff

Reid-Henry, D and Harrison, C, 1988 *The history of the birds of Britain*, London

Renfrow, C, 1990 *Take a thousand eggs or more*, vol II, USA

Renn, D, 1961 'The round keeps of the Brecon Region', *Archaeologia Cambrensis* 110, 129–143

Renn, D, 1967–68 'The donjon at Pembroke Castle', *Transactions of the Ancient Monuments Society* (new series) 15, 35–47

Renn, D, 1993 *Goodrich Castle*, London

Rhys, M, 1936 *Ministers' accounts for West Wales 1277 to 1306*, Cymmrodorion Record Series 13, London

Richards, J, 2001 *The vicars choral of York Minster: the College of Bedern*, The Archaeology of York 10/5, York

Rice, P, 1987 *Pottery analysis: a sourcebook*, Edinburgh

Rigold, S, 1977 'Small change in the light of medieval site-finds', in N Mayhew (ed), *Edwardian monetary affairs (1279–1344)*, BAR 36, 59–80

Roberts, E, 1982, *Food of the Bards*, Cardiff

Robinson, D M, 2006 *The Cistercians in Wales: architecture and archaeology 1130–1540*, London

Rooney, A, 1993 *Hunting in middle English literature*, Cambridge

Rottlander, R C A, 1990 'Die Resultate der modernen Fettanalytik und ihre Anwendung auf die prähistorische Forschung', in G Bauchhenss (ed), *Naturwissenschaftliche Beiträge zur Archäologie 2, Archaeo-Physika* 12, 1–354

Rouse, E C, 1991 *Medieval wall paintings*, Princes Risborough

Rowland, I W, 1996 'William Marshal, Pembroke castle and the historian', *Chateau Gaillard* 17, 151–155

Ryder, M L, 1983 *Sheep and man*, London

Salisbury and South Wiltshire Museum, 2001 *Salisbury Museum Medieval Catalogue*, Salisbury

Salzman, L F, 1952 *Building in England down to 1540: a documentary history*, Oxford

Samson, R, 1982 'Finds from Urquhart Castle', *Proceedings of Society of Antiquaries of Scotland*, 112, 466–469

Savory, N H, 1960 'Excavations at Dinas Emrys, Beddgelert, Caernarvonshire 1954–1956', *Archaeologia Cambrensis* 109, 13–77

Schweingruber, F H, 1990 *Anatomy of European woods*, Berne and Stuttgart

Schweingruber, FH, 1978 *Microscopic wood anatomy*, Zurich

Scott, S, 1992 'The animal bones', in D H Evans and D G Tomlinson, *Excavations at 33–35 Eastgate, Beverley, 1983–6*, Sheffield Excavation Reports 3, 236–251

Scully, T, 1995 *The art of cookery in the Middle Ages*, Woodbridge

Sealy, J, 2001 'Body tissue chemistry and paleodiet', in D R Brothwell and A M Pollard (eds), *Handbook of archaeological sciences*, London, 269–279

Seddon, B, 1960 'Report on the organic deposits in the pool at Dinas Emrys', in N H Savory, 'Excavations at Dinas Emrys, Beddgelert, Caernarvonshire 1954–1956', *Archaeologia Cambrensis* 109, 72–77 (13–77)

Serjeantson, D, 1989 'Animal remains and the tanning trade', in D Serjeantson and T Waldron (eds), *Diet and crafts in towns*, BAR 199, 129–146

Simon, A L, 1952 *A concise encyclopaedia of gastronomy*, London

Simoons, F J, 1994 *Eat not this flesh*, Madison, Wisconsin and London (2nd ed)

Simpson, D, Breeze, D J and Hume, J R, 1990 *Bothwell Castle*, Edinburgh

Smith, G H, 1979 'The excavation of the Hospital of St Mary of Ospringe, commonly called Mason Dieu', *Archaeologia Cantiana* 95, 81–184

Smith, J B, 1964 'The 'Chronica de Wallia' and the Dynasty of Dinefwr', *Bulletin of the Board of Celtic Studies* 20, 261–282

Smith, J B, 1965 'The origins of the revolt of Rhys ap Maredudd', *Bulletin of the Board of Celtic Studies* 21 (II), 151–163

Smith, J B, 1998 *Llywelyn ap Gruffudd*, Cardiff

Smith, J B, and O'Neil, B H St J, 1967 *Talley Abbey, Dyfed*, Cardiff

Smith, J B and Knight, J K, 1981 *Bronllys Castle*, Cardiff

Smith, M J, Hooper, A P and Bartley, D, 1983 'An investigation of the charcoal samples', in P Mayes and L Butler, *Sandal Castle excavations 1964–1973: a detailed archaeological report*, Wakefield, 356–357

Smith, P, 1975 *Houses of the Welsh countryside*, London

Solomon, A, 1982 *The last siege of Dryslwyn Castle*, Carmarthen (private publication)

Soulsby, I, 1983 *The towns of medieval Wales*, Phillimore

Spencer-Gregson, F, 1990 *Investigation into the components of mortar from Dryslwyn Castle, Dyfed, by means of x-ray spectroscopy*, unpublished BSc dissertation, University of Durham

Spry, C, 1956 *The Constance Spry cookery book*, London

Stace, C, 1997 *New flora of the British Isles*, Cambridge (2nd ed)

Stallibrass, S, 1990 'Canid damage to animal bones: two current lines of research', in D E Robinson (ed), *Experimentation and reconstruction in environmental archaeology*, Oxford, 151–166

Steane, J M, 1985 *The archaeology of medieval England and Wales*, London

Steane, J M and Foreman, M, 1988 'Medieval fishing tackle', in M. Aston (ed), *Medieval fish, fisheries and fishponds*, BAR 182, Oxford, 137–186

Stephenson, D, 1984 *The governance of Gwynedd*, Cardiff

Stocker, D, 1992 'The shadow of the general's armchair', *Archaeological Journal* 149, 415–420

Strahan, A, Cantrill, T C and Thomas, H H, 1907 *Memoirs of the Geological Survey: England and Wales, Sheet 230: the Geology of the South Wales Coal-Field, Part VII: The Country around Ammanford*, London

Strahan, A, Cantrill, T C, Dixon, E E L and Thomas, H H, 1909 *Memoirs of the Geological Survey: England and Wales, Sheet 229: the Geology of the South Wales Coal-Field, Part X: The Country around Carmarthen*, London

Tabraham, C, 1986 *Kildrummy Castle*, Edinburgh

Tapper, S C, 1991 'Brown Hare', in G B Corbet and S Harris (eds), *The handbook of British mammals*, Oxford, 154–160

Taylor, A J, 1976 'Who was John Pennardd, leader of the men of Gwynedd?', *English Historical Review* 91, 79–97 (republished in 1985a)

Taylor, A, 1985a 'Who was John Pennardd, leader of the men of Gwynedd?', *Studies in castles and castle building*, 209–227

Taylor, A, 1985b *Beaumaris Castle*, Cardiff (2nd ed)

Taylor, A, 1987 'The Beaumaris Castle Building Account of 1295–1298', in J R Kenyon and R Avent (eds), *Castles in Wales and the Marches*, Cardiff, 125–142

Taylor, C, 1975 *Fields in the English landscape*, London

Thienpont, D, Rochette, F and Vanparijs, O F J, 1986 *Diagnosing Helminthiasis by Coprological Examination*, Beerse, Belgium

Thomas, C, 1968 'Thirteenth-century farm economies in North Wales', *Agricultural History Review* 16, 1–14

Thomas, C, 1975 'Peasant agriculture in medieval Gwynedd', *Folk Life* 13, 24–37

Thomas, T M, 1961 *The mineral wealth of Wales and its exploitation*, London

Thompson, A, 1994 *A study of nails from the excavation of Dryslwyn Castle 1980–1993*, unpublished report, Dryslwyn Castle Excavation Archive

Thompson, A, 1990 *A study of nails from the Excavation of Dryslwyn Castle 1980–89*, unpublished BA dissertation, University of Durham

Thompson, M W, 1991a *Kennilworth Castle*, London (2nd ed)

Thompson, M W, 1991b *The rise of the castle*, Cambridge

Thompson, M W, 1987 *The decline of the castle*, Cambridge

Thomson, R, 1981 'Leather manufacture in the post-medieval period with special reference to Northamptonshire', *Post-Medieval Archaeology* 15, 161–175

Thorpe, L, (ed and trans) 1978 *Gerald of Wales: journey through Wales, description of Wales*, Harmondsworth

Tristram, E W, 1950 *English wall painting: the thirteenth century*, Oxford

Tristram, E W, 1955 *English wall painting of the fourteenth century*, London

Trow-Smith, R, 1957 *A history of British livestock husbandry to 1700*, London

Turner, R, 2000a 'St Davids Bishop's Palace, Pembrokeshire', *The Antiquaries Journal* 80, 87–194

Turner, R, 2000b *Lamphey Bishop's Palace, Llawhadden Castle, Carswell medieval house, Carew Cross*, Cardiff (2nd ed)

Turner, R, 2002a *Chepstow Castle*, Cardiff

Turner, R, 2002b 'Fish weirs and fish traps', in A Davidson (ed), *The coastal archaeology of Wales*, CBA Research Report 131, York, 95–107

Turner, R, 2006 *Llangibby Castle, Cas Troggy and Castell Coch: three Marcher lord's lodges from early 14th century Wales*, lecture delivered to the Society of Antiquaries and the Castle Studies Group, September 2006

Turner, R and Johnson, A, 2006 *Chepstow Castle its history and buildings*, Logaston

Turvey, R, 1997 'The castle strategy of the Lord Rhys', *Archaeologia Cambrensis* 144, 103–132

Turvey, R, 2002 *The Welsh Princes 1063–1283*, London

Tweddle, D, 1992 *The Anglian helmet from 16–22 Coppergate*, The Archaeology of York 17/8

Tyson, R, 2002 *The glass from Dryslwyn Castle*, unpublished report, Dryslwyn Castle Excavation Archive

Tyson, R, 2000 *Medieval glass vessels found in England c. AD 1200–1500*, York

Van Geersdaele, P C and Goldsworthy, L J, 1978 'The restoration of wall painting fragments from St Stephen's Chapel, Westminster', *The Conservator* 2, 9–12

Vaughan, D, 1983 *Plant remains from Prudhoe Castle*, AMLR 3924

Veale, E M, 1966 *The English fur trade in the Later Middle Ages*, Oxford

Velander, K A, 1991 'Pine Marten', in G B Corbet and S Harris (eds), *The handbook of British mammals*, Oxford, 367–376

Vinson, C, 2001 *Quill pen*, unpublished report, Dryslwyn Castle Excavation Archive

Wade Labarge, M, 1965 *A baronial household of the thirteenth century*, London

Wade, M, 1990 *An x-ray fluorescence spectroscopy study of mortar from Dryslwyn Castle, South Wales*, unpublished BSc dissertation, University of Durham.

Wade-Evans, A W, 1909 *Welsh medieval law*, Oxford

Walker, R F, 1992 'The fourteenth-century surveys of Newcastle Emlyn and the building programme of 1347–8', *Carmarthenshire Antiquary* 28, 37–50

Ward Perkins, J B, 1940 *London Museum medieval catalogue*, London

Warner, P, 1968 *Sieges of the Middle Ages*, London

Warner, R, 1791 *Antiquitates Culinariae*, London (facsimile edition)

Waterman, D M, 1954 'Excavations at Clough Castle, Co. Down', *Ulster Journal of Archaeology* 17, 103–163

Waterman, D M, 1955 'Excavations at Seafin Castle and Bally Roney Motte and Bailey', *Ulster Journal of Archaeology* 18, 83–104

Watkin, J, 1987 'Objects of stone, fired clay, jet and mica', in P Armstrong and B Ayers (eds), *Excavations in High Street & Black Friaridge, Hull*, East Riding Archaeologist 8, 190–191

Webster, P, 1980 'Dryslwyn Castle', *Archaeology in Wales* 20, 56–58

Webster, P, 1981a 'Dryslwyn Castle', *Medieval Archaeology* 25, 203

Webster, P, 1981b 'Dryslwyn Castle 1980', in R Avent and P Webster (eds), *Interim reports of excavations at Laugharne Castle, Dyfed, 1976–1980, and Dryslwyn Castle, Dyfed, 1980*, Cardiff, 34–54

Webster, P, 1982a 'Dryslwyn Castle', *Medieval Archaeology* 26, 223–224

Webster, P, 1982b 'Dryslwyn Castle', *Archaeology in Wales* 22, 30–33

Webster, P, 1982c 'Dryslwyn, Dyfed', *CBA Newsletter and Calendar* 5, 144

Webster, P, 1983a 'Dryslwyn Castle 1981–2', in C Arnold, R Avent, L A S Butler and P Webster (eds), *Interim reports on excavations at three castles in Wales 1981–1982*, Cardiff, 12–22

Webster, P, 1983b 'Dryslwyn, Dyfed', *CBA Newsletter and Calendar* 6, 154

Webster, P, 1984 'Dryslwyn Castle', *Medieval Archaeology* 28, 263

Webster, P, 1987 'Dryslwyn Castle', in J R Kenyon and R Avent (eds), *Castles in Wales and the Marches*, Cardiff, 89–104

Webster, P, 2000 *The pottery*, unpublished report, Dryslwyn Castle Excavation Archive

Webster, P and Caple, C, 1983 'Dryslwyn Castle', *Archaeology in Wales* 23, 55–57

Webster, P and Caple, R, 1980 'Radyr Deserted Medieval Settlement, 1975–8', Bulletin of the Board of Celtic Studies 29, 190–200

Wells, H W, 1938 *The vision of Piers Plowman*, London

West, I and Anderson, F, 1975 'Stone objects', in C Platt and R Coleman-Smith, *Excavations in medieval Southampton. Volume 2: the finds*, Leicester, 311–312

Wheatley, A, 2004, *The idea of the castle in medieval England*, Woodbridge

Wheeler, A, 1975 'The fish bones', in C Platt and R Coleman-Smith, *Excavations in Medieval Southampton 1953–1969. Volume 1*, Leicester, 342

Wheeler, A, 1977 'Fish bones', in D S Neal, 'Excavations at the Palace of Kings Langley, Herefordshire 1974–1976', *Medieval Archaeology* 21, 163 (124–165)

Wheeler, A, 1978 *Key to the fishes of northern Europe*, London

Wheeler, A, 1993 'Fish remains', in J M Lewis, 'Excavations at Loughor Castle, West Glamorgan 1969–1973', *Archaeologia Cambrensis* 142, 172 (99–180)

Wheeler, A and Jones, A, 1976 'Fish remains', in A Rogerson, 'Excavations at Fullers Hill, Great Yarmouth', *East Anglian Archaeology Report No 2*, Norwich, 208–224 (131–245)

White, M, 2002 *The lithic artefacts (flint)*, unpublished report, Dryslwyn Castle Excavation Archive

Whitehead, G K, 1953 *The ancient white cattle of Britain and their descendants*, London

Wiggins, K, 2001 *Anatomy of a siege, King John's Castle, Limerick 1662*, Woodbridge

van Wijngaarden-Bakker, L H, 1990 'Replication of butchering marks on pig mandibles', in D E Robinson (ed), *Experimentation and reconstruction in environmental archaeology*, Oxford, 167–174

William, E, 1987 *The historical farm nuildings of Wales*, Edinburgh

Williams, D, 1992 'Plant macrofossils', in K Lightfoot, 'Rumney Castle, a ringwork and manorial centre in South Glamorgan', *Medieval Archaeology* 36, 155–156 (96–163)

Williams, E, 1993 *The cleaning and conservation of a copper-alloy macehead from Dryslwyn Castle, Wales*, unpublished report, Dryslwyn Castle Excavation Archive

Williams, J H, 1979 *St Peter's Street Northampton; Excavations 1973–1976*, Northampton

Willis-Bund, J W (trans), 1902 *The Black Book of St Davids*, Cymmrodorion Record Series 5, London

Wilson, B and Edwards, P, 1993 'Butchery of horse and dog at Witney Palace, Oxfordshire, and the knackering and feeding of meat to hounds during the post-medieval period', *Post-Medieval Archaeology* 27, 43–56

Wood, M, 1983 *The English mediaeval house*, London (revised edition)

Woods, H, 1982 'Excavations at Eltham Place 1975–9', *Transactions of the London and Middlesex Archaeological Society* 33, 214–265

Zalkin, V I, 1960 'Metapodial variation and its significance for the study of ancient horned cattle', *Bull. D. Mosk. Ges. D. Nat'Forscher. Abt. Biol.* 65, 109–126 (Russian with English Summary)

INDEX

Rebecca Brown